FOURTH EDITION

Active Directory Cookbook

Brian Svidergol and Robbie Allen

O'REILLY®

Beijing · Cambridge · Farnham · Köln · Sebastopol · Tokyo

Active Directory Cookbook, Fourth Edition

by Brian Svidergol and Robbie Allen

Printed in the United States of America.

Published by O'Reilly Media, Inc., 1005 Gravenstein Highway North, Sebastopol, CA 95472.

O'Reilly books may be purchased for educational, business, or sales promotional use. Online editions are also available for most titles (*http://my.safaribooksonline.com*). For more information, contact our corporate/institutional sales department: 800-998-9938 or *corporate@oreilly.com*.

Editors: Maria Gulick and Rachel Roumeliotis

Production Editor: Melanie Yarbrough

Copyeditor: Audrey Doyle

Proofreader: BIM Publishing Services

Indexer: Ellen Troutman-Zaig

Cover Designer: Randy Comer

Interior Designer: David Futato

Illustrator: Rebecca Demarest

June 2013:   Fourth Edition

Revision History for the Fourth Edition:

2013-05-24:   First release

See *http://oreilly.com/catalog/errata.csp?isbn=9781449361426* for release details.

ISBN: 978-1-449-36142-6

[LSI]

Table of Contents

Preface

In 1998, when Robbie first became involved with the Microsoft Windows 2000 Joint Development Program (JDP), very little data was available on Active Directory (AD). In the following months, and even after the initial release of Windows 2000, there were very few books or white papers to help early adopters of Active Directory get started. And some of the information that had been published was often inaccurate or misleading. Many early adopters had to learn by trial and error. As time passed, a greater number of informative books were published, which helped fill the information gap.

By the end of the second year of its release, there was an explosion of information on Active Directory. Not only were there more than 50 books published, but Microsoft also cleaned up its documentation on MSDN (*http://msdn.microsoft.com*) and its AD website (*http://www.microsoft.com/ad*). Now those sites have numerous white papers, many of which could serve as mini booklets. Other websites have popped up as well that contain a great deal of information on Active Directory. With Windows Server 2008, Windows Server 2008 R2, and Windows Server 2012, Microsoft has taken its level of documentation a step further. Extensive information on Active Directory is available directly from any Windows Server 2008 or 2012 computer in the form of the built-in help information. So, with all this data available on Active Directory in the form of published books, white papers, websites, and even from within the operating system, why would you want to purchase this book?

In the summer of 2002, Robbie was thumbing through Tom Christiansen and Nathan Torkington's *Perl Cookbook* (O'Reilly), looking for help with an automation script that he was writing for Active Directory. It just so happened that there was a recipe that addressed the specific task he was trying to perform. In Cookbook parlance, a recipe provides instructions on how to solve a particular problem. We thought that since Active Directory is such a task-oriented environment, the Cookbook approach might be a very good format. After a little research, Robbie found there were books (often several) on nearly every facet of Active Directory, including introductory books, design guides, books that focused on migration, programming books, and reference books. The one type of book that he didn't see was a task-oriented "how to" book, which is exactly what the Cookbook format provides. With this was born the first edition of *Active Directory Cookbook*, covering Active Directory tasks in Windows 2000 and Windows Server 2003 Active Directory.

In 2005 and again in 2008, Laura E. Hunter revised the already popular *Active Directory Cookbook* to include an updated range of automation options, including the use of command-line tools and scripts that had been created by active members of the Directory Services community in the years since AD was first introduced.

Based on our experience, hours of research, and nearly a decade of hanging out on Active Directory newsgroups and mailing lists, we've compiled more than 500 recipes that should answer the majority of "How do I do *X*?" questions one could pose about Active Directory. And just as in the Perl community, where the *Perl Cookbook* was a great addition, we believe *Active Directory Cookbook*, Fourth Edition, will also be a great addition to any Active Directory library.

Who Should Read This Book?

As with many of the books in the Cookbook series, *Active Directory Cookbook*, Fourth Edition, can be useful to anyone who wants to deploy, administer, or automate Active Directory. This book can serve as a great reference for those who have to work with Active Directory on a day-to-day basis. For those without much programming background, the command-line and PowerShell solutions are straightforward and provide an easy way to automate repetitive administrative tasks for any administrator.

The companion to this book, *Active Directory*, Fifth Edition, by Brian Desmond et al. (O'Reilly), is a great choice for those wanting a thorough description of the core concepts behind Active Directory, how to design an Active Directory infrastructure, and how to automate that infrastructure using Active Directory Service Interfaces (ADSI) and Windows Management Instrumentation (WMI). *Active Directory*, Fifth Edition, does not necessarily detail the steps needed to accomplish every possible task within Active Directory; that is more the intended purpose of this book. These two books, along with the supplemental information referenced within each, should be sufficient to answer most questions you have about Active Directory.

What's in This Book?

This book consists of 21 chapters. Here is a brief overview of each chapter:

Chapter 1, Getting Started
Sets the stage for the book by covering where you can find the tools used in the book, PowerShell issues to consider, and where to find additional information.

Chapter 2, Forests, Domains, and Trusts

Covers how to create and remove forests and domains, update the domain mode or functional levels, create different types of trusts, and perform other administrative trust tasks.

Chapter 3, Domain Controllers, Global Catalogs, and FSMOs

Covers promoting and demoting domain controllers, finding domain controllers, enabling the global catalog, and finding and managing Flexible Single Master Operation (FSMO) roles.

Chapter 4, Searching and Manipulating Objects

Covers the basics of searching Active Directory: creating, modifying, and deleting objects; using LDAP controls; and importing and exporting data using LDAP Data Interchange Format (LDIF) and comma-separated value (CSV) files.

Chapter 5, Organizational Units

Covers creating, moving, and deleting organizational units (OUs), and managing the objects contained within them.

Chapter 6, Users

Covers all aspects of managing user objects, including creating, renaming, and moving user objects, resetting passwords, unlocking and modifying the profile attributes, and locating users that have certain criteria (e.g., password is about to expire).

Chapter 7, Groups

Covers how to create groups, modify group scope and type, and manage membership.

Chapter 8, Computer Objects

Covers creating computers, joining computers to a domain, resetting computers, and locating computers that match certain criteria (e.g., have been inactive for a number of weeks).

Chapter 9, Group Policy Objects

Covers how to create, modify, link, copy, import, back up, restore, and delete GPOs using the Group Policy Management snap-in and scripting interface.

Chapter 10, Schema

Covers basic schema administration tasks, such as generating object identifiers (OIDs) and schemaIDGUIDs, how to use LDIF to extend the schema, and how to locate attributes or classes that match certain criteria (e.g., all attributes that are indexed).

Chapter 11, Site Topology

Covers how to manage sites, subnets, site links, and connection objects.

Chapter 12, Replication

Covers how to trigger and disable the Knowledge Consistency Checker (KCC), and how to query metadata, force replication, and determine which changes have yet to replicate between domain controllers.

Chapter 13, DNS and DHCP

Covers how to create zones and resource records, modify DNS server configuration, query DNS, and customize the resource records a domain controller dynamically registers.

Chapter 14, Security and Authentication

Covers how to delegate control, view and modify permissions, view effective permissions, and manage Kerberos tickets.

Chapter 15, Logging, Monitoring, and Quotas

Covers how to enable auditing, diagnostics, DNS, NetLogon, and Kerberos and GPO logging; obtain LDAP query statistics; and manage quotas.

Chapter 16, Backup, Recovery, DIT Maintenance, and Deleted Objects

Covers how to back up Active Directory, perform authoritative and nonauthoritative restores, check DIT file integrity, perform online and offline defrags, and search for deleted objects.

Chapter 17, Application Partitions

Covers how to create and manage application partitions.

Chapter 18, Active Directory Lightweight Directory Service

Covers application partitions including Active Directory Lightweight Directory Services (AD LDS).

Chapter 19, Active Directory Federation Services

Covers Active Directory Federation Services (AD FS) that are included with Windows Server 2012.

Chapter 20, Microsoft Exchange Server 2013

Covers common administrative tasks for Exchange Server 2013.

Chapter 21, Microsoft Forefront Identity Manager

Provides an introduction to Microsoft's Forefront Identity Manager (FIM), a service that can be used to synchronize multiple directories, enforce data integrity within a single or multiple stores, and provide self-service password reset for end users.

Conventions Used in This Book

The following typographical conventions are used in this book:

Constant width

> Indicates classes, attributes, cmdlets, methods, objects, command-line elements, computer output, and code examples

Constant width italic

> Indicates placeholders (for which you substitute an actual name) in examples and in registry keys

Constant width bold

> Indicates user input

Italic

> Introduces new terms and example URLs, commands, file extensions, filenames, directory or folder names, and UNC pathnames

> This icon indicates a tip, suggestion, or general note. For example, we'll tell you if you need to use a particular version or if an operation requires certain privileges.

> This icon indicates a warning or caution. For example, we'll tell you if Active Directory does not behave as you'd expect or if a particular operation has a negative impact on performance.

Using Code Examples

This book is here to help you get your job done. In general, if this book includes code examples, you may use the code in this book in your programs and documentation. You do not need to contact us for permission unless you're reproducing a significant portion of the code. For example, writing a program that uses several chunks of code from this book does not require permission. Selling or distributing a CD-ROM of examples from O'Reilly books *does* require permission. Answering a question by citing this book and quoting example code does not require permission. Incorporating a significant amount of example code from this book into your product's documentation *does* require permission.

We appreciate, but do not require, attribution. An attribution usually includes the title, author, publisher, and ISBN. For example: *Active Directory Cookbook*, Fourth Edition, by Brian Svidergol and Robbie Allen. Copyright 2013 O'Reilly Media, Inc., 978-1-449-36142-6.

If you feel your use of code examples falls outside fair use or the permission given here, feel free to contact us at *permissions@oreilly.com*.

Safari® Books Online

 Safari Books Online (*www.safaribooksonline.com*) is an on-demand digital library that delivers expert content in both book and video form from the world's leading authors in technology and business.

Technology professionals, software developers, web designers, and business and creative professionals use Safari Books Online as their primary resource for research, problem solving, learning, and certification training.

Safari Books Online offers a range of product mixes and pricing programs for organizations, government agencies, and individuals. Subscribers have access to thousands of books, training videos, and prepublication manuscripts in one fully searchable database from publishers like O'Reilly Media, Prentice Hall Professional, Addison-Wesley Professional, Microsoft Press, Sams, Que, Peachpit Press, Focal Press, Cisco Press, John Wiley & Sons, Syngress, Morgan Kaufmann, IBM Redbooks, Packt, Adobe Press, FT Press, Apress, Manning, New Riders, McGraw-Hill, Jones & Bartlett, Course Technology, and dozens more. For more information about Safari Books Online, please visit us online.

How to Contact Us

Please address comments and questions concerning this book to the publisher:

O'Reilly Media, Inc.
1005 Gravenstein Highway North
Sebastopol, CA 95472
800-998-9938 (in the United States or Canada)
707-829-0515 (international or local)
707-829-0104 (fax)

We have a web page for this book, where we list errata, examples, and any additional information. You can access this page at *http://oreil.ly/active_directory_cb_4*.

To comment or ask technical questions about this book, send email to *bookquestions@oreilly.com*.

For more information about our books, courses, conferences, and news, see our website at *http://www.oreilly.com*.

Find us on Facebook: *http://facebook.com/oreilly*

Follow us on Twitter: *http://twitter.com/oreillymedia*

Watch us on YouTube: *http://www.youtube.com/oreillymedia*

Acknowledgments

First, let me thank the authors of the original editions—Robbie and Laura—as without you guys, my job of updating the book for the Fourth Edition would not have been possible! Thankfully, I was able to start with a fantastic and well-regarded book!

Everybody from O'Reilly has been great. Special thanks go to Rachel Roumeliotis and Maria Gulick for being easy to work with and helping to move this project along. They were able to recruit some fantastic technical reviewers. Mike Kline (Directory Services MVP) provided great practical feedback to bring real-world thinking into every chapter. I really appreciated his way of looking at the solutions from an administrator's perspective because it helped to ensure that the solutions were real-world and that the solutions involved the tools that the typical administrator uses. While I hadn't worked with Mike before, I was familiar with his extensive work in the community. The other reviewer was Marcin Policht (Directory Services MVP). I've worked with Marcin on quite a few projects in the past and knew that he would be a valuable addition to the team. His technical depth and his attention to detail are really incredible, and it showed in his chapter reviews. Thanks, Mike and Marcin—without you guys, the overall quality of this edition wouldn't have been possible!

Other people contributed in other ways. To Ken Jones, thanks for the party invite; without it, this project never would've come to fruition! By the way, Ken, I still often think back to our first meeting. There were eight SMEs in the room; you were running the show for the first time. The room was loud and everybody was shouting out instructions like backseat drivers. You showed incredible poise in that situation! Charles Pluta was my number-one resource when I needed anything. Charles, keep doing what you are doing and you will go far! Thanks to Elias Mereb—Elias gave me extra motivation a few years ago and that has helped to fuel me ever since. Evan Hanna—if there was something strange or unknown, he was always the man to go to. Jonathan Hopp was there for me even when he didn't want to be! Of course, I also have to thank my wife, Lindsay, and my son, Jack, for putting up with me working seven days and seven nights a week juggling multiple projects. We can now get back to our regularly scheduled programming!

## CHAPTER 1

Getting Started

1.1. Approach to the Book

If you are familiar with the O'Reilly Cookbook format, which can be seen in other popular books such as the *Perl Cookbook*, *Java Cookbook*, and *DNS and BIND Cookbook*, then the layout of this book will be familiar to you. The book is composed of 21 chapters, each containing 10 to 30 recipes for performing a specific Active Directory task. Within each recipe are three sections: "Problem," "Solution," and "Discussion." The "Problem" section briefly describes the task that the recipe focuses on. The "Solution" section contains step-by-step instructions on how to accomplish the task. The "Discussion" section contains detailed information about the problem or solution. A fourth section, "See Also," is included in most recipes and contains references to additional sources of information that can be useful if you still need more information after reading the discussion. The "See Also" section may reference other recipes, MS Knowledge Base (*http://support.microsoft.com*) articles or documentation from the Microsoft Developer Network (MSDN) (*http://msdn.microsoft.com*).

At Least Three Ways to Do It!

When we first began developing the content for the book, we struggled with how to capture the fact that you can do things in multiple ways with Active Directory. You may be familiar with the famous computer science motto: TIMTOWTDI, or There Is More Than One Way To Do It. With Active Directory, there are often At Least Three Ways To Do It! You can perform a task with a graphical user interface (GUI), such as ADSI Edit, LDP, Active Directory Administrative Center, or the Active Directory Users and Computers snap-in; you can use a command-line interface (CLI), such as the *ds* utilities (i.e., *dsadd*, *dsmod*, *dsrm*, *dsquery*, and *dsget*), *nltest*, *netdom*, or *ldifde*, or freeware tools such as *adfind* and *admod* from joeware (*http://www.joeware.net*); and finally, you can perform the same task using a scripting language, such as VBScript, Perl, or PowerShell. Since people prefer different methods, and no single method is necessarily better than another, we decided to write solutions to the recipes using one of each. This means that instead of just a single solution per recipe, we include up to three solutions using GUI, CLI, and programmatic examples; in some cases you'll find more than one option for a given solution, as in the case where there is more than one command-line utility to perform a particular task. However, in cases where one of the methods cannot be used or would be too difficult to use to accomplish a given recipe, only the applicable methods are covered.

A special note regarding PowerShell coverage in this text: *PowerShell* is a command-line and scripting language introduced by Microsoft. PowerShell's claim to fame is its use of a predictable *Verb-Noun* syntax that can be leveraged regardless of the technology that it is managing: `Get-Object`, `Get-ChildItem`, `Get-Mailbox`, and so on. This predictable syntax is driven by the use of *cmdlets* (pronounced "command-lets") that can be created by individuals and software vendors alike. The first Microsoft product to rely on PowerShell was Exchange 2007, which includes a rich set of cmdlets to perform Exchange management tasks. In fact, there are certain tasks in Exchange 2007 that can *only* be performed using PowerShell! Since Exchange 2007, virtually every major product released by Microsoft includes a PowerShell module for management.

The challenge that Active Directory administrators faced with PowerShell, prior to the release of Windows Server 2008 R2, was that a set of PowerShell cmdlets had not yet been produced by Microsoft to support Active Directory administration tasks. However, that issue was fixed with the introduction of the PowerShell module for Active Directory. Microsoft initially released 76 cmdlets specific to Active Directory administration. Then, with the release of Windows Server 2012, additional cmdlets were introduced. In total, there are now 145 cmdlets for Active Directory administration! PowerShell has come a long way since the previous version of this book. As such, all of the Quest PowerShell cmdlets that were used in the previous version have been replaced with native cmdlets. Most of the VBScript solutions have also been replaced with simpler PowerShell solutions.

Readers who are looking for more in-depth programming coverage of these topics should consult *The .NET Developer's Guide to Directory Services Programming* referenced in the Recipe 1.5 section at the end of this chapter.

Windows Server 2008, Windows Server 2008 R2, and Windows Server 2012

Another challenge with writing this book is that there are now multiple versions of Active Directory deployed on most corporate networks. The initial version released with Windows 2000 was followed by Windows Server 2003 and an incremental update to Windows Server 2003 R2, and then Microsoft released Windows Server 2008 and Windows Server 2008 R2, which provided a lot of updates and new features. With the release of Windows Server 2012, administration has changed and new functionality has been introduced again. We've decided to go with the approach of making everything work under the most recent version of Active Directory first, and earlier versions of Windows second. In fact, the majority of the GUI solutions will work unchanged all the way back to Windows 2000. The PowerShell solutions will work out of the box with Windows Server 2008 R2 or newer domain controllers. By using the Active Directory Management Gateway Service, the PowerShell solutions will work with domain controllers running Windows Server 2003 SP2 or Windows Server 2008. For the recipes or solutions that are specific to a particular version, we include a note mentioning the version it is targeted for. In particular, because so much has changed since the introduction of Windows Server 2008 R2, the majority of our focus will be on Windows Server 2008 R2 and later.

1.2. Where to Find the Tools

You'll find a number of references to third-party command-line tools such as *adfind*, *admod*, *oldcmp*, *findexpacc*, and *memberof*. These tools were developed by Microsoft Directory Services MVP joe Richards, and he has made them available for free download from his website (*http://www.joeware.net/freetools*). While these tools are not native to the Windows operating system, they have become an invaluable addition to many Active Directory system administrators' toolkits, and we include them here to showcase their capabilities.

Once you have the tools at your disposal, there are a couple of other issues to be aware of while trying to apply the solutions in your environment, which we'll describe in the following sections.

Running Tools with Alternate Credentials

A best practice for managing Active Directory is to create separate administrator accounts to which you grant elevated privileges, instead of letting administrators utilize the user account to access other Network Operating System (NOS) resources. This is beneficial because an administrator who wants to use elevated privileges has to log on with his administrative account explicitly instead of having the rights implicitly, which could lead to accidental changes in Active Directory. Assuming you employ this method, you must provide alternate credentials when using tools to administer Active Directory unless you log on to a machine, such as a domain controller, with the administrative credentials.

There are several options for specifying alternate credentials. Many GUI and CLI tools have an option to specify a user and password with which to authenticate. If the tool you want to use does not have that option, you can use the `runas` command instead. The following command will run the `enumprop` command under the credentials of the administrator account in the *adatum.com* domain:

```
> runas /user:administrator@adatum.com
/netonly "enumprop "LDAP://dc1/dc=adatum,dc=com""
```

You can also open a Windows command prompt using alternate credentials, which will allow you to run commands using these elevated credentials until you close the command prompt window. To open a command prompt using the runas command, simply type runas /user:administrator@adatum.com cmd.

To run a Microsoft Management Console (MMC) with alternate credentials, simply use mmc as the command to run from runas:

```
> runas /user:administrator@adatum.com /netonly "mmc"
```

This will create an empty MMC from which you can add consoles for any snap-ins that have been installed on the local computer.

 The /netonly switch is necessary if the user with which you are authenticating does not have local logon rights on the machine from which you are running the command, such as a user ID from a nontrusted domain.

There is another option for running MMC snap-ins with alternate credentials. In Windows Explorer, hold down the Shift key and then right-click on the tool you want to open. If you select Run As Different User, you will be prompted to enter credentials under which to run the tool.

Targeting Specific Domain Controllers

Another issue to be aware of when following the instructions in the recipes is whether you need to target a specific domain controller. In the solutions in this book, we typically do not target a specific domain controller. When you don't specify a domain controller, you are using a *serverless bind*, and there is no guarantee as to precisely which server you will be hitting. Depending on your environment and the task you need to do, you may want to target a specific domain controller so that you know where the query or change will be taking place. Also, serverless binding can work only if the DNS for the Active Directory forest is configured properly and your client can query it. If you have a standalone Active Directory environment that has no ties to your corporate DNS, you may need to target a specific domain controller for the tools to work.

1.3. Getting Familiar with LDIF

Native support for modifying data within Active Directory using a command-line tool is relatively weak. The *dsmod* tool can modify attributes on a limited set of object classes.

One reason for the lack of native command-line tools to do this is that the command line is not well suited for manipulating numerous attributes of an object simultaneously. If you want to specify more than just one or two values that need to be modified, a single command could get quite long. It would be easier to use a GUI editor, such as ADSI Edit, to do the task instead.

The LDAP Data Interchange Format (LDIF) was designed to address this issue. Defined in RFC 2849 (*http://www.rfc-editor.org*), LDIF allows you to represent directory additions, modifications, and deletions in a text-based file, which you can import into a directory using an LDIF-capable tool.

The *ldifde* utility has been available since Windows 2000, and it allows you to import and export Active Directory content in LDIF format. LDIF files are composed of blocks of entries. An entry can add, modify, or delete an object. The first line of an entry is the distinguished name. The second line contains a changetype, which can be add, modify, or delete. If it is an object addition, the rest of the entry contains the attributes that should be initially set on the object (one per line). For object deletions, you do not need to specify any other attributes. And for object modifications, you need to specify at least three more lines. The first should contain the type of modification you want to perform on the object. This can be add (to set a previously unset attribute or to add a new value to a multivalued attribute), replace (to replace an existing value), or delete (to remove a value). The modification type should be followed by a colon and the attribute you want to modify. The next line should contain the name of the attribute followed by a colon and the value for the attribute. For example, to replace the last name attribute with the value Smith, you'd use the following LDIF:

```
dn: cn=jsmith,cn=users,dc=adatum,dc=com
changetype: modify
replace: sn
sn: Smith
-
```

Modification entries must be followed by a line that contains only a hyphen (-). You can add additional modification actions after the hyphen, each separated by another hyphen. Here is a complete LDIF example that adds a jsmith user object and then modifies the givenName and sn attributes for that object:

```
dn: cn=jsmith,cn=users,dc=adatum,dc=com
changetype: add
objectClass: user
samaccountname: jsmith
sn: JSmith

dn: cn=jsmith,cn=users,dc=adatum,dc=com
changetype: modify
add: givenName
givenName: Jim
-
```

```
replace: sn
sn: Smith
```

See Recipes 4.28 and 4.29 for more details on how to use the *ldifde* utility to import and export LDIF files.

1.4. Replaceable Text

This book is filled with examples. Every recipe consists of one or more examples that show how to accomplish a task. Most CLI- and PowerShell-based solutions use parameters that are based on the domain, forest, OU, user, and so on, that is being added, modified, queried, and so on. Instead of using fictitious names, in most cases we use replaceable text. This text should be easily recognizable because it is in italics and surrounded by angle brackets (<>). Instead of describing what each replaceable element represents every time we use it, we've included a list of some of the commonly used ones here:

<DomainDN>
> Distinguished name of the domain (e.g., dc=amer,dc=adatum,dc=com)

<ForestRootDN>
> Distinguished name of the forest root domain (e.g., dc=adatum,dc=com)

<DomainDNSName>
> Fully qualified DNS name of the domain (e.g., amer.adatum.com)

<ForestDNSName>
> Fully qualified DNS name of the forest root domain (e.g., adatum.com)

<DomainControllerName>
> Single-label or fully qualified DNS hostname of the domain controller (e.g., dc01.adatum.com)

<UserDN>
> Distinguished name of the user (e.g., cn=administrator,cn=users,dc=adatum,dc=com)

<GroupDN>
> Distinguished name of the group (e.g., cn=DomainAdmins,cn=users,dc=adatum,dc=com)

<ComputerName>
> Single-label DNS hostname of the computer (e.g., adatum-xp)

1.5. Where to Find More Information

While it is our hope that this book provides you with enough information to perform most of the tasks you need to do to maintain your Active Directory environment, it is not realistic to think that we have covered every possible task. In fact, working on this book has made us realize just how much Active Directory administrators need to know.

Now that Active Directory has been around for a number of years, a significant user base has been built, which has led to other great resources of information. This section contains some of the valuable sources of information that we use on a regular basis.

Command-Line Tools

If you have any questions about the complete syntax or usage information for any of the command-line tools we use, you should first take a look at the help information for the tools. The vast majority of CLI tools provide syntax information by simply passing /? as a parameter. For example:

```
> dsquery /?
```

Microsoft Knowledge Base

The Microsoft Support website is a great source of information and is home to the Microsoft Knowledge Base (MS KB) articles. Throughout the book, we include references to pertinent MS KB articles where you can find more information on the topic. You can find the complete text for a KB article by searching on the KB number at *support.microsoft.com/default.aspx*. You can also append the KB article number to the end of this URL to go directly to the article: *http://support.microsoft.com/kb/<Article-Number>*.

Microsoft Developer Network

MSDN contains a ton of information on Active Directory and the programmatic interfaces to Active Directory, such as ADSI and LDAP. We sometimes reference MSDN pages in recipes. Unfortunately, there is no easy way to reference the exact page we're talking about unless we provide the URL or navigation to the page, which would more than likely change by the time the book is printed. Instead, we provide the title of the page, which you can use to search on via *msdn.microsoft.com/library*.

Websites

While the Web is often changing, the following websites are a mainstay for Active Directory–related material:

Microsoft Active Directory home page (http://www.microsoft.com/ad)
> This site is the starting point for Active Directory information provided by Microsoft. It contains links to white papers, case studies, and tools.

Microsoft PowerShell home page (http://www.microsoft.com/PowerShell)
> This site is the starting point for PowerShell information provided by Microsoft. This will be an interesting site to keep an eye on as the various Microsoft product groups release new and updated PowerShell support.

Microsoft forum for Directory Services on the Social Technet Microsoft forum site (http://bit.ly/124Nejc)
> This forum is a great place to ask a question and confer with other Active Directory administrators and experts. It is frequented by some of the top Active Directory experts in the business.

Microsoft webcasts (http://bit.ly/YsUSXp)
> Webcasts are on-demand audio/video technical presentations that cover a wide range of Microsoft products. There are several Active Directory–related webcasts that cover such topics as disaster recovery, upgrading to Windows Server 2003 Active Directory, and Active Directory tools.

DirTeam blogs (http://blogs.dirteam.com)
> The DirTeam collection of blogs features content from very active members of the Directory Services MVP community.

joe Richards' home page (http://www.joeware.net)
> This is the home of the *joeware* utilities that you'll see referenced throughout this book; you can always download the latest version of *adfind*, *admod*, and so on, from joe's site, as well as browse FAQs and forums discussing each utility.

Petri.co.il by Daniel Petri (http://www.petri.co.il/ad.htm)
> This is another site that is run by a Microsoft MVP and that contains a number of valuable links and tutorials.

Ask the Directory Services Team (http://blogs.technet.com/askds)
> This site features regularly updated content from members of the Directory Services support organization within Microsoft.

ActiveDir home page (http://www.activedir.org)
> This is the home page for the ActiveDir Active Directory mailing list. It includes links to Active Directory Services blogs, as well as articles, tutorials, and links to third-party tools.

Directory Programming (http://www.directoryprogramming.net)
> Just as the ActiveDir list is crucial for AD administrators, this site is extremely valuable for AD developers. It also includes user forums where participants can post questions about AD programming topics.

Mailing List

ActiveDir (http://www.activedir.org)
> The ActiveDir mailing list is where the most advanced Active Directory questions can get answered. The list owner, Tony Murray, does an excellent job of not allowing topics to get out of hand (as can sometimes happen on large mailing lists). The list is very active, and it is rare for a question to go unanswered. Some of Microsoft's Active Directory program managers and developers also participate on the list and are very helpful with the toughest questions. Keeping track of this list is crucial for any serious Active Directory administrator.

Additional Resources

In addition to the Resource Kit books, the following are good sources of information:

Active Directory, Fifth Edition, by Brian Desmond et al. (O'Reilly)
> This is a good all-purpose book on Active Directory. A few of the topics the Fifth Edition covers are new Windows Server 2012 features, designing Active Directory, upgrading from Windows 2000, Active Directory Lightweight Directory Services (AD LDS), Exchange 2013, and Active Directory automation.

The .NET Developer's Guide to Directory Services Programming by Joe Kaplan and Ryan Dunn (Addison-Wesley)
> Written by two notables in the Directory Services programming community, this book is a practical introduction to programming directory services, using both versions 1.1 and 2.0 of the .NET Framework.

Windows IT Pro (http://windowsitpro.com)
> This is a general-purpose monthly magazine for system administrators who support Microsoft products. The magazine isn't devoted to Active Directory, but generally, related topics are covered every month.

## CHAPTER 2

Forests, Domains, and Trusts

2.0. Introduction

To the layperson, the title of this chapter may seem like a hodgepodge of unrelated terms. For the seasoned Active Directory administrator, however, these terms represent the most fundamental and, perhaps, most important concepts within Active Directory. In simple terms, a *forest* is a collection of data partitions and domains; a *domain* is a hierarchy of objects in a data partition that is replicated between one or more domain controllers; and a *trust* is an agreement between two domains or forests to allow security principals (i.e., users, groups, and computers) from one domain or forest to access resources in the other domain or forest.

Active Directory domains are named using the Domain Name System (DNS) namespace. You can group domains that are part of the same contiguous DNS namespace within the same domain tree. For example, the *marketing.adatum.com*, *sales.adatum.com*, and *adatum.com* domains are part of the *adatum.com* domain tree. A single domain tree is sufficient for most implementations, but one example in which multiple domain trees might be necessary is with large conglomerate corporations. Conglomerates are made up of multiple individual companies in which each company typically wants to maintain its own identity and, therefore, its own namespace. If you need to support noncontiguous namespaces within a single forest, you will need to create multiple domain trees. For example, *adatum.com* and *treyresearch.com* can form two separate domain trees within the same forest.

Assuming that each company within the conglomerate wants its Active Directory domain name to be based on its company name, you have two choices for setting up this type of environment. You could either make each company's domain(s) a domain tree within a single forest, or you could implement multiple forests. One of the biggest differences between the two options is that all the domains within the forest trust each other, whereas separate forests, by default, do not have any trust relationships set up between them. Without trust relationships, users from one forest cannot access resources located in the other forest. In our conglomerate scenario, if you want users in each company to be able to access resources within their own domain, as well as the domains belonging to other companies in the organization, using separate domain trees can create an easier approach than separate forests. However, it's important to keep in mind when designing your network that forests form the *security boundary* for Active Directory, as we'll cover in the next section. This is because transitive trusts are established between the root domains of each domain tree within a forest. As a result, every domain within a forest, regardless of which domain tree it is in, is trusted by every other domain. Figure 2-1 illustrates an example with three domain trees in a forest called *adatum.com*.

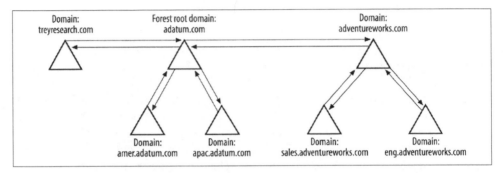

Figure 2-1. Multiple domain trees in a forest

Each domain increases the support costs of Active Directory due to the need for maintaining additional domain controllers, as well as the time you must spend configuring and maintaining the domain. When designing an Active Directory forest, your goal should be to keep the number of domains that you deploy to an absolute minimum. Since the forest constitutes the security boundary for an Active Directory environment, the minimalist approach toward the number of domains you use in an AD design becomes all the more sensible.

With Windows 2000, if you implement the alternative approach and create multiple Active Directory forests, you would have to create individual trusts between the domains in every forest to create the fully trusted model. This can get out of hand pretty quickly if there are numerous domains. Fortunately, with Windows Server 2003 and newer versions, you can use a trust type called a *cross-forest trust* to create a single transitive trust between two forest root domains. This single trust allows all of the domains in both forests to fully trust one another.

There are many more issues to consider when deciding how many forests, domains, and domain trees to implement. For a thorough explanation of Active Directory design considerations, we recommend reading *Active Directory*, Fifth Edition, by Brian Desmond et al. (O'Reilly).

In this chapter, we cover the most common tasks that you would need to do with forests, domains, and trusts. First, we're going to review how each item is represented within Active Directory.

The Anatomy of a Forest

A forest is a logical structure that is a collection of one or more interconnected domains, plus the configuration and schema naming contexts, as well as any application partitions that have been configured. This means that all domains in a forest share a common configuration and schema between them. Forests are considered the security boundary in Active Directory; by this we mean that if you need to definitively restrict access to a resource within a particular domain so that administrators from other domains do not have any access to it whatsoever, you need to implement a separate forest instead of using an additional domain within the current forest. This security concern is due to the transitive trust relationship that exists between all domains in a forest, the writable naming contexts (NCs) that exist on all domain controllers in a forest, and the extensive rights and permissions that are granted to members of the *Administrators* group. In the earliest days of Windows 2000 Active Directory, Microsoft advocated an "empty forest root" design with the intention of protecting the enterprise-wide security principals in the forest root domain from being accessible by domain administrators in the child domains. However, subsequent discoveries have indicated that it is in fact the forest, not the domain, that truly provides security separation between distinct groups of resources and administrators.

Active Directory relies on naming contexts to divide the AD database into separate partitions, each of which contains information that is replicated together as a logical unit. At a minimum, an Active Directory forest consists of three naming contexts: the Domain NC for the forest root domain, the Configuration NC, and the Schema NC. Here is a description of the types of partitions that can be part of a forest:

Configuration NC
> This contains data that is applicable across all domains in a forest, and thus is replicated to all domain controllers in the forest. Some of this data includes the site topology, list of partitions, published services, display specifiers, and extended rights.

Schema NC

>This contains the objects that describe how data can be structured and stored in Active Directory. The classSchema objects in the Schema NC represent class definitions for objects. The attributeSchema objects describe what data can be stored with classes. The Schema NC is replicated to all domain controllers in a forest.

Domain NC

>A domain is a naming context that holds domain-specific data, including user, group, and computer objects. This forms a collection of objects that is replicated between one or more domain controllers.

Application partitions

>These are configurable partitions that can be rooted anywhere in the forest and can be replicated to any domain controller in the forest, or to a subset of domain controllers. These are not available with Windows 2000.

The Partitions container in the Configuration NC contains the complete list of all partitions associated with a particular forest.

The Anatomy of a Domain

Although forests constitute the security boundary in an Active Directory environment, you can split up your AD infrastructure into separate domains to create smaller administrative or replication boundaries within a large-scale network. In Active Directory, domains can also constitute a policy boundary, as certain Group Policy settings such as password policies and account lockout policies can be applied only to domain user accounts at the domain level. However, Windows Server 2008 introduced the concept of a Fine-Grained Password Policy, which allows administrators to configure multiple password and account lockout policies within a single domain.

Domains are represented in Active Directory by domainDNS objects. The distinguished name (DN) of a domainDNS object directly corresponds to the fully qualified DNS name of the domain. For example, the *amer.adatum.com* domain would have a DN of dc=amer,dc=adatum,dc=com.

In Active Directory, each domain is a naming context and is also represented under the Partitions container in the Configuration NC as a crossRef object, which allows each domain controller in a forest to be aware of every partition in the forest and not just those that are held by one particular DC. In this case, the relative distinguished name (RDN) of the crossRef object is the NetBIOS name of the domain as defined by the netBIOSName attribute of the domain object.

In our previous example of *amer.adatum.com*, the corresponding crossRef object for the domain (assuming the forest name was *adatum.com*) would be located at cn=AMER,cn=Partitions,cn=Configuration,dc=adatum,dc=com.

The Anatomy of a Trust

Microsoft has relied on trust relationships to provide resource access across domain boundaries since the early days of Windows NT. Before Active Directory, all trust relationships were *one-way* and *nontransitive* in nature. A one-way trust relationship, as the name suggests, enables resource access only in a single direction: a single trust relationship will enable resource access only from *DomainA* to *DomainB*, but a separate trust would need to be created to enable access in the other direction. A nontransitive trust relationship means that if you create a trust from *DomainA* to *DomainB* and a second one from *DomainB* to *DomainC*, *DomainA* does *not* trust *DomainC* by default. This one-way nontransitive trust relationship was the only type that was available in Windows NT. Active Directory improved on this by automatically creating *two-way transitive* trust relationships between every parent and child domain in a domain tree, and between the root domains of all trees in every forest. Thus, all of the domains in a forest effectively trust all of the other domains in the forest.

Trusts are stored as `trustedDomain` objects within the `System` container of a domain. Table 2-1 lists some of the important attributes of `trustedDomain` objects.

Table 2-1. Attributes of trustedDomain objects

Attribute	Description
cn	Relative distinguished name of the trust. This is the name of the target domain that is trusted. For Windows NT domains, it is the NetBIOS name. For Active Directory domains, it is the DNS name.
trustDirection	Flag that indicates whether the trust is disabled, inbound, outbound, or both inbound and outbound. See Recipes 2.18 and 2.19 for more information.
trustType	Flag that indicates if the trust is to a down-level (NT4), up-level (Windows 2000 or later), or Kerberos (e.g., MIT) domain. See Recipe 2.18 for more information.
trustAttributes	Contain miscellaneous properties that can be enabled for a trust. See Recipe 2.18 for more information.
trustPartner	The name of the trust partner. See Recipe 2.18 for more information.

A trust also has a corresponding `user` object in the `Users` container of a domain. This is where the trust password is stored. The RDN of this `user` object is the same as the `cn` attribute for the corresponding `trustedDomain` object with a $ appended.

2.1. Creating a Forest

Problem

You want to create a new forest by creating a new forest root domain.

Solution

Using a graphical user interface

On a Windows Server 2008 R2 computer:

1. Open the Server Manager utility. In the lefthand pane, click Roles.
2. In the righthand pane, click Add Roles.
3. Click Next. Place a checkmark next to Active Directory Domain Services.
4. Click Next, click Add Required Features if applicable, click Next twice, and then click Install.
5. Click Close and then click the Active Directory Domain Services link in the left pane.
6. In the righthand pane, click the "Run the Active Directory Domain Services Installation Wizard (dcpromo.exe)" link.
7. Click Next twice to continue. Click the "Create a new domain in a new forest" radio button and click Next.
8. Follow the rest of the configuration steps to complete the wizard.

On a Windows Server 2012 computer:

1. Add the Active Directory Domain Services role. After the role installation, a notification will appear within Server Manager.
2. Click Notifications, and then click "Promote this server to a domain controller."
3. The Active Directory Domain Services Configuration Wizard will appear.
4. Click "Add a new forest."
5. Enter the root domain name and then click Next.
6. Select the forest and domain functional levels or leave the defaults of Windows Server 2012.
7. Confirm the options to install a DNS server and a global catalog server (not optional for a new forest and a new forest root domain).
8. Enter the Directory Services Restore Mode (DSRM) password and then click Next.
9. Specify the DNS delegation creation, if necessary, and then click Next.
10. Verify the NetBIOS domain name and then click Next.
11. Specify the location of the database, or accept the defaults, and then click Next.

12. Review the selections given while using the wizard. Optionally, click "View script" to see the PowerShell command and then click Next.

13. After the prerequisites have been successfully validated, click Install to begin the process. After promotion, the server will automatically reboot.

Using PowerShell

The Install-ADDSForest cmdlet is used to create a new forest, as shown in the following examples. The first example installs a new forest, a new forest root domain, and DNS.

```
> Install-ADDSForest -DomainName <DomainName> -InstallDNS
```

The following example installs a new forest, installs a new forest root domain, sets the file locations, sets the domain and forest functional levels, and installs DNS.

```
> Install-ADDSForest -DatabasePath "D:\ADDS\DB" -DomainMode "Win2012"↵
  -DomainName <DomainName> -DomainNetBIOSName <NetBIOSName> -ForestMode↵
  "Win2012" -InstallDNS:$true -LogPath "E:\ADDS\logs" -SYSVOLPath↵
  "F:\ADDS\SYSVOL" -Force:$true
```

Discussion

The act of creating a forest consists of creating a forest root domain. To do this, you need to promote a Windows Server 2008 R2 or Windows Server 2012 server to be a domain controller for a new domain. When using the GUI method, the promotion process has a wizard interface that requires you to answer several questions about the forest and domain into which you want to promote the server. After it finishes, you will be asked to reboot the computer to complete the promotion process. When using the PowerShell method, the only information needed after running the PowerShell command is the desired Directory Services Restore Mode (DSRM) password.

As you have probably noticed since Windows Server 2008, Microsoft has changed the nomenclature surrounding Active Directory. What used to simply be called "Active Directory" is now "Active Directory Domain Services," as a number of other server services have been rebranded under the Active Directory umbrella, including Active Directory Certificate Services, Active Directory Rights Management Services, Active Directory Federated Services, and Active Directory Lightweight Directory Services.

See Also

"Install a New Windows Server 2012 Active Directory Forest (Level 200)" (*http://bit.ly/ 166coUa*); Recipe 3.7 for automating the promotion of a domain controller; MS KB 238369 (How to Promote and Demote Domain Controllers in Windows 2000); MS KB 324753 (How to Create an Active Directory Server in Windows Server 2003)

2.2. Removing a Forest

Problem

You want to tear down a forest and decommission any domains contained within it because you no longer need it.

Solution

To remove a forest, you need to demote all the domain controllers in the forest. When you demote an existing domain controller, you will be given the option to demote the machine to a member server (unless the domain controller is the last domain controller in the domain, in which case the server will become part of a workgroup instead). After that is completed, and depending on how your environment is configured, you may need to remove WINS and DNS entries that were associated with the domain controllers and domains, unless they were automatically removed via WINS deregistration and dynamic DNS (DDNS) during demotion. The following commands can help determine if all entries have been removed:

```
> netsh wins server \\<WINSServerName> show name <DomainNetBiosName> 1b
> netsh wins server \\<WINSServerName> show name <DomainNetBiosName> 1c
> nslookup <DomainControllerDNSName>
> nslookup -type=SRV _ldap._tcp.dc._msdcs.<ForestDNSName>
> nslookup <ForestDNSName>
```

 You should run the first two commands for every domain in the forest if the forest contained more than one. The preceding list is not meant to be exhaustive, so be sure to check DNS across all domains and watch for entries for RODCs, if the domain controller that was demoted was an RODC.

Discussion

The method described in this solution is the graceful way to tear down a forest. You can also use a brute-force method to remove a forest by simply reinstalling the operating system on all domain controllers in the forest. This method is not recommended except in lab or test environments. You'll also need to make sure any DNS resource records for the domain controllers are removed from your DNS servers since the domain controllers will not dynamically remove them like they do during the demotion process.

You will also want to remove any trusts that have been established for the forest (see Recipe 2.21 for more details). For more information on how to demote a domain controller, see Recipe 3.6.

To fully remove all traces of an Active Directory forest in Windows Server 2008 and later, you should also remove the Active Directory Domain Services role that has been installed on any of the domain controllers. This will remove the actual system files associated with the AD DS server role. You may also want to remove any associated infrastructure roles from the servers in question, such as the DNS server role or the WINS server role. If you need to forcibly remove a single domain from an AD forest, you can also use the *ntdsutil* command-line utility; see Recipe 2.4 for more information.

See Also

Recipe 2.18 for viewing the trusts for a domain; Recipe 2.21 for removing a trust; Recipe 3.6 for demoting a domain controller

2.3. Creating a Domain

Problem

You want to create a new domain that may be part of an existing domain tree or the root of a new domain tree.

Solution

Using a graphical user interface

On Windows Server 2008 R2, add the Active Directory Domain Services role and then run *dcpromo* from a command line. Place a checkmark next to "Use advanced mode installation." You can then select one of the following:

- Existing forest
  - Create a new domain in an existing forest
  - Create a new domain tree root instead of a new child domain
- Create a new domain in a new forest

On Windows Server 2012, add the Active Directory Domain Services role. After the role installation completes, a notification will appear within Server Manager. Click Notifications and then click "Promote this server to a domain controller." The Active Directory Domain Services Configuration Wizard appears. Select the desired deployment operation ("Add a domain controller to an existing domain," "Add a new domain to an existing forest," or "Add a new forest"). Then, configure the remaining options in the wizard to complete the process.

Using PowerShell

The `Install-ADDSDomain` cmdlet is used to create a new domain. The following example installs a new child domain in an existing forest and installs DNS:

```
> Install-ADDSDomain -NewDomainName <newdomainname> -ParentDomainName↵
contoso.com; -DomainMode Win2012 -DomainType ChildDomain -InstallDNS:$true↵
-NewDomainNetBiosName <newNetBIOSname>
```

Note that the `Install-ADDSDomain` cmdlet is available only if the Active Directory Domain Services role has been installed on the server where the cmdlet will be run.

Discussion

The options to create a new domain allow you a great deal of flexibility in creating an Active Directory infrastructure that maps to your organization's business requirements. You can add a new domain to an existing domain tree, or else create a new domain tree entirely. If you want to create a new domain that is a child domain of a parent domain (for example, contained within the same contiguous namespace), then you are creating a domain in an existing domain tree. If you are creating the first domain in a forest or a domain that is outside the namespace of the forest root, then you are creating a domain in a new domain tree. For example, if you have already created the *treyresearch.com* domain and then you install the first DC in the *amer.treyresearch.com* domain, then *amer.treyresearch.corp* is a *child domain*. Conversely, if you want to create a domain that is part of the *treyresearch.com* forest but uses an entirely different naming convention (such as *treyresearchasia.com*), then you are creating a new domain tree within an existing forest.

See Also

Recipe 3.1 for promoting a domain controller; Recipe 3.7 for automating the promotion or demotion of a domain controller

2.4. Removing a Domain

Problem

You want to remove a domain from a forest. You may need to remove a domain during test scenarios or if you are collapsing or reducing the number of domains in a forest.

Solution

Removing a domain consists of demoting each domain controller in the domain, which can be accomplished by running the Remove Roles and Features Wizard on the domain controllers and following the steps to demote the domain controllers. For the last domain controller in the domain, be sure to select the "Last domain controller in the domain" option in the wizard so that the objects associated with the domain get removed. If you do not select this option for the last domain controller in the domain, take a look at Recipe 2.5 for how to remove an orphaned domain.

 If the domain you want to remove has child domains, you must remove the child domains before proceeding.

You can also demote domain controllers by using PowerShell, as shown in the following example:

```
> Uninstall-ADDSDomainController -LastDomainControllerInDomain↵
  -RemoveApplicationPartitions
```

In the preceding example, two optional parameters have been specified. The `-LastDomainControllerInDomain` parameter is used when demoting the last domain controller, while the `-RemoveApplicationPartitions` parameter should be specified to delete all data associated with any application partitions in the domain.

After all domain controllers have been demoted, depending on how your environment is configured you may need to remove any WINS and DNS entries that were associated with the domain controllers and domain that were automatically removed via WINS deregistration and DDNS during the demotion process. The following commands can help determine if all entries have been removed:

```
> netsh wins server \\<WINSServerName> show name <DomainNetBiosName> 1b
> netsh wins server \\<WINSServerName> show name <DomainNetBiosName> 1c
> nslookup <DomainControllerName>
> nslookup -type=SRV _ldap._tcp.dc._msdcs.<DomainDNSName>
> nslookup <DomainDNSName>
```

You will also want to remove any trusts that have been established for the domain (see Recipe 2.21 for more details). For more information on how to demote a domain controller, see Recipe 3.6.

Discussion

The brute-force method for removing a forest, as described in the discussion for Recipe 2.2, is not a good method for removing a domain. Doing so will leave all of the domain controller and server objects, along with the domain object and associated domain naming context, hanging around in the forest. If you used that approach, you would eventually see numerous replication and file replication service errors in the event log caused by failed replication events from the nonexistent domain. You would need to remove the metadata associated with the removed domain using *ntdsutil* to correct these errors.

To fully remove all traces of an Active Directory forest in Windows Server 2008 and later, you should also remove the Active Directory Domain Services role that has been installed on any of the Windows Server 2008 or later domain controllers. This will remove the actual system files associated with the AD DS server role. You may also want to remove any associated infrastructure roles from the servers in question, such as the DNS server role or the WINS server role.

See Also

Recipe 2.2; Recipe 2.5; Recipe 2.18 for viewing the trusts for a domain; Recipe 2.21 for removing a trust; Recipe 3.6 for demoting a domain controller; and TechNet (*http://bit.ly/166ePG5*) for details on removing Active Directory Domain Services

2.5. Removing an Orphaned Domain

Problem

You want to completely remove a domain that was orphaned because the domain was forcibly removed, or the last domain controller in the domain failed or was otherwise decommissioned improperly.

Solution

Using a command-line interface

The following commands will forcibly remove an orphaned domain from a forest. Replace *<DomainControllerName>* with the hostname of the Domain Naming Master Flexible Single Master Operation (FSMO; pronounced *fiz-mo*) for the forest.

```
1    NTDSUTIL
2    metadata cleanup
3    connections
4    connect to server <DomainControllerName>
5    quit
6    select operation target
7    list sites
8    select site <# of site>
9    list servers in site
10   select server <# of domain controller>
11   list domains
12   select domain <# of domain>
13   quit
14   remove selected server (confirm when prompted)
15   list naming context
16   select naming context <# of the DNS Naming Context>
17   quit
18   remove selected naming context (confirm when prompted)
```

```
19   select operation target
20   list naming context
21   select naming context <# of the domain DN>
22   quit
23   remove selected naming context (confirm when prompted)
```

Discussion

Removing an orphaned domain consists of removing the domain object for the domain (e.g., dc=emea,dc=adatum,dc=com), all of its child objects, and the associated cross Ref object in the Partitions container. You need to target the Domain Naming FSMO when using *ntdsutil* because that server is responsible for creation and removal of domains.

Before you can use *ntdsutil* to remove an orphaned domain, you must first forcibly remove any domain controllers in that domain that were not gracefully demoted. (Forcibly removing individual domain controllers will be discussed in Chapter 3.) You must also remove the DomainDNSZones application partition associated with the orphaned domain, if this was not gracefully removed. (Forcibly removing the DomainDNSZones application partition will be discussed in Chapters 13 and 17.)

See Also

Recipe 3.10 for removing an unsuccessfully demoted domain controller; MS KB 230306 (How to Remove Orphaned Domains from Active Directory); MS KB 251307 (How to Remove Orphaned Domains from Active Directory Without Demoting the Domain Controllers); MS KB 255229 (Dcpromo Demotion of Last Domain Controller in Child Domain Does Not Succeed); Chapter 3 for information on performing a metadata cleanup of individual domain controllers; Chapters 13 and 17 for information on manually removing the DomainDNSZones application partition

2.6. Finding the Domains in a Forest

Problem

You want a list of all domains in an Active Directory forest.

Solution

Using a graphical user interface

Open the Active Directory Domains and Trusts snap-in (*domain.msc*). The list of the domains in the default forest can be browsed in the left pane.

Using PowerShell

You can retrieve this information using the Get-ADForest command, as shown here:

```
> Get-ADForest | Select Domains
```

Discussion

Using a graphical user interface

If you want to view the domains for a forest other than the one you are logged in to, right-click on Active Directory Domains and Trusts in the left pane and select Change Forest. Enter the forest root domain name in which you want to browse. In the left pane, expand the forest root domain to see any subdomains.

Using PowerShell

In the PowerShell solution, we are relying on the Active Directory module. The Get-ADForest cmdlet has been available since Windows Server 2008 R2 and the usage remains identical in Windows Server 2012.

See Also

Recipe 3.12 for finding the domain controllers for a domain

2.7. Finding the NetBIOS Name of a Domain

Problem

You want to find the NetBIOS name of a domain. Although Windows primarily uses DNS for name resolution, the NetBIOS name of a domain is still important. Some users still rely on the NetBIOS name to log on to a domain or to applications by using the down-level logon name. The down-level logon name uses the *<domainname>\<user name>* format.

Solution

Using a graphical user interface

1. Open the Active Directory Users and Computers snap-in.
2. Right-click the domain you want to view in the left pane and select Properties.

The NetBIOS name will be shown in the "Domain name (pre-Windows 2000)" field.

You can also retrieve this information by using the Active Directory Administrative Center, as follows:

1. Open the Active Directory Administrative Center.
2. Right-click the domain in the left pane and then select Properties. The NetBIOS name will be shown in the "Pre-Windows 2000 domain name" field.

Using a command-line interface

To find the NetBIOS name of a Windows domain, use the following command while logged on as a domain user from a computer joined to the domain:

```
> set userdomain
```

Using PowerShell

In a single-domain environment, run the following command:

```
> Get-ADDomain | FL NetBIOSName
```

In a multidomain environment, run the following command:

```
> Get-ADDomain -identity <domainname> | FL NetBIOSName
```

Discussion

Obtaining the NetBIOS name of a domain is easier today than it was before the introduction of the Active Directory module for Windows PowerShell. Prior to the module, third-party PowerShell modules had to be used, and the solution was a multiline PowerShell script. Today, we have the Get-ADDomain cmdlet, which outputs 29 properties. Running the Get-ADDomain cmdlet without specifying the desired property will show the output with all 29 properties.

The NetBIOS name of a domain is often referred to with alternative names. In the command-line example in this recipe, Windows uses the USERDOMAIN environment variable to store the NetBIOS name of the domain to which the user logged on. By running just the set command, you can display all of the Windows environment variables. This can be helpful when you need to find out if specific information is already stored within an environment variable.

2.8. Renaming a Domain

Problem

You want to rename a domain—for example, due to organizational changes, due to legal restrictions, or because of a merger, acquisition, or divestiture. Renaming a domain is a very involved process and should be done only when absolutely necessary. Changing the name of a domain can have an impact on everything from DNS, replication, and GPOs to DFS and Certificate Services. A domain rename also requires rebooting all domain controllers, member servers, and client computers in the domain!

Solution

A domain rename procedure is supported if a forest is running Windows Server 2003 domain controllers or later and is at the Windows Server 2003 forest functional level or later. Microsoft provides a rename tool (*rendom.exe*) that is used for the process. Here are the commands for a domain rename in Server 2012:

```
1   rendom /list (this command will produce a file named DomainList.xml)
2   Edit DomainList.xml (Change the domain name to the desired name.)
3   rendom /upload
4   rendom /prepare
5   rendom /execute
6   gpfixup /olddns:adatum.com /newdns:contoso.com
7   gpfixup /oldnb:adatum /newnb:contoso
8   rendom /end
```

We highly recommend reading additional material on TechNet before attempting the procedure, as well as attempting the procedure in a test lab before performing it against a production environment.

Discussion

The domain rename process can accommodate very complex changes to your domain model. You can perform the following types of renames:

- Rename a domain to a new name without repositioning it in the domain tree.
- Reposition a domain within a domain tree.
- Create a new domain tree with a renamed domain.

One thing you cannot do with the domain rename procedure is to reposition the forest root domain. You can rename the forest root domain, but you cannot change its status as the forest root domain. Another important limitation to note is that you cannot rename any domain in a forest that has had Exchange 2007 or Exchange 2010 installed, though an environment with Exchange Server 2003 SP1 is capable of handling domain renames. The *rendom.exe* utility also includes the *gpfixup.exe* utility, which corrects references to Group Policy objects after the domain name changes. When working with Exchange 2003, you can also use the *xdr-fixup* tool to correct Exchange attributes to match the new domain name.

See Also

"Introduction to Administering Active Directory Domain Rename" (*http://bit.ly/ 135P9q8*)

2.9. Raising the Domain Functional Level to Windows Server 2012

Problem

You want to change the functional level of a Windows Server 2008 R2 Active Directory domain to the Windows Server 2012 functional level.

Solution

Using a graphical user interface

1. Open the Active Directory Domains and Trusts snap-in (*domain.msc*).
2. Browse to the domain you want to change in the left pane.
3. Right-click on the domain and select Properties. The current level will be shown in the dialog box.
4. To change the level, click the Raise button at the bottom.

Using PowerShell

To change the functional level, use the Set-ADDomainMode cmdlet:

```
> Set-ADDomainMode -Identity <DomainDNSName> -DomainMode Windows2012
```

Discussion

Since Windows Server, Active Directory functional levels have replaced the domain mode that was used in Windows 2000 to signify what operating systems are allowed to run on the domain controllers in the domain. With Windows Server 2003 and later, there are functional levels for both domains and forests, whereas with Windows 2000, the domain mode applied only to domains. The msDS-Behavior-Version attribute of the domainDNS object (e.g., dc=amer,dc=adatum,dc=com) holds the current domain functional level. Table 2-2 shows the six functional levels, their associated msDS-Behavior-Version values, and the operating systems that can be used on domain controllers in each.

Table 2-2. Active Directory domain functional levels

Functional level	msDS-Behavior-Version	Valid operating systems for domain controllers
Windows Server 2003	2	Windows Server 2003 and later
Windows Server 2008	3	Windows Server 2008 and later
Windows Server 2008 R2	4	Windows Server 2008 R2 and later
Windows Server 2012	5	Windows Server 2012

Various new features of Active Directory are enabled with each domain functional level. See *Active Directory*, Fifth Edition, by Brian Desmond et al. (O'Reilly) for more details.

The value contained in msDS-Behavior-Version is mirrored in the attribute domain Functionality of the RootDSE. That means you can perform anonymous queries against the RootDSE of a domain to quickly determine its current functional level.

 One of the benefits of the GUI solution is that if a problem is encountered, you can save and view the output log, which will contain information on any errors that were found.

See Also

"Raise the Domain Functional Level" (*http://bit.ly/14IZBD9*)

2.10. Raising the Functional Level of a Windows Server 2008 or 2008 R2 Forest

Problem

You want to raise the functional level of a forest to Windows Server 2012. You should raise the functional level to take advantage of the new features and enhancements available in the latest functional level.

Solution

Using a graphical user interface

1. Open the Active Directory Domains and Trusts snap-in (*domain.msc*).

2. In the left pane, right-click on Active Directory Domains and Trusts and select Raise Forest Functional Level.

3. Ensure that "Windows Server 2012" is displayed in the available forest functional level drop-down list and then click Raise. A warning dialog box will appear that mentions that the process may not be reversible. Click OK to proceed.

After a few seconds, you should see a message stating whether the operation was successful.

Using PowerShell

To retrieve the current forest functional level, run the following command:

```
> Get-ADForest | FL Name,ForestMode
```

Discussion

The Windows Server 2012 forest functional level is very similar to a domain functional level. Even if just one of the domains in the forest is at the domain functional level of Windows Server 2008 R2, you cannot raise the forest above the Windows Server 2008 R2 forest functional level. If you attempt to do so, you will receive an error that the operation cannot be completed. After you raise the last Windows Server 2008 R2 domain functional level to Windows Server 2012, you can then raise the forest functional level as well.

You may be wondering why there is a need to differentiate between forest and domain functional levels. The primary reason is new features. Some new features of Windows Server 2008 R2 require that all domain controllers in the forest are running the appropriate operating system. To ensure that all domain controllers are running a certain operating system throughout a forest, Microsoft had to apply the functional-level concept to forests as well as domains. Windows Server 2012 requires a minimum forest functional level of Windows Server 2003. The Windows Server 2012 forest functional level does not offer any new features, although the Windows Server 2012 domain functional level does offer a couple of new Kerberos authentication options.

The forest functional level is stored in the msDS-Behavior-Version attribute of the Partitions container in the Configuration NC. For example, in the *adatum.com* forest, it would be stored in cn=partitions,cn=configuration,dc=adatum,dc=com. The value contained in msDS-Behavior-Version is mirrored to the forestFunctionality attribute of the RootDSE, which means you can find the functional level of the forest by querying the RootDSE.

 One of the benefits of the GUI solution is that if a problem occurs, you can save and view the output log, which will contain information on any errors that were encountered.

See Also

"Upgrade Domain Controllers to Windows Server 2012" (*http://bit.ly/18ACNps*) for information about the forest and domain functional levels and other prerequisites; Recipe 2.11 for preparing a forest with AdPrep

2.11. Using AdPrep to Prepare a Domain or Forest for Windows Server 2012

Problem

You want to upgrade your existing Active Directory domain controllers to Windows Server 2012.

Solution

You can run the AdPrep tool, which extends the schema and adds several objects in Active Directory. For instance, to prepare a domain or forest for a Windows Server 2012 upgrade, you can first run the following command on the Schema FSMO with the credentials of an account that is in both the *Enterprise Admins* and *Schema Admins* groups:

```
> adprep /forestprep
```

After the updates from `/forestprep` have replicated throughout the forest (see Recipe 2.10), run the following command on the Infrastructure FSMO in each domain with the credentials of an account in the *Domain Admins* group:

```
> adprep /domainprep
```

If the updates from `/forestprep` have not replicated to at least the Infrastructure FSMO servers in each domain, an error will be returned when running `/domainprep`. To debug any problems you encounter, check out the AdPrep logfiles located at *%SystemRoot% \System32\Debug\Adprep\Logs*.

 AdPrep can be found in the *\support\adprep* directory on the Windows Server 2012 installation media. The tool relies on several files in that directory, so you cannot simply copy that file out to a server and run it. You must run it from a CD or from a location where the entire directory has been copied.

To prepare to add the first Windows Server 2012 domain controller to an existing domain, you will need to run the version of AdPrep contained on Windows Server 2012 installation media. The preparation also includes a third AdPrep switch that will update

permissions on existing Group Policy Objects (GPOs) to allow for updated functionality in the Group Policy Management Console (GPMC):

```
> adprep /domainprep /gpprep
```

The Windows Server 2012 preparation, in addition to /forestprep, /domainprep, and /domainprep /gpprep, also includes /rodcprep to allow for the installation of Read-Only Domain Controllers (RODCs), which we will discuss in Chapter 3.

Discussion

The adprep command prepares a forest and domains for Windows Server 2012. Both /forestprep and /domainprep must be run before you can upgrade any domain controllers to Windows Server 2012 or install new Windows Server 2012 domain controllers.

The adprep command serves a similar function to the Exchange 2010 setup /forest prep and /domainprep commands, which prepare an Active Directory forest and domains for Exchange 2010. The adprep /forestprep command extends the schema and modifies some default security descriptors, which is why it must run under the credentials of someone in both the *Schema Admins* and *Enterprise Admins* groups. In addition, the adprep /forestprep and /domainprep commands add new objects throughout the forest.

 Although not mandatory, it is helpful to run /domainprep from the server hosting the Infrastructure Master FSMO since this is the DC that controls the /domainprep process.

See Also

Recipe 2.10; Recipe 2.12 for determining whether AdPrep has completed; the Microsoft TechNet site for information about the Windows Server 2008 AdPrep process

2.12. Determining Whether AdPrep Has Completed

Problem

You want to determine whether the AdPrep process, described in Recipe 2.11, has successfully prepared a domain or forest for Windows Server 2012. After AdPrep has completed, you will then be ready to start promoting Windows Server 2012 domain controllers.

Solution

To determine whether adprep /forestprep has completed for a Windows Server 2012 upgrade, run ADSI Edit and then follow these steps:

1. In the left pane, right-click on ADSI Edit and then click Connect To.
2. In the Connection Settings window, click the "Select a well known Naming Context" radio button and then click Schema.
3. In the left pane, double-click "Schema [*<FQDN of domain controller>*]".
4. Right-click the DN of the schema and then click Properties.
5. Read the value of the objectVersion attribute. If the objectVersion attribute shows a value of 56, then the adprep /forestprep command completed successfully.

To determine whether adprep /domainprep has completed for a Windows Server 2012 upgrade, run ADSI Edit and then follow these steps:

1. In the left pane, right-click on ADSI Edit and click Connect To.
2. In the Connection Settings window, click the "Select a well known Naming Context" radio button, and then click "Default naming context."
3. In the left pane, double-click "Default naming context [*<FQDN of domain controller>*]."
4. Expand the DN of the domain.
5. Expand the CN=System container.
6. Expand the CN=DomainUpdates container.
7. Right-click on CN=ActiveDirectoryUpdate and then click Properties.
8. Read the value of the revision attribute. If the revision attribute has a value of 9, then the adprep /domainprep command completed successfully.

Discussion

As described in Recipe 2.11, the AdPrep utility is used to prepare an Active Directory forest for the upgrade to Windows Server 2012. One of the nice features of AdPrep is that it stores its progress in Active Directory. For /forestprep, the objectVersion attribute of the schema indicates the level of the forest. For /domainprep, a container with a distinguished name of cn=DomainUpdates,cn=System,<DomainDN> is created. After all of the operations have completed successfully, the objectVersion attribute should show a value of 56 (see Figure 2-2).

Figure 2-2. ADSI Edit showing the objectVersion attribute of an AD DS forest that was updated to Windows Server 2012 by running adprep /forestprep

For /domainprep, a container with a distinguished name of cn=ActiveDirectoryUpdate,cn=DomainUpdates,cn=System,<DomainDN> is created. After all of the operations have completed successfully, the revision attribute of the ActiveDirectoryUpdate object should show a value of 9 (see Figure 2-3).

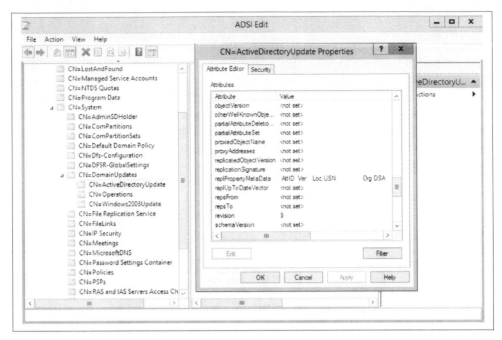

Figure 2-3. ADSI Edit showing the revision attribute of an AD DS domain that was updated to Windows Server 2012 by running adprep /domainprep

See Also

Recipe 2.11 for running AdPrep; the Microsoft TechNet site for additional information about the Windows Server 2012 AdPrep process

2.13. Checking Whether a Windows Domain Controller Can Be Upgraded to Windows Server 2003 or 2008

Problem

You want to determine whether a domain controller is ready to be upgraded to Windows Server 2003 or Windows Server 2008.

Solution

Using a graphical user interface

For Windows Server 2008, Windows Server 2008 R2, and Windows Server 2012, download and run the Microsoft Assessment and Planning Solution Accelerator from the Microsoft website, which will generate upgrade readiness reports to help your organization prepare for an upgrade to Windows Server 2008, Windows Server 2008 R2, and Windows Server 2012.

Discussion

Prior to Windows Server 2008, the WINNT32 command with the /checkupgradeon ly switch could be used to assess whether a domain controller could be upgraded. Windows Server, since 2008, has eliminated the /checkupgradeonly switch in the installation media, instead opting to provide a free inventory and analysis tool in the form of the Microsoft Assessment and Planning (MAP) tools.

See Also

"Microsoft Assessment and Planning Toolkit" (*http://bit.ly/10gkxlm*)

2.14. Creating an External Trust

Problem

You want to create a one-way or two-way nontransitive trust from an AD domain to a Windows NT domain, or to a domain within an untrusted Active Directory forest.

Solution

Using a graphical user interface

1. Open the Active Directory Domains and Trusts snap-in (*domain.msc*).
2. In the left pane, right-click the forest root domain and select Properties.
3. Click on the Trusts tab.
4. Click the New Trust button. Then click Next.
5. Enter the name of the domain and then click Next.
6. Verify that External trust is selected and then click Next.
7. Verify that a two-way trust direction is selected and then click Next.
8. Verify that "This domain only" is selected to create the trust and then click Next.
9. Verify that "Domain-wide authentication" is selected and then click Next.
10. Enter a complex password for the trust password and then click Next. Note that the password must meet the domain password policy.
11. Review the trust settings summary and then click Next.

12. A message indicating that the trust relationship was created successfully will appear. Click Next to configure the new trust.

13. Perform the same steps on the trusted domain. Then, on both sides, select Yes to confirm the incoming trust and then click Next.

14. A success message will appear. Click Finish.

15. A message will appear from AD DS that mentions that security identifier (SID) filtering is enabled. Click OK.

    The external trust should now appear in the Trusts tab of the domain properties.

Using a command-line interface

```
> netdom trust TrustingDomainName/d:TrustedDomainName/add
```

For example, to create a trust from the NT4 domain ADATUM_NT4 to the AD domain ADATUM, use the following command:

```
> netdom trust ADATUM_NT4 /d:ADATUM /add↵
/UserD:ADATUM\administrator /PasswordD:*↵
/UserO:ADATUM_NT4\administrator /PasswordO:*
```

You can make the trust bidirectional (i.e., two-way) by adding a /TwoWay switch to the example.

Discussion

It is common when migrating a single domain within a large, multidomain forest, as in the case of a corporate merger or divestiture, to set up trusts to down-level master account domains or resource domains, or to create a trust relationship with a single AD domain in a remote, untrusted forest. This allows AD users to access resources in the remote domain without providing alternate credentials. In the case of a remote Active Directory forest, you might choose to establish an external trust in order to limit access to and from only the specific domain that you specify, rather than allowing implicit access between all domains on both sides of a transitive trust. In the GUI solution, each side of the trust is completed independently to simulate a typical real-world situation where a distinct administrative team manages each side of the trust.

See Also

"Understanding When to Create an External Trust" (*http://bit.ly/15eRL8D*) for details about external trusts; "Understanding Trust Types" (*http://bit.ly/12xBIvv*) for a detailed explanation of the available trust types

2.15. Creating a Transitive Trust Between Two AD Forests

 This recipe requires at least the Windows Server 2003 forest functional level in both forests.

Problem

You want to create a transitive trust between two AD forests. This causes all domains in both forests to trust each other without the need for additional trusts.

Solution

Using a graphical user interface

1. Open the Active Directory Domains and Trusts snap-in (*domain.msc*).
2. In the left pane, right-click the forest root domain and select Properties.
3. Click on the Trusts tab.
4. Click the New Trust button. Then click Next.
5. Enter the name of the domain and then click Next.
6. Select Forest Trust and then click Next.
7. Verify that a two-way trust direction is selected and then click Next.
8. Verify that "This domain only" is selected to create the trust and then click Next.
9. Verify that "Domain-wide authentication" is selected and then click Next.
10. Enter a complex password for the trust password and then click Next. Note that the password must meet the domain password policy.
11. Review the trust settings summary and then click Next.
12. A message indicating that a trust relationship was created successfully will appear. Click Next to configure the new trust.
13. Perform the same steps on the trusted domain. Then, on both sides, select Yes to confirm the incoming trust and then click Next.
14. A success message will appear. Click Finish.

    The trust should now appear in the Trusts tab of the domain properties.

Using a command-line interface

```
> netdom trust <Forest1DNSName> /Domain:<Forest2DNSName> /Twoway /Transitive↵
/ADD [/UserD:<Forest2AdminUser> /PasswordD:*]↵
[/UserO:<Forest1AdminUser> /PasswordO:*]
```

For example, to create a two-way forest trust from the AD forest *adatum.com* to the AD forest *othercorp.com*, use the following command:

```
> netdom trust adatum.com /Domain:othercorp.com /Twoway /Transitive
/ADD /UserD:administrator@othercorp.com /PasswordD:*↵
/UserO:administrator@adatum.com /PasswordO:*↵
```

Discussion

A new type of trust called a *forest trust* was introduced in Windows Server 2003. With a forest trust, you can define a single one-way or two-way transitive trust relationship that extends to all the domains in both forests. You may want to implement a forest trust if you merge with or acquire a company and you want all of the new company's Active Directory resources to be accessible for users in your Active Directory environment and vice versa. Figure 2-4 shows a cross-forest trust scenario. To create a forest trust, you need to use accounts from the *Enterprise Admins* group in each forest.

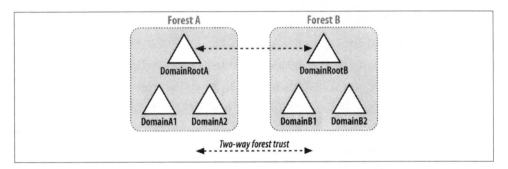

Figure 2-4. Forest trust

2.16. Creating a Shortcut Trust Between Two AD Domains

Problem

You want to create a shortcut trust between two AD domains that are in the same forest. Shortcut trusts can make the authentication process more efficient between two domains in a forest.

Solution

Using a graphical user interface

1. Open the Active Directory Domains and Trusts snap-in (*domain.msc*).
2. In the left pane, right-click the forest root domain and select Properties.
3. Click on the Trusts tab.
4. Click the New Trust button. Then click Next.
5. Enter the name of the domain and then click Next.
6. Verify that a two-way trust direction is selected and then click Next.
7. Verify that "This domain only" is selected to create the trust and then click Next.
8. Verify that "Domain-wide authentication" is selected and then click Next.
9. Enter a complex password for the trust password and then click Next. Note that the password must meet the domain password policy.
10. Review the trust settings summary and then click Next.
11. A message indicating that a trust relationship was created successfully will appear. Click Next to configure the new trust.
12. Perform the same steps on the trusted domain. Then, on both sides, select Yes to confirm the incoming trust and then click Next.
13. A success message will appear. Click Finish.
14. The trust should now appear in the Trusts tab of the domain properties.

Using a command-line interface

```
> netdom trust <Domain1DNSName> /Domain:<Domain2DNSName /Twoway /ADD↵
[/UserD:<Domain2AdminUser> /PasswordD:*]↵
[/UserO:<Domain1AdminUser> /PasswordO:*]
```

To create a shortcut trust from the *emea.adatum.com* domain to the *apac.adatum.com* domain, use the following netdom command:

```
> netdom trust emea.adatum.com /Domain:apac.adatum.com /Twoway /ADD↵
/UserD:administrator@apac.adatum.com /PasswordD:*↵
/UserO:administrator@emea.adatum.com /PasswordO:*
```

Discussion

Consider the forest shown in Figure 2-5. It has five domains in a single domain tree. For authentication requests for Domain 3 to be processed by Domain 5, the request must traverse the path from Domain 3 to Domain 2 to Domain 1 to Domain 4 to Domain 5. If you create a shortcut trust between Domain 3 and Domain 5, the authentication path is just a single hop from Domain 3 to Domain 5. To create a shortcut trust, you must be a member of the *Domain Admins* group in both domains, or a member of the *Enterprise Admins* group.

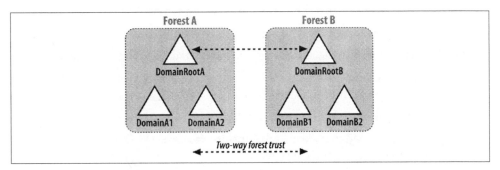

Figure 2-5. Shortcut trust

2.17. Creating a Trust to a Kerberos Realm

Problem

You want to create a trust to a Kerberos realm.

Solution

Using a graphical user interface

1. Open the Active Directory Domains and Trusts snap-in (*domain.msc*).

2. In the left pane, right-click the forest root domain and select Properties.

3. Click on the Trusts tab.

4. Click the New Trust button. Click Next.

5. Enter the name of the realm and then click Next.

6. Verify that "Realm trust" is selected and then click Next.

7. Select Transitive for the trust transitivity and then click Next.

8. Verify that a two-way trust is selected for the direction of the trust and then click Next.

9. Enter a complex password for the trust password; click Next. Note that the password must meet the domain password policy.

10. Review the trust settings summary and then click Next.

11. A success message will appear. Click Finish.

12. The trust should now appear in the Trusts tab of the domain properties.

Using a command-line interface

```
> netdom trust <ADDomainDNSName> /Domain:<KerberosRealmDNSName>↵
/Realm /ADD /PasswordT:<TrustPassword>↵
[/User0:<ADDomainAdminUser> /Password0:*]
```

The *<TrustPassword>* has to match what was set on the Kerberos side. To create a realm trust from the *adatum.com* domain to the Kerberos realm called *kerb.adatum.com*, use the following command:

```
> netdom trust adatum.com /Domain:kerb.adatum.com↵
/Realm /ADD /PasswordT:MyKerbRealmPassword↵
/User0:administrator@adatum.com /Password0:*
```

Discussion

You can create a Kerberos realm trust between an Active Directory domain and a non-Windows Kerberos v5 realm. A realm trust can be used to allow clients from the non-Windows Kerberos realm to access resources in Active Directory, and vice versa. See Recipe 15.4 for more information on MIT Kerberos interoperability with Active Directory.

See Also

"Understanding When to Create a Realm Trust" (*http://bit.ly/105Emwp*) for information about realm trusts; "Understanding Trust Types" (*http://bit.ly/12xBIvv*) for a detailed explanation of the available trust types

2.18. Viewing the Trusts for a Domain

Problem

You want to view the trusts that have been configured for a domain.

Solution

Using a graphical user interface

1. Open the Active Directory Domains and Trusts snap-in (*domain.msc*).
2. In the left pane, right-click the domain you want to view and select Properties.
3. Click on the Trusts tab.

Using a command-line interface

To enumerate domain trusts using the *netdom* utility, use the following syntax:

```
> netdom query trust /Domain:<DomainDNSName>
```

You can also use *nltest*, available from the Windows Support Tools, as follows:

```
> nltest /domain_trusts /All_Trusts
```

Using PowerShell

```
Get-ADTrust -filter *
```

If the *adatum.com* domain is configured with a two-way external trust with the *barcelona.corp* domain, running this script from *dc1.adatum.com* would produce the following output:

```
Direction                 : BiDirectional
DisallowTransivity        : False
DistinguishedName         : CN=barcelona.corp,CN=System,dc=adatum,dc=com
ForestTransitive          : True
IntraForest               : False
IsTreeParent              : False
IsTreeRoot                : False
Name                      : barcelona.corp
ObjectClass               : trustedDomain
ObjectGUID                : 98616652-c2ec-4057-a7ea-f639e1ec2680
SelectiveAuthentication   : False
SIDFilteringForestAware   : False
SIDFilteringQuarantined   : False
Source                    : dc=adatum,dc=com
Target                    : barcelona.corp
TGTDelegation             : False
TrustAttributes           : 8
TrustedPolicy             :
TrustingPolicy            :
TrustType                 : Uplevel
UplevelOnly               : False
UsesAESKeys               : False
UsesRC4Encryption         : False
```

Discussion

Using a graphical user interface

You can view the properties of a particular trust by clicking on a trust and clicking the Properties button.

Using a command-line interface

You can include the /Direct switch with *netdom* if you want to view only direct-trust relationships. If you don't use /Direct, implicit trusts that occur due to transitive trust relationships will also be listed.

The nltest command can take the following additional switches to modify the default behavior of the /domain_trusts switch:

/Primary
> Returns only the domain that the computer account you're running nltest from belongs to

/Forest
> Returns domains that are in the same forest as the primary domain

/Direct_Out
> Returns only those domains that are trusted by the primary domain

/Direct_In
> Returns only those domains that trust the primary domain

/v
> Displays domain SIDs and GUIDs

See Also

"Understanding Trusts" (*http://bit.ly/ZFEba1*) for a deep dive into Active Directory trusts

2.19. Verifying a Trust

Problem

You want to verify that a trust is working correctly. This is the first diagnostic step to take if users notify you that authentication to a remote domain appears to be failing.

Solution

Using a graphical user interface

For the Windows Server 2003, Windows Server 2008, and Windows Server 2012 versions of the Active Directory Domains and Trusts snap-in:

1. In the left pane, right-click on the trusting domain and select Properties.
2. Click the Trusts tab.
3. Click the domain that is associated with the trust you want to verify.
4. Click the Properties button.
5. Click the Validate button and select the option to validate the incoming trust or validate only the outgoing trust.

Using a command-line interface

```
> netdom trust <TrustingDomain> /Domain:<TrustedDomain> /Verify /verbose↵
[/UserO:<TrustingDomainUser> /PasswordO:*]↵
[/UserD:<TrustedDomainUser> /PasswordD:*]
```

Discussion

Verifying a trust consists of checking connectivity between the domains and determining if the shared secrets of a trust are synchronized between the two domains. It is recommended that you validate both sides of the trust. You can validate both sides of the trust by selecting the option to validate the incoming trust during the verification. Otherwise, you have to perform verification from each side independently.

Using a graphical user interface

The Active Directory Domains and Trusts screens have not changed between Windows 2003 and Windows Server 2012.

Using a command-line interface

If you want to verify a Kerberos trust, use the /Kerberos switch with the netdom command.

See Also

"Understanding Trusts" (*http://bit.ly/ZFEba1*) for a deep dive into Active Directory trusts

2.20. Resetting a Trust

Problem

You want to reset a trust password. If you've determined a trust is broken, you need to reset it, which will allow users to authenticate across it again.

Solution

Using a graphical user interface

Follow the same directions as in Recipe 2.19. The option to reset the trust will be presented only if the verification/validation did not succeed. In Windows Server 2012, if the trust validation process fails, you will be prompted to reset the trust passwords.

Using a command-line interface

```
> netdom trust <TrustingDomain> /Domain:<TrustedDomain> /Reset /verbose↵
[/UserO:<TrustingDomainUser> /PasswordO:*]↵
[/UserD:<TrustedDomainUser> /PasswordD:*]
```

Discussion

Resetting a trust synchronizes the shared secrets (i.e., passwords) for the trust. The PDC Emulators in both domains are used to synchronize the password, so they must be reachable during the reset process.

Using a command-line interface

If you are resetting a Kerberos realm trust, you'll need to specify the /PasswordT option with netdom.

See Also

Recipe 2.19 for verifying a trust

2.21. Removing a Trust

Problem

You want to remove a trust. This is commonly done when the remote domain has been decommissioned or access to it is no longer required.

Solution

Using a graphical user interface

1. Open the Active Directory Domains and Trusts snap-in (*domain.msc*).
2. In the left pane, right-click on the trusting domain and select Properties.
3. Click the Trusts tab.
4. Click on the domain that is associated with the trust you want to remove.
5. Click the Remove button.
6. Select the option to remove the trust from both domains, or the option to delete the trust only from the local domain, and then click OK.

Using a command-line interface

To remove a trust relationship using the netdom utility, use the following syntax:

```
> netdom trust <TrustingDomain> /Domain:<TrustedDomain> /Remove /verbose↵
[/UserO:<TrustingDomainUser> /PasswordO:*]↵
[/UserD:<TrustedDomainUser> /PasswordD:*]
```

To remove a trust using a combination of AdFind and AdMod, issue the following two commands:

```
> adfind -b cn=<Trusted Domain>,cn=system,<Domain DN> -dsq | admod -rm
> adfind -b cn=<TrustName>$,cn=users,<Domain DN> -dsq | admod -rm
```

> Both of these commands first use AdFind to return the object that needs to be deleted, and then use the | operator to send that object to AdMod to perform the actual deletion.

Discussion

Trusts are stored in Active Directory as two objects: a trustedDomain object in the System container and a user object in the Users container. Both of these objects need to be removed when deleting a trust. The GUI and netdom solutions take care of that in one step, but in the AdMod example, both objects needed to be explicitly deleted.

2.22. Enabling SID Filtering for a Trust

Problem

You want to enable Security Identifier (SID) filtering for a trust. By enabling SID filtering, you can keep a hacker from spoofing an SID across a trust.

Solution

Using a command-line interface

```
> netdom trust <TrustingDomain> /Domain:<TrustedDomain> /EnableSIDHistory:No↵
[/UserO:<TrustingDomainUser> /PasswordO:*]↵
[/UserD:<TrustedDomainUser> /PasswordD:*]
```

Using PowerShell to view SID filtering settings

The following PowerShell command retrieves the current SID filtering settings on a trust configured with the remote *treyresearch.net* domain:

```
Get-ADTrust treyresearch.net | FL *SID*
```

Discussion

A security vulnerability exists with the use of SID history, which is described in detail in MS KB 289243. An administrator in a trusted domain can modify the SID history for a user, which could grant her elevated privileges in the trusting domain. The risk of this exploit is relatively low due to the complexity of forging an SID, but nevertheless, you should be aware of it. To prevent this from happening you can enable SID filtering for a trust. When SID filtering is enabled, the only SIDs that are used as part of a user's token are from those domains in the trust path of the trusted domain—so if the trusted domain is *adatum.com*, which has a child domain called *emea.adatum.com*, SID filtering would accept SIDs from both the *adatum.com* domain and its child domain, *emea*. SIDs that are not a part of the trusted domain's trust path are not included, so an SID from the *barcelona.corp* would be stripped from the user's access token. SID filtering makes things more secure, but it prevents the use of SID history and can cause problems with transitive trusts and domain migrations. For example, if we migrated a user from *barcelona.corp* to *adatum.com*, that user's *barcelona.corp* SID history entry would be ignored as long as SID filtering was in place. You would need to update the access control lists (ACLs) on resources in *barcelona.corp* to point to the migrated user's *adatum.com* SID, which would allow the user to access them with SID filtering in place.

SID filtering is enabled by default on all trust relationships created in Windows 2000 Service Pack 4 and later. This can cause unexpected behavior if you create a trust relationship under an earlier Service Pack version, but then delete and re-create the trust under SP4 or later. You can disable SID filtering by running the `netdom` command with the `/EnableSIDHistory:Yes` switch.

See Also

MS KB 289243 (MS02-001: Forged SID Could Result in Elevated Privileges in Windows 2000)

2.23. Enabling Quarantine for a Trust

Problem

You want to enable Quarantine for a trust. By enabling Quarantine, you can greatly restrict the acceptable domain SIDs in a trust relationship.

Solution

Using a command-line interface

```
> netdom trust <TrustingDomain> /Domain:<TrustedDomain> /Quarantine:Yes↵
[/UserO:<TrustingDomainUser> /PasswordO:*]↵
[/UserD:<TrustedDomainUser> /PasswordD:*]
```

Discussion

A security vulnerability exists with the use of SID history, which is described in detail in MS KB 289243. An administrator in a trusted domain can modify the SID history for a user, which could grant him elevated privileges in the trusting domain. The risk of this exploit is relatively low due to the complexity in forging an SID, but nevertheless, you should be aware of it. You can put in strong restrictions in order to minimize the risk of privilege elevation by enabling Quarantine for a trust. When Quarantine is enabled, the only SIDs that are used as part of a user's token are from those domains in the trusted domain itself. So if the trusted domain is *adatum.com*, which has a child domain called *emea.adatum.com*, Quarantine will only accept SIDs from *adatum.com* itself. Even domain SIDs that are a part of the trusted domain's trust path are not included, so an SID from *emea.adatum.com* would be stripped from the user's access token. Enabling Quarantine for a trust effectively removes the transitivity of a forest trust relationship, restricting the trust relationship to only the domain that you specified when you created the trust. (This causes a forest trust to emulate the default behavior of an external trust instead.)

You can disable Quarantine on a trust relationship by running the `netdom` command again and specifying the `/Quarantine:No` switch.

2.24. Managing Selective Authentication for a Trust

Problem

You want to enable or disable Selective Authentication for a trust. By enabling Selective Authentication, you can control which computers—in a trusting domain—users in a trusted domain can access. Disabling Selective Authentication will allow users in the trusted domain to authenticate to any computer in the trusting domain.

Solution

Using a graphical user interface

To enable Selective Authentication:

1. Open the Active Directory Domains and Trusts snap-in (*domain.msc*).

2. To enable Selective Authentication for a forest trust, right-click on the forest root domain and select Properties. To enable Selective Authentication for an external trust, right-click on the domain you wish to configure and select Properties.

3. On the Trusts tab, right-click on the trust that you wish to administer and select Properties.

4. On the Authentication tab, click Selective Authentication.

5. Click OK to finish.

To disable Selective Authentication:

1. Open the Active Directory Domains and Trusts snap-in (*domain.msc*).

2. To enable forest-wide authentication for a forest trust, right-click on the forest root domain and select Properties. To enable domain-wide authentication for an external trust, right-click on the domain you wish to configure and select Properties.

3. On the Trusts tab, right-click on the trust that you wish to administer and select Properties.

4. In the case of a forest trust, on the Authentication tab click Forest-Wide Authentication. For an external trust, on the Authentication tab click Domain-Wide Authentication.

5. Click OK to finish.

To grant permissions on individual computers in the trusting domain:

1. Open the Active Directory Users and Computers snap-in (*dsa.msc*).

2. Right-click on the computer object on which you wish to grant permissions and select Properties.

3. On the Security tab, select the user or group that you want to authorize, and select the Allow checkbox next to the Allowed to Authenticate permission.

4. Click OK to finish.

Using a command-line interface

To enable Selective Authentication, use the following syntax:

```
> netdom trust <TrustingDomain> /Domain:<TrustedDomain> /SelectiveAUTH:Yes
[/UserO:<TrustingDomainUser> /PasswordO:*]
[/UserD:<TrustedDomainUser> /PasswordD:*]
```

 Use the /SelectiveAUTH:No switch to enable domain- or forest-wide authentication.

Discussion

Trust relationships since Windows Server 2003, by default, allow users in a trusted domain to authenticate to and access shared resources on any computer in the trusting domain. Selective Authentication, also known as the Authentication Firewall, will restrict access to only those computers in the trusted domain that you specifically designate. This level of increased security is particularly useful when you need to grant access to shared resources in your forest, but you need to restrict that access to only a limited set of users in the remote forest.

For users in a trusted domain or forest to be able to access resources in a trusting domain or forest, where the trust authentication setting has been set to Selective Authentication, each user must be explicitly granted the Allowed to Authenticate permission on the security descriptor of the computer objects (resource computers) that reside in the trusting domain or forest. By default, only members of the *Account Operators*, *Administrators*, *Domain Admins*, *Enterprise Admins*, and *SYSTEM* groups in the trusting domain have the ability to modify this permission.

 Enabling Selective Authentication has the potential to create a huge increase in your AD administrative overhead, and should only be enabled when the security risks justify the administrative implications.

2.25. Finding Duplicate SIDs in a Domain

Problem

You want to find any duplicate SIDs in a domain. Generally, duplicate SIDs in a domain should not exist, but it is possible in some situations, such as when the relative identifier (RID) FSMO role owner has to be seized.

Solution

Using a command-line interface

To find duplicate SIDs, run the following command, replacing *<DomainController Name>* with a domain controller or domain name:

```
> ntdsutil "sec acc man" "co to se <DomainControllerName" "check dup sid" q q
```

The following message will be returned:

```
Duplicate SID check completed successfully. Check dupsid.log for any duplicates
```

The *dupsid.log* file will be in the directory where you started *ntdsutil*.

If you want to delete any objects that have duplicate SIDs, you can use the following command:

```
> ntdsutil "sec acc man" "co to se <DomainControllerName>" "clean dup sid" q q
```

Like the check command, the clean command will generate a message like the following upon completion:

```
Duplicate SID cleanup completed successfully. Check dupsid.log for any duplicates
```

Discussion

All security principals in Active Directory have an SID, which is used to uniquely identify the object in the Windows security system. There are two parts of an SID: the domain identifier and the RID. Domain controllers are allocated a RID pool from the RID FSMO for the domain. When a new security principal (user, group, or computer) is created, the domain controller takes an RID from its pool to generate an SID for the account.

In some rare circumstances, such as when the RID master role is seized, overlapping RID pools can be allocated, which can ultimately lead to duplicate SIDs. Having duplicate SIDs is a potentially hazardous problem because a user, group, or computer could gain access to sensitive data it was never intended to have access to.

See Also

MS KB 816099 (How to Find and Clean Up Duplicate Security Identifiers with Ntdsutil in Windows Server 2003)

2.26. Adding Additional Fields to Active Directory Users and Computers

Problem

You want to add to the list of attributes by which you can search and sort records within the ADUC (Active Directory Users and Computers) MMC snap-in (*dsa.msc*).

Solution

Using a graphical user interface

In this example, we will add the operating system service-pack-level attributes of computer objects to ADUC to allow you to search and sort by these fields:

1. Open ADSI Edit.
2. If an entry for the Configuration NC is not already displayed, do the following:
   a. Right-click on ADSI Edit in the right pane and click "Connect to."
   b. Under "Select a well-known naming context," select Configuration. Click Advanced if you need to specify alternate credentials, and then click OK to create the connection.
   c. In the left pane, click on cn=DisplaySpecifiers and then cn=409. Right-click on the container and select Properties.

 If you are using a locale other than one that uses US English, specify the appropriate locale number in place of cn=409, using the reference listed by Microsoft (*http://bit.ly/10xdxLV*).

3. Right-click on cn=computerDisplay and select Properties.
4. Double-click on attributeDisplayNames. Type operatingSystemServicePack, Operating System Service Pack, and click Add.
5. Click Apply, followed by OK.

Using a command-line interface

First create an LDIF file containing the following information and save it as *modi fy_display_specifiers.ldif*:

```
dn: cn=computer-display,cn=409,cn=DisplaySpecifiers,
    cn=Configuration, <ForestRootDN>
changetype: modify
add: attributeDisplayNames
attributeDisplayNames: operatingSystemServicePack,Operating System Service Pack
-
```

Then run the following command:

```
> ldifde -v -i -f modify_display_specifiers.ldf
```

You can also modify this information using a combination of AdFind and AdMod, as follows:

```
> adfind -config -rb cn=computer-display,cn=409,cn=DisplaySpecifiers |↵
admod "attributeDisplayNames:+:operatingSystemServicePack,Operating System↵
Service Pack"
```

Discussion

When working within the Active Directory Users and Computers MMC snap-in, there are a number of default attributes for each type of object that you can use to either search or sort on. Computer objects, for example, allow you to search and sort by the computer name, description, manager, operating system, and pre-Windows 2000 computer name. Once you add a new attribute to the display specifiers, you can access it by opening ADUC, right-clicking on a container, and clicking on Find. Select Computers in the drop-down box next to Find, and click on Advanced. When you click on Field, you'll see the new field that you just added; you can now use it to search for objects within the ADUC snap-in.

See Also

Recipe 4.14 for more on modifying an object; MSDN: Attribute-Display-Names [AD Schema]; MSDN: PutEx Method [ADSI]

## CHAPTER 3

Domain Controllers, Global Catalogs, and FSMOs

3.0. Introduction

Domain controllers are servers that host an Active Directory domain and provide authentication and directory services to clients. A domain controller (DC) can only be authoritative (i.e., it can only process authentication requests) for a single domain, but it can store partial read-only copies of objects in other domains in the forest if it is enabled as a global catalog server. All domain controllers in a forest also host a copy of the Configuration and Schema naming contexts (NCs), which are replicated to all domain controllers in a forest.

Active Directory domain controllers are fully multimaster in nature, meaning that updates to the directory (with a few exceptions, which we'll discuss next) can originate on any domain controller in a forest. However, some tasks are sufficiently sensitive in nature that they cannot be distributed to all DCs, due to the potential of significant issues arising from more than one DC performing the same update simultaneously. For example, if two different domain controllers made conflicting updates to the schema, the impact could be severe and could result in data loss or an unusable directory. For this reason, Active Directory uses Flexible Single Master Operation (FSMO, pronounced "fiz-mo") roles. For each FSMO role, only one domain controller acts as the role owner and performs the tasks associated with the role. These roles are termed "single master" because only a single DC can hold a FSMO role at any one time, but they are "flexible" because a single physical server can host multiple FSMOs, and a FSMO role can be transferred from one DC to another, largely without repercussion. In each Active Directory forest there are two FSMO roles that are unique across an entire forest and three FSMO roles that appear within each domain. So, in the case of a forest containing three domains, there would be two forest-wide FSMO role holders and *nine* domain-wide FSMO role holders, three for each of the three domains. See Recipe 3.29 for more information on FSMO roles.

In Windows Server 2008, Microsoft introduced the Read-Only Domain Controller, or RODC, to improve security for organizations that need to deploy DCs in branch offices or other remote locations where the physical or logical security of the DC might not be completely assured. An RODC will receive replication updates from writable DCs in the same domain, but domain controllers will not replicate from an RODC. See Recipe 3.2 for more information on RODCs.

The Anatomy of a Domain Controller

Each domain controller is represented in Active Directory by several objects; the two main ones are a computer object and an nTDSDSA object. The computer object is necessary because a domain controller needs to be represented as a security principal just like any other type of computer in Active Directory. The default location in a domain for domain controller computer objects is the Domain Controllers organizational unit (OU) at the root of the domain. They can be moved to a different OU, but it is highly recommended that you don't move them. One of the reasons not to move them is because any DCs that you move outside the domain controller's OU will not receive the same Group Policy Object settings as those within the OU, which can lead to unpredictable behavior on your network. Table 3-1 contains some useful attributes of domain controller computer objects.

Table 3-1. Attributes of domain controller computer objects

Attribute	Description
dnsHostName	Fully qualified DNS name of the DC.
msDS-AdditionalDnsHostName	Contains the old DNS name of a renamed DC.
msDS-AdditionalSamAccountName	Contains the old NetBIOS name of a renamed DC.
operatingSystem	Text description of the operating system running on the DC.
operatingSystemServicePack	Service pack version installed on the DC.
operatingSystemVersion	Numeric version of the operating system installed on the DC.
sAMAccountName	NetBIOS-style name of the DC.
serverReferenceBL	DN of the DC's server object contained under the Sites container in the Configuration NC.
servicePrincipalName	List of SPNs supported by the DC.

Domain controllers are also represented by several objects under the `Sites` container in the Configuration NC. The `Sites` container stores objects that are needed to create a site topology, including `site`, `subnet`, `sitelink`, and `server` objects. The site topology is necessary so that domain controllers can replicate data efficiently around the network as well as localize authentication traffic. See Chapter 11 for more information on sites and replication.

Each domain controller has an `nTDSDSA` object that is subordinate to the domain controller's `server` object in the site it is a member of. For example, if the DC1 domain controller were part of the RTP site, its `nTDSDSA` object would be located here:

```
cn=NTDS Settings,cn=DC1,cn=RTP,cn=sites,cn=configuration,dc=adatum,dc=com
```

Table 3-2 lists some of the interesting attributes that are stored with `nTDSDSA` objects.

Table 3-2. Attributes of domain controller nTDSDSA objects

Attribute	Description
hasMasterNCs	List of DNs for the naming contexts the DC is authoritative for. This does not include application partitions.
hasPartialReplicaNCs	List of DNs for the naming contexts the DC has a partial read-only copy of.
msDS-HasDomainNCs	The DN of the domain the DC is authoritative for.
msDS-HasMasterNCs	List of DNs for the naming contexts (domain, configuration, and schema) and application partitions the DC is authoritative for.
options	If the low-order bit of this attribute is set, the domain controller stores a copy of the global catalog.
invocationID	GUID that is assigned to the Active Directory database itself when the first domain controller is initially installed. When the first DC is initially installed, the `invocationID` value is the same as the `objectGUID` for the DC itself; however, the `invocationID` changes whenever a restore operation is performed or when the DC is configured to host an application partition.

RODCs also maintain a number of RODC-specific attributes, primarily relating to the Password Replication Policy (PRP) that is configured for each RODC in an Active Directory forest. As discussed previously, writable DCs will store an entire copy of the Domain NC on the hard drive of each DC, which creates a significant liability if the physical or logical security of one of these DCs is compromised. By contrast, an RODC will store *most* information from the Domain NC, but by default will not store passwords and other security secrets for any Active Directory user account. (A default RODC will contain only secrets for the local Administrator and the local krbtgt accounts, both of which are required for the RODC to function.) An Active Directory administrator can configure a Password Replication Policy for a single RODC or for all RODCs in a domain that will specify the following:

- Users and computers whose password secrets are permitted to be cached on individual RODCs or on all RODCs in a domain
- Users and computers whose password secrets are *never* permitted to be cached on individual RODCs, or on all RODCs in a domain

In order to maintain this information, each RODC contains a number of attributes relating to the Password Replication Policy. Each RODC will also maintain information pertaining to which user and computer accounts' password secrets have *actually* been cached by a particular RODC, instead of merely being *permitted* to do so.

Table 3-3 lists some of the interesting attributes pertaining to Password Replication Policy that are stored within an RODC's computer object.

Table 3-3. Interesting attributes of a Read-Only Domain Controller

Attribute	Description
msDS-Reveal-OnDemandGroup	Accounts that are allowed to be cached on the RODC.
msDS-NeverRevealGroup	Accounts that are not allowed to be cached on the RODC.
msDS-AuthenticatedAtDC	A forward link indicating a list of RODCs through which a user has successfully authenticated to a full DC.
msDS-AuthenticatedToAccountList	A backlink indicating a list of accounts that have successfully authenticated to a full DC through the RODC.

3.1. Promoting a Server to a Domain Controller

Problem

You want to promote a server to a domain controller. You may need to promote a server to a domain controller to initially create a domain in an Active Directory forest, or to add additional domain controllers to a domain for load balancing and fault tolerance.

Solution

The following process will promote a server as an additional domain controller in an existing domain. On a Windows Server 2012 computer:

1. Add the Active Directory Domain Services role. After the role installation, a notification will appear within Server Manager.
2. Click Notifications and then click "Promote this server to a domain controller."
3. Select the "Add a domain controller to an existing domain" option. Specify the desired domain and credentials (or accept the default values if appropriate) and then click Next.

4. Select the desired domain controller options: "Domain Name System (DNS) server," "Global Catalog (GC)," and/or "Read only domain controller (RODC)."

5. Type a Directory Services Restore Mode (DSRM) password and then click Next.

6. Select the desired additional options: install from media—if installing from media—and replication from a specific domain controller. Then click Next.

7. Specify the desired database, logfiles, and *SYSVOL* paths and then click Next.

8. Review all of the options and then click Next.

9. After a successful prerequisite check, click Install to complete the promotion. Note that the server will automatically reboot after completing the promotion process.

Discussion

Promoting a server to a domain controller is the process where the server becomes authoritative for an Active Directory domain. When you initiate the promotion, a wizard interface walks you through a series of screens that collect information about the forest and domain into which to promote the server. There are several options for promoting a server to domain controller status:

- Promoting into a new forest (see Recipe 2.1)
- Promoting into a new domain tree or child domain (see Recipe 2.3)
- Promoting into an existing domain

A server can also be promoted by using PowerShell. See the following section for links to some recipes with PowerShell steps for domain controller promotion.

See Also

Recipe 2.1 for creating a new forest; Recipe 2.3 for creating a new domain; Recipe 3.2; Recipe 3.7

3.2. Promoting a Server to a Read-Only Domain Controller

Problem

You want to promote a server to an RODC in a Windows Server 2012 domain.

 This recipe requires that at least one writable Windows Server 2008 or newer domain controller is present in the domain.

Solution

1. First, add the Active Directory Domain Services role using Server Manager.
2. Click "Promote this server to a domain controller" in the notification area.
3. Verify that the "Add a domain controller to an existing domain" option is selected.
4. Type the domain name and domain credentials and then click Next.
5. Select the "Read only domain controller (RODC)" option, enter the Directory Services Restore Mode (DSRM) password, and then click Next.
6. Select a user account for delegation. Verify the accounts that are allowed to replicate passwords and the accounts that are denied from replicating passwords. Click Next.
7. Select a domain controller to replicate from and then click Next.
8. Verify the AD DS database locations and then click Next.
9. Review the summary and then click Next.
10. After the prerequisites have been verified, click Install to begin the promotion.

    The server will automatically restart after replication is complete.

Discussion

In order to add a Read-Only Domain Controller to an Active Directory domain, the domain must be running at the Windows Server 2003 or later domain functional mode, and at least one writable Windows Server 2008 or later domain controller must be available, since an RODC will only accept replication traffic from a 2008 or later writable DC.

To further customize the behavior of an RODC installation, you can select the Advanced installation option, which will allow you to install an RODC using IFM media, as well as customizing the Password Replication Policy. You can also automate RODC installation by using an *unattend.txt* file as described in a later recipe.

You can also use the `Install-ADDSDomainController` PowerShell cmdlet to promote a server as an RODC.

See Also

Recipe 3.3; Recipe 3.4; Recipe 3.5; Recipe 3.7

3.3. Performing a Two-Stage RODC Installation

Problem

You want to perform a two-stage promotion of a server to an RODC in a Windows Server 2012 domain.

 This recipe requires that at least one writable Windows Server 2008 or later domain controller is present in the domain.

Solution

The first stage of the two-stage installation process is performed from a writable Windows Server 2012 domain controller, using the following steps.

 The server designated for configuration as an RODC must be joined to a workgroup prior to the start of this process; if the computer is joined to the domain as a member server, these steps will fail. The server must also be configured with the same name that you will specify in the following steps.

1. From Active Directory Users and Computers, right-click the Domain Control lers OU and then click "Pre-create Read only Domain Controller account."
2. When the Active Directory Domain Services Installation Wizard appears, click Next to begin.
3. Specify the account credentials or accept the default settings by using the currently logged on user credentials, and then click Next.
4. Enter the desired computer name of the RODC and then click Next.
5. Select the site location for the RODC and then click Next.
6. Select the additional options for DNS server and global catalog services and then click Next.
7. Add the user or group that will have local administrative rights to the RODC and then click Next.
8. Review the selections on the summary screen and then click Next.
9. After the successful installation of the RODC, click Finish to close the wizard.

The second stage of the RODC installation will be completed from the console of the server that is to be configured as an RODC, using the following steps:

1. Click "Promote this server to a domain controller" in the Server Manager notification area and then click Next.

2. Enter the parent domain name and credentials and click Next.

3. Verify that the "Use existing RODC account" option is selected. Enter a password for DSRM and then click Next.

4. Specify a DC to replicate from and then click Next.

5. Specify the locations for the database, logfiles, and *SYSVOL*, and then click Next.

6. Review the options and then click Next.

7. After the prerequisites have been successfully checked, click Install to begin promotion.

8. The server will automatically reboot after completion.

Discussion

When deploying RODCs to remote locations, you have the ability to perform a two-stage installation in which you pre-create the RODC's domain controller account. Once this first stage is completed, an on-site administrator can complete the installation without requiring elevated rights within Active Directory. This *Admin Role Separation* feature allows you to configure one or more users or groups as local administrators of an individual RODC, without granting administrative privileges within the Active Directory domain itself.

When pre-creating the RODC computer account, you can select the Advanced installation option to customize the Password Replication Policy for the RODC prior to deployment.

See Also

Recipe 3.4; Chapters 6 and 7 for more on managing users and groups

3.4. Modifying the Password Replication Policy

Problem

You wish to modify the Password Replication Policy on a Read-Only Domain Controller to control which user and computer passwords can and cannot be cached on a particular RODC.

Solution

Using a graphical user interface

1. Open Active Directory Users and Computers and then select the built-in `Domain Controllers` OU.
2. Locate the desired RODC, right-click it, and then click Properties.
3. Select the Password Replication Policy tab.
4. Click Add. Then click the "Allow passwords for the account to replicate to this RODC" option. Click OK.
5. Enter the user or group that you will cache passwords on the RODC and then click OK.
6. Click OK to complete the process.

Using a command-line interface

To add a user or group to the "Allowed to Cache" list, use the following syntax:

```
repadmin /prp add <DomainControllerName> allow "<GroupName>"
```

To remove a user or group from the "Allowed to Cache" list, use the following syntax:

```
repadmin /prp delete <DomainControllerName> allow "<GroupName>"
```

To add a user or group to the "Denied to Cache" list, use the following syntax:

```
repadmin /prp add <DomainControllerName> deny "<GroupName>"
```

Discussion

A separate Password Replication Policy can be maintained individually on each Read-Only Domain Controller; this is implemented by the addition of several attributes on each RODC that control which users' passwords can and cannot be cached on the RODC in question. It is good practice to manage these attributes using security groups rather than individual users or computers, as this makes for a much more simplified management model. By default, the following domain groups are added to the Password Replication Policy of each RODC in the domain:

- `msDS-NeverRevealGroup`
  - Account operators
  - Administrators
  - Backup operators
  - Denied RODC Password Replication Group

— Server operators

- msDS-RevealOnDemandGroup

  — Allowed RODC Password Replication Group

When Windows evaluates the Password Replication Policy, a "Deny" setting would override an "Allow" setting; for example, if a user is a member of two security groups that are configured with contradictory settings. As with most aspects of Windows security, the "Keep It Simple" principle should be followed whenever possible.

Using a command-line interface

You can modify the password caching policy on all RODCs in a single command by using an asterisk (*) in place of the RODC hostname. The asterisk is a wildcard character that represents any hostname. It can be combined with characters before or after. An example is using DC* to represent all RODCs that have a hostname starting with "DC."

See Also

TechNet article on the repadmin command (*http://bit.ly/121zl6A*); Chapter 4 for more on searching and updating Active Directory; Chapters 6 and 7 for more on managing users and groups

3.5. Promoting a Server to a Windows Server 2012 Domain Controller from Media

 This recipe requires that the server being promoted is running Windows Server 2012.

Problem

You want to promote a server to be a new domain controller using a backup from another domain controller as the initial source of the Active Directory database instead of replicating the entire *NTDS.DIT* file and *SYSVOL* over the network.

Solution

From a DC, run the *ntdsutil* program.

1. From *ntdsutil*, run the following commands:

   a. activate instance ntds

b. `ifm`

c. `create sysvol full <PathToSaveData>`

2. Copy the media from the saved located to the new server that will be promoted.

3. Add the Active Directory Domain Services role. After the role installation, a notification will appear within Server Manager.

4. Click Notifications and then click "Promote this server to a domain controller."

5. Select the "Add a domain controller to an existing domain" option. Specify the desired domain and credentials (or accept the default values if appropriate) and then click Next.

6. Select the desired domain controller options: "Domain Name System (DNS) server," "Global Catalog (GC)," and/or "Read only domain controller (RODC)." Note that a full backup is not necessary if you are planning to promote a server to an RODC (instead, you would use `create sysvol RODC` rather than `create sysvol full`).

7. Type a Directory Services Restore Mode (DSRM) password and then click Next.

8. Select the desired additional options, including the Install from Media option. Type the path to the IFM files and then specify the replication from a specific domain controller if desired. Then click Next.

9. Specify the desired database, logfiles, and *SYSVOL* paths and then click Next.

10. Review all of the options and then click Next.

11. After a successful prerequisite check, click Install to complete the promotion. Note that the server will automatically reboot after completing the promotion process.

Discussion

The ability to promote a domain controller using the System State backup of another domain controller was first introduced in Windows Server 2003. Without the Install from Media option, a new domain controller has to replicate the entire *NTDS.DIT* Active Directory database file and *SYSVOL* folder over a network connection, object by object, from an existing domain controller. For organizations with a sizeable Active Directory DIT file and/or very poor network connectivity to a remote site, replicating the full contents over the network presented challenges. Under these conditions, the promotion process could take a prohibitively long time to complete. With the Install from Media option, the initial domain controller promotion process can be substantially quicker. After you've done the initial installation from media, the new domain controller will replicate any changes that have been made to the Active Directory database since the backup media was created.

Be sure that the age of the backup files you are using is significantly less than your AD forest's tombstone lifetime. If you install a domain controller using backup files that are older than the tombstone lifetime value, you could run into issues with deleted objects being reinjected into the Active Directory database after their tombstone lifetime has expired.

See Also

Chapter 16 for more on backing up Active Directory; Recipe 16.24 for modifying the tombstone lifetime of a domain; MS KB 216993 (Useful Shelf Life of a System-State Backup of Active Directory)

3.6. Demoting a Domain Controller

Problem

You want to demote a Windows Server 2012 domain controller from a domain.

Solution

Using a graphical user interface

1. In Server Manager, click the Manage menu and then click Remove Roles and Features.

2. Click Next on the "Before you begin" page, if applicable.

3. Select the destination server that you want to demote and then click Next.

4. Deselect the Active Directory Domain Services role. In the corresponding pop-up dialog box, click Remove Features to also remove the management tools.

5. A validation process will display an error indicating that the domain controller must be demoted before the Active Directory Domain Services role can be removed. Click "Demote this domain controller" in the validation box.

6. Specify credentials to perform the operation or accept the default of the currently logged on user, and then click Next.

7. Click to select the "Proceed with removal" option and then click Next.

8. If you want to retain the domain controller metadata, select the option to retain. Click Next.

9. Type in and confirm a new password for the local Administrator account. Click Next.

10. Review the options and then click Demote.

Using PowerShell

1. Open PowerShell on the domain controller to be demoted.
2. Run the `Uninstall-ADDSDomainController` command.
3. Supply a new password for the local Administrator account.
4. Type Y and press Enter to confirm the operation. Note that the server will reboot after completing the demotion process.

Discussion

Before demoting a domain controller, you first need to ensure that all of the FSMO roles have been transferred to other servers; otherwise, they will be transferred to random domain controllers that may not be optimal for your installation. (Managing FSMO role holders is discussed in Recipe 3.29.) Also, if the DC is a global catalog server or running a service such as DNS, WINS, DHCP, and so on, ensure that you have sufficient GCs and other infrastructure servers elsewhere in your forest that can handle the increased load.

It is important to demote a domain controller before decommissioning or rebuilding it so that its associated objects in Active Directory are removed, its SRV locator resource records are dynamically removed, and replication with the other domain controllers is not interrupted. If a domain controller does not successfully demote, or if you do not get the chance to demote it because of some type of hardware failure, see Recipe 2.4 for removing a domain from Active Directory and Recipe 3.6 for instructions on manually removing a domain controller from Active Directory.

See Also

Recipe 2.4; Recipe 3.6; Recipe 3.10 for removing an unsuccessfully demoted domain controller; Recipe 3.22 for disabling the global catalog; Recipe 3.29; Recipe 3.30 for transferring FSMO roles

3.7. Automating the Promotion or Demotion of a Domain Controller

Problem

You want to automate the installation or removal of a domain controller.

Solution

You can automate the promotion of a domain controller by using PowerShell. Use the
`Install-ADDSDomainController` cmdlet, as shown in the following example:

```
Import-Module ADDSDeployment
Install-ADDSDomainController↵
-CreateDNSDelegation↵
-Credential (Get-Credential)↵
-CriticalReplicationOnly:$false↵
-DatabasePath "D:\NTDS\DB"↵
-LogPath "E:\NTDS\Logs"↵
-DomainName "adatum.com"↵
-InstallDNS:$true↵
-SiteName "Default-First-Site-Name"↵
-SYSVOLPath "C:\Windows\SYSVOL"↵
-Force:$true
```

You can automate the demotion of a domain controller by using the `Uninstall-ADDSDomainController` cmdlet. The cmdlet can be run locally, with the only requirement being to enter a local administrator password, or it can be run against a remote domain controller as noted in the following section.

Discussion

To remotely install a domain controller by using PowerShell, use the `Invoke-Command` cmdlet to kick off a command on a remote computer, as shown in the following syntax:

```
Invoke-Command {<PowerShell command>} -ComputerName <RemoteHost>
```

See Also

"Create an Answer File for Unattended Domain Controller Installation" (*http://bit.ly/YjNVWk*)

3.8. Troubleshooting Domain Controller Promotion or Demotion Problems

Problem

You are having problems promoting or demoting a domain controller and you want to troubleshoot it.

Solution

The best sources of information about the status of promotion or demotion problems are the *Dcpromo.log* and *Dcpromoui.log* files contained in the *%SystemRoot%\Debug* folder on the server. The *Dcpromo.log* file captures the input entered into *dcpromo* and logs the information that is displayed as *dcpromo* progresses. The *Dcpromoui.log* file is much more detailed and captures discrete actions that occur during *dcpromo* processing, including any user input. A sample *dcpromoui.log* file might look something like this:

```
dcpromoui 404.554 0000 11:09:01.479 opening log file↵
C:\Windows\debug\dcpromoui.log dcpromoui 404.554 0001 11:09:01.479↵
C:\Windows\system32\wsmprovhost.exe dcpromoui 404.554 0002 11:09:01.479↵
file timestamp 07/25/2012 20:08:53.059 dcpromoui 404.554 0003 11:09:01.479↵
C:\Windows\system32\dcpromocmd.dll dcpromoui 404.554 0004 11:09:01.479↵
file timestamp 07/25/2012 20:05:25.050 dcpromoui 404.554 0005 11:09:01.479↵
local time 09/27/2012 11:09:01.479 dcpromoui 404.554 0006 11:09:01.480↵
running Windows NT 6.2 build 9200  (BuildLab:9200.win8_rtm.120725-1247) amd64↵
...
dcpromoui AD0.BD0 087D 20:03:51.337    exitCode = 55
dcpromoui AD0.BD0 087E 20:03:51.337   Enter State::UnbindFromReplicationPartnetDC
dcpromoui AD0.BD0 087F 20:03:51.368 closing log
```

Additionally, *dcdiag* contains two tests that can aid in troubleshooting promotion problems. The *dcpromo* test reports anything it finds that could impede the promotion process. The *RegisterInDNS* test checks whether the server can register records in DNS. Here is an example of running both commands to test against the *adatum.com* domain (note that the /ReplicaDC parameter is specific to a scenario where you want to add an additional domain controller to an existing domain):

```
> dcdiag /test:dcpromo /DnsDomain:adatum.com /ReplicaDC /test:RegisterInDNS
```

Discussion

In most cases, the level of detail provided by *Dcpromoui.log* should be sufficient to pinpoint any problems, but you can increase logging if necessary. To enable the highest level of logging available, set the following registry value to FF0003: HKLM\Software\Microsoft\Windows\CurrentVersion\AdminDebug. You can confirm that this mask took effect by running a promotion again, checking *Dcpromoui.log*, and searching for "logging mask."

If *dcdiag* does not return sufficient information, the Network Monitor (*netmon*) program is very handy for getting a detailed understanding of the network traffic that is being generated and any errors that are being returned. Network Monitor is available as a free download from the Microsoft website. Using Network Monitor, you can identify what other servers a DC is communicating with or if it is timing out when attempting to perform certain queries or updates.

See Also

MS KB 221254 (Registry Settings for Event Detail in the Dcpromoui.log File); "Active Directory Diagnostic Logging" (*http://bit.ly/166jhF1*)

3.9. Verifying the Promotion of a Domain Controller

Problem

You want to verify that a domain controller has been successfully promoted within an Active Directory domain.

Solution

Using a command-line interface

```
> dcdiag  /test:replications
> dcdiag  /s:<DCName> /test:knowsofroleholders
> dcdiag  /s:<DCName> /test:fsmocheck
```

Discussion

Once you've installed a domain controller, there are several steps that you can take to ensure that the promotion process has completed successfully. Since Windows Server 2008, *dcdiag.exe* has been built directly into the AD DS binaries; *netdiag.exe* is no longer supported. Regardless of the version of the server operating system, *dcdiag* and *netdiag* can perform a number of diagnostic tests, including the following:

- Verify that all necessary DNS records have been registered and are present on the DNS server.
- Check the domain membership for the newly promoted computer.
- Confirm that the new DC can communicate with other DCs in the domain.
- Confirm that the new DC is replicating with other DCs.
- Verify that the new DC can communicate with all of the FSMO role holders.

In addition, you can verify a successful domain controller promotion by verifying that it is responding on TCP ports 389 and 3268, running *dcdiag /replsum*, confirming that the *SYSVOL* directory has been shared, as well as checking the Directory Service log in the Event Viewer for any errors or warnings.

See Also

"Dcdiag" (*http://bit.ly/100DTKj*)

3.10. Removing an Unsuccessfully Demoted Domain Controller

Problem

You want to manually remove a domain controller from Active Directory if the demotion process was unsuccessful or you are unable to bring a domain controller back online after a hardware or software failure.

Solution

Use the following steps to remove a domain controller:

1. Go to the Windows command line and type `ntdsutil`.

2. From the *ntdsutil* menu, type **metadata cleanup**.

3. Type `remove selected server cn=<ServerName>,cn=Servers,cn=<SiteName>, cn=Sites,cn=Configuration,dc=<ForestRootDomain>` to remove the server metadata associated with *dc1.adatum.com*.

If successful, a message will state that the removal was complete. However, if you receive an error message, check to see if the server's nTDSDSA object (e.g., `cn=NTDSSet tings,cn=DC5,cn=Servers,cn=MySite1,cn=Sites,cn=Configuration,dc=ada tum,dc=com`) is present. If so, the demotion process may have already removed it, and it will take time for the change to replicate. If it is still present, try the *ntdsutil* procedure again, and if that doesn't work, manually remove that object and the parent object (e.g., `cn=DC5`) using ADSI Edit or another tool. (Deleting Active Directory objects is discussed in Recipe 4.24.)

Follow these additional steps to remove all traces of the domain controller:

1. Delete the CNAME record from DNS for *<GUID>*._msdcs.*<RootDomainDNSName>*, where *<GUID>* is the objectGUID for the server's nTDSDSA object as obtained via ADSI Edit or a command-line tool such as AdFind. You'll need to manually check and delete any associated SRV records. Delete any A and PTR records that exist for the server. When using Microsoft DNS, you can use the DNS MMC snap-in to accomplish these tasks.

2. Delete the computer object for the server under `ou=DomainControl lers,<DomainDN>`. This can be done using the Active Directory Users and Computers snap-in or PowerShell. (Deleting objects is described in Chapter 4.)

3. Delete the FRS Member object for the computer contained under `cn=DomainSys temVolume (SYSVOL share),cn=file replication service,cn=sys tem,<DomainDN>`. This can be done using the Active Directory Users and Computers

snap-in when Advanced Features has been selected from the View menu (so the System container will be displayed), or with the AdMod tool.

4. Delete the server object associated with the failed domain controller in the Active Directory Sites and Services MMC.

Discussion

If the domain controller that you are forcibly removing from Active Directory is the last one in an Active Directory domain, you'll need to manually remove the domain from the forest as well. See Recipe 2.5 for more information on removing orphaned domains.

Here are some additional issues to consider when you forcibly remove a domain controller:

- Seize any FSMO roles the DC may have had to another domain controller. (Managing FSMO roles is discussed later in this chapter.)
- If the DC was a global catalog server, ensure there is another global catalog server configured in the site that can handle the increased workload.
- If the DC was a DNS server, ensure that there is another DNS server that can handle the additional name resolution queries, and be sure that your clients are configured to use the correct name server.
- If the DC was the RID FSMO master, check to make sure duplicate SIDs have not been issued (see Recipe 2.25).
- Check to see if the DC hosted any application partitions, and if so, consider making another server a replica server for those application partitions (see Recipe 16.8).

If the (former) domain controller that you forcibly removed is still active or otherwise returns to your network, you should strongly consider reinstalling the operating system to avoid potential conflicts from the server trying to reinsert itself back into Active Directory.

See Also

Recipe 2.5 for removing an orphaned domain; Recipe 2.25; Recipe 3.31 for seizing FSMO roles; Recipe 4.24; Recipe 16.8

3.11. Renaming a Domain Controller

Problem

You want to rename a domain controller.

Solution

Your first step in renaming a domain controller is as follows, where *<NewName>* is a fully qualified domain name (FQDN):

```
> netdom computername <CurrentName> /Add:<NewName>
```

The new name will be automatically replicated throughout Active Directory and DNS. Once you've verified that the new name has replicated (which may take some time depending on your replication topology), you can designate it as the domain controller's primary name as follows, and then reboot the domain controller:

```
> netdom computername <CurrentName> /MakePrimary:<NewName>
```

 See Chapter 12 for information on verifying Active Directory replication.

Once you're satisfied that your clients are accessing the domain controller using its new name, you can remove the old computer name using the following syntax:

```
> netdom computername <NewName> /remove:<OldName>
```

Discussion

An option in the *netdom* utility allows an alternate computer name to be associated with a computer in Active Directory. Once you've added a new name, you can then set that name to be the primary name, thereby renaming the computer.

The old name effectively remains with the domain controller until you remove it, which can be done using the `netdom computername /Remove:<Name>` command. You should reboot the server before removing the old name. The old names are stored in the `msDS-AdditionalDnsHostName` and `msDS-AdditionalSamAccountName` attributes on the domain controller's `computer` object.

If the domain controller has any version of Microsoft Exchange installed on it, renaming the domain controller is unsupported.

3.12. Finding the Domain Controllers for a Domain

Problem

You want to find the domain controllers in a domain.

Solution

Using a graphical user interface

1. Open the Active Directory Users and Computers snap-in (*dsa.msc*).
2. Right-click on the target domain and select Find.
3. In the Find drop-down box, select Computers.
4. In the Role drop-down box, select Writable Domain Controllers or Read-Only Domain Controllers.
5. Click Find Now. The list of domain controllers for the domain will be present in the search results pane.

Using PowerShell

To find all of the domain controllers in the *adatum.com* domain, use the following command:

```
Get-ADDomainController -Filter { domain -eq "adatum.com" } | select Name
```

Discussion

There are several ways to get a list of domain controllers for a domain. The GUI solution simply uses the built-in "Find" functionality of the Active Directory Users and Computers MMC. The PowerShell solution uses a dedicated cmdlet for getting information about domain controllers.

For yet another solution, see Recipe 3.26 to find out how to query DNS to get the list of domain controllers for a domain.

See Also

Recipe 3.26 for finding domain controllers via DNS

3.13. Finding the Closest Domain Controller

Problem

You want to find the closest domain controller for a particular domain.

Solution

Using a command-line interface

The following command finds the closest domain controller in the specified domain (*<DomainDNSName>*); that is, a domain controller that is located in the same site or in the closest site if a local DC is not available. By default, it will return the closest DC for the computer from which *nltest* is being run, but you can optionally use the /server option to target a remote host. If you are interested in finding a DC within a particular site regardless of whether it is the closest DC to you, you can also optionally specify the /site option to find a domain controller that belongs to a particular site:

```
> nltest/dsgetdc:<DomainDNSName> [/site:<SiteName>] [/server:<ClientName>]
```

Using PowerShell

```
Get-ADDomainController -Discover
```

The preceding command will discover the closest domain controller from the computer where the command is run.

Discussion

The DC locator process defines how clients find the closest domain controller. The process uses the site topology stored in Active Directory to calculate the site a particular client is in. After the client site has been identified, it is a matter of finding a domain controller that is a member of that same site or that is covering for that site.

The Microsoft DsGetDcName Directory Services API method implements the DC Locator process, but unfortunately it cannot be used directly from a scripting language, such as VBScript. The nltest /dsgetdc command is also a wrapper around the DsGetDcName method, and it is a handy tool when troubleshooting client issues related to finding an optimal domain controller.

Using a command-line interface

You can use *nltest* to return the closest domain controller that is serving a particular function. Some of the available functions include a global catalog server (/GC switch), time server (/TIMESERV switch), KDC (/KDC switch), and PDC (/PDC switch). Run nltest /? from a command line for the complete list.

Using PowerShell

Similar to *nltest*, you can specify additional criteria for finding a domain controller by using the -Filter parameter. The following are some of the most used filters:

```
IsGlobalCatalog
IsReadOnly
Site
Service
```

3.14. Finding a Domain Controller's Site

Problem

You need to determine the site of which a domain controller is a member.

Solution

Using a command-line interface

To retrieve the site for a particular DC, use the following command syntax:

```
> nltest /dsgetsite /server:<DomainControllerName>
```

 The nltest /dsgetsite command is a wrapper around the DsGetSi teName method.

Using PowerShell

```
Get-ADDomainController -Server <DomainControllerName> | FL Name,Site
```

Discussion

Domain controllers are represented in the site topology by a server object and a child nTDSDSA object. Actually, any type of server can conceivably have a server object; it is the nTDSDSA object that differentiates domain controllers from other types of servers. You'll often see the nTDSDSA object of a domain controller used to refer to that domain controller elsewhere in Active Directory. For example, the fSMORoleOwner attribute that represents the FSMO owners contains the distinguished name of the nTDSDSA object of the domain controller that is holding the role.

Finding a domain controller's site using a GUI solution is time-consuming but can be accomplished by using LDP or Active Directory Sites and Services.

See Also

Recipe 3.13

3.15. Moving a Domain Controller to a Different Site

Problem

You want to move a domain controller to a different site.

Solution

Using a graphical user interface

1. Open the Active Directory Sites and Services snap-in (*dssite.msc*).
2. In the left pane, expand the site that contains the domain controller.
3. Expand the `Servers` container.
4. Right-click on the domain controller you want to move and select Move.
5. In the Move Server box, select the site to which the domain controller will be moved and click OK.

Using a command-line interface

When using DSMove, you must specify the DN of the object you want to move. In this case, it needs to be the distinguished name of the `server` object for the domain controller. The value for the `-newparent` option is the distinguished name of the `Servers` container you want to move the domain controller to:

```
> dsmove "<ServerDN>" -newparent "<NewServersContainerDN>"
```

For example, the following command would move *dc2* from the `Default-First-Site-Name` site to the Raleigh site:

```
> dsmove "cn=dc2,cn=servers,cn=Default-First-Site-Name,cn=sites,↵
cn=configuration,cn=adatum,dc=com" -newparent↵
"cn=servers,cn=Raleigh,cn=sites,cn=configuration,cn=adatum,dc=com"
```

You can also move an object using AdMod, as follows:

```
> admod -b cn=<ServerName>,cn=servers,cn=<OldSite>,cn=sites,↵
cn=configuration,<ForestRootDN> -move cn=servers,cn=<NewSite>,↵
cn=sites,cn=configuration,<ForestRootDN>
```

Using PowerShell

```
Move-ADDirectoryServer -Identity <DomainControllerName> -Site <NewSite>
```

Discussion

When you install a new domain controller, a `server` object and `nTDSDSA` object for the domain controller get added to the site topology. The Knowledge Consistency Checker (KCC) and Intersite Topology Generator (ISTG) use these objects to determine whom the domain controller should replicate with.

A domain controller is assigned to the site that has been mapped to the subnet it is located on. If there is no `subnet` object that has an address range that contains the domain controller's IP address, the `server` object is added to the `Default-First-Site-Name` site. If the domain controller should be in a different site, you'll then need to manually move it. It is a good practice to ensure that a `subnet` object that matches the domain controller's subnet is already in Active Directory before promoting the server into the forest. That way you do not need to worry about moving it after the fact.

 When moving a `server` object, remember that it has to be moved to a `Servers` container within a site, not directly under the site itself.

Using a command-line interface

In the solution provided, you need to know the current site of the domain controller you want to move. If you do not know the site it is currently in, you can use DSQuery to find it. In fact, you can use DSQuery in combination with DSMove in a single command line:

```
> for /F "usebackq" %i in ('dsquery server↵
    -name"<DomainControllerName>"') do dsmove -newparent "cn=servers,↵
    cn=Default-First-Site,cn=sites, cn=configuration,<ForestDN>" %i
```

This command is long, so we'll break it up into three parts to clarify it. The first part contains the `for` command extension that is built into the *cmd.exe* shell. When the `/F` `"usebackq"` syntax is specified, it is typically used to iterate over output from a command and perform certain functions on the output.

```
for /F "usebackq" %i in
```

The next part of the `for` loop contains the data to iterate over. In this case, we use DSQuery to return the distinguished name of the `server` object for *dc2*:

```
('dsquery server -name "<DomainControllerName>"')
```

The last part executes a command for each result returned from DSQuery. In this case, there should only be one result, so this command will run only once:

```
do dsmove -newparent "cn=servers,cn=Default-First-↵
Site,cn=sites,cn=configuration,<ForestDN>" %i
```

See Also

Recipe 3.14 for finding a domain controller's site; Recipe 4.20 for moving objects to different containers

3.16. Finding the Services a Domain Controller Is Advertising

Problem

You want to find the services that a domain controller is advertising.

Solution

The following command will display the list of services a domain controller is advertising:

```
> dcdiag /v /s:<DomainControllerName> /test:advertising
```

Running this command on a typical domain controller will produce the following output:

```
Starting test: Advertising
   The DC dc1 is advertising itself as a DC and having a DS.
   The DC dc1 is advertising as an LDAP server
   The DC dc1 is advertising as having a writable directory
   The DC dc1 is advertising as a Key Distribution Center
   The DC dc1 is advertising as a time server
   The DS dc1 is advertising as a GC.
```

You can also use *nltest* to get similar information:

```
> nltest /server:<DomainControllerName> /dsgetdc:<DomainName>
```

Running this command on a domain controller in the *adatum.com* domain will produce the following output:

```
       DC: \\dc1.adatum.com
  Address: \\10.0.0.1
 Dom Guid: ac0e4884-cf79-4c9d-8cd9-817e3bfdab54
 Dom Name: adatum.com
Forest Name: adatum.com
Dc Site Name: Raleigh
Our Site Name: Raleigh
    Flags: PDC GC DS LDAP KDC TIMESERV GTIMESERV WRITABLE DNS_DC DNS_DOMAIN
DNS_FOREST CLOSE_SITE
```

In the previous example, GTIMESERV denotes a DC that is a master time server. WRITABLE denotes a DC that holds a writable copy of the Active Directory database. Prior to Windows Server 2008, only NT 4.0 BDCs would not possess this flag. Since 2008, Read-Only Domain Controllers will also lack the WRITABLE flag.

Discussion

The `dcdiag /test:advertising` command is a wrapper around the `DsGetDcName` method. `DsGetDcName` returns a structure called `DOMAIN_CONTROLLER_INFO` that contains the list of services a domain controller provides. Table 3-4 contains the possible values returned from this call.

Table 3-4. DOMAIN_CONTROLLER_INFO flags

Value	Description
DS_DS_FLAG	Directory server for the domain.
DS_GC_FLAG	Global catalog server for the forest.
DS_KDC_FLAG	Kerberos Key Distribution Center for the domain.
DS_PDC_FLAG	Primary domain controller of the domain.
DS_TIMESERV_FLAG	Time server for the domain.
DS_WRITABLE_FLAG	Hosts a writable directory service.

See Also

MSDN: DsGetDcName; MSDN: DOMAIN_CONTROLLER_INFO

3.17. Restoring a Deleted Domain Controller in Windows Server 2012

Problem

You want to restore the computer account of a domain controller that has been accidentally deleted.

Solution

Using a graphical user interface

The following solution requires that the Active Directory Recycle Bin feature has been enabled and that the feature was enabled prior to the deletion of the domain controller computer object.

---

1. Launch the Active Directory Administrative Center.

2. In the left pane, select the domain and then double-click the `Deleted Objects` container in the right pane.

3. In the Filter box near the top of the Active Directory Administrative Center, enter the domain controller name to narrow down the displayed objects to the domain controller object.

4. Right-click the domain controller object and then click Restore.

Using a command-line interface

This command-line solution uses a traditional restoration approach by performing an authoritative restore. To restore the computer account, use the following sequence of commands in Windows Server 2012:

```
> ntdsutil
> activate instance ntds
> authoritative restore> restore object <DomainControllerDN>
> quit
> exit
```

Restart the domain controller after running these commands.

Using PowerShell

The PowerShell solution requires that the Active Directory Recycle Bin feature be enabled and that the feature was enabled prior to the deletion of the domain controller computer object. To restore the computer account for a domain controller named DC1, use the following PowerShell command:

```
Get-ADObject -Filter {Name -eq "dc1" -and ObjectClass -eq "computer"}↲
   -IncludeDeletedObjects | Restore-ADObject
```

Discussion

The Active Directory Recycle Bin has greatly simplified the restoration of AD objects. Now, deleted objects can be restored in their entirety without rebooting a domain controller or recovering data from backup media. In addition, the restore process is much faster, literally just minutes.

Without the use of the Active Directory Recycle Bin, when you restore a deleted object within Active Directory you have the option of performing an *authoritative* or a *nonauthoritative* restore. In both cases, any changes that have been made to the AD database subsequent to the time that the backup was taken will be replicated back to the restored DC. With an authoritative restore, the version number of the object(s) being restored is incremented so that the restored objects will "win" in the case of any replication collisions. In a case where you want to restore an object that has been inadvertently deleted, you need to perform an authoritative restore to prevent the deletion from re-propagating to the restored domain controller. You can mark an entire restore as authoritative, or any subtree of your AD environment down to a single object (in this case, the computer object for the DC that was deleted).

Using PowerShell

The PowerShell solution uses two filters: one for Name and one for ObjectClass. Although filtering by just the name will find and restore the object, it may also restore noncomputer objects as well (e.g., an object in the msDFSR-Member object class will have the same name). Instead of using two filters, you can also find the specific object that you want to recover and then recover it directly by specifying the object GUID.

See Also

Chapter 16 for more on recovering and restoring Active Directory

3.18. Resetting the TCP/IP Stack on a Domain Controller

Problem

You want to uninstall and reinstall the TCP/IP stack on a domain controller as part of a disaster recovery or troubleshooting operation.

Solution

Using a command-line interface

```
> netsh int tcp reset <Log_File_Name>
```

Discussion

Resetting the TCP/IP stack using *netsh* will remove all configuration information, including the default gateway and any configured DNS and WINS servers. This procedure might be necessary during a disaster recovery situation where you're restoring System State data to a server with a dissimilar hardware configuration, for example, as the restore process might corrupt the TCP/IP stack on the destination computer.

Using a command-line interface

In addition to resetting the TCP/IP stack, you can also reset Winsock using the following command:

```
> netsh winsock reset
```

Use this command with care, though, as resetting Winsock can cause network applications such as antivirus scanners to malfunction and require reinstallation. A reboot is required to complete the Winsock reset.

See Also

MS KB 299357 (How to reset Internet Protocol (TCP/IP)) (*http://support.micro soft.com/kb/299357*)

3.19. Configuring a Domain Controller to Use an External Time Source

Problem

You want to set the reliable time source for a domain controller.

Solution

Using the Registry

To configure a domain controller to sync to an external time provider, set the following Registry keys:

```
[HKLM\System\CurrentControlSet\Services\W32Time\Parameters\]
Type: REG_SZ - "NTP"

[HKLM\System\CurrentControlSet\Services\W32Time\Config\]
AnnounceFlags: REG_DWORD - 10

[HKLM\System\CurrentControlSet\Services\W32Time\TimeProviders\]
NTPServer: REG_DWORD - 1

[HKLM SYSTEM\CurrentControlSet\Services\W32Time\Parameters\]
NTPServer: REG_SZ -<Peers>

[HKLM \SYSTEM\CurrentControlSet\Services\W32Time\TimeProviders\
NtpClient\]
SpecialPollInterval: REG_DWORD -<TimeBetweenPollsInSeconds>

[HKLM \SYSTEM\CurrentControlSet\Services\W32Time\Config\]
MaxPosPhaseCorrection: REG_DWORD -<MaximumForwardOffsetInSeconds>

[HKLM \SYSTEM\CurrentControlSet\Services\W32Time\Config\]
MaxNegPhaseCorrection: REG_DWORD -<MaximumBackwardOffsetInSeconds>
```

<Peers> in the preceding code refers to a space-separated list of FQDNs of external time servers. Each DNS name must be followed by ,0x1 for the rest of these settings to take effect.

Once you have made these changes to the Registry, stop and restart the W32time service by issuing the following commands:

```
> net stop w32time
> net start w32time
```

Using a command line

```
w32tm /config /syncfromflags:manual /manualpeerlist:<FQDNofTimeServer>
w32tm /config /update
```

Discussion

You should set a reliable time source on the PDC Emulator FSMO for only the forest root domain. All other domain controllers sync their time either from that server, from a PDC within their own domain, or from a designated time server on another domain controller. The list of external time servers is stored in the Registry under the W32Time Service Registry key: `HKLM\SYSTEM\CurrentControlSet\Services\W32Time\Parame ters\ntpserver`.

If you want a domain controller such as the PDC to use an external time source, you have to set the `ntpserver` Registry value along with the `type` value. The default value for `type` on a domain controller is `Nt5DS`, which means that the domain controller will use the Active Directory domain hierarchy to find a time source. You can override this behavior and have a domain controller contact a non-DC time source by setting `type` to NTP.

After setting the time server, the W32Time service should be restarted for the change to take effect. You can check that the server was set properly by running the following command:

```
> w32tm /query /computer:localhost /configuration
```

Since the PDC Emulator is the time source for the other domain controllers, you should also make sure that it is advertising the time service, which you can do with the following command:

```
> nltest /server:<DomainControllerName> /dsgetdc:<DomainDNSName> /TIMESERV
```

To configure the PDC Emulator to use its own internal clock as a time source instead of relying on an external clock, modify the `HKLM\SYSTEM\CurrentControlSet\Services\W32Time\Config\AnnounceFlags` DWORD value to contain a value of `0x0A`.

The algorithm used by domain controllers to sync time gets quite complex. See the next section for links to additional details on how the Windows time service works.

See Also

"Configure the Time Source for the Forest" (*http://bit.ly/ZFHPAS*); "How Windows Time Service Works" (*http://bit.ly/11HGpng*)

3.20. Finding the Number of Logon Attempts Made Against a Domain Controller

Problem

You want to find the number of logon requests a domain controller has processed.

Solution

The following query returns the number of logon requests processed:

```
> nltest /server:<DomainControllerName> /LOGON_QUERY
```

This will produce output similar to the following:

```
Number of attempted logons: 10542526
```

Discussion

The `nltest /LOGON_QUERY` command is a wrapper around the `I_NetLogonControl2` method, and it can be useful to determine how many logon requests are being processed by a server. Viewing the results of the command over a period of time and comparing them against another DC in the same domain can also tell you if one domain controller is being used significantly more or less than the others.

See Also

MSDN: I_NetLogonControl2

3.21. Enabling the /3GB Switch to Increase the LSASS Cache

Problem

You have installed more than 1 GB of memory on your 32-bit domain controllers and want to enable the /3GB switch so that the LSASS process can use more memory.

Solution

Using a command-line interface

On a 32-bit Windows Server 2008 server, run the following command:

```
> bcdedit /set IncreaseUserVA 3072
```

Restart the computer.

Discussion

When computers are referred to as 32- or 64-bit computers, it means they support memory addresses that are 32 or 64 bits long. This is the total available memory (virtual and real) that can be processed by the system. Since the days of Windows NT, Microsoft has split memory allocation in half by giving applications up to 2 GB and the Windows kernel 2 GB of memory to use (32 bits of address space = 2^32 = 4 GB). In many cases, administrators would rather allocate more memory to applications than to the kernel. For this reason, Microsoft developed the /3GB switch to allow applications running on 32-bit versions of Windows to use up to 3 GB of memory, leaving the kernel with 1 GB.

 This configuration is not necessary for 64-bit versions of Windows.

3.22. Enabling and Disabling the Global Catalog

Problem

You want to enable or disable the global catalog (GC) on a particular server.

Solution

Using a graphical user interface

1. Open the Active Directory Sites and Services snap-in (*dssite.msc*).
2. Browse to the nTDSDSA object (NTDS Settings) underneath the server object for the domain controller for which you want to enable or disable the global catalog.
3. Right-click on NTDS Settings and select Properties.
4. Under the General tab, check (to enable) or uncheck (to disable) the box beside Global Catalog.
5. Click OK.

Using a command-line interface

In the following command, *<ServerObjectDN>* should be the server object DN, not the DN of the nTDSDSA object:

```
> dsmod server "<ServerObjectDN>" -isgc yes|no
```

For example, the following command will enable the global catalog on DC1 in the Raleigh site:

```
> dsmod server
"cn=DC1,cn=servers,cn=Raleigh,cn=sites,cn=configuration,dc=adatum,dc=com"↵
-isgc Yes
```

You can also use AdMod with the following syntax and output to disable the GC; to enable it, use options::{{.:CLR:1}}:

```
> adfind -b "cn=NTDS
Settings,cn=dc1,cn=Servers,cn=Raleigh,cn=Sites,cn=Configuration,dc=adatum,↵
dc=com" options -adcsv | admod options::{{.:SET:1}}
```

 See Chapter 4 for information on safely modifying bitwise operators.

Using PowerShell

```
Set-ADObject "cn=NTDS Settings,cn="<DomainControllerName>,cn=Servers,↵
cn=<SiteName>,;cn=Sites,cn=Configuration,dc="<DomainName>,dc=<TopLevelDomain>"↵
 -Replace @{Options='1'}
```

Discussion

The first domain controller promoted into a forest is also made a global catalog (GC) server by default. In a single-domain environment, the global catalog server incurs no memory or bandwidth overhead beyond that of a domain controller, so you could configure each DC in a single-domain forest as a GC without any ill effects. In a multidomain environment, however, each global catalog server will require additional disk space to store a partial replica of other domains in the forest, and will require additional network bandwidth to replicate with other GCs. For more details on DC and GC placement planning, see *Active Directory*, Fifth Edition, by Brian Desmond et al. (O'Reilly).

The global catalog on a domain controller becomes enabled when the low-order bit on the options attribute on the nTDSDSA object under the server object for the domain controller is set to 1; it becomes disabled when it is set to 0. The DN of this object for DC1 in the Default-First-Site-Name site looks like this:

```
cn=NTDSSettings,cn=DC1,cn=Default-First-Site-Name,cn=Sites,cn=Configuration,↵
dc=adatum,dc=com
```

After enabling the global catalog, it can take some time before the domain controller can start serving as a global catalog server. The length of time is based on the amount of data that needs to replicate and the type of connectivity between the domain controller's replication partners. This is also dependent on the Global Catalog Partition Occupancy setting, which is set in the HKLM\System\CurrentControlSet\Services \NTDS\Parameters key on the GC itself, which specifies how many directory partitions must be fully replicated to the GC before it is considered ready; this can range from no occupancy requirement whatsoever, to requiring that all partitions be fully synchronized before the GC can begin servicing requests. After replication is complete, you should see Event 1119 in the Directory Services log stating the server is advertising itself as a global catalog. At that point you should also be able to perform LDAP queries against port 3268 on that server. See Recipe 3.23 for more information on how to determine whether global catalog promotion is complete.

See Also

Recipe 3.23 for determining whether global catalog promotion is complete; "Understanding the Global Catalog" (*http://bit.ly/100F4JG*)

3.23. Determining Whether Global Catalog Promotion Is Complete

Problem

You want to determine whether a domain controller is a global catalog server. After you initially enable the global catalog on a domain controller, it can take some time for all of the read-only naming contexts to replicate to it, depending on the number of domains, the volume of directory data, and the underlying network topology.

Solution

Query the isGlobalCatalogReady attribute on the RootDSE for the domain controller. A TRUE value means the server is a global catalog, and a FALSE value indicates it is not.

For more information on how to query the RootDSE, see Recipe 4.1.

You can also check the Directory Services Event Log in the Event Viewer MMC for the presence of Event ID 1119, whose text reads as follows:

```
"This Windows Domain Controller is now a Global Catalog Server"
```

Using a command-line interface

To confirm that a domain controller in the *adatum.com* domain named dc1 is functioning as a global catalog server, use *nltest* with the following syntax:

```
> nltest /server:dc1.adatum.com /dsgetdc:adatum.com
```

If the DC in question is functioning as a GC, you'll see output similar to the following:

```
> C:\>nltest /dsgetdc:adatum.com
>             DC: \\dc1.adatum.com
>       Address: \\10.0.0.1
>      Dom Guid: ac0e4884-cf79-4c9d-8cd9-817e3bfdab54
>      Dom Name: adatum.com
>   Forest Name: adatum.com
> Dc Site Name: Raleigh
> Our Site Name: Raleigh
>         Flags: PDC GC DS LDAP KDC TIMESERV GTIMESERV WRITABLE DNS_DC DNS_DOMAIN
> DNS_FOREST CLOSE_SITE
> The command completed successfully
```

Using PowerShell

```
Get-ADDomainController -Server <DomainControllerName> |
  FT Name,IsGlobalCatalog -AutoSize
```

Discussion

Once a server has completed initial replication of the global catalog, the attribute is GlobalCatalogReady in the RootDSE will be set to TRUE. Another way to determine if a domain controller has been at least flagged to become a global catalog is by checking whether the options attribute on the nTDSDSA object for the server has been set to 1. (Note that this does not necessarily mean the server is accepting requests as a global catalog.) An additional query to the RootDSE as described in the "Solution" on page 89 or directly to port 3268 (the global catalog port) could also confirm that the appropriate flag has been set.

See Also

Recipe 4.1 for viewing the RootDSE

3.24. Finding the Global Catalog Servers in a Forest

Problem

You want a list of the global catalog servers in a forest.

Solution

Using a command-line interface

To enumerate all GCs in a forest using DSQuery, use the following syntax:

```
> dsquery server -forest -isgc
```

Using PowerShell

To find all global catalogs in the current domain, use the following syntax:

```
Get-ADDomainController -Filter { IsGlobalCatalog -eq $true } | Select Name
```

To find all global catalogs in the forest, use the following two PowerShell commands:

```
$GCs = Get-ADForest
$GCs.GlobalCatalogs
```

Discussion

To find the global catalog servers in a forest, you need to query for NTDS Settings objects that have the low-order bit of the options attribute equal to 1 under the Sites container in the Configuration naming context. That attribute determines whether a domain controller should be a global catalog server, but it does not necessarily mean it is a global catalog server yet. See Recipe 3.23 for more information on how to tell whether a server marked as a global catalog is ready to accept requests as one.

See Also

Recipe 3.23 for determining whether global catalog promotion is complete

3.25. Finding the Domain Controllers or Global Catalog Servers in a Site

Problem

You want a list of the domain controllers or global catalog servers in a specific site.

Solution

Using a graphical user interface

1. Open the Active Directory Administrative Center.
2. In the left pane, double-click the domain name.
3. Double-click the Domain Controllers OU.
4. In the right pane, you can view the Domain Controller Type column to see if a domain controller is a global catalog server.

   Global catalog servers will have the appropriate box checked beside Global Catalog.

Using PowerShell

To find all of the domain controllers in SiteA for the current domain, use the following syntax:

```
Get-ADDomainController -Filter { Site -eq "SiteA" } | FL Name
```

To find all GCs in SiteA for the current domain, use the following syntax:

```
Get-ADDomainController -Filter { Site -eq "SiteA" -and↵
( IsGlobalCatalog -eq "True" )} | FL Name
```

To find all global catalogs in SiteA in the entire forest, use the following syntax:

```
$for = [System.DirectoryServices.ActiveDirectory.Forest]::getCurrentForest()
$dom.FindAllGlobalCatalogs("SiteA")
```

Discussion

Each domain controller has a server object within the Servers container for the site it is a member of (e.g., cn=DC1,cn=Servers,cn=MySite,cn=site,cn=configura tion,dc=adatum,dc=com). Since other types of servers can have server objects in a site's Servers container, domain controllers are differentiated by the nTDSDSA object that is a child of the server object (e.g., cn=NTDSSettings,cn=DC1,cn=Servers,cn=My Site,cn=site,cn=configuration,dc=adatum,dc=com). Querying for this nTDSDSA object will return a list of domain controllers in the site. Locating global catalog servers consists of the same query, except where the low-order bit of the options attribute of the nTDSDSA object is equal to 1. Note that this may not be available if replication has not completed after enabling the GC.

3.26. Finding Domain Controllers and Global Catalogs via DNS

Problem

You want to find domain controllers or global catalogs using DNS lookups.

Solution

Domain controllers and global catalog servers are represented in DNS as SRV records. You can query SRV records using *nslookup* by setting type=SRV, such as in the following:

```
> nslookup
Default Server: dns01.adatum.com
Address: 10.1.2.3

> set type=SRV
```

You then need to issue the following query to retrieve all writable domain controllers for the specified domain:

```
> _ldap._tcp.<DomainDNSName>
```

You can issue a similar query to retrieve global catalogs:

```
> _gc._tcp
```

You can even find the domain controllers or global catalogs that are in a particular site or that *cover* a particular site by querying the following:

```
> _ldap._tcp.<SiteName>._sites
> _gc._tcp.<SiteName>._sites
```

See Recipe 11.20 for more information on site coverage.

Discussion

One of the benefits of Active Directory over its predecessor, Windows NT, is that it relies on DNS for name resolution, which is the standard for name resolution on the Internet and on most TCP/IP-based networks. Active Directory uses DNS to locate servers that serve a particular function, such as a domain controller for a domain, global catalog server, PDC Emulator, or KDC. It also uses the site topology information stored in Active Directory to populate site-specific records for domain controllers.

The DC locator process relies on this information in DNS to direct clients to the most optimal server when logging in. Reliance on DNS makes it easy to troubleshoot problems related to clients finding domain controllers. If you know the site a client is in, you can make a few DNS queries to determine which domain controller they should be using to authenticate.

The resource records that a domain controller registers in DNS can be restricted, if you have a lag site configured, for example, so querying DNS may return only a subset of the actual domain controllers that are available. See Recipes 12.13 and 12.14 for more information.

See Also

Recipe 12.13; Recipe 12.14; Recipe 3.32 for finding the PDC Emulator via DNS; MS KB 267855 (Problems with Many Domain Controllers with Active Directory Integrated DNS Zones); RFC 2782, "A DNS RR for Specifying the Location of Services (DNS SRV)"

3.27. Changing the Preference for a Domain Controller

Problem

You want a particular domain controller to be used less frequently for client requests, or not at all. This may be necessary if a particular domain controller is overloaded, perhaps due to numerous application requests.

Solution

You can modify the `Priority` or `Weight` field in SRV resource records by modifying the registry on the domain controller. Open *regedit* or *regedit32* on the domain controller and browse to the following key: `HKLM\SYSTEM\CurrentControlSet\Services\Netlo gon\Parameters`. To configure the priority, add a `REG_DWORD` with the name `LdapSrv Priority`. To configure the weight, add a `REG_DWORD` with the name `LdapSrvWeight`.

After you make the change, the *%SystemRoot%\System32\Config\netlogon.dns* file should be updated and the DDNS updates sent to the DNS server within an hour. You can also restart the NetLogon service to expedite the process.

Discussion

Each domain controller registers several SRV records that clients use as part of the DC locator process to find the closest domain controller. Two fields of the SRV record let clients determine which server to use when multiple possibilities are returned. The Priority field is used to dictate whether a specific server or set of servers should always be contacted over others unless otherwise unavailable. A server with a higher priority (i.e., lower Priority field value) will always be contacted before a server with a lower priority. For example, if DC1 has an SRV priority of 5 and DC2 has an SRV priority of 10, DC1 will always be used unless it is unavailable.

The Weight field, on the other hand, determines the percentage of time clients should use a particular server. You can easily calculate the percentage by dividing the weight by the sum of all weights for servers with the same priority. If servers DC1, DC2, and DC3 have weights of 1, 2, and 3, respectively, then DC1 will be contacted one out of six times or (1 / (3 + 2 + 1)), DC2 will be contacted two out of every six times or 1/3 (2 / (3 + 2 + 1)), and DC3 will be contacted three out of every six times or 1/2 (3 / (3 + 2 + 1)). Here is an example of how the SRV records look with these weights:

```
C:\> nslookup -type=SRV _ldap._tcp.dc._msdcs.adatum.com
Server: dns01.adatum.com
Address: 172.16.168.183

_ldap._tcp.dc._msdcs.adatum.com SRV service location:
        priority       = 0
        weight         = 1
        port           = 389
        svr hostname   = dc1.adatum.com
_ldap._tcp.dc._msdcs.adatum.com SRV service location:

priority       = 0

weight         = 2
        port           = 389
        svr hostname   = dc2.adatum.com
_ldap._tcp.dc._msdcs.datum.com SRV service location:
        priority       = 0
        weight         = 3
        port           = 389
        svr hostname   = dc3.datum.com
```

In certain situations, having this capability can come in handy. For example, the server acting as the PDC FSMO role owner typically receives more traffic from clients simply because of the nature of tasks that the PDC FSMO has to handle. If you find a certain server, like the PDC FSMO, has considerably higher load than the rest of the servers, you could change the priority or weight of the SRV records so that the server is used less often during the DC locator process. You can increase the Priority to eliminate its use unless all other domain controllers fail, or modify the Weight to reduce how often it will be used.

You can modify this information manually within the DNS Management Console, or for multiple DCs using Group Policy Objects in the Computer Configuration\Administrative Templates\System\Net Logon\DC Locator DNS Records GPO node.

See Also

MS KB 232025 (Description of the DNS SRV Resource Record Type)

3.28. Disabling the Global Catalog Requirement for User Logon

Problem

You want to disable the requirement for a global catalog server to be reachable when a user logs in to a Windows domain.

Solution

See Recipe 7.12 for information on enabling universal group caching, which can reduce the need to contact a global catalog server during logon for universal group expansion.

3.29. Finding the FSMO Role Holders

Problem

You want to find the domain controllers that are acting as one of the FSMO roles.

Solution

Using a graphical user interface

For the Schema Master:

1. Open the Active Directory Schema snap-in.
2. Right-click on Active Directory Schema in the left pane and select Operations Master.

For the Domain Naming Master:

1. Open the Active Directory Domains and Trusts snap-in (*domain.msc*).

2. Right-click on Active Directory Domains and Trusts in the left pane and select Operations Master.

For the PDC Emulator, RID Master, and Infrastructure Master:

1. Open the Active Directory Users and Computers snap-in (*dsa.msc*).
2. Make sure you've targeted the correct domain.
3. Right-click on Active Directory Users and Computers in the left pane and select Operations Masters.
4. Work your way through the individual tabs for the PDC, RID, and Infrastructure roles.

Using a command-line interface

In the following command, you can leave out the `/Domain <DomainDNSName>` option to query the domain you are currently logged in to:

```
> netdom query fsmo /Domain:<DomainDNSName>
```

To query the owner of an individual FSMO role, you can use the `dsquery server` command shown here, where `<Role>` can be schema, name, infr, pdc, or rid:

```
> dsquery server -hasfsmo <Role>
```

Using PowerShell

The following command will query the forest-level FSMO roles:

```
Get-ADForest | FL DomainNamingMaster,SchemaMaster
```

The following command will query the domain-level FSMO roles for the specified domain:

```
Get-ADDomain -Identity <DomainDNSName> |↵
FL InfrastructureMaster,PDCEmulator,RIDMaster
```

Discussion

Several Active Directory operations are sensitive, such as updating the schema, and therefore need to be restricted to a single domain controller to prevent corruption of the AD database. This is because Active Directory cannot guarantee the proper evaluation of these functions in a situation where they may be invoked from more than one DC. The FSMO mechanism is used to limit these functions to a single DC.

Five designated FSMO roles correspond to these sensitive functions. A FSMO role can apply either to an entire forest or to a specific domain. Each role is stored in the fSMOR oleOwner attribute on various objects in Active Directory depending on the role. Table 3-5 contains a list of FSMO roles.

Table 3-5. FSMO roles

Role	Description	fSMORoleOwner location	Domain- or forest-wide?
Schema	Processes schema updates.	cn=Schema,cn=Configura tion,*<ForestDN>*	Forest
Domain Naming	Processes the addition, removal, and renaming of domains.	cn=Partitions cn=Configu ration,*<ForestDN>*	Forest
Infrastructure	Maintains references to objects in other domains.	cn=Infrastructure,*<Do mainDN>*	Domain
RID	Handles RID pool allocation for the domain controllers in a domain.	cn=RidManager$,cn=Sys tem,*<DomainDN>*	Domain
PDC Emulator	Receives preferential password replication, handles user authentication after another DC reports bad password, handles account lockouts.	*<DomainDN>*	Domain

Using PowerShell

For a quick method of retrieving the FSMO role holders in a forest or domain, simply retrieve the properties of the forest or domain object, as follows:

```
Get-ADForest
```

or:

```
Get-ADDomain
```

See Also

Recipe 3.13; "Using Ntdsutil.exe to transfer or seize FSMO roles to a domain controller" (*http://support.microsoft.com/kb/255504*)

3.30. Transferring a FSMO Role

Problem

You want to transfer a FSMO role to a different domain controller. This may be necessary if you need to take a current FSMO role holder down for maintenance.

Solution

Using a graphical user interface

1. Use the same directions as described in Recipe 3.29 for viewing a specific FSMO, except target (i.e., right-click and select Connect to Domain Controller) the domain controller you want to transfer the FSMO *to* before selecting Operations Master.

2. Click the Change button.

3. Click OK twice.

   You should then see a message stating whether the transfer was successful.

Using a command-line interface

The following will transfer the PDC Emulator role to *<NewRoleOwner>* (see "Discussion" on page 96 section for information on transferring the other roles):

```
> ntdsutil roles conn "co t s <NewRoleOwner>" q "transfer PDC" q q
```

Using PowerShell

The following command will transfer the PDC Emulator role to a DC named DC1:

```
Move-ADDirectoryServerOperationMasterRole DC1 -PDCEmulator
```

The following will transfer the RID Master role to another DC named DC1; this syntax can be used for all FSMO role holders except for the PDC Emulator:

```
Move-ADDirectoryServerOperationMasterRole DC1 -RIDMaster
```

Discussion

The first domain controller in a new forest is assigned the two forest-wide FSMO roles (schema and domain naming). The first domain controller in a new domain gets the other three domain-wide roles. It is very likely you'll need to move the roles around to different domain controllers at some point. Also, when you need to decommission a domain controller that is currently a FSMO role owner (either permanently or for a significant period of time), you'll want to transfer the role beforehand.

If you plan to install a hotfix or do some other type of maintenance that only necessitates a quick reboot, you may not want to go to the trouble of transferring the FSMO role. This is because some FSMO roles are more time-critical than others, and some come into use on a far more frequent basis. For example, the PDC Emulator role is used extensively (and therefore should be transferred to a domain controller of equal or better capacity as a best practice), but the Schema Master is needed only when you are extending the schema by installing a new software package, such as Microsoft Exchange.

If a FSMO role owner becomes unavailable before you can transfer it, you'll need to seize the role (see Recipe 3.31).

Using a command-line interface

Any role can be transferred using *ntdsutil* by replacing `"transfer PDC"` in the solution with one of the following:

- `"transfer domain naming master"`
- `"transfer infrastructure master"`
- `"transfer RID master"`
- `"transfer schema master"`

Using PowerShell

The FSMO roles can be shortened to simplify the commands to move the roles. Because each role starts with a unique letter, you can transfer them by just referring to them by the first letter of the role name. In addition, you can transfer multiple roles in one command. The following command will transfer all five roles to DC1:

```
Move-ADDirectoryServerOperationMasterRole DC1 -S,D,I,P,R
```

See Also

Recipe 3.29 for finding FSMO role holders; Recipe 3.31 for seizing a FSMO role; "Using Ntdsutil.exe to transfer or seize FSMO roles to a domain controller" (*http://support.microsoft.com/kb/255504*)

3.31. Seizing a FSMO Role

Problem

You need to seize a FSMO role because the current role holder is down and will not be restored.

Solution

Using a command-line interface

The following will seize the PDC Emulator role to *<NewRoleOwner>*:

```
> ntdsutil roles conn "co t s <NewRoleOwner>" q "seize PDC" q q
```

Any of the other roles can be transferred as well using *ntdsutil* by replacing `"seize PDC"` in the previous solution with one of the following:

- "seize domain naming master"
- "seize infrastructure master"
- "seize RID master"
- "seize schema master"

Using PowerShell

The following will seize the PDC Emulator role to *<NewRoleOwner>*:

```
> Move-ADDirectoryServerOperationMasterRole <NewRoleOwner> -PDCEmulator -Force
```

Discussion

Seizing a FSMO role should not be taken lightly. The general recommendation is to seize a FSMO role only when you cannot possibly bring the previous role holder back online. One reason that seizing a role is problematic is that you could possibly lose data. For example, let's say that you extended the schema and immediately after it was extended the Schema FSMO went down. If you could not bring that server back online, those extensions may not have replicated before the server went down. You would need to determine whether any of the schema extensions replicated and, if not, reextend the schema. Other issues can result from losing the RID FSMO, where duplicate RID pools may be allocated. See Recipe 3.29 for more information.

See Also

Recipe 3.29 for finding FSMO role holders; Recipe 3.30 for transferring a FSMO role; "Using Ntdsutil.exe to transfer or seize FSMO roles to a domain controller" (*http://support.microsoft.com/kb/255504*)

3.32. Finding the PDC Emulator FSMO Role Owner via DNS

Problem

You want to find the PDC Emulator for a domain using DNS.

Solution

Using a command-line interface

```
> nslookup -type=SRV _ldap._tcp.pdc._msdcs.<DomainDNSName>
```

Discussion

The PDC Emulator FSMO role is the only FSMO role that is stored in DNS. Like many of the other Active Directory–related DNS records, the PDC record is stored as an SRV record under `_ldap._tcp.pdc._msdcs.`*`<DomainDNSName>`* where *`<DomainDNSName>`* is the domain the PDC is in. This allows your Active Directory clients to use normal DNS name resolution to locate the PDC Emulator for their domain.

See Also

Recipe 3.26 for finding domain controllers via DNS

## CHAPTER 4

Searching and Manipulating Objects

4.0. Introduction

Active Directory is based on Lightweight Directory Access Protocol (LDAP) and supports the LDAP version 3 specification defined in RFC 2251. And while many of the AD tools and interfaces, such as ADSI, abstract and streamline LDAP operations to make things easier, any good AD administrator or developer must have a thorough understanding of LDAP to fully utilize Active Directory. This chapter will cover some of the LDAP-related tasks you may need to perform when working with Active Directory, along with other tasks related to searching and manipulating objects within the directory.

The Anatomy of an Object

The Active Directory schema is composed of a hierarchy of classes that define the types of objects that can be created within Active Directory, as well as the different attributes they can possess. These classes support *inheritance*, which enables developers to reuse existing class definitions for more than one type of object; for example, the `description` attribute is available with every type of AD object, but the attribute itself is defined only *once* within the schema. At the top of the inheritance tree is the `top` class, from which every class in the schema is derived. Table 4-1 contains a list of some of the attributes that are available from the `top` class, and subsequently are defined on every object that is created in Active Directory.

Table 4-1. *Common attributes of objects*

Attribute	Description
cn	RDN attribute for most object classes, also referred to as the *common name.*
whenCreated	Timestamp when the object was created. See Recipe 4.26 for more information.
description	Multivalued attribute that can be used as a generic field for storing a description of the object. Although this attribute is multivalued, objects such as users and groups can have only one value populated due to legacy support requirements.
displayName	Name of the object displayed in administrative interfaces.
distinguishedName	Distinguished name of the object.
whenChanged	Timestamp when the object was last changed by the local server. See Recipe 4.26 for more information.
name	RDN of the object. The value of this attribute will mirror the naming attribute (e.g., cn, ou, dc).
nTSecurityDescriptor	Security descriptor assigned to the object.
objectCategory	Used as a grouping mechanism for objects with a similar purpose (e.g., Person).
objectClass	List of classes from which the object's class was derived.
objectGUID	Globally unique identifier for the object.
uSNChanged	Update sequence number (USN) assigned by the local server after the last change to the object (can include creation).
uSNCreated	USN assigned by the local server when the object was created.

4.1. Viewing the RootDSE

Problem

You want to view attributes of the RootDSE, which can be useful for discovering basic information about a forest, domain, or domain controller without hardcoding the name of a particular naming context into a query.

Solution

Using a graphical user interface

1. Open LDP.
2. From the menu, select Connection→Connect.
3. For Server, enter a domain controller or domain name, or leave it blank to do a serverless bind.
4. For Port, enter 389.
5. Click OK.

6. The contents of the RootDSE will be shown in the right pane.

Using a command-line interface

To display the RootDSE of a domain controller using AdFind, use the following syntax:

```
> adfind -rootdse
```

Using PowerShell

```
Get-ADRootDSE
```

You'll see results similar to the following (truncated for readability):

```
configurationNamingContext: cn=Configuration,dc= adatum,dc=com
currentTime: 10/9/2012 9:27:38 AM
defaultNamingContext: dc=adatum,dc=com
dnsHostName: dc1.adatum.com
domainControllerFunctionality: Windows2012
domainFunctionality: Windows2012Domain
dsServiceName: cn=NTDS Settings,cn=DC1,cn=Servers,cn=Default-First-Site-Name,↵
cn=Sites,cn=Configuration,dc=adatum,dc=com
forestFunctionality: Windows2012Forest
highestCommittedUSN: 28013
isGlobalCatalogReady: {TRUE}
isSynchronized: {TRUE}
ldapServiceName: adatum.com:dc1$@ADATUM.COM
namingContexts: {dc=adatum,dc=com, cn=Configuration,dc=adatum,dc=com,
cn=Schema,cn=Configuration,dc=adatum,dc=com,dc=DomainDnsZones,dc=adatum,↵
dc=com...}
rootDomainNamingContext: dc=adatum,dc=com
schemaNamingContext: cn=Schema,cn=Configuration,dc=adatum,dc=com
serverName: cn=dc1,cn=Servers,cn=Default-First-Site-Name,cn=Sites,↵
cn=Configuration,dc=adatum,dc=com
subschemaSubentry: cn=Aggregate,cn=Schema,cn=Configuration,dc=adatum,dc=com
supportedCapabilities: {1.2.840.113556.1.4.800 (LDAP_CAP_ACTIVE_DIRECTORY_OID),↵
;1.2.840.113556.1.4.1670(LDAP_CAP_ACTIVE_DIRECTORY_V51_OID),↵
;1.2.840.113556.1.4.1791(LDAP_CAP_ACTIVE_DIRECTORY_LDAP_INTEG_OID),↵
;1.2.840.113556.1.4.1935(LDAP_CAP_ACTIVE_DIRECTORY_V61_OID)...}
supportedControl: {1.2.840.113556.1.4.319(LDAP_PAGED_RESULT_OID_STRING),↵
;1.2.840.113556.1.4.801(LDAP_SERVER_SD_FLAGS_OID),↵
;1.2.840.113556.1.4.473(LDAP_SERVER_SORT_OID),↵
;1.2.840.113556.1.4.528(LDAP_SERVER_NOTIFICATION_OID)...}
supportedLDAPPolicies: {MaxPoolThreads, MaxDatagramRecv, MaxReceiveBuffer,↵
; InitRecvTimeout...}
supportedLDAPVersion: {3, 2}
supportedSASLMechanisms: {GSSAPI, GSS-SPNEGO, EXTERNAL, DIGEST-MD5}
```

Discussion

The RootDSE was originally defined in RFC 2251 as part of the LDAPv3 specification. It is not part of the Active Directory namespace per se. It is a synthetic object that is maintained separately by each domain controller.

The RootDSE can be accessed anonymously using LDP; the command-line and PowerShell solutions use the credentials of the currently logged-on user unless you specify an alternate username and password. In the CLI and PowerShell solutions, serverless binds were used against the RootDSE. In that case, the DC Locator process is used to find a domain controller in the domain you authenticate against. This can also be accomplished with LDP by not entering a server name from the Connect dialog box.

The RootDSE is key to writing portable AD-enabled applications. It provides a mechanism to programmatically determine the distinguished names of the various naming contexts (among other things), which means that you do not need to hardcode that information in scripts and programs.

See Also

RFC 2251; MS KB 219005 (Windows 2000: LDAPv3 RootDSE); MSDN: IADsPropertyEntry; MSDN: IADsProperty Value; MSDN: IADs::Get MSDN: IADs::GetEx

4.2. Viewing the Attributes of an Object

Problem

You want to view one or more attributes of an object.

Solution

Using a graphical user interface

1. Open LDP.
2. From the menu, select Connection→Connect.
3. For Server, enter the name or IP address of a domain controller or domain that contains the object.
4. For Port, enter 389.
5. Click OK.
6. From the menu, select Connection→Bind.
7. Accept the default and bind as the currently logged on user or select the option to bind with credentials and then enter the credentials.

---

8. Click OK.

9. From the menu, select View→Tree.

10. For BaseDN, type the DN of the object you want to view.

11. For Scope, select Base.

12. Click OK.

Using a command-line interface

To obtain a list of attributes for a particular object using DSQuery, use the following syntax:

```
> dsquery * "<ObjectDN>" -scope base -attr *
```

To query for an object using AdFind, use the following syntax:

```
> adfind -b <Parent Container DN> -f cn=<Object CN> -tdcgt
```

Using PowerShell

To get the attributes of the built-in Administrator account, run the following PowerShell command:

```
Get-ADUser -Identity Administrator -Properties *
```

An example of the output is shown here:

```
AccountExpirationDate                  :
accountExpires                         : 0
AccountLockoutTime                     :
AccountNotDelegated                    : False
adminCount                             : 1
AllowReversiblePasswordEncryption      : False
BadLogonCount                          : 0
badPasswordTime                        : 129934507947486667
badPwdCount                            : 0
CannotChangePassword                   : False
CanonicalName                          : adatum.com/Users/Administrator
Certificates                           : {}
City                                   :
CN                                     : Administrator
codePage                               : 0
Company                                :
CompoundIdentitySupported              : {}
Country                                :
countryCode                            : 0
Created                                : 9/27/2012 11:16:45 AM
createTimeStamp                        : 9/27/2012 11:16:45 AM
Deleted                                :
Department                             :
```

```
Description                            : Built-in account for administering the
                                         computer/domain
DisplayName                            :
DistinguishedName                      : cn=Administrator,cn=Users,dc=adatum,dc=com
Division                               :
DoesNotRequirePreAuth                  : False
dSCorePropagationData                  : {9/27/2012 11:34:42 AM,↵
                                           9/27/2012 11:34:42 AM,↵
                                           9/27/2012 11:19:31 AM,↵
                                           1/1/1601 10:12:16 AM}

EmailAddress                           :
EmployeeID                             :
EmployeeNumber                         :
Enabled                                : True
Fax                                    :
GivenName                              :
HomeDirectory                          :
HomedirRequired                        : False
HomeDrive                              :
HomePage                               :
HomePhone                              :
Initials                               :
instanceType                           : 4
isCriticalSystemObject                 : True
isDeleted                              :
KerberosEncryptionType                 : {}
LastBadPasswordAttempt                 : 9/29/2012 8:53:14 PM
LastKnownParent                        :
lastLogoff                             : 0
lastLogon                              : 129942736428265971
LastLogonDate                          : 10/9/2012 9:27:17 AM
lastLogonTimestamp                     : 129942736379503412
LockedOut                              : False
logonCount                             : 29
logonHours                             : {255, 255, 255, 255...}
LogonWorkstations                      :
Manager                                :
MemberOf                               : {cn=Group Policy Creator
          Owners,cn=Users,dc=adatum,dc=com, cn=Domain
          Admins,cn=Users,dc=adatum,dc=com, cn=Enterprise
          Admins,cn=Users,dc=adatum,dc=com, cn=Schema
          Admins,cn=Users,dc=adatum,dc=com...}
MNSLogonAccount                        : False
MobilePhone                            :
Modified                               : 10/9/2012 9:27:17 AM
modifyTimeStamp                        : 10/9/2012 9:27:17 AM
msDS-AuthenticatedAtDC                 : {cn=2012-DC05,OU=Domain
                                           Controllers,dc=adatum,dc=com}
msDS-User-Account-Control-Computed     : 0
Name                                   : Administrator
nTSecurityDescriptor                   : System.DirectoryServices.↵
                                         ActiveDirectorySecurity
```

```
ObjectCategory                          : cn=Person,cn=Schema,cn=Configuration,↵
                                          dc=adatum,dc=com
ObjectClass                             : user
ObjectGUID                              : c897bc0a-b5d4-4025-8c10-b696e45ce780
objectSid                               : S-1-5-21-3384837461-4027165227-↵
                                          453512602-500
Office                                  :
OfficePhone                             :
Organization                            :
OtherName                               :
PasswordExpired                         : False
PasswordLastSet                         : 9/27/2012 10:18:17 AM
PasswordNeverExpires                    : False
PasswordNotRequired                     : False
POBox                                   :
PostalCode                              :
PrimaryGroup                            : cn=Domain Users,cn=Users,dc=adatum,dc=com
primaryGroupID                          : 513
PrincipalsAllowedToDelegateToAccount    : {}
ProfilePath                             :
ProtectedFromAccidentalDeletion         : False
pwdLastSet                              : 129932398979898472
SamAccountName                          : Administrator
sAMAccountType                          : 805306368
ScriptPath                              :
sDRightsEffective                       : 15
ServicePrincipalNames                   : {}
SID                                     : S-1-5-21-3384837461-4027165227-↵
                                          453512602-500
SIDHistory                              : {}
SmartcardLogonRequired                  : False
State                                   :
StreetAddress                           :
Surname                                 :
Title                                   :
TrustedForDelegation                    : False
TrustedToAuthForDelegation              : False
UseDESKeyOnly                           : False
userAccountControl                      : 512
userCertificate                         : {}
UserPrincipalName                       :
uSNChanged                              : 28008
uSNCreated                              : 8196
whenChanged                             : 10/9/2012 9:27:17 AM
whenCreated                             : 9/27/2012 11:16:45 AM
```

Discussion

Objects in Active Directory are made up of a collection of attributes. Attributes can be single- or multivalued. Each attribute also has an associated syntax that is defined in the schema. See Recipe 10.6 for a complete list of syntaxes.

Using a graphical user interface

You can customize the list of attributes returned from a search with LDP by modifying the Attributes: field under Options→Search. To include all attributes, enter an asterisk (*). To modify the default subset of attributes that are returned, enter a semicolon-separated list of attributes. You can also use the numeric attribute ID instead of the attribute name, such as using 1.1 in place of distinguishedName.

Using a command-line interface

The -attr option for the dsquery command accepts a whitespace-separated list of attributes to display. Using an asterisk (*) will return all default attributes.

When using AdFind, you have several shortcut switches to reduce the amount of typing you need to do. If you are searching for an object in the default container, you can use the -default switch rather than something like -b dc=contoso,dc=com. Likewise, if you are querying the Configuration NC, you can use the -config switch, -root for the root partition, or -schema for the Schema partition. If you want to query a subcontainer of one of these partitions, you can add the -rb switch, which stands for *Relative Base*.

See Also

Recipe 10.6; MSDN: IADsPropertyEntry; MSDN: IADsPropertyList; MSDN: ADSTY-PEENUM; MSDN: IADs::GetInfo; *Active Directory*, Fifth Edition, by Brian Desmond et al. (O'Reilly)

4.3. Counting Objects in Active Directory

Problem

You want to retrieve the number of directory objects that meet the result of an LDAP query.

Solution

Using a graphical user interface

1. Open LDP.
2. From the menu, select Connection→Connect.
3. For Server, enter the name or IP address of a domain controller or the domain that contains the object.
4. For Port, enter 389.
5. Click OK.

6. From the menu, select Connection→Bind.

7. Accept the default and bind as the currently logged on user or select the option to bind with credentials and then enter the credentials.

8. Click OK.

9. From the menu, select Browse→Search.

10. Enter the base DN, scope, and LDAP filter of the objects that you're looking for.

11. Click Options and remove the checkmark next to Display Results. This will display the number of objects returned by the query without displaying the details of the items that are returned.

12. Click OK and then click Run to perform the query.

Using a command-line interface

To retrieve a count of objects that match a particular query, use the following syntax:

```
> adfind -b <Search Base> -s <Scope> -f <Search Filter> -c
```

For example, retrieving the number of user objects in the *adatum.com* domain would use the following syntax:

```
> adfind -default -f "(&(objectclass=user)(objectcategory=person))" -c
>
> AdFind V01.46.00cpp Joe Richards (joe@joeware.net) March 2012
>
> Using server: dc1.adatum.com:389
> Directory: Windows Server 8
> Base DN: dc=adatum,dc=com
>
> 5 Objects returned
```

Using PowerShell

The following example will query Active Directory for a list of user objects in the current domain and return the count:

```
Get-ADObject -Filter {(objectClass -eq "user") -and ↵
(objectCategory -eq "person")} | Measure-Object | FL Count
```

To retrieve a count of all of the computer objects in the current domain, run the following command:

```
Get-ADObject -Filter {(objectClass -eq "user") -and ↵
(objectCategory -eq "computer")} | Measure-Object | FL Count
```

Discussion

Using PowerShell

The PowerShell commands can target a specific container or OU, as follows:

```
Get-ADObject -SearchBase "OU=Branches,dc=adatum,dc=com"↵
 -Filter {(objectClass -eq "user") -and (objectCategory -eq "person")} |↵
Measure-Object | FL Count
```

Be careful with the filtering. The class and category of the object must be combined to accurately target user objects.

There are other ways to filter, too. In this recipe, we've used an efficient filtering method while keeping the commands easy to use. However, in large environments, using LDAP filtering can be a bit faster than standard filtering. The following command counts all of the user objects in the current domain and uses LDAP filtering:

```
Get-ADObject -LDAPFilter "(&(objectCategory=Person)(objectClass=User)) "↵
Measure-Object | FL Count
```

4.4. Using LDAP Controls

Problem

You want to use an LDAP control as part of an LDAP operation.

Solution

Using a graphical user interface

1. Open LDP.
2. From the menu, select Options→Controls.
3. Under Load Predefined, select the control you want to use. The control should automatically be added to the list of Active Controls.
4. Under Value, enter the value for the control.
5. Under Control Type, select whether the control is server-side or client-side.
6. Check the box beside Critical if the control is critical.
7. Click OK.
8. At this point, you will need to invoke the LDAP operation (such as Search) that will use the control. In the dialog box for any operation, click Options and ensure that the Extended option is checked before initiating the operation.

Using a command-line interface

The AdFind and AdMod utilities will enable a number of LDAP controls, either by default or through the use of various command-line switches. For example, the `-show del` switch will invoke the Show Deleted Objects LDAP control, and `-stats` will invoke the Show Stats control.

Using PowerShell

PowerShell leverages LDAP controls in some built-in parameters of various cmdlets. For example, the `Get-ADObject` cmdlet has a parameter to include deleted objects in searches. The `-IncludeDeletedObjects` parameter uses LDAP controls as part of the command.

Discussion

LDAP controls were defined in the LDAPv3 specification as a way to extend LDAP and its operations without breaking the protocol. Many controls have been implemented, some of which are used when searching the directory (e.g., paged searching, Virtual List View [VLV], finding deleted objects, and attribute scoped query), and some are needed to do certain modifications to the directory (e.g., cross-domain object moves, tree delete, and permissive modify). Controls can be marked as critical, which means they must be processed with the request or an error is returned. If an unsupported control is not flagged as critical, the server can continue to process the request and ignore the control.

The complete list of controls supported by Active Directory is included in Table 4-2.

Table 4-2. LDAP controls supported by Active Directory

Name	OID	Description
Permit No-Opt Modify	1.2.840.113556.1.4.1413	Allows duplicate adds of the same value for an attribute or deletion of an attribute that has no values to succeed (normally, it would fail in that situation).
Return Deleted Objects	1.2.840.113556.1.4.417	Used to inform the server to return any deleted objects that matched the search criteria.
Cross Domain Move	1.2.840.113556.1.4.521	Used to move objects between domains.
Set change notifications	1.2.840.113556.1.4.528	Used by clients to register for notification of when changes occur in the directory.
Delayed Write	1.2.840.113556.1.4.619	Used to inform the server to return after directory modifications have been written to memory, but before they have been written to disk. This can speed up processing of a lot of modifications.
Security Descriptor Flags	1.2.840.113556.1.4.801	Used to pass flags to the server to control certain security descriptor options.
Subtree Delete	1.2.840.113556.1.4.805	Used to delete portions of the directory tree, including any child objects.
Verify Name Existence	1.2.840.113556.1.4.1338	Used to target a specific GC server that is used to verify DN-valued attributes that are processed during addition or modification operations.

Name	OID	Description
No referrals generated	1.2.840.113556.1.4.1339	Informs the server not to generate any referrals in a search response.
Domain or phantom scope	1.2.840.113556.1.4.1340	Used to pass flags to the server to control search options.
Search Stats	1.2.840.113556.1.4.970	Used to return statistics about an LDAP query. See Recipe 15.8 for an example.
Attribute Scoped Query	1.2.840.113556.1.4.1504	Used to force a query to be based on a specific DN-valued attribute. This control is new to Windows Server 2003. See Recipe 4.8 for an example.
Extended DN	1.2.840.113556.1.4.529	Used to return an object's GUID and SID (for security principals) as part of its distinguished name.
Quota SID	1.2.840.113566.1.4.1852	Used to pass the SID of a security principal in order to query constructed attributes such as ms-DS-Quota-Effective and ms-DS-Quota-Used.
Paged Results	1.2.840.113556.1.4.319	Instructs the server to return search results in "pages."
DIRSYNC	1.2.840.113556.1.4.841	Used to find objects that have changed over a period of time.
Server-side Sort Request	1.2.840.113556.1.4.473	Used to inform the server to sort the results of a search.
Server-side Sort Response	1.2.840.113556.1.4.474	Returned by the server in response to a sort request.
Show deactivated links	1.2.840.113556.1.4.2065	Used to request deactivated links to be included in a search.
Show deleted objects	1.2.840.113556.1.4.417	Used to request deleted objects to be included in a search.
VLV Request	2.16.840.1.113730.3.4.9	Used to request a virtual list view of results from a search. This control is new to Windows Server 2003.
VLV Response	2.16.840.1.113730.3.4.10	Response from a server returning a virtual list view of results from a search. This control is new to Windows Server 2003.

See Also

Recipe 4.8; Recipe 15.8; RFC 2251 (Lightweight Directory Access Protocol [v3]) for a description of LDAP controls; 3.1.1.3.4.1 LDAP Extended Controls (*http://bit.ly/ 10a5zth*); MSDN: Using Controls

4.5. Using a Fast or Concurrent Bind

Problem

You want to perform an LDAP bind using a concurrent bind, also known as a fast bind. Concurrent binds are typically used in situations where you need to authenticate a lot of users, and either those users do not need to directly access the directory or the directory access is done with another account.

Solution

Using a graphical user interface

1. Open LDP.
2. From the menu, select Connection→Connect.
3. For Server, enter the name of a DC.
4. For Port, enter 389.
5. Click OK.
6. From the menu, select Options→Connection Options.
7. Under Option Name:, select LDAP_OPT_FAST_CONCURRENT_BIND.
8. Click the Set button. Then click the Close button.
9. From the menu, select Connection→Bind.
10. Accept the default and bind as the currently logged on user or select the option to bind with credentials and then enter the credentials.
11. Click OK.

Discussion

Unlike simple binding, concurrent binding does not generate a security token or determine a user's group memberships during the authentication process. It determines only whether the authenticating user has a valid enabled account and password, which makes it much faster than a typical bind. This is usually used programmatically for AD-enabled applications to improve the speed of AD authentication; it's not something that you'll typically do on the fly. Concurrent binding is implemented as a session option that is set after you establish a connection to a domain controller, but before any bind attempts are made. After the option has been set, any bind attempt made with the connection will be a concurrent bind.

There are a couple of caveats when using concurrent binds. First, you cannot enable signing or encryption, which means that all data for concurrent binds will be sent over the network in clear text. Second, because the user's security token is not generated, access to the directory is done anonymously and access restrictions are based on the ANONYMOUS LOGON principal.

It is worth mentioning that there is another type of fast bind that is completely different from the procedure just described. This fast bind is implemented within ADSI, and it simply means that when you fast-bind to an object, the objectClass attribute for the object is not retrieved; therefore, the object-specific IADs class interfaces are not available. For example, if you bind to a user object using an ADSI fast bind, then only the basic IADs interfaces will be available, not the IADsUser interfaces.

This is the complete list of interfaces that are available for objects retrieved with fast binds:

- IADs
- IADsContainer
- IDirectoryObject
- IDirectorySearch
- IADsPropertyList
- IADsObjectOptions
- ISupportErrorInfo
- IADsDeleteOps

You must use the IADsOpenDSObject::OpenDSObject interface to enable fast binds. If you call IADsContainer::GetObject on a child object of a parent you used a fast bind with, the same fast bind behavior applies. Unlike concurrent binds, ADSI fast binds do not impose any restrictions on the authenticating user. This means that the object-specific IADs interfaces will not be available. Also, no check is done to verify the object exists when you call OpenDSObject.

ADSI fast binds are useful when you need to make a lot of updates to objects that you know exist (perhaps from an ADO query that returned a list of DNs) and you do not need any IADs-specific interfaces. Instead of two trips over the network per object binding, there would be only one.

See Also

MSDN: Using Concurrent Binding; MSDN: ADS_AUTHENTICATION_ENUM

4.6. Connecting to an Object GUID

Problem

You want to bind to a container using its globally unique identifier (GUID).

Solution

Using a graphical user interface

1. Open LDP.

---

2. From the menu, select Connection→Connect.

3. For Server, enter the name of a domain controller (or leave it blank to do a serverless bind).

4. For Port, enter 389.

5. Click OK.

6. From the menu, select Connection→Bind.

7. Accept the default and bind as the currently logged on user or select the option to bind with credentials and then enter the credentials.

8. Click OK.

9. From the menu, select Browse→Search.

10. For BaseDN, enter the GUID of the object that you're searching for in the following format:

   ```
   <GUID=758A39F4A44A0C48A16016457C1AE9E9>
   ```

11. For Scope, select the appropriate scope.

12. For Filter, enter an LDAP filter.

13. Click Run.

Discussion

Each object in Active Directory has a GUID associated with it, stored in the object GUID attribute. The GUID is, for most purposes, a unique identifier that retains its value even if an object is updated, renamed, or moved. This makes the GUID the preferable means of binding to an object, rather than hardcoding a reference to an object name that might change or by using a potentially complex LDAP query.

See Also

"'GUIDs' or 'Having unique in the name doesn't make it so...'" (*http://blog.joeware.net/2005/06/19/42/*) for a more in-depth discussion of the objectGUID attribute; MSDN: IADs.GUID; MSDN: Using objectGUID to Bind to an Object; Recipe 4.7

4.7. Connecting to a Well-Known GUID

Problem

You want to connect to LDAP using one of the well-known GUIDs in Active Directory.

Solution

Using a graphical user interface

1. Open LDP.
2. From the menu, select Connection→Connect.
3. For Server, enter the name of a domain controller (or leave it blank to do a serverless bind).
4. For Port, enter 389.
5. Click OK.
6. From the menu, select Connection→Bind.
7. Accept the default and bind as the currently logged on user or select the option to bind with credentials and then enter the credentials.
8. Click OK.
9. From the menu, select View→Tree.
10. For the DN, enter:

    `<WKGUID=<WKGUID>,<DomainDN>>`

    where `<WKGUID>` is the well-known GUID that you want to connect to, and `<DomainDN>` is the distinguished name of a domain.

11. Click OK. In the lefthand menu, you can now browse the container corresponding to the well-known GUID that you specified.

Using a command-line interface

To enumerate the well-known GUIDs in the Domain NC, use the following syntax:

```
> adfind -default -s base wellknownObjects
```

To display the WKGUIDs in the Configuration NC, replace `-default` with `-config` in the previous syntax.

To connect to a well-known GUID in the Domain NC using AdFind, use the following syntax:

```
> adfind -b "<WKGUID=<WKGUID>,<DomainDN>>" -s base -dn
```

 Because of additional security settings attached to the `Deleted Objects` container, if you specify the GUID you must also use the `-showdel` switch in AdFind.

Using PowerShell

```
Get-ADObject (Get-ADRootDSE).DefaultNamingContext -Properties wellKnownObjects↵
| Select wellKnownObjects -ExpandProperty wellknownobjects
```

Discussion

The Domain NC in Active Directory contains a number of well-known GUIDs that correspond to containers that exist in every AD implementation. These GUIDs are stored as wellKnownObjects attributes within the *<DomainDN>* object, and they allow administrators and developers to consistently connect to critical containers even if they are moved or renamed. The *<DomainDN>* container possesses the following objects that correspond to well-known GUIDs:

- cn=NTDS Quotas,*<DomainDN>*
- cn=Microsoft,cn=Program Data,*<DomainDN>*
- cn=Program Data,*<DomainDN>*
- cn=ForeignSecurityPrincipals,*<DomainDN>*
- cn=Deleted Objects,*<DomainDN>*
- cn=Infrastructure,*<DomainDN>*
- cn=LostAndFound,*<DomainDN>*
- cn=System,*<DomainDN>*
- OU=Domain Controllers,*<DomainDN>*
- cn=Computers,*<DomainDN>*
- cn=Users,*<DomainDN>*

The Configuration NC adds these additional WKGUIDs:

- cn=NTDS Quotas,cn=Configuration,*<ForestRootDN>*
- cn=LostAndFoundConfig,cn=Configuration,*<ForestRootDN>*
- cn=Deleted Objects,cn=Configuration,*<ForestRootDN>*

See Also

MSDN: Binding to Well-Known Objects Using WKGUID

4.8. Searching for Objects in a Domain

Problem

You want to find objects in a domain that match certain criteria.

Solution

Using a graphical user interface

1. Open LDP.
2. From the menu, select Connection→Connect.
3. For Server, enter the name of a domain controller (or leave it blank to do a serverless bind).
4. For Port, enter 389.
5. Click OK.
6. From the menu, select Connection→Bind.
7. Accept the default and bind as the currently logged on user or select the option to bind with credentials and then enter the credentials.
8. Click OK.
9. From the menu, select Browse→Search.
10. For BaseDN, type the base distinguished name where the search will start. (You can leave this blank if you wish to connect to the Domain NC as the base DN.)
11. For Scope, select the appropriate scope.
12. For Filter, enter an LDAP filter.
13. Click Run.

Using a command-line interface

To run a query using the built-in DSQuery tool, use the following syntax:

```
> dsquery * <BaseDN> -scope <Scope> -filter "<Filter>" -attr "<AttrList>"
```

To retrieve the SAM account name for all user objects within the *adatum.com* domain, for example, use the following syntax:

```
> dsquery * dc=adatum,dc=com -filter
"(&(objectclass=user)(objectcategory=person))" -attr sAMAccountName
```

To run a query using `adfind`, use the following syntax:

```
> adfind -b <BaseDN> -s <Scope> -f <Filter> <Attributes>
```

Querying for SAM account names of user objects with `adfind` takes the following syntax:

```
> adfind -b dc=adatum,dc=com -f↵
  "(&(objectclass=user)(objectcategory=person))" sAMAccountName
```

 Both DSQuery and AdFind assume a default search scope of subtrees; you need only to specify the search scope if you want to use a different one.

Using PowerShell

The following example will search for user objects within the current Active Directory domain:

```
Get-ADObject -Filter {(objectClass -eq "user") -and ↵
(objectCategory -eq "person")}
```

Discussion

Most tools that can be used to search Active Directory require a basic understanding of how to perform LDAP searches using a base DN, search scope, and search filter, as described in RFC 2251 and RFC 2254. The base DN is where the search begins in the directory tree. The search scope defines how far down in the tree to search from the base DN. The search filter is a prefix notation string that contains equality comparisons of attribute and value pairs.

The scope can be `base`, `onelevel` (or `one`), or `subtree` (or `sub`). A `base` scope will match only the base DN, `onelevel` will match only objects that are contained directly under the base DN, and `subtree` will match everything from the base DN and any objects beneath it.

 There are no LDAP query scopes that will walk backward "up" the tree.

The search filter syntax is a powerful way to represent simple and complex queries. For example, a filter that matches all of the user objects would be `(&(objectclass=user)(objectcategory=Person))`. For more information on filters, see RFC 2254.

Using a graphical user interface

To customize the list of attributes returned for each matching object, look at the GUI discussion in Recipe 4.2.

Using a command-line interface

<AttrList> should be a space-separated list of attributes to return. To return all attributes that have been populated with a value, leave this field blank or use an asterisk (*).

See Also

Recipe 4.2 for viewing attributes of objects; Recipe 4.9 for setting advanced ADO options; RFC 2251 (Lightweight Directory Access Protocol [v3]); RFC 2254 (Lightweight Directory Access Protocol [v3]); "LDAP Query Basics" (*http://bit.ly/166mR1P*)

4.9. Searching the Global Catalog

Problem

You want to perform a forest-wide search using the global catalog.

Solution

Using a graphical user interface

1. Open LDP.
2. From the menu, select Connection→Connect.
3. For Server, enter the name of a global catalog server.
4. For Port, enter 3268.
5. Click OK.
6. From the menu, select Connection→Bind.
7. Accept the default and bind as the currently logged on user or select the option to bind with credentials and then enter the credentials.
8. Click OK.
9. From the menu, select Browse→Search.
10. For BaseDN, type the base distinguished name of where to start the search.
11. For Scope, select the appropriate scope.
12. For Filter, enter an LDAP filter.
13. Click Run.

Using a command-line interface

To query the global catalog using DSQuery, use the following syntax:

```
> dsquery * <BaseDN> -gc -scope <Scope> -filter "<Filter>" -attr "<AttrList>"
```

To run a query using AdFind, use the following syntax:

```
> adfind -gc -b <BaseDN> -s <Scope> -f <Filter> <Attributes>
```

Using PowerShell

To query the global catalog server named *dc1.adatum.com* for all computer objects in the *adatum.com* domain, run the following command:

```
Get-ADObject -Filter {ObjectClass -eq "computer"} -Server dc1.adatum.com:3268↵
  -SearchBase "dc=adatum,dc=com" -Properties Name | FT Name
```

Discussion

The global catalog facilitates forest-wide searches. When you perform a normal LDAP search over port 389, you are searching against a particular partition within Active Directory, whether that is the Domain naming context, Configuration naming context, Schema naming context, or an application partition. If you have multiple domains in your forest, this type of search will not search against all domains; it will search only the domain that you specify.

The global catalog, by contrast, contains a subset of the attributes for all objects in the forest (excluding objects in application partitions). Think of it as a subset of all the naming contexts combined. Every object in the directory will be contained in the global catalog (except for objects contained within application partitions), but only some of the attributes of those objects will be available. For that reason, if you perform a global catalog search and do not get values for attributes you were expecting to, make sure those attributes are included in the global catalog, also known as the partial attribute set (PAS). See Recipe 10.13 for more information on adding information to the PAS. As an alternative, you can query a DC within the domain containing the object to return a list of all attributes configured for that object. Note that the Active Directory Administrative Center provides a method to easily change the scope of a search to be a global catalog search.

Using a graphical user interface

The only difference between this solution and the one in Recipe 4.8 is that the port has changed to 3268, which is the standard GC port.

Using a command-line interface

The only difference between this solution and the one in Recipe 4.8, both for DSQuery and AdFind, is the addition of the -gc flag.

See Also

Recipe 4.8 for searching for objects; Recipe 10.13

4.10. Searching for a Large Number of Objects

Problem

Your search is returning exactly 1,000 objects, which is only a subset of the objects you expected, and you want it to return all matching objects.

Solution

You might notice, when using some tools, that searches with large numbers of matches stop displaying after 1,000. By default, domain controllers return a maximum of 1,000 entries from a search unless paging is enabled. This is done to prevent queries from consuming excessive resources on domain controllers by retrieving the results all at once instead of in pages or batches. The following examples are variations of Recipe 4.8, which will show how to enable paging and return all matching entries.

Using a graphical user interface

1. Open LDP.
2. From the menu, select Connection→Connect.
3. For Server, enter the name of a domain controller (or leave it blank to do a serverless bind).
4. For Port, enter 389.
5. Click OK.
6. From the menu, select Connection→Bind.
7. Accept the default and bind as the currently logged on user or select the option to bind with credentials and then enter the credentials.
8. Click OK.
9. From the menu, select Browse→Search.
10. For BaseDN, type the base distinguished name of where the search will start. (You can leave this blank if you wish to connect to the domain NC as the base DN.)
11. For Scope, select the appropriate scope.

12. For Filter, enter an LDAP filter.

13. Click Options to customize the options for this query.

14. For "Time limit," enter a value such as 120.

15. For "Size limit," enter the number of objects to be returned with each page (e.g., 1,000).

16. Under Search Call Type, select Paged.

17. Click OK and then Run to perform the query. A page of results (i.e., 1,000 entries) will be displayed each time you click Run until all results have been returned.

Using a command-line interface

```
> dsquery * <BaseDN> -limit 0 -scope <Scope> -filter "<Filter>" ↵
-attr "<AttrList>"
```

Using PowerShell

The following PowerShell command will search the default Users container and return all objects while limiting results to 12,000 objects:

```
Get-ADObject -SearchBase "cn=users,dc=adatum,dc=com" -Filter * -ResultSetSize ↵
12000
```

Discussion

Paged searching support is implemented via an LDAP control. LDAP controls were defined in RFC 2251 and the Paged control in RFC 2696. Controls are extensions to LDAP that were not built into the protocol, so not all directory vendors support the same ones.

 In Active Directory, you can change the default maximum page size of 1,000 by modifying the LDAP query policy. See Recipe 4.27 for more information.

Active Directory will return a maximum of 256 KB of data even when paged searching is enabled. This value is defined in the LDAP query policy and can be modified like the maximum page size (see Recipe 4.27).

Using a graphical user interface

A word of caution when using LDP to display a large number of entries: by default, only 2,048 lines will be displayed in the right pane. To change that value, go to Options→General and change the number of lines under Buffer Size to a larger number.

Note that newer tools aren't as limited as some of the tools that have been around a long time. For example, the Active Directory Administrative Center displays up to 20,000 objects in a search by default.

Using a command-line interface

The only difference between this solution and the one in Recipe 4.8 is the addition of the -limit 0 flag. With -limit set to 0, paging will be enabled according to the default LDAP query policy; matching objects will be returned within those parameters. If -limit is not specified, a maximum of 100 entries will be returned.

 AdFind enables paged searches by default; it will return any number of objects from a query without any modification.

See Also

Recipe 4.8 for searching for objects; Recipe 4.27 for viewing the default LDAP policy; RFC 2251 (Lightweight Directory Access Protocol [v3]); RFC 2696 (LDAP Control Extension for Simple Paged Results Manipulation)

4.11. Searching with an Attribute-Scoped Query

Problem

You want to perform a search using an individual value within a multivalued attribute as part of the search criteria. An attribute-scoped query can do this in a single query, instead of the previous method, which required multiple queries.

Solution

Using a graphical user interface

1. Follow the steps in Recipe 4.4 to enable an LDAP control.
2. Select the Attribute Scoped Query control.
3. For Value, enter the multivalued attribute name (e.g., member).
4. Click the "Check in" button.
5. Click OK.
6. From the menu, select Browse→Search.
7. For BaseDN, type the DN of the object that contains the multivalued attributes.

8. For Scope, select Base.

9. For Filter, enter an LDAP filter to match against the objects that are part of the multivalued DN attribute.

10. Click Run.

 Attribute-scoped queries can only be performed using a Base scope.

Using a command-line interface

AdFind allows attribute-scoped queries by using the -asq switch. For example:

```
adfind -b cn=somegroup,cn=users,dc=domain,dc=group -asq member ↵
-f objectclass=user
samaccountname
```

Using PowerShell

The PowerShell pipeline will allow you to perform an attribute-scoped query as follows:

```
Get-ADGroup "Domain Admins" | Get-ADGroupMember |↵
Get-ADUser -Properties sAMAccountName | Select samaccountname
```

Discussion

When dealing with group objects, you may have encountered the problem where you wanted to search against the members of a group to find a subset or to retrieve certain attributes about each member. This normally involved performing a query to retrieve all of the members, and additional queries to retrieve whatever attributes you needed for each member. This was less than ideal, so an alternative was developed.

With an attribute-scoped query, you can perform a single query against the group object and return whatever properties you need from the member's object, or return only a subset of the members based on certain criteria. Let's look at the LDAP search parameters for an attribute-scoped query:

Attribute-scoped query control value
  The value to set for this control should be the DN attribute that you want to iterate over (for example, member).

Base DN
  This must be the DN of the object that contains the DN attribute (e.g., cn=Domain Admins,cn=users,dc=adatum,dc=com).

Scope
  This must be set to Base to query only the group object itself.

Filter

The filter will match against objects defined in the Control Value. For example, a filter of (objectClass=computer) would match computer objects only. You can also use any other attributes that are available with those objects. The following filter would match all computer objects that have a Description attribute equal to "Sales":

```
(&(objectclass=computer)(Description=Sales))
```

Attributes

This should contain the list of attributes to return for the objects matched in the DN attribute.

When performing an attribute-scoped query against a member attribute, it's important to remember that primary group membership is handled as a special case; as such you may experience unpredictable results in this situation.

See Also

Recipe 4.4; MSDN: Performing an Attribute Scoped Query

4.12. Searching with a Bitwise Filter

Problem

You want to search against an attribute that contains a *bit flag*, which requires you to use a bitwise filter to perform the search.

Solution

Using a graphical user interface

1. Open LDP.
2. From the menu, select Connection→Connect.
3. For Server, enter the name of a domain controller (or leave it blank to do a serverless bind).
4. For Port, enter 389.
5. Click OK.
6. From the menu, select Connection→Bind.
7. Accept the default and bind as the currently logged on user or select the option to bind with credentials and then enter the credentials.
8. Click OK.

---

9. From the menu, select Browse→Search.

10. For Base DN, type the base distinguished name of where the search will start. (You can leave this blank if you wish to connect to the domain NC as the base DN.)

11. For Scope, select the appropriate scope.

12. For the Filter, enter the bitwise expression, such as the following, which will find all universal groups:

```
(&(objectCategory=group)(groupType:1.2.840.113556.1.4.804:=8))
```

13. Click Run.

Using a command-line interface

The following query finds universal groups in the *adatum.com* domain by using a bitwise AND filter:

```
> dsquery * dc=adatum,dc=com -scope subtree -attr "name" -filter↵
"(&(objectclass=group)(objectCategory=group)↵
(groupType:1.2.840.113556.1.4.804:=8) )"
```

The following query finds disabled user accounts in the *adatum.com* domain by using a bitwise AND filter:

```
> dsquery * dc=adatum,dc=com -attr name -scope subtree -filter
"(&(objectclass=user)(objectcategory=person)↵
(useraccountcontrol:1.2.840.113556.1.4.
803:=2))"
```

You can also perform queries that use bitwise filters using AdFind. The following will find all disabled user accounts in the *adatum.com* domain:

```
> adfind -default -bit -f useraccountcontrol:AND:=2
```

Similarly, the following will return all universal groups in the *adatum.com* domain using a bitwise filter:

```
> adfind -default -bit -f groupType:AND:=8
```

Using PowerShell

The following command will find all universal groups in the current domain:

```
Get-ADObject -LDAPFilter {(groupType:1.2.840.113556.1.4.803:=8)} | Select Name
```

Discussion

Many attributes in Active Directory are composed of bit flags. A bit flag is often used to encode properties about an object into a single attribute. For example, the group Type attribute on group objects is a bit flag that is used to determine the group scope and type.

The `userAccountControl` attribute on user and `computer` objects is used to describe a whole series of properties, including account status (i.e., enabled or disabled), account lockout, password not required, smartcard authentication required, and so on.

The `searchFlags` and `systemFlags` attributes on `attributeSchema` objects define, among other things, whether an attribute is constructed, indexed, and included as part of Ambiguous Name Resolution (ANR).

To search against these types of attributes, you need to use bitwise search filters. There are two types of bitwise search filters you can use, one that represents a logical OR and one that represents a logical AND. This is implemented within a search filter as a *matching rule*. A matching rule is simply a way to inform the LDAP server (in this case, a domain controller) to treat part of the filter differently. Here is an example of what a matching rule looks like:

```
(userAccountControl:1.2.840.113556.1.4.803:=514)
```

The format is (*attributename:MatchingRuleOID:=value*), though AdFind allows you to use an easier syntax for bitwise queries. As mentioned, there are two bitwise matching rules, which are defined by OIDs. The logical AND matching rule OID is 1.2.840.113556.1.4.803, and the logical OR matching rule OID is 1.2.840.113556.1.4.804. These OIDs instruct the server to perform special processing on the filter. A logical OR filter will return success if any bit specified by *value* is stored in *attributename*. Alternatively, the logical AND filter will return success if all bits specified by *value* match the value of *attributename*. Perhaps an example will help clarify this.

To create a normal user account, you have to set `userAccountControl` to 514. The number 514 was calculated by adding the normal user account flag of 512 together with the disabled account flag of 2 (512 + 2 = 514). If you use the following logical OR matching rule against the 514 value, as shown here:

```
(useraccountcontrol:1.2.840.113556.1.4.804:=514)
```

then all normal user accounts (flag 512) OR disabled accounts (flag 2) would be returned. This would include enabled user accounts (from flag 512), disabled computer accounts (from flag 2), and disabled user accounts (from flag 2). In the case of `userAc countControl`, flag 2 can apply to both user and computer accounts, which is why both would be included in the returned entries.

One of the benefits of bitwise matching rules is that they allow you to combine a bunch of comparisons into a single filter. In fact, it may help to think that the OR filter could also be written using two expressions:

```
(|(useraccountcontrol:1.2.840.113556.1.4.804:=2)
(useraccountcontrol:1.2.840.113556.1.4.804:=512))
```

Just as before, this will match `userAccountControl` attributes that contain either the 2 or 512 flag; we're performing two OR operations against the same value, first ORing the value against 2, then against 512.

For the logical AND operator, similar principles apply. Instead of any of the bits in the flag being a possible match, *all* of the bits in the flag must match for it to return a success. If the `userAccountControl` example was changed to use logical AND, it would look like this:

```
(useraccountcontrol:1.2.840.113556.1.4.803:=514)
```

In this case, only normal user accounts that are also disabled would be returned. The same filter could be rewritten using the & operator instead of | as in the following:

```
(&(useraccountcontrol:1.2.840.113556.1.4.803:=2)
(useraccountcontrol:1.2.840.113556.1.4.803:=512))
```

An important subtlety to note is that when you are comparing only a single bit-flag value, the logical OR and logical AND matching rules would return the same result. So, if you wanted to find any normal user accounts, you could search on the single bit flag of 512 using either of the following:

```
(useraccountcontrol:1.2.840.113556.1.4.803:=512)
```

```
(useraccountcontrol:1.2.840.113556.1.4.804:=512)
```

Using PowerShell

Searching on a bitwise operator in PowerShell is done using the appropriate LDAP filter, as you can see. In other chapters we will look at individual AD cmdlets that mask the bitwise search into a more human-readable operation, such as the `Enable-ADAccount` and `Disable-ADAccount` cmdlets.

See Also

MSDN: Enumerating Groups by Scope or Type in a Domain; MSDN: Determining Which Properties Are Non-Replicated, Constructed, Global Catalog, and Indexed; MS KB 305144 (How to Use the UserAccountControl Flags to Manipulate User Account Properties)

4.13. Creating an Object

Problem

You want to create an object.

Solution

In each solution in this recipe, an example of adding a user object is shown. Modify the examples as needed to include whatever class and attributes you need to create.

Using a graphical user interface

1. Open ADSI Edit.
2. If an entry for the naming context you want to browse is not already displayed, do the following:
   a. Right-click on ADSI Edit in the right pane and click "Connect to."
   b. Fill in the information for the naming context, container, or OU you want to add an object to. Click on the Advanced button if you need to enter alternate credentials.
3. In the left pane, browse to the container or OU you want to add the object to. Once you've found the parent container, right-click on it and select New→Object.
4. Under Select a Class, select user.
5. For the cn, enter jsmith and click Next.
6. For sAMAccountName, enter jsmith and click Next.
7. Click the More Attributes button to enter additional attributes.
8. Click Finish.

Using a command-line interface

Create an LDAP Data Interchange Format (LDIF) file called *create_object.ldf* with the following contents:

```
dn: cn=jsmith,cn=users,dc=adatum,dc=com
changetype: add
objectClass: user
samaccountname: jsmith
```

Then run the following command:

```
> ldifde -v -i -f create_object.ldf
```

It is also worth noting that you can add a limited number of object types with the dsadd command. Run dsadd /? from a command line for more details.

You can also create objects using AdMod; to create a new user object in the *adatum.com* domain use the following syntax:

```
> admod -b "cn=Joe Smith,cn=users,dc=adatum,dc=com"↵
  objectclass::user samaccountname::jsmith -add
```

Using PowerShell

To create a new computer object named Kiosk2 in the Workstations OU, use the following PowerShell command:

```
New-ADObject -Path "OU=Workstations,dc=adatum,dc=com" -Type Computer ↵
-Name "Kiosk2" -Description "Computer in lobby" -OtherAttributes ↵
@{SamAccountName="Kiosk2"}
```

Discussion

To create an object in Active Directory, you have to specify the objectClass, RDN value, and any other mandatory attributes that are not automatically set by Active Directory. Some of the automatically generated attributes include objectGUID, instanceType, and objectCategory.

In the jsmith example, the object class was user, the RDN value was jsmith, and the only other attribute set was sAMAccountName. Admittedly, this user object is unusable in its current state because it will be disabled by default and no password was set, but it should give you an idea of how to create an object. In the case of a user object, you'll need to configure a password that meets any existing password complexity requirements before enabling the user.

Using a graphical user interface

Other tools, such as Active Directory Administrative Center and AD Users and Computers, could be used to do the same thing, but ADSI Edit is useful as a generic object editor.

One attribute that you will not be able to set via ADSI Edit is the password (unicodePwd attribute). It is stored in binary form and needs to be edited using a secure connection. If you want to set the password for a user through a GUI, you can do it with the AD Users and Computers snap-in or Active Directory Administrative Center.

Using a command-line interface

For more on *ldifde*, see Recipe 4.28.

With DSAdd, you can set numerous attributes when creating an object. The downside is that you can create only the following object types: computer, contact, group, OU, quota, and user.

See Also

Recipe 4.28; Recipe 4.29 for importing objects with LDIF; MSDN: IADsContainer:: GetObject; MSDN: IADsContainer::Create; MSDN: IADs::Put; MSDN: IADs::SetInfo

4.14. Modifying an Object

Problem

You want to modify one or more attributes of an object.

Solution

The following example sets the employeeID attribute for a user object.

Using a graphical user interface

1. Open Active Directory Administrative Center.
2. In the bottom-right pane, enter the search criteria of the desired object and then click the Search button.
3. In the search results, locate the object, right-click it, and then click Properties.
4. Scroll down to the Extensions section and then click the Attribute Editor tab.
5. Scroll down and click the employeeID attribute and then click the Edit button.
6. Enter the value and then click OK.
7. Click OK again to close the object properties.

Using a command-line interface

Create an LDIF file called *modify_object.ldf* with the following contents:

```
dn: cn=jsmith,cn=users,dc=adatum,dc=com
changetype: modify
replace: employeeID
employeeID: 17320
-
```

Then run the following command:

```
> ldifde -v -i -f modify_object.ldf
```

To modify an object using AdMod, you'll use the following general syntax:

```
> admod -b <ObjectDN> <attribute>:<operation>:<value>
```

For example, you can add a description to a user object using the following syntax:

```
> admod -b cn="Joe Smith,cn=Users,dc=adatum,dc=com" description::Consultant
```

You can modify a limited number of object types with the dsmod command. Run dsmod /? from a command line for more details.

Using PowerShell

To modify an object using PowerShell, use the following syntax:

```
Set-ADObject -Identity <"ObjectDN"> -Replace @{<property>=<"value">}
```

Discussion

Using a command-line interface

For more on *ldifde*, see Recipe 4.28.

As of the publication of this book, the only types of objects you can modify with DSMod are the following: computer, contact, group, OU, server, quota, partition, and user.

As you saw in this recipe, the basic format of the AdMod command when used to modify an attribute is as follows:

```
> admod -b <ObjectDN> <attribute>:<operation>:<value>
```

The value used for *<operation>* can be any one of the following:

<blank>
:   Updates the attribute with the new value. (In practical terms, this leads to a syntax of *<attribute>*::*<value>*, with nothing included between the two colons.)

+
:   Adds a value to an attribute.

−
:   Clears an attribute.

++
:   Adds multiple values to an attribute.

−−
:   Removes multiple values from an attribute.

 To change a user's password via AdMod, encrypt the connection by using the -kerbenc switch and then modify the unicodepwd attribute.

See Also

MSDN: IADs::Put; MSDN: IADs::PutEx; MSDN: IADs::SetInfo; MSDN: ADS_ PROP-ERTY_OPERATION_ENUM

4.15. Modifying a Bit-Flag Attribute

Problem

You want to safely modify an attribute that contains a bit flag, without blindly overwriting its existing contents. The solutions in this recipe modify a new attribute named adatum-UserProperties that was previously added to the schema.

Solution

Using VBScript

```
' This code safely modifies a bit flag attribute
' ------ SCRIPT CONFIGURATION ------
strObject = "<ObjectDN>" ' e.g. cn=jsmith,cn=users,dc=adatum,dc=com
strAttr = "<AttrName>" ' e.g. adatum-UserProperties
boolEnableBit = <TRUEorFALSE> ' e.g. FALSE
intBit = <BitValue> ' e.g. 16
' ------ END CONFIGURATION --------

set objObject = GetObject("LDAP://" & strObject)
intBitsOrig = objObject.Get(strAttr)
intBitsCalc = CalcBit(intBitsOrig, intBit, boolEnableBit)

if intBitsOrig <> intBitsCalc then
   objObject.Put strAttr, intBitsCalc
   objObject.SetInfo
   WScript.Echo "Changed " & strAttr & " from " & intBitsOrig &↵
" to " & intBitsCalc
else
   WScript.Echo "Did not need to change " & strAttr & " (" & intBitsOrig & ")"
end if

Function CalcBit(intValue, intBit, boolEnable)

   CalcBit = intValue

   if boolEnable = TRUE then
      CalcBit = intValue Or intBit
   else
      if intValue And intBit then
         CalcBit = intValue Xor intBit
      end if
   end if

End Function
```

Using PowerShell

To set the `adatum-UserProperties` value using PowerShell, use the following example script:

```
$user = Get-ADObject "cn=jsmith,cn=users,dc=adatum,dc=com"↵
 -Properties adatum-UserProperties
if (!$user.adatum-UserProperties) {
Set-ADObject $user -Add @{"adatum-UserProperties"=4}
Write-Host "Changed from NULL to 4."
} else {
$value = $user.adatum-UserProperties + 4
Set-ADObject $user -Replace @{"adatum-UserProperties"=$value}
Write-Host "Changed value from" $user.adatum-UserProperties "to" $value"."
}
```

Discussion

Recipe 4.12 described how to search against attributes that contain a bit flag, which is used to encode various settings about an object in a single attribute. As a quick recap, you need to use a logical OR operation to match any bits being searched against, and a logical AND to match a specific set of bits. If you want to set an attribute that is a bit flag, you need to take special precautions to ensure that you don't overwrite an existing bit. Let's consider an example. Adatum wants to secretly store some politically incorrect information about their users, such as whether the user is really old or has big feet. They don't want to create attributes such as `adatum-UserHasBigFeet`, so they decide to encode the properties in a single bit-flag attribute. They decide to call the attribute `adatum-UserProperties` with the possible bit values shown in Table 4-3.

Table 4-3. Sample bit-flag attribute values

Value	Description
1	User is overweight.
2	User is very tall.
4	User has big feet.
8	User is very old.

After they extend the schema to include the new attribute, Adatum needs to initially populate the attribute for all their users. To do so they can simply logically OR the values together that apply to each user. So, if settings 4 and 8 apply to the `jsmith` user, his `adatum-UserProperties` would be set to 12 (4 OR 8). No big deal so far. The issue comes in when they need to modify the attribute in the future.

You will, however, find that searching for information based on a bit-flag attribute is not terribly efficient. This is because bit flags cannot be indexed; you need to calculate the value for every object populated with the bit-flag attribute in question.

They later find out that jsmith was a former basketball player and is 6'8". They need to set the 2 bit (for being tall) in his adatum-UserProperties attribute. To set the 2 bit they need to first determine whether it has already been set. If it has already been set, then there is nothing to do. If the 2 bit hasn't been set, they need to logical OR 2 with the existing value of jsmith's adatum-UserProperties attribute. If they simply set the attribute to 2, it would overwrite the 4 and 8 bits that had been set previously. In the VBScript solution, they could use the CalcBit function to determine the new value:

```
intBitsCalc = CalcBit(intBitsOrig, 2, TRUE)
```

The result would be 14 (12 OR 2).

The same logic applies if they want to remove a bit, except the XOR logical operator is used.

 Active Directory contains numerous bit-flag attributes, most notably options (which is used on several different object classes) and userAc countControl (which is used on user objects). We do not recommend blindly setting those attributes unless you know what you are doing. It is preferable to use a script from this recipe so that it calculates the new value based on the existing value.

You should note that it's certainly possible to modify bitwise attributes using a GUI tool like ADSI Edit or a command-line tool like DSMod. However, it will require a certain amount of manual effort, as you'll first need to make note of the existing attribute value and then calculate the new value using a calculator or some other method. The VBScript solution presented here simply automates that process by performing the lookup and calculations for you.

Using PowerShell

The PowerShell solution looks at the existing adatum-UserProperties attribute value. If it is null, it changes it to 4. If it contains a value already, it takes that value and adds 4 to it, and then replaces the existing value with the new value.

See Also

Recipe 4.12 for searching with a bitwise filter

4.16. Dynamically Linking an Auxiliary Class

Problem

You want to dynamically link an auxiliary class to an existing object instance.

Solution

In each solution in this recipe, an example of adding the custom `adatum-SalesUser` auxiliary class to the `jsmith` user object will be described.

Using a graphical user interface

1. Open ADSI Edit.
2. If an entry for the naming context you want to browse is not already displayed, do the following:
   a. Right-click on ADSI Edit in the right pane and click "Connect to."
   b. Fill in the information for the naming context, container, or OU you want to add an object to. Click the Advanced button if you need to enter alternate credentials.
3. In the left pane, browse to the container or OU that contains the object you want to modify. Once you've found the object, right-click on it and select Properties.
4. Edit the values for the `objectClass` attribute.
5. For "Value to add," enter `adatum-SalesUser`.
6. Click Add.
7. Click OK twice.

Using a command-line interface

Create an LDIF file called *dynamically_link_class.ldf* with the following contents:

```
dn: cn=jsmith,cn=users,dc=adatum,dc=com
changetype: modify
add: objectClass
objectClass: adatum-SalesUser
-
```

Then run the following command:

```
> ldifde -v -i -f dynamically_link_class.ldf
```

Alternatively, you can use AdMod as follows:

```
> admod -b <ObjectDN> objectClass:+:<Dynamic Object Class>
```

Using PowerShell

```
Set-ADObject -Identity "cn=jsmith,cn=users,dc=adatum,dc=com"↵
  -Add @{ObjectClass="adatum-SalesUser"}
```

Discussion

Dynamically linking an auxiliary class to an object is an easy way to use new attributes without modifying the existing object class definition in the schema.

A situation in which it makes more sense to dynamically link auxiliary classes than to link them statically is when several organizations or divisions within a company maintain their own user objects and want to add new attributes to the user class.

It is also worth mentioning that extensive use of dynamically linked auxiliary classes can lead to problems. If several groups are using different auxiliary classes, it might become hard to determine what attributes you can expect on your user objects. Essentially, you could end up with many variations of a user class that each group has implemented through the use of dynamic auxiliary classes. For this reason, use of dynamic auxiliary classes should be closely monitored. In addition, some tools that access Active Directory may not work properly with auxiliary classes.

See Also

Recipe 4.14 for modifying an object

4.17. Creating a Dynamic Object

Problem

You want to create an object that is automatically expired and removed from the directory after a period of time.

Solution

Using a graphical user interface

1. Open LDP.
2. Click Connection→Connect and click OK.
3. Click Connection→Bind.
4. Accept the default and bind as the currently logged on user or select the option to bind with credentials and then enter the credentials.
5. Click View→Tree. Enter the DN of the parent container of the object you want to create and then click OK.

6. Click Browse→Add Child. The Add window will appear.

7. In the DN text box, enter the DN of the new object.

8. In the Attribute text box, enter objectClass. In the Values text box, enter the object class of the object you are creating, such as 'user'. Click Enter. In the Values text box, type **dynamicObject** and click Enter.

9. In the Attribute text box, type **entryTTL**. In the Values text box, enter the time to live (TTL) of the object you are creating, such as '3600'. Click Enter.

10. Enter any other attributes and values that you wish to populate in the Attribute and Values text boxes.

11. Click Run.

Using a command-line interface

Create an LDIF file called *create_dynamic_object.ldf* with the following contents:

```
dn: cn=jsmith,cn=users,dc=adatum,dc=com
changetype: add
objectClass: user
objectClass: dynamicObject
entryTTL: 1800
sAMAccountName: jsmith
```

Then run the following command:

```
> ldifde -v -i -f create_dynamic_object.ldf
```

Discussion

The ability to create dynamic objects allows you to create objects that have a limited lifespan before they are automatically removed from the directory. To create a dynamic object, you simply need to specify the objectClass to have a value of dynamicObject in addition to its structural objectClass (e.g., user) value when instantiating the object. The entryTTL attribute can also be set to the number of seconds before the object is automatically deleted. If entryTTL is not set, the object will use the dynamicObjectDefaultTTL attribute specified in the domain. The entryTTL cannot be lower than the dynamicObjectMinTTL for the domain. See Recipe 4.19 for more information on how to view and modify these default values.

Dynamic objects have a few special properties worth noting:

- A static object cannot be turned into a dynamic object. The object must be marked as dynamic when it is created.
- Dynamic objects cannot be created in the Configuration NC and Schema NC.
- Dynamic objects do not leave behind tombstone objects.

- Dynamic objects that are containers cannot have static child objects.
- A dynamic container will not expire prior to any child objects contained within it. If the dynamic container has a lower TTL value than any of the children, once the container's TTL expires it will be reset to the highest TTL value of the children plus one second.

See Also

Recipe 4.18 for refreshing a dynamic object; Recipe 4.19 for modifying the default dynamic object properties

4.18. Refreshing a Dynamic Object

Problem

You want to refresh a dynamic object to keep it from expiring and getting deleted from Active Directory.

Solution

In each solution in this recipe, an example of adding a user object is used. Modify the examples as needed to refresh whatever object is needed.

Using a graphical user interface

1. Open LDP.
2. From the menu, select Connection→Connect.
3. For Server, enter the name of a domain controller (or leave it blank to do a serverless bind).
4. For Port, enter 389.
5. Click OK.
6. From the menu, select Connection→Bind.
7. Accept the default and bind as the currently logged on user or select the option to bind with credentials and then enter the credentials.
8. Click OK.
9. Select Browse→Modify.
10. For DN, enter the DN of the dynamic object you want to refresh.
11. For Attribute, enter entryTTL.

12. For Values, enter the new time to live (TTL) for the object in seconds.

13. Under Operation, select Replace.

14. Click Enter.

15. Click Run.

Using a command-line interface

Create an LDIF file called *refresh_dynamic_object.ldf* with the following contents:

```
dn: cn=jsmith,cn=users,dc=adatum,dc=com
changetype: modify
replace: entryTTL
entryTTL: 1800
-
```

Then run the following command:

```
> ldifde -v -i -f refresh_dynamic_object.ldf
```

You can also use AdMod with the following syntax:

```
> admod -b <ObjectDN> entryTTL::<TTL in Seconds>
```

Using PowerShell

To refresh a dynamic object using PowerShell, use the following command:

```
Set-ADObject -Identity "cn=jsmith,cn=users,dc=adatum,dc=com"↵
  -Replace @{entryTTL="1800"}
```

Discussion

Dynamic objects expire after their TTL becomes 0. You can determine when a dynamic object will expire by looking at the current value of an object's entryTTL attribute or by querying msDS-Entry-Time-To-Die, which contains the seconds remaining until expiration. If you've created a dynamic object and need to refresh it so that it will not get deleted, you must reset the entryTTL attribute to a new value. There is no limit to the number of times you can refresh a dynamic object. As long as the entryTTL value does not reach 0, the object will remain in Active Directory.

See Also

Recipe 4.14 for modifying an object; "Dynamic Objects (Windows)" (*http://bit.ly/ 16F5QvE*); Recipe 4.17 for creating a dynamic object

4.19. Modifying the Default TTL Settings for Dynamic Objects

Problem

You want to modify the minimum and default TTLs for dynamic objects.

Solution

In each solution in this recipe, we'll show how to set the `DynamicObjectDefaultTTL` setting to `172800`. Modifying the `DynamicObjectMinTTL` can be done in the same manner.

Using a graphical user interface

1. Open ADSI Edit.
2. If an entry for the Configuration naming context is not already displayed, do the following:
   a. Right-click on ADSI Edit in the right pane and click "Connect to."
   b. Fill in the information for the naming context for your forest. Click on the Advanced button if you need to enter alternate credentials.
3. In the left pane, browse to the following path under the Configuration naming context: Services→Windows NT→Directory Service.
4. Right-click `cn=Directory Service` and select Properties.
5. Edit the `msDS-Other-Settings` attribute.
6. Click on `DynamicObjectDefaultTTL= <xxxxx>` and click Remove.
7. The attribute/value pair should have been populated in the "Value to add" field.
8. Edit the number part of the value to be `172800`.
9. Click Add.
10. Click OK twice.

Using a command-line interface

The following `ntdsutil` command connects to *<DomainControllerName>*, displays the current values for the dynamic object TTL settings, sets the `DynamicObjectDefaultTTL` to `172800`, commits the change, and displays the results:

```
> ntdsutil "config settings" connections "connect to server↵
<DomainControllerName>" q "show values" "set DynamicObjectDefaultTTL to 172800"↵
```

```
"commit changes"
"show values" q q
```

Discussion

Two configuration settings apply to dynamic objects:

dynamicObjectDefaultTTL
> Defines the default TTL that is set for a dynamic object at creation time unless another one is set via entryTTL

dynamicObjectMinTTL
> Defines the smallest TTL that can be configured for a dynamic object

Unfortunately, these two settings are not stored as discrete attributes. Instead, they are stored as attribute value assertions (AVAs) in the msDS-Other-Settings attribute on the cn=DirectoryServices,cn=WindowsNT,cn=Configuration,<ForestRootDN> object. AVAs are used occasionally in Active Directory on multivalued attributes, in which the values take the form of Setting1=Value1,Setting2=Value2, and so on.

For this reason, you cannot simply manipulate AVA attributes as you would another attribute. You have to be sure to add or replace values with the same format, as they existed previously.

Using a command-line interface

You can use *ntdsutil* in interactive mode or in single-command mode. In this solution, we've included all the necessary commands on a single line. You can, of course, step through each command by simply running *ntdsutil* in interactive mode and entering each command one by one.

See Also

Recipe 4.14 for modifying an object; MSDN: Regular Expression (RegExp) Object

4.20. Moving an Object to a Different OU or Container

Problem

You want to move an object to a different container or OU.

Solution

Using a graphical user interface

1. Open Active Directory Administrative Center.

2. In the bottom-right pane, enter the search criteria of the desired object and then click the Search button.

3. In the search results, locate the object, right-click it, and then click Move.

4. In the dialog box, browse to the destination container, click to highlight it, and then click OK to move the object.

 You can also move objects by using the ADSI Edit tool or the Active Directory Users and Computers snap-in.

Using a command-line interface

To move an object to a new parent container within the same domain, you can use either dsmove or admod, as follows:

```
> dsmove "<ObjectDN>" -newparent "<NewParentDN>"
```

or:

```
> admod -b <ObjectDN> -move "<NewParentDN>"
```

Using PowerShell

To move an Active Directory object using PowerShell, use the following syntax:

```
Move-ADObject -Identity <ObjectDN> -TargetPath <NewParentDN>
```

Discussion

Using a command-line interface

The DSMove utility can work against any type of object (it has no limitations, as with DSAdd and DSMod). The first parameter is the DN of the object to be moved. The second parameter is the new parent container of the object. The -s parameter can additionally be used to designate a specific server to work against.

 Regardless of the method you use to move objects, you need to ensure that the user who is performing the move has the appropriate permissions to create objects in the destination container and delete objects from the source container.

See Also

Recipe 4.23; MSDN: IADsContainer::MoveHere

4.21. Moving an Object to a Different Domain

Problem

You want to move an object to a different domain.

Solution

Using a graphical user interface (ADMT 3.2)

To migrate a `computer` object between domains in the same forest, use the following steps:

1. Open the ADMT MMC snap-in.
2. Right-click on the Active Directory Migration Tool folder and select the Computer Migration Wizard.
3. On the Welcome screen, click Next.
4. On the Domain Selection page, enter the DNS or NetBIOS name of the source and target domains. Click Next.
5. On the Computer Selection Option screen, select the option to select computer from the domain and then click Next.
6. On the Computer Selection screen, click Add and use the object picker to select a computer object. Click OK to return to the Computer Selection screen and then click Next.
7. On the Organizational Unit Selection screen, enter the destination OU in the new domain and then click Next.
8. On the Translate Objects screen, specify which objects should have new ACLs applied in the new domain. Select any, none, or all of the following, and then click Next to continue:

   - Files and folders
   - Local groups
   - Printers
   - Registry
   - Shares
   - User profiles

- User rights

9. On the Computer Options screen, click Next to maintain the default reboot time of 5 minutes.

10. On the Object Property Exclusion screen, select any object properties that you do not want to migrate and then click Next.

11. On the Conflict Management screen, click Next to accept the default that will not migrate the computer if there is a conflict.

12. On the Completing the Computer Migration Wizard screen, review the migration settings and then click Finish to complete the move.

Using PowerShell

In the following example, the `cn=jsmith` object in the *amer.adatum.com* domain will be moved to the *emea.adatum.com* domain:

```
Move-ADObject -Identity "cn=jsmith,cn=users,dc=amer,dc=adatum,dc=com"↵
 -TargetPath "ou=MigratedUsers,dc=emea,dc=adatum,dc=com"↵
 -TargetServer dc-emea1.emea.adatum.com -Credential "emea\Administrator"
```

Discussion

At the time of this writing, the current version of ADMT, version 3.2, is not supported on Windows Server 2012. Therefore, you should install it on a previous version of Windows Server as part of the migration to Windows Server 2012. You can move objects between domains assuming you follow a few guidelines:

- The user performing the move operation must have permission to modify objects in the parent container of both domains.

- You need to explicitly specify the target DC (serverless binds usually do not work). This is necessary because the "Cross Domain Move" LDAP control is being used behind the scenes. For more information on controls, see Recipe 4.4.

- The move operation must be performed against the RID master for both domains.

- When you move a `user` object to a different domain, its `objectSID` is replaced with a new SID (based on the new domain), and the old SID is optionally added to the `sIDHistory` attribute.

See Also

Recipe 4.4 for more information on LDAP controls; MS KB 238394 (How to Use the MoveTree Utility to Move Objects Between Domains in a Single Forest); MSDN: IADs-

Container::MoveHere; "ADMT Guide: Migrating and Restructuring Active Directory Domains" (*http://bit.ly/YmmzPD*)

4.22. Referencing an External Domain

Problem

You need to create a reference to an external Active Directory domain.

Solution

Using a graphical user interface

1. Open ADSI Edit.
2. If an entry for the naming context you want to browse is not already displayed, do the following:
    a. Right-click on ADSI Edit in the right pane and click "Connect to."
    b. Fill in the information for the naming context, container, or OU you want to add an object to. Click on the Advanced button if you need to enter alternate credentials.
3. Right-click on the top-level node and open a connection to the Configuration NC.
4. Right-click on the `Partitions` container and select New→Object. Click Next.
5. Right-click on `crossRef` and click Next.
6. For the `cn` attribute, enter the FQDN of the external domain—*othercorp.com*, for example. Click Next.
7. For the `nCName` attribute, enter the DN of the external domain, such as `dc=other corp,dc=com`. Click Next.
8. For the `dnsRoot` attribute, enter the DNS name of a server that can respond to LDAP queries about the domain in question, such as *dc1.othercorp.com*.
9. Click Next and then Finish to create the `crossRef` object.

Using a command-line interface

Create an LDIF file called *create_crossref.ldf* with the following contents:

```
dn: cn=othercorp.com,cn=partitions,cn=configuration,dc=adatum,dc=com
changetype: add
objectClass: crossRef
cn: othercorp.com
nCName: dc=othercorp,dc=com
dnsRoot: dc1.othercorp.com
```

Then run the following command:

```
> ldifde -v -i -f create_crossref.ldf
```

You can also create a `crossRef` using AdMod as follows:

```
> admod -config -rb cn=othercorp.com,cn=partitions↵
objectClass::crossRef cn::othercorp.com nCName::dc=othercorp,dc=com↵
dnsRoot::dc1.othercorp.com -add
```

Discussion

Similar to the way in which DNS servers use iterative queries to resolve hostnames that can be resolved only by remote servers, LDAP uses *referrals* to resolve queries for objects contained in naming contexts that are not hosted by the local DC. When a DC receives any query, it will search the `Partitions` container for a `crossRef` object containing the DN that's being used as the Base DN of the query. If the DC locates a `crossRef` that matches the search base of the query, and that `crossRef` indicates a naming context that's hosted by the domain controller itself, then the DC will perform the search locally. If the `crossRef` refers to an NC that's hosted on a remote server, the DC generates a *referral* to the server that is pointed to by the `crossRef` object. If the DC can't locate a relevant `crossRef` object, it will use DNS to attempt to generate an additional location to refer the client to.

In most cases, Active Directory will generate LDAP referrals automatically. However, you should manually create a `crossRef` object to generate LDAP referrals for an external domain, such as referrals to *othercorp.com* that are generated by the *adatum.com* domain.

See Also

MS KB 241737 (How to Create a Cross-Reference to an External Domain in Active Directory); MS KB 817872 (How to Create crossRef Objects for a DNS Namespace Subordinate of an Existing Active Directory Forest); MSDN: Referrals [Active Directory]; MSDN: When Referrals Are Generated [Active Directory]

4.23. Renaming an Object

Problem

You want to rename an object and keep it in its current container or OU.

Solution

Using a graphical user interface

1. Open ADSI Edit.

2. If an entry for the naming context you want to browse is not already displayed, do the following:

   a. Right-click on ADSI Edit in the right pane and click "Connect to."

   b. Fill in the information for the naming context, container, or OU that contains the object you want to rename. Click on the Advanced button if you need to enter alternate credentials.

3. In the left pane, browse to the container or OU that contains the object you want to modify. Once you've found the object, right-click on it and select Rename.

4. Enter the new name and click OK.

You can also rename a leaf object by using LDP as follows:

1. Open LDP.

2. From the menu, select Connection→Connect.

3. For Server, enter the name of a domain controller (or leave it blank for a serverless bind).

4. For Port, enter 389.

5. Click OK.

6. From the menu, select Connection→Bind.

7. Accept the default and bind as the currently logged on user or select the option to bind with credentials and then enter the credentials.

8. Click OK.

9. Click Browse→Modify RDN. For Old DN, enter the Distinguished Name of the object that you want to rename. For New DN, enter the object's new name.

10. Click Run to rename the object.

Using a command-line interface

To rename an object using the built-in DSMove utility, use the following syntax:

```
> dsmove "<ObjectDN>"  newname "<NewName>"
```

To use AdMod, use the following:

```
> admod -b "<ObjectDN>" -rename "<NewName>"
```

Using PowerShell

To rename an object using PowerShell, use the following syntax:

```
Rename-ADObject -Identity "<Object DN>" -NewName "<New Value of 'name'
attribute>"
```

Discussion

Before you rename an object, you should ensure that no applications reference it by name. You can make objects rename-safe by requiring all applications that must store a reference to an object to use the GUID of the object, rather than the name.

The GUID (stored in the `objectGUID` attribute) is effectively unique and does not change when an object is renamed.

 Keep in mind that you may wish to perform other cleanup tasks when renaming an object. In the case of a user who is changing her name, you may wish to update her Display Name and `sn` attributes to match the new CN.

Using a graphical user interface

If the parent container of the object you want to rename has a lot of objects in it, you may want to add a new connection entry for the DN of the object you want to rename. This may save you time searching through the list of objects in the container. You can do this by right-clicking ADSI Edit and selecting "Connect to" under Connection Point; select Distinguished Name and enter the DN of the object you want to rename.

You can also rename most objects within the Active Directory Users and Computers MMC snap-in (*dsa.msc*) by navigating to the object in question, right-clicking on it, and selecting Rename.

Using a command-line interface

The two parameters that are needed to rename an object are the original DN of the object and the new RDN (`-newname`). The `-s` option can also be used to specify a server name to work against.

See Also

MSDN: IADsContainer::MoveHere

4.24. Deleting an Object

Problem

You want to delete an individual object.

Solution

Using a graphical user interface

1. Open ADSI Edit.
2. If an entry for the naming context you want to browse is not already displayed, do the following:
   a. Right-click on ADSI Edit in the right pane and click "Connect to."
   b. Fill in the information for the naming context, container, or OU that contains the object you want to delete. Click on the Advanced button if you need to enter alternate credentials.
3. In the left pane, browse to the object you want to delete.
4. Right-click on the object and select Delete.
5. Click Yes to confirm.

You can also delete an object using LDP, as follows:

1. Open LDP.
2. From the menu, select Connection→Connect.
3. For Server, enter the name of a domain controller (or leave it blank for a serverless bind).
4. For Port, enter 389.
5. Click OK.
6. From the menu, select Connection→Bind.
7. Accept the default and bind as the currently logged on user or select the option to bind with credentials and then enter the credentials.
8. Click OK.
9. Click Browse→Delete. For DN, enter the Distinguished Name of the object that you want to delete.
10. Click Run to delete the object.

Using a command-line interface

You can delete an object using the built-in *dsrm* utility, as well as AdMod. For *dsrm*, use the following syntax:

```
> dsrm "<ObjectDN>"
```

For AdMod, enter the following:

```
> admod -b "<ObjectDN>" -del
```

Using PowerShell

To delete the "Branches" OU in the *adatum.com* domain, use the following command:

```
Remove-ADObject -Identity "ou=Branches,dc=adatum,dc=com" -Confirm:$false
```

Discussion

This recipe covers deleting individual objects. If you want to delete a container or OU and all the objects in it, take a look at Recipe 4.25.

Using a graphical user interface

If the parent container of the object you want to delete has a lot of objects in it, you may want to add a new connection entry for the DN of the object you want to delete. This can save you time searching through the list of objects in the container and could help avoid accidental deletions. You can do this by right-clicking ADSI Edit and selecting "Connect to." Under Connection Point, select Distinguished Name and enter the DN of the object you want to delete.

You can also delete most objects within the Active Directory Users and Computers MMC snap-in (*dsa.msc*) by navigating to the object in question, right-clicking on it, and selecting Delete.

Using a command-line interface

The *dsrm* utility can be used to delete any type of object (there are no limitations based on object type, as with dsadd and dsmod). The only required parameter is the DN of the object to delete. You can also specify -noprompt to keep it from asking for confirmation before deleting. The -s parameter can be used as well to designate a specific server to target. AdMod will not prompt you in this manner.

See Also

Recipe 4.25 for deleting a container; MS KB 258310 (Viewing Deleted Objects in Active Directory); MSDN: IADsContainer::Delete; MSDN: IADsDeleteOps:: DeleteObject

4.25. Deleting a Container That Has Child Objects

Problem

You want to delete a container or organizational unit and all child objects contained within.

Solution

Using a graphical user interface

Open ADSI Edit and follow the same steps as in Recipe 4.24. The only difference is that you'll be prompted to confirm twice instead of once before the deletion occurs.

Using a command-line interface

You can delete a container and its child objects using the built-in *dsrm* utility, as well as AdMod. For *dsrm*, use the following syntax:

```
> dsrm "<ObjectDN>" -subtree
```

For AdMod, enter the following:

```
> admod -b "<ObjectDN>" -del -treedelete
```

Using PowerShell

The "Branches" OU in the *adatum.com* domain contains child objects. To delete it without a confirmation prompt, use the following command:

```
Remove-ADObject -Identity "ou=Branches,dc=adatum,dc=com" -Recursive↵
 -Confirm:$false
```

Discussion

As you can see from the solutions, there is not much difference between deleting a leaf node and deleting a container that has child objects. However, there is a distinction in what is happening in the background.

Deleting an object that has no children can be done with a simple LDAP delete operation. On the other hand, to delete a container and its children, the tree-delete LDAP control has to be used. If you were to do the deletion from an LDAP-based tool like LDP (the Active Directory Administration Tool), you would first need to enable the Subtree Delete control, which has an OID of 1.2.840.113556.1.4.805. LDP provides another option to do a Recursive Delete from the client side. That will essentially iterate through all the objects in the container, deleting them one by one. The Subtree Delete is much more efficient, especially when dealing with large containers.

As with the other operations we've discussed in this chapter (create, rename, move, and so on), the user performing the delete operation needs to have the necessary permissions to delete the object or objects in question. Active Directory permissions are discussed more extensively in Chapter 14.

See Also

Recipe 4.24 for information about deleting objects; Recipe 8.19; Recipe 6.39; MSDN: IADsDeleteOps::DeleteObject

4.26. Viewing the Created and Last-Modified Timestamp of an Object

Problem

You want to determine when an object was either created or last updated.

Solution

Using a graphical user interface

1. Follow the steps in Recipe 4.2.
2. Ensure that `createTimestamp` and `modifyTimestamp` are included in the list of attributes to be returned by looking at Attributes under Options→Search.

Using a command-line interface

You can view the created and modified timestamps using the built-in DSQuery utility, as well as AdFind. For DSQuery, use the following syntax:

```
> dsquery * "<ObjectDN>" -attr name createTimestamp modifyTimestamp
```

For AdFind, use the following:

```
> adfind -default -rb cn=Users -f "cn=Joe Smith"↵
createTimestamp modifyTimestamp
```

Using PowerShell

The following command gets the creation date and the last-modified date for a user object:

```
Get-ADUser <sAMAccountName> -Properties * | Select Name,whenCreated,Modified
```

Discussion

When an object is created or modified in Active Directory, the `createTimestamp` and `modifyTimestamp` attributes get set with the current time. The `createTimestamp` attribute is replicated between domain controllers, so assuming the latest modification of the object in question has replicated to all domain controllers, they will all contain the timestamp when the object was created. `whenChanged` and `modifyTimestamp` are not replicated, which means that their values will be local to an individual domain controller. Additionally, `modifyTimestamp` is a constructed attribute.

See Also

Recipe 4.2 for viewing the attributes of an object; Chapter 12 for a more detailed description of the Active Directory replication process

4.27. Modifying the Default LDAP Query Policy

Problem

You want to view or modify the default LDAP query policy of a forest. The query policy contains settings that restrict search behavior, such as the maximum number of entries that can be returned from a search.

Solution

Using a graphical user interface

1. Open ADSI Edit.
2. In the Configuration partition, browse to Services→Windows NT→Directory Service→Query Policies.
3. In the left pane, click on the `Query Policies` container, then right-click on the Default Query Policy object in the right pane and select Properties.
4. Double-click on the `lDAPAdminLimits` attribute.
5. Click on the attribute you want to modify and click Remove.
6. Modify the value in the "Value to add" box and click Add.
7. Click OK twice.

Using a command-line interface

To view the current settings, use the following command:

```
> ntdsutil "ldap pol" conn "con to server <DomainControllerName>" q "show values"
```

To change the `MaxPageSize` value to 2,000, you can do the following:

```
> ntdsutil "ldap pol" conn "con to server <DomainControllerName>" q
ldap policy: set MaxPageSize to 2000
ldap policy: Commit Changes
```

Discussion

The LDAP query policy contains several settings that control how domain controllers handle searches. By default, one query policy is defined for all domain controllers in a forest, but you can create additional ones and apply them to a specific domain controller or even at the site level (so that all domain controllers in the site use that policy).

Query policies are stored in the Configuration NC as `queryPolicy` objects. The default query policy is located at `cn=Default Query Policy,cn=Query-Policies,cn=Direc tory Service,cn=Windows NT,cn=Services, <ConfigurationPartitionDN>`. The attribute `lDAPAdminLimits` of a `queryPolicy` object is multivalued and contains each setting for the policy in name/value pairs. Table 4-4 contains the available settings.

Table 4-4. LDAP query policy settings

Name	Default value	Description
MaxPoolThreads	4 per proc	Maximum number of threads that are created by the DC for query execution.
MaxDatagramRecv	4096	Maximum number of datagrams that can be simultaneously processed by the DC.
MaxReceiveBuffer	10485760	Maximum size in bytes for an LDAP request that the server will attempt to process. If the server receives a request that is larger than this value, it will close the connection.
InitRecvTimeout	120 secs	Initial receive timeout.
MaxConnections	5000	Maximum number of open connections.
MaxConnIdleTime	900 secs	Maximum amount of time a connection can be idle.
MaxPageSize	1000	Maximum number of records that will be returned by LDAP responses.
MaxQueryDuration	120 secs	Maximum length of time the domain controller can execute a query.
MaxTempTableSiz	10000	Maximum size of temporary storage that is allocated to execute queries.
MaxResultSetSize	262144	Controls the total amount of data that the domain controller stores for this kind of search. When this limit is reached, the domain controller discards the oldest of these intermediate results to make room to store new intermediate results.
MaxNotificationPer Conn	5	Maximum number of notifications that a client can request for a given connection.

Instead of modifying the default LDAP query policy, you can create a new one from scratch. In the `Query Policies` container (where the default query policy object is located), create a new `queryPolicy` object and set the `lDAPAdminLimits` attribute as just described based on the settings you want configured. Then modify the attribute `query PolicyObject` on the `nTDSDSA` object of a domain controller you want to apply the new policy to. This can be done via the Active Directory Sites and Services snap-in by browsing to the nTDSDSA object of a domain controller (cn=NTDS Settings), right-clicking on it, and selecting Properties. You can then select the new policy from a drop-down menu beside Query Policy. Click OK to apply the new policy.

 You should not change the default query policy in production unless you've done plenty of testing. Changing some of the settings may result in unexpected application or domain controller behavior, such as a significant failure of your Active Directory domain controllers.

See Also

Recipe 4.19; MS KB 315071 (How to View and Set LDAP Policy in Active Directory by Using Ntdsutil.exe)

4.28. Exporting Objects to an LDIF File

Problem

You want to export objects to an LDIF file.

Solution

Using a graphical user interface

None of the standard Microsoft tools support exporting LDIF from a GUI.

Using a command-line interface

```
> ldifde -f output.ldf -l <AttrList> -p <Scope> -r "<Filter>" -d "<BaseDN>"
```

Discussion

The LDIF specification defined in RFC 2849 describes a well-defined file-based format for representing directory entries. The format is intended to be both human- and machine-parseable, which adds to its usefulness. LDIF is the de facto standard for importing and exporting a large number of objects in a directory and is supported by virtually every directory vendor, including Microsoft.

Using a command-line interface

The -f switch specifies the name of the file to use to save the entries to, -s is the DC to query, -l is the comma-separated list of attributes to include, -p is the search scope, -r is the search filter, and -d is the base DN. If you encounter any problems using ldifde, the -v switch enables verbose mode and can help identify problems.

See Also

Recipe 4.29 for importing objects using LDIF; RFC 2849 (The LDAP Data Interchange Format [LDIF]—Technical Specification); MS KB 237677 (Using LDIFDE to Import and Export Directory Objects to Active Directory)

4.29. Importing Objects Using an LDIF File

Problem

You want to import objects into Active Directory using an LDIF file. The file could contain object additions, modifications, and deletions.

Solution

Using a command-line interface

To import objects using the *ldifde* utility, you must first create an LDIF file with the objects to add, modify, or delete. Here is an example LDIF file that adds a user:

```
dn: cn=jsmith,cn=users,dc=adatum,dc=com
changetype: add
objectClass: user
samaccountname: jsmith
sn: JSmith
```

Once you've created the LDIF file, you just need to run the ldifde command to import the new objects:

```
> ldifde -i -f input.ldf
```

Discussion

For more information on the LDIF format, check RFC 2849.

Using a command-line interface

To import with *ldifde*, simply specify the -i switch to turn on import mode and -f *<filename>* for the file. It can also be beneficial to use the -v switch to turn on verbose mode to get more information in case of errors. The Windows Server 2003 version of *ldifde* also includes the -j switch that will create a logfile for troubleshooting purposes. The LDIF file can specify a deletion or a modification instead of an addition. To modify a user, set the changetype to modify. To delete a user, set the changetype to delete.

See Also

Recipe 4.28 for information on LDIF; RFC 2849 (The LDAP Data Interchange Format [LDIF]—Technical Specification); MS KB 237677 (Using LDIFDE to Import and Export Directory Objects to Active Directory)

4.30. Exporting Objects to a CSV File

Problem

You want to export objects to a comma-separated values (CSV) file. The CSV file can then be opened and manipulated from a spreadsheet application or with a text editor.

Solution

Using a graphical user interface

You can export objects to a CSV file using Active Directory Users and Computers, as follows:

1. Open Active Directory Users and Computers.
2. Browse to the desired container or OU.
3. Right-click on the container or OU and click Export List.
4. Choose the CSV file type, name the file, and then click Save to save the file.

Using a command-line interface

You can export objects to a CSV file using the built-in *csvde* utility, as well as AdFind. For *csvde*, use the following syntax:

```
> csvde -f output.csv -l <AttrList> -p <Scope> -r "<Filter>" -d "<BaseDN>"
```

You can also export information to a CSV file using `adfind`:

```
> adfind -b <SearchBase> -f <Filter> -csv <Attr1> <Attr2> <Attr3>
```

Using PowerShell

You can also export objects to a CSV file by using PowerShell. In the following command, all user objects in the Users OU in the *adatum.com* domain will be exported to *c:\temp\users.csv*:

```
Get-ADUser -SearchBase "cn=users,dc=adatum,dc=com" -Filter * |↵
  Select Name,UserPrincipalName,samAccountName |↵
  Export-Csv c:\temp\users.csv
```

Discussion

Once you have a CSV file containing entries, you can use a spreadsheet application such as Excel to view, sort, and manipulate the data.

Using a graphical user interface

Before performing the export, add any needed columns to the view in Active Directory Users and Computers. To add columns, click on View and then click Add/Remove Columns.

Using a command-line interface

The parameters used by *csvde* are nearly identical to those used by *ldifde*. The -f switch specifies the name of the file to use to save the entries to, -s is the DC to query, -l is the comma-separated list of attributes to include, -p is the search scope (base, onelevel, or subtree), -r is the search filter, and -d is the base DN. If you encounter any issues, the -v switch enables verbose mode and can help identify problems.

AdFind offers a number of additional switches to customize the behavior of CSV file output, including the following:

-csv xxx
> CSV output. xxx is an optional string that specifies the value to use for empty attributes.

-csvdelim x
> Delimiter to use for separating attributes in CSV output. The default is (,).

-csvmvdelim x
> Delimiter to use for separating multiple values in output. The default is (;).

-csvq x
> Character to use for quoting attributes. The default is (").

See Also

Recipe 4.31 for importing objects using a CSV file

4.31. Importing Objects Using PowerShell and a CSV File

Problem

You want to import objects into Active Directory using a CSV file.

Solution

Using PowerShell

You must first create a CSV file containing the objects to add. The first line of the file should contain a comma-separated list of attributes you want to set, with DN being the first attribute. Here is an example:

```
DN,objectClass,cn,sn,userAccountControl,sAMAccountName,userPrincipalName
```

The rest of the lines should contain entries to add. If you want to leave one of the attributes unset, then leave the value blank (followed by a comma). Here is a sample CSV file that would add two user objects:

```
DN,objectClass,sn,userAccountControl,sAMAccountName,userPrincipalName
"cn=jim,cn=users,dc=adatum,dc=com",user,Smith,512,jim,jim@adatum.com
"cn=john,cn=users,dc=adatum,dc=com",user,,512,john,john@adatum.com
```

Once you've created the CSV file, you just need to import the new objects by using PowerShell:

```
> -Import-CSV c:\temp\input.csv | New-ADUser
```

Discussion

Prior to the New-ADUser cmdlet, CSVDE was often used to import objects from a CSV file. However, starting with Windows Server 2008, it became much more difficult to use CSVDE due to the inability to meet password complexity requirements of a domain. CSVDE creates users with a blank password, which usually doesn't meet password complexity requirements of a domain. With the New-ADUser cmdlet, new disabled users can be created without a password, even if there is a password complexity requirement.

See Also

Recipe 4.30 for exporting objects in CSV format; Recipe 6.2; Recipe 6.3

CHAPTER 5

Organizational Units

5.0. Introduction

An LDAP directory such as Active Directory stores data in a hierarchy of *containers* and *leaf nodes* called the directory information tree (DIT). Leaf nodes are end points in the tree, while containers can store other containers and leaf nodes. In Active Directory, the two most common types of containers are organizational units (OUs) and container objects. The *container objects* are generic containers that do not have any special properties about them other than the fact that they can contain objects. *Organizational units*, on the other hand, have some special properties, such as the ability to link a Group Policy Object (GPO) to an OU. In most cases when designing a hierarchy of objects in Active Directory, especially users and computers, you should use OUs instead of containers. There is nothing you can do with a container that you can't do with an OU, but the reverse is certainly not the case.

The Anatomy of an Organizational Unit

Organizational units can be created as a child of a domain object or another OU; by default, OUs cannot be added as a child of a container object. (See Recipe 5.13 for more on how to work around this.) OUs themselves are represented in Active Directory by `organizationalUnit` objects. Table 5-1 contains a list of some interesting attributes that are available on `organizationalUnit` objects.

Table 5-1. Attributes of organizationalUnit objects

Attribute	Description
`description`	Text description of the OU.
`gPLink`	List of GPOs that have been linked to the OU.
`gPOptions`	Contains `1` if GPO inheritance is blocked and `0` otherwise.

Attribute	Description
msDS-Approx-Immed-Subordinates	Approximate number of direct child objects in the OU. See Recipe 5.11 for more information.
managedBy	DN of user or group that is in charge of managing the OU.
ou	Relative distinguished name of the OU.
modifyTimestamp	Timestamp of when the OU was last modified.
createTimeStamp	Timestamp of when the OU was created.

5.1. Creating an OU

Problem

You want to create an OU.

Solution

Using a graphical user interface

1. Open the Active Directory Administrative Center.
2. In the left pane, click to highlight the domain.
3. In the right pane, click New and then click Organizational Unit.
4. Enter a name for the OU, enter a description, fill in any of the desired fields, and then click OK to create the OU.

Using a command-line interface

You can create a new OU using the built-in DSAdd utility, as well as AdMod. To create an OU using DSAdd, use the following syntax:

```
> dsadd ou "<OrgUnitDN>" -desc "<Description>"
```

To create an OU with AdMod, use the following syntax:

```
> admod -b "<OrgUnitDN>" objectclass::organizationalUnit↵
  description::"<Description>" -add
```

For example, creating the Finance OU with the description of "Finance OU" in the *adatum.com* domain would look like this:

```
> admod -b ou=Finance,dc=adatum,dc=com objectclass::organizationalUnit↵
  description::"Finance OU" -add

> AdMod V01.18.00cpp Joe Richards (joe@joeware.net) March 2012

>
```

```
> DN Count: 1
> Using server: dc1.adatum.com
> Adding specified objects...
>    DN: ou=Finance,dc=adatum,dc=com...
>
> The command completed successfully
```

Using PowerShell

To create an organizational unit named "Finance," create a description of "Finance OU," and not protect the OU from accidental deletion, use the following command:

```
New-ADOrganizationalUnit "Finance" -ProtectedFromAccidentalDeletion $False↵
 -Description "Finance OU"
```

Discussion

OUs are used to structure data within Active Directory. Typically, there are three reasons you might need to create an OU:

Segregate objects

It is common practice to group related data into an OU. For example, user objects and computer objects are typically stored in separate containers (in fact, this is the default configuration with Active Directory). One reason for this is to make searching the directory easier.

Delegate administration

One of two primary reasons for creating an OU is to delegate administration. With OUs you can give a person or group of people rights to perform certain administrative functions on objects within an OU.

Apply a GPO

An OU is the lowest-level container object that a GPO can be applied to. If you have different types of users within your organization that need to apply different GPOs, the easiest way to set that up is to store the users in different OUs and apply GPOs accordingly.

In each solution in this recipe, the description attribute of the new OU was set. This is not a mandatory attribute, but it is good practice to set it so that others browsing the directory have a general understanding of the purpose of the OU. Also, consider setting the managedBy attribute to reference a user or group that is the owner of the OU. The -ProtectedFromAccidentalDeletion parameter configures the OU so that it cannot be deleted by using the traditional deletion methods (e.g., right-clicking on it and then selecting Delete from the menu).

See Also

"Create an Organizational Unit Design" (*http://bit.ly/10za7Zf*)

5.2. Enumerating the OUs in a Domain

Problem

You want to enumerate all containers and OUs in a domain, which effectively displays the structure of the domain.

Solution

Using a graphical user interface

1. Open the Active Directory Users and Computers snap-in (*dsa.msc*).
2. If you need to change domains, right-click on Active Directory Users and Computers in the left pane, select Change Domain, enter the domain name, and click OK.
3. In the left pane, you can browse the directory structure.

Using a command-line interface

The following command will enumerate all OUs in the current domain of the user running the command using the built-in DSQuery utility:

```
> dsquery ou
```

You can also retrieve this information with AdFind, using the following syntax:

```
> adfind -default -f "objectcategory=organizationalUnit" -dn
```

This `adfind` syntax can be shortened as follows:

```
> adfind -default -sc oudmp
```

Output from the `adfind` command will resemble the following:

```
> adfind -default -f "objectcategory=organizationalUnit" -dn
>
> AdFind V01.46.00cpp Joe Richards (joe@joeware.net) March 2012
>
> Using server: dc1.adatum.com:389
> Directory: Windows Server 8
> Base DN: dc=adatum,dc=com
>
> dn:ou=Domain Controllers,dc=adatum,dc=com
> dn:ou=Finance,dc=adatum,dc=com
> dn:ou=FinanceTemps,ou=Finance,dc=adatum,dc=com
>
> 3 Objects returned
```

Using PowerShell

To enumerate all OUs in the current domain using PowerShell, run the following command:

```
Get-ADOrganizationalUnit -Filter * | Select DistinguishedName
```

Discussion

Using a graphical user interface

If you want to expand all containers and OUs within an OU, you have to manually expand each one within ADUC or the Active Directory Administrative Center; there is no "expand all" option.

Using a command-line interface

To enumerate both OUs and containers, you have to use a more generic dsquery command. The following command will display all containers and OUs in the domain of the user running the command:

```
> dsquery * domainroot -filter↵
"(|(objectcategory=container)(objectcategory=organizationalunit))"↵
-limit 0
```

5.3. Finding an OU

Problem

You want to find a specific OU within an Active Directory domain.

Solution

Using a graphical user interface

1. Open the ADUC snap-in (*dsa.msc*).

2. If you need to change domains, right-click on the Active Directory Users and Computers label in the left pane, select Change Domain, enter the domain name, and click OK.

3. Right-click on the domain node and select Find.

4. In the Find drop-down box, select Organizational Units. In the Name: text box, enter the name of the OU.

5. Click Find Now.

Using a command-line interface

```
> adfind -f "ou=<OU Name>"
```

Using PowerShell

To find any OU with "Test" in the name under the EMEA OU, run the following command:

```
Get-ADOrganizationalUnit -SearchBase "ou=emea,dc=adatum,dc=com"↵
 -LDAPFilter {(ObjectCategory=OrganizationalUnit)} |↵
 Where {$_.Name -Match "Test"}
```

The command can be shortened to omit the search base, which will then search the current domain, as shown in the following command:

```
Get-ADOrganizationalUnit -LDAPFilter {(ObjectCategory=OrganizationalUnit)} |↵
 Where {$_.Name -Match "Test"}
```

Discussion

In a heavily nested environment, you may need to locate an OU based on its name when you don't necessarily know its location. By using the ADUC GUI or a command-line tool with a search scope of subtree, you can easily recurse through the entire domain structure to find an OU based on its name, description, or any other attribute. In AdFind, you can use wildcards.

> When designing your Active Directory structure, you should try to keep OU nesting from becoming too deep, since processing many levels of Group Policy Objects can greatly increase the logon times for your clients. In the interests of keeping things simple, it's often a good idea to keep your OU structure shallow whenever possible.

See Also

Recipe 5.2; Recipe 5.4

5.4. Enumerating the Objects in an OU

Problem

You want to enumerate all the objects in an OU.

Solution

The following solutions will enumerate all the objects directly under an OU. Refer to "Discussion" section for more on how to display all objects under an OU regardless of the number of objects involved.

Using a graphical user interface

1. Open the ADUC snap-in (*dsa.msc*).
2. If you need to change domains, right-click on Active Directory Users and Computers in the left pane, select Change Domain, enter the domain name, and click OK.
3. In the left pane, browse to the OU you want to view.
4. The contents of the OU will be displayed in the right pane.

Using a command-line interface

To list the contents of an OU using the built-in DSQuery utility, use the following syntax:

```
> dsquery * "<OU DN>" -limit 0 -scope onelevel
```

You can also use AdFind, as follows:

```
> adfind -b "<OU DN>" -s one -dn
```

Using PowerShell

To enumerate the contents of the Users container in the *adatum.com* domain, run the following command:

```
Get-ADObject -SearchBase "cn=users,dc=adatum,dc=com" -Filter *
```

Discussion

Using a graphical user interface

By default, ADUC will display only 2,000 objects. To view more than 2,000 objects, click View→Filter Options. Then modify the maximum number of items displayed per folder.

Using a command-line interface

Using -limit 0, all objects under the OU will be displayed. If -limit is not specified, 100 objects will be shown by default. You can also specify your own number if you want to display only a limited number of objects.

The -scope onelevel or -s one (for AdFind) option causes only direct child objects of the OU to be displayed. Displaying all objects regardless of depth is referred to as the *subtree scope*, which is the default search scope for AdFind and DSQuery. If you want to return all objects regardless of depth, including the OU being searched, simply omit the -scope switch entirely.

To save on typing, you can use the -default switch with AdFind, which automatically uses the Domain DN as its search base. You can use this in combination with the -rb (Relative Base) switch, which will only require you to type in the relative DN of the OU that you want to search. So to list the objects in the cn=Finance,dc=adatum,dc=com OU, you can use the following abbreviated AdFind syntax:

```
> adfind -default -rb ou=Finance -s one -dn
```

Another option would be to use the -incldn switch, which will return objects that contain a particular search string anywhere within the Distinguished Name. So specifying -incldn "ou=Finance" would return the cn=Finance,dc=adatum,dc=com OU, as well as the cn=FinanceTemps,cn=Finance,dc=adatum,dc=com OU.

Using PowerShell

The command uses a default search scope of subtree, which will return the OU being searched and all child objects recursively. To restrict the search to only the immediate children of the OU, add the -searchscope 'onelevel' switch to the command.

See Also

Recipe 5.2

5.5. Deleting the Objects in an OU

Problem

You want to delete all child objects in an OU, but not the OU itself.

Solution

Using a graphical user interface

1. Open the ADUC snap-in (*dsa.msc*).
2. If you need to change domains, right-click on Active Directory Users and Computers in the left pane, select Change Domain, enter the domain name, and click OK.
3. In the left pane, browse to and select the OU that contains the objects you want to delete.

4. Highlight all the objects in the right pane and press the Delete key on your keyboard.

5. Press F5 to refresh the contents of the OU. If objects still exist, repeat step 4.

Using a command-line interface

To delete all objects within an OU, but not the OU itself, you need to use the `-subtree` and `-exclude` options with the `dsrm` command:

```
> dsrm "<OrgUnitDN>" -subtree -exclude
```

You can also perform this task by piping the results of an `adfind` query into `admod`, as follows:

```
>adfind -default -rb ou=<OU Name> -s one -dsq | admod -unsafe -del
```

Using PowerShell

To delete the child objects within the Test OU without a confirmation, use the following command:

```
Get-ADObject -SearchBase "ou=test,dc=adatum,dc=com" -Filter *↵
  -SearchScope OneLevel | Remove-ADObject -Confirm:$False
```

Discussion

If you want to delete the objects in an OU and re-create the OU, you can delete the OU itself, which will delete all child objects, or you could just delete the child objects. The benefit to the latter approach is that you do not need to reconfigure the ACL on the OU or relink any Group Policy Objects after you've re-created the OU.

See Also

Recipe 5.4 for enumerating objects in an OU; Recipe 5.6 for deleting an OU; MSDN: IADsDeleteOps::DeleteObject

5.6. Deleting an OU

Problem

You want to delete an OU that is not protected from accidental deletion along with all of the objects in it.

Solution

Using a graphical user interface

1. Open the ADUC snap-in (*dsa.msc*).
2. If you need to change domains, right-click on Active Directory Users and Computers in the left pane, select Change Domain, enter the domain name, and click OK.
3. In the left pane, browse to the OU you want to delete, right-click on it, and select Delete.
4. Click Yes for the confirmation prompt.
5. If the OU contains child objects, you will be asked for confirmation again before deleting it. Click Yes to continue.

Using a command-line interface

To delete an OU and all objects contained within, use the `-subtree` option with the `dsrm` command. If you don't use `-subtree` and the object you are trying to delete has child objects, the deletion will fail:

```
> dsrm "<OrgUnitDN>" -subtree
```

You can also delete an OU and all of its contents using the following `admod` command:

```
> admod -b "<OrgUnitDN>" -del -treedelete
```

Using PowerShell

To delete an OU named Test and its contents without a confirmation prompt, run the following command:

```
Remove-ADObject -Identity "ou=test,dc=adatum,dc=com" -Recursive -Confirm:$False
```

Discussion

Deleting OUs that do not contain objects is just like deleting any other type of object. Deleting an OU that contains objects, however, requires a special type of delete operation. The Tree Delete LDAP control (OID: 1.2.840.113556.1.4.805) must be used by the application or script to inform AD to delete everything contained in the OU. All three solutions in this case use the control behind the scenes, but if you were going to perform the operation via an LDAP utility such as LDP, you would need to enable the control first.

In Windows Server 2008 R2 and Windows Server 2012, the Active Directory Users and Computers console adds an option to the delete confirmation prompt to use the Delete Subtree server control. By using the control, you can delete all child objects in an OU, even if the objects are protected from accidental deletion.

See Also

Recipe 4.4 for using LDAP controls; MSDN: IADsDeleteOps::DeleteObject

5.7. Moving the Objects in an OU to a Different OU

Problem

You want to move some or all of the objects in an OU to a different OU. You may need to do this as part of a domain restructuring effort.

Solution

Using a graphical user interface

1. Open the ADUC snap-in (*dsa.msc*).

2. If you need to change domains, right-click on the Active Directory Users and Computers node in the lefthand pane, select Change Domain, enter the domain name, and click OK.

3. In the left pane, browse to and select the OU that contains the objects you want to move.

4. Highlight the objects you want to move in the right pane, right-click on them, and select Move.

5. Browse to and select the parent container you want to move the objects to, and then click OK.

6. Press F5 to refresh the contents of the OU. If objects still exist, repeat steps 3–5.

Using a command-line interface

To move each object from one OU to another, you can pipe the results of an `adfind` query into `admod` using the following syntax:

```
> adfind -b "<Old OU DN>" -s one -dsq | admod -move "<New OU DN>"
```

Using PowerShell

To move all users from the Test OU to the Test2 OU using PowerShell, use the following command:

```
Get-ADObject -Filter {(ObjectClass -eq "User") -and↵
  (ObjectCategory -eq "Person")} -SearchBase "ou=test,dc=adatum,dc=com" |↵
  Move-ADObject -TargetPath "ou=test2,dc=adatum,dc=com"
```

Discussion

When you move objects from one OU to another, you need to be aware of two significant Active Directory design factors that can affect the behavior of the objects that you're moving: delegation and Group Policy Object inheritance.

The first factor to be aware of is *delegation*. As an administrator, you can delegate permissions at the OU level so that specific users and groups can (or cannot) access or modify information concerning the objects contained within that OU. When you move an object from one OU to another, that object inherits the delegation settings from its new parent OU. This means that a user or group who had rights to an object before it was moved may no longer have rights to it afterward, and a user or group who did not have rights to the object before may have been delegated rights to the destination OU. You need to be aware of this setting to be sure that you do not allow or prevent object access unintentionally. Active Directory security and delegation is discussed further in Chapter 14.

The second factor to keep in mind is that of GPO inheritance. You can link a GPO at the site, domain, or OU level; any child objects that you move to a new OU will cease to receive the GPO settings that were applied to the old OU and will receive those settings associated with the new OU instead (unless the GPO is linked to the source OU and the destination OU).

The one exception to this would be if you were moving an object from a parent OU to its child OU—for example, moving from `ou=Finance,dc=adatum,dc=com` to `ou=FinanceTemps,ou=Finance,dc=adatum,dc=com`. In this example, the rules of GPO inheritance would cause the moved objects to receive any GPO settings linked to the Finance OU, followed by any GPO settings linked to the Finance Temps OU. Again, you need to be certain that moving an object from one OU to another does not create any unintended effects.

 You can use the Group Policy Management Console's Resultant Set of Policy (Modeling) Wizard to simulate the effect that the move will have on objects within the originating OU before you actually perform the move.

Using a graphical user interface

If you want to move more than 2,000 objects at one time, you will need to modify the default number of objects displayed, as described in the "Discussion" section of Recipe 5.4.

Using a command-line interface

AdMod will move only 10 objects at a time by default. To move more objects than this, you need to either specify the `-safety` *xx* option, where *xx* is the maximum number of objects to modify, or else use `-unsafe` to move an unlimited number of objects.

See Also

Recipe 4.20 for moving objects; Recipe 5.4 for enumerating objects in an OU; MSDN: IADsContainer::MoveHere

5.8. Moving an OU

Problem

You want to move an OU and all its child objects to a different location in the directory tree. Note that this scenario covers OUs and child objects that are not protected from accidental deletion.

Solution

Using a graphical user interface

1. Open the ADUC snap-in (*dsa.msc*).
2. If you need to change domains, right-click on Active Directory Users and Computers in the left pane, select Change Domain, enter the domain name, and click OK.
3. In the left pane, browse to the OU you want to move.
4. Right-click on the OU and select Move.
5. Select the new parent container for the OU and click OK.

Using a command-line interface

You can move an OU from one location to another by using either DSMove or AdMod. The DSMove syntax is as follows:

```
> dsmove "<OrgUnitDN>" -newparent "<NewParentDN>"
```

If you wish to move an OU with AdMod, use the following syntax:

```
> admod -b "<OrgUnitDN>" -move "<NewParentDN>"
```

Using PowerShell

To move the Test OU to the Test2 OU, use the following command:

```
Move-ADObject -Identity "ou=test,dc=adatum,dc=com"↵
 -TargetPath "ou=test2,dc=adatum,dc=com"
```

Discussion

One of the benefits of Active Directory is the ability to structure and restructure data easily. Moving an OU, even one that contains a complex hierarchy of other OUs and objects, can be done without impacting the child objects.

If any applications have a dependency on the location of specific objects, you need to ensure that either they are updated with the new location or, preferably, they reference the objects by GUID, not by distinguished name.

You should also be mindful of the impact of inherited ACLs and the effect of any new GPOs that are linked to the new parent OU. Keep in mind that any GPOs that were already linked to the OU will stay intact, and the link will follow the OU to its new location in the directory structure.

See Also

"Move an Organizational Unit" (*http://bit.ly/17ErtKm*)

5.9. Renaming an OU

Problem

You want to rename an organizational unit in your domain.

Solution

Using a graphical user interface

1. Open the ADUC snap-in (*dsa.msc*).
2. If you need to change domains, right-click on Active Directory Users and Computers in the left pane, select Change Domain, enter the domain name, and click OK.
3. In the left pane, browse to the OU you want to rename.

4. Right-click on the OU and select Rename.

5. Type in the new name for the OU and press Enter.

Using a command-line interface

To rename an object using the built-in DSMove utility, use the following syntax:

```
> dsmove "<ObjectDN>" -newname "<NewName>"
```

To use admod, use the following:

```
> admod -b "<ObjectDN>" -rename "<NewName>"
```

Using PowerShell

You can rename the Test OU to Test2 by using the following PowerShell command:

```
Rename-ADObject -Identity "ou=test,dc=adatum,dc=com" -NewName "Test2"
```

Discussion

Before you rename an OU, ensure that none of your production applications references it by name. You can make objects rename-safe by requiring all applications that must store a reference to an object to use the GUID of the object, rather than the name. The GUID (stored in the objectGUID attribute) is effectively unique within a forest and does not change when an object is renamed.

Using a command-line interface

The two parameters needed to rename an object are the original DN of the object and the new RDN (-newname). The -s option can also be used to specify a server name to work against.

See Also

Recipe 4.23; MSDN: IADsContainer::MoveHere

5.10. Modifying an OU

Problem

You want to modify one or more attributes of an OU.

Solution

The following examples set the description (description) attribute for the Finance OU.

Using a graphical user interface

1. Open the ADUC snap-in (*dsa.msc*).

2. If you need to change domains, right-click on Active Directory Users and Computers in the left pane, select Change Domain, enter the domain name, and click OK.

3. In the left pane, browse to the OU you want to modify.

4. Right-click on the OU and select Properties.

5. Modify the Description field and then click OK.

Using a command-line interface

To modify an object using AdMod, you'll use the following general syntax:

```
> admod -b <ObjectDN> <attribute>:<operation>:<value>
```

For example, you can add a description to an OU object using the following syntax:

```
> admod -b cn="ou=Finance,dc=adatum,dc=com" description::"Finance Department"
```

You can modify a limited number of object types with DSMod. Run `dsmod /?` from a command line for more details.

Using PowerShell

```
Set-ADObject -Identity "ou=finance,dc=adatum,dc=com" -Description↵
  "Finance Department"
```

Discussion

Modifying the attributes of an OU is a relatively straightforward process that's similar to modifying other types of objects within Active Directory. You can modify most attributes of an OU using the Active Directory Computers and Users MMC snap-in, but some attributes will be available for editing only by using ADSI Edit or a command-line or scripting utility.

See Also

MSDN: IADs::Put; MSDN: IADs::PutEx; MSDN: IADs::SetInfo; MSDN: ADS_PROPERTY_OPERATION_ENUM

5.11. Determining Approximately How Many Child Objects an OU Has

Problem

You want to quickly determine a rough approximation of how many child objects, if any, an OU contains.

Solution

Using a graphical user interface

1. Open LDP.
2. From the Menu, select Browse→Search.
3. For Base DN, enter *<OrgUnitDN>*.
4. For Filter, enter (objectclass=*).
5. For Scope, select Base.
6. Click the Attributes input area and enter msDS-Approx-Immed-Subordinates for attributes.
7. Click Run.

   The results will be displayed in the righthand pane.

 Another option would be to run a search using the onelevel scope and count the number of objects returned by the query. In LDP you can suppress the display of results so that it displays only the number of objects returned rather than displaying the specifics of each item.

Using a command-line interface

You can retrieve the number of child objects that are contained in an OU using either DSQuery or AdFind. To perform this task using DSQuery, use the following syntax:

```
> dsquery * "<OrgUnitDN>" -scope base -attr msDS-Approx-Immed-Subordinates
```

The syntax for AdFind is as follows:

```
> adfind -b "<OrgUnitDN>" -s base msDS-Approx-Immed-Subordinates
```

Using PowerShell

You can retrieve the number of child objects that are contained in an OU by using the following PowerShell command:

```
Get-ADObject -SearchBase "ou=test,dc=adatum,dc=com" -Filter * |↵
Measure-Object | FL Count
```

Discussion

The msDS-Approx-Immed-Subordinates attribute was introduced in Windows Server 2003. It contains the approximate number of direct child objects in a container or organizational unit. Note that this is an approximation and can be off by 10% or more, sometimes significantly more, of the actual total for large containers. (For instance, we ran this query for a container with 2,008 objects in it that reported a value of 1306 for the msDS-Appox-Immed-Subordinates attribute.) The main reason for adding this attribute was to give applications an idea of the rough order of magnitude of how many objects a container has so that it can display them accordingly.

msDS-Approx-Immed-Subordinates is a constructed attribute—that is, the value is not actually stored in Active Directory like other attributes. Rather, Active Directory computes the value when an application asks for it.

Using PowerShell

The PowerShell solution relies on the Measure-Object cmdlet, which counts the number of objects. The PowerShell solution will return an accurate count of objects, which makes it the best choice when you need more accuracy than an estimate.

See Also

MSDN: GetInfoEx

5.12. Delegating Control of an OU

Problem

You want to delegate administrative access of an OU to allow a group of users to manage objects in the OU.

Solution

Using a graphical user interface

1. Open the ADUC snap-in (*dsa.msc*).

2. If you need to change domains, right-click on Active Directory Users and Computers in the left pane, select Change Domain, enter the domain name, and click OK.

3. In the left pane, browse to and select the target OU, and then select Delegate Control.

4. Click Next and then click Add to select the users and/or groups to delegate control. Click OK to close the selection window and then click Next.

5. Select the type of task to delegate to the users or groups you selected in step 4 and then click Next.

6. Click Finish.

Using a command-line interface

ACLs can be set via the command line with the *dsacls* utility. See Recipe 14.12 for more information.

Discussion

Although you can delegate control of an OU to a particular user, it is almost universally a better practice to use a group instead. Even if there is only one user to delegate control to, you should create a group, add that user as a member, and use that group in the ACL. That way, in the future when you have to replace that user with someone else, you can simply make sure the new person is in the correct group instead of modifying ACLs again. The Delegation of Control Wizard is discussed further in Recipe 14.5.

See Also

Recipe 14.12 for changing the ACL on an object; Recipe 14.5

5.13. Assigning or Removing a Manager for an OU

Problem

You want to assign or remove a manager for an OU.

Solution

Using a graphical user interface

1. Open the ADUC snap-in (*dsa.msc*).

2. If you need to change domains, right-click on Active Directory Users and Computers in the left pane, select Change Domain, enter the domain name, and click OK.

3. Locate the OU in the left pane and then right-click on the OU and select Properties.

4. Select the Managed By tab.

5. Click the Change button.

6. Locate the group or user to delegate control to and click OK.

7. Click OK again to close the OU properties window and apply the changes.

8. To remove a manager from an OU, follow the same steps but click Clear instead of Change on the Managed By tab.

Using a command-line interface

To add a manager for an OU, use the following syntax:

```
> admod -b <ObjectDN> managedBy::<ManagerDN>
```

To clear the managedBy attribute, use the following:

```
> admod -b <ObjectDN> managedBy:-
```

Using PowerShell

You can use the following command to configure the Test OU to be managed by the account with a CN of Administrator:

```
Set-ADOrganizationalUnit "ou=test,dc=adatum,dc=com" -ManagedBy "Administrator"
```

Or, you can also specify the DN in place of the CN as shown in the following example:

```
Set-ADOrganizationalUnit "ou=test88,dc=woodgrovebank,dc=com"↵
  -ManagedBy "cn=aministrator,cn=users,dc=adatum,dc=com"
```

Discussion

In the case of an OU, specifying a user, group, computer, or another OU in the Managed By tab does not confer any particular rights onto the manager; this is used as a strictly informational field. When you configure a manager for an OU, the manager's DN is placed in the OU's managedBy attribute, and the OU's DN is placed in the manager's managedObjects attribute. managedObjects is the backlink attribute of managedBy, showing all objects where that manager is specified.

See Also

MSDN: Managed-by attribute [AD Schema]; MSDN: Managed-Objects [AD Schema]

5.14. Linking a GPO to an OU

Problem

You want to apply the settings in a GPO to the users and/or computers within an OU, also known as linking the GPO to the OU.

Solution

Using a graphical user interface

1. Open the Group Policy Management snap-in (*gpmc.msc*).
2. Expand Forest in the left pane.
3. Expand Domains, expand the targeted domain name, and then navigate down to the OU in the domain you want to link the GPO to.
4. Right-click on the OU and select either "Create a GPO in this domain, and Link it here" (if the GPO does not already exist) or "Link an Existing GPO" (if you have already created the GPO).
5. To unlink a GPO, right-click on an existing link and remove the checkmark next to Link Enabled.

Using PowerShell

To link the "Marketing" Group Policy Object to the Marketing OU in *adatum.com*, use the following PowerShell command:

```
New-GPLink -Name "Marketing" -Target "ou=marketing,dc=adatum,dc=com"
```

Discussion

The GPOs that are linked to an OU are stored in the gpLink attribute of the OU. The format of the gpLink attribute is kind of strange, so you have to be careful when programmatically or manually setting that attribute. Since multiple GPOs can be linked to an OU, the gpLink attribute has to store multiple values; unfortunately, it does not store them in a multivalued attribute as you might expect. Instead, the links are stored as part of the single-valued gpLink attribute. The ADsPath of each linked GPO is concatenated into a string, with each enclosed in square brackets. The ADsPath for each GPO is followed by ; 0 to signify the link is enabled or ; 1 to signify the link is disabled. Here is an example gpLink with two GPOs linked:

```
[LDAP://cn={6491389E-C302-418C-8D9D-
BB24E65E7507},cn=policies,cn=system,dc=adatum,dc=com;0]
```

```
[LDAP://cn={6AC1786C-016F-
11D2-945F-00C04fB984F9},cn=policies,cn=system,dc=adatum,dc=com;0]
```

See Also

Recipe 9.14 for more information on the Group Policy Management snap-in

5.15. Protecting an OU Against Accidental Deletion

Problem

You want to prevent an organizational unit object from being accidentally deleted.

Solution

Using a graphical user interface

1. Open Active Directory Users and Computers (dsa.mc). Click on View and confirm that Advanced Features is selected.

2. Drill down to the current domain. To connect to a different domain, right-click on the top-level node and click "Change domain"; select the appropriate domain and then drill down to it.

3. Right-click on the OU that you want to modify and click Properties.

4. Click on the Object tab.

5. Place a checkmark next to "Protect object from accidental deletion."

6. Click OK.

Using a command-line interface (all versions)

```
dsacls <OU DN> /d EVERYONE:SDDT
```

Using PowerShell

```
Set-ADOrganizationalUnit -Identity "ou=test,dc=adatum,dc=com"↵
  -ProtectedFromAccidentalDeletion:$True
```

Discussion

One of the challenges in delegating permissions within Active Directory is the potential for accidental deletions, particularly when administrators delete an entire organizational unit when they had only intended to delete a single object within that OU. Since Windows Server 2008, a new option is exposed in the Active Directory Users and Computers and Active Directory Sites and Services MMCs that will prevent an object from being deleted by means of a "fat-finger" deletion. By default, all new OUs that are created via the Active Directory Users and Computers MMC will have this protection enabled; however, any preexisting OUs or OUs created through other methods will not unless you enable it manually using one of the methods shown in this recipe. Additionally, built-in Active Directory containers, such as the BUILTIN, Computers, and Users containers, as well as the Domain Controllers OU and other built-in containers, do *not* have this protection enabled by default. If you attempt to delete an OU that is protected using this option, even when signed on as a Domain Admin or other similarly elevated account, you will receive an "Access Denied" message until you manually remove the checkbox or manually remove the deny ACE associated with it.

If you wish to enable this protection for all OUs that were present in your environment, you can automate the use of dsacls with a for do loop, as follows:

```
for /f "tokens=*" %i in ('dsquery ou -limit 0') do dsacls %i /d everyone:SDDT
```

You can also automate the process through PowerShell by piping the results of a Get-ADOrganizationalUnit query into the Set-ADOrganizationalUnit cmdlet, as follows:

```
Get-ADOrganizationalUnit -Filter * |↵
 Set-ADOrganizationalUnit -ProtectedFromAccidentalDeletion:$True
```

One advantage to using the command-line or PowerShell method is that this protection can be applied to container and leaf objects in *all* versions of Windows Server, even though the GUI checkbox is available only in Windows Server 2008 and later.

## CHAPTER 6

Users

6.0. Introduction

User accounts are some of the most frequently used objects in Active Directory; they create the means of authenticating and authorizing someone to access resources on your network. Because Windows server systems authenticate and authorize users primarily through Active Directory, many key issues that system administrators deal with are covered in this chapter. In particular, Active Directory manages information regarding user passwords; group membership; enabling, disabling, or expiring user accounts; and keeping track of when users have logged on to the network.

The Anatomy of a User

The default location for user objects in a domain is the cn=Users container directly off the domain root. You can, of course, create user objects in other containers and organizational units in a domain, or move them to these containers after they've been created. Table 6-1 contains a list of some of the interesting attributes that are available on user objects. This is by no means a complete list. There are many other informational attributes that we haven't included.

Table 6-1. Attributes of user objects

Attribute	Description
accountExpires	Large integer representing when the user's account is going to expire. See Recipe 6.31 for more information.
cn	Relative distinguished name of user objects. This is commonly the username or the display name of the user.
displayName	Typically the full name of a user. This attribute is used in administrative tools to display a user's descriptive name.
givenName	First name of the user.

Attribute	Description
homeDirectory	Local or UNC path of user's home directory. See Recipe 6.31 for more information.
homeDrive	Defines the drive letter to map the user's home directory to. See Recipe 6.31 for more information.
lastLogon	The last time that a user logged on to a particular DC. This information is not replicated among domain controllers.
lastLogonTimestamp	Approximate last logon timestamp, which is replicated among domain controllers. See Recipe 6.37 for more information.
managedObjects	Multivalued, linked attribute (with managedBy) that contains a list of DNs of objects the user manages.
lockoutTime	Large integer representation of the timestamp for when a user was locked out. See Recipe 6.13 for more information.
memberOf	Backlink listing of DNs of the groups the user is a member of. See Recipe 6.21 for more information.
objectSid	Octet string representing the SID of the user.
primaryGroupID	ID of the primary group for the user. See Recipe 6.23 for more information.
profilePath	UNC path to profile directory. See Recipe 6.31 for more information.
pwdLastSet	Large integer denoting the last time the user's password was set. See Recipe 6.27 for more information.
sAMAccountName	NetBIOS-style name of the user; limited to 20 characters to support legacy applications.
sIDHistory	Multivalued attribute that contains a list of SIDs that are associated with the user.
scriptPath	Path and filename of logon script. See Recipe 6.33 for more information.
sn	Last name of user.
tokenGroups	List of SIDs for the groups in the domain the user is a member of (both directly and via nesting).
unicodePwd	Octet string that contains a hash of a user's password. This attribute cannot be directly queried.
userAccountControl	Account flags that define such things as account status and password change status.
userPrincipalName	Internet-style account name for a user, which the user can use to log on to a computer. In most cases this should map to the user's email address, but this does not always need to be the case.
userWorkstations	List of computers a user can log on to, stored as a Unicode string.
msDS-PSOApplied	New since Windows Server 2008. A backlink that lists the Password Settings Objects that are applied to a user object.
msDS-ResultantPSO	New since Windows Server 2008. A constructed attribute that indicates which PSO is in effect for a user object.
msDS-UserPasswordExpiryTimeComputed	New since Windows Server 2008. A constructed attribute that indicates when a user's password is going to expire.
msDS-FailedInteractiveLogonCount	New since Windows Server 2008. Indicates the number of failed interactive logons for a user account since the Interactive Logon Count feature was enabled.

Attribute	Description
msDS-FailedInteractiveLogonCountAtLastSuccessfulLogon	New since Windows Server 2008. Indicates the number of failed interactive logons for a user account since the last time the user successfully logged on interactively.
msDS-LastFailedInteractiveLogonTime	New since Windows Server 2008. Indicates the last time and date that the user performed an unsuccessful interactive logon.
msDS-LastSuccessfulInteractiveLogonTime	New since Windows Server 2008. Indicates the last time and date that the user performed a successful interactive logon.
msDS-AuthenticatedAtDC	New since Windows Server 2008. A multivalued attribute listing the RODCs through which a user has successfully authenticated to a full DC.
msDS-RevealedDSAs	New since Windows Server 2008. Backlink indicating which RODCs have cached a user's password secrets.
msDS-ManagedPassword	New since Windows Server 2012. Contains password information for group-managed service accounts.

6.1. Modifying the Default Display Name Used When Creating Users in ADUC or ADAC

Problem

You want to modify how the default display name gets generated when you create a new user through the ADUC snap-in or through the Active Directory Administrative Center.

Solution

Using a graphical user interface

1. Open ADSI Edit.
2. In the Configuration Naming Context, browse to DisplaySpecifiers→<Locale> where <Locale> is the locale for your language (e.g., the U.S. English locale is 409).
3. Double-click on cn=user-Display.
4. Edit the createDialog attribute with the value you want the new default to be (e.g., %<sn>, %<givenName>).
5. Click OK.

Using a command-line interface

```
> admod -config -rb cn=user-Display,cn=409,cn=DisplaySpecifiers↵
  createDialog::"%<sn>, %<givenName>"
```

Using PowerShell

To modify display specifiers using PowerShell, run the following command:

```
Set-ADObject↵
 -Identity "cn=user-Display,cn=409,cn=DisplaySpecifiers,cn=configuration,↵
dc=adatum,dc=com"; -Add @{createDialog="%<sn>, %<givenname>"}
```

Discussion

When you create a new user object in ADUC or ADAC, it will automatically fill in the Full Name field as you type in the First Name, Initials, and Last Name fields. As a convenience, you may want to alter that behavior so that it automatically fills in a different value. To do that, you need to modify the User-Display display specifier, which has the following distinguished name:

```
cn=user-Display,cn=<Locale>,cn=DisplaySpecifiers,cn=Configuration,<ForestRootDN>
```

<Locale> should be replaced with your language-specific locale, and *<ForestRootDN>* should contain the distinguished name for your forest root domain. You need to modify the createDialog attribute, which by default has no value. Replacement variables are presented by *%<attribute>*, where *attribute* is an attribute name. For example, if you wanted the default to be "LastName, FirstName", you would use the following value:

```
%<sn>, %<givenName>
```

See Also

MS KB 250455 (XADM: How to Change Display Names of Active Directory Users)

6.2. Creating a User

Problem

You want to create a user object.

Solution

Using a graphical user interface

1. Open the Active Directory Administrative Center.
2. In the left pane, click to highlight the domain.
3. In the right pane, click New and then click User.

4. The two required fields are Full Name and sAMAccountName. The Full Name field will automatically be populated if you enter at least a first or a last name. Fill out any of the remaining fields and then click OK to complete the new-user creation.

Using a command-line interface

You can create a user with the built-in DSAdd utility or by using AdMod. Use the following DSAdd syntax:

```
> dsadd user "<UserDN>" -upn <UserUPN> -fn "<UserFirstName>"↵
-ln "<UserLastName>" -display "<UserDisplayName>" -pwd <UserPasswd>
```

To create a user account with AdMod, use the following syntax:

```
> admod -b "<UserDN>" -add objectClass::user sAMAccountName::<SAMAccount>
```

Using PowerShell

To create a new Active Directory user with PowerShell, use the following syntax:

```
New-ADUser -Name "<User CN>" -Path "<Parent DN>" -GivenName "<User First Name>"↵
 -Surname "<User Last name>" -sAMAccountName "<User sAMAccountName>"
```

Discussion

To make a user account immediately available for a user, you'll need to make sure the account is enabled, which is accomplished by setting userAccountControl to 512 after you've set a password that follows any password complexity rules in place for the user (order is important in this case). If you set only the attributes shown in the command-line and PowerShell examples, then the user accounts will be disabled by default.

You can also create user accounts using the inetOrgPerson class, which is described in Recipe 6.4. inetOrgPerson objects can be used for user authentication and restricting access to resources in much the same way as user objects.

Using a graphical user interface

To set additional attributes, double-click on the user account after it has been created. There are several tabs to choose from that contain attributes that are grouped together based on function (e.g., Profile).

Using a command-line interface

Several additional attributes can be set with the dsadd user command. Run dsadd user /? for the complete list. When creating a user with AdMod, you must specify the objectClass and sAMAccount attributes at a minimum. You can add additional attributes with the admod command by using the <attributename>::<value> syntax.

Using PowerShell

When using the `New-ADUser` cmdlet, there are about 50 common switches that can be used. In addition, you can specify the `-OtherAttributes` switch to set less common attributes. Here is a list of some of the common switches:

- `-Name`
- `-AccountPassword`
- `-City`
- `-Company`
- `-Department`
- `-Description`
- `-DisplayName`
- `-GivenName`
- `-HomeDirectory`
- `-HomeDrive`
- `-Manager`
- `-OfficePhone`
- `-PostalCode`
- `-SamAccountName`
- `-State`
- `-StreetAddress`
- `-Surname`
- `-Title`

See Also

Recipe 6.3 for creating users in bulk; Recipe 6.4 for creating an `inetOrgPerson` user; Recipe 6.31; MSDN: ADS_USER_FLAG_ENUM

6.3. Creating a Large Number of Users

Problem

You want to create a large number of `user` objects, either for testing purposes or to initially populate Active Directory with your employee, customer, or student user accounts.

Solution

Using a command-line interface

The following example uses a `for` do loop in combination with `dsadd` to create 1,000 users under the bulk OU in the *adatum.com* domain with usernames following the naming convention of *User1*, *User2*, *User3*, etc. The password is set, but other attributes are not configured. However, you can modify the `dsadd` command to populate additional attributes, as well.

```
> for /L %i in (1,1,1000) do dsadd user "cn=User%i,ou=bulk,dc=adatum,dc=com"↵
  -samid User%i -pwd N78ie.%i
```

You can also use the *ldifde* utility to perform a bulk import of unique usernames. Create an *.ldf* file using the following syntax (separate multiple entries with a blank line in between):

```
dn: cn=Joe Richards, ou=Engineering, dc=adatum, dc=com
changetype: add
cn: Joe Richards
objectClass: user
samAccountName: jrichards
```

Once you've created the LDIF file containing your user records, import the file using the following command:

```
> ldifde -i -f <filename.ldf> -s <servername>
```

You may notice that the LDIF file does not specify the user's password; this attribute must be modified after the user object has been created.

You can also use `admod` to automate this task. The following code will create 4,000 users named "TestUser_1", "TestUser_2", "TestUser_3", etc.:

```
> admod -sc adau:4000;MyPassword1!;cn=testuser,ou=testou,dc=adatum,dc=com
```

Using PowerShell

The following PowerShell example will create 1,000 users with the Name1, Name2, Name3 naming convention.

```
$i=1
do {New-ADUser -Name User$i
$i++
} while ($i -le 1000)
```

Discussion

Using ADSI, PowerShell, and the command-line utilities, you can create hundreds and even thousands of users far more easily and quickly than you would be able to do through a graphical user interface. You can also modify the examples to pull real data from a data source, such as an employee database.

Using a command-line interface

The AdMod syntax makes use of the `-adau` shortcut, which will add *X* number of users with *Y* as their starting password, so that `"-adau:4000;MyPassword1"` will create 4,000 users with a starting password of `"MyPassword1"`. If the starting password is not specified, a unique random complex password will be generated for each user.

Using PowerShell

The PowerShell example contains multiple lines. After the do command, PowerShell will drop down to a `>>` prompt, which indicates that the command is not complete. After entering the final line of the script, you need to press the Enter key twice to execute the script. Once complete, the configured PowerShell prompt will return.

See Also

Recipe 6.2 for creating a user; MS KB 263911 (How to Set a User's Password using LDIFDE)

6.4. Creating an inetOrgPerson User

Problem

You want to create an `inetOrgPerson` object, which is the standard LDAP object class to represent users.

Solution

Using a graphical user interface

1. Open the ADUC snap-in (*dsa.msc*).
2. If you need to change domains, right-click on Active Directory Users and Computers in the left pane, select Change Domain, enter the domain name, and click OK.
3. In the left pane, browse to the parent container of the new user, right-click on it, and select New→InetOrgPerson.
4. Enter text in the First Name, Last Name, and User Logon Name fields as appropriate and click Next.
5. Enter and confirm the password, set any of the password flags, and click Next.

6. Click Finish.

Using a command-line interface

DSAdd does not support creating `inetOrgPerson` objects, so use *ldifde* or AdMod instead. First, you need to create an LDIF file called *create_inetorgperson.ldf* with the following contents:

```
dn: <UserDN>
changetype: add
objectclass: inetorgperson
sAMAccountName: <UserName>

dn: <UserDN>
changetype: modify
add: userAccountControl
userAccountControl: 512
```

Be sure to replace *<UserDN>* with the distinguished name of the user you want to add and *<UserName>* with the user's username. Then run the following command:

```
> ldifde -i -f create_inetorgperson.ldf
```

You can also use the *admod* utility to create an `inetOrgPerson` object, as follows:

```
> admod -b "cn=inetOrgPerson,cn=Users,dc=adatum,dc=com"↵
  objectclass::inetOrgPerson sAMAccountName::inetOrgPerson -add
```

Using PowerShell

To create an `inetOrgPerson` object by using PowerShell, use the following syntax:

```
New-ADObject -Type inetOrgPerson -Name "<UserName>"↵
 -Path "ou=users,dc=adatum,dc=com" -OtherAttributes↵
 @{SamAccountName="<UserName>";UserPrincipalName="<UserUPN>"}
```

Discussion

The `inetOrgPerson` object class was defined in RFC 2798. It is the closest thing in the LDAP world to a standard representation of a user, and most LDAP vendors support the `inetOrgPerson` class. Unfortunately, Microsoft did not support `inetOrgPerson` with the initial release of Active Directory. Even though it provided an add-on later to extend the schema to support it, the damage had been done. Most Active Directory implementations were already using the user object class and were unlikely to convert, which required vendors to build in support for the user class.

You can create `inetOrgPerson` objects for your users, who can use them to authenticate just like accounts of the user object class. If you haven't deployed Active Directory yet and you plan to integrate a lot of third-party LDAP-based applications that rely on `inetOrgPerson`, you may want to consider using it instead of the user class. You won't be losing any information or functionality because the inetOrgPerson class inherits directly from the user class. For this reason, the inetOrgPerson class has even more attributes than the Microsoft user class.

The one potential downside is that some of the Microsoft tools, such as the DS utilities, do not support modifying inetOrgPerson objects. (You can, however, use AdMod to perform these modifications.)

See Also

Recipe 6.2 for creating a user; MS KB 314649; RFC 2798 (Definition of the InetOrg-Person LDAP Object Class)

6.5. Converting a user Object to an inetOrgPerson Object (or Vice Versa)

Problem

You want to convert one or more user objects to inetOrgPerson objects to improve interoperability in a heterogeneous environment.

Solution

Using a graphical user interface

1. Open ADSI Edit.

2. If an entry for the naming context you want to browse is not already displayed, do the following:

   a. Right-click on ADSI Edit in the right pane and click "Connect to."

   b. Fill in the information for the domain naming context, container, or OU that contains the object you want to modify. Click the Advanced button if you need to enter alternate credentials.

3. In the left pane, browse to the naming context, container, or OU containing the user object that you want to view. Once you've found the object, right-click on it and select Properties.

4. Scroll to objectClass and select Edit.

5. Under "Value to add," enter inetOrgPerson and click Add.

6. Click OK twice to save your changes.

Using a command-line interface

To convert a user object to an inetOrgPerson object, use the following syntax:

```
> admod -b "<UserDN>" objectClass:+:inetOrgPerson
```

 To revert the object back to a regular user, replace + with - in the previous syntax.

Using PowerShell

To convert a user object to an inetOrgPerson object, use the following syntax:

```
Set-ADObject -Identity "<UserDN>" -Add @{objectClass="inetOrgPerson"}
```

Discussion

In a heterogeneous environment, you may wish to convert one or more Active Directory user objects to inetOrgPerson objects. Since the inetOrgPerson class inherits from the user class, making this modification is a simple matter of adding the "inetOrgPerson" value to an object's objectClass attribute. It's important to note that this is the only instance in which you can modify structural classes in this manner; you can't simply modify a user object with whatever class you wish, even if that class inherits from the user class.

You can easily modify the command-line and PowerShell solutions to convert all user accounts in your domain (or just in a particular OU) to inetOrgPerson objects. For example, the following combination of adfind and admod will search for all user accounts in the Marketing OU and convert each one to an inetOrgPerson object (the -unsafe switch is necessary if you need to modify more than 10 objects at a time; you can also use the -safety X switch and specify the actual number of objects that you expect to modify for X):

```
adfind -default -rb "ou=Marketing" -f↵
"(&(objectcategory=person)(objectclass=User))" | admod↵
objectcategory:+:inetOrgPerson -unsafe
```

See Also

MS KB 307998 (Changing the Naming Attribute of the inetOrgPerson Class)

6.6. Modifying an Attribute for Several Users at Once

Problem

You want to modify an attribute for several users at once.

Solution

Using a graphical user interface

1. Open the ADUC snap-in (*dsa.msc*).
2. If you need to change domains, right-click on Active Directory Users and Computers in the left pane, select Change Domain, enter the domain name, and click OK.
3. In the left pane, browse to the parent container of the objects you want to modify.
4. In the right pane, highlight each object you want to modify, right-click, and select Properties.
5. Check the box beside the attribute(s) you want to modify and edit the fields for the attributes.
6. Click OK.

Using a command-line interface

The following command sets the home directory of all users under a parent container (*<ParentDN>*) to be on a particular fileserver (*<FileServer>*). The folder name is automatically replaced with the sAMAccountName for the user by using the $username$ syntax:

```
> dsquery user "<ParentDN>" -limit 0 -scope onelevel | dsmod user -hmdir↵
"\\<FileServerName>\$username$"
```

Using PowerShell

```
Get-ADuser -SearchBase "<ParentDN>" -Filter * |↵
  Set-ADUser -HomeDirectory "\\<FileServerName>\%username%"
```

Discussion

It is often necessary to update several users at once due to an organizational, geographic, or fileserver change. In each solution, we showed how to modify all users within a parent container, but you may need to use different criteria for locating the users.

Within ADUC, it may appear that you are limited to modifying multiple users that reside in the same container. However, you can create a saved query that returns users based on any criteria you specify. You can then highlight those users and modify them as described in the GUI solution.

With the CLI solution, you can modify the dsquery user command to search on whatever criteria you want. The same applies in the PowerShell solution by using a filter or an LDAP filter.

See Also

Recipe 4.8 for more information on searching AD

6.7. Deleting a User

Problem

You want to delete a user object.

Solution

Using a graphical user interface

1. Open the Active Directory Administrative Center.
2. In the right pane, enter the name of the user in the Global Search box, select the desired domain in the scope, and then click the search icon.
3. In the search results, right-click the name of the user and then click Delete.
4. Click Yes to confirm the deletion, which will complete the deletion process.

Using a command-line interface

You can delete a user using the built-in *dsrm* utility, as well as AdMod. For *dsrm*, use the following syntax:

```
> dsrm "<UserDN>"
```

For AdMod, enter the following:

```
> admod -b "<UserDN>" -del
```

Using PowerShell

To delete an object using PowerShell, use the following syntax:

```
Remove-ADUser -Identity "<UserDN>" -Confirm:$False
```

Discussion

This recipe covers deleting individual users. If you want to delete a container or OU and all the objects in it, take a look at Recipe 4.25.

Using PowerShell

Using the –Confirm:$False parameter allows the deletion to occur without a confirmation message from PowerShell.

See Also

Recipe 4.25 for deleting a container; MSDN: IADsContainer::Delete; MSDN: IADsDeleteOps:: DeletesObject

6.8. Setting a User's Profile Attributes

Problem

You want to set one or more of the user profile attributes.

Solution

Using a graphical user interface

1. Open the ADUC snap-in (*dsa.msc*).
2. In the left pane, right-click on the domain and select Find.
3. Select the appropriate domain beside In.
4. Beside Name, type the name of the user and click Find Now.
5. In the Search Results window, double-click on the user.
6. Click the Profile tab.
7. Modify the various profile settings as necessary.
8. Click OK.

Using a command-line interface

You can update a user's profile attributes using either DSMod or AdMod. DSMod uses the following syntax:

```
> dsmod user "<UserDN>" -loscr <ScriptPath> -profile <ProfilePath>↵
 -hmdir <HomeDir> -hmdrv <DriveLetter>
```

AdMod uses the following syntax:

```
> admod -b "<UserDN>" <attribute>::<NewValue>
```

Using PowerShell

To modify user profile attributes using PowerShell, use the following syntax:

```
Set-ADUser -Identity "<User DN>" -HomeDirectory "<HomeDir>"↵
 -HomeDrive "<DriveLetter>" -ProfilePath "<ProfilePath>"↵
 -ScriptPath "<ScriptPatch>"
```

Discussion

The four attributes that make up a user's profile settings are:

homeDirectory
> UNC path to home directory

homeDrive
> Drive letter (e.g., Z:) to map home directory

profilePath
> UNC path to profile directory

scriptPath
> Path to logon script

When you set the homeDirectory attribute, the folder being referenced needs to already exist. For an example on creating shares for users, see MS KB 234746.

See Also

Recipe 6.6 for methods to modify the attributes for multiple users

6.9. Moving a User

Problem

You want to move a user object to a different container or OU.

Solution

Using a graphical user interface

1. Open the ADUC snap-in (*dsa.msc*).
2. If you need to change domains, right-click on Active Directory Users and Computers in the left pane, select Change Domain, enter the domain name, and click OK.

3. In the left pane, right-click on the domain and select Find.

4. Type the name of the user and click Find Now.

5. In the Search Results window, right-click on the user and select Move.

6. Browse to and select the new parent container or OU.

7. Click OK.

 You can also drag and drop objects from one container or OU into another.

Using a command-line interface

You can move an object using either the built-in DSMove utility or AdMod. DSMove takes the following syntax:

```
> dsmove "<UserDN>" -newparent "<NewParentDN>"
```

To move an object using AdMod, do the following:

```
> admod -b "<CurrentUserDN>" -move "<NewParentDN>"
```

Using PowerShell

To move a user with PowerShell, use the following syntax:

```
Move-ADObject -Identity "<UserDN>" -TargetPath "<NewParentDN>"
```

Discussion

Moving a user object between OUs in the same domain has no direct impact on the actual user in terms of any security or distribution groups that the user is a member of. The things to be cautious of when moving the user to a new OU are different security settings, different GPOs, and the possibility of breaking applications that have the user's DN hardcoded into them.

See Also

Recipe 4.20 for moving objects between OUs

6.10. Redirecting Users to an Alternative OU

Problem

You want to redirect all new users from the default location (cn=Users) into a different location that you specify.

Solution

Using a graphical user interface

1. Open LDP.
2. From the menu, select Connection→Connect.
3. For Server, enter the name of a domain controller (or leave it blank to do a serverless bind).
4. For Port, enter 389.
5. Click OK.
6. From the menu, select Connection→Bind.
7. Accepted the default and bind as the currently logged on user or select the option to bind with credentials and then enter the credentials.
8. Click OK.
9. From the menu, select Browse→Modify.
10. For DN, enter the distinguished name of the domainDNS object of the domain you want to modify.
11. For Attribute, type **wellKnownObjects**.
12. For Values, enter the following:

        B:32:A9D1CA15768811D1ADED00C04FD8D5CD:cn=Users,<DomainDN>

    where *<DomainDN>* is the same as the DN you enter for the DN field.
13. Select Delete for the Operation and click the Enter button.
14. Go back to the Values field and enter the following:

        B:32:A9D1CA15768811D1ADED00C04FD8D5CD:<NewUsersParent>,<DomainDN>

    where *<NewUsersParent>* is the new parent container for new computer objects (e.g., "ou=Adatum Users").
15. Select Add for the Operation and click the Enter button.

16. Click the Run button.

17. The result of the operations will be displayed in the right pane of the main LDP window.

Using the command-line interface

To redirect the default OU that new users will be created into, use the following syntax:

```
> redirusr "<DestinationDN>"
```

Discussion

Most modern methods for creating user accounts, including the Active Directory Administrative Center, ADUC MMC snap-in, AdFind, and DSAdd, allow you to specify which OU a new user should be created in. However, some utilities, such as net user or the WinNT ADSI provider, still rely on a legacy API that will create a user only in its default location until an administrator manually moves it to another OU. The default location is the cn=Users container; this can create issues applying Group Policy to new user objects since the Users container cannot have a GPO linked to it. To ensure that all newly created users receive the necessary Group Policy settings as soon as they are created, use the *redirusr.exe* utility to redirect all new users that are not otherwise placed into a designated OU into the destination OU that you specify. You need to run this utility only once per domain, and the destination OU needs to exist before you run the utility.

See Also

"Redirect Users and Computers" (*http://bit.ly/13UYD6u*)

6.11. Renaming a User

Problem

You want to rename a user.

Solution

Using a graphical user interface

1. Open the ADUC snap-in (*dsa.msc*).

2. In the left pane, right-click on the domain and select Find.

3. Type the name of the user and click Find Now.

4. In the Search Results window, right-click on the user and select Rename.

5. You can modify the Full Name, First Name, Last Name, Display Name, User Logon Name, and User Logon Name (pre-Windows 2000) fields.

6. Click OK after you are done.

Using a command-line interface

The following command will rename the RDN of the user:

```
> dsmove "<UserDN>" -newname "<NewUserName>"
```

You can modify the UPN (-upn), first name (-fn), last name (-ln), and display name (-display) using the dsmod user command. For example, the following command will change the user's UPN and last name:

```
> dsmod user "<UserDN>" -upn "<NewUserUPN>" -ln "<NewUserLastName>"
```

You can also rename a user by using AdMod with the following syntax:

```
> admod -b "<UserDN>" -rename "<NewUserName>"
```

Using PowerShell

To rename a user object using PowerShell, use the following syntax:

```
Rename-ADObject -Identity "<UserDN>" -NewName "<NewCN>"
```

Discussion

Renaming a user object can have a couple of different meanings in Active Directory. In the generic object sense, renaming an object consists of changing the RDN for the object to something else, as when cn=jsmith becomes cn=joe. Typically, though, you need to rename more than that with users. For example, let's say you had a username naming convention of FirstInitialLastName, so Joe Smith's username would be jsmith. Let's pretend that Joe decides one day that Smith is way too common and he wants to be unique by changing his last name to Einstein. Now his username should be jeinstein. The following attributes would need to change to complete a rename of his object:

- His RDN should change from cn=jsmith to cn=jeinstein.

- His sAMAccountName should change to jeinstein.

- His userPrincipalName (UPN) should change to jeinstein@adatum.com.

- His mail (email address) attribute should change to jeinstein@adatum.com.

- His sn (last name) attribute should change to Einstein.

While this example may be contrived, it shows that renaming Joe Smith to Joe Einstein can take up to five attribute changes in Active Directory, or more if you include updates to proxy addresses and other attributes that are typically tied to the user's name. It is also important to note that if you change any of the first three in the bulleted list (RDN, SAM Account Name, or UPN), you should have the user log off and log back on after the changes have replicated. Since most applications and services rely on user GUID or SID, which doesn't change during a user rename, the person should not be affected, but you want to have him log off and back on anyway, just in case.

See Also

Recipe 4.23 for renaming objects

6.12. Copying a User

Problem

You want to copy an existing user account, which may be serving as a template, to create a new account.

Solution

Using a graphical user interface

1. Open the ADUC snap-in (*dsa.msc*).
2. In the left pane, browse to the parent container of the template user object.
3. In the right pane, right-click on the user and select Copy.
4. Enter the name information for the new user and click Next.
5. Enter a password, check any options you want enabled, and click Next.
6. Click Finish.

Using PowerShell

To create a new user from a template with PowerShell, use the following syntax:

```
$user = Get-ADUser -Identity <TemplateUserDN>↵
  -Properties department, co, title, l, c, st, countrycode
New-ADUser -Instance $user -Name "<NewUserName>" -DisplayName↵
  "<NewDisplayName>" -GivenName "<NewGivenname>" -Surname "<NewSuname>"↵
  -UserPrincipalName "<NewUPN>" -SamAccountName "<NewSamAccountName>"↵
  -PasswordNotRequired $true -Enable $true
```

Discussion

Copying a user consists of copying the attributes that are common among a certain user base, which can include department, address, and perhaps even organizational information. ADUC actually uses attributes that are marked in the schema as "Copied when duplicating a user" to determine which attributes to copy. If you are interested in finding the attributes that are configured in the schema to get copied, see Recipe 10.11.

Using a graphical user interface

To copy a user in ADUC, you have to browse to the user object. If you locate the user by using Find instead, the Copy option is not available when right-clicking a user in the Search Results window.

See Also

Recipe 10.11 for finding the attributes that should be copied when duplicating a user

6.13. Finding Locked-Out Users

Problem

You want to find users whose accounts are locked out.

Solution

Using a command-line interface

The following command finds all locked-out users in the domain of the specified domain controller:

```
> unlock <DomainControllerName> * -view
```

Using PowerShell

The following command finds all locked-out users in the current domain:

```
Search-ADAccount -LockedOut -UsersOnly | FT Name,LockedOut -AutoSize
```

Discussion

Despite the deceptively simple commands just shown, finding the accounts that are currently locked out is a surprisingly complicated task. You would imagine that you could run a query using DSQuery or AdFind (similar to the one to find disabled users in Recipe 6.20), but unfortunately, it is not that easy.

The lockoutTime attribute is populated with a timestamp when a user is locked. One way to find locked-out users would be to find all users that have something populated in lockoutTime (i.e., lockoutTime=*). That query would definitely find all the currently locked users, but it would also find all the users that subsequently became unlocked and have yet to log in since being unlocked; the lockoutTime attribute doesn't get reset until the next time the user logs on successfully. This is where the complexity comes into play.

To determine the users that are currently locked out, you have to query the attribute lockoutDuration stored on the domain object (e.g., dc=adatum,dc=com). This attribute defines the number of minutes that an account will stay locked before becoming automatically unlocked. You need to take this value and subtract it from the current time to derive a timestamp that would be the outer marker for which users could still be locked. You can then compare this timestamp with the lockoutTime attribute of the user object. The search filter to find all locked users once you've determined the locked timestamp would look something like this:

```
(&(objectcategory=Person)(objectclass=user)(lockoutTime>DerivedTimestamp))
```

For any users that have a lockoutTime that is less than the derived timestamp, their account has already been automatically unlocked per the lockoutDuration setting.

None of the current standard GUI or CLI tools incorporates this kind of logic, but fortunately joe Richards wrote the *unlock.exe* utility, which does. And as its name implies, you can also unlock locked accounts with it. Thanks, joe!

See Also

"Details of Account Lockout Settings and Processes" (*http://bit.ly/16MeWGN*)

6.14. Unlocking a User

Problem

You want to unlock a locked-out user.

Solution

Using a graphical user interface

1. Open the ADUC snap-in (*dsa.msc*).
2. In the left pane, right-click on the domain and select Find.
3. Select the appropriate domain.
4. Type the name of the user and click Find Now.
5. In the Search Results window, right-click on the user and select Properties.

6. Click the Account tab and then click Unlock account.

7. Click OK.

Using a command-line interface

To unlock all locked user accounts in your domain, use *unlock.exe* with the following syntax:

```
> unlock . *
```

To unlock a specific user object, replace * with the user's sAMAccountName or distinguished name, as follows:

```
> unlock . joe.smith
```

Using PowerShell

```
Unlock-ADAccount -Identity <UserDN>
```

To unlock all locked user accounts in your domain, use the following syntax:

```
Search-ADAccount -LockedOut -UsersOnly | Unlock-ADAccount
```

Discussion

If you've enabled account lockouts for an Active Directory domain (see Recipe 6.13), some users may eventually get locked out. A user can get locked out for a number of reasons, but generally it is because a user mistypes her password a number of times, changes her password and does not log off and log on again, or has services or scheduled tasks running under the security context of her individual user account rather than a service account.

You can use ADSI's IADsUser::IsAccountLocked method to determine whether a user is locked out. You can set IsAccountLocked to FALSE to unlock a user. You can also query the msDS-User-Account-Control-Computed attribute of an object.

See Also

Recipe 6.13 for finding locked-out users; Recipe 6.15 for viewing the account lockout policy; MSDN: Account Lockout

6.15. Troubleshooting Account Lockout Problems

Problem

A user is having account lockout problems and you need to determine from where and how the account is getting locked out.

Solution

Using a graphical user interface

LockoutStatus is a program available for Windows that can help identify the domain controller that handled the lockout. It works by querying the lockout status of a user against all domain controllers in the user's domain.

To determine the lockout status of a user:

1. Launch LockoutStatus and select File→Select Target from the menu.

2. Enter the target username and the domain of the user.

3. Click OK.

At this point, each domain controller in the domain will be queried and the results will be displayed. To dive deeper and figure out which computer the lockout occurred on, you need to use the EventCombMT utility and point it at the domain controller that handled the lockout. EventCombMT can query the domain controller with the specific lockout event IDs that will allow you to find the computer.

Discussion

The *lockoutstatus.exe* utility is just one of many that is available in the Account Lockout and Management tool set provided by Microsoft. These lockout tools are intended to help administrators with account lockout problems that were very difficult to trouble-shoot in the past. Along with the tool mentioned in "Solution", here are a few others that are included in the set:

ALockout.dll
> A script that uses this DLL, called *EnableKerbLog.vbs* (included with the tool set), can be used to enable logging of application authentication. This can help identify applications that are using bad credentials and causing account lockouts.

ALoInfo.exe
> This displays services and shares that are using a particular account name. It can also print all the users and their password ages.

NLParse.exe
> This is a filter tool for the *netlogon.log* files. You can use it to extract just the lines that relate to account lockout information.

EventCombMT
> This utility parses event logs from multiple servers, either to collect all entries to-gether or to search for individual events across multiple computers. This is

extremely useful when troubleshooting user account lockouts, for example, by determining which computer is causing the account lockout.

All the Account Lockout tools are available for download from the Microsoft Download Center (*http://bit.ly/ZKV5nC*).

See Also

Account Lockout Best Practices White Paper (*http://bit.ly/ZKV8jf*) and Troubleshooting Account Lockout the PSS Way (*http://bit.ly/9ZHtSK*)

6.16. Viewing the Domain-Wide Account Lockout and Password Policies

Problem

You want to view the domain-wide account lockout and password policies for a domain.

Solution

Using a graphical user interface

1. Open the Group Policy Management snap-in (*gpmc.msc*).
2. In the left pane, expand the forest, expand Domains, expand the desired domain, expand Group Policy Objects, and then click the Default Domain Policy.
3. In the right pane, click the Settings tab to generate a report of all of the GPO settings.
4. Click "show" to the right of Security Settings and then click "show" to the right of Accounts Policies/Password Policy to view the password policy.
5. Click "show" to the right of Account Policies/Account Lockout Policy to view the account lockout policy.

Using PowerShell

To retrieve the minimum password length, number of passwords remembered, password properties, and lockout threshold of the domain-wide password policy for the *adatum.com* domain using PowerShell, run the following command:

```
Get-ADObject "dc=adatum,dc=com" -Properties * |↵
  FL minPwdLength,pwdHistoryLength,pwdProperties,lockoutThreshold
```

To retrieve the maximum password age, minimum password age, lockout duration, and lockout observation of the domain-wide password policy for the *adatum.com* domain using PowerShell, use the following script:

```
$DOMAIN = Get-ADObject "dc=adatum,dc=com" -Properties *
$MAXPWDAGE = [System.TimeSpan]::FromTicks([System.Math]↵
::ABS($DOMAIN.maxPwdAge)).Days
$MINPWDAGE = [System.TimeSpan]::FromTicks([System.Math]↵
::ABS($DOMAIN.minPwdAge)).Days
$LOCKOUTDURATION =↵
; [System.TimeSpan]::FromTicks([System.Math]::ABS($DOMAIN.lockoutDuration)).Days
$LOCKOUTOBSERVATION =↵
; [System.TimeSpan]::FromTicks([System.Math]::↵
;ABS($DOMAIN.lockoutObservationWindow)).Days
Write-Host "Maximum password age:",↵
;$MAXPWDAGE;Write-Host "Minimum password age:",↵
;$MINPWDAGE;Write-Host "Lockout duration:",↵
;$LOCKOUTDURATION;Write-Host "Lockout observation:",$LOCKOUTOBSERVATION
```

Discussion

Several parameters controlling account lockout and password complexity can be set on a domain-linked Group Policy Object such as the Default Domain Policy. The properties that can be set for the password and account lockout policies include:

Account lockout duration
> Number of minutes an account will be locked before being automatically unlocked. A value of 0 indicates accounts will be locked out indefinitely—that is, until an administrator manually unlocks them.

Account lockout threshold
> Number of failed logon attempts after which an account will be locked.

Reset account lockout counter after
> Number of minutes after a failed logon attempt that the failed logon counter for an account will be reset to 0.

The properties that can be set for the Password Policy include:

Enforce password history
> Number of passwords to remember before a user can reuse a previous password.

Maximum password age
> Maximum number of days a password can be used before a user must change it.

Minimum password age
> Minimum number of days a password must be used before it can be changed.

Minimum password length
> Minimum number of characters a password must be.

Password must meet complexity requirements
  If enabled, passwords must meet all of the following criteria:

  - Not contain all or part of the user's account name

  - Be at least six characters in length

  - Contain characters from three of the following four categories:

    a. English uppercase characters (A–Z)

    b. English lowercase characters (a–z)

    c. Base 10 digits (0–9)

    d. Nonalphanumeric characters (e.g., !, $, #, %)

Store passwords using reversible encryption
  If enabled, passwords are stored in such a way that they can be retrieved and de-crypted. This is essentially the same as storing passwords in plain text, and should be avoided unless it is absolutely necessary.

In Windows Server 2003 and legacy versions of Windows, administrators can configure only one password and account lockout policy for domain users, per domain. If a group of users requires a different policy, a separate domain (and all of the hardware require-ments and administrative overhead associated with managing that separate domain) is needed. Windows Server 2008 and later versions of Windows allow for the creation of Fine-Grained Password Policies (FGPPs), which allow you to configure multiple pass-word policies within a single domain.

Using a graphical user interface

On a domain controller or any computer that has the Remote Server Administration Tools (RSAT) installed, the Group Policy Management snap-in is available from the Start menu under Administrative Tools.

Using PowerShell

In the first example, the `pwdProperties` attribute returns a value that indicates some of the general settings of the password policy. For example, a 1 indicates that password complexity is enabled. A 0 indicates that password complexity is disabled. The number 16 indicates that passwords are stored using reversible encryption.

In the second example, we have to deal with conversion from 100-nanosecond intervals, which is how the values are stored.

See Also

"Account Lockout Best Practices White Paper" (*http://bit.ly/1068cQ1*); MSDN: DO-MAIN_PASSWORD_INFORMATION; "Pwd–Properties attribute (Windows)" (*http://bit.ly/YpxDvo*)

6.17. Applying a Fine-Grained Password Policy to a User Object

Problem

You want to apply a Fine-Grained Password Policy (FGPP) to a user object.

Solution

Using a graphical user interface (steps specific to Windows Server 2012)

1. Open Active Directory Administrative Center.
2. In the top-left pane, click the tree view icon.
3. Expand the System container.
4. Scroll down and right-click Password Settings Container, expand the New menu, and then click Password Settings.
5. Fill in the desired password settings in the top pane. Note that the fields with a red asterisk are required fields.
6. In the Directly Applies To section, click the Add button to add a user object that will be the target of the FGPP.
7. Click OK to create the FGPP.

Using a command-line interface

The following will add the 'cn=joer' user to the list of groups that a PSO will apply to:

```
psomgr -applyto cn=joer,cn=Users,dc=ADATUM,dc=COM -pso TestPSO -forreal
```

Using PowerShell

To ensure that a user will be a target of an FGPP, use the following syntax:

```
Add-ADFineGrainedPasswordPolicySubject -Identity "<Name of FGPP>"↵
  -Subjects "<User Object sAMAccountName>"
```

Discussion

Once an FGPP has been created, you can modify the password and account lockout settings controlled by the object, as well as the users and groups that it should apply to. Since the `PasswordSettingsObject` is an Active Directory object class, these modifications can be made using any interface that can modify objects. When working from the command line, the *psomgr* tool from joeware (*http://www.joeware.net/freetools*) allows you to modify one or multiple PSOs at a time, and can also create "starter" PSOs using the `-quickstart` command-line switch. The full syntax for *psomgr.exe* can be obtained by typing `psomgr.exe /?` at a command prompt, or by visiting the *joeware* website.

See Also

Chapter 9

6.18. Viewing the Fine-Grained Password Policy That Is in Effect for a User Account

Problem

You want to determine which FGPP is in effect for a particular user.

Solution

Using a graphical user interface

1. Open Active Directory Users and Computers. Click View and confirm that there is a checkmark next to Advanced Features.

2. Browse to the user or group in question; right-click on the object and click Properties.

3. Click on the Attribute Editor tab. Click Filter and confirm that there is a checkmark next to "Show read-only attributes: Constructed and Backlinks."

4. Scroll to the `msDS-PSOApplied` attribute. If an FGPP is applied directly to the user, it will be shown in the value.

5. Scroll to the `msDS-ResultantPSO` attribute. If an FGPP is applied to a group that the user is a member of, it will be shown in the value.

6. Click OK.

Using a command prompt

```
psomgr.exe -effective <User DN>
```

Using PowerShell

```
Get-ADObject -Identity "<UserDN>" -Properties "msDS-PSOApplied",↵
"msDS-ResultantPSO" | FL Name,msDS-PSOApplied,msDS-ResultantPSO
```

Discussion

Within a domain, each `user` object contains a constructed backlink attribute called `msDS-ResultantPSO` that indicates which `PasswordSettingsObject` is in effect for that user. The precedence rules for `PasswordSettingsObjects` are as follows:

1. If a PSO has been applied directly to the user object, this PSO will take precedence. If multiple PSOs have been applied to a single user, the following tiebreakers will be used:

   - A PSO with a lower-numbered Precedence attribute (e.g., 5) will be applied over a higher-numbered one (e.g., 50).

   - If multiple PSOs have been configured with the same Precedence attribute, the PSO with the lowest GUID will take final precedence.

2. If no PSOs have been applied directly to the user, any PSO that has been applied to a group that the user is a member of, whether directly or indirectly, will be applied. The same tiebreakers will be used here as in rule 1.

3. If no PSOs have been applied to the user or any groups that the user is a member of, the default domain PSO will be applied.

See Also

Recipe 6.18; Recipe 9.29

6.19. Enabling and Disabling a User

Problem

You want to enable or disable a user account.

Solution

Using a graphical user interface

1. Open the ADUC snap-in (*dsa.msc*).
2. In the left pane, right-click on the domain and select Find.
3. Select the appropriate domain.
4. Type the name of the user beside Name and click Find Now.
5. In the Search Results window, right-click on the user and select Enable Account to enable, or Disable Account to disable.
6. Click OK.

Using a command-line interface

To enable a user, use the following command:

```
> dsmod user "<UserDN>" -disabled no
```

To disable a user, use the following command:

```
> dsmod user "<UserDN>" -disabled yes
```

Using PowerShell

To use PowerShell to enable or disable a user account, use the following syntax:

```
Set-ADUser "<User DN>" -Enabled $False
Set-ADUser "<User DN>" -Enabled $True
```

Discussion

Account status is used to control whether a user is allowed to log on or not. When an account is disabled, the user is not allowed to log on to his workstation with the account or to access AD controlled resources. Much like the lockout status, the account status is stored as a flag in the userAccountControl attribute (see Recipe 6.31).

There is an IADsUser::AccountDisabled property that allows you to determine and change the status. Set the method to FALSE to enable the account or to TRUE to disable it.

See Also

Recipe 6.20 for finding disabled users; Recipe 6.31 for more on the attribute userAccountControl

6.20. Finding Disabled Users

Problem

You want to find disabled users in a domain.

Solution

Using a graphical user interface

1. Open the ADUC snap-in (*dsa.msc*).
2. In the left pane, connect to the domain you want to query.
3. Right-click on the domain and select Find.
4. In the Find dropdown box, select Common Queries.
5. Click the "Disabled accounts" option box.
6. Click the Find Now button.

Using a command-line interface

You can enumerate all disabled user objects in your domain by using the built-in DSQuery utility, as follows:

```
> dsquery user <DomainDN> -disabled
```

You can also use a bitwise query in AdFind to produce the same output, using the following syntax:

```
> adfind -bit -b <DomainDN> -f↵
"&(objectcategory=person)(objectclass=user)(useraccountcontrol:AND:=2)"
```

 You can replace *<DomainDN>* with the DN of a specific organizational unit if you wish to restrict the results of your AdFind query.

Using PowerShell

To locate all disabled users in a domain by using PowerShell, run the following command:

```
Get-ADUser -Filter {Enabled -eq "False"} | FL Name
```

Discussion

Users in Active Directory can be either enabled or disabled. A disabled user cannot log in to the domain. Unlike account lockout, which is an automatic process that is based on the number of times a user incorrectly enters a password, an account has to be manually enabled or disabled.

All disabled user accounts have the bit that represents 2 (0010 base 2) set in their userAccountControl attribute. This doesn't mean that the attribute will be equal to 2, it just means that the bit that equals 2 will be enabled—other bits may also be set. See Recipe 4.12 and Recipe 4.15 for a more detailed explanation of bit flags.

See Also

Recipe 4.12; Recipe 4.15; Recipe 6.19 for enabling and disabling users

6.21. Viewing a User's Group Membership

Problem

You want to view the group membership of a user.

Solution

Using a graphical user interface

1. Open the ADUC snap-in (*dsa.msc*).
2. In the left pane, right-click on the domain and select Find.
3. Select the appropriate domain.
4. Type the name of the user beside Name and click Find Now.
5. In the Search Results window, double-click on the user.
6. Click the Member Of tab.
7. To view all indirect group membership (from nested groups), you'll need to double-click on each group.

Using a command-line interface

The following command displays the groups that *<UserDN>* is a member of. Use the -expand switch to list nested group membership as well:

```
> dsget user <UserDN> -memberof [-expand]
```

You can also use the GetUserInfo tool (*http://www.joeware.net*) with the following syntax:

```
> getuserinfo \\<Domain>\<Username>
```

A third option would be to use the *whoami* tool, as follows:

```
> whoami /groups
```

To round out the command-line options for viewing group memberships, you can use the MemberOf *joeware* utility with the following syntax:

```
> memberof -u <Domain>\<User>
```

 To query group membership from a specific domain controller using MemberOf, use the -s switch followed by the name of the DC.

Using PowerShell

```
Get-ADUser "<User DN>" -Properties MemberOf | select -ExpandProperty MemberOf
```

Discussion

The memberOf attribute on user objects is multivalued and contains the list of distinguished names for groups of which the user is a member. memberOf is actually linked with the member attribute on group objects, which holds the distinguished names of its members. For this reason, you cannot directly modify the memberOf attribute; you must instead modify the member attribute on the group.

The primary group of a user, which the user is technically a member of, will not be shown in the CLI or solutions except in the case of the MemberOf utility. This is due to the fact that the primary group is not stored in the memberOf attribute like the rest of the groups. See Recipes 6.23 and 7.11 for more on finding the primary group of a user.

Using PowerShell

The example command will display only the direct members of a group.

See Also

Recipe 6.23; Recipe 7.4 for more on viewing the nested members of a group; Recipe 7.11; Recipe 10.15 for more information on linked attributes

6.22. Removing All Group Memberships from a User

Problem

You want to remove all group membership information from a user object.

Solution

Using a graphical user interface

1. Open the ADUC snap-in (*dsa.msc*).
2. In the left pane, right-click on the domain and select Find.
3. Select the appropriate domain.
4. Type the name of the user beside Name and click Find Now.
5. In the Search Results window, double-click on the user.
6. Click the Member Of tab.
7. Highlight all groups listed in the Member Of tab and select Remove. Click Yes to confirm.
8. Click OK.

Using a command-line interface

You can accomplish this task at the command line using a combination of AdFind and AdMod:

```
> adfind -b <DomainDN> -f  member=<UserDN> -dsq | admod member:-:<UserDN> -unsafe
```

Using PowerShell

To remove group memberships using PowerShell, use the following syntax:

```
Get-ADGroup -Filter {Name -ne "Domain Users"} |↵
  ForEach-Object {Remove-ADGroupMember $_ -Members "<User DN>" -Confirm:$False}
```

Discussion

Using PowerShell

The example command filters out the Domain Users group. By default, the Domain Users group is the primary group for user objects. You can't remove a user from her primary group. In some cases, a different group may be the primary group and, in such situations, should be substituted for Domain Users in the command.

See Also

MSDN: Adding Members to Groups in a Domain [Active Directory]; MSDN: Group Objects [Active Directory]

6.23. Changing a User's Primary Group

Problem

You want to change the primary group of a user.

Solution

Using a graphical user interface

1. Open the ADUC snap-in (*dsa.msc*).
2. In the left pane, right-click on the domain and select Find.
3. Select the appropriate domain.
4. Type the name of the user beside Name and click Find Now.
5. In the Search Results window, double-click on the user.
6. Click the Member Of tab.
7. Click on the name of the group you want to set as the primary group.
8. Click the Set Primary Group button.
9. Click OK.

Using PowerShell

First, obtain the `primarygroupToken` of the desired primary group by using the following syntax:

```
Get-ADGroup -Identity "<GroupDN>" -Properties primarygroupToken |↵
  FL primarygroupToken
```

Next, use the following syntax to replace the `primaryGroupID` attribute on a user back to the Domain Users group (change the ID to the desired group ID based on the first PowerShell command if the goal is to change the primary group to something else):

```
Set-ADObject "<UserDN>" -Replace @{PrimaryGroupID="513"}
```

Discussion

The primary group is a holdover from Windows NT that was used to support Macintosh and POSIX clients. That being said, you might have some legacy applications that depend on the primary group, and therefore you may have to change some users' primary groups.

Changing the primary group is not difficult, but it is not straightforward, either. The primary group is stored on `user` objects in the `primaryGroupID` attribute, which contains the RID of the primary group. You can obtain this value by querying the `primary GroupToken` attribute on the target `group` object. Before you can set the `primaryGrou pID` on the user object, you have to first make sure the user is a member of the group. If you try to set the `primaryGroupID` for a group in which the user is not a member, you will get an error.

The default `primaryGroupID` is set to 513 (Domain Users) for all users.

See Also

Recipe 7.11 for determining the group name given a group ID; MS KB 297951 (How to Use the PrimaryGroupID Attribute to Find the Primary Group for a User)

6.24. Copying a User's Group Membership to Another User

Problem

You want to copy one user's group membership to another user.

Solution

Using a graphical user interface

1. Open the ADUC snap-in (*dsa.msc*).
2. In the left pane, right-click on the domain and select Find.
3. Select the appropriate domain.
4. Beside Name, type the name of the user you want to transfer groups from and click Find Now.
5. In the Search Results window, double-click on the user.
6. Click the Member Of tab.
7. For each group you want to add another user in, do the following:
   a. Double-click on the group.

b. Click the Members tab.

c. Click the Add button.

d. Find the user you want to add in the object picker and click OK.

e. Click OK.

Using a command-line interface

The following command line will add *<NewUserDN>* to all of the groups that *<CurrentU serDN>* is a member of:

```
> for /F "usebackq delims=""" %i in ('dsget user↵
"<CurrentUserDN>" -memberof') do dsmod group %i -addmbr "<NewUserDN>"
```

If you want to get fancy and remove *<CurrentUserDN>* from each of the groups in the same operation, simply add an -rmmbr option on the end:

```
> for /F "usebackq delims=""" %i in ('dsget user↵
"<CurrentUserDN>" -memberof') do dsmod group %i -addmbr "<NewUserDN>"↵
-rmmbr "<CurrentUserDN>"
```

You can also add *<NewUserDN>* to all of the groups that *<CurrentUserDN>* is a member of by using a combination of AdFind and AdMod, as follows:

```
> adfind -b <DomainDN> -f member=<Source User DN> -dsq |↵
admod member:+:<Dest. UserDN> -unsafe
```

Using PowerShell

To copy group memberships using PowerShell, use the following syntax:

```
$SOURCE=Get-ADUser -Identity "<SourceUserDN>" -Properties *
$DESTINATION="<DestinationUserDN>"
foreach ($group in $SOURCE.MemberOf)
{
Add-ADGroupMember -Identity $group -Members $destination
}
```

Discussion

Employees come and go; people take on new responsibilities and move on to new jobs. It is common to have movement within an organization. When this happens, typically someone is replacing the person who is moving on. The administrator needs to get the new person up to speed as quickly as possible, including setting up accounts and granting access to any necessary resources. A big part of this process includes adding the new user to the correct groups. You can help facilitate this by using one of the processes outlined in the "Solution" section to help the user gain access to the exact same groups that the former employee was a member of.

One important issue to point out is that the memberOf attribute, which was used in the command-line solutions to determine a user's group membership, contains only the groups that are visible to the DC that's being queried; this can vary depending on whether the DC in question is a global catalog and whether the user belongs to any universal groups. Any groups the user is a member of outside of the user's domain will not be transferred. To transfer universal group membership outside of a domain, you will need to perform a query against the global catalog for all group objects that have a member attribute that contains the DN of the user. You can also search the global catalog for the memberOf attribute for a given user to determine a user's universal group memberships.

See Also

Recipe 7.5 for adding and removing members of a group

6.25. Setting a User's Password

Problem

You want to set the password for a user.

Solution

Using a graphical user interface

1. Open the ADUC snap-in (*dsa.msc*).
2. In the left pane, right-click on the domain and select Find.
3. Select the appropriate domain.
4. Type the name of the user beside Name and click Find Now.
5. In the Search Results window, right-click on the user and select Reset Password.
6. Enter and confirm the new password.
7. Click OK.

Using a command-line interface

This command changes the password for the user specified by *<UserDN>*. Using * after the -pwd option prompts you for the new password. You can replace * with the password you want to set, but it is not a good security practice since other users that are logged in to the machine may be able to see it:

```
> dsmod user <UserDN> -pwd *
```

You can modify the `unicodepwd` attribute directly by encrypting the `admod` connection using the `-kerbenc` switch:

```
> admod -b "<UserDN>" unicodepwd::<Password> -kerbenc
```

You can also use `admod` with the `#setpwd#` switch:

```
> admod -b "<UserDN>" #setpwd#::<NewPassword>
```

Using PowerShell

To set a user's password with PowerShell, use the following syntax:

```
$newPassword = (Read-Host -Prompt "Provide New Password" -AsSecureString)
Set-ADAccountPassword -Identity <UserDN> -NewPassword $newPassword -Reset
```

Discussion

The PowerShell solution follows the command-line solution model, which prompts for the password instead of entering the password in plain text in the command. PowerShell supports converting a plain text string as part of the command, but that method isn't considered as secure. You can use a plain text password in the password reset by using the `ConvertTo-SecureString -AsPlainText "<NewPassword>"` option in place of the password prompt. The following example shows the full command:

```
Set-ADAccountPassword -Identity "<UserDN>" -Reset↵
 -NewPassword (ConvertTo-SecureString -AsPlainText "<NewPassword>" -Force)
```

See Also

MS KB 225511 (New Password Change and Conflict Resolution Functionality in Windows); MSDN: IADsUser::SetPassword; MSDN: IADsUser::Change-Password

6.26. Preventing a User from Changing a Password

Problem

You want to disable a user's ability to change his password.

Solution

Using a graphical user interface

1. Open the ADUC snap-in (*dsa.msc*).
2. In the left pane, right-click on the domain and select Find.
3. Select the appropriate domain.

4. Beside Name, type the name of the user you want to modify and click Find Now.

5. In the Search Results window, double-click on the user.

6. Click the Account tab.

7. Under Account options, check the box beside "User cannot change password."

8. Click OK.

Using a command-line interface

```
> dsmod user <UserDN> -canchpwd no
```

Using PowerShell

```
> Set-ADAccountControl -Identity "<UserDN>" -CannotChangePassword $True
```

Discussion

Using a graphical user interface

Even though in the GUI solution you check and uncheck the "User cannot change password" setting, actually making the change in Active Directory is a little more complicated. Not allowing a user to change his password consists of setting two deny Change Password ACEs on the target user object. One deny ACE is for the Everyone account and the other is for Self.

To perform this change across multiple users, you can multiselect users in Active Directory Users and Computers and then perform the remaining steps in the GUI solution.

See Also

"How to use the UserAccountControl flags to manipulate user account properties" (*http://support.microsoft.com/kb/305144*)

6.27. Requiring a User to Change a Password at Next Logon

Problem

You want to require a user to change her password the next time she logs on to the domain.

Solution

Using a graphical user interface

1. Open the ADUC snap-in (*dsa.msc*).

2. In the left pane, right-click on the domain and select Find.

3. Select the appropriate domain.

4. Beside Name, type the name of the user you want to modify and click Find Now.

5. In the Search Results window, double-click on the user.

6. Click the Account tab.

7. Under Account options, check the box beside "User must change password at next logon."

8. Click OK.

Using a command-line interface

You can configure the "User must change password" setting using either DSMod or AdMod. To modify this setting using DSMod, use the following syntax:

```
> dsmod user "<UserDN>" -mustchpwd yes
```

For AdMod, do the following:

```
> admod -b "<UserDN>" pwdLastSet::0
```

Using PowerShell

To flag a user's password to change on next logon with PowerShell, use the following syntax:

```
Set-ADUser -Identity <UserDN> -ChangePasswordAtLogon $True
```

Discussion

Be careful when forcing users to change their password at next logon by using the PowerShell solution. Active Directory Users and Computers will not allow you to force a user to change her password at next logon if the user is already configured not to be able to change her password. However, you can set both of those options by using PowerShell. In such a situation, the user would not be able to log on.

6.28. Preventing a User's Password from Expiring

Problem

You want to prevent a user's password from expiring.

Solution

Using a graphical user interface

1. Open the ADUC snap-in (*dsa.msc*).
2. In the left pane, right-click on the domain and select Find.
3. Select the appropriate domain.
4. Beside Name, type the name of the user you want to modify and click Find Now.
5. In the Search Results window, double-click on the user.
6. Click the Account tab.
7. Under Account options, check the box beside "Password never expires."
8. Click OK.

Using a command-line interface

```
> dsmod user "<UserDN>" -pwdneverexpires yes
```

Using PowerShell

To prevent a user's password from expiring with PowerShell, use the following syntax:

```
Set-ADUser -Identity "<UserDN>" -PasswordNeverExpires $True
```

Discussion

Setting a user's password to never expire overrides any password-aging policy you've defined in the domain. To disable password expiration, you need to set the bit equivalent of 65,536 (i.e., 10000000000000000) in the userAccountControl attribute of the target user.

See Also

Recipe 4.15 for more on modifying a bit flag attribute; Recipe 6.31 for more on setting the userAccountControl attribute

6.29. Finding Users Whose Passwords Are About to Expire

Problem

You want to find the users whose passwords are about to expire.

Solution

Using a command-line interface

```
> dsquery user -stalepwd <NumDaysSinceLastPwdChange>
```

You can also use the FindExpAcc *joeware* tool with the following syntax:

```
> findexpacc -pwd -days <NumDaysUntilExpiration>
```

Using PowerShell

The following script finds users whose passwords will expire within seven days:

```
$Policy = (Get-ADDefaultDomainPasswordPolicy).MaxPasswordAge.days
$DaysUntil = 7
Get-ADUser -Filter {(Enabled -eq "True") -and (PasswordNeverExpires↵
 -eq "False")} -Properties * | Select Name,@{Name="Expires";↵
Expression={$Policy - ((Get-Date) - ($_.PasswordLastSet)).days}} |↵
 Where-Object {$_.Expires -gt 0 -AND $_.Expires -le $DaysUntil}
```

Discussion

When a Windows-based client logs on to Active Directory, a check is done against the effective password policy and the user's pwdLastSet attribute to determine whether the user's password has expired. If it has, the user is prompted to change it. In a pure Windows-based environment, this notification process may be adequate, but if you have a lot of non-Windows-based computers that are joined to an Active Directory domain (e.g., Kerberos-enabled Unix clients), or you have a lot of application and service accounts, you'll need to develop your own user password expiration notification process. Even in a pure Windows environment, cached logins present a problem because when a user logs in to the domain with cached credentials (i.e., when the client is not able to reach a domain controller), this password expiration notification check is not done.

The process of finding users whose passwords are about to expire is a little complicated. Fortunately, the dsquery user command helps by providing an option for searching for users that haven't changed their password for a number of days (-stalepwd). The downside to the dsquery user command is that it will find users whose passwords are about to expire, users who are configured so that their passwords never expire, and users that must change their passwords at next logon (i.e., pwdLastSet = 0).

Using a command-line interface

You can use the FindExpAcc tool to query Active Directory for expired user or computer accounts, as well as active accounts with expired passwords. It also includes switches that are familiar from AdFind and AdMod, such as -b to specify the Base DN, -f to specify an LDAP filter, and so on.

The *findexpacc* utility can also be used to query for user accounts that are about to expire, in addition to accounts with expiring passwords.

See Also

Recipe 6.16 for more on the password policy for a domain; Recipe 6.20; Recipe 6.25 for how to set a user's password; Recipe 6.28 for how to set a user's password to never expire

6.30. Viewing the RODCs That Have Cached a User's Password

Problem

You wish to view the RODCs that have cached a user account's password secrets.

Solution

Using a graphical user interface

1. Open ADSI Edit and connect to the default naming context.
2. In the left pane, navigate to the container or the OU that contains the user object.
3. In the right pane, right-click the user and click Properties.
4. Scroll down the list of attributes until you find the msDS-RevealedDSAs attribute.
5. View the value of msDS-RevealedDSAs to view the RODCs that have cached the user's password.
6. Click OK or Cancel to close the Properties window.

Using a command-line interface

```
> adfind -b <UserDN> msDS-RevealedDSAs
```

Using PowerShell

```
> Get-ADUser -Identity "<UserDN>" -Properties "msDS-RevealedDSAs" |↵
  FL msDS-RevealedDSAs
```

Discussion

Read-Only Domain Controllers (RODCs) improve the security of branch offices and other remote environments. One of the security measures introduced by the RODC is the Password Replication Policy (PRP), which specifies a list of users and groups that can and cannot have their password secrets cached on one or more DCs. Each RODC maintains a forward-link attribute called msDS-RevealedUsers, which lists the user accounts for whom each RODC has cached password secrets. Each user account, in turn, maintains a backlink called msDS-RevealedDSAs. This backlink can be queried to determine which RODCs have stored password information for a particular user account; however, like all backlinks, this attribute cannot be modified directly.

See Also

Recipe 3.2; Recipe 3.4

6.31. Setting a User's Account Options (userAccountControl)

Problem

You want to view or update the userAccountControl attribute for a user. This attribute controls various account options, such as whether the user must change her password at next logon and whether the account is disabled.

Solution

Using a graphical user interface

1. Open the ADUC snap-in (*dsa.msc*).
2. In the left pane, right-click on the domain and select Find.
3. Select the appropriate domain.
4. Beside Name, type the name of the user and click Find Now.
5. In the Search Results window, double-click on the user.
6. Select the Account tab.
7. Many of the userAccountControl flags can be set under Account options.
8. Click OK when you're done.

Using a command-line interface

The dsmod user command has several options for setting various userAccountControl flags, as shown in Table 6-2. Each switch accepts yes or no as a parameter to either enable or disable the setting.

Table 6-2. dsmod user options for setting userAccountControl

dsmod user switch	Description
-mustchpwd	Sets whether the user must change his password at next logon.
-canchpwd	Sets whether the user can change his password.
-disabled	Sets account status to enabled or disabled.
-reversiblepwd	Sets whether the user's password is stored using reversible encryption.
-pwdneverexpires	Sets whether the user's password never expires.

Using PowerShell

To modify user properties associated with the userAccountControl attribute, you have several switches available through the set-ADUser cmdlet, including the following:

```
Set-ADUser -Identity <UserDN> -PasswordNeverExpires
Set-ADUser -Identity <UserDN> -ChangePasswordAtLogon
Set-ADUser -Identity <UserDN> -Enabled
```

To see all of the available properties that can be modified, run the following command:

```
Get-Command Set-ADUser -Syntax
```

Discussion

The userAccountControl attribute on user (and computer) objects could be considered the kitchen sink of miscellaneous and sometimes completely unrelated user account properties. If you have to work with creating and managing user objects very much, you'll need to become intimately familiar with this attribute.

The userAccountControl attribute is a bit flag, which means you have to take a couple of extra steps to search against it or modify it. See Recipe 4.12 for more on searching with a bitwise filter and Recipe 4.15 for modifying a bit flag attribute.

The dsmod user command can be used to modify a subset of userAccountControl properties, as shown in Table 6-2, and Table 6-3 contains the complete list of userAccountControl properties as defined in the ADS_USER_FLAG_ENUM enumeration.

Table 6-3. ADS_USER_FLAG_ENUM values

Name	Value	Description
ADS_UF_SCRIPT	1	Logon script is executed.
ADS_UF_ACCOUNTDISABLE	2	Account is disabled.

Name	Value	Description
ADS_UF_HOMEDIR_REQUIRED	8	View-only attribute. Indicates that Home Directory is required.
ADS_UF_LOCKOUT	16	Account is locked out.
ADS_UF_PASSWD_NOTREQD	32	A password is not required.
ADS_UF_PASSWD_CANT_CHANGE	64	Read-only flag that indicates if the user cannot change her password.
ADS_UF_ENCRYPTED_TEXT_PASSWORD_ALLOWED	128	Store password using reversible encryption.
ADS_UF_NORMAL_ACCOUNT	512	Enabled user account.
ADS_UF_INTERDOMAIN_TRUST_ ACCOUNT	2048	A permit to trust account for a system domain that trusts other domains.
ADS_UF_WORKSTATION_TRUST_ACCOUNT	4096	Enabled computer account.
ADS_UF_SERVER_TRUST_ACCOUNT	8192	Computer account for backup domain controller.
ADS_UF_DONT_EXPIRE_PASSWD	65536	Password will not expire.
ADS_UF_MNS_LOGON_ACCOUNT	131072	MNS logon account.
ADS_UF_SMARTCARD_REQUIRED	262144	Smart card is required for logon.
ADS_UF_TRUSTED_FOR_DELEGATION	524288	Allow Kerberos delegation.
ADS_UF_NOT_DELEGATED	1048576	Do not allow Kerberos delegation even if ADS_UF_TRUSTED_FOR_DELEGATION is enabled.
ADS_UF_USE_DES_KEY_ONLY	2097152	Requires DES encryption for keys.
ADS_UF_DONT_REQUIRE_PREAUTH	4194304	Account does not require Kerberos preauthentication for logon.
ADS_UF_PASSWORD_EXPIRED	8388608	Read-only flag indicating account's password has expired. Only used with the WinNT provider.
ADS_UF_TRUSTED_TO_AUTHENTICATE_FOR_DELEGATION	16777216	Account is enabled for delegation.
ADS_UF_PARTIAL_SECRETS_ACCOUNT	67108864	Account is an RODC.

See Also

Recipe 4.12; Recipe 4.15 for setting a bit flag attribute; "How to use the UserAccount-Control flags to manipulate user account properties" (*http://bit.ly/19VlLTK*)

6.32. Setting a User's Account to Expire

Problem

You want a user's account to expire at some point in the future.

Solution

Using a graphical user interface

1. Open the ADUC snap-in (*dsa.msc*).
2. In the left pane, right-click on the domain and select Find.
3. Select the appropriate domain.
4. Beside Name, type the name of the user you want to modify and click Find Now.
5. In the Search Results window, double-click on the user.
6. Click the Account tab.
7. Under "Account expires," select the radio button beside "End of."
8. Select the date the account should expire.
9. Click OK.

Using a command-line interface

Valid values for the -acctexpires flag include a positive number of days in the future when the account should expire—for instance, at the end of the day, or to never expire the account:

```
> dsmod user "<UserDN>" -acctexpires <NumDays>
```

Using PowerShell

```
Set-ADUser -Identity "<UserDN>" -AccountExpirationDate 12/31/2014
```

Discussion

User accounts can be configured to expire on a certain date. Account expiration is stored in the accountExpires attribute on a user object. This attribute contains a large integer representation of the date on which the account expires, expressed in 100-nanosecond intervals since January 1, 1601. If you set this attribute to 0, it disables account expiration for the user (i.e., the account will never expire). Note that this is different from the dsmod user command, where a value of 0 with -acctexpires will cause the account to expire at the end of the day.

See Also

MSDN: Account Expiration

6.33. Determining a User's Last Logon Time

Problem

You want to determine the last time a user logged in to a domain.

Solution

Using a graphical user interface

To view the last logon timestamp in ADUC, do the following:

1. Open the ADUC snap-in (*dsa.msc*).
2. Click View and confirm that Advanced Features has a checkmark next to it.
3. Right-click on the domain and select Find.
4. Select the appropriate domain.
5. Beside Name, type the name of the user you want to locate and click Find Now.
6. In the Search Results window, double-click on the user.
7. Click the Attribute Editor tab.
8. View the value for the lastLogonTimestamp attribute.

Using a command-line interface

```
> adfind -b <UserDN> lastLogonTimestamp -tdc
```

The -tdc and -tdcs switches will display attributes such as lastLogon Timestamp in a human-readable format.

Discussion

Trying to determine when a user last logged on has always been a challenge in the Microsoft NOS environment. In Windows NT, you could retrieve a user's last logon timestamp from a PDC or BDC, but this timestamp was the last time the user logged on to the individual PDC or BDC itself. That means to determine the actual last logon, you'd have to query every domain controller in the domain. In large environments, this wasn't practical. With Windows 2000 Active Directory, things did not improve. A lastLogon attribute is used to store the last logon timestamp, but unfortunately, this attribute isn't replicated. So again, to get an accurate picture, you'd have to query every domain controller in the domain for the user's last logon attribute and keep track of the most recent one.

Since the Windows Server 2003 forest functional level became available, we have had a viable solution. A new attribute called lastLogonTimestamp was added to the schema for user objects. This attribute is similar to the lastLogon attribute that was available previously, with two distinct differences. First, and most importantly, this attribute is replicated. That means when a user logs in, the lastLogonTimestamp attribute will get populated and then replicate to all domain controllers in the domain.

The second difference is that since lastLogonTimestamp is replicated, special safeguards needed to be put in place so that users who logged in repeatedly over a short period of time did not cause unnecessary replication traffic. So, the lastLogonTimestamp is updated only if the last update occurred between 9 and 14 days ago by default. (This window is configurable by modifying the msDS-LogonTimeSyncInterval on the domain NC.) This means that the lastLogonTimestamp attribute could be more than a week off in terms of accuracy with a user's actual last logon. Ultimately, this shouldn't be a problem for most situations because lastLogonTimestamp is intended to address the common problem where administrators want to run a query and determine which users have not logged in over the past month or more.

See Also

Recipe 6.34 for finding users who have not logged on recently; "The LastLogonTimeStamp Attribute—What it was designed for and how it works" (*http://bit.ly/13lpvg7*)

6.34. Finding Users Who Have Not Logged On Recently

Problem

You want to determine which users have not logged on recently.

Solution

Using a graphical user interface

1. Open the ADUC snap-in (*dsa.msc*).
2. In the left pane, right-click on the domain and select Find.
3. Beside Find, select Common Queries.
4. Select the number of days beside "Days since last logon."
5. Click the Find Now button.

Using a command-line interface

You can locate users who have not logged on for a certain amount of time using either the built-in DSQuery tool or the OldCmp utility from joeware (*http://www.joeware.net*):

```
> dsquery user -inactive <NumWeeks>
```

OldCmp can create a report of all user objects based on several criteria. To create a report of all users in the *adatum.com* domain who haven't logged on in more than 90 days, for example, use the following syntax:

```
> oldcmp -report -users -b dc=adatum,dc=com -llts -age 90 -sh
```

Using PowerShell

You can also locate users who have not logged on for a certain amount of time using PowerShell, as shown in the following command that finds users that have not logged on in 60 days:

```
$DaysSince = (Get-Date).AddDays(-60)
Get-ADUser -Filter * -Properties LastLogonDate |↵
 Where-Object {($_.LastLogonDate -le $DaysSince) ↵
 -and ($_.Enabled -eq $True) -and ($_.LastLogonDate -ne $NULL)} |↵
 Select Name,LastLogonDate
```

Discussion

An attribute on user objects called lastLogonTimestamp contains the approximate last time the user logged on. However, the lastLogonTimestamp attribute has a certain amount of latency associated with it to cut down on replication traffic; the date contained in this attribute can be anywhere from nine to 14 days off in a default domain. This latency can be made longer or shorter by modifying the attribute msDS-LogonTimeSyncInterval of the Domain NC.

Using PowerShell

PowerShell has a property named LastLogonDate that is a human-friendly conversion of the lastLogonTimestamp attribute. This allows for easy PowerShell queries involving finding inactive users.

See Also

Recipe 6.29 for more on computing large integer timestamps; Recipe 6.33 for more on finding a user's last logon timestamp

6.35. Viewing and Modifying a User's Permitted Logon Hours

Problem

You want to see the hours that a user is permitted to log on to the network.

Solution

Using a graphical user interface

1. Open the ADUC snap-in (*dsa.msc*).

2. If you need to change domains, right-click on Active Directory Users and Computers in the left pane, select Connect to Domain, enter the domain name, and click OK.

3. Right-click on the user and select Properties. From the Account tab, click on Logon Hours.

4. Select the hours that you want to allow or disallow, and click Logon Permitted or Logon Denied. Click OK.

5. Click OK.

Using PowerShell

```
## user DN
$userDN = "LDAP://<UserDN>"

## powers of two in a single byte
## can use [System.Math]::Pow(), but this is faster
$pow2 = @(1, 2, 4, 8, 16, 32, 64, 128)

## bit-state - a bit is either off (0) or on (1)
$onoff = @("0", "1")

function dump($byte)
{
    $result = ""
    for ($i = 0; $i -lt 8; $i++)
    {
        $result += $onoff[($byte -band $pow2[$i]) -ne 0]
    }
    return $result
}

# days of the week, zero based
$days = @("Sunday", "Monday", "Tuesday", "Wednesday", "Thursday",↵
```

```
"Friday", "Saturday")
$day = 0

# main
$obj  = [ADSI]$userDN
$arr = $obj.logonHours.Value

for ($i = 0; $i -lt $arr.Length; $i += 3)
{
    $days[$day]
    (dump $arr[$i]) + " " + (dump $arr[$i+1]) + " " + (dump $arr[$i+2])
    $day += 1
}
```

Discussion

Using PowerShell

The logonHours attribute of a user object is represented as an octet string, rather than a simple string like most of the other attributes we've discussed. As a result, manipulating it directly is a bit trickier than simply inserting a new string in place of an old one. An octet string is just another name for an array of bytes containing arbitrary binary data. For the logonHours attribute, each hour of a day is represented as a single bit within a byte. Each byte contains eight (8) bits, so it takes three bytes to represent all of the hours in a day. It goes from low-order to high-order (i.e., the low-order bit in the lowest byte for a given day is midnight to 1:00 a.m.). The information is stored in the logonHours attribute in UTC and translated by the user interface into local time. Finally, since there are seven days in a week, and each day takes three bytes of information, the attribute will have 21 elements.

In the PowerShell example, we pregenerate an array containing the powers-of-2 contained with a byte and process each day as a subarray of the entire attribute. Using the bitwise and function in PowerShell allows us to map binary values directly into array subscripts, which reduces the complexity of the routine.

See Also

MS KB 816666 (How to Limit User Logon Time in a Domain in Windows Server 2003); MSDN: Logon-Hours attribute [AD Schema]

6.36. Viewing a User's Managed Objects

Problem

You want to view the objects that are managed by a user.

Solution

Using a graphical user interface

1. Open ADSI Edit.
2. If an entry for the naming context you want to browse is not already displayed, do the following:
   a. Right-click on ADSI Edit in the right pane and click "Connect to."
   b. Fill in the information for the naming context, container, or OU you want to add an object to. Click on the Advanced button if you need to enter alternate credentials.
3. In the left pane, browse to the naming context, container, or OU of the object you want to view. Once you've found the object, right-click on it and select Properties.
4. View the managedObjects attribute.

Using a command-line interface

```
> adfind -b "<UserDN>" managedObjects
```

Using PowerShell

To retrieve a user's managedObjects property with PowerShell, use the following syntax:

```
Get-ADUser -Identity "<UserDN>" -Properties managedObjects |↵
  Select -ExpandProperty managedObjects
```

Discussion

The managedObjects attribute is linked to the managedBy attribute that can be set on certain objects in Active Directory, such as computers, OUs, and groups. Setting the managedBy attribute provides a quick way to define who owns an object. If you do use it, you can use the managedObjects attribute on user, contact, or group objects to get the list of objects for which the user has been configured in the managedBy attribute.

6.37. Creating a UPN Suffix for a Forest

Problem

You want users to have a different UPN suffix from the default provided by your forest.

Solution

Using a graphical user interface

1. Open the Active Directory Domains and Trusts snap-in (*domain.msc*).

2. In the left pane, right-click Active Directory Domains and Trusts and select Properties.

3. Under Alternative UPN suffixes, type the name of the suffix you want to add.

4. Click Add and then click OK.

Using a command-line interface

```
> admod -config -rb cn=Partitions uPNSuffixes:+:treyresearch.com
```

 The *attributeName:+:attributeValue* syntax will add an additional value to an existing list of values in a multivalued attribute. Using *attributeName::attributeValue* would overwrite the existing values with the value you specify.

Using PowerShell

```
Set-ADForest -Identity <ForestRootDomainName> -UPNSuffixes @{Add="<NewSuffix>"}
```

Discussion

The UPN allows users to log on with a friendly name that may even correspond to their email address. UPN logons also do not require the domain to be known so that it can be abstracted away from the user. You may need to create an additional UPN suffix (e.g., @*adatum.com*) if you want UPNs to map to email addresses, but your AD forest is rooted at a different domain name (e.g., *ad.adatum.com*) from the domain name used in email addresses (e.g., *treyresearch.com*).

See Also

MS KB 243280 (Users Can Log On Using User Name or User Principal Name); "Add User Principal Name Suffixes" (*http://bit.ly/10BIIWw*); MS KB 269441 (How to Use ADSI to List the UPN Suffixes that Are Defined in Active Directory)

6.38. Restoring a Deleted User

Problem

You want to restore a user object that has been inadvertently deleted.

 This recipe assumes that the Active Directory Recycle Bin was enabled prior to the deletion. If you have not enabled the AD Recycle Bin, you can do so from the Tasks pane in the Active Directory Administrative Center.

Solution

Using a graphical user interface (steps specific to Windows Server 2012)

1. Launch the AD Administrative Center.
2. Select the domain and navigate to the `Deleted Objects` container.
3. Locate the deleted object in the container.
4. Right-click the object and select Restore.

Discussion

In most cases, it is sufficient when restoring a deleted object within Active Directory to simply perform an *authoritative* restore of the individual object. Performing this authoritative restore will allow the restored user object to be replicated to other DCs within the domain along with all attributes that were present at the time that the System State backup was taken.

See Also

MS KB 216993 (Useful Shelf Life of a System-State Backup of Active Directory); MS KB 840001 (How to Restore Deleted User Accounts and Their Group Memberships in Active Directory); Chapter 16 for more on recovering and restoring Active Directory

6.39. Protecting a User Against Accidental Deletion

Problem

You want to prevent a user object from being accidentally deleted by an administrator who selects the incorrect option in Active Directory Users and Computers.

Solution

Using a graphical user interface

1. Open Active Directory Users and Computers. Click on View and confirm that Advanced Features is selected.
2. Drill down to the current domain. To connect to a different domain, right-click on the top-level node and click "Change domain"; select the appropriate domain and then drill down to it.
3. Right-click on the object that you want to modify and click Properties.
4. Click on the Object tab.
5. Place a checkmark next to "Protect object from accidental deletion."
6. Click OK.

Using a command-line interface (all versions)

```
dsacls <User DN> /d EVERYONE:SDDT
```

Using PowerShell

```
Set-ADObject -Identity "<User DN>" -ProtectedFromAccidentalDeletion $True
```

Discussion

By default, all new OUs that are created in Windows Server 2008 and later will have this protection enabled; however, no other object types are configured with this default protection. If you attempt to delete a group that is protected using this option, even when signed on as a Domain Admin or other similarly elevated account, you will receive an "Access Denied" message until you manually remove the checkbox or manually remove the deny ACE associated with it.

By using the command-line or PowerShell method, you can apply this protection to group objects in *all* versions of Windows Server, even though the GUI checkbox is available only in Windows Server 2008 and later.

## CHAPTER 7

Groups

7.0. Introduction

A group is a simple concept that has been used in many different types of standalone and networked systems over the years. In generic terms, a group is just a collection of objects. Groups are often used to apply security in an efficient manner, where you create a collection of users and assign certain permissions or rights to that group, rather than to each individual user within the group. When applying security settings, it's much easier to use a group than to use individual users, because you only need to apply the security setting once per group instead of once per user. In addition, groups are also frequently used to send email messages to an entire group of users at once rather than requiring the sender to address each person individually.

In Active Directory, groups are flexible objects that can contain virtually any other type of object as a member, although they'll generally contain only users, inetOrgPersons, computers, and other groups. Active Directory groups can be used for many different purposes, including controlling access to resources, defining a filter for the application of group policies, and serving as an email distribution list.

The ways in which a group can be used in an Active Directory forest are defined by the group's *scope* and *type*. The *type* of a group can be either *security* or *distribution*. Security groups can be used to grant or restrict access to Windows resources, whereas distribution groups can be used only as a simple grouping mechanism for sending email messages or for some other non-Windows security-related function. Both security and distribution groups can be used as email lists, but only security groups can be used to assign access to resources.

The *scope* of a group determines where members of the group can be located within the forest and where in the forest you can use the group in an ACL. The supported group scopes include *universal*, *global*, and *domain local*. Universal groups and domain local groups can have members that are part of any domain in the same forest (or, in the case of domain local groups, a separate forest if a cross-forest trust exists), whereas global groups can only have members that are part of the same domain that the group is contained in. When assigning permissions to group objects, universal and global groups can be assigned permissions to resources anywhere in the forest (or any trusted forest), whereas domain local groups can only be assigned permissions to resources in the same domain. (In this way, domain local and global groups are functional opposites of each other.)

The Anatomy of a Group

Groups are represented in Active Directory by group objects. Table 7-1 contains a list of some of the noteworthy attributes that are available on group objects.

Table 7-1. Attributes of group objects

Attribute	Description
cn	Relative distinguished name of group objects.
whenCreated	Timestamp of when the OU was created.
description	Text description of the group.
groupType	Flag containing the group scope and type. See Recipe 7.8 for more information.
info	Additional notes about a group.
primaryGroupToken	Local RID for the group. This matches the primaryGroupID attribute that is set on user objects.
managedBy	DN of a user or group that is the owner of the group.
managedObjects	List of DNs of objects for which this group is listed in the managedBy attribute.
Member	List of DNs of members of the group.
memberOf	List of DNs of the groups this group is a member of.
whenChanged	Timestamp of when the OU was last modified.
sAMAccountName	Down-level account name for the group. Typically this is the same as the cn attribute.
wWWHomePage	URL of the home page for the group.
sAMAccountType	Describes the type of account that was created for an object, such as a domain object, a group object, a normal user account, and so on.

7.1. Creating a Group

Problem

You want to create a group.

Solution

Using a graphical user interface

1. Open the Active Directory Administrative Center.

2. In the left pane, click to highlight the desired domain.

3. In the right pane, click New and then click Group.

4. Enter the name of the group, enter the sAMAccountName, select the group scope (Domain local, Global, or Universal), and select the group type (Security or Distribution).

5. Enter any other desired information into the optional fields and then click OK.

Using a command-line interface

In the following example, *<GroupDN>* should be replaced with the DN of the group to create, *<GroupScope>* should be l, g, or u for domain local, global, and universal groups, respectively, and -secgroup should be set to yes if the group is a security group or no otherwise. Another recommended option is to set -desc for specifying a group description:

```
> dsadd group "<GroupDN>" -scope <GroupScope> -secgrp yes|no -desc "<GroupDesc>"
```

You can also create a group object with admod, using the following syntax:

```
> admod -b "<GroupDN>" objectClass::group groupType::↵
"<GroupType>" sAMAccountName::"<Pre-Windows2000Name>" -add
```

For example, to create a global security group called "Finance Users" in the Finance OU of the *adatum.com* domain, you can use either of the following commands:

```
> dsadd group "cn=Finance Users,ou=Finance,dc=adatum,dc=com"-scope g -secgrp yes
```

```
> admod-b "cn=Finance Users,ou=Finance,dc=adatum,dc=com" groupType::-2147483646↵
sAMAccountName::"Finance Users" -add
```

In the case of AdMod, you must specify the numeric value for the group type, which can be any one of those listed in Table 7-2.

Table 7-2. Numeric values for group types

Group type	Numeric value
Universal Distribution Group	8
Universal Security Group	−2147483640
Domain Local Distribution Group	4
Domain Local Security Group	−2147483644
Global Distribution Group	2
Global Security Group	−2147483646

These values are defined in the ADS_GROUP_TYPE_ENUM enumeration; see Recipe 7.8 for more information.

 If you omit the sAMAccountName attribute when creating the group, it will be automatically populated with a random string.

Using PowerShell

To create a group using PowerShell, run the following command:

```
New-ADGroup -Name "Finance Users" -SamAccountName FinanceUsers↵
  -GroupCategory Security -GroupScope Global -DisplayName "Finance Users"↵
  -Path "ou=Finance,dc=adatum,dc=com" -Description "Finance Department Users"
```

Discussion

In each solution, a group was created with no members. For more information on how to add and remove members, see Recipe 7.5.

The groupType attribute contains a flag indicating both group scope and type. The available flag values are defined in the ADS_GROUP_TYPE_ENUM enumeration. Recipe 7.8 contains more information on setting the group scopes and types.

Using a graphical user interface

The Active Directory Administrative Center is used to perform this solution. This allows you to completely configure the group during the creation process (whereas, if you used ADUC to create the group, you would have had to create the group and then go back into the properties to completely configure it).

See Also

Recipe 7.5 for adding and removing group members; "Understanding Group Accounts" (*http://bit.ly/16MrGgI*); MSDN: ADS_ GROUP_TYPE_ENUM

7.2. Viewing the Permissions of a Group

Problem

You want to list the AD object permissions that have been assigned to a group object.

Solution

Using a graphical user interface

1. Open the Active Directory Users and Computers (ADUC) snap-in (*dsa.msc*). Click on View and ensure that there is a checkmark next to Advanced Features.

2. If you need to change domains, right-click on Active Directory Users and Computers in the left pane, select Connect to Domain, enter the domain name, and click OK.

3. In the left pane, right-click on the domain and select Find.

4. Enter the name of the group and click Find Now.

5. Double-click on the group in the bottom results pane.

6. Click on the Security tab. The users and groups that have been assigned permissions to the object are listed in the bottom pane; select each entry to view the permissions that have been assigned to it.

7. Click on Advanced to view the owner of the group, as well as any auditing that has been configured.

Using a command-line interface

```
> dsacls "<GroupDN>"
```

You can also obtain this information using AdFind, as follows:

```
adfind -gcb -f name=<Group Name> ntsecuritydescriptor -sddl++ -resolvesids
```

Using PowerShell

If you have Exchange 2007 or later management tools installed on your workstation, you can retrieve DACL and SACL information using the following Exchange cmdlet:

```
Get-ADPermission -Identity <Group Name>
```

Discussion

In an Active Directory environment, you can set permissions on an object within the directory in much the same way that you can set NTFS permissions on files and folders.

Each AD object has a Security Descriptor (SD) associated with it that is made up of a Discretionary Access Control List (DACL) that dictates which users and groups can access an object, and a System Access Control List (SACL) that controls which users' or groups' activities should be audited. The DACL and SACL are each made up of one or more Access Control Entries (ACEs), one for each user or group and its associated permission.

See Also

MSDN: Creating a DACL [Security]; MSDN: Order of ACEs in a DACL [Security]; MSDN: SACL Access Right [Security]; MSDN: Retrieving an Object's SACL [Security]

7.3. Viewing the Direct Members of a Group

Problem

You want to view the direct members of a group.

Solution

Using a graphical user interface

1. Open the Active Directory Administrative Center.
2. In the right pane, enter the name of the group in the Global Search box, select the desired domain in the scope, and then click the search icon.
3. In the search results, double-click the name of the group to open the group properties.
4. Scroll down to the Members area to view the members.

Using a command-line interface

You can enumerate the direct members of a group using the built-in DSGet utility, or AdFind. Use the following DSGet syntax to view the members:

```
> dsget group "<GroupDN>" -members
```

To list group members with AdFind, use the following syntax:

```
> adfind -b "<GroupDN>" member
```

Using PowerShell

To enumerate the direct group membership of the Domain Admins group, run the following PowerShell command:

```
Get-ADGroupMember -Identity "Domain Admins" | Select Name
```

Discussion

The member attribute of a group object contains the distinguished names of the direct members of the group. By direct members, we mean the members that have been directly added to the group. This is in contrast to indirect group members, which are members of the group due to nested group membership. See Recipe 7.4 for how to find the nested membership of a group.

The memberOf attribute is a *backlink* to member. This means that, for each group membership listed in a group's member attribute, the DN of the group itself appears in that user/computer/group's memberOf attribute. Think of it this way: if the *FinanceUsers* group has Jane as a member, then Jane is a member of the *FinanceUsers* group. In this way, Active Directory uses forward links and backlinks to maintain consistency between groups and their membership.

See Also

Recipe 7.4 for viewing nested group membership

7.4. Viewing the Nested Members of a Group

Problem

You want to view the nested membership of a group.

Solution

Using a graphical user interface

1. Open the ADUC snap-in (*dsa.msc*).
2. If you need to change domains, right-click on Active Directory Users and Computers in the left pane, select Connect to Domain, enter the domain name, and click OK.
3. In the left pane, right-click on the domain and select Find.
4. Enter the name of the group and click Find Now.
5. Double-click on the group in the bottom results pane.

6. Click the Members tab.

7. Double-click on each group member to view its membership.

Using a command-line interface

```
> dsget group "<GroupDN>" -members -expand
```

You can also obtain this information using the *joeware* MemberOf utility:

```
> memberof -group <GroupDN>
```

Using PowerShell

The simplest method of listing nested group membership in PowerShell is to use the -recursive switch, as shown in the following command:

```
Get-ADGroupMember -Identity "Domain Admins" -recursive | Select Name
```

Discussion

As described in Recipe 7.3, group membership is stored in the multivalued member attribute on group objects. But the member attribute will not show the complete picture because of group nesting. To view the complete group membership, you have to recursively search through the group membership of each group. (The exception to this is the memberof command-line utility, which correctly displays primary group memberships.)

See Also

Recipe 7.3 for viewing group membership; MSDN: IADsMember

7.5. Adding and Removing Members of a Group

Problem

You want to add or remove members of a group.

Solution

Using a graphical user interface

1. Open the ADUC snap-in (*dsa.msc*).

2. If you need to change domains, right-click on Active Directory Users and Computers in the left pane, select Connect to Domain, enter the domain name, and click OK.

3. In the left pane, right-click on the domain and select Find.

4. Enter the name of the group and click Find Now.

5. Double-click on the group in the bottom results pane.

6. Click the Members tab.

7. To remove a member, click on the member name, click the Remove button, click Yes, and click OK.

8. To add a member, click on the Add button, enter the name of the member, and click OK twice.

Using a command-line interface

The -addmbr option in dsmod adds a member to a group:

```
> dsmod group "<GroupDN>" -addmbr "<MemberDN>"
```

To add a group member with admod, use the following syntax:

```
> admod -b "<GroupDN>" member:+:"<MemberDN>"
```

The -rmmbr option in dsmod removes a member from a group:

```
> dsmod group "<GroupDN>" -rmmbr "<MemberDN>"
```

To remove a group member with admod, use the following syntax:

```
> admod -b "<GroupDN>" member:-:"<MemberDN>"
```

The -chmbr option in dsmod replaces the complete membership list:

```
> dsmod group "<GroupDN>" -chmbr "<Member2DN Member2DN ... >"
```

To replace the membership of a group with admod, use the following command:

```
> admod -b "<GroupDN>" member:+-:"<Member1DN>;<Member2DN>;<Member3DN>"
```

Using PowerShell

To add and remove users from groups using PowerShell, use the following syntax:

```
Add-ADGroupMember -Identity "<GroupDN>" -Members "<UserDN>"
Remove-ADGroupMember -Identity "<GroupDN>" -Members "<UserDN>" -Confirm:$False
```

Discussion

Since there are no restrictions on what distinguished names you can put in the mem ber attribute, you can essentially have any type of object as a member of a group. Although OUs are typically used to structure objects that share certain criteria, group objects can be used to create loose collections of objects.

The benefit of using group objects as a collection mechanism is that the same object can be a member of multiple groups, whereas an object can only be a part of a single OU. Another key difference is that you can assign permissions on resources to groups because they are considered security principals in Active Directory, whereas OUs are not.

See Also

Recipe 7.3 for viewing group membership; MSDN: IADsGroup::Add; MSDN: IADsGroup::Remove

7.6. Moving a Group Within a Domain

Problem

You want to move a group to a different OU or container within the same domain.

Solution

Using a graphical user interface

1. Open the Active Directory Administrative Center.
2. In the right pane, enter the name of the group in the Global Search box, select the desired domain in the scope, and then click the search icon.
3. In the search results, right-click the name of the group and then click Move.
4. In the Move dialog box, browse to the desired destination container, click to highlight it, and then click OK to complete the move.

Using a command-line interface

To move an object to a new parent container within the same domain, you can use either DSMove or AdMod, as follows:

```
> dsmove "<GroupDN>" -newparent "<NewParentDN>"
```

or:

```
> admod -b "<GroupDN>" -move "<NewParentDN>"
```

Using PowerShell

To move a group with PowerShell, use the following syntax:

```
Move-ADObject -Identity "<GroupDN>" -TargetPath "<New OU DN>"
```

Discussion

Using a command-line interface

The DSMove utility can work against any type of object, including groups. The first parameter is the DN of the group that you want to move. The second parameter is the new parent container of the group. The -s parameter can additionally be used to designate a specific server to work against.

See Also

Recipe 4.20 for moving an object to a different OU; Recipe 4.21 for moving an object to a different domain; Recipe 7.8 for changing group scope and type; "Understanding Group Accounts" (*http://bit.ly/16MrGgI*); MSDN: IADsContainer::MoveHere

7.7. Moving a Group to Another Domain

Problem

You want to move a group to a different domain in the same forest.

Solution

Using a graphical user interface

To migrate user, computer, group, or OU objects between domains in the same forest, use the following steps:

1. Open the ADMT MMC snap-in (migrator.msc).
2. Right-click on the Active Directory Migration Tool folder and select the Group Account Migration Wizard.
3. Click Next on the welcome screen.
4. On the Domain Selection screen, enter the DNS or NetBIOS name of the source and target domains and click Next.
5. On the Group Select Option screen, select the option to select the group from the domain and click Next.
6. On the Group Selection screen, add the group objects that you wish to migrate and click Next. (You cannot migrate built-in or well-known groups such as Domain Users or Domain Admins using this process.)
7. On the Organizational Unit Selection screen, enter the name of the target OU or select Browse to open an object picker in the target domain. Click Next to continue.

8. On the Group Options screen, select one or more of the following and click Next:

"Update user rights"
> Copies any user rights that are assigned in the source domain to the target domain.

"Copy group members"
> Specifies whether the user objects that belong to the group should be migrated along with the group. If you don't select this option, the group will be created in the target domain with no members.

"Update previously migrated objects"
> Supports migrations that take place over time by comparing the source and target groups and migrating any changes that have taken place.

"Fix membership of group"
> Adds any migrated user accounts to groups in the target domain if the user accounts were members of the source groups in the source domain.

"Migrate group SIDs to target domain"
> Adds the security identifiers (SIDs) of the migrated group accounts in the source domain to the SID history of the new group in the target domain.

9. On the Naming Conflicts screen, select whether you want to migrate group objects that conflict with objects in the target domain and click Next.

10. Click Finish to complete the migration.

Using a command-line interface

To migrate a group from the command line using the ADMT utility, use the following syntax:

```
> ADMT GROUP /N "<GroupName>" /IF:YES /SD:"<SourceDomainDN>"↵
/TD:"<TargetDomainDN>" /TO:"<TargetOUName>"
```

Using PowerShell

To migrate a group by using PowerShell, use the following syntax:

```
Move-ADObject -Identity "<GroupDN>" -TargetPath "<TargetOUDN>"↵
 -TargetServer "<TargetServerFQDN>"
```

Discussion

The only type of group that can be moved between domains using the built-in operating system tools is universal groups; additionally, the RID Master for both the source and the target domains needs to be available in order to complete the move. If you want to move a global or domain local group to a different domain, first convert it to a universal group, move the group, and then convert it back to a global or domain local group.

When you convert a group between types, you may encounter problems because different groups have different membership restrictions. See the Recipe 7.0 section of this chapter for more information on group type membership restrictions.

Another way to accomplish interdomain (intraforest or interforest) group moves is by using ADMT, which might be quite useful if you need to move a large number of groups. With ADMT, you can move and restructure groups without needing to go to all the trouble of converting the group to a universal group and then modifying the group membership. For more on the latest version of ADMT, see "Active Directory Migration Tool (ADMT) Guide: Migrating and Restructuring Active Directory Domains" (*http://bit.ly/YzyAUa*).

7.8. Changing the Scope or Type of a Group

Problem

You want to change the scope or type of a group.

Solution

Using a graphical user interface

1. Open the ADUC snap-in (*dsa.msc*).
2. If you need to change domains, right-click on Active Directory Users and Computers in the left pane, select Connect to Domain, enter the domain name, and click OK.
3. In the left pane, right-click on the domain and select Find.
4. Enter the name of the group you want to modify and click Find Now.
5. Double-click on the group in the results pane.
6. In the group properties dialog box, select the new scope or type, and click OK.

Using a command-line interface

The following example changes the group scope for *<GroupDN>* to *<NewScope>*, which should be l for domain local group, g for global group, or u for universal group:

```
> dsmod group "<GroupDN>" -scope <NewScope>
```

The following example changes the group type for *<GroupDN>*. For the -secgrp switch, specify yes to change to a security group or no to make the group a distribution group:

```
> dsmod group "<GroupDN>" -secgrp yes|no
```

To change the scope and/or type of a group using AdMod, use the following syntax:

```
> admod -b "<GroupDN>" groupType::<GroupType>
```

Just as when you created a group using AdMod, you must specify the numeric value for the group type. Refer to Recipe 7.1 for more information.

Using PowerShell

To modify a group's type or scope with PowerShell, use the following syntax. Use `'Security'` or `'Distribution'` as the group category, and `'Global'`, `'Universal'`, or `'DomainLocal'` as the group scope:

```
Set-ADGroup "<Group Name>" -GroupCategory <GroupCategory> -GroupScope <GroupScope>
```

Discussion

Group scope and type are stored as a flag in the `groupType` attribute on `group` objects. To directly update `groupType`, you must logically OR the values associated with each type and scope, as shown in the API solution, or use the raw numeric values listed in Recipe 7.1 when using AdMod. Note that there is no specific value for the distribution list type. If you want to create a distribution list, just do not include the `ADS_GROUP_TYPE_SECURITY_ENABLED` flag when setting `groupType`. Additional group types also are available through Authorization Manager.

 For a good description of the usage scenarios for each group type, see *Active Directory*, Fifth Edition, by Brian Desmond et al. (O'Reilly).

See Also

Recipe 7.1; "Understanding Group Accounts" (*http://bit.ly/16MrGgI*); MSDN: ADS_GROUP_TYPE_ENUM; MSDN: What Type of Group to Use

7.9. Modifying Group Attributes

Problem

You want to modify one or more attributes of an object.

Solution

Using a graphical user interface

1. Open the Active Directory Administrative Center.

2. In the right pane, enter the name of the group in the Global Search box, select the desired domain in the scope, and then click the search icon.

3. In the search results pane, double-click the group to display the group properties.

4. Scroll down to the Extensions section and then click the Attribute Editor tab.

5. Find the attribute that you want to modify, click to highlight the attribute, and then click Edit.

6. Enter the new value for the attribute and then click OK.

7. Click OK in the group properties window to complete the modification.

Using a command-line interface

Create an LDIF file called *modify_object.ldf* with the following contents:

```
dn: cn=Finance Users,cn=users,dc=adatum,dc=com
changetype: modify
add: description
description: Members of the Finance Department
-
```

Then run the following command:

```
> ldifde -v -i -f modify_object.ldf
```

To modify a group using AdMod, you'll use the following general syntax:

```
> admod-b "<GroupDN>" <attribute>:<operation>:<value>
```

For example, you can add a description to a group object using the following syntax:

```
> C:\>admod -b cn="Finance Users,cn=Users,dc=adatum,dc=com"↵
description::"Members of the Finance Department"
```

You can also modify group objects with the dsmod group command using the following syntax:

```
> dsmod group "<GroupDN>" <options>
```

The available options for dsmod include the following:

-samid <NewSAMName>
: Updates the sAMAccountName attribute of the group object

-desc <NewDescription>
: Updates the description attribute of the group object

-secgrp {yes | no}
: Configures the group object as a security group (yes) or a distribution group (no)

-scope {l | g | u}
: Configures the group scope as domain local (l), global (g), or universal (u)

```
{-addmbr | -rmmbr | -chmbr} <MemberDN1> <MemberDN2>
```
> Adds the specified objects to the group (addmbr), removes the specified objects (rmmbr), or replaces the membership list wholesale with only the specified objects (chmbr)

Using PowerShell

You can modify a group's properties by using the Set-ADGroup cmdlet, as shown in the following example:

```
Set-ADGroup -Identity "<GroupDN>" -GroupType "<GroupType>"↵
  -GroupScope "<GroupScope>" -Description "<Description>"
```

Discussion

Using a graphical user interface

If the parent container of the object you want to modify has a lot of objects in it, you may want to add a new connection entry for the DN of the target object. This will be easier than trying to hunt through a container full of objects. You can do this by right-clicking ADSI Edit and selecting "Connect to" under Connection Point, then selecting Distinguished Name and entering the DN of the object.

Using a command-line interface

For more on *ldifde*, see Recipe 4.28.

Using PowerShell

The Set-ADGroup cmdlet has the following parameters that allow you to modify specific attributes of a group object:

- -ManagedBy
- -Notes
- -Email
- -GroupCategory
- -GroupScope
- -SamAccountName
- -Description
- -DisplayName
- -HomePage

See Also

Recipe 4.14; Recipe 4.28

7.10. Delegating Control for Managing Membership of a Group

Problem

You want to delegate the ability to manage the membership of a group.

Solution

Using a graphical user interface

1. Open the ADUC snap-in (*dsa.msc*).

2. If you need to change domains, right-click on Active Directory Users and Computers in the left pane, select Connect to Domain, enter the domain name, and click OK.

3. In the left pane, right-click on the domain and select Find.

4. Enter the name of the group and click Find Now.

5. Double-click on the group in the results pane.

6. Select the Managed By tab.

7. Click the Change button.

8. Locate the group or user to delegate control to and click OK.

9. Check the box beside "Manager can update membership list."

10. Click OK.

Using a command-line interface

```
> dsacls <GroupDN> /G <GroupName>@DomainName:WP;member;
```

In the following example, the *SalesAdmin* group will be given rights to modify membership of the *PreSales* group:

```
> dsacls cn=presales,ou=sales,dc=adatum,dc=com /G salesadmins@adatum.com:↵
WP;member;
```

Using PowerShell

In PowerShell, you can change the person or group who is listed as the manager of a group. However, note that the following example does not set the permissions for the manager to manage the group's membership:

```
Set-ADGroup <Group Name> -ManagedBy "<GroupDN>"
```

You can use a PowerShell console on a computer where the Exchange Server 2007 or later management tools have been installed to grant the right to manage group membership:

```
Add-ADPermission -Identity <Group Name> -User <User or Group Name>↵
 -AccessRights WriteProperty -Properties "members"
```

Discussion

To grant a user or group the ability to manage group membership, you have to grant the write property (WP) permission on the member attribute of the target group. You can add this ACE directly using dsacls, or more indirectly with ADUC. ADUC also has a feature that allows you to simply check a box to grant the ability to modify group membership to the object represented by the managedBy attribute.

If you want to configure additional permissions, such as the ability to modify the description attribute for the group, you will need to go to the Security tab in ADUC or specify the appropriate attribute with the /G switch with dsacls. For example, this will grant the write property on the description attribute:

```
/G <GroupName>@DomainDNSName:WP;description;
```

See Also

Recipe 14.5 for delegating control in Active Directory

7.11. Resolving a Primary Group ID

Problem

You want to find the name of a user's primary group.

Solution

Using a graphical user interface

1. Open the ADUC snap-in (*dsa.msc*).

2. If you need to change domains, right-click on Active Directory Users and Computers in the left pane, select Connect to Domain, enter the domain name, and click OK.

3. In the left pane, right-click on the domain and select Find.

4. Type the name of the user and click Find Now.

5. In the Search Results window, double-click on the user.

6. Click the Member Of tab.

7. The Primary Group name is shown on the bottom half of the dialog box.

Using PowerShell

To find the primary group for a user with PowerShell, use the following syntax:

```
Get-ADUser -Identity "<UserDN>" -Properties PrimaryGroup | Select PrimaryGroup
```

Discussion

In the past, when trying to determine a user's group membership you had to look at the user's memberOf attribute, which contains a list of DNs for each group the user is a member of, as well as the user's primary group. By default, all users are assigned *Domain Users* as their primary group. Therefore, by default all users in a domain are implicitly members of the *Domain Users* group. Unfortunately, a user's primary group does not show up in the memberOf attribute.

 Services for Macintosh and POSIX-based applications are the main users of primary groups. If you don't use either of those, you usually don't need to worry about changing a user's primary group.

The primary group is stored in the primaryGroupID attribute on user objects. Unfortunately, the information that's stored in that attribute is the relative identifier (RID) of the group, not the DN or even sAMAccountName as you might expect. group objects have a primaryGroupToken attribute, which contains the same value but is a constructed attribute. Because Active Directory dynamically constructs it, you cannot utilize it in search filters. So even if you have the primaryGroupID of a user (e.g., 513), you cannot do a simple query to find out which group it is associated with. However, with Power-Shell and Active Directory Users and Computers, this task is very straightforward.

Using PowerShell

The PowerShell solution uses the calculated property named `PrimaryGroup`, which allows the solution to be straightforward and similar to querying for typical user attributes.

See Also

MS KB 297951 (How to Use the PrimaryGroupID Attribute to Find the Primary Group for a User)

7.12. Enabling Universal Group Membership Caching

Problem

You want to enable universal group membership caching so that a global catalog server is not needed during most user logins.

Solution

Using a graphical user interface

1. Open the Active Directory Sites and Services snap-in (dssite.msc).
2. In the left pane, browse to the site you want to enable group caching for and click on it.
3. In the right pane, double-click on the `NTDS Site Settings` object.
4. Under Universal Group Membership Caching, check the box beside Enable Universal Group Membership Caching.
5. If you want to force the cache refresh from a particular site, select a site or else leave the default set to `<Default>`.
6. Click OK.

Using a command-line interface

You can use a combination of the `dsquery site` and `dsget site` commands to determine whether a site has group caching enabled:

```
> dsquery site -name <SiteName> | dsget site -dn -cachegroups -prefGCSite
```

You can use *ldifde* to enable group caching. Create a file called *enable_univ_cache.ldf* with the following contents, but change `<SiteName>` to the name of the site you want to enable and `<ForestRootDN>` to the distinguished name of the forest root domain:

```
dn: cn=NTDS Site Settings,cn=<SiteName>,cn=sites,cn=configuration,<ForestRootDN>
changetype: modify
replace: options
options: 32
-
```

Then use the following command to import the change:

```
> ldifde -i -f enable_univ_cache.ldf
```

You can also perform this change in the *adatum.com* domain by using AdMod with the following syntax:

```
> admod -b "cn=NTDS Site Settings,cn=<SiteName>,cn=sites,cn=configuration,↵
  dc=adatum,dc=com" options::32
```

Using PowerShell

You can use the following PowerShell syntax to find out whether a site has universal group membership caching enabled:

```
Get-ADReplicationSite "<Site Name>" -Properties UniversalGroupCachingEnabled |↵
  FL UniversalGroupCachingEnabled
```

To enable universal group membership caching on a site by using PowerShell, use the following syntax:

```
Set-ADReplicationSite "<Site Name>" -UniversalGroupCachingEnabled $True
```

Discussion

When a client logs on, the domain controller that authenticates the user needs to contact a global catalog server in order to fully authenticate the client (however, if the DC that authenticates the user is itself a GC, then it does not need to contact any other servers to complete the authentication process). This is necessary because global catalogs are the only servers that store universal group information, which is needed to completely determine a user's group memberships upon logon.

Universal groups can be created and used anywhere in a forest. Objects located anywhere in a forest can be added as members of a universal group. Since a universal group could be created in a domain other than where the user object resides, it is necessary to store universal group membership in the global catalog. That way, during logon, domain controllers can query a global catalog to determine all universal groups a user is a member of. Microsoft's primary reason for making this a requirement during logon is that a user could be part of a universal group that has been explicitly denied access to certain resources. If universal groups aren't evaluated, a user could gain access to resources that are supposed to be restricted.

To remove this limitation, Microsoft introduced *universal group caching*. Universal group caching can be enabled on a per-site basis and allows domain controllers to cache universal group information locally, thus removing the need to query the global catalog during client logon.

You can enable universal group caching manually by enabling the 10000 bit (32 in decimal) on the `options` attribute of the `NTDS Site Settings` object. See Recipe 4.15 for more information on properly setting a bit flag attribute. The Sites and Services snap-in just requires you to check a box. Another setting can also be configured that relates to universal group caching. By default, domain controllers will use the site topology to determine the optimal site to use to query a global catalog server for universal group information. You can override this feature and explicitly set which site domain controllers should use by selecting the site in the Sites and Services snap-in or by setting the attribute `msDS-Preferred-GC-Site` on the `NTDS Site Settings` object to the DN of the target site.

See Also

Recipe 4.15

7.13. Restoring a Deleted Group

Problem

You want to restore a `group` object that has been inadvertently deleted, as well as restore its members.

 These solutions assume that the Active Directory Recycle Bin was enabled prior to the deletion. If you have not enabled the AD Recycle Bin, you can do so from the Tasks pane in the Active Directory Administrative Center.

Solution

Using a graphical user interface (steps specific to Windows Server 2012)

1. Launch the Active Directory Administrative Center.

2. Select the domain and navigate to the `Deleted Objects` container.

3. Locate the deleted group in the container.

4. Right-click the group and select Restore.

Using PowerShell

To restore the `group` object and membership, use the following PowerShell command syntax:

```
Get-ADObject -Filter {isDeleted -eq $true} -IncludeDeletedObjects |↵
Where-Object {$_.DistinguishedName -match "<GroupName>"} |↵
Restore-ADObject
```

Discussion

Prior to the introduction of the Active Directory Recycle Bin, the most common way to restore a deleted object was to perform an authoritative restore by using `ntdsutil`. However, the Active Directory Recycle Bin and PowerShell have greatly simplified the process. While legacy restore methods are still valid and occasionally necessary, many restores can use the newer and more efficient methods.

Note that in both the GUI solution and the PowerShell solution, the group membership is restored along with the `group` object. In situations where you have deleted `user` objects and a deleted `group` object that contained some of the deleted `user` objects as members, restore the `user` objects first before restoring the `group` object. This will ensure that an accurate group membership is maintained after the group restore.

See Also

MS KB 216993 (Useful Shelf Life of a System-State Backup of Active Directory); "Rebooting Windows Server 2012-based Domain Controllers into Directory Services Restore Mode" (*http://bit.ly/18MAlwj*); Chapter 16 for more on recovering and restoring Active Directory

7.14. Protecting a Group Against Accidental Deletion

Problem

You want to prevent a `group` object from being accidentally deleted by an administrator who selects the incorrect option in Active Directory Users and Computers.

Solution

Using a graphical user interface

1. Open Active Directory Users and Computers. Click on View and confirm that Advanced Features is selected.

2. Drill down to the current domain. To connect to a different domain, right-click on the top-level node and click "Change domain"; select the appropriate domain and then drill down to it.

3. Right-click on the group that you want to modify and click Properties.

4. Click on the Object tab.

5. Place a checkmark next to "Protect object from accidental deletion."

6. Click OK.

Using a command-line interface (all versions)

```
dsacls "<GroupDN>" /d EVERYONE:SDDT
```

Using PowerShell (all versions)

```
Set-ADObject "<GroupDN>" -ProtectedFromAccidentalDeletion $True
```

If you have Exchange 2007 or later installed in your environment, you can also use the following Exchange cmdlet to modify this information:

```
Add-ADPermission -Identity <Group Name> -User <User or Group Name>↵
  -AccessRights Delete,DeleteTree -Deny $true
```

Discussion

By default, all new OUs that are created in Windows Server 2008 or later will have this protection enabled; however, no other object types are configured with this default protection. If you attempt to delete a group that is protected using this option, even when signed on as a Domain Admin or other similarly elevated account, you will receive an "Access Denied" message until you manually remove the checkbox or manually remove the deny ACE associated with it.

By using the command-line or PowerShell method, you can apply this protection to group objects in *all* versions of Windows Server, even though the GUI checkbox is available only in Windows Server 2008 or later.

7.15. Applying a Fine-Grained Password Policy to a Group Object

Problem

You want to apply a Fine-Grained Password Policy to a group object in a domain.

Solution

Using a graphical user interface

1. Open Active Directory Administrative Center.
2. In the top-left pane, click the tree view icon.
3. Expand the System container.
4. Scroll down and right-click Password Settings Container, expand the New menu, and then click Password Settings.
5. Fill in the desired password settings in the top pane. Note that the fields with a red asterisk are required fields.
6. In the Directly Applies To section, click the Add button to add a security group that will be the target of the FGPP.
7. Click OK to create the FGPP.

Using a command-line interface

The following will add the Marketing group to the list of groups that a PSO will apply to:

```
psomgr -applyto cn=Marketing,cn=Users,dc=ADATUM,dc=COM -pso TestPSO -forreal
```

Using PowerShell

To add a group to the list of groups that a FGPP will apply to, use the following syntax:

```
Add-ADFineGrainedPasswordPolicySubject -Identity "<Name of FGPP>"↵
 -Subjects "<Security Group sAMAccountName>"
```

Discussion

Once a PasswordSettingsObject has been created, you can modify the password and account lockout settings controlled by the object, as well as the users and groups that the PSO should apply to. Since the PasswordSettingsObject is an Active Directory object class, these modifications can be made using any interface that can modify objects. When working from the command line, the *psomgr* tool (*http://www.joeware.net/free tools*) allows you to modify one or multiple PSOs at a time, and can also create "starter" PSOs using the -quickstart command-line switch. The full syntax for *psomgr.exe* can be obtained by typing psomgr.exe /? at a command prompt or by visiting the *joeware* website.

See Also

"AD DS Fine-Grained Password and Account Lockout Policy Step-by-Step Guide" (*http://bit.ly/12b2ona*)

## CHAPTER 8

Computer Objects

8.0. Introduction

As far as Active Directory is concerned, computers are very similar to users. In fact, computer objects inherit directly from the user object class, which is used to represent user accounts. This means that computer objects possess all of the attributes of user objects and then some. Computers need to be represented in Active Directory for many of the same reasons users do, including the need to access resources securely, utilize GPOs, and have permissions assigned to them.

To participate in a domain, computers need a *secure channel* to a domain controller. A secure channel is an authenticated connection that can transmit encrypted data. To set up the secure channel, a computer must present a password to a domain controller. Similar to the way in which it authenticates a user account, Active Directory will use Kerberos authentication to verify the identity of a computer account. Without the com puter object and, by association, the password stored with it that the operating system changes behind the scenes on a regular basis, there would be no way for the domain controller to verify a computer is what it claims to be.

The Anatomy of a Computer

The default location for computer objects in a domain is the cn=Computers container located directly off the domain root. You can, however, create computer objects anywhere in a domain. You can also modify the default location for computer objects as described in Recipe 8.13. Table 8-1 contains a list of some of the interesting attributes that are available on computer objects.

Table 8-1. Attributes of computer objects

Attribute	Description
cn	Relative distinguished name of computer objects.
dnsHostName	Fully qualified DNS name of the computer.
lastLogonTimestamp	The approximate timestamp of the last time the computer logged in to the domain.
managedBy	The distinguished name (DN) of the user or group that manages the computer.
memberOf	List of DNs of the groups the computer is a member of.
msDS-AuthenticatedToAccountList	This attribute was introduced in Windows Server 2008. It is a backlink attribute that identifies users who have successfully authenticated to a full DC via a particular RODC.
msDS-IsPrimaryComputerFor	This attribute was introduced in Windows Server 2012. It indirectly identifies the primary user of a computer.
msDS-RevealedUsers	This attribute was introduced in Windows Server 2008. It identifies the list of users and computers whose secrets have been replicated to an RODC.
operatingSystem	Text description of the operating system running on the computer. See Recipe 8.14 for more information.
operatingSystemHotFix	Currently not being used, but will hopefully be populated at some point.
operatingSystemServicePack	Service pack version installed on the computer. See Recipe 8.14 for more information.
operatingSystemVersion	Numeric version of the operating system installed on the computer. See Recipe 8.14 for more information.
pwdLastSet	Large integer that can be translated into the last time the computer's password was set. See Recipe 8.10 for more information.
sAMAccountName	NetBIOS-style name of the computer. This is typically the name of the computer with a $ at the end.
userAccountControl	Account flag that defines various account properties. In the case of a computer object, this specifies whether the computer is a member computer or a domain controller.

8.1. Creating a Computer

Problem

You want to create a computer account.

Solution

Using a graphical user interface

1. Open the Active Directory Administrative Center.
2. In the left pane, click to highlight the desired domain.

3. In the right pane, click New and then click Computer.

4. Type a name for the computer, fill in the desired optional fields, and then click OK to create the computer object.

Using a command-line interface

You can create a computer object using either the built-in DSAdd utility or AdMod. To create an account using DSAdd, use the following syntax:

```
> dsadd computer "<ComputerDN>" -desc "<Description>"
```

To create a computer account using AdMod, enter the following:

```
> admod -b "<ComputerDN>" objectclass::computer↵
sAMAccountName::<ComputerName>$ userAccountControl::4096↵
description::"<Description>" -add
```

Using PowerShell

To create a computer account using PowerShell, use the new-ADComputer cmdlet as follows:

```
New-ADComputer -Name "<ComputerName>" -SamAccountName "<SamAccountName>"↵
-Path <OU DN>
```

Discussion

Creating a computer object in Active Directory is not much different from creating a user object. We set the description attribute in the CLI solutions, but it is not a mandatory attribute. The only mandatory attribute is sAMAccountName, which should be set to the name of the computer with a $ appended. Note that ADAC and ADUC will both populate the sAMAccountName automatically based on the name given to the computer during the creation process. Also note that these solutions simply create a computer object. This does not mean any user can join a computer to the domain with that computer account. For more information on creating a computer object and allowing a specific user or group to join the computer to the domain, see Recipe 8.2.

See Also

Recipe 8.2 for creating a computer for a user; "New-ADComputer" (*http://bit.ly/ 10gmmQ5*); MSDN: ADS_USER_FLAG_ENUM

8.2. Creating a Computer for a Specific User or Group

Problem

You want to create a computer account for a specific user or group to join to the domain. This requires setting permissions on the computer account so that the user or group can modify certain attributes.

Solution

Using a graphical user interface

1. Open the Active Directory Administrative Center.
2. In the left pane, click to highlight the desired domain.
3. In the right pane, click New and then click Computer.
4. Type a name for the computer and fill in the desired optional fields.
5. In the top-right corner of the Computer section, click the Change button near the text that says, "The above user or group can join this computer to a domain."
6. Use the Object Picker to select a user or group to join the computer to the domain and then click OK.
7. Click OK to create the `computer` object.

Using a command-line interface

In the following solution, replace *<ComputerDN>* with the distinguished name of the computer object and *<UserOrGroup>* with the user principal name or NT-style name of a user or group you want to manage the computer:

```
> dsadd computer <ComputerDN>
> dsacls <ComputerDN> /G <UserOrGroup>:CALCGRSDDTRC;;
> dsacls <ComputerDN> /G <UserOrGroup>:WP;description;
> dsacls <ComputerDN> /G <UserOrGroup>:WP;sAMAccountName;
> dsacls <ComputerDN> /G <UserOrGroup>:WP;displayName;
> dsacls <ComputerDN> /G <UserOrGroup>:WP;userAccountControl;
> dsacls <ComputerDN> /G <UserOrGroup>:WS;"Validated write to service↵
  principalname";
> dsacls <ComputerDN> /G <UserOrGroup>:WS;"Validated write to DNS host name";
```

 You can replace the first line of this code with the AdMod code from Recipe 8.1 if you choose.

Discussion

By default, members of the *Authenticated Users* group can join up to 10 computers to an Active Directory domain. If you've modified this default behavior or need to allow a user to add computers to the domain on a regular basis, you need to grant certain permissions so that the user has rights to modify the computer object. When you create a computer via ADAC or the ADUC snap-in (*dsa.msc*), you have the option to select a user or group to manage the computer object and join a computer to the domain using that object. When you use that method, eight ACEs are added to the ACL of the computer object. They are:

- List Contents, Read All Properties, Delete, Delete Subtree, Read Permissions, All Extended Rights (i.e., Allowed to Authenticate, Change Password, Send As, Receive As, Reset Password)
- Write Property for description
- Write Property for sAMAccountName
- Write Property for displayName
- Write Property for Logon Information
- Write Property for Account Restrictions
- Validated write to DNS hostname
- Validated write for service principal name

Using a graphical user interface

If you want to modify the default permissions that are applied when you select a user or group through the GUI, double-click on the computer object after you've created it and go to the Security tab. For the Security tab to be visible, you have to select View→Advanced Features.

Using a command-line interface

With the *dsacls* utility, you can specify either a UPN (*user@domain*) or a down-level-style (*DOMAIN\user*) account name when applying permissions. Also, *dsacls* requires that the displayName of the attribute, property set, or extended right you are setting the permission on be used instead of the lDAPDisplayName, as you might expect. That is why we had to use "Validated write to service principal name," which is the display Name for the Validated-SPN controlAccessRight object, with the ACE for the SPN-validated write. *dsacls* is also case-sensitive, so be sure to specify the correct case for the words in the displayName.

See Also

Recipe 8.1 for creating a computer account

8.3. Deleting a Computer

Problem

You want to delete a computer account.

Solution

Using a graphical user interface

1. Open the Active Directory Administrative Center.
2. In the right pane, type the name of the computer in the Global Search box, select the desired domain in the scope, and then click the search icon.
3. In the search results, right-click the name of the computer and then click Delete.
4. In the Delete Confirmation dialog box, click Yes to complete the deletion of the computer object.

Using a command-line interface

You can delete a computer using the built-in *dsrm* utility, as well as AdMod. For *dsrm*, use the following syntax:

```
> dsrm "<Computer DN>"
```

For AdMod, enter the following:

```
> admod -b "<Computer DN>" -del
```

Using PowerShell

To delete an object using PowerShell, use the following syntax:

```
Remove-ADComputer -Identity "<Computer DN>" -Confirm:$False
```

8.4. Joining a Computer to a Domain

Problem

You want to join a computer to a domain after the computer object has already been created in Active Directory.

Solution

Using a graphical user interface (steps specific to Windows 7, Windows 8, and Windows Server 2012)

1. Log on to the computer that you want to join to the domain, and then open the Control Panel.

2. Open the System applet.

3. In the "Computer name, domain, and workgroup settings section," click "Change settings."

4. Click the Change button.

5. Under "Member of," select Domain.

6. Enter the domain name that you want to join and click OK.

7. You may be prompted to enter credentials in order to join the computer to the domain.

8. Reboot the computer.

Using a command-line interface

```
> netdom join <ComputerName> /Domain <DomainName> /UserD <DomainUserUPN>↵
/PasswordD * /UserO <ComputerAdminUser> /PasswordO * /Reboot
```

Using a command-line interface with PowerShell

```
Add-Computer -DomainName <DomainName> -Restart
```

Discussion

When trying to add a computer to Active Directory, either you can pre-create the computer object as described in Recipes 8.1 and 8.2 before joining it to the domain, or you can perform both operations at the same time.

Using a graphical user interface

If you have the correct permissions in Active Directory, you can actually create a computer object at the same time as you join it to a domain via the instructions described in the GUI solution. Since the System applet doesn't allow you to specify an OU for the computer object, if it needs to create a computer object it will do so in the default Computers container. See Recipe 8.16 for more information on the default Computers container and how to change it.

Using a command-line interface

The netdom command will attempt to create a computer object for the computer during a join if one does not already exist. An optional /OU switch can be added to specify the OU in which to create the computer object.

You can unjoin a computer from a domain at the command line by using *unjoin.exe*, another free download from the *joeware* website. *unjoin.exe* will not remove the computer account from the Active Directory domain; it will merely change the domain membership locally on the machine itself.

See Also

Add-Computer cmdlet reference (*http://bit.ly/18plWso*)

8.5. Moving a Computer Within the Same Domain

Problem

You want to move a computer object to a different container or OU within the same domain.

Solution

Using a graphical user interface

1. Open the ADUC snap-in (*dsa.msc*).
2. If you need to change domains, right-click on Active Directory Users and Computers in the left pane, select Connect to Domain, enter the domain name, and click OK.
3. In the left pane, right-click on the domain and select Find.
4. Beside Find, select Computers.
5. Type the name of the computer and click Find Now.
6. In the Search Results window, right-click on the computer and select Move.
7. Browse to and select the new parent container or OU.
8. Click OK.

 You can also use drag-and-drop functionality to move computers and other objects.

Using a command-line interface

You can move a `computer` object to a new container using the built-in DSMove utility or AdMod. To use DSMove, enter the following syntax:

```
> dsmove "<ComputerDN>" -newparent "<NewParentDN>"
```

To move a `computer` object using AdMod, use the following:

```
> admod -b "<ComputerDN>" -move "<NewParentDN>"
```

Using PowerShell

To move an Active Directory computer account using PowerShell, use the following syntax:

```
Move-ADObject -Identity "<ComputerDN>" -TargetPath "<NewParentDN>"
```

Discussion

You can move `computer` objects around a domain without much impact on the computer itself. You just need to be cautious of the security settings on the new parent OU, which may impact a user's ability to manage the `computer` object in Active Directory. Also, if GPOs are used differently on the new parent, it could impact booting and logon times, and how the computer's operating system behaves after a user has logged on.

See Also

Recipe 4.20 for moving an object to a different OU; Recipe 8.6 for moving a computer to a different domain

8.6. Moving a Computer to a New Domain

Problem

You want to move a `computer` object to a different domain.

Solution

Using a graphical user interface (ADMT 3.2)

To migrate a `computer` object between domains, use the following steps:

1. Open the ADMT MMC snap-in (*migrator.msc*).
2. Right-click on the Active Directory Migration Tool folder and select the Computer Migration Wizard.
3. On the Welcome screen, click Next.

4. On the Domain Selection page, enter the DNS or NetBIOS name of the source and target domains. Click Next.

5. On the Computer Selection Option screen, select the option to select the computer from the domain and then click Next.

6. On the Computer Selection screen, click Add and use the object picker to select a computer object. Click OK to return to the Computer Selection screen and then click Next.

7. On the Organizational Unit Selection screen, enter the destination OU in the new domain and then click Next.

8. On the Translate Objects screen, specify which objects should have new ACLs applied in the new domain. Select any, none, or all of the following, and then click Next to continue:

   - Files and folders
   - Local groups
   - Printers
   - Registry
   - Shares
   - User profiles
   - User rights

9. On the Computer Options screen, click Next to maintain the default reboot time of 5 minutes.

10. On the Object Property Exclusion screen, select any object properties that you do not want to migrate and then click Next.

11. On the Conflict Management screen, click Next to accept the default, which will not migrate the computer if there is a conflict.

12. On the Completing the Computer Migration Wizard screen, review the migration settings and then click Finish to complete the move.

Using a command-line interface

The following command migrates a computer object from the *adatum.com* domain to the *emea.adatum.com* domain. It will place the migrated object in the Finance OU and will wait two minutes before rebooting the target computer:

```
ADMT COMPUTER /IF /N "FIN101-A" "FIN101-A" /SD:"adatum.com"↵
/TD:"emea.adatum.com"
/TO:"Finance" /RDL:2
```

Discussion

You can move objects between domains assuming you follow a few guidelines:

- The user requesting the move must have permission to modify objects in the parent container of both domains.

- You should explicitly specify the target DC (serverless binds usually do not work). This is necessary because the Cross Domain Move LDAP control is being used behind the scenes. (For more information on controls, see Recipe 4.4.)

- The move operation must be performed against the RID master for both domains. This is done to ensure that two objects that are being moved simultaneously don't somehow get assigned the same RID.

See Also

Recipe 4.4 for more on LDAP controls; MSDN: IADsContainer::MoveHere; "Active Directory Migration Tool (ADMT) Guide: Migrating and Restructuring Active Directory Domains" (*http://bit.ly/YpE959*)

8.7. Renaming a Computer

Problem

You want to rename a computer.

Solution

Using a graphical user interface (steps specific to Windows 7, Windows 8, and Windows Server 2012)

1. Log on to the computer either directly or with a remote console application, such as Remote Desktop Connection.

2. Open the Control Panel and double-click on the System applet.

3. In the "Computer name, domain, and workgroup settings section," click the Change Settings button.

4. On the Computer Name tab, click Change.

5. Under Computer Name, type the new name of the computer and click OK until you are out of the System applet.

6. Reboot the computer.

Using a command-line interface

You can rename a `computer` object by using the built-in *netdom* utility with the following syntax:

```
> netdom renamecomputer <ComputerName> /NewName <NewComputerName>↵
/UserD<DomainUserUPN> /PasswordD * /UserO <ComputerAdminUser> /PasswordO *↵
 /Reboot
```

Using PowerShell

You can rename a computer by using PowerShell. After running the following command on the computer that will be renamed, reboot the computer to complete the process.

```
Rename-Computer <NewComputerName>
```

Discussion

Renaming a computer consists of two operations: renaming the `computer` object in Active Directory and renaming the hostname on the machine itself. To do it in one step —an option that each of the three solutions offers—you must have permission in Active Directory to rename the account and administrator permissions on the target machine. For the rename operation to be complete, you must reboot the computer.

 In some cases, renaming a computer can adversely affect services running on the computer. For example, you cannot rename a machine that is a domain controller, Exchange Server, or a Windows Certificate Authority without taking additional (and often significant) steps and precautions.

Using a graphical user interface

After you rename the computer, you will be prompted to reboot. You can cancel if necessary, but you'll need to reboot at some point to complete the rename operation.

Using a command-line interface

The `renamecomputer` option in *netdom* can run remotely and includes a `/Reboot` switch that allows you to automatically reboot the computer after the rename is complete.

See Also

Recipe 4.23 for renaming objects; "Netdom renamecomputer" (*http://bit.ly/10gninB*)

8.8. Adding or Removing a Computer Account from a Group

Problem

You want to add or remove a computer account from an Active Directory security group.

Solution

Using a graphical user interface

1. Open the ADUC snap-in (*dsa.msc*).

2. If you need to change domains, right-click on Active Directory Users and Computers in the left pane, select Connect to Domain, enter the domain name, and click OK.

3. In the left pane, browse to the parent container of the objects you want to modify.

4. In the right pane, highlight each object you want to modify, right-click, and select Properties.

5. On the "Member of" tab, click Add.

6. Click the group to which you want to add the computer, and then click Add. To add the computer to more than one group, press Ctrl while selecting the groups you want to add the computer to, and then click Add.

7. To remove a group, select the group object and click Remove.

8. Click OK to finish.

Using a command-line interface

To add a computer object to a group, use the following syntax:

```
> admod -b "<GroupDN>" member:+:"<ComputerDN>"
```

> To remove an object, replace :+: with :-: in the previous syntax.

Using PowerShell

To add a computer account to a group using PowerShell, use the following syntax:

```
Add-ADGroupMember -Identity "<GroupDN>" -Members "<ComputerDN>"
```

Discussion

In Active Directory, both user and computer objects are security principals that can be assigned rights and permissions in a domain. As such, computer objects can be added to or removed from group objects to make for simpler resource administration. You can make this change through ADAC, ADUC, or ADSI Edit, or by manually editing the member attribute of the appropriate group object.

See Also

MSDN: NT-Group-Members attribute [AD Schema]; MSDN: Member Attribute [AD Schema]

8.9. Testing the Secure Channel for a Computer

Problem

You want to test the secure channel of a computer.

Solution

Using a command-line interface

```
> nltest /server:<ComputerName> /sc_query:<DomainName>
```

Using PowerShell

```
Test-ComputerSecureChannel -Server <ComputerName> -Verbose
```

Discussion

Every member computer in an Active Directory domain establishes a secure channel with a domain controller. The computer's password is stored locally in the form of an LSA secret and in Active Directory. The NetLogon service uses this password to establish the secure channel with a domain controller. If for some reason the LSA secret and computer password become out of sync, the computer will no longer be able to authenticate in the domain. The nltest /sc_query command can query a computer to verify its secure channel is working. Here is sample output from the command when things are working:

```
Flags: 30 HAS_IP HAS_TIMESERV
Trusted DC Name \\dc1.adatum.com
Trusted DC Connection Status Status = 0 0x0 NERR_Success
The command completed successfully
```

If a secure channel is failing, you'll need to reset the computer as described in Recipe 8.10. Here is sample output when things are not working:

```
Flags: 0
Trusted DC Name
Trusted DC Connection Status Status = 1311 0x51f ERROR_NO_LOGON_SERVERS
The command completed successfully
```

Using PowerShell

If the -Verbose parameter is not specified, the command only returns True when the secure channel is working properly. By specifying verbose output, the command returns "The secure channel between 'Client Computer', 'Domain Controller', and 'Domain Name' is alive and working correctly."

See Also

Recipe 8.10 for resetting a computer

8.10. Resetting a Computer Account

Problem

You want to reset a computer because its secure channel is failing.

Solution

Using a graphical user interface

1. Open the ADUC snap-in (*dsa.msc*).
2. If you need to change domains, right-click on Active Directory Users and Computers in the left pane, select Connect to Domain, enter the domain name, and click OK.
3. In the left pane, right-click on the domain and select Find.
4. Beside Find, select Computers.
5. Type the name of the computer and click Find Now.
6. In the Search Results window, right-click on the computer and select Reset Account.
7. Click Yes to confirm the reset.
8. Click OK.
9. Rejoin the computer to the domain.

Using a command-line interface

You can use the DSMod utility to reset a computer's password. You will need to rejoin the computer to the domain after doing this:

```
> dsmod computer "<ComputerDN>" -reset
```

Another option is to use the `netdom` command, which can reset the secure channel between the computer and the domain controller without affecting the computer's password, so that you do not need to rejoin it to the domain:

```
> netdom reset <ComputerName> /Domain <DomainName> /UserO <UserUPN> /PasswordO *
```

You can also use the `nltest` command to reset a secure channel using the following syntax:

```
> nltest /sc_reset:<DomainName>\<DCName>
```

Using PowerShell

To reset the local computer's secure channel by using PowerShell, run the following command:

```
Test-ComputerSecureChannel -Repair
```

Discussion

When you've identified that a computer's secure channel has failed, you'll need to reset the computer object, which consists of setting the computer object password to the name of the computer. This is the default initial password for new computers. Every 30 days, Windows computers automatically change their passwords in the domain. After you've set the password, you'll need to rejoin the computer to the domain since it will no longer be able to communicate with a domain controller due to unsynchronized passwords. However, the `netdom reset` command and the `Test-ComputerSecureChannel` command will try to reset the password both on the computer and in Active Directory, which will not necessitate rejoining it to the domain if successful.

From a practical standpoint, you should first attempt to reset the secure channel between the computer and the domain using the `netdom`, `Test-ComputerSecureChannel`, or `nltest` syntax, since doing so will not require you to unjoin and rejoin the computer to the domain; in particular, this will save you from performing the associated reboots involved with rejoining the domain. If resetting the secure channel does not correct the issue you're facing, you can then resort to resetting the computer's password.

A new utility from joe Richards, named MachinePwd, is another way to change computer passwords from the command line. See joeware (*http://bit.ly/1OBO1Fv*) for more detail.

See Also

Recipe 8.4 for joining a computer to a domain

8.11. Finding Inactive or Unused Computers

Problem

You want to find inactive computer accounts in a domain.

Solution

> These solutions might apply only to Windows-based machines. Other types of machines—for example, Unix, Mac, and Network Attached Storage (NAS)—that have accounts in Active Directory might not update their login timestamps or passwords, which are used to determine inactivity.

Using a command-line interface

The following query will locate all inactive computers in the current forest:

```
> dsquery computer forestroot -inactive <NumWeeks>
```

You can also use `domainroot` in combination with the `-d` option to query a specific domain:

```
> dsquery computer domainroot -d <DomainName> -inactive <NumWeeks>
```

Or you can target your query at a specific container:

```
> dsquery computer ou=MyComputers,dc=adatum,dc=com -inactive <NumWeeks>
```

You can also use the OldCmp *joeware* utility to create a report of all computer accounts whose passwords are older than a certain number of days (90 by default) by using the following syntax:

```
> oldcmp -report
```

> To specify an alternate password age with `oldcmp`, use the `-age` x switch. You can also use the `-llts` switch to use the `lastLogonTimeStamp` attribute to perform the age calculations. (Without this switch, `oldcmp` will use `pwdLastSet` by default, which will work against any version of Active Directory in any domain mode.)

Using PowerShell

You can also locate computers that have not been logged on to for a certain amount of time using PowerShell, as shown in the following example that finds computers that have not been logged on to in 60 days:

```
$DaysSince = (Get-Date).AddDays(-60)
Get-ADComputer -Filter * -Properties LastLogonDate |↵
  Where-Object {($_.LastLogonDate -le $DaysSince) -and ($_.Enabled -eq $True)↵
  -and ($_.LastLogonDate -ne $NULL)} | Select Name,LastLogonDate
```

Discussion

Using a command-line interface

The dsquery computer command is very handy for finding inactive computers that have not logged in to the domain for a number of weeks or months. You can pipe the results of the query to the *dsrm* command-line utility if you want to remove the inactive computer objects from Active Directory in a single command.

You can also use OldCmp to disable inactive accounts, and then either delete them or move them to an alternate OU. OldCmp has a number of safeties built into the utility to prevent you from deleting a large number of computer accounts without meaning to. For example, OldCmp will not delete an account unless it has first been disabled, it will not modify more than 10 objects at a time unless you manually specify a higher limit, and it simply will not do anything at all to a domain controller computer account under any circumstances. Unless you have a requirement for quickly removing unused computer objects, we'd recommend allowing them to remain inactive for at least three months before removing them. If you don't really care when the objects get removed, use a year (i.e., 52 weeks) to be on the safe side.

See Also

Recipe 6.28 for finding users whose passwords are about to expire; "Find Inactive Users using Powershell" (*http://bit.ly/15keyjn*) (can be used with the -computersonly switch)

8.12. Changing the Maximum Number of Computers a User Can Join to the Domain

Problem

You want to grant users the ability to join more or fewer than 10 computers to a domain. This limit is called the *machine account quota*.

Solution

Using a graphical user interface

1. Open the ADSI Edit MMC snap-in (*adsiedit.msc*) and connect to the Domain Naming Context.
2. Right-click on the domainDNS object for the domain you want to change and select Properties.
3. Edit the ms-DS-MachineAccountQuota attribute and enter the new quota value.
4. Click OK twice.

Using a command-line interface

In the following LDIF code, replace *<DomainDN>* with the distinguished name of the domain you want to change, and replace *<Quota>* with the new machine account quota:

```
dn: <DomainDN>
changetype: modify
replace: ms-DS-MachineAccountQuota
ms-DS-MachineAccountQuota: <Quota>
-
```

If the LDIF file was named *change_computer_quota.ldf*, you would then run the following command:

```
> ldifde -v -i -f change_computer_quota.ldf
```

You can also make this change using AdMod, as follows:

```
> admod -b <DomainDN> ms-DS-MachineAccountQuota::<Quota>
```

Using PowerShell

You can modify the MachineAccountQuota attribute using PowerShell, as follows:

```
Set-ADDomain -Identity <DomainName>↵
 -Replace @{"ms-DS-MachineAccountQuota"="<NewQuota>"}
```

Discussion

In a default Active Directory installation, members of the Authenticated Users group can add and join up to 10 computer accounts in the default Computers container. The number of computer accounts that can be created is defined in the attribute ms-DS-MachineAccountQuota on the domainDNS object for a domain. The default setting is 10, but you can easily change that to whatever number you want, including 0, via the methods described in this recipe. If you set it to 0, users have to be granted explicit permissions

---

in Active Directory to join computers; refer to Recipe 8.4 for instructions on granting these permissions.

Another method for granting users the right to add computer objects, although not recommended, is via Group Policy. If you grant the "Add workstation to domain" right via Computer Configuration→Windows Settings→Security Settings→Local Policies→User Rights Assignment on a GPO that's been linked to the Domain Controllers OU, then users will be able to create computer accounts even if they do not have create child permissions on the default Computers container. This is a holdover from Windows NT to maintain backward compatibility and should not be used unless absolutely necessary. In fact, a good security best practice would be to remove this user right from any user or group objects that do not require it.

See Also

Recipe 8.4 for permissions needed to join computers to a domain; MS KB 251335 (Domain Users Cannot Join Workstation or Server to a Domain); "Default limit to number of workstations a user can join to the domain" (*http://support.microsoft.com/kb/243327*)

8.13. Modifying the Attributes of a computer Object

Problem

You want to modify one or more attributes of a computer object.

Solution

Using a graphical user interface

1. Open the Active Directory Administrative Center.
2. In the right pane, enter the name of the computer in the Global Search box, select the desired domain in the scope, and then click the search icon.
3. In the search results, double-click the name of the computer to open the computer properties.
4. Scroll down to the Extension section and then click the Attribute Editor tab.
5. Click the attribute that you want to modify and then click the Edit button.
6. Modify or set the desired value for the attribute and then click OK.
7. Click OK to finalize the attribute change.

Using a command-line interface

Create an LDIF file called *modify_object.ldf* with the following contents:

```
dn: <ComputerDN>
changetype: modify
add: <AttributeName><AttributeName>: <AttributeValue>
-
```

Then run the following command:

```
> ldifde -v -i -f modify_object.ldf
```

To modify an object using AdMod, you'll use the following general syntax:

```
> admod -b <ComputerDN> <attribute>:<operation>:<value>
```

For example, you can add a location to a computer object using the following syntax:

```
> admod -b cn="Fin101,cn=Computers,dc=adatum,dc=com" location::"Berlin, Germany"
```

Using PowerShell

The Set-ADComputer cmdlet allows you to set commonly used attributes by using the following syntax:

```
Set-ADComputer -Identity <ComputerDN> -<ObjectAttribute> "<Value>"
```

To set attributes that are not supported by the Set-ADComputer cmdlet natively, use the following syntax:

```
Set-ADComputer -Identity <ComputerDN> -Replace @{<ObjectAttribute>="<Value>"}
```

Discussion

Like all objects within Active Directory, computer objects have various attributes that can be queried, modified, and deleted during the day-to-day management of your domain. Because computer objects inherit from the user class, they include similar informational attributes to the user objects, as well as attributes that are specific to computer objects, including:

- Location
- Description
- operatingSystemVersion
- operatingSystemServicePack
- sAMAccountName
- pwdLastSet
- primaryGroupID

Using PowerShell

See the full help file for the `Set-ADComputer` cmdlet to view the options and detailed usage of the `Add`, `Replace`, `Clear`, and `Remove` parameters.

See Also

Recipe 8.11 for finding inactive or unused computers; Recipe 8.14 for finding computers with a particular OS; MSDN: Computer System Hardware Classes [WMI]

8.14. Finding Computers with a Particular OS

Problem

You want to find computers that have a certain OS version, release, or service pack in a domain.

Solution

Using a graphical user interface

You can perform this search using the Active Directory Users and Computers MMC snap-in, as follows:

1. Open the ADUC MMC snap-in (*dsa.msc*).
2. Right-click on the domain, OU, or container that you wish to search and click Find.
3. In the Find drop-down box, select Computers.
4. Click on the Advanced tab. Click on Field and select Operating System.
5. Select the Condition that you want to search on from one of the following:

   - Starts with
   - Ends with
   - Is (exactly)
   - Is not
   - Present
   - Not present

6. In the Value field, enter the value that you want to search for, such as "Windows Server 2012 Datacenter."
7. Click Find Now.

Using a command-line interface

You can query for `computer` objects of a particular operating system using either DSQuery or AdFind. To perform the query with DSQuery, use the following syntax:

```
> dsquery * <DomainDN> -scope subtree -attr "*" -filter "(&(↵
objectcategory=computer)(operatingSystem=Windows Server 2012 Datacenter))"
```

To use AdFind, enter the following:

```
> adfind -b <DomainDN> -f  "(&(objectcategory=computer)↵
(operatingSystem=Windows Server 2012 Datacenter))"
```

Using PowerShell

To search for computers based on operating system version using PowerShell, use the `get-ADComputer` cmdlet. The following example finds all computers that are running Windows Server 2012 Datacenter without regard for the service pack level:

```
Get-ADComputer -Filter {OperatingSystem -eq "Windows Server 2012 Datacenter"} |↵
Select Name
```

The following example searches for all computers that are running Windows Server 2008 R2 Enterprise with Service Pack 1:

```
Get-ADComputer -Filter {OperatingSystem -eq "Windows Server 2008 R2 Enterprise"↵
-and OperatingSystemVersion -eq "6.1 (7601)"} | Select Name
```

Discussion

When a computer joins an Active Directory domain, the operating system attributes are updated for the `computer` object. There are three of these attributes, which can be used in queries to find computers that match certain OS-specific criteria, such as service pack level.

These attributes include the following:

operatingSystem
> Descriptive name of the installed operating system—for example, Windows Server 2008, Windows Server 2008 R2, and Windows Server 2012. The values of this attribute sometimes include special characters such as the copyright symbol, which makes this attribute a poor choice for searching. However, if you know the descriptive name, it can still be a logical choice in a filter.

operatingSystemVersion
> Numerical representation of the operating system—for example, 6.1 (7601) and 6.2 (9200). The version corresponds to the current service pack level, if one is installed. For instance, 6.1 (7600) represents Windows Server 2008 R2 without a service pack, while 6.1 (7601) represents Windows Server 2008 R2 with Service Pack 1. Windows Server 2012 is represented by 6.2 (9200).

`operatingSystemServicePack`

Current service pack level if one is installed—for example, Service Pack 2 and Service Pack 3.

 This recipe typically applies only to Windows-based machines. Other types of machines (e.g., Unix) that have accounts in Active Directory might not automatically update their OS attributes, though some newer Unix or Linux-based NAS devices have been configured to do so.

See Also

"Operating System Version (Windows)" (*http://bit.ly/10j4krJ*)

8.15. Binding to the Default Container for Computers

Problem

You want to bind to the default container that new `computer` objects are created in.

Solution

Using a graphical user interface

1. Open LDP.
2. From the menu, select Connection→Connect.
3. For Server, enter the name of a domain controller (or leave it blank to do a serverless bind).
4. For Port, enter 389.
5. Click OK.
6. From the menu, select Connection→Bind.
7. Enter the credentials of a domain user or accept the default setting and bind as the currently logged on user.
8. Click OK.
9. From the menu, select View→Tree.
10. For the DN, enter:

    `<WKGUID=aa312825768811d1aded00c04fd8d5cd,<DomainDN>>`

    where *<DomainDN>* is the distinguished name of a domain.

11. Click OK.

12. In the lefthand menu, you can now browse the default `Computers` container for the domain.

Using a command-line interface

By default, all `computer` objects created in an Active Directory domain are placed into the built-in `Computers` container. This default container has a significant limitation, in that you are unable to link Group Policy Objects (GPOs) to the built-in container. If you have one or more GPOs that you wish to apply to all `computer` objects in your domain, you should modify the default location for computer accounts in AD. You can use the *redircmp* utility to change this default location, as we will discuss in Recipe 8.16.

Using PowerShell

```
$strDomain = "<DomainDNSName>"

Set-Variable ADS_GUID_COMPUTERS_CONTAINER aa312825768811d1aded00c04fd8d5cd

$rootDSE = [ADSI]("LDAP://" + $strDomain + "/RootDSE")
$container = [ADSI]("LDAP://<WKGUID=" + $ADS_GUID_COMPUTERS_CONTAINER + "," +
$rootDSE.defaultNamingContext + ">")
$container.distinguishedName
```

Discussion

In much the same way that the TCP/IP protocol defines a list of well-known ports that are commonly used by industry applications (TCP ports 20 and 21 for FTP, TCP port 80 for HTTP, and so on), Active Directory defines Well-Known GUIDs that map to `container` objects that are present in every AD installation. The Domain NC defines the following WKGUIDs:

- `Users`
- `Computers`
- `System`
- `Domain Controllers`
- `Infrastructure`
- `Deleted Objects`
- `Lost and Found`

The Configuration NC also defines its own `Deleted Objects` WKGUID.

For example, the default `Computers` container has the following WKGUID:

```
aa312825768811d1aded00c04fd8d5cd
```

You can use the GUID to bind to the default `Computers` container in the domain using the following ADsPath:

```
LDAP://<WKGUID=aa312825768811d1aded00c04fd8d5cd,dc=apac,dc=adatum,dc=com>
```

The list of well-known objects for a domain is contained in the `wellKnownObjects` attribute of the `domainDNS` object for the domain. The `wellKnownObjects` attribute is multivalued with `DNWithBinary` syntax. The following is an example of what that attribute looks like for the *adatum.com* domain:

```
B:32:AA312825768811D1ADED00C04FD8D5CD:cn=Computers,dc=adatum,dc=com;
B:32:F4BE92A4C777485E878E9421D53087DB:cn=Microsoft,cn=Program
Data,dc=adatum,dc=com;
B:32:09460C08AE1E4A4EA0F64AEE7DAA1E5A:cn=Program Data,dc=adatum,dc=com;
B:32:22B70C67D56E4EFB91E9300FCA3DC1AA:
cn=ForeignSecurityPrincipals,dc=adatum,dc=com;
B:32:18E2EA80684F11D2B9AA00C04F79F805:cn=Deleted Objects,dc=adatum,dc=com;
B:32:2FBAC1870ADE11D297C400C04FD8D5CD:cn=Infrastructure,dc=adatum,dc=com;
B:32:AB8153B7768811D1ADED00C04FD8D5CD:cn=LostAndFound,dc=adatum,dc=com;
B:32:AB1D30F3768811D1ADED00C04FD8D5CD:cn=System,dc=adatum,dc=com;
B:32:A361B2FFFFD211D1AA4B00C04FD7D83A:ou=Domain Controllers,dc=adatum,dc=com;
B:32:A9D1CA15768811D1ADED00C04FD8D5CD:cn=Users,dc=adatum,dc=com;
```

Each value has the format of:

```
B:NumberofBytes:GUID:DistinguishedName
```

As you can see, the GUID for the first value is the same as the one we used in the ADsPath earlier to bind to the default `Computers` container.

See Also

Recipe 8.16 for changing the default `Computers` container; MSDN: Binding to Well-Known Objects Using WKGUID

8.16. Changing the Default Container for Computers

Problem

You want to change the container that computers are created in by default.

Solution

Using a graphical user interface

1. Open LDP.

2. From the menu, select Connection→Connect.

3. For Server, enter the name of a domain controller (or leave it blank to do a serverless bind).

4. For Port, enter 389.

5. Click OK.

6. From the menu, select Connection→Bind.

7. Enter the credentials of a domain user.

8. Click OK.

9. From the menu, select Browse→Modify.

10. For DN, enter the distinguished name of the domainDNS object of the domain you want to modify.

11. For Attribute, enter wellKnownObjects.

12. For Values, enter the following:

    B:32:AA312825768811D1ADED00C04FD8D5CD:cn=Computers,<DomainDN>

    where <DomainDN> is the same as the DN you enter for the DN field.

13. Select Delete for the Operation and click the Enter button.

14. Go back to the Values field and enter the following:

    B:32:AA312825768811D1ADED00C04FD8D5CD:<NewComputersParent>,<DomainDN>

    where <NewComputersParent> is the new parent container for new computer objects (e.g., ou=Adatum Computers).

15. Select Add for the Operation and click the Enter button.

16. Click the Run button.

The result of the operations will be displayed in the right pane of the main LDP window.

Using a command-line interface

```
> redircmp "<NewParentDN>"
```

Discussion

Many Active Directory administrators do not use the Computers container within the Domain Naming context as their primary computer repository. One reason is that since it is a container and not an OU, you cannot apply Group Policy Objects to it. If you have another location where you store computer objects, you might want to consider changing the default container used to bind to the Computers container by changing the well-known objects attribute, as shown in this recipe. This can be beneficial if you want to ensure computers cannot sneak into Active Directory without having the appropriate group policies applied to them. While you can also apply GPOs at the site or the domain level, forcing new computers into a particular organizational unit ensures that those computers receive the Group Policy settings that you want them to receive through GPOs linked at the OU level. However, this does not protect you from an administrator (whether intentionally or accidentally) explicitly creating a computer object in the incorrect OU; this only protects you from applications or utilities that do not allow or do not require you to specify an OU when creating the computer.

 See Recipe 8.15 for more information on how well-known objects are specified in Active Directory.

See Also

"Redirecting the users and computers containers in Active Directory domains" (KB 324949) (*http://support.microsoft.com/kb/324949*)

8.17. Listing All the Computer Accounts in a Domain

Problem

You want to obtain a list of all computer accounts in an Active Directory domain.

Solution

Using a graphical user interface

1. Open the Active Directory Users and Computers MMC snap-in.
2. Right-click on the domain node and select Find.
3. In the Find drop-down box, select Computers and click Find Now.

   All computer objects in the domain will be displayed in the Search Results window.

Using a command-line interface

```
> adfind -default -f objectCategory=computer
```

Using PowerShell

You can obtain a listing of computer accounts using PowerShell, as shown in the following two examples:

```
Get-ADComputer -Filter * | Select Name
```

or

```
Get-ADObject -Filter {objectCategory -eq "Computer"} | Select Name
```

Discussion

Using PowerShell

The `Get-ADComputer` cmdlet simplifies the process of finding computers by removing the need to know about the `object` class and object category. However, both methods end up with the exact same results.

See Also

`Get-ADComputer` cmdlet reference (*http://bit.ly/YzD7pE*); MSDN: Object Class and Object Category [Active Directory]; MSDN: Object-Class Attribute [AD-Schema]

8.18. Identifying a Computer Role

Problem

You want to identify the role that a particular computer serves in an Active Directory domain.

Solution

Using a graphical user interface

1. Open the Active Directory Users and Computers MMC snap-in (*dsa.msc*).
2. Right-click on the domain node and select Find.
3. In the Find drop-down box, select Computers and click Find Now.

   The role of each computer will be displayed in the Machine Role column in the Search Results window.

Using a command-line interface

```
> wmic computersystem get domainrole
```

For a domain controller that holds the PDC Emulator FSMO role, this will return the following output:

```
DomainRole
5
```

For a DC that doesn't hold the PDCe FSMO, this command will return a value of 4.

Using PowerShell

```
Get-WmiObject Win32_ComputerSystem -ComputerName <ComputerFQDN>↵
 -Property Name,DomainRole
```

Discussion

The DomainRole attribute returns a numeric value that identifies the role, as shown in the following list:

- 0 is a standalone workstation.
- 1 is a member workstation.
- 2 is a standalone server.
- 3 is a member server.
- 4 is a backup domain controller.
- 5 is a primary domain controller.

Using a command-line interface

WMIC is the command-line component of the Windows Management Instrumentation that uses aliases to enable you to easily access WMI namespaces from the command line. To run wmic against a remote computer, specify the /node:"<ComputerFQDN>" switch.

8.19. Protecting a Computer Against Accidental Deletion

Problem

You want to prevent a computer object from being accidentally deleted by an administrator who selects the incorrect option in Active Directory Users and Computers.

Solution

Using a graphical user interface (steps specific to Windows Server 2008 and later)

1. Open Active Directory Users and Computers. Click on View and confirm that Advanced Features is selected.

2. Drill down to the current domain. To connect to a different domain, right-click on the top-level node and click "Change domain"; select the appropriate domain and then drill down to it.

3. Right-click on the computer that you want to modify and click Properties.

4. Click on the Object tab.

5. Place a checkmark next to "Protect object from accidental deletion."

6. Click OK.

Using a command-line interface (all versions)

```
dsacls <Computer DN> /d EVERYONE:SDDT
```

Using PowerShell (all versions)

```
Set-ADObject -Identity "<Computer DN>" -ProtectedFromAccidentalDeletion $True
```

Discussion

By default, all new OUs that are created in Windows Server 2008 and later will have this protection enabled; however, no other object types are configured with this default protection. If you attempt to delete a computer object that is protected using this option, even when signed on as a Domain Admin or other similarly elevated account, you will receive an "Access Denied" message until you manually remove the checkbox or manually remove the deny ACE associated with it.

Using the command-line or PowerShell method, you can apply this protection to group objects in *all* versions of Windows Server, even though the GUI checkbox is available only in Windows Server 2008 and later.

8.20. Viewing the RODCs That Have Cached a Computer's Password

Problem

You wish to view the RODCs that have cached a computer account's password secrets.

Solution

Using a graphical user interface

1. Open the ADUC snap-in (*dsa.msc*).

2. Click View→Advanced Features. In the left pane, right-click on the domain and select Find.

3. In the Find drop-down box, select Computers. Select the appropriate domain.

4. Beside Name, type the name of the computer account and click Find Now.

5. In the Search Results window, double-click on the computer.

6. Select the Attribute Editor tab. Click Filter and ensure that there is a checkmark next to Backlinks.

7. Scroll to the msDS-RevealedDSAs attribute to view a list of RODCs that have cached this computer's password secrets.

8. Click OK.

Using a command-line interface

```
> adfind -b <ComputerDN> msDS-RevealedDSAs
```

Using PowerShell

```
Get-ADComputer -Identity "<UserDN>" -Properties "msDS-RevealedDSAs" |↵
  FL msDS-RevealedDSAs
```

Discussion

As discussed in Chapter 3, Windows Server 2008 introduced the Read-Only Domain Controller (RODC) to improve the security of branch office and other remote environments. One of the security measures introduced by the RODC is the Password Replication Policy (PRP), which specifies a list of users, computers, and groups that can and cannot have their password secrets cached on one or more DCs. Each RODC maintains a forward-link attribute called msDS-RevealedUsers, which lists the user and computer accounts for whom each RODC has cached password secrets. Each computer account, in turn, maintains a backlink called msDS-RevealedDSAs. This backlink can be queried to determine which RODCs have stored password information for a particular user account; however, like all backlinks, this attribute cannot be modified directly.

See Also

Recipe 3.2; Recipe 3.4

## CHAPTER 9

Group Policy Objects

9.0. Introduction

Active Directory Group Policy Objects (GPOs) can customize virtually any aspect of a computer or user's desktop. They can also be used to install applications, secure a computer, run logon/logoff or startup/shutdown scripts, and much more. You can assign a GPO to a local computer, site, domain, or organizational unit. This is called *scope of management* (SOM), because only the users or computers that fall under the scope of the computer, OU, site, or domain will process the GPO. Assigning a GPO to a SOM is referred to as *linking* the GPO. You can restrict the application of GPOs further by using security groups to filter which users or groups they will apply to or by using inheritance blocking.

You can also use a WMI filter to restrict the application of a GPO. A WMI filter is simply a WMI query that can search against any information on a client's computer. If the WMI filter returns a true value (i.e., the client computer matches the conditions that are specified in the filter), the GPO will be processed; otherwise, it will not. So not only do you have all of the SOM options for applying GPOs, but also you can use any WMI information available on the client's computer to determine whether GPOs should be applied. For more on the capabilities of GPOs, we recommend reading *Active Directory*, Fifth Edition, by Brian Desmond et al. (O'Reilly).

Group Policies are defined by a set of files that are replicated to each domain controller in a domain and a `groupPolicyContainer` (GPC) object that is stored in the `cn=Poli cies,cn=System,<DomainDN>` container. GPC objects contain information related to software deployment, wireless deployments, IPSec assignments, and metadata about the version of the GPO. GPC objects are used for linking to OUs, sites, and domains. The guts of GPOs are stored on the filesystem of each domain controller in Group Policy Template (GPT) files and can be found in the *%SystemRoot%\SYSVOL\sysvol \<DomainDNSName>\Policies* directory.

So why are there two storage points for GPOs? The need for the Active Directory object is obvious: to be able to link GPOs to other types of objects, the GPOs need to be represented in Active Directory. Group Policy Templates are stored in the OS filesystem to reduce the amount of data that needs to be replicated within Active Directory.

For legacy Windows computers, each Group Policy Object stores individual copies of Administrative templates (*.adm* files) in the *SYSVOL* folder. In an environment containing numerous GPOs, this can add significantly to the amount of data that must be replicated to the SYSVOL share on all domain controllers in a domain. However, since Windows Vista, GPO settings are deployed using a new XML-based *.admx* format, and administrators have the option to configure a single Central Store to provide a storage instance for all GPOs in a domain.

Furthermore, Windows Server 2008 introduced Group Policy Preferences (GPPs), a new group of GPO settings that can be used to manage configuration items that could not be managed previously (or that could not be managed particularly well) via GPOs, including managing the creation of file shortcuts, ODBC connections, drive mappings, printer connections, and more.

Managing GPOs

While the new capabilities of GPOs were significant when first introduced with Active Directory, the obvious things that were lacking were good tools for managing them. The dual storage nature of GPOs creates a lot of problems. Initially, Microsoft did not provide a scriptable interface for accessing and manipulating GPO settings. Additionally, there were no tools for copying or migrating GPOs from a test environment to production. Back then the primary tool for managing GPOs was the Group Policy Editor (GPE), now known as the Group Policy Management Editor (GPME). The main function of the GPME is to modify GPO settings; it does not provide any other management capabilities.

Microsoft realized these were major issues for Group Policy adoption, so it developed the Group Policy Management Console (GPMC) with the release of Windows Server 2003. The GPMC is an MMC snap-in that provides the kitchen sink of GPO management capabilities: you can create, delete, import, copy, back up, restore, and model GPO processing from a single interface. Perhaps what is even better is the scriptable API that comes with the GPMC. Pretty much every function you can accomplish with the GPMC tool, you can do via a script.

The only major feature that is still lacking is the ability to modify the settings of a GPO directly via command line or script (although there is some ability to modify specific types of settings, improvement is needed). Previously, this could be done with only the GPOE, but there are third-party options that can provide this type of functionality. The GPMC still provides numerous options for migrating GPOs, which addresses the majority of the problems people face today.

In versions prior to Windows Server 2008, GPMC is an out-of-band download that can be obtained from Microsoft (*http://bit.ly/YFv199*). In Windows Server 2008 and later, Group Policy Management is a feature, and it can be installed on Windows client computers as part of the Remote Server Administration Tools (RSAT). Note that throughout the book we use the name "Group Policy Management" instead of GPMC in order to match up with the shortcut and menu names used by Windows.

Another tool that you can download from the Microsoft website is GPInventory. This is an incredibly useful tool that will allow you to perform a software inventory for users and computers in a domain or OU, and to track information about the rollout of GPOs in AD, such as computers that have not applied new GPO information. Additionally, the Group Policy Best Practice Analyzer (GP BPA) is a free download that can help you identify Group Policy configuration errors within your environment.

The majority of solutions presented in this chapter use the Group Policy Management snap-in. Most of the command-line solutions we provide will use one of the scripts provided in the Group Policy Management Console Sample Scripts install available from the Microsoft Download Center (*http://bit.ly/17HD3EI*). A whole host of precanned scripts have been written already, in a mix of VBScript and JScript, which serve as great command-line tools and good examples to start scripting GPOs. These scripts are available by default in the *C:\Program Files (x86)\Microsoft Group Policy\GPMC Sample Scripts* directory on a Windows Server 2012 server that has had the sample scripts installed on it. You can execute them in one of two ways, either by using *cscript*:

```
> cscript listallgpos.wsf
```

or, if you make *cscript* your default WSH interpreter, by executing the file directly. To make *cscript* your default interpreter, run this command:

```
> cscript //H:cscript
```

9.1. Finding the GPOs in a Domain

Problem

You want to find all of the GPOs that have been created in a domain.

Solution

Using a graphical user interface

1. Open the Group Policy Management snap-in (*gpmc.msc*).
2. In the left pane, expand the `Forest` container.
3. Expand the `Domains` container.
4. Browse to the desired domain.
5. Expand the domain and then expand the `Group Policy Objects` container. All of the GPOs in the domain will be listed under that container.

Using a command-line interface

You can generate a list of all GPOs in a domain using the *listastallgpos.wsf* script, as well as DSQuery and AdFind:

```
> listallgpos.wsf [/domain:<DomainDNSName>] [/v]

> dsquery * domainroot -filter (objectcategory=grouppolicycontainer)
-attr displayname

> adfind -default -f (objectcategory=grouppolicycontainer)↵
 displayname
```

Using PowerShell

To get all of the GPOs in the current domain and return their display name, run the following PowerShell command:

```
Get-GPO -All | Select DisplayName
```

Discussion

See Recipe 9.0 for more on how GPOs are stored in Active Directory.

Using PowerShell

You can obtain the details from a single GPO by replacing `-All` with the `-Name` parameter, followed by the friendly name of the GPO, such as `Get-GPO -Name "Default Domain Policy"`.

See Also

`Get-GPO` cmdlet reference (*http://bit.ly/17HDn6g*); "Group Policy Cmdlets in Windows PowerShell" (*http://bit.ly/17HDqPx*)

9.2. Creating a GPO

Problem

You want to create a Group Policy Object within Active Directory.

Solution

Using a graphical user interface

1. Open the Group Policy Management snap-in (*gpmc.msc*).
2. In the left pane, expand the Forest container, expand the Domains container, and browse to the domain that will contain the new GPO.
3. Expand the domain and then right-click on the Group Policy Objects container and select New.
4. Enter the name of the GPO, ensure that the Source Start GPO is set to (none), and then click OK.

Using a command-line interface

```
> creategpo.wsf <GPOName> [/domain:<DomainDNSName>]
```

Using PowerShell

To create a GPO called "Marketing GPO" in the current domain, use the following syntax:

```
New-GPO -Name "Marketing GPO"
```

If the GPO is successfully created, the cmdlet will output the display name of the GPO, along with the GUID and other information.

Discussion

When you create a GPO through the Group Policy Management snap-in, it is initially empty with no settings or links configured. See Recipe 9.6 for more on modifying GPO settings, and Recipe 9.14 for more on creating a link.

See Also

New-GPO cmdlet reference (*http://bit.ly/11bbggS*); "Group Policy Cmdlets in Windows PowerShell" (*http://bit.ly/17HDqPx*)

9.3. Copying a GPO

Problem

You want to copy the properties and settings of one GPO into another GPO.

Solution

Using a graphical user interface

1. Open the Group Policy Management snap-in (*gpmc.msc*).
2. In the left pane, expand the Forest container, expand the Domains container, browse to the domain of the source GPO, expand the domain, and then expand the Group Policy Objects container.
3. Right-click on the source GPO and select Copy.
4. Right-click on the Group Policy Objects container and select Paste.
5. Select whether you want to use the default permissions or to preserve the existing permissions from the GPO being copied, and click OK.
6. A status window will pop up that will indicate whether the copy was successful. Click OK to close.
7. Rename the new GPO by right-clicking it in the left pane and selecting Rename.

Using a command-line interface

```
> copygpo.wsf <SourceGPOName> <TargetGPOName>
```

Using PowerShell

```
Copy-GPO -SourceName "<SourceGPOName>" -TargetName "<TargetGPOName>"
```

Discussion

Prior to the GPMC tool, two of the biggest problems with managing GPOs in large environments were migrating GPOs from one forest to another and copying GPOs from one domain to another within the same forest. It is common to have a test forest where GPOs are initially created, configured, and tested before moving them into production. The problem before GPMC was that once you had the GPO the way you wanted it in the test forest, there was no easy or well-publicized way to move it to the production forest.

With the GPMC and the Group Policy Management snap-in, you can simply copy GPOs between domains. You can also import GPOs, which is similar to a copy operation. A

GPO import uses a backup of the source GPO in order to create the new GPO. See Recipe 9.7 for more information on importing a GPO.

Some properties of GPOs, such as security group filters, UNC paths, and Restricted Groups, may vary slightly from domain to domain; for example, a logon script that runs from \\SERVERA\share in the source domain may need to run on \\SERVERB\share in the target domain. In that case, you can use a GPMC migration table to help facilitate the transfer of those types of references to the target domain. For more information on migration tables, see the GPMC help file and Recipe 9.8.

Using PowerShell

PowerShell has greatly simplified the process of managing GPOs. With PowerShell, you can copy all of the GPOs in one domain to a different domain in a single line of PowerShell.

See Also

Recipe 9.7 for importing a GPO; Recipe 9.8; Copy-GPO cmdlet reference (*http://bit.ly/ 13lLILe*)

9.4. Deleting a GPO

Problem

You want to delete a GPO.

Solution

Using a graphical user interface

1. Open the Group Policy Management snap-in (*gpmc.msc*).
2. In the left pane, expand the Forest container, expand the Domains container, browse to the domain of the target GPO, expand the domain, and then expand the Group Policy Objects container.
3. Right-click on the target GPO and select Delete.
4. Click OK to confirm.

Using a command-line interface

```
> deletegpo.wsf <GPOName> [/domain:<DomainDNSName>]
```

To retain the links to the deleted GPO, use the `/keeplinks` switch. Otherwise, all links will be deleted along with the GPO.

Using PowerShell

```
Remove-GPO -Name "<GPO Friendly Name>" -KeepLinks
```

Discussion

When you delete a GPO through the Group Policy Management snap-in, it attempts to find all links to the GPO in the domain and will delete them if the user has permissions to delete the links. If the user does not have the necessary permissions to remove the links, the GPO will still get deleted, but the links will remain intact. Any links external to the domain the GPO is in are not automatically deleted. For this reason, it is a good practice to view the links to the GPO before you delete it. Links to deleted GPOs show up as "Not Found" in the Group Policy Management snap-in.

Using PowerShell

To delete a GPO in a remote domain, use the `-DomainName` switch, followed by the FQDN of the domain.

See Also

Recipe 9.13 for viewing the links for a GPO; `Remove-GPO` cmdlet reference (*http://bit.ly/12b6TxQ*)

9.5. Viewing the Settings of a GPO

Problem

You want to view the settings that have been defined in a GPO.

Solution

Using a graphical user interface

1. Open the Group Policy Management snap-in (*gpmc.msc*).
2. In the left pane, expand the `Forest` container, expand the `Domains` container, browse to the domain of the target GPO, expand the domain, and then expand the `Group Policy Objects` container.
3. Click on the target GPO.

4. In the right pane, click on the Settings tab.

5. Click the Show All link to display all configured settings.

Using a command-line interface

```
> getreportsforgpo.wsf "<GPOName>" <ReportLocation> [/domain:<DomainDNSName>]
```

Using PowerShell

```
Get-GPOReport -Name "<GPO Friendly Name>" -Path <Path With File Name>↵
 -ReportType HTML
```

Discussion

The Group Policy Management snap-in can generate an XML or HTML report that contains all of the settings in a GPO. See Recipe 9.6 for more information on how to modify GPO settings.

Using PowerShell

The Get-GPOReport cmdlet can produce output in either HTML or XML format, by using the –ReportType HTML or –ReportType XML switch, respectively.

See Also

Get-GPOReport cmdlet reference (*http://bit.ly/10dROZJ*)

9.6. Modifying the Settings of a GPO

Problem

You want to modify the settings associated with a GPO.

Solution

Using a graphical user interface

1. Open the Group Policy Management snap-in (*gpmc.msc*).

2. In the left pane, expand the Forest container, expand the Domains container, browse to the domain of the target GPO, expand the domain, and then expand the Group Policy Objects container.

3. Right-click on the target GPO and select Edit. This will bring up the Group Policy Management Editor.

4. Browse through the Computer Configuration or User Configuration settings and modify them as necessary.

Using PowerShell

You can modify a registry-based setting in a GPO by using PowerShell. The following example modifies the IE High Sec GPO by disabling the Flash add-in:

```
Set-GPRegistryValue -Name "IE High Sec"↵
 -key "HKLM\Software\Policies\Microsoft\Internet Explorer"↵
 -ValueName "DisableFlashInIE" -Type String -Value "1"
```

Discussion

Modifying GPOs has historically been performed from a GUI. Up until the `Set-GPRegistryValue` cmdlet was introduced, there wasn't an easy way to modify a GPO from a command-line environment. Note that the `Set-GPRegistryValue` cmdlet is restricted to registry settings only and thus isn't as fully featured as the Group Policy Management Editor.

See Also

Recipe 9.3 for copying a GPO; Recipe 9.5 for viewing the settings of a GPO; Recipe 9.7 for importing settings into a GPO; `Set-GPRegistryValue` cmdlet reference (*http://bit.ly/18MKx7T*)

9.7. Importing Settings into a GPO

Problem

You want to import settings from one GPO to another.

Solution

Using a graphical user interface

1. Open the Group Policy Management snap-in (*gpmc.msc*).
2. In the left pane, expand the `Forest` container, expand the `Domains` container, expand the domain of the target GPO, and expand the `Group Policy Objects` container.
3. Right-click on the target GPO and select Import Settings.
4. Click Next.

5. Click the Backup button if you want to take a backup of the GPO you are importing into.

6. Click Next.

7. Select the backup folder location and click Next.

8. Select the backed-up GPO you want to import from and click Next.

9. The Import wizard then will scan to see whether there are any security principals or UNC paths in the GPO being imported from. If there are, it will give you an option to modify those settings.

10. Click Next.

11. Click Finish.

Using a command-line interface

```
> importgpo.wsf "<GPOBackupLocation>" "<OrigGPOName>" "<NewGPOName>"
```

Using PowerShell

```
Import-GPO -BackupGpoName "<Friendly Name of Source GPO>"↵
 -TargetName "<Friendly Name of Target GPO>" -Path "<Path to backed up GPO>"
```

Discussion

The Group Policy Management import function uses a backup of the source GPO to create the new "imported" GPO. This means you must first back up the source GPO. You can then import the settings from that GPO into a new GPO, which may be in the same domain or in a completely different forest. Importing a GPO is a great way to help facilitate transferring GPO settings from a test environment to production.

Some properties of GPOs, such as security group filters and UNC paths, may vary slightly from domain to domain; a logon script that runs from \\SERVERA\share in the source domain may need to run on \\SERVERB\share in the target domain, for example. In this case, you can use a migration table to help facilitate the transfer of those kinds of references to the target domain. For more information on migration tables, see Recipe 9.8.

Using PowerShell

Be aware that the target GPO will be overwritten by the contents of the GPO backup during the import operation.

See Also

Recipe 9.3 for copying a GPO; Recipe 9.8; Recipe 9.23 for backing up a GPO; Import-GPO cmdlet reference (*http://bit.ly/10gu2C2*)

9.8. Creating a Migration Table

Problem

You want to create a migration table to assist in copying or migrating a GPO from one domain or forest to another.

Solution

Using a graphical user interface

1. Open the Group Policy Management snap-in (*gpmc.msc*). Navigate to the forest and domain containing the GPOs you wish to migrate or copy.

2. Right-click on the Group Policy Objects node and select Open Migration Table Editor.

3. You will begin with a blank migration table. To populate the source fields from existing data, click on Tools→Populate from GPO or Tools→Populate from Backup. Select the GPO or the backup that you wish to import. Optionally, place a checkmark next to "During scan, include security principals from the DACL on the GPO." Click OK.

4. Modify the Destination Name column of any entries to match their format in the destination forest or domain.

5. To add a new entry, enter the name of the item in the Source Name column. In the Source Type column, select one of the following:

   - User
   - Computer
   - Domain Local Group
   - Domain Global Group
   - Universal Group
   - UNC Path
   - Free Text or SID

6. To delete an entry, right-click on the entry and select Delete.

7. To configure an entry to use the same information as configured in the source GPO, right-click on the entry and select Set Destination→Same As Source.

8. To configure an entry to use the relative name of the destination, right-click on the entry and select Set Destination→Map by Relative Name. For example, if you have an entry for the *salesuser@adatum.com* user in a GPO that you wish to copy to the *mycompany.com* forest, selecting Map by Relative Name will populate the entry in the destination GPO as *salesuser@mycompany.com*.

9. To ensure that you have properly formatted all entries in the table, click Tools→Validate Table, then click File→Save or File→Save As to save the migration table.

Using a command-line interface

```
> createmigrationtable.wsf <DestinationFileName> /GPO:<GPO> /MapByName
```

Discussion

One of the convenient features of the Group Policy Management snap-in is the ability to copy a GPO's settings from one GPO to another, or to migrate GPOs between domains or forests. In some cases, certain entries in the GPO may need to be modified to suit the needs of the destination domain or forest. For example, a UNC for user home directories will likely need to be modified to correspond to a server or DFS share in the destination, as well as individual user or group names. To address this need, you can create and populate a migration table to automatically transform the necessary entries on one or more GPOs.

Using a command-line interface

To create a migration table from the command line, use the *createmigrationtable.wsf* script that is included in the *~\GPMC Sample Scripts* folder. The script requires two arguments: the destination filename and the GPO that it should be populated from.

As an alternative to the /GPO: switch, you can use /BackupLocation: to populate the migration table from a GPO backup. By default, a migration table that you create using this script will use Same As Source mapping, or you can specify the /MapByName parameter to use relative name mapping.

See Also

Recipe 9.3 for more on copying a GPO; Recipe 9.7 for information on importing settings into a GPO

9.9. Creating Custom Group Policy Settings

Problem

You want to deploy settings via Group Policy that are not covered by the default set of GPO templates that come with Active Directory.

Solution

Windows comes preloaded with a number of default *templates* that define a number of settings that can be controlled via GPO. To control and deploy settings for additional or third-party applications, you'll need to create your own custom ADM or ADMX file to manage the settings you require. You'll create this file in Notepad or another simple text editor, and save it as *<FileName>.adm* or *<FileName>.admx*. For example, the following ADMX file will add a new search provider to Internet Explorer using a customized ADMX file:

```xml
<?xml version="1.0" encoding="utf-8"?> <policyDefinitions
  xmlns:xsd="http://www.w3.org/2001/XMLSchema"
  xmlns:xsi="http://www.w3.org/2001/XMLSchema-instance" revision="1.0"
  schemaVersion="1.0"
xmlns="http://www.microsoft.com/GroupPolicy/PolicyDefinitions">
  <policyNamespaces>
    <target prefix="search" namespace="Microsoft.Policies.search" />
    <using prefix="inetres" namespace="Microsoft.Policies.InternetExplorer" />
  </policyNamespaces>
  <resources minRequiredRevision="1.0" />
  <policies>
    <policy name="PopulateSearchProviderList_1" class="User"
      displayName="$(string.PopulateSearchProviderList)"
      explainText="$(string.IE_Explain_PopulateSearchProviderList)"
      key="Software\Policies\Microsoft\Internet Explorer\SearchScopes">
      <parentCategory ref="inetres:InternetExplorer" />
      <supportedOn ref="inetres:SUPPORTED_IE7Vista"/>
      <enabledList>
        <item key="Software\Policies\Microsoft\Internet Explorer\SearchScopes"
          valueName="Version">
          <value>
            <decimal value="VERSION" />
          </value>
        </item>
        <item key="Software\Policies\Microsoft\Internet
          Explorer\SearchScopes\SUBKEY1" valueName="DisplayName">
          <value>
            <string>NAME1</string>
          </value>
        </item>
        <item key=" Software\Policies\Microsoft\Internet
          Explorer\SearchScopes\SUBKEY1" valueName="URL">
```

```
          <value>
            <string>URL1</string>
          </value>
        </item>
      </enabledList>
    </policy>
    <policy name="PopulateSearchProviderList_2" class="Machine"
      displayName="$(string.PopulateSearchProviderList)"
      explainText="$(string.IE_Explain_PopulateSearchProviderList)"
      key="Software\Policies\Microsoft\Internet Explorer\SearchScopes">
      <parentCategory ref="inetres:InternetExplorer" />
      <enabledList> Insert same as user policy above </enabledList>
    </policy>
  </policies>
</policyDefinitions>
```

In addition to the ADMX file, you will need to create an ADML file using a format similar to the following:

```
<?xml version="1.0" encoding="utf-8"?>
  <policyDefinitionResources xmlns:xsd=http://www.w3.org/2001/XMLSchema
    xmlns:xsi="http://www.w3.org/2001/XMLSchema-instance" revision="1.0"
schemaVersion="1.0"
    xmlns="http://www.microsoft.com/GroupPolicy/PolicyDefinitions">
    <displayName>enter display name here</displayName>
    <description>enter description here</description>
    <resources>
      <stringTable>
        <string id="PopulateSearchProviderList">Populate List of search
providers</string>
        <string id="IE_Explain_PopulateSearchProviderList">
This policy setting will allow you to populate a list of search providers that
will be displayed in Internet Explorer's search box. If you enable this policy
setting and if the "Restrict search providers to a specific list of search
providers" Group Policy setting is enabled, this list will be the only list
that appears in the Internet Explorer drop-down list. If the "Add a specific
list of search providers to the user's search provider list" Group Policy
setting is enabled, this list will be added to the user's list of search
providers. If you disable this policy setting or do not configure it,
users will have complete freedom to create their own search provider list.
</string>
      </stringTable>
    </resources>
  </policyDefinitionResources>
```

Discussion

When you create a custom ADMX file, save it to the *%windir%\policydefinitions* folder, the ADML file will be saved in the *%windir%\policydefinitions\<Definition Language>* folder. After saving the files, you can edit a GPO to use the new settings. The templates will automatically populate in the Administrative Templates section of the GPO.

See Also

"Managing Group Policy ADMX Files Step-by-Step Guide" (*http://bit.ly/18MLixS*)

9.10. Assigning Logon/Logoff and Startup/Shutdown Scripts in a GPO

Problem

You want to assign either user logon/logoff scripts or computer startup/shutdown scripts in a GPO.

Solution

Using a graphical user interface (steps specific to Windows Server 2008 and later)

1. Open the Group Policy Management snap-in (*gpmc.msc*).
2. In the left pane, expand the Forest container, expand the Domains container, expand the domain of the target GPO, and expand the Group Policy Objects container.
3. Right-click on the target GPO and select Edit. This will bring up the Group Policy Management Editor.
4. Browse to Computer Configuration→Policies→Windows Settings→Scripts. If you want to assign a user logon or logoff script, browse to User Configuration→Policies→Windows Settings→Scripts.
5. In the right pane, double-click on the type of script you want to add.
6. Click the Add button.
7. Select the script by typing its name or browsing to its location.
8. Optionally, type any script parameters in the Script Parameters field.
9. Click OK twice.

Discussion

When you assign a script in a GPO, you can reference a script that either is stored locally on the domain controller somewhere under the *SYSVOL* share or is stored in a UNC path to a remote fileserver. The default storage location is in the *<DomainName>\SYS*

VOL\<DomainName>\scripts folder—for example, *\\adatum.com\sysvol\adatum.com\scripts.*

9.11. Installing Applications with a GPO

Problem

You want to install an application on a group of computers using a GPO.

Solution

Using a graphical user interface

1. Open the Group Policy Management snap-in (*gpmc.msc*).

2. In the left pane, expand the `Forest` container, expand the `Domains` container, expand the domain of the target GPO, and expand the `Group Policy Objects` container.

3. Right-click on the target GPO and select Edit. This will bring up the Group Policy Management Editor.

4. Expand Software Settings under Computer Configuration or User Configuration, depending on which you want to target the installation for.

5. Right-click on Software Installation and select New→Package.

6. Browse to the network share that has the MSI package for the application and click OK. Be sure to specify a UNC path such as *\\servername\share\installer.msi*. If you enter a local file path on the DC, such as *c:\packages\pro.msi*, the client will not be able to access the installer.

7. Select whether you want to assign the application or publish it, and click OK. You can also click Advanced to define further how you want to deploy the software installation package.

Discussion

Installing applications with a GPO is a powerful feature, but you must be careful about the impact it can have on your network throughput and clients. If the MSI package you are installing is large in size, it will take a while for it to download to the client computer. This can result in sluggish performance on the client, especially over a heavily utilized connection. (Software installation does not occur over slow links, by default.) You'll also want to make sure you've thoroughly tested the application before deployment. After you've configured the GPO to install an application, it will be only a short period of time before it has been installed on all targeted clients. If there is a bug in the application or the installer program is faulty, the impact could be severe to your user base and support staff alike.

Your two options for deploying an application are to assign it or to publish it. If you assign an application using the "deploy at logon" option, it will be installed automatically on the targeted clients when users log on to those machines. If you publish an application or assign it without choosing this option, it will be installed the first time a user double-clicks on a shortcut to the application or attempts to open a file that requires the application. A published application also can be installed manually from the Programs and Features applet in the Control Panel on the target computers. You can assign an application to both user and computer objects, but you can publish applications only to users.

 If you need to exert more granular control over your software installations than is enabled by Group Policy, you should investigate leveraging the additional capabilities of dedicated deployment software such as Microsoft's System Center Configuration Manager (ConfigMgr).

9.12. Disabling the User or Computer Settings in a GPO

Problem

You want to disable either the user or the computer settings of a GPO.

Solution

Using a graphical user interface

1. Open the Group Policy Management snap-in (*gpmc.msc*).
2. In the left pane, expand the Forest container, expand the Domains container, expand the domain of the target GPO, and expand the Group Policy Objects container.
3. Right-click on the target GPO and select GPO Status.
4. You can select User Configuration Settings Disabled to disable the user settings, Computer Configuration Settings Disabled to disable the computer settings, or All Settings Disabled to disable both user and computer settings.

Using PowerShell

```
$gpm = New-Object -ComObject GPMgmt.GPM
$gpmConstants = $gpm.GetConstants()
```

```
$objDomain = $gpm.GetDomain("<Domain FQDN>", "", $gpmConstants.UseAnyDC)
$objGpo = $objDomain.GetGPO("{<GPO GUID>}")
$objGpo.SetComputerEnabled($true)
$objGpo.SetUserEnabled($false)
```

Discussion

GPOs consist of two parts, a user section and a computer section. The user section contains settings that are specific to a user that logs in to a computer, while the computer section defines settings that apply to the computer regardless of which user logs in. You can enable or disable either the user configuration or the computer configuration section of a GPO, or both. By disabling both, you effectively disable the GPO. This can be useful if you want to stop a GPO from applying settings to clients, but you do not want to delete it, remove the links, or clear the settings.

Disabling the user configuration or the computer configuration is useful in environments that have separate OUs for computers and users. Typically, you would disable the computer configuration for GPOs linked to the users' OU, and vice versa. Disabling half of the GPO in this way makes GPO processing a tiny bit more efficient but likely will have almost no impact on overall performance.

Using PowerShell

Although 26 cmdlets are dedicated to managing Group Policy, none of them can be used to enable or disable computer or user settings. Instead, we utilize a COM object in PowerShell.

See Also

"Group Policy Cmdlets in Windows PowerShell" (*http://bit.ly/17HDqPx*); MSDN: GPMGPO.SetUserEnabled; MSDN: GPMGPO.SetComputerEnabled

9.13. Listing the Links for a GPO

Problem

You want to list all of the links for a particular GPO.

Solution

Using a graphical user interface

1. Open the Group Policy Management snap-in (*gpmc.msc*).

2. In the left pane, expand the `Forest` container, expand the `Domains` container, expand the domain of the target GPO, and expand the `Group Policy Objects` container.

3. Click on the GPO you want to view the links for.

   In the right pane, the defined links for the GPO will be listed under the Scope tab.

Using a command-line interface

```
> dumpgpoinfo.wsf "<GPOName>"
```

Using PowerShell

```
Get-ADOrganizationalUnit -Filter * -Properties * |↵
Where {$_.gPLink -match "<GPO GUID>"} | Select Name
```

Discussion

See Recipe 9.0 for more information on GPO linking.

Using PowerShell

The built-in PowerShell cmdlets are not useful for retrieving links. Instead, we rely on searching the other direction: the OUs themselves. In the PowerShell solution, we get all of the OUs in the current domain and then filter them for any that have the specified GPO GUID stored in the `gpLink` attribute. This indicates that the GPO is linked to the OU. Finally, we select only the name of the OUs.

See Also

Recipe 9.0; Recipe 9.14 for creating a GPO link to an OU

9.14. Creating a GPO Link to an OU

Problem

You want to apply the GPO settings to the users and/or computers in an OU. This is called *linking* a GPO to an OU.

Solution

Using a graphical user interface

1. Open the Group Policy Management snap-in (*gpmc.msc*).

2. In the left pane, expand the `Forest` container, expand the `Domains` container, and expand the target domain.

3. Right-click on the OU you want to link and select Link an Existing GPO.

4. Select from the list of available GPOs and click OK.

Using PowerShell

```
New-GPLink -Name "<GPO Display Name>" -Target "<Container DN>"
```

Discussion

Linking a GPO is the process whereby you assign a scope of management (SOM), which can be an OU, site, or domain. The solutions show how to link a GPO to an OU, but they easily could be modified to link to a site or domain.

See Recipe 5.14 for details on how to link an OU by modifying the `gpLink` attribute, instead of using the Group Policy Management interface.

Using PowerShell

During the creation of the new link, you can also specify the link order by using the `-Order <Number>` parameter.

See Also

`New-GPLink` cmdlet reference (*http://bit.ly/17HE6V8*); MSDN: GPM-SOM.CreateGPOLink

9.15. Blocking Inheritance of GPOs on an OU

Problem

You want to block inheritance of GPOs on an OU.

Solution

Using a graphical user interface

1. Open the Group Policy Management snap-in (*gpmc.msc*).

2. In the left pane, expand the `Forest` container, expand the `Domains` container, and expand the target domain.

3. Right-click on the OU you want to block inheritance for and select Block Inheritance.

Using PowerShell

Below are two ways to block inheritance by using PowerShell. The first example uses one of the cmdlets from the Group Policy module, whereas the other relies on a COM object.

```
Set-GPInheritance -Target "<OU DN>" -IsBlocked Yes

$gpm = New-Object -ComObject GPMgmt.GPM
$gpmConstants = $gpm.GetConstants()
$objDomain = $gpm.GetDomain("<Domain FQDN>", "", $gpmConstants.UseAnyDC)
$objOU = $objDomain.GetSOM("<OU DN>")
$objOU.GPOInheritanceBlocked = $true
```

Discussion

By default, GPOs are inherited down through the directory tree. If you link a GPO to a top-level OU, that GPO will apply to any objects within the child OUs. Sometimes that may not be what you want, and you can disable inheritance as described in the solutions.

Try to avoid blocking inheritance when possible because it can make determining what settings should be applied to a user or computer difficult. If someone sees that a GPO is applied at a top-level OU, he may think it applies to any object under it. Using the Resultant Set of Policies (RSoP) snap-in can help identify what settings are applied to a user or computer (see Recipe 9.25).

See Also

Recipe 9.25; `Set-GPInheritance` cmdlet reference (*http://bit.ly/ZAO6KG*); MSDN: GPMSOM; MSDN: GPOInheritanceBlocked; MSDN: GPMDomain.GetSOM

9.16. Enforcing the Settings of a GPO Link

Problem

You want to ensure that a GPO's settings are enforced regardless of any Block Inheritance settings that have been enforced farther down the scope of management.

Solution

Using a graphical user interface

1. Open the Group Policy Management snap-in (*gpmc.msc*).

2. In the left pane, expand the Forest container, expand the Domains container, expand the domain of the target GPO, and expand the container containing the link you want to enforce.

3. Right-click on the link you want to configure and place a checkmark next to Enforced. To remove the Enforced setting, right-click on the link and remove the checkmark.

Using PowerShell

```
Set-GPLink -Guid "<GPOGUID>" -Target "<SiteName>" -Enforced Yes
```

Discussion

As a counterpoint to the ability to block inheritance of a GPO for a particular site, domain, or OU, an administrator can configure a particular GPO link as Enforced, meaning that the settings contained in that GPO will be configured for that SOM regardless of the presence of any Block Inheritance configuration. This is useful in a decentralized environment, for example, where a central IT department has configured a certain Group Policy baseline that it wishes to enforce regardless of what individual departments may have configured on their own. Just like security filtering and Block Inheritance, though, we recommend that you use this function sparingly, as it can create complex troubleshooting issues when trying to determine where and how the Group Policy application is failing.

 Remember that the Enforced setting is configured against a particular *link* to a GPO, not against the GPO itself. This means that one GPO can be linked to several locations, but not all of those links need to be enforced.

See Also

Recipe 9.15 ; Set-GPLink cmdlet reference (*http://bit.ly/ZAO99i*); MSDN:IGPMSearchCriteria; MSDN:GPMC Obje

9.17. Applying a Security Filter to a GPO

Problem

You want to configure a GPO so that it applies only to members of a particular security group.

Solution

Using a graphical user interface

1. Open the Group Policy Management snap-in (*gpmc.msc*).
2. In the left pane, expand the Forest container, expand the Domains container, expand the target domain, and expand the Group Policy Objects container.
3. Click on the GPO you want to modify.
4. In the right pane under Security Filtering, click the Add button.
5. Use the Object Picker to select a group and click OK.
6. Highlight Authenticated Users and click the Remove button.
7. Click OK to confirm.

Using a command-line interface

```
> setgpopermissions.wsf "<GPOName>" "<GroupName>" /permission:Apply
> setgpopermissions.wsf "<GPOName>" "Authenticated Users" /permission:None
```

Using PowerShell

```
Set-GPPermission -Name <GPO Display Name> -TargetName "<Group Name>"↵
 -TargetType Group -PermissionLevel GpoApply"
```

Discussion

You can use security filtering to restrict the users, groups, or computers that a GPO applies to by granting or denying the Apply Group Policy permission on the ACL of the GPO. By default, *Authenticated Users* are granted the Apply Group Policy right on all new GPOs, so you will also need to remove this right if you want to restrict the GPO to be applied only to members of one specific group.

As a rule, you should avoid using Deny permissions as part of any custom security filter, because this can lead to confusion with accounts that are members of groups with conflicting filter settings. For example, if a user is a member of a group that has Deny set in the filter and is also a member of a group that is allowed to apply the policy, the Deny setting will always win. This can be difficult to troubleshoot, particularly if nested group memberships are involved.

 Be very careful when changing permissions on GPOs. If you create a very restricted GPO and apply a security filter to it, also be sure to put tight controls on who can modify the GPO and how. If for some reason that security filter were removed (resulting in no security filters), the restrictive GPO could be applied to every user or computer in the domain.

Using PowerShell

The Set-GPPermission cmdlet allows you to apply one of the following preconfigured permissions:

- GpoRead
- GpoApply
- GpoEdit
- GpoEditDeleteModifySecurity
- None

See Also

Set-GPPermission cmdlet reference (*http://bit.ly/YpI55Z*);MSDN: GPM.CreatePermission; MSDN: GPMGPO.GetSecurityInfo

9.18. Delegating Administration of GPOs

Problem

You want to delegate permissions on GPOs and related tasks within Active Directory.

Solution

Using a graphical user interface

To delegate the ability to create GPOs, do the following:

1. Open the Group Policy Management snap in (*gpmc.msc*).
2. Navigate to the Group Policy Objects node and click on the Delegation tab.

3. To add permissions for a new user or group to create GPOs, click Add. Use the object picker to select the object you want and click OK.

To delegate permissions on a particular GPO, follow these steps:

1. Open the Group Policy Management snap-in (*gpmc.msc*).

2. Navigate to the GPO that you want to delegate permissions for and click on the Delegation tab.

3. To add permissions for a new user or group, click Add. Use the object picker to select the object you want and click OK.

4. In the Permissions drop-down box, select "Read", "Edit settings," or "Edit settings, delete, and modify security," then click OK.

To delegate Group Policy–related tasks on a particular site, domain, or OU, do the following:

1. Open the Group Policy Management snap-in (*gpmc.msc*).

2. Navigate to the site, domain, or OU that you want to delegate permissions for and click on the Delegation tab.

3. In the Permission drop down, select "Link GPOs," "Perform Group Policy Modeling analyses," or "Read Group Policy Results data."

4. To add permissions for a new user or group, click Add. Use the object picker to select the object you want and click OK.

5. In the Permissions drop-down box, select "This container only" or "This container and all child containers"; then click OK.

Discussion

In addition to using Active Directory users and groups to control how GPOs are applied within a site, domain, or OU, you can also use ACLs to delegate permissions over GPOs to allow you to decentralize the administration of them in your organization.

You can delegate the ability to do the following:

- Create GPOs
- Manage the settings of an individual GPO
- Link GPOs to a site, domain, or OU
- Create WMI filters
- Manage an individual WMI filter

While the ability to delegate administration in this manner is quite simple to implement, it's critical that you fully understand the security implications that it carries. For example, the ability to link GPOs to an entire site or domain should be granted only to highly trusted administrators as it can have far-reaching implications for the performance and behavior of your network.

See Also

MS KB 250842 (Troubleshooting Group Policy Application Problems); Recipe 9.17 for more on using security filtering to control GPO behavior

9.19. Importing a Security Template

Problem

You want to import a security template into a GPO.

Solution

Using a graphical user interface

1. Open the Group Policy Management snap-in (*gpmc.msc*).
2. In the left pane, expand the `Forest` container, expand the `Domains` container, expand the domain of the GPO you want to target, and expand the `Group Policy Objects` container.
3. Right-click on the target GPO and select Edit.
4. Navigate to Computer Configuration→Policies→Windows Settings.
5. Right-click on Security Settings and select Import Policy.
6. Browse to the template you want to import and click Open.

Discussion

Rather than manually configuring the plethora of security settings available in Windows, you can use a template. Windows 2003 shipped with several templates, including templates for high-security workstations and high-security domain controllers. However, Windows 2008 and later have scaled back the number of default templates and now only include three templates: a default base template, a default domain controller template, and a default member server template. Each template is useful in a scenario where you need to reset security settings back to the default state.

9.20. Creating a WMI Filter

Problem

You want to create a WMI filter.

Solution

Using a graphical user interface

1. Open the Group Policy Management snap-in (*gpmc.msc*).
2. In the left pane, expand the Forest container, expand the Domains container, expand the target domain, and click the WMI Filters container.
3. Right-click on the WMI Filters container and select New.
4. Enter a name and description for the filter.
5. Click the Add button.
6. Select the appropriate namespace, enter a WQL query, and click OK.
7. Repeat steps 5 and 6 for as many queries as you need to add.
8. Click the Save button.

Discussion

WMI filters provide another way to filter how GPOs are applied to clients. WMI filters live in Active Directory as objects under the WMIPolicy container within the System container for a domain. A WMI filter consists of a WMI Query Language (WQL) query that, when linked to a GPO, will be run against all clients that the GPO applies to. If the WQL returns a true value (i.e., it returns nonempty results from the WQL query), the GPO will continue to process. If the WQL query returns false (nothing is returned from the query), the GPO will not be processed.

The great thing about WMI filters is that the vast amount of information that is available in WMI on a client becomes available to filter GPOs. You can query against CPU, memory, disk space, hotfixes installed, service packs installed, applications installed, running processes—the list goes on and on.

For example, creating a GPO that applies only to computers that are running a specific version of Windows would have been really difficult to accomplish without a WMI filter. Either you would have had to create a security group that contained all of those computers as members (and apply a security filter) or you would have had to move all of those workstations to a particular OU. With a WMI filter, this becomes trivial to create. Bear in mind, however, that there is client performance overhead associated with WMI queries, as each computer will need to process the WMI query to determine whether a particular GPO should or should not be applied. Here is a sample WQL query that would return `true` when run on a Windows Server 2012 Datacenter server:

```
select * from Win32_OperatingSystem↵
where Caption = "Microsoft Windows Server 2012 Datacenter"
```

The introduction of Group Policy Preferences created significant new options in terms of how GPOs can be targeted and filtered. Prior to the introduction of Group Policy Preferences, you were limited to filtering using only WMI filters to control whether the entire GPO is applied. With WMI filters, you cannot specify individual settings within a GPO. Group Policy Preferences, on the other hand, support item-level targeting, where individual settings can be targeted based on criteria such as IP address, whether that machine is a laptop or desktop, security group membership, and so on.

See Also

Recipe 9.21 for applying a WMI filter to a GPO; MSDN: Querying with WQL

9.21. Applying a WMI Filter to a GPO

Problem

You want to apply a WMI filter to a GPO.

Solution

Using a graphical user interface

1. Open the Group Policy Management snap-in (*gpmc.msc*).
2. In the left pane, expand the Forest container, expand the Domains container, expand the domain of the GPO you want to target, and expand the Group Policy Objects container.
3. Click on the target GPO.
4. At the bottom of the right pane, on the Scope tab, select a WMI filter from the list of WMI filters.
5. After you've selected the WMI filter, click Yes to change the filter.

Discussion

You can link only one WMI filter to a GPO at any time. This is not an overly restrictive limitation, though, because you still can link more than one GPO to a site, domain, or

OU. If you need multiple WMI filters to apply to a GPO, copy the GPO and apply a different WMI filter to it. See Recipe 9.20 for more information on WMI filters.

 Keep in mind that requiring your clients to process multiple WMI filters will have an impact on their performance at logon time and during the GPO background refresh process.

9.22. Configuring Loopback Processing for a GPO

Problem

You want to configure a GPO to use loopback processing that will enforce consistent computer settings regardless of which user logs on to a computer.

Solution

Using a graphical user interface

1. Open the Group Policy Management snap-in (*gpmc.msc*).
2. Navigate to the GPO that you want to configure. Right-click on the GPO and select Edit Settings.
3. Navigate to Computer Configuration→Policies→Administrative→Templates System→Group Policy. Double-click on "Configure user Group Policy loopback processing mode". Select the radio button next to Enabled.
4. In the Mode drop-down box, select either Merge or Replace. (See this recipe's "Discussion" for more information on these two options.)
5. Click OK.

Discussion

GPOs are applied to user/computer combinations on an Active Directory network based on the site, domain, and OU that the user and computer objects belong to. If the user and computer are located in two separate locations, the user will receive the GPOs that apply to the user's container combined with those that apply to the computer's container. However, there may be cases where you want a user to receive GPOs based solely on the location of the computer objects. In this case, you will enable loopback processing in one of two modes:

Merge mode

In this mode, any GPOs that are associated with the user will be applied first. The GPOs associated with the computer object will be applied after the GPOs associated with the user object, thereby giving them a higher precedence than the user GPOs. In this case, the user will still receive any GPO settings associated with her user object, but settings configured for the computer will override in the case of any conflicts.

Replace mode

In this mode, only the list of GPOs that apply to the computer object will be applied.

See Also

MS KB 231287 (Loopback Processing of Group Policy)

9.23. Backing Up a GPO

Problem

You want to back up a GPO.

Solution

Using a graphical user interface

1. Open the Group Policy Management snap-in (*gpmc.msc*).
2. In the left pane, expand the Forest container, expand the Domains container, expand the domain of the GPO you want to back up, and expand the Group Policy Objects container.
3. Right-click on the GPO you want to back up and select Back Up.
4. For Location, enter the folder path to store the backup files.
5. For Description, enter a descriptive name for the backup.
6. Click the Back Up button.
7. You will see a progress bar and status message that indicates whether the backup was successful.
8. Click OK to exit.

Using a command-line interface

```
> backupgpo.wsf "<GPOName>" "<BackupFolder>" /comment:"<BackupComment>"
```

Using PowerShell

```
Backup-Gpo -Name <GPO Display Name> -Path <Path to Backup Folder>↵
  -Comment "<Backup Description>"
```

Discussion

The Group Policy Management snap-in and the Backup-Gpo cmdlet both provide a way to back up individual (or all) GPOs. A GPO backup consists of a set of folders and files that catalog the GPO settings, filters, and links, and is created in the backup location you specify. You can back up a GPO to a local drive or over the network to a fileserver. Restoring a GPO is just as easy and is described in Recipe 9.24.

In legacy versions of Windows, the only way to back up GPOs was by backing up the System State on a domain controller. The System State includes Active Directory and the SYSVOL share (both components are needed to completely back up a GPO). To restore a GPO using this method, you'd have to boot into DS Restore mode and perform an authoritative restore of the GPO(s) you were interested in. Needless to say, the methods are significantly easier now.

A good practice is to back up your GPO backups. Since all the backup information is captured in a series of files, you can back up that information to media, which provides two levels of restore capability. You could restore the last backup taken, which could be stored on a domain controller or fileserver, or you could go to tape and restore a previous version.

In the folder you specify to store the GPO backups is a list of folders that have GUIDs for names. This does not make it very easy to distinguish which backups are for which GPOs. A quick way to find that out is to use the *querybackuplocation.wsf* script. This will list each folder GUID name and the corresponding GPO it is for:

```
> querybackuplocation.wsf "c:\gpmc backups"
```

Using PowerShell

The -Path switch allows you to back up GPOs to either a local file location such as *C: \GPOBackups* or a remote UNC path such as *\\SERVER1\GPOBackups.*

See Also

Recipe 9.24 for restoring a GPO; Backup-GPO cmdlet reference (*http://bit.ly/10j84JQ*); and MSDN: GPMGPO.Backup

9.24. Restoring a GPO

Problem

You want to restore a GPO.

Solution

Using a graphical user interface

1. Open the Group Policy Management snap-in (*gpmc.msc*).
2. In the left pane, expand the Forest container, expand the Domains container, expand the domain of the GPO you want to restore, and expand the Group Policy Objects container.
3. Right-click on the GPO you want to restore and select Restore from Backup.
4. Click Next.
5. Select the backup folder location and click Next.
6. Select the backup you want to restore and click Next.
7. Click Finish.
8. You will see the restore status window. After it completes, click OK to close the window.

Using a command-line interface

```
> restoregpo.wsf "<BackupFolder>" "<GPOName>"
```

Using PowerShell

```
Restore-GPO -Name "<GPO Display Name>" -Path <Backup Location>
```

Discussion

To restore a GPO using the Group Policy Management snap-in, you first need a valid backup of the GPO. The procedure for backing up a GPO is described in Recipe 9.23. You can then restore the GPO, even if the GPO has been deleted. To restore a deleted GPO, use the following steps:

1. Right-click on the Group Policy Objects container in the target domain and select Manage Backups.
2. Highlight the GPO you want to restore and click the Restore button.
3. Click Yes to confirm.

4. Click OK after the restore completes.

If you don't have a valid backup of the GPO, but you do have another GPO that is identical or similar to the one you want to restore (perhaps in another forest), you can copy that GPO to replace the one you want to restore.

Keep in mind that restoring a GPO does not restore the links that were associated with that GPO, since the `gpLink` attribute is configured on the container that the GPO was linked to and not the container itself. See Recipe 9.3 for more on copying GPOs.

See Also

Recipe 9.3 for copying a GPO; Recipe 9.23 for backing up a GPO; `Restore-GPO` cmdlet reference (*http://bit.ly/13ct0q4*); MSDN: GPMDomain.RestoreGPO

9.25. Simulating the RSoP

Problem

You want to simulate the Resultant Set of Policies (RSoP) based on OU, site, and security group membership. This is also referred to as Group Policy Modeling.

Solution

Using a graphical user interface

1. Open the Group Policy Management snap-in (*gpmc.msc*).
2. In the left pane, right-click Group Policy Modeling and select Group Policy Modeling Wizard.
3. Click Next.
4. Select a domain controller to process the query and click Next.
5. Under User Information and/or Computer Information, either select the container you want to simulate to contain the user or computer, or select a specific user or computer account, and click Next.
6. Select a site if necessary, and specify whether you wish to simulate a slow network connection or loopback processing, and then click Next.
7. If you selected a target user container or user account in step 5, you will be presented with an option to simulate different group membership. Click Next when you are done.

8. If you selected a target computer container or computer account in step 5, you will be presented with an option to simulate different group membership. Click Next when you are done.

9. If you selected a target user container or user account in step 5, you will be presented with an option to simulate any additional WMI filters. Click Next when you are done.

10. If you selected a target computer container or computer account in step 5, you will be presented with an option to simulate any additional WMI filters. Click Next when you are done.

11. Click Next to start the simulation.

12. Click Finish.

13. In the right pane of the Group Policy Management snap-in window, the results of the simulation will be displayed.

Discussion

You can simulate the RSoP based on user-defined OU, site, group, and domain membership. This is very powerful because it allows you to create one or more GPOs, simulate them being applied to a user and computer, and determine whether any changes are necessary before deployment.

See Also

Recipe 9.26 for viewing the RSoP

9.26. Viewing the RSoP

Problem

You want to view the actual RSoP for a user and computer. This is a great tool for determining whether policies are being applied correctly on a client.

Solution

Using a command-line interface

To display summary RSoP data to the screen, use the following command:

```
> gpresult /R
```

To generate an RSoP in HTML format, use the following command:

```
> gpresult /H RSoP.htm
```

You can specify a /S option and the name of a computer to target, which allows you to run the command remotely. For a complete list of options with either version, run gpresult /? from a command line.

Discussion

If you implement more than a few GPOs, it can get confusing as to what settings will apply to users. To address this problem, you can query the resultant set of policies on a client to determine which settings have been applied.

The registry on the target computer is another source of information. You can view the list of policies that were applied to the computer by viewing the subkeys under this key:

```
HKEY_CURRENT_USER\Software\Microsoft\Windows\CurrentVersion\Group Policy\History
```

The settings that were applied are not stored in the registry, but you can obtain the GPO name, distinguished name, SYSVOL location, version, and where the GPO is linked.

Finally, you can also rely on the Windows Event Logs for troubleshooting. Since Windows Vista, the logs have been improved greatly and now include a Group Policy operational log. Additionally, the source name for events now uses "Group Policy," which makes it easier to track down Group Policy events.

See Also

Recipe 9.25 for simulating the RSoP

9.27. Refreshing GPO Settings on a Computer

Problem

You've made some changes to a GPO and want to apply them to a computer by refreshing the group policies for the computer.

Solution

Using a command-line interface

On a Windows XP or later computer, use this command:

```
> gpupdate [/target:{Computer | User}]
```

Using PowerShell

```
Invoke-GPUpdate -Computer "<Machine FQDN>"
```

Discussion

By default, Group Policy settings will refresh automatically every five minutes on a domain controller and every 90 minutes (with an additional random offset between zero and 30 minutes) on clients and member servers. To force GPO settings to refresh sooner than that, you will need to run the *gpupdate* utility on the client computer. With *gpupdate*, you can force all settings to be applied with the /force option (the default is only changed settings). You can apply the computer or user settings of GPOs using the /target option, and you can force a logoff or reboot after the settings have been applied using the /logoff or /boot option. Windows Server 2012 introduced a remote Group Policy update feature built into the Group Policy Management snap-in. (Right-click on an OU and you can force a Group Policy update on all computers in the OU.)

Using PowerShell

The Invoke-GPUpdate cmdlet includes a number of optional switches that map to the *gpupdate.exe* command-line option, including -Computer, -User, -Force, -Logoff, -Boot, and -Sync.

See Also

Invoke-GPUpdate cmdlet reference (*http://bit.ly/10dTYbP*)

9.28. Restoring a Default GPO

Problem

You've made changes to the Default Domain Security Policy, Default Domain Controller Security Policy, or both, and now you want to reset them to their original configuration.

Solution

Using a command-line interface

The following command will replace both the Default Domain Security Policy and the Default Domain Controller Security Policy on a domain controller. You can specify Domain or DC instead of Both, to only restore one or the other:

```
> dcgpofix /target:Both
```

Note that this must be run from a domain controller in the target domain where you want to reset the GPO.

Discussion

If you've made changes to the default GPOs in the Windows Server 2003 or later version of Active Directory and would like to revert back to the original settings, the *dcgpofix* utility is your solution. *dcgpofix* works with a particular version of the schema. If the version it expects to be current is different from what is in Active Directory, it will not restore the GPOs. You can work around this by using the /ignoreschema switch, which will restore the GPO according to the version *dcgpofix* thinks is current. The only time you might experience this issue is if you install a service pack on a domain controller (DC1) that extends the schema but the changes have not yet replicated to a second domain controller (DC2). If you try to run *dcgpofix* from DC2, you will receive the error since a new version of the schema and the *dcgpofix* utility were installed on DC1. Note that this tool isn't a panacea. It doesn't always return permissions to the exact state after the domain controller promotion process. Because of this, backups of Group Policy should be relied on first.

9.29. Creating a Fine-Grained Password Policy

Problem

You want to create a Fine-Grained Password Policy (FGPP).

Solution

Using a graphical user interface (steps specific to Windows 7, Windows 8, and Windows Server 2012)

1. Open Active Directory Administrative Center.
2. At the top of the left pane, click the tree view icon.
3. Browse to the desired domain and then expand the domain, expand System, and then highlight the Password Settings container.
4. Right-click the Password Settings container in the left pane, click New, and then click Password Settings.
5. Type in a name for the settings, enter a precedence value, and then fill in the desired password settings. Note that settings with a red asterisk are mandatory.
6. In the Directly Applies To section near the bottom, click the Add button to specify users or groups to apply the password settings to.
7. When finished, click OK to save the settings and apply the settings to the specified users or groups.

Using PowerShell

Fine-Grained Password Policy objects can also be created in PowerShell, as follows:

```
New-ADFineGrainedPasswordPolicy -Name "HighSec2" -Precedence 1↵
 -ComplexityEnabled $true -Description "High Security Password Policy"↵
 -DisplayName "Domain Users PSO" -PasswordHistoryCount "12" -MinPasswordLength↵
 "15" -MinPasswordAge "1" -MaxPasswordAge "180" -LockoutDuration "30"↵
 -LockoutObservationWindow "1" -LockoutThreshold "999"
```

Discussion

Prior to Windows Server 2008, only one password and account lockout policy functioned per domain (note that we are only talking about domain user accounts); this has been updated since Windows Server 2008 once you reach the Windows Server 2008 domain functional level. Fine-Grained Password Policies are controlled by creating one or more msDS-PasswordSettingsObjects, or PSOs for short, in the cn=Password Settings Container,cn=System,cn=<Domain DN> container. Each PSO can apply to one or more user or group objects, and each is assigned a precedence that will allow Active Directory to determine which PSO to enforce if more than one can apply to a particular user.

See Also

Recipe 9.31; Recipe 9.30; New-ADFineGrainedPasswordPolicy cmdlet reference (*http:// bit.ly/13ctwEI*)

9.30. Editing a Fine-Grained Password Policy

Problem

You want to modify a Fine-Grained Password Policy.

Solution

Using a graphical user interface

1. Open Active Directory Administrative Center.
2. At the top of the left pane, click the tree view icon.
3. Browse to the desired domain, expand the domain, expand System, and then highlight the Password Settings container.
4. In the right pane, right-click on the desired policy and then click Properties.
5. Update the desired settings and click OK to save the new settings.

Using a command-line interface

The following command renames a `PasswordSettingsObject`:

```
psomgr -rename newname -pso oldname -forreal
```

The following modifies a PSO's maximum password age to 60 days:

```
psomgr -mod -pso TestPSO -pwdlen 60 -forreal
```

The following adds the *Marketing* group to the list of groups that a PSO will apply to:

```
psomgr -applyto cn=Marketing,cn=Users,dc=ADATUM,dc=COM -pso TestPSO -forreal
```

The following removes the *Marketing* group from the list of groups that a PSO will apply to:

```
psomgr -unapplyto cn=Marketing,cn=Users,dc=ADATUM,dc=COM -pso TestPSO -forreal
```

 You can also use the *Domain\sAMAccountName* syntax instead of a distinguished name.

Using PowerShell

The following modifies a PSO's maximum password length:

```
Set-ADFineGrainedPasswordPolicy -Identity "<PSO Name>" -MinPasswordLength 20
```

To rename a PSO, use the following syntax:

```
Set-ADFineGrainedPasswordPolicy -Identity "<PSO Name>" -DisplayName "HighSec2"
```

Discussion

Once a `PasswordSettingsObject` has been created, you can modify the password and account lockout settings controlled by the object, as well as the users and groups that the PSO should apply to. Since the `PasswordSettingsObject` is an Active Directory object class, these modifications can be made using any interface that can modify objects.

When working from the command line, the *psomgr* tool (*http://www.joeware.net/free tools*) allows you to modify one or multiple PSOs at a time, and can also create "starter" PSOs using the `psomgr -quickstart -forreal` syntax. The `-quickstart` switch creates a PSO that replicates the domain-linked password policy, as well as the following two PSOs:

cn=pwd_policy_admin
: Creates a PSO with a minimum password length of 15, with passwords that expire every 35 days and that are subject to a 30-minute lockout after 25 bad-password attempts

```
cn=pwd_policy_serviceid
```
Creates a PSO with a minimum length of 15, with passwords that expire every 364 days and that are not subject to account lockout

The full syntax for *psomgr.exe* can be obtained by typing `psomgr.exe /?` at a command prompt, or by visiting the *joeware* website.

See Also

Recipe 9.31; Recipe 9.29; Recipe 6.17

9.31. Viewing the Effective PSO for a User

Problem

You want to determine which PSO is in effect for a particular user.

Solution

Using a graphical user interface

1. Open Active Directory Users and Computers. Click on View and confirm that there is a checkmark next to Advanced Features.

2. Browse to the user or group in question; right-click on the object and click Properties.

3. Click on the Attribute Editor tab. Click Filter and confirm that there is a checkmark next to "Show read-only attributes: Constructed and Backlinks".

4. Scroll to `msDS-PSOApplied`.

5. Click OK.

Using a command-line interface

```
psomgr.exe -effective <User DN>
```

Using PowerShell

```
Get-ADUser -Identity "<UserDN>" -Properties msDS-ResultantPSO |↵
FL Name, msDS-ResultantPSO
```

Discussion

Within a Windows Server 2008 or later domain, each user object contains a constructed backlink attribute called msDS-ResultantPSO that indicates which PasswordSettingsObject is in effect for that user. The precedence rules for PasswordSettingsObjects are as follows:

1. If a PSO has been applied directly to the user object, it will take precedence. If multiple PSOs have been applied to a single user, the following tiebreakers will be used:

   - A PSO with a lower-numbered Precedence attribute (e.g., 5) will be applied over a higher-numbered one (e.g., 50).

   - If multiple PSOs have been configured with the same Precedence attribute, the PSO with the lowest GUID will take final precedence.

2. If no PSOs have been applied directly to the user, any PSO that has been applied to a group that the user is a member of, whether directly or indirectly, will be applied. The same tiebreakers will be used here as in rule 1.

3. If no PSOs have been applied to the user or any groups that the user is a member of, the default domain PSO will be applied.

See Also

Recipe 9.29; 3.1.1.4.5.36 msDSResultantPSO (*http://bit.ly/10dUp5Y*)

## CHAPTER 10

Schema

10.0. Introduction

The Active Directory schema contains the blueprint for how objects are structured and secured, what data they can contain, and even how they can be viewed. Having a good understanding of the schema is paramount for any Active Directory administrator, designer, or architect. Understanding key concepts, such as class inheritance, class types, attribute syntax, and attribute indexing options is critical to being able to adequately design an Active Directory infrastructure and should be considered mandatory for any developer who is writing applications or automation scripts that utilize Active Directory.

If you are one of the lucky few who is designated as a schema administrator (i.e., a member of the *Schema Admins* group), then the importance of the schema is already well known to you. This chapter serves as a guide to accomplishing many of the day-to-day tasks of schema administrators. For a more in-depth discussion of the schema, we suggest reading *Active Directory*, Fifth Edition, by Brian Desmond et al. (O'Reilly).

The Anatomy of Schema Objects

An interesting feature of Active Directory not common among other LDAP implementations is that the schema is stored within Active Directory itself as a set of objects. This means that you can use similar interfaces and programs to manage the schema as you would any other type of object without any need to shut down or restart Active Directory.

All schema objects are stored in the Schema container (cn=schema,cn=configura tion,<*ForestRootDN*>). The schema consists of two classes of objects, classSchema and attributeSchema. Not surprisingly, the classSchema objects define classes and attrib uteSchema objects define attributes. The Schema container contains a third type of object called subSchema, also known as the abstract schema, which is defined in the LDAP version 3 specification (RFC 2251). There is only a single subSchema object in the Schema container, named cn=Aggregate, and it contains a summary of the entire schema.

Table 10-1 and Table 10-2 contain useful attributes of classSchema objects and attrib uteSchema objects, respectively.

Table 10-1. Attributes of classSchema objects

Attribute	Description
adminDescription	Description of the class.
auxiliaryClass	Multivalued attribute containing any auxiliary classes defined for the class.
cn	Relative distinguished name of the class.
defaultHidingValue	Boolean that determines whether objects of this class are hidden by default in administrative GUIs.
defaultSecurityDescriptor	Default security descriptor applied to objects of this class.
governsID	OID for the class.
isDefunct	Boolean that indicates whether the class is defunct (i.e., deactivated).
lDAPDisplayName	Name used when referencing the class in searches or when instantiating or modifying objects of this class.
mayContain	Multivalued attribute that contains a list of attributes that can be optionally set on the class.
mustContain	Multivalued attribute that contains a list of attributes that must be set on the class.
objectClassCategory	Integer representing the class's type. Can be one of 1 (structural), 2 (abstract), 3 (auxiliary), or 0 (88).
possibleInferiors	Multivalued list of other object classes this object can contain.
possSuperiors	Multivalued list of object classes this object can be subordinate to.
rDNAttID	Naming attribute (i.e., RDN) of instances of the class.
schemaIDGUID	GUID of the class.
showInAdvancedViewOnly	Boolean that indicates whether instances of this class should be shown only in Advanced mode in the administrative GUIs.
subClassOf	Parent class.
systemAuxiliaryClass	Multivalued attribute containing any auxiliary classes defined for the class. This can be modified only internally by Active Directory.
systemFlags	Integer representing additional properties of the class.
systemMayContain	Multivalued attribute that contains a list of attributes that can be optionally set on the class. This can be modified only internally by Active Directory.
systemMustContain	Multivalued attribute that contains a list of attributes that must be set on the class. This can be modified only internally by Active Directory.
systemPossSuperiors	Multivalued list of object classes this object can be subordinate to. This can be modified only internally by Active Directory.

Table 10-2. Attributes of attributeSchema objects

Attribute	Description
adminDescription	Description of the attribute.
attributeID	OID for the attribute.
attributeSecurityGUID	GUID of the property set (if any) that an attribute is a member of.
attributeSyntax	OID representing the syntax of the attribute. This is used in conjunction with oMSyntax to define a unique syntax.
cn	Relative distinguished name of the attribute.
isDefunct	Boolean that indicates if the attribute is defunct (i.e., deactivated).
isMemberOfPartialAttributeSet	Boolean that indicates if the attribute is a member of the partial attribute set (i.e., the global catalog).
isSingleValued	Boolean that indicates whether the attribute is single-valued or multivalued.
linkID	If populated, will contain an integer that represents a link (either forward or backward) to another attribute.
LDAPDisplayName	Name used when referencing the attribute in searches or when populating it on objects. Note that this value may not be the same as cn.
oMSyntax	An integer representing the OSI Abstract Data Manipulation (OM) type of the attribute. This is used in conjunction with attributeSyntax to determine a unique syntax for the attribute.
schemaIDGUID	GUID of the attribute.
searchFlags	Integer representing special properties related to searching with the attribute. This includes how the attribute is indexed and if it is used in ANR searches.
systemFlags	Integer representing additional properties of the attribute.

10.1. Registering the Active Directory Schema MMC Snap-in

Problem

You want to use the Active Directory Schema MMC snap-in for the first time on an administrative computer.

Solution

Before you can use the Active Directory Schema MMC snap-in, you have to register the *.dll* associated with it. This can be done with the *regsvr32* utility using the following command:

```
> regsvr32 schmmgmt.dll
```

If the command is successful, you'll see the following message:

```
DllRegisterServer in schmmgmt.dll succeeded.
```

Discussion

Most of the Active Directory MMC snap-ins do not require that you manually register the associated *.dll*. Microsoft requires this with the Active Directory Schema snap-in, however, due to the sensitive nature of modifying the schema. This doesn't actually do much to prevent users from using it, but at least it isn't available by default. And regardless, only members of the *Schema Admins* group have permission to modify the schema anyway, so making this snap-in available should not pose any risk.

The *schmmgmt.dll* file is installed as part of the AD DS Tools feature (specifically, the AD DS Snap-Ins and Command-Line Tools subfeature), or else it is installed by default on domain controllers when they are first promoted. If you want to use the Schema snap-in on a domain member server or workstation machine and you have not installed the feature, you'll need to specify the full path to *schmmgmt.dll* when using *regsvr32*.

10.2. Generating an OID to Use for a New Class or Attribute

Problem

You want to generate an OID to use with a new class or attribute that you intend to add to the schema.

Solution

To implement schema extensions for production use, you should use an OID from your company or organization's OID branch. To determine whether your company already has an assigned OID, see these sites:

- *www.iana.org/assignments/enterprise-numbers*
- *www.alvestrand.no/objectid/* (*http://www.alvestrand.no/objectid/*)

If your organization does not have an assigned OID, go to your country's national registry to request one.

Once you have a base OID, you can create branches from that OID however you want. For example, if you had a base OID of 1.2.3.4, you could start new class OIDs under 1.2.3.4.1 and new attributes under 1.2.3.4.2. In that case, the first class OID you would create would be 1.2.3.4.1.1, and the first attribute OID would be 1.2.3.4.2.1.

Discussion

An OID is nothing more than a string of numbers separated by periods (.). OIDs were initially defined by the ITU-T in X.208 and have been used to uniquely identify a variety of things, including SNMP MIB objects and LDAP schema classes and attributes. OIDs are hierarchical, and the national registries are responsible for managing and assigning OID branches.

10.3. Extending the Schema

Problem

You want to extend the schema to support new classes and attributes in Active Directory.

Solution

Extending the schema is a straightforward process that consists of adding new classes or attributes, or modifying existing ones in the schema. While extending the schema is not hard, due to the sensitive nature of the schema you should implement a schema extension process that thoroughly tests any extensions before you put them in your production forest. Here is a suggested summary of what your schema extension process should entail:

1. Meet with staff and determine whether there is a business justification for integrating the application with Active Directory. Determine whether there are any existing attributes that would fulfill the desired requirements instead.
2. Examine the extensions and determine what impact, if any, they will have on your Active Directory environment (e.g., adding an attribute to the global catalog).
3. Update your test environment with the extensions and then test your core applications and services.
4. Document the extensions.
5. Extend the schema in your production Active Directory.

For more information on defining a schema extension process, see *Active Directory*, Fifth Edition, by Brian Desmond et al. (O'Reilly).

Discussion

One thing to be cautious of when developing a schema extension process is not to make it an overly bureaucratic process that can require months to complete. At the same time, you want to ensure that any schema changes that you make are well thought out, tested, and documented thoroughly to avoid encountering issues later. While some organizations may want to strictly limit schema extensions, there is nothing inherently bad about properly extending the schema.

See Also

Recipe 10.6 for adding a new attribute; Recipe 10.8 for adding a new class; "Extending the schema" (*http://bit.ly/16bLo5w*)

10.4. Preparing the Schema for an Active Directory Upgrade

Problem

You want to prepare the Active Directory schema for an Active Directory upgrade.

Solution

From a graphical user interface

To prepare your Active Directory forest for a Windows upgrade, do the following:

1. Log on to a server or a domain controller in the AD forest. Copy the installation media of the new Windows operating system to the domain controller.

2. Open an elevated command prompt and navigate to the installation media. For example, if the installation media is at the root of the *D:* volume, you would navigate to *D:\support\adprep*.

3. Run the command `adprep /forestprep`. Read the warning message that appears and press C, followed by Enter.

To determine whether `adprep /forestprep` has completed, see Recipe 2.12.

To extend an Active Directory domain to prepare for an upgrade, follow these steps:

1. Log on to a server or domain controller in the domain. Copy the installation media of the new Windows operating system to the domain controller.

2. Open an elevated command prompt and navigate to the installation media. For example, if the installation media is at the root of the *D:* volume, you would navigate to *D:\support\adprep*.

3. Run the command `adprep /domainprep`. Read the warning message that appears and press C, followed by Enter.

Discussion

Major upgrades to the Windows operating system on domain controllers will usually require that the Active Directory schema be extended with new classes and attributes.

To automate this process, Active Directory includes the *adprep* utility to perform these modifications. *adprep* needs to be run once for the entire forest using the /forest prep switch and once for each domain that will be upgraded using the /domainprep switch. In the case of a Windows Server 2012 upgrade, you can view the schema extensions that will be performed by this utility by looking at the *.ldf* files in the *support* *adprep* directory in the installation media. These files contain LDIF entries for adding and modifying new and existing classes and attributes. Since the /forestprep process extends and modifies the schema, you must perform this task using credentials that belong to both the *Schema Admins* and *Enterprise Admins* groups.

After /forestprep has completed, /domainprep will create new containers and objects within each Domain NC, as well as modify ACLs on some objects and the behavior of the *Everyone* security principal. Before you can run /domainprep, you need to ensure that the updates from /forestprep have replicated to all domain controllers in the forest using the method described in this recipe. /domainprep needs to have connectivity to the *Infrastructure Master* of the domain, using *Domain Admin* credentials.

One major change that Windows Server 2012 introduced is the integration of *adprep* into the domain controller promotion process. For some environments, this is seen as a nifty new feature that saves time and hassle. For large enterprise environments, this is sometimes seen as a dangerous thing and a potential violation of change control. Some enterprise environments are opting to prepare the forest and domain ahead of time, prior to the promotion of the first Windows Server 2012 server.

See Also

Recipe 3.9 for more on verifying the promotion of a domain controller

10.5. Documenting Schema Extensions

Problem

You want to document your schema extensions.

Solution

There are several different ways you can document schema extensions. If you require LDIF files of the schema extensions before you extend the schema, you can use the files themselves as a simple self-documenting system. You can put comments in LDIF files by putting # at the beginning of a line, or else use the AD Schema Analyzer available with Active Directory Lightweight Directory Service (AD LDS). We recommend a combination of these options, and recommend that any company that needs to extend its schema include LDIF files, regardless of whether you use that method to actually extend the schema.

The AD Schema Analyzer is a useful tool that can document your existing schema, as well as create a file to help you modify the schema. To use the Schema Analyzer to create an LDIF file, do the following:

1. Open a command prompt and navigate to the *Windows\ADAM* directory. Run the program *adschemaanalyzer.exe* from the command prompt.

2. Click File→Load target schema. To load the current Active Directory schema, enter your username, password, and domain name, and then click OK.

3. Place a checkmark next to each class, attribute, and property set that you wish to export.

4. Click File→Create LDIF file. Enter a path and name of the file to export, and click Save.

Discussion

There are no hard-and-fast rules for documenting schema extensions. Documenting schema extensions in some fashion, even a rudimentary one, should be a requirement of any schema extension process you adopt. If you have the resources and time, you can even develop a much more elaborate documentation system.

See Also

RFC 2849 (The LDAP Data Interchange Format (LDIF)—Technical Specification); "Windows Server 2012: Changes to Adprep.exe" (*http://bit.ly/12baI6g*)

10.6. Adding a New Attribute

Problem

You want to add a new attribute to the schema.

Solution

Using a graphical user interface

1. Open the Active Directory Schema snap-in.

2. In the left pane, expand Active Directory Schema, and then right-click on the Attributes folder and select Create Attribute.

3. Click the Continue button to confirm that you want to extend the schema.

4. Enter the information for the new attribute.

5. Click OK.

Using a command-line interface

You can create new attributes by using *ldifde* and an LDIF file that contains the properties to be set on the attribute. The following code shows a sample LDIF file called *cre ate_attr.ldf* that creates an attribute called adatum-LanguagesSpoken:

```
dn: cn=adatum-LanguagesSpoken,cn=schema,cn=configuration,<ForestRootDN>
changetype: add
objectclass: attributeSchema
lDAPDisplayName: adatumLanguagesSpoken
attributeId: 1.3.6.1.4.1.999.1.1.28.3
oMSyntax: 20
attributeSyntax: 2.5.5.4
isSingleValued: FALSE
searchFlags: 1
description: "Languages a user speaks"
```

Then run the following command:

```
> ldifde -v -i -f create_attr.ldf
```

You can also use AdMod to add a schema attribute as follows:

```
> admod -schema -rb cn=adatumLanguagesSpoken
  objectClass::attributeSchema
      lDAPDisplayName::adatumLanguagesSpoken
      attributeId::1.3.6.1.4.1.999.1.1.28.3
      omSyntax::20
      attributeSyntax::2.5.5.4
      isSingleValued::FALSE
      searchFlags::1
      description::"Languages a user speaks"
      -add
```

Using PowerShell

To create a schema attribute by using PowerShell, use the following syntax:

```
New-ADObject -Name "Custom60" -Type "attributeSchema" -OtherAttributes↵
 @{distinguishedName="cn=Custom60,cn=Schema,cn=Configuration,<ForestRootDN>"↵
;LDAPDisplayName="Custom60";attributeId="1.3.6.1.4.1.999.1.1.28.3";oMSyntax="20"↵
;attributeSyntax="2.5.5.4";isSingleValued=$false↵
;Description="Custom class #60";searchFlags="1"}
```

Discussion

The GUI solution requires that the *.dll* file for the Active Directory Schema snap-in has been registered. See Recipe 10.1 for more information.

To create an attribute, you need to add an `attributeSchema` object to the Schema container. Typically, when you extend the schema you perform several additions or modifications at once. The order of your extensions is very important. You can't create a class, assign an attribute, and then create the attribute; you obviously need to create the attribute before it can be assigned to the class. Even if you create the attribute before you assign it to a class, you must reload the schema before doing the class assignment. Reloading the schema is described in more detail in Recipe 10.23.

Most of the attributes that can be set on `attributeSchema` objects are pretty straightforward, but a couple of them require a little explanation. The `attributeSyntax` and `oMSyntax` attributes together define the syntax, or the type of data that can be contained in the attribute. Table 10-3 shows the possible combinations of these two attributes and the resultant syntax.

Table 10-3. attributeSyntax and oMSyntax combinations

Name	attributeSyntax	oMSyntax	Description
AccessPointDN	2.5.5.14	127	Type of distinguished name taken from X.500.
Boolean	2.5.5.8	1	TRUE or FALSE value.
CaseExactString	2.5.5.3	27	Case-sensitive string.
CaseIgnoreString	2.5.5.4	20	Case-insensitive string.
DirectoryString	2.5.5.12	64	Case-insensitive Unicode string.
DN	2.5.5.1	127	String representing a distinguished name.
DNWithBinary	2.5.5.7	127	Octet string that has the following format: B:*CharCount*:*BinaryValue*:*ObjectDN*, where *CharCount* is the number of hexadecimal digits in *BinaryValue*, *BinaryValue* is the hexadecimal representation of the binary value, and *ObjectDN* is a distinguished name.
DNWithString	2.5.5.14	127	Octet string that contains a string value and a DN. A value with this syntax has the following format: S:*CharCount*:*StringValue*:*ObjectDN*, where *CharCount* is the number of characters in the *StringValue* string and *ObjectDN* is a distinguished name of an object in Active Directory.
Enumeration	2.5.5.9	10	Defined in X.500 and treated as an integer.
GeneralizedTime	2.5.5.11	24	Time-string format defined by ASN.1 standards. See ISO 8601 and X.680.
IA5String	2.5.5.5	22	Case-sensitive string containing characters from the IA5 character set.
Integer	2.5.5.9	2	32-bit integer.
Integer8	2.5.5.16	65	64-bit integer, also known as a large integer.
NTSecurityDescriptor	2.5.5.15	66	Octet string that contains a security descriptor.
NumericString	2.5.5.6	18	String that contains digits.

Name	attributeSyntax	oMSyntax	Description
OctetString	2.5.5.10	4	Array of bytes used to store binary data.
OID	2.5.5.2	6	String that contains digits (0-9) and decimal points (.).
ORName	2.5.5.7	127	Taken from X.400; used for X.400 to RFC 822 map ping.
PresentationAddress	2.5.5.13	127	String that contains OSI presentation addresses.
PrintableString	2.5.5.5	19	Case-sensitive string that contains characters from the printable character set.
ReplicaLink	2.5.5.10	127	Used by Active Directory internally.
Sid	2.5.5.17	4	Octet string that contains a security identifier (SID).
UTCTime	2.5.5.11	23	Time-string format defined by ASN.1 standards.

The `searchFlags` attribute is a bit flag that defines special properties related to searching with the attribute. Table 10-4 contains the values that can be set for this attribute. The values are cumulative, so to index an attribute and include it in ANR searches, you would set a value of 5 (1 + 4).

Table 10-4. searchFlags bit values

Value	Description
1	Index over attribute. See Recipe 10.10 for more information.
2	Index over container and attribute.
4	Include as part of Ambiguous Name Resolution (ANR). Should be used in addition to 1. See Recipe 10.12 for more information.
8	Preserve attribute in tombstone objects. This will ensure that the value of a particular attribute will be retained when the object is tombstoned, so that it will be repopulated automatically if you need to reanimate the object.
16	Copy attribute when duplicating an object. See Recipe 10.11 for more information.
32	Create a tuple index for this attribute. This improves the response time for searches that put a wildcard in front of the search string for the attribute (e.g., `givenname=*on`).
64	Create an index on which to assist with VLV performance.
128	Set the confidential bit on this attribute, which requires normal users to be assigned additional permissions to be able to read its contents.
256	Disable security auditing for the attribute. Applicable to Windows Server 2008 and later.
512	Attribute should be added to the Read-Only Filtered Attribute Set (RO-FAS), preventing the attribute from being replicated to any RODCs in the environment.

See Also

Recipe 4.15 for setting a bit flag; Recipe 10.8 for adding a new class; Recipe 10.23 for reloading the schema

10.7. Viewing an Attribute

Problem

You want to view the properties of an attribute.

Solution

Using a graphical user interface

1. Open the Active Directory Schema snap-in.
2. In the left pane, expand Active Directory Schema and then click on the Attributes folder.
3. In the right pane, double-click the attribute you want to view.
4. Click on each tab to view the available properties.

Using a command-line interface

In the following command, replace *<AttrCommonName>* with the common name (not the LDAP display name) of the attribute you want to view:

```
> dsquery * cn=schema,cn=configuration,<ForestRootDN> -scope onelevel -attr *↵
  -filter "(&(objectcategory=attributeSchema)(cn=<AttrCommonName>))"
```

For example, to view the properties of the Surname attribute in the *adatum.com* domain, you would run the following command:

```
> dsquery * cn=schema,cn=configuration,dc=adatum,dc=com -scope onelevel -attr *↵
  -filter "(&(objectcategory=attributeSchema)(cn=surname))"
```

You can also use AdFind to view the properties of an attribute, as follows:

```
> adfind -schema -f (ldapdisplayname=<AttributeName>)
```

You can also use shortcut syntax for this command, as follows:

```
> adfind -sc s:<AttributeName>
```

Using PowerShell

You can view the properties of a schema attribute using PowerShell, as follows:

```
Get-ADObject -Identity "<ObjectDN>" -Properties * | FL
```

For example, to view the properties of the Surname attribute, you would run the following PowerShell command:

```
Get-ADObject -Identity "cn=surname,cn=schema,cn=configuration,dc=adatum,dc=com"↵
  -Properties * | FL
```

Discussion

The GUI solution requires that the *.dll* file for the Active Directory Schema snap-in has been registered. See Recipe 10.1 for more information.

In the CLI solutions, we mention that you need to specify the common name (or cn) of the attribute you want to view. The common name is a source of confusion for many people. For example, the surname attribute has the following distinguished name in the *adatum.com* forest:

```
cn=surname,cn=schema,cn=configuration,dc=adatum,dc=com
```

The problem is that most applications refer to attributes by their LDAP display name as defined in the lDAPDisplayName attribute for the attributeSchema object, which is typically different from the cn attribute. As an example, the surname attribute uses surname for its common name (cn), but sn for its LDAP display name (lDAPDisplay Name).

In the CLI solution, to use the LDAP display name instead of cn when using DSQuery, simply change (cn=*<AttrCommonName>*) to (lDAPDisplayName= *<AttrLDAPName>*).

AdFind includes the shortcut adfind -sc s:<name>, which will check both the LDAP Display Name and the cn automatically. Additionally, this shortcut will decode various properties when it produces its output.

One attribute of note that is defined on attributeSchema objects is the systemFlags bit flag, which is used to define a few miscellaneous properties about an attribute. Table 10-5 contains the bits associated with systemFlags. The values are cumulative, so a value of 17 (1 + 16) would indicate that the attribute is part of the base Active Directory installation and is not replicated.

Table 10-5. systemFlags bit values

Value	Description
1	Not replicated among domain controllers.
4	Dynamically constructed by Active Directory.
16	Part of the base Active Directory installation. This value cannot be set.

See Also

Recipe 4.2 for viewing the attributes of an object; Recipe 4.12 for searching with a bitwise filter

10.8. Adding a New Class

Problem

You want to add a new class to the schema.

Solution

Using a graphical user interface

1. Open the Active Directory Schema snap-in.
2. In the left pane, expand Active Directory Schema and then right-click on the Classes folder and select "Create Class".
3. Click the Continue button to confirm that you want to extend the schema.
4. Enter the information for the new class and click Next.
5. Enter any mandatory and optional attributes and click Finish.

Using a command-line interface

You can create new classes by using *ldifde* and an LDIF file that contains the properties to be set on the class. The following code shows a sample LDIF file called *create_class.ldf* that creates a class called adatum-SalesUser:

```
dn: cn=adatum-SalesUser,cn=schema,cn=configuration,<ForestRootDN>
changetype: add
objectclass: classSchema
lDAPDisplayName: adatum-SalesUser
governsId: 1.3.6.1.4.1.999.1.1.28.4
objectClassCategory: 3
subClassOf: top
description: Auxiliary class for Sales user attributes
adminDescription: Auxiliary class for Sales user
attributes
mayContain: adatum-Building
mayContain: adatum-Theatre
```

Then run the following command:

```
> ldifde -v -i -f create_class.ldf
```

You can also add a new class using AdMod, as follows:

```
> admod -schema -rb cn=adatum-SalesUser↵
objectclass::classSchema lDAPDisplayName::adatum-SalesUser↵
governsId::1.3.6.1.4.1.999.1.1.28.4 objectClassCategory::3↵
subClassOf::top↵
description::"Auxiliary class for Sales user"↵
```

```
adminDescription::"Auxiliary class for Sales user"↵
mayContain::adatum-Building;adatum-Theatre↵
-add
```

Using PowerShell

To create a schema class by using PowerShell, use the following syntax:

```
New-ADObject -Name "adatum-SalesUser " -Description "Custom Class"↵
 -Type "classSchema" -OtherAttributes↵
 @{distinguishedname="cn=Custom24,cn=Schema,cn=Configuration,<ForestRootDN>"↵
 ;LDAPDisplayName="adatum-SalesUser";governsId="1.3.6.1.4.1.999.1.1.28.4"↵
 ;objectCategory="3";subClassOf="top"↵
 ;adminDescription="Auxilliary class for Sales user attributes"}
```

Discussion

To create a new class, you need to create a classSchema object in the Schema container. The important attributes to set include:

governsId
: Defines the OID for the class

objectClassCategory
: Defines the class type

subClassOf
: Defines the parent class

mayContain *and* mustContain
: Define any optional and mandatory attributes for instantiated objects of the class

The LDAPDisplayName also needs to be set and should be equal to the common name (cn) as a general rule. Even though many of the default classes do not use the same name for the common name and LDAP display name, using the same name is highly recommended to avoid confusion when referencing the class. Another good practice is to set the schemaIDGUID of the class.

See Also

See Recipe 10.0 for attributes of classSchema objects; Recipe 10.2 for generating an OID; Recipe 10.16 for more on object class type; Recipe 10.18 for setting the default security for a class; Recipe 10.23 for reloading the schema cache

10.9. Viewing a Class

Problem

You want to view the attributes of a class.

Solution

Using a graphical user interface

1. Open the Active Directory Schema snap-in.

2. In the left pane, expand Active Directory Schema and then click on the Classes folder.

3. In the right pane, double-click the class you want to view.

4. Click on each tab to view the available properties.

Using a command-line interface

In the following command, replace *<ClassCommonName>* with the common name (not LDAP display name) of the class you want to view:

```
> dsquery * cn=<ClassCommonName>,cn=schema,cn=configuration,<ForestRootDN>↵
  -scope base -attr *
```

You can also use AdFind to view the properties of a class, as follows:

```
> adfind -schema -rb cn=<ClassCommonName>
```

In addition, you can use shortcut syntax for this command, as follows:

```
> adfind -sc s:<ClassCommonName or ClassLDAPDisplayName>
```

Using PowerShell

```
Get-ADObject -Identity "cn=<ClassName>,cn=schema,cn=configuration,↵
<ForestRootDN>" -Properties * | FL
```

Discussion

The GUI solution requires that the *.dll* file for the Active Directory Schema snap-in has been registered. See Recipe 10.1 for more information.

See Table 10-1, at the beginning of this chapter, for a list of the important classSche ma attributes and their descriptions.

See Also

Recipe 4.2 for viewing the attributes of an object

10.10. Indexing an Attribute

Problem

You want to index an attribute so that searches using that attribute are faster.

Solution

Using a graphical user interface

1. Open the Active Directory Schema snap-in.
2. In the left pane, expand Active Directory Schema and then click on the Attributes folder.
3. In the right pane, double-click the attribute you want to index.
4. Check the box beside "Index this attribute."
5. Click OK.

Using a command-line interface

You can index an attribute by using the *ldifde* utility and an LDIF file that contains the following:

```
dn: cn=<AttrCommonName>,cn=schema,cn=configuration,<ForestRootDN>
changetype: modify
replace: searchFlags
searchFlags: 1
-
```

If the LDIF file were named *index_attribute.ldf*, you would run the following command:

```
> ldifde -v -i -f index_attribute.ldf
```

You can also enable the appropriate searchFlags value using admod, as follows:

```
> admod -schema -rb cn=<AttrCommonName> searchFlags::1
```

 The CLI solution and the PowerShell solution assume that search Flags wasn't previously set; if a value is present, it just blindly overwrites it. See Recipe 4.15 for a better solution that will enable the bit value you want without overwriting any previous settings.

Using PowerShell

To set the `searchFlags` bit value by using PowerShell, use the following syntax:

```
Set-ADObject "<AttributeDN>" -Replace @{"searchFlags"="1"}
```

Discussion

To index an attribute, you need to set bit 0 (0001) in the `searchFlags` attribute for the `attributeSchema` object.

`searchFlags` is a bit-flag attribute that is used to set various properties related to searching with the attribute. Table 10-5, earlier in this chapter, contains the various bit flags that can be set with `searchFlags`. When setting `searchFlags`, you may often need to set a couple of bits together. For example, all Ambiguous Name Resolution (ANR) attributes must also be indexed, which means `searchFlags` should be set to 5 (1 + 4).

You can find the attributes that are indexed in the schema by using the following search criteria:

Base
```
cn=Schema,cn=Configuration,<ForestRootDN>
```

Filter
```
(&(objectcategory=attributeSchema)(searchFlags:
1.2.840.113556.1.4.803:=1))
```

Scope
```
onelevel
```

Alternatively, to find attributes that aren't indexed, change the previous search filter to the following:

```
(&(objectcategory=attributeSchema)(!(searchFlags:1.2.840.113556.1.4.803:=1)))
```

 Since Windows Server 2008, the `objectClass` attribute is now indexed by default. This allows you to perform simpler searches by querying directly against `objectClass`, rather than using the more complex query of `"(&(objectCategory=ABC)(objectClass=XYZ))"`. Note that some searches require a more complex query as the results may differ if only relying on the `objectClass` attribute.

You can also find indexed attributes using AdFind, as follows:

```
adfind -sc indexed
```

See Also

Recipe 4.15 for modifying a bit-flag attribute; Recipe 10.6 for adding a new attribute

10.11. Modifying the Attributes That Are Copied When Duplicating a User

Problem

You want to add an attribute to the list of attributes that are copied when duplicating a user with the ADUC snap-in.

Solution

Using a graphical user interface

1. Open the Active Directory Schema snap-in.
2. In the left pane, expand Active Directory Schema and then click on the Attributes folder.
3. In the right pane, double-click the attribute you want to edit.
4. Check the box beside "Attribute is copied when duplicating a user."
5. Click OK.

Using a command-line interface

You can cause an attribute to get copied when duplicating a user by using the *ldifde* utility and an LDIF file that contains the following:

```
dn: cn=adatum-LanguagesSpoken,cn=schema,cn=configuration,<ForestRootDN>
changetype: modify
replace: searchFlags
searchFlags: 16
-
```

If the LDIF file were named *add_dup_user_attr.ldf*, you would run the following command:

```
> ldifde -v -i -f add_dup_user_attr.ldf
```

You can also modify the searchFlags attribute using AdMod, as follows:

```
> admod -b <AttributeDN> searchFlags::16
```

The CLI solution and the PowerShell solution assume that search Flags wasn't previously set; if a value is present, it just blindly overwrites it. See Recipe 4.15 for a better solution that will enable the bit you want without overwriting any previous settings.

Using PowerShell

To set the searchFlags bit value by using PowerShell, use the following syntax:

```
Set-ADObject "<AttributeDN>" -Replace @{"searchFlags"="16"}
```

Discussion

The GUI solution requires that the *.dll* file for the Active Directory Schema snap-in has been registered. See Recipe 10.1 for more information.

The Active Directory Users and Computers snap-in queries the schema for the list of attributes that should be copied whenever you right-click on a user and select Copy. This flag is purely informational and does not impose any restrictions.

To find out which attributes are copied when duplicating a user, use the following search criteria:

Base
> cn=Schema,cn=Configuration,<ForestRootDN>

Filter
> (&(objectcategory=attributeSchema)(searchFlags:
> 1.2.840.113556.1.4.803:=16))

Scope
> onelevel

Alternatively, to find attributes that aren't copied, change the previous search filter to the following:

```
(&(objectcategory=attributeSchema)(!(searchFlags:1.2.840.113556.1.4.803:=16)))
```

You can also find a list of these attributes using AdFind, as follows:

```
adfind -sc copy
```

See Also

Recipe 4.15 for modifying a bit-flag attribute; Recipe 10.6 for adding a new attribute

10.12. Modifying the Attributes Included with ANR

Problem

You want to modify the attributes that are included as part of ANR.

Solution

Using a graphical user interface

1. To proceed, you must have first indexed the attribute.
2. Open the Active Directory Schema snap-in.
3. In the left pane, click on the Attributes folder.
4. In the right pane, double-click the attribute you want to edit.
5. Check the box beside Ambiguous Name Resolution (ANR).
6. Click OK.

Using a command-line interface

You can include an attribute as part of ANR by using the *ldifde* utility and an LDIF file that contains the following:

```
dn: cn=adatum-LanguagesSpoken,cn=schema,cn=configuration,<ForestRootDN>
changetype: modify
replace: searchFlags
searchFlags: 5
-
```

If the LDIF file were named *add_anr_attr.ldf*, you'd run the following command:

```
> ldifde -v -i -f add_anr_attr.ldf
```

You can also modify the searchFlags attribute using AdMod, as follows:

```
> admod -b <AttributeDN> searchFlags::5
```

 The CLI solution and the PowerShell solution assume that search Flags wasn't previously set; if a value is present, it just blindly overwrites it. Check out Recipe 4.15 for a better solution that will enable the bit you want without overwriting any previous settings.

Using PowerShell

To set the ANR bit value by using PowerShell, use the following syntax:

```
Set-ADObject "<AttributeDN>" -Replace @{"searchFlags"="5"}
```

Discussion

ANR is an efficient search algorithm that allows for a complex search filter to be written using a single comparison. For example, a search for (anr=Jim Smith) would translate into the following query:

- An OR filter with every attribute in the ANR set against Jim Smith*
- A filter for givenName = Jim* and sn = Smith*
- A filter for givenName = Smith* and sn = Jim*

These filters are ORed together and then processed by Active Directory. Since all ANR attributes are also indexed, the query return should come back quickly.

Here is a list of the default attributes that are included as part of ANR searches. The LDAP display name of the attribute is shown first, with the common name in parentheses:

- displayName (Display-Name)
- givenName (Given-Name)
- legacyExchangeDN (Legacy-Exchange-DN)
- msDS-AdditionalSamAccountName (ms-DS-Additional-Sam-Account-Name)
- physicalDeliveryOfficeName (Physical-Delivery-Office-Name)
- name (RDN)
- sAMAccountName (SAM-Account-Name)
- sn (Surname)

One requirement of any new ANR attribute is that the attribute must also be indexed. ANR searches are intended to be very fast, so if a nonindexed attribute were added to the set, it could dramatically impact the performance of the searches. Therefore, Active Directory requires that each added attribute be indexed. The PowerShell solution can be run for a nonindexed attribute, but the result will be that the attribute will be set to index and will be set for ANR. The Active Directory Schema snap-in will show the ANR option as grayed out unless an attribute is already set to be indexed. Once an attribute is set to be indexed, the Active Directory Schema snap-in will allow the ANR option to be enabled.

You can use adfind with the -stats+only switch to verify what the ANR expansion actually looks like. You can find out which attributes are included in the ANR set by using the following search criteria:

Base

```
cn=Schema,cn=Configuration,<ForestRootDN>
```

Filter

```
(&(objectcategory=attributeSchema)(searchFlags:
1.2.840.113556.1.4.803:=4))
```

Scope

```
onelevel
```

You can also find attributes that are included in ANR using AdFind, as follows:

```
adfind -sc anr
```

Alternatively, to find attributes that aren't included in ANR, change the previous search filter to the following:

```
(&(objectcategory=attributeSchema)(!(searchFlags:1.2.840.113556.1.4.803:=4)))
```

See Also

Recipe 4.15 for modifying a bit-flag attribute; Recipe 10.6 for adding a new attribute; "Ambiguous Name Resolution for LDAP in Windows 2000" (*http://support.micro soft.com/kb/243299*)

10.13. Modifying the Set of Attributes Stored on a Global Catalog

Problem

You want to add or remove an attribute in the global catalog.

Solution

Using a graphical user interface

1. Open the Active Directory Schema snap-in.

2. In the left pane, expand Active Directory Schema and then click on the Attributes folder.

3. In the right pane, double-click the attribute you want to edit.

4. Check the box beside "Replicate this attribute to the Global Catalog" to add the attribute to the global catalog, or uncheck to remove the attribute from the global catalog.

5. Click OK.

Using a command-line interface

You can add an attribute to the global catalog by using the *ldifde* utility and an LDIF file that contains the following:

```
dn: cn=<AttrCommonName>,cn=schema,cn=configuration,<ForestRootDN>
changetype: modify
replace:
isMemberOfPartialAttributeSet
isMemberOfPartialAttributeSet: TRUE
-
```

If the LDIF file were named *add_gc_attr.ldf*, you would run the following command:

```
> ldifde -v -i -f add_gc_attr.ldf
```

You can also modify this property using AdMod, as follows:

```
> admod -schema -rb cn=<AttrCommonName> isMemberOfPartialAttributeSet::TRUE
```

Using PowerShell

To add an attribute to the Partial Attribute Set by using PowerShell, use the following syntax:

```
Set-ADObject "<AttributeDN>" -Replace @{"isMemberOfPartialAttributeSet"=$True}
```

Discussion

The GUI solution requires that the *.dll* file for the Active Directory Schema snap-in has been registered. See Recipe 10.1 for more information.

Each domain controller in a forest replicates a copy of the Domain naming context for its own domain, as well as copies of the forest-wide Configuration and Schema partitions. However, domain controllers do not replicate Domain naming contexts for other domains in the forest. When enabled as a global catalog server, a domain controller will make partial, read-only replicas of all the objects in other domains in the forest.

Searching against the global catalog is useful when you need to perform a single search across several naming contexts at once. The global catalog stores only a subset of each object's attributes, which is why it is considered a partial replica. Attributes stored in the global catalog are considered part of the PAS. Any attributes that you add to the PAS should be ones you'd want to use as part of global catalog searches that are not present already.

You can add to the attributes that are stored in the global catalog by setting the isMemberOfPartialAttributeSet attribute of an attributeSchema object to TRUE. Likewise, to remove an attribute from the PAS, set isMemberOfPartialAttributeSet to FALSE for the target attribute.

You can find which attributes are included in the global catalog by using a query with the following criteria:

Base
> `cn=Schema,cn=Configuration,<ForestRootDN>`

Filter
> `(&(objectcategory=attributeSchema)(isMemberOfPartialAttribute`
> `Set=TRUE))`

Scope
> `onelevel`

You can also find attributes that are included in the PAS using AdFind, as follows:

> `adfind -sc pas`

Alternatively, to find attributes that aren't in the global catalog, you only need to change part of the previous filter to the following:

> `(isMemberOfPartialAttributeSet=FALSE)`

See Also

"How to Modify Attributes That Replicate to the Global Catalog" (*http://support.micro soft.com/kb/248717*)

10.14. Finding Nonreplicated and Constructed Attributes

Problem

You want to find the attributes that are not replicated or that are constructed by Active Directory.

Solution

Using a graphical user interface

1. Open LDP.
2. From the menu, select Connection→Connect.
3. For Server, enter the name or IP address of a domain controller or domain that contains the object.
4. For Port, enter 389.
5. Click OK.
6. From the menu, select Connection→Bind.

---

7. Accept the default and bind as the currently logged on user or select the option to bind with credentials and then enter the credentials.

8. Click OK.

9. From the menu, select Browse→Search.

10. For Base DN, enter the `Schema` container DN (e.g., `cn=schema,cn=configuration,dc=adatum,dc=com`).

11. For Scope, select One Level.

12. To find nonreplicated attributes, use the following for Attributes:

    ```
    (&(objectcategory=attributeSchema)(systemFlags:1.2.840.113556.1.4.803:=1))
    ```

13. To find constructed attributes, use the following for Attributes:

    ```
    (&(objectcategory=attributeSchema)(systemFlags:1.2.840.113556.1.4.803:=4))
    ```

14. Click Run to display the results.

Using a command-line interface

To find the nonreplicated attributes using DSQuery, use the following command:

```
> dsquery * cn=schema,cn=configuration,<ForestRootDN> -attr "cn" -filter↵
"(&(objectcategory=attributeSchema)(systemFlags:1.2.840.113556.1.4.803:=1))"↵
 -limit 0
```

To find the nonreplicated attributes using AdFind, use the following:

```
> adfind -sc norepl
```

To find the constructed attributes using DSQuery, use the following command:

```
> dsquery * cn=schema,cn=configuration,<ForestRootDN> -attr "cn" -filter↵
"(&(objectcategory=attributeSchema)(systemFlags:1.2.840.113556.1.4.803:=4))"
```

To find the constructed attributes using AdFind, use the following:

```
> adfind -sc constructed
```

Using PowerShell

You can obtain information about nonreplicated attributes by using PowerShell, as follows:

```
Get-ADObject -SearchBase "cn=schema,cn=configuration,<ForestRootDN>"↵
 -LDAPFilter "(&(objectCategory=attributeSchema)↵
(systemFlags:1.2.840.113556.1.4.803:=1))" | FL
```

You can obtain information about constructed attributes by using PowerShell, as follows:

```
Get-ADObject -SearchBase "cn=schema,cn=configuration,<ForestRootDN>"↵
 -LDAPFilter "(&(objectCategory=attributeSchema)↵
(systemFlags:1.2.840.113556.1.4.803:=4))" | FL
```

Discussion

The systemFlags attribute of attributeSchema objects defines a few special attribute properties, including whether an attribute is not replicated between domain controllers and whether Active Directory constructs it dynamically.

Most attributes are replicated after they are updated on an object, but some never replicate between domain controllers. These attributes are considered nonreplicated. An example of a nonreplicated attribute you may be familiar with is the lastLogon attribute, which stores the last logon time for user and computer objects. Whenever a user or computer logs in to Active Directory, the authenticating domain controller updates the user or computer's lastLogon attribute, but the update does not get replicated out to other domain controllers.

Constructed attributes are automatically maintained by Active Directory and cannot be set manually. A good example of a constructed attribute is the msDS-Approx-Immed-Subordinates attribute. The attribute contains the approximate number of child objects within a container. Obviously this attribute wouldn't be of much value if you had to maintain it, so Active Directory does it automatically.

One of the downsides to constructed attributes is that you cannot search against them. For example, we cannot perform a search to find all containers that have more than 10 objects in them (i.e., msDS-Approx-Immed-Subordinates>10). This would return an operations error. Constructed attributes can be returned only as part of the attribute set for a query and cannot be used as part of the query itself.

To find the nonreplicated or constructed attributes, you have to use a bitwise LDAP filter against attributeSchema objects. A bit value of 1 indicates the attribute is nonreplicated, and a value of 4 indicates the attribute is constructed.

See Also

Recipe 4.12 for searching with a bitwise filter

10.15. Finding the Linked Attributes

Problem

You want to find attributes that are linked.

Solution

Using a graphical user interface

1. Open LDP.

2. From the menu, select Connection→Connect.

3. For Server, enter the name or IP address of a domain controller or domain that contains the object.

4. For Port, enter 389.

5. Click OK.

6. From the menu, select Connection→Bind.

7. Accept the default and bind as the currently logged on user or select the option to bind with credentials and then enter the credentials.

8. Click OK.

9. From the menu, select Browse→Search.

10. For Base DN, enter the Schema container DN (e.g., cn=schema, cn=configura tion,dc=adatum,dc=com).

11. For Scope, select One Level.

12. To find linked attributes, use the following for Filter:

        (&(objectcategory=attributeSchema)(linkid=*))

13. Click Run.

Using a command-line interface

You can return a list of linked attributes using either the built-in DSQuery tool or Ad-Mod. To use DSQuery, use the following syntax:

```
> dsquery * cn=schema,cn=configuration,<ForestRootDN> -scope onelevel -filter↵
"(&(objectcategory=attributeSchema)(linkid=*))" -attr cn linkID
```

To return a list of linked attributes with AdFind, use the following:

```
> adfind -sc linked
```

Using PowerShell

You can obtain linked attribute information by using PowerShell, as follows:

```
Get-ADObject -SearchBase "cn=schema,cn=configuration,<ForestRootDN>"↵
 -LDAPFilter "($(objectCategory=attributeSchema)(linkID=*))"
```

Discussion

The values of some attributes in Active Directory are linked. For example, if you set the `manager` attribute on one `user` object to be the DN of a second `user` object, the `reports` attribute on the second `user` object will automatically contain the first `user` object's DN. In this example, the `manager` attribute, or the attribute that gets set, is considered the *forward link*, and the `reports` attribute, or the attribute that automatically gets calculated, is called the *backlink*. Another common example is group membership. The `member` attribute of the `group` object represents the forward link, while the `memberOf` attribute of the corresponding object (e.g., *user*) represents the backlink.

You can identify which attributes are linked in the schema by searching for `attributeSchema` objects that have a `linkID` attribute that contains some value. The `linkID` value for a forward-link attribute will be an even, positive number. The corresponding backlink attribute will be the forward `linkID` plus 1. For example, the `manager` attribute `linkID` is 42, and the backlink `reports` attribute has a `linkID` of 43.

LDP, by default, only returns 100 entries in a search. To display more results, modify the page size in the LDP search options (click the Options menu and then click Search to modify the search options).

10.16. Finding the Structural, Auxiliary, Abstract, and 88 Classes

Problem

You want to list the structural, auxiliary, abstract, and 88 classes.

Solution

Using a graphical user interface

1. Open the Active Directory Schema snap-in.
2. In the left pane, expand Active Directory Schema and then click on the Classes folder.
3. In the right pane, view the list of the classes.

Using a command-line interface

You can return the list of Active Directory classes using either DSQuery or AdFind. DSQuery takes the following syntax:

```
> dsquery * cn=schema,cn=configuration,<ForestRootDN> -limit 0 -scope onelevel↵
-filter "(objectcategory=classSchema)" -attr lDAPDisplayName objectclasscategory
```

AdFind requires the following syntax:

```
> adfind -schema -f "(objectcategory=classSchema)" LDAPDisplayName↵
objectClassCategory
```

Using PowerShell

You can obtain information about different class types using PowerShell.

To obtain structural class type objects, use the following syntax:

```
Get-ADObject -SearchBase "cn=schema,cn=configuration,<ForestRootDN>"↵
-LDAPFilter "(&(objectcategory=classSchema)(objectClassCategory=1))"
```

To obtain auxiliary class type objects, use the following syntax:

```
Get-ADObject -SearchBase "cn=schema,cn=configuration,<ForestRootDN>"↵
-LDAPFilter "(&(objectcategory=classSchema)(objectClassCategory=3))"
```

To obtain abstract class type objects, use the following syntax:

```
Get-ADObject -SearchBase "cn=schema,cn=configuration,<ForestRootDN>"↵
-LDAPFilter "(&(objectcategory=classSchema)(objectClassCategory=2))"
```

To obtain 88 class type objects, use the following syntax:

```
Get-ADObject -SearchBase "cn=schema,cn=configuration,<ForestRootDN>"↵
-LDAPFilter "(&(objectcategory=classSchema)(objectClassCategory=0))"
```

Discussion

The GUI solution requires that the *.dll* file for the Active Directory Schema snap-in has been registered. See Recipe 10.1 for more information.

There are four supported class types in the Active Directory schema. The class type is defined by the objectClassCategory attribute on classSchema objects. Each class type is used for a different purpose relating to organizing and inheriting classes. Table 10-6 describes each type.

Table 10-6. Object class category values

Name	Value	Description
88	0	Legacy class type defined by the original X.500 standards. It should not be used for new classes.
Structural	1	Used for instantiating objects. Can consist of abstract, auxiliary, and other structural classes.
Abstract	2	Used to define a high-level grouping of attributes that can be used as part of other abstract or structural class definitions. Objects cannot be instantiated using an abstract class.
Auxiliary	3	Used as a collection of attributes that can be applied to other abstract, auxiliary, or structural classes.

10.17. Finding the Mandatory and Optional Attributes of a Class

Problem

You want to view the mandatory and optional attributes of a class.

Solution

Using a graphical user interface

1. Open the Active Directory Schema snap-in.
2. In the left pane, expand Active Directory Schema and then click on the Classes folder.
3. In the right pane, double-click the class you want to view.
4. Click on the Attributes tab and then view the mandatory and optional attributes.

Using a command-line interface

You can enumerate the mandatory and optional attributes of a class using either DSQuery or AdFind. DSQuery takes the following syntax:

```
> dsquery * cn=<ClassCommonName>,cn=schema,cn=configuration,<ForestRootDN> -l↵
-attr mayContain mustContain systemMayContain systemMustContain
```

To list these attributes using AdFind, use the following syntax:

```
> adfind -schema -rb cn=<ClassCommonName> mayContain mustContain↵
systemMayContain systemMustContain
```

Using PowerShell

To view the mandatory and optional attributes with PowerShell, use the following syntax:

```
Get-ADObject -Identity "cn=<ClassName>,cn=schema,cn=configuration,↵
<ForestRootDN>" -Properties * | foreach {(Write-Output "mayContain:"↵
$_.mayContain " "), (Write-Output "systemMayContain:" $_.systemMayContain " "),↵
(Write-Output "mustContain:" $_.mustContain " "),↵
(Write-Output "systemMustContain:" $_.systemMustContain " ")}
```

Discussion

The GUI solution requires that the *.dll* file for the Active Directory Schema snap-in has been registered. See Recipe 10.1 for more information.

The mayContain and systemMayContain attributes define the optional attributes for a class, while the mustContain and systemMustContain attributes contain the mandatory attributes. The systemMayContain and systemMustContain attributes are set by Active Directory itself and cannot be modified. You can only populate the mustContain attribute when a class is first created; you cannot add attributes to it after the fact. This is so that you are not inadvertently able to modify a class such that existing instances of that class become invalid.

It is also worth noting that each solution displays only the attributes defined directly on the class. It will not show any inherited attributes that are defined by inherited classes.

10.18. Modifying the Default Security of a Class

Problem

You want to modify the default security that is applied to objects instantiated from a particular structural class.

Solution

Using a graphical user interface

1. Open the Active Directory Schema snap-in.
2. In the left pane, expand Active Directory Schema and then click on the Classes folder.
3. In the right pane, double-click the class you want to modify the security for.
4. Click the Default Security tab.
5. Modify the security as necessary.
6. Click OK.

Using a command-line interface

```
> admod -schema -rb cn=<ClassShortName>↵
defaultSecurityDescriptor::"O:AOG:DAD:(A;;RPWPCCDCLCSWRCWDWOGA;;;S-1-0-0)"
```

Using PowerShell

```
Set-ADObject "cn=<ClassName>,cn=schema,cn=configuration,<ForestRootDN>" -Replace↵
@{"defaultSecurityDescriptor"="O:AOG:DAD:(A;;RPWPCCDCLCSWRCWDWOGA;;;S-1-0-0)"}
```

Discussion

Whenever a new object is created in Active Directory, if a security descriptor is not specified in the object creation, a default security descriptor (SD) is applied to it. Then any inherited security from its parent container is applied. The default security descriptor is stored in the `defaultSecurityDescriptor` attribute of the `classSchema` object. If you modify the default SD, every new object will get that SD, but it does not affect any existing objects.

Using a command-line interface

The `defaultSecurityDescriptor` attribute is stored in Active Directory using the Security Descriptor Definition Language (SDDL) format and will return data formatted similar to the following:

```
"O:AOG:DAD:(A;;RPWPCCDCLCSWRCWDWOGA;;;S-1-0-0)"
```

For more information on formulating SDDL strings, see the Platform Software Development Kit (SDK) or MSDN.

 When creating Active Directory classes, we recommend against setting a default security descriptor, as this feature can create issues when working with delegated permissions.

When modifying the `defaultSecurityDescriptor` attribute, it's important to remember that this is a single-valued attribute. This means that if you put any value into this attribute, it will overwrite all existing security descriptors that have been defined on the object. If you wish to append a new entry onto the default security descriptor, you will need to retrieve the existing value in the attribute, append the new entry that you wish to add, and then write the full string back to the attribute.

See Also

MS KB 265399 (How to Change Default Permissions for Objects That Are Created in the Active Directory); MSDN: Security Descriptor String Format

10.19. Managing the Confidentiality Bit

Problem

You want to manage the confidentiality of a schema attribute.

Solution

Using a command-line interface

```
admod -schema -rb cn=<AttrName> searchFlags::128
```

Using PowerShell

To set the searchFlags bit value by using PowerShell, use the following syntax:

```
Set-ADObject "cn=<AttrName>,cn=schema,cn=configuration,dc=<ForestRootDN>"↵
 -Replace @{"searchFlags"="128"}
```

Discussion

The confidentiality bit is a feature that allows you to restrict access to attributes that should not be accessible to all users. For example, you may have created an attribute to store users' Social Security number information. Even though this attribute may be populated for every user object in the directory, you likely will wish to restrict access to that specific attribute to only a subset of your personnel. The confidentiality bit is set in the searchFlags attribute by setting bit 7 (128) to a value of 1. Once you've done this, the Read permission on that attribute will not be sufficient to access the information stored in it; you'll need to grant the Control_Access permission to allow a user or group to view the contents of the attribute using LDP.

While the confidentiality bit is a great improvement in Active Directory security, it does have two significant limitations. First, there is no supported mechanism to set the confidentiality bit on any attributes that are a part of the base schema; you can, however, obtain a list of these attributes by searching for attributes that have bit 4 (16 in decimal) set to 1.

Second, certain default permissions included with Active Directory still will allow certain security principals to access the information stored in confidential attributes; these groups include the *Administrators*, *Account Operators*, and any user or group who has the Full Control permission on an object containing a confidential attribute.

See Also

Recipe 4.15 for more on modifying a bit-flag attribute; "How the Active Directory Schema Works" (*http://bit.ly/18psTd2*)

10.20. Adding an Attribute to the Read-Only Filtered Attribute Set (RO-FAS)

Problem

You want to add an attribute to the RO-FAS to prevent it from being replicated to any Read-Only Domain Controllers (RODCs) in your environment.

Solution

Using a command-line interface

```
admod -schema -rb cn=<AttrName> searchFlags::512
```

Using PowerShell

To set the searchFlags bit value by using PowerShell, use the following syntax:

```
Set-ADObject "cn=<AttrName>,cn=schema,cn=configuration,dc=<ForestRootDN>"↵
  -Replace @{"searchFlags"="512"}
```

Discussion

As discussed in Chapter 3, Read-Only Domain Controllers contain a read-only copy of all partitions that are held by a writable domain controller, with the exception of attributes that are configured as part of the RO-FAS, as well as user credentials, except for those that are specifically configured so that they are allowed to be cached to one or more RODCs.

Attributes that are configured as part of the RO-FAS are not replicated to any RODCs within an Active Directory forest. Because this data is not replicated to RODCs, the data will not be resident on an RODC if it is compromised or stolen. Administrators can add any attribute to the RO-FAS that is not a system-critical attribute; that is, any attribute that does not have a schemaFlagsEx attribute of TRUE.

Microsoft recommends that the forest functional level be set to Windows Server 2008 or later before configuring the RO-FAS, and that any attributes destined for the RO-FAS be configured as such before any RODCs are deployed in the environment. Both of these recommendations will ensure that data contained in the RO-FAS will never be replicated to an RODC. Additionally, any attribute that is configured as part of the RO-FAS should also be configured with the confidentiality bit for further security.

For additional information on Read-Only Domain Controllers and the RO-FAS, we suggest reading *Active Directory*, Fifth Edition, by Brian Desmond et al. (O'Reilly).

See Also

Recipe 10.19 for more on managing confidential data in Active Directory

10.21. Deactivating Classes and Attributes

Problem

You want to deactivate a class or attribute in the schema because you no longer need it.

Solution

Using a graphical user interface

1. Open the Active Directory Schema snap-in.
2. In the left pane, expand Active Directory Schema and then click on the Classes folder or the Attributes folder.
3. In the right pane, double-click the class or attribute you want to deactivate.
4. Uncheck the box beside "Class is active" or "Attribute is active."
5. Click OK.

Using a command-line interface

You can deactivate a class using the *ldifde* utility and an LDIF file that contains the following lines:

```
dn: cn=<SchemaObjectCommonName>,cn=schema,cn=configuration,<ForestRootDN>
changetype: modify
replace: isDefunct
isDefunct: TRUE
-
```

If the LDIF file were named *deactivate_class.ldf*, you would run the following command:

```
> ldifde -v -i -f deactivate_class.ldf
```

You can also deactivate a class using AdMod, as follows:

```
> admod -schema -rb cn=<SchemaObjectCommonName> isDefunct::TRUE
```

Using PowerShell

To deactivate a schema attribute or class by using PowerShell, use the following syntax:

```
Set-ADObject "cn=<ObjectName>,cn=schema,cn=configuration,<ForestRootDN>"↵
 -Replace @{"isDefunct"=$True}
```

Discussion

The GUI solution requires that the *.dll* file for the Active Directory Schema snap-in has been registered. See Recipe 10.1 for more information.

There is no supported way to delete classes or attributes defined in the schema. You can, however, deactivate them, also known as making them *defunct*. Before you deactivate a class, make sure that no instantiated objects of that class exist. If you want to deactivate an attribute, you should make sure no object classes define the attribute as mandatory. After you've verified the class or attribute is no longer being used, you can deactivate it by setting the isDefunct attribute to TRUE. You can always reactivate it at a later time by simply setting isDefunct to FALSE. You can even redefine the class or attribute while it is defunct. This gives you some flexibility over reusing classes or attributes you may have added before but no longer want.

See Also

Recipe 10.22 for more on redefining classes and attributes

10.22. Redefining Classes and Attributes

Problem

You want to redefine a class or attribute that was created previously.

Solution

To redefine a class or attribute, you must first deactivate it by setting the isDefunct attribute to TRUE (see Recipe 10.21 for more details). If you are deactivating a class, make sure that no objects are instantiated that use the class. If you are deactivating an attribute, make sure that it isn't populated on any objects and remove it from any classes that have it defined as part of mayContain and mustContain. After the class or attribute has been deactivated, you can modify (i.e., redefine) the LDAP display name (lDAPDisplay Name), the OID (governsID or attributeID), the syntax (attributeSyntax and oMSyn tax), and the schemaIDGUID. The one attribute that you cannot modify is the common name.

Discussion

Although you cannot delete schema objects, you can work around many of the reasons that would cause you to want to delete a schema object by redefining it instead. Redefining schema objects comes in handy if you accidentally mistype an OID (governsID/ attributeID) or lDAPDisplayName, or no longer need an attribute you created previously. You can reuse it by renaming the attribute and giving it a different syntax.

See Also

Recipe 10.21 for more on deactivating classes and attributes

10.23. Reloading the Schema Cache

Problem

You want to reload the schema cache so that schema extensions will take effect immediately.

Solution

Using a graphical user interface

1. Open the Active Directory Schema snap-in.

2. In the left pane, right-click on Active Directory Schema and select Reload the Schema.

Using a command-line interface

You can reload the schema by using the *ldifde* utility and an LDIF file that contains the following:

```
dn:
changetype: modify
add: schemaUpdateNow
schemaUpdateNow: 1
-
```

If the LDIF file were named *reload.ldf*, you would run the following command:

```
> ldifde -v -i -f reload.ldf
```

You can also reload the schema cache using AdMod, as follows:

```
> admod -sc refreshschema
```

Using PowerShell

```
$objRootDSE = [ADSI] "LDAP://<DCName>/RootDSE" # Specify the Schema Master FSMO
$objRootDSE.put("schemaUpdateNOW", 1)
$objRootDSE.SetInfo()
```

Discussion

Each domain controller maintains a complete copy of the schema in memory to make access to the schema very fast. This is called the *schema cache*. When you extend the schema on the Schema FSMO role owner, the change is written to the schema cache and is not committed to disk yet. The schema automatically commits any changes to the schema every five minutes if a change has taken place, but you can also do it manually/programmatically by writing to the schemaUpdateNow operational attribute of the RootDSE on the Schema FSMO role owner. Once that is done, any changes to the schema cache are written to disk.

It is necessary to force a schema cache update if your schema extensions reference newly created attributes or classes. For example, let's say that you want to create one new auxiliary class that contains one new attribute. To do that, you would first need to create the attribute and then create the auxiliary class. As part of the auxiliary class's definition, you would need to reference the new attribute, but unless you reload the schema cache, an error would be returned stating that the attribute does not exist. For this reason, you need to add an additional step. First create the attribute, then reload the schema cache, and finally create the auxiliary class. Here is what an LDIF representation would look like:

```
dn: cn=adatum-TestAttr,cn=schema,cn=configuration,dc=adatum,dc=com
changetype: add
objectclass: attributeSchema
lDAPDisplayName: adatum-TestAttr
attributeId: 1.3.6.1.4.1.999.1.1.28.312
oMSyntax: 20
attributeSyntax: 2.5.5.4
isSingleValued: FALSE
searchFlags: 1

dn:
changetype: modify
add: schemaUpdateNow
schemaUpdateNow: 1
-

dn: cn=adatum-TestClass,cn=schema,cn=configuration,dc=adatum,dc=com
changetype: add
objectclass: classSchema
lDAPDisplayName: adatum-TestClass
governsId: 1.3.6.1.4.1.999.1.1.28.311
subClassOf: top
objectClassCategory: 3
mayContain: adatum-TestAttr
```

See Also

Recipe 10.6 for adding a new attribute to the schema; Recipe 10.8 for adding a new class to the schema

10.24. Managing the Schema Master FSMO

Problem

You want to view, transfer, or seize the Schema Master FSMO for your Active Directory forest.

Solution

Using a graphical user interface

To view the current Schema Master FSMO role holder, do the following:

1. Open the Active Directory Schema snap-in.
2. Right-click on Active Directory Schema in the left pane and select Operations Master.

To transfer the Schema Master to another server, follow these steps:

1. Open the Active Directory Schema snap-in. Right-click on Active Directory Schema in the left pane and select Change Active Directory Domain Controller. Select the DC that you wish to transfer the FSMO role to.
2. Right-click on Active Directory Schema in the left pane and select Operations Master.
3. Click the Change button.
4. Click OK twice.

   You should see a message stating whether the transfer was successful.

Using a command-line interface

To query the owner of the Schema Master FSMO role, you can use the dsquery server or adfind command shown here:

```
> dsquery server -hasfsmo schema
> adfind -sc fsmo:schema
```

To transfer the Schema Master to another server, use the following syntax:

```
> ntdsutil roles conn "co t s <NewRoleOwner>" q "transfer Schema Master" q q
```

To forcibly seize the Schema Master to another DC, do the following:

```
> ntdsutil roles conn "co t s <NewRoleOwner>" q "seize Schema Master" q q
```

Using PowerShell

To move the Schema Master to another DC by using PowerShell, use the following syntax:

```
Move-ADDirectoryServerOperationMasterRole -Identity <NewRoleOwner>↵
  -OperationMasterRole schemaMaster
```

Discussion

The GUI solution requires that the *.dll* file for the Active Directory Schema be registered. See Recipe 10.1 for more information.

Several Active Directory operations, such as updating the schema, are sensitive and therefore need to be restricted to a single domain controller to prevent corruption of the AD database. This is because Active Directory cannot guarantee the proper evaluation of these functions in a situation where they may be invoked from more than one DC. The FSMO mechanism is used to limit these functions to a single DC.

The first domain controller in a new forest is assigned the two forest-wide FSMO roles, the Schema Master and Domain Naming Master. The first domain controller in a new domain gets the other three domain-wide roles. If you need to decommission the domain controller that is currently the Schema Master role owner (either permanently or for a significant period of time), you'll want to transfer the role beforehand.

If the Schema Master becomes unavailable before you can transfer it, you'll need to seize the role (see Recipe 3.31).

See Also

Recipe 3.29, Recipe 3.30, and Recipe 3.31 for more on viewing, transferring, and seizing FSMO roles; "How to view and transfer FSMO roles in Windows Server 2003" (*http://support.microsoft.com/kb/324801*)

## CHAPTER 11

Site Topology

11.0. Introduction

Active Directory needs information about the underlying network to determine how domain controllers should replicate and what domain controller(s) are optimal for a given client to authenticate with. This network information is often referred to as the site or replication *topology*, and it consists of numerous object types that represent various aspects of the network.

At a high level, a site is a logical collection of high-speed LAN segments. One or more subnets can be associated with a site, and this mapping is used to determine which site a client belongs to, based on its IP address. Sites are connected via site links, which are analogous to WAN connections. Finally, each domain controller in a site has one or more `connection` objects, which define a replication connection to other domain controllers.

These site topology objects are contained under the `Sites` container within the Configuration naming context. Figure 11-1 shows an example of the site topology hierarchy using the Active Directory Sites and Services snap-in.

Directly under the `Sites` container are the individual site containers, plus containers that store the site link objects (`cn=Inter-site Transports`) and subnets (`cn=Sub nets`). Three objects are included within a site:

- An `NTDS Site Settings` (`nTDSSiteSettings`) object that contains attributes that can customize replication behavior for the whole site
- A `License Site Settings` (`licensingSiteSettings`) object that can be used to direct hosts within the site to the appropriate licensing server
- A `Servers` container

The `Servers` container contains a `server` object for each domain controller that is a member of the site, along with any other servers that need to be represented in the site topology (e.g., DFS servers). Figure 11-1 shows a site topology hierarchy.

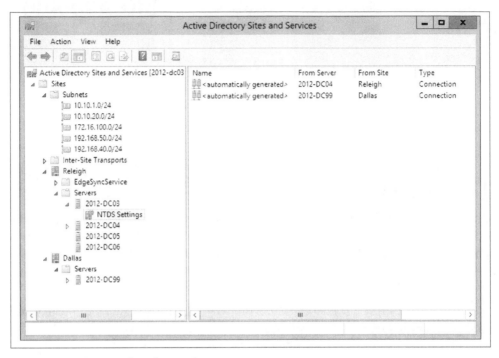

Figure 11-1. Site topology hierarchy

A `server` object can contain an `NTDS Settings` (`nTDSDSA`) object, which distinguishes domain-controller `server` objects from other `server` objects. The `NTDS Settings` object stores several attributes that are used to customize replication behavior for a specific domain controller. The `NTDS Settings` object can contain one or more `nTDSConnection` objects, which define the replication connections between domain controllers.

The Anatomy of Site Topology Objects

Table 11-1 through Table 11-7 contain some of the important attributes of the various site topology objects.

Table 11-1. Attributes of site objects

Attribute	Description
cn	RDN of the object. This is the name of the site (e.g., Raleigh).
gpLink	Contains a prioritized list of GPOs that are linked to the site.
siteObjectBL	Multivalued attribute that contains a list of distinguished names for each subnet that is associated with the site.

Table 11-2. Attributes of nTDSSiteSettings objects

Attribute	Description
cn	RDN of the object, which is always equal to NTDS Site Settings.
interSiteTopologyGenerator	Distinguished name of the NTDS Settings object of the current ISTG.
msDS-Preferred-GC-Site	If universal group caching is enabled, contains the distinguished name of the site that domain controllers should refresh their cache from. See Recipe 7.12 for more information.
options	Bit flag that determines if universal group caching is enabled, whether site link transitivity is disabled, and if replication schedules should be ignored. For more information see Recipe 11.6.
schedule	Octet string that represents the default replication schedule for the site.

Table 11-3. Attributes of subnet objects

Attribute	Description
cn	RDN of the object. Contains the network number and bit mask for the subnet (e.g., 10.10.1.0/24).
siteObject	Distinguished name of the site object the subnet is associated with.

Table 11-4. Attributes of siteLink objects

Attribute	Description
cn	RDN of the object. Contains the name of the link.
cost	Number that represents the site link cost. See Recipe 11.15 for more information.
replInterval	Interval in minutes that replication occurs over the site link.
schedule	Octet string that represents the replication schedule for the site link.
siteList	Multivalued list of distinguished names of each site that is associated with the site link. See Recipe 11.13 for more information.

Table 11-5. Attributes of server objects

Attribute	Description
bridgeheadTransportList	Multivalued attribute that contains the list of transports (e.g., IP or SMTP) for which the server is a preferred bridgehead server.
cn	RDN of the object. This is set to the hostname of the associated server.
dNSHostName	Fully qualified domain name of the server. This attribute is automatically maintained for domain controllers.
serverReference	Distinguished name of the corresponding computer object contained within one of the domain-naming contexts.

Table 11-6. Attributes of nTDSDSA (NTDS Settings) objects

Attribute	Description
cn	RDN of the object, which is always equal to NTDS Settings.
invocationID	GUID that represents the DIT (*ntds.dit*) on the domain controller.
hasMasterNCs	Multivalued attribute containing the list of writable naming contexts (does not include application partitions) stored on the domain controller.
hasPartialReplicaNCs	Multivalued attribute containing the list of read-only naming contexts stored on the domain controller. This will be populated only if the domain controller is a global catalog server.
msDS-Behavior-Version	Number that represents the functional level (i.e., operating system) of the domain controller.
msDS-HasDomainNCs	Contains the distinguished name of the writable domain-naming context stored on the domain controller.
msDs-HasInstantiatedNCs	A combination of all available read-only and writable naming contexts stored on the domain controller.
msDS-hasPartialReplicaNCs	Multivalued attribute that contains distinguished names of each read-only naming context stored on the domain controller. This will be populated only if the domain controller is a global catalog server.
msDS-hasMasterNCs	Multivalued attribute that contains distinguished names of each writable naming context and application partition stored on the domain controller.
options	Bit flag that determines whether the domain controller is a global catalog server.
queryPolicyObject	If set, the distinguished name of the LDAP query policy object to be used by the domain controller.

Table 11-7. Attributes of nTDSConnection objects

Attribute	Description
cn	RDN of the object. For KCC-generated connections, this is a GUID.
enabledConnection	Boolean that indicates whether the connection is available to be used.
fromServer	Distinguished name of the NTDS Settings object of the domain controller this connection replicates with.
ms-DS-ReplicatesNCReason	Multivalued attribute that stores reason codes for why the connection exists. There will be one entry per naming context the connection is used for.
options	Bit flag where a value of 1 indicates the connection was created by the KCC and a value of 0 means the connection was manually created. See Recipe 11.29 for more information.
schedule	Octet string that represents the replication schedule for the site link.
transportType	Distinguished name of the transport type (e.g., IP or SMTP) that is used for the connection.

11.1. Creating a Site

Problem

You want to create a site.

Solution

Using a graphical user interface

1. Open the Active Directory Sites and Services snap-in (*dssite.msc*).
2. Right-click on the Sites container and select New Site.
3. Beside Name, enter the name of the new site.
4. Under Link Name, select a site link for the site.
5. Click OK twice.

Using a command-line interface

Create an LDIF file called *create_site.ldf* with the following contents:

```
dn: cn=<SiteName>,cn=sites,cn=configuration,<ForestRootDN>
changetype: add
objectclass: site

dn: cn=Licensing Site Settings,cn=<SiteName>,cn=sites,cn=configuration,↵
<ForestRootDN>
changetype: add
objectclass: licensingSiteSettings
```

```
dn: cn=NTDS Site Settings,cn=<SiteName>,cn=sites,cn=configuration,<ForestRootDN>
changetype: add
objectclass: nTDSSiteSettings

dn: cn=Servers,cn=<SiteName>,cn=sites,cn=configuration,<ForestRootDN>
changetype: add
objectclass: serversContainer
```

Then run the following command:

```
> ldifde -v -i -f create_site.ldf
```

You also can create a site by issuing the following three AdMod commands:

```
> admod -config -rb "cn=<SiteName>,cn=sites" -add objectclass::site
> admod -config -rb "cn=NTDS Site Settings,cn=<SiteName>,cn=sites" -add↵
  objectclass::nTDSSiteSettings
> admod -config -rb cn=Servers,cn=<SiteName>,cn=sites" -add↵
  objectclass::serversContainer
```

Using PowerShell

To create a new site by using PowerShell, use the following syntax:

```
New-ADReplicationSite -Name "<SiteName>" -Description "<SiteDescription>"
```

Discussion

To create a site in Active Directory, a few objects must be created. The first is a `site` object, which is the root of all the other objects. The `site` object contains the following:

nTDSSiteSettings
> This object stores replication-related properties about a site, such as the replication schedule, current ISTG role holder, and whether universal group caching is enabled.

serversContainer
> This container is the parent of the `server` objects that are part of the site. All the domain controllers that are members of the site will be represented in this container.

After a site is created in PowerShell, you've essentially got an empty site. If you didn't do anything else, the site would not be of much value. To make it usable, you need to assign `subnet` objects to it (see Recipe 11.11), and add the site to a `siteLink` object to link the site to other sites (see Recipe 11.14). At that point, you can promote or move domain controllers into the site, and it should be fully functional.

Using PowerShell

The PowerShell solution obfuscates the creation of the `site` objects. Running the PowerShell command syntax automatically creates the three `site` objects.

See Also

Recipe 11.11; Recipe 11.14

11.2. Listing Sites in a Domain

Problem

You want to obtain the list of sites in a domain.

Solution

Using a graphical user interface

1. Open the Active Directory Sites and Services snap-in (*dssite.msc*).
2. Click on the Sites container.

   The list of sites will be displayed in the right pane.
3. Double-click on a site to view its properties.

Using a command-line interface

Run one of the following commands to list the sites in a forest:

```
> dsquery site
```

or:

```
> adfind -sites -f (objectcategory=site)
```

Run one of the following commands to view the properties for a particular site:

```
> dsget site "<SiteName>"
```

or:

```
> adfind -sites -rb "cn=<SiteName>"
```

Using PowerShell

You can obtain a list of sites in a domain by using PowerShell, as follows:

```
Get-ADReplicationSite -Filter * | Select Name
```

Discussion

Site objects are stored in the Sites container (e.g., cn=sites,cn=configura
tion,dc=adatum,dc=com) in the Configuration naming context. For more information
on creating sites, see Recipe 11.1.

11.3. Renaming a Site

Problem

You want to rename a site.

Solution

Using a graphical user interface

1. Open the Active Directory Sites and Services snap-in (*dssite.msc*).
2. Click on the Sites container.
3. In the right pane, right-click the site you want to rename and select Rename.
4. Enter the new name of the site and press Enter.

Using a command-line interface

The following command will change the cn of a site:

```
> dsmove "<SiteDN>" -newname "<NewSiteName>"
```

You can also rename a site with AdMod, using the following syntax:

```
> admod -b "<SiteDN>" -rename "<NewSiteName>"
```

Using PowerShell

To rename a site by using PowerShell, use the following syntax:

```
Rename-ADObject -Identity "<Site DN>" -NewName "<NewSiteName>"
```

Discussion

Renaming a site in Active Directory involves changing the cn of the site object. The largest concern with renaming a site, as with any other AD object, is to ensure that no applications reference the site by name. A best practice to avoid this pitfall is to reference AD objects by their GUIDs, which will not change even when the object is renamed.

See Also

MSDN: Object Names and Identities; MSDN: Using objectGUID to Bind to an Object

11.4. Deleting a Site

Problem

You want to delete a site.

Solution

Using a graphical user interface

1. Open the Active Directory Sites and Services snap-in (*dssite.msc*).
2. Click on the Sites container.
3. In the right pane, right-click the site you want to delete and select Delete.
4. Click Yes twice.

Using a command-line interface

You can remove a site and its associated objects by issuing the following AdMod command syntax:

```
> admod -b "cn=<SiteName>,cn=sites,cn=configuration,<ForestRootDN>" -del↵
  -treedelete
```

Using PowerShell

To delete a site by using PowerShell without confirmation, use the following syntax:

```
Remove-ADReplicationSite -Identity "<SiteName>" -Confirm:$False
```

Discussion

When deleting a site, be very careful to ensure that no active server objects exist within it. If you delete a site that contains domain controllers, it will disrupt replication for all domain controllers in that site. A more robust solution would be to first perform a query for all server objects using the distinguished name of the site as the base DN. If no servers were returned, then you could safely delete the site. If server objects were found, you should move them before deleting the site.

It is also worth noting that deleting a site does not delete any of the subnets or site links that are associated with the site.

See Also

Recipe 11.1 for more on creating a site; Recipe 11.7 for creating a subnet

11.5. Delegating Control of a Site

Problem

You want to delegate permission of an AD site to allow it to be administered by another user or group.

Solution

Using a graphical user interface

The following example will delegate administration of the managedBy attribute of a site:

1. Open the Active Directory Sites and Services snap-in (*dssite.msc*).

2. Click on the Sites container.

3. In the right pane, right-click the site you want to delegate and select Delegate Control.

4. Click Next to bypass the initial Welcome screen of the Delegation of Control Wizard.

5. Click Add to select the users or groups that you want to delegate control to. Click Next to continue.

6. Select "Create a custom task to delegate" and click Next.

7. Click "Only the following objects in the folder." Place a checkmark next to site objects and click Next.

8. Deselect the General permissions and then select the Property-specific permissions.

9. Place a checkmark next to "Write managedBy." Click Next to continue.

10. Click Finish.

Using a command-line interface

The following code will allow a group called *SiteAdmins* to manage the managedBy attribute of sites within *adatum.com*:

```
> dsacls cn=Sites,cn=Configuration,dc=adatum,dc=com /I:S↵
/G adatum.com\SiteAdmins:WP;;managedBy
```

Discussion

Using a graphical user interface

You can delegate control over a site via the Delegation of Control Wizard or by using *dsacls* at the command line. The Delegation of Control Wizard allows you to delegate one preconfigured task—managing Group Policy links—or create a custom task to delegate. When delegating a custom task, first you must determine whether you are delegating permission over the entire site and all objects contained therein or whether you only are going to delegate control over specific child objects. For example, you can delegate control over all computer objects within a site. Once you've made this determination, then you'll designate the specific permissions that you're delegating; you can delegate anything from full control of the entire object down to granting read permissions on a single attribute.

11.6. Configuring Universal Group Caching for a Site

Problem

You want to configure a site so that it does not require access to a global catalog server during most user logins.

Solution

Using a graphical user interface

1. Open the Active Directory Sites and Services snap-in (*dssite.msc*).
2. In the left pane, browse to the site you want to enable group caching for and click on it.
3. In the right pane, double-click on the NTDS Site Settings object.
4. Under Universal Group Membership Caching, check the box beside Enable Universal Group Caching.
5. If you want to force the cache refresh from a particular site, select a site; otherwise, leave the default set to <Default>.
6. Click OK.

Using a command-line interface

You can use *ldifde* to enable universal group caching. Create a file called *enable_univ_cache.ldf* with the following contents, but change <SiteName> to the name of the site you want to enable, and *<ForestRootDN>* to the distinguished name of the forest root domain:

```
dn: cn=NTDS Site Settings,cn=<SiteName>,cn=sites,cn=configuration,<ForestRootDN>
changetype: modify
replace: options
options: 32
-
```

Then use the following command to import the change:

```
> ldifde -i -f enable_univ_cache.ldf
```

You also can perform this change using a combination of AdFind and AdMod, using the following syntax:

```
> adfind -config -rb "cn=NTDS Site Settings,cn=<SiteName>,cn=Sites"↵
 options -adcsv | admod options::{{.:SET:32}}
```

 To explicitly set the site that domain controllers in this site should use to refresh universal group membership, configure the msDS-Preferred-GC-Site attribute on the NTDS Site Settings object with the DN of the desired site.

Using PowerShell

To enable a site for universal group membership caching, use the following syntax:

```
Set-ADReplicationSite -Identity <SiteName> -UniversalGroupCachingEnabled:$True
```

To enable a site for universal group membership caching while also setting the site to refresh the cache from, use the following syntax:

```
Set-ADReplicationSite -Identity <SiteName> -UniversalGroupCachingEnabled:$True↵
 -UniversalGroupCachingRefreshSite:<RefreshSiteName>
```

Discussion

An authenticating domain controller is required to contact a global catalog server (if it is not one itself) in order to process any client authentication requests. This is necessary because of the need to verify universal group memberships for any clients attempting to access the domain. *Universal group caching* was introduced in Windows Server 2003 to reduce the impact of this requirement. Universal group caching can be enabled on a site-by-site basis and allows domain controllers to cache universal group information locally. This largely removes the need to query the global catalog during client logon, though a global catalog will still need to be contacted the first time a new user logs on because no membership information will be cached in that case. The local DC will also need to contact a GC at regular intervals to update its cached information.

You can enable universal group caching manually by enabling bit 5 (32 in decimal) on the options attribute of the NTDS Site Settings object. The *ldifde* solution blindly writes a value of 32 to that attribute, which is not ideal since it will overwrite any existing values that may already be in place.

See Also

Recipe 4.12 for more on viewing bitwise attributes; Recipe 4.15 for information on configuring bitwise values; Set-ADReplicationSite cmdlet reference (*http://bit.ly/ 18ptHi2*)

11.7. Creating a Subnet

Problem

You want to create a subnet.

Solution

Using a graphical user interface

1. Open the Active Directory Sites and Services snap-in (*dssite.msc*).
2. Right-click on the Subnets container and select New Subnet.
3. In the Prefix dialog box, enter the Address and Mask (e.g., for IPv4 enter 192.168.1.0/24 and for IPv6 enter 3FFE:FFFF:0:C000::/64) and then select the site the subnet is part of.
4. Click OK.

Using a command-line interface

Create an LDIF file called *create_subnet.ldf* with the following contents:

```
dn: cn=<Subnet>,cn=subnets,cn=sites,cn=configuration,<ForestRootDN>
changetype: add
objectclass: subnet
siteObject: cn=<SiteName>,cn=sites,cn=configuration,<ForestRootDN>
```

Then run the following command:

```
> ldifde -v -i -f create_subnet.ldf
```

You can also create a subnet using AdMod. The following command creates a subnet for 10.1.1.0/24 in the *adatum.com* domain and associates the subnet with the Dallas site:

```
> admod -b "cn=10.1.1.0/24,cn=subnets,cn=sites,cn=configuration,↵
dc=adatum,dc=com" objectClass::subnet↵
 siteObject::"cn=Dallas,cn=sites,cn=configuration,dc=adatum,dc=com" -add
```

Using PowerShell

You can create a subnet object and associate it with an existing site by using PowerShell. The following command creates a new subnet for 10.1.1.0/24 and associates the subnet to the Dallas site:

```
New-ADReplicationSubnet -Name 10.1.1.0/24 -Site Dallas
```

Discussion

Subnet objects reside in the Subnets container in the Configuration NC (e.g., cn=subnets,cn=sites,cn=configuration,dc=adatum,dc=com). The RDN of the subnet should be the subnet address and bit-mask combination (e.g., 10.1.1.0/24). The other important attribute to set is siteObject, which should contain the DN of the site that the subnet is associated with.

See Also

New-ADReplicationSubnet cmdlet reference (*http://bit.ly/18ptJGP*)

11.8. Listing the Subnets

Problem

You want to list the subnet objects in Active Directory.

Solution

Using a graphical user interface

1. Open the Active Directory Sites and Services snap-in (*dssite.msc*).
2. Click on the Subnets container in the left pane.

   The list of subnets will be displayed in the right pane.
3. To view the properties of a specific subnet, right-click on the one you want to view and then click Properties.

Using a command-line interface

The following command will list all subnets:

```
> dsquery subnet
```

You can also list all configured subnets with AdFind, as follows:

```
> adfind -subnets -f (objectCategory=subnet)
```

To display the properties of a particular subnet with AdFind, use this syntax:

```
> adfind -subnets -rb "cn=<Subnet>"
```

Using PowerShell

To list all of the subnets with PowerShell, use the following command:

```
Get-ADReplicationSubnet -Filter * | Select Name
```

To get all of the properties of a specific subnet, use the following syntax:

```
Get-ADReplicationSubnet -Identity <Subnet> -Properties *
```

Discussion

Using PowerShell

To display the site that subnets are associated with, use the following command:

```
Get-ADReplicationSubnet -Filter * | Select Name,Site
```

See Also

Get-ADReplicationSubnet cmdlet reference (*http://bit.ly/13m2gm4*)

11.9. Finding Missing Subnets

Problem

You want to find the subnets that are missing from your site topology. Missing subnets can result in clients not authenticating against the most optimal domain controller, which can degrade performance.

Solution

Having all of your subnets in Active Directory is important because a client that attempts to log on from a subnet that is not associated with any site may authenticate with any domain controller in the domain. This can result in the logon process taking longer to complete.

One way to dynamically determine missing subnets is to query each domain controller for 5807 events and then to look at the *netlogon.log* file. Each IP address that has a

`NO_CLIENT_SITE` entry needs to be addressed by adding a subnet to a corresponding site.

Here is an example of a 5807 event log entry:

```
Event Type:          Warning
Event Source:        NETLOGON
Event Category:      None

Event ID:            5807
Date:                12/11/2012
Time:                4:42:20 AM
User:                N/A
Computer:            DC1
Description:
During the past 4.18 hours there have been 48 connections to this Domain
Controller from client machines whose IP addresses don't map to any of the
existing sites in the enterprise. Those clients, therefore, have undefined
sites and may connect to any Domain Controller including those that are in
far distant locations from the clients.
A client's site is determined by the mapping of its subnet to one of the existing
sites. To move the above clients to one of the sites, please consider creating
subnet object(s) covering the above IP addresses with mapping to one of the
existing sites.
The names and IP addresses of the clients in question have been logged on this
computer in the following log file '%SystemRoot%\debug\netlogon.log' and,
potentially, in the log file '%SystemRoot%\debug\netlogon.bak' created if the
former log becomes full. The log(s) may contain additional unrelated debugging
information.
To filter out the needed information, please search for lines which contain text
'NO_CLIENT_SITE:'. The first word after this string is the client name and the
second word is the client IP address. The maximum size of the log(s) is
controlled by the following registry DWORD value
'HKEY_LOCAL_MACHINE\SYSTEM\CurrentControlSet\Services\
Netlogon\Parameters\LogFileMaxSize'; the default is 20000000 bytes. The current
maximum size is 20000000 bytes. To set a different maximum size, create the
above registry value and set the desired maximum size in bytes.
```

Instead of scraping the event logs on every domain controller, you can look directly at the *%SystemRoot%\debug\netlogon.log* file on each domain controller and parse out all of the `NO_CLIENT_SITE` entries.

Here is an example of some of the `NO_CLIENT_SITE` entries from the *netlogon.log* file:

```
12/11 20:02:35 [1316] ADATUM: NO_CLIENT_SITE: WIN8-CLIENT02 192.168.0.143
12/11 20:09:25 [1316] ADATUM: NO_CLIENT_SITE: 2012-SERVER05 192.168.10.245
12/11 20:12:08 [1316] ADATUM: NO_CLIENT_SITE: WIN8-CLIENT14 172.16.0.14
12/11 20:17:35 [1316] ADATUM: NO_CLIENT_SITE: WIN8-CLIENT02 192.168.0.143
12/11 20:17:37 [1316] ADATUM: NO_CLIENT_SITE: WIN8-CLIENT02 192.168.0.143
12/11 20:20:51 [4156] ADATUM: NO_CLIENT_SITE: 2012-SERVER09 192.168.1.8
12/11 20:32:38 [1316] ADATUM: NO_CLIENT_SITE: WIN8-CLIENT01 10.16.0.77
```

If you wanted to get creative and automate a solution to do this, you could write a script that goes out to each domain controller, opens the *netlogon.log* file, and retrieves NO_CLIENT_SITE entries. Then you could examine all of the IP addresses and create subnets in Active Directory that would contain them. You could associate all of those subnets with a placeholder site or even use the Default-First-Site-Name site (if it still exists). Then, once a week (or another desired length of time), you could look at the sites that were created or that were associated with the default site and determine what site they should actually be associated with.

Using PowerShell

You can get a list of all 5807 events from the System event log on the local computer by running the following command:

```
Get-WinEvent -LogName System | where {$_.ID -eq "5807"}
```

You can also get the events on a remote computer by using the following syntax:

```
Get-WinEvent -ComputerName <NameOfDC> -LogName System | where {$_.ID -eq "5807"}
```

See Also

Get-WinEvent cmdlet reference (*http://bit.ly/ZAVntH*); "Freaky neat Active Directory site links with PowerShell" (*http://bit.ly/13m2BVX*)

11.10. Deleting a Subnet

Problem

You want to delete a subnet object.

Solution

Using a graphical user interface

1. Open the Active Directory Sites and Services snap-in (*dssite.msc*).
2. Click on the Subnets container.

   The list of subnets will be displayed in the right pane.
3. Right-click on the subnet you wish to remove and select Delete.
4. Click Yes to confirm.

Using a command-line interface

You can delete a subnet object using the built-in *dsrm* utility or AdMod. The *dsrm* utility takes the following syntax (note the parameter at the end to avoid being prompted for confirmation):

```
> dsrm cn=<SubnetName>,cn=subnets,cn=sites,cn=configuration,<ForestRootDN>↵
-noprompt
```

To remove a subnet using AdMod, use this syntax:

```
> admod -b cn=<SubnetName>,cn=subnets,cn=sites,cn=configuration,<ForestRootDN>↵
-del
```

Using PowerShell

To delete a site without a confirmation prompt, use the following syntax:

```
Remove-ADReplicationSubnet <SubnetName> -Confirm:$False
```

Discussion

Before removing a subnet, you should confirm that it is not in use by examining the *netlogon.log* file on domain controllers. If IP addresses within the subnet range appear in the logfile, it may point to activity from the subnet.

See Also

Remove-ADReplicationSubnet cmdlet reference (*http://bit.ly/12be8px*)

11.11. Changing a Subnet's Site Assignment

Problem

You want to change the site object that a particular subnet is associated with.

Solution

Using a graphical user interface

1. Open the Active Directory Sites and Services snap-in (*dssite.msc*).
2. Click on the Subnets container.
3. Locate the desired subnet and then right-click it and click Properties.
4. In the Site drop-down box, select the name of the site that the subnet should be associated with and click OK.

Using a command-line interface

```
> admod -b cn=<SubnetName>,cn=Subnets,cn=Sites,cn=Configuration,<ForestRootDN>↵
  objectClass::subnet siteObject::<NewSiteDN>
```

 For *<SubnetName>*, use the format "192.168.1.0/24", for example.

Using PowerShell

```
Set-ADReplicationSubnet -Identity <SubnetName> -Site <SiteName>
```

Discussion

Since the site topology that you create in Active Directory is meant to map to your physical network topology, an Active Directory subnet object can be associated with only a single AD site at any one time. If you modify your site configuration or need to delete a site object for any reason, you should configure any subnets associated with that site that are still active on your network so that they are associated with another Active Directory site. This will ensure that any clients that reside on those subnets will be able to locate resources such as domain controllers appropriately, without sending authentication requests across site links unnecessarily.

See Also

Recipe 11.9 to find missing subnets on your network; Recipe 11.10 for more on deleting subnet objects

11.12. Creating a Site Link

Problem

You want to create a site link to connect two or more sites together.

Solution

Using a graphical user interface

1. Open the Active Directory Sites and Services snap-in (*dssite.msc*).
2. Expand the Sites container.
3. Expand the Inter-Site Transports container.
4. Right-click on IP (or SMTP) and select New Site Link.

5. For Name, enter the name for the site link.

6. Under "Sites not in this site link", select at least two sites and click the Add button.

7. Click OK.

Using a command-line interface

The following LDIF would create a site link connecting the SJC and Dallas sites:

```
dn: cn=Dallas-SJC,cn=IP,cn=inter-site
transports,cn=sites,cn=configuration,<ForestRootDN>
changetype: add
objectclass: siteLink
siteList: cn=SJC,cn=sites,cn=configuration,<ForestRootDN>
siteList: cn=Dallas,cn=sites,cn=configuration,<ForestRootDN>
```

If the LDIF file were named *create_site_link.ldf*, you'd then run the following command:

```
> ldifde -v -i -f create_site_link.ldf
```

You also can also create a site link using AdMod, as follows:

```
> admod -b "cn=<SiteLinkName>,cn=IP,cn=inter-site transports, ↵
cn=sites,cn=configuration,<ForestRootDN>" objectclass::sitelink↵
 "sitelist:++:cn=<FirstSite>,cn=sites,cn=configuration,<ForestRootDN>↵
;cn=<SecondSite>,cn=sites,cn=configuration,<ForestRootDN>"↵
 cost::50 replInterval::180 -add
```

Using PowerShell

You can create a site link object by using PowerShell, as shown in the following syntax:

```
New-ADReplicationSiteLink -Name <SiteLinkName> -SitesIncluded <Site1Name>,↵
<Site2Name> -ReplicationFrequencyInMinutes <NumberOfMinutesForReplication>↵
 -Cost <SiteLinkCost>
```

Discussion

Without site links, domain controllers would not be able to determine the optimal partners to replicate with. The cost that is associated with a site defines how expensive the link is. A lower cost is less expensive (or faster) than a higher cost. Link costs are inversely proportional to bandwidth, so a faster link should be configured with a lower cost than a low-speed one. (Sometimes bandwidth costs can play a role, too.) Site link costs are manually configured items, which means that the administrator can control how inter-site replication should take place on the network.

Using PowerShell

By default, a new site link created with `New-ADReplicationSiteLink` will utilize the IP transport protocol. If SMTP is needed, the `-InterSiteTransportProtocol` parameter can be used and SMTP can be specified.

See Also

"Active Directory Replication Concepts" (*http://bit.ly/15qGEJA*); `New-ADReplicationSiteLink` cmdlet reference (*http://bit.ly/13YxeR7*)

11.13. Finding the Site Links for a Site

Problem

You want to list the site links that are associated with a site.

Solution

Using a command-line interface

You can list the site links associated with a particular site using DSQuery or AdFind. DSQuery uses the following syntax:

```
> dsquery * "cn=inter-site transports,cn=sites,cn=configuration,<ForestRootDN>"↵
-filter "(&(objectcategory=siteLink)(siteList=cn=<SiteName>,↵
cn=sites,cn=configuration,<ForestRootDN>))" -scope subtree -attr name
```

To obtain this information using AdFind, use the following:

```
> adfind -config -f "(&(objectcategory=siteLink)(siteList=cn=<SiteName>,↵
cn=sites,cn=configuration,<ForestRootDN>))" name
```

Using PowerShell

```
Get-ADObject -SearchBase "cn=sites,cn=configuration,<ForestRootDN>"↵
 -Filter {objectCategory -eq "siteLink" -and↵
 siteList -eq "cn=<SiteName>,cn=sites,cn=configuration,<ForestRootDN>"}
```

Discussion

A site can be included as a part of zero or more site links. A site with no site links would be considered orphaned from the site topology, since there is no way to determine how and where it connects into the topology. Branch office sites may have only a single site link back to a hub, while a hub site may have numerous links that connect it to the rest of the world.

Finding the site links associated with a site consists of performing a query for all `site Link` objects that have the DN of the site included in the `siteList` attribute for a link. The `siteList` attribute is a multivalued attribute that contains all the sites that are connected via the site link.

11.14. Modifying the Sites That Are Part of a Site Link

Problem

You want to modify the sites associated with a site link.

Solution

Using a graphical user interface

1. Open the Active Directory Sites and Services snap-in (*dssite.msc*).
2. In the left pane, expand Sites→Inter-Site Transports.
3. Click either the IP or SMTP folder, depending on where the site link is stored.
4. In the right pane, double-click on the link you want to modify.
5. Under the General tab, you can add and remove sites that are associated with the site link.
6. Click OK.

Using a command-line interface

Create an LDIF file called *modify_site_link.ldf* with the following contents. Replace *<LinkName>* with the name of the link and *<SiteName>* with the site to add to the link:

```
dn: cn=<LinkName>,cn=IP,cn=inter-site transports,cn=sites,cn=configuration,↵
<ForestRootDN>
changetype: modify
add: siteList

siteList: cn=<SiteName>,cn=sites,cn=configuration,<ForestRootDN>
-
```

Then run the following command:

```
> ldifde -v -i -f modify_site_link.ldf
```

You can also add sites to a site link using AdMod, as follows:

```
> admod -b "cn=<LinkName>,cn=IP,cn=inter-site transports,cn=sites,↵
cn=configuration, <ForestRootDN>" siteList:+:"cn=<SiteName>,cn=sites,↵
cn=configuration,<ForestRootDN>"
```

Using PowerShell

To add one or more sites to a site link by using PowerShell, use the following syntax:

```
Set-ADReplicationSiteLink "<SiteLinkName>"↵
  -SitesIncluded @{Add="<SiteName1>","<SiteName2>"}
```

To remove one or more sites from a site link by using PowerShell, use the following syntax:

```
Set-ADReplicationSiteLink "<SiteLinkName>"↵
  -SitesIncluded @{Remove="<SiteName1>","<SiteName2>"}
```

Discussion

To associate a site with a site link, add the DN of the site to the `siteList` attribute of the `siteLink` object that represents the link. To remove a site from a link, remove the DN associated with the site from the `siteList` attribute. For example, to remove a site from a site link using AdMod, replace `siteList:+:` with `siteList:-:`.

See Also

Recipe 11.13 for finding the links associated with a site

11.15. Modifying the Cost for a Site Link

Problem

You want to modify the cost for a site link.

Solution

Using a graphical user interface

1. Open the Active Directory Sites and Services snap-in (*dssite.msc*).
2. In the left pane, expand Sites→Inter-Site Transports.
3. Click either the IP or SMTP folder, depending on where the site link is stored.
4. In the right pane, double-click on the link you want to modify.
5. Under the General tab, you can change the cost for the site link.
6. Click OK.

Using a command-line interface

Create an LDIF file called *modify_site_link_cost.ldf* with the following contents. Replace *<LinkName>* with the name of the link you want to modify and *<LinkCost>* with the cost:

```
dn: cn=<LinkName>,cn=IP,cn=inter-site
transports,cn=sites,cn=configuration,<ForestRootDN>
changetype: modify
replace: cost
cost: <LinkCost>
-
```

Then run the following command:

```
> ldifde -v -i -f modify_site_link_cost.ldf
```

You can also modify the cost of a site link using AdMod, as follows:

```
> admod -b "cn=<LinkName>,cn=IP,cn=inter-site transports,cn=sites,↵
cn=configuration,<ForestRootDN>" cost::<LinkCost>
```

Using PowerShell

You can modify the cost of a site link using the Quest cmdlets or ADSI, as follows:

```
Set-ADReplicationSiteLink "<LinkName>" -Cost <LinkCost>
```

Discussion

The cost attribute is one of the most important attributes of siteLink objects. cost is used by the KCC to determine what connection objects should be created to allow domain controllers to replicate data.

cost is inversely proportional to bandwidth—the lower the cost, the greater the bandwidth. (Don't forget about looking at the bandwidth costs, too.) The number you use for the cost is also arbitrary; the default is 100. You could use 100–1,000 as the range for your site link costs, or you could use 1–10. The actual number isn't important, so long as you configure the values to be relative based on the other site links you've configured. The costs that you assign to your site links should be configured according to the physical topology of your network, where you assign the lowest costs to the highest-speed links (or lowest-cost links), and higher costs to lower-speed links between two sites.

11.16. Enabling Change Notification for a Site Link

Problem

You want to enable change notification between sites so that replication will occur as changes occur rather than according to a set schedule.

Solution

Using a graphical user interface

1. Open the Active Directory Sites and Services snap-in (*dssite.msc*).
2. In the left pane, expand Sites→Inter-Site Transports.
3. Click either the IP or SMTP folder, depending on where the site link is stored.
4. In the right pane, double-click on the link you want to modify.
5. On the Attribute Editor tab, scroll to the options attribute and then click Edit.
6. Enter a 1 to enable change notification and then click OK.
7. Click OK to close the site link properties window.

Using a command-line interface

```
> adfind -b cn=<SiteLinkName>,cn=IP,cn=Inter-site Transports,cn=Sites, ↵
cn=Configuration,cn=<ForestRootDN>" options -adcsv | admod options::{{.:SET:1}}
```

Using PowerShell

```
Set-ADReplicationSiteLink <SiteLinkName> -Add @{Options=1}
```

Discussion

By default, intra-site replication occurs on the basis of change notifications where replication occurs almost immediately after a change occurs, while domain controllers in different sites will, by default, only replicate with each other on a set schedule. To configure a particular site link to use the change-notification mechanism for replication, you can set bit 1 of its options attribute. Keep in mind that this will create more frequent replication traffic on the site link in question, but it will ensure that changes made in one site can be replicated to the other site much more quickly than by using the default inter-site replication schedules.

See Also

Recipe 4.15 for more on modifying bitwise attributes; Recipe 11.17 for more on modifying replication schedules

11.17. Modifying Replication Schedules

Problem

You want to change the times of day or week that a particular site link (IP or SMTP) is available for replication.

Solution

1. Open the Active Directory Sites and Services snap-in (*dssite.msc*).
2. In the left pane, expand Sites→Inter-Site Transports.
3. Click either the IP or SMTP folder, depending on where the site link is stored.
4. In the right pane, double-click on the link you want to modify.
5. On the General tab, click Change Schedule.
6. Select the times and days of the week that you wish to allow or disallow replication, and select the Replication Available or Replication Not Available radio button, as appropriate.
7. Click OK twice to save the changes.

Using a command-line interface

To configure a site link to be available 24 hours a day, seven days a week, use the following syntax:

```
> admod -b cn=<SiteLinkName>,cn=<TransportName>,cn=Inter-site↵
Transports,cn=sites,cn=configuration,<ForestRootDN> schedule::0
```

Using PowerShell

The following PowerShell command will configure a site link to allow replication Monday through Friday from midnight to 7:45 a.m. and from 5:00 p.m. to 11:45 p.m. while allowing replication all day and night on Saturday and Sunday:

```
$schedule = New-Object -TypeName System.DirectoryServices.ActiveDirectory.↵
ActiveDirectorySchedule;$schedule.ResetSchedule();$schedule.SetSchedule↵
 ("Monday","Zero","Zero","Seven","FortyFive");$schedule.SetSchedule↵
 ("Monday","Seventeen","Zero","TwentyThree","FortyFive");$schedule.SetSchedule↵
 ("Tuesday","Zero","Zero","Seven","FortyFive");$schedule.SetSchedule↵
 ("Tuesday","Seventeen","Zero","TwentyThree","FortyFive");↵
$schedule.SetSchedule ("Wednesday","Zero","Zero","Seven","FortyFive");↵
$schedule.SetSchedule ("Wednesday","Seventeen","Zero","TwentyThree","FortyFive")↵
;$schedule.SetSchedule ("Thursday","Zero","Zero","Seven","FortyFive");↵
$schedule.SetSchedule ("Thursday","Seventeen","Zero","TwentyThree","FortyFive")↵
;$schedule.SetSchedule ("Friday","Zero","Zero","Seven","FortyFive")↵
;$schedule.SetSchedule ("Friday","Seventeen","Zero","TwentyThree","FortyFive")↵
```

```
;$schedule.SetSchedule ("Saturday","Zero","Zero","TwentyThree","FortyFive")↵
;$schedule.SetSchedule ("Sunday","Zero","Zero","TwentyThree","FortyFive");↵
Set-ADReplicationSiteLink "<SiteLinkName>" -ReplicationSchedule $schedule
```

Discussion

When you configure an inter-site replication link, you can specify a particular schedule during which the link will be available for replication. By default, inter-site links can pass replication traffic 24 hours a day, seven days a week, but you can restrict this so that it is only available for specific hours of the day and/or days of the week. This might be useful for a heavily utilized link that you do not want to have overloaded with replication traffic. For example, a bank headquarters may wish to prevent replication traffic from being initiated during a two-hour time period at the end of every day while its branch offices are transmitting daily report information.

Using PowerShell

The SetSchedule method is used, which allows each day of the week to have a different schedule, if desired. This is handy when, for example, replication is available all day and all night on weekends. An alternative is to use the SetDailySchedule method, which will use the same replication schedule for every day of the week.

See Also

Recipe 12.4 to force replication from one DC to another; MSDN: ActiveDirectory-Schedule Class

11.18. Disabling Site Link Transitivity or Site Link Schedules

Problem

You want to disable site link transitivity to control replication manually.

Solution

Using a graphical user interface

1. Open the Active Directory Sites and Services snap-in (*dssite.msc*).
2. In the left pane, expand Sites→Inter-Site Transports.
3. Right-click either the IP or SMTP folder, depending on which protocol you want to disable transitivity or ignore schedules for.
4. Select Properties.

5. To disable site link transitivity, uncheck "Bridge all site links".

6. To ignore site link schedules, check "Ignore schedules".

7. Click OK.

Using PowerShell

To disable site link transitivity and site link schedules, use the following syntax:

```
Set-ADObject "cn=ip,cn=inter-site transports,cn=sites,cn=configuration,↵
<ForestRootDN>" -Replace @{Options=2}
```

Discussion

Active Directory site links, by default, are transitive, which means that if site A is linked to site B, and site B is linked to site C, then site A is also linked (through site B) to site C. The KCC uses transitivity when making decisions about creating connection objects. You can, however, disable this behavior if you so choose. Typically, this is not something you'll want to do without a very good reason. Disabling transitivity may be necessary, for example, in some legacy deployments that have a lot of sites and find that the KCC is having a hard time keeping up. Since Windows Server 2003, the KCC has been greatly improved, and site link transitivity should not cause these problems.

The other reason you might want to disable transitivity is if you need to make replication more deterministic—that is, you want to exert more manual control over the process. Disabling transitivity makes it much easier to determine where the KCC will attempt to establish connection objects, because the KCC on a domain controller will not be able to replicate with domain controllers that are not in sites that are directly linked. There can be other reasons, one of which is when you have nonroutable networks.

We mention site link schedules here primarily because the same attribute (i.e., op tions) that determines site link transitivity also determines whether link schedules are enforced. If you enable the ignore schedules option for a particular transport (i.e., IP or SMTP), the KCC ignores any preconfigured link schedules. If you later disable this setting, link schedules will go back into effect.

Using PowerShell

There are multiple value variations for the options attribute. By setting the value to 4, it reverts the settings to the default (all site links bridged with schedules enabled). By setting the value to 3, it disables site link bridging while ignoring schedules. By setting the value to 1, it enables site link bridging and ignores schedules.

See Also

Recipe 4.15 for more on setting a bit-flag attribute

11.19. Creating a Site Link Bridge

Problem

You want to create a site link bridge because you've disabled site link transitivity.

Solution

Using a graphical user interface

1. Open the Active Directory Sites and Services snap-in (*dssite.msc*).
2. In the left pane, expand Sites→Inter-Site Transports.
3. Right-click either the IP or SMTP folder, depending on which protocol you want to create a site link bridge for.
4. Select New Site Link Bridge.
5. Enter a name for the bridge.
6. Highlight two or more site links in the left box.
7. Click the Add button.
8. Click OK.

Using a command-line interface

Create an LDIF file called *create_site_link_bridge.ldf* with the following contents, where *<Link1>* and *<Link2>* refer to the site links to be bridged:

```
dn: cn=<BridgeName>,cn=IP,cn=inter-site transports,cn=sites,cn=configuration,↵
;<ForestRootDN>
changetype: add
objectclass: siteLinkBridge
siteLinkList: cn=<Link1>,cn=IP,cn=Inter-site
Transports,cn=sites,cn=configuration,<ForestRootDN>
siteLinkList: cn=<Link2>,cn=IP,cn=Inter-site
Transports,cn=sites,cn=configuration,<ForestRootDN>
```

Then run the following command:

```
> ldifde -v -i -f create_site_link_bridge.ldf
```

You can also create a site link bridge using AdMod, as follows:

```
> admod -b "cn=<BridgeName>,cn=IP,cn=inter-site transports,cn=sites,↵
cn=configuration,<ForestRootDN>" objectclass::siteLinkBridge↵
 "sitelinklist:++:cn=<FirstSiteLink>,cn=IP,cn=inter-site transports,↵
cn=sites,cn=configuration,<ForestRootDN>;cn=<SecondSiteLink>,cn=IP,↵
 cn=inter-site transports,cn=sites,cn=configuration,<ForestRootDN>" -add
```

Using PowerShell

To create a site link bridge by using PowerShell, use the following syntax:

```
New-ADReplicationSiteLinkBridge "<BridgeName>" -SiteLinksIncluded↵
"<SiteLink1>","<SiteLink2>"
```

Discussion

If you've disabled site link transitivity or have networks that lack direct routes between sites, you should create *site link bridges*. Creating a site link bridge to link several links is analogous to creating a site link to link several sites. Let's take an example where site link transitivity is disabled and we have four sites, among which site A has a link to site B and site C has a link to site D. If site link transitivity has been disabled and we want domain controllers in sites A and B to replicate with sites C and D, we need to create a site link bridge to bridge the A–B link with the C–D link.

See Also

Recipe 11.18 for disabling site link transitivity

11.20. Finding the Bridgehead Servers for a Site

Problem

You want to find the bridgehead servers for a site.

Solution

Using a graphical user interface

1. The *replmon.exe* utility is no longer available in Windows Server 2008 and later; for 2008 and later servers the command-line interface option is appropriate. Open the Replication Monitor from the Support Tools (*replmon.exe*)

2. From the menu, select View→Options.

3. In the left pane, right-click on Monitored Servers and select Add Monitored Server.

4. Use the Add Monitored Server Wizard to add a server in the site you want to find the bridgehead server(s) for.

5. In the left pane, right-click on the server and select Show BridgeHead Servers→In This Server's Site.

Using a command-line interface

```
> repadmin /bridgeheads [<ServerName>] [/verbose]
```

Using PowerShell

To search for all bridgehead servers in a site, use the following syntax:

```
Get-ADObject -Filter {objectClass -eq "server"} -SearchBase↵
"cn=<SiteName>,cn=sites,cn=configuration,<ForestRootDN>"↵
-SearchScope subtree -Properties * |↵
Where {$_.bridgeheadTransportList -ne $NULL} |↵
Select Name,bridgeheadTransportList
```

To search for all bridgehead servers across all sites in the domain, use the following syntax:

```
Get-ADObject -Filter {objectClass -eq "server"} -SearchBase↵
"cn=sites,cn=configuration,<ForestRootDN>" -SearchScope subtree -Properties *↵
| Where {$_.bridgeheadTransportList -ne $NULL} |↵
Select Name,bridgeheadTransportList
```

Discussion

Bridgehead servers are responsible for replicating data between sites. Instead of all domain controllers replicating the same naming contexts outside of the site, the bridgehead servers act as a funnel for replication into and out of a site. Any domain controller in a site can become a bridgehead server, and bridgeheads are designated by the KCC for each writable partition in the site. You can control which servers are designated as bridgehead servers by defining preferred bridgehead servers (see Recipe 11.21 for more on how to do this).

See Also

"Active Directory Replication Concepts" (*http://bit.ly/15qGEJA*); "Bridgehead Server Selection" (*http://bit.ly/10gT9EM*)

11.21. Setting a Preferred Bridgehead Server for a Site

Problem

You want to set a preferred bridgehead server for a site.

Solution

Using a graphical user interface

1. Open the Active Directory Sites and Services snap-in (*dssite.msc*).

---

2. In the left pane, expand Sites, expand the site where the server you want to set as a bridgehead is contained, and expand the Servers container.

3. Right-click on the server you want to set as the bridgehead and select Properties.

4. Highlight IP, SMTP, or both, depending on the protocol(s) for which you want the server to be a bridgehead.

5. Click the Add button.

6. Click OK.

Using a command-line interface

Create an LDIF file called *set_bridgehead_server.ldf* with the following contents:

```
dn: cn=<DCName>,cn=servers,cn=<SiteName>,cn=sites,cn=configuration,<ForestRootDN>
changetype: modify
add: bridgeheadTransportList
bridgeheadTransportList: cn=IP,cn=Inter-site
Transports,cn=sites,cn=configuration,<ForestRootDN>
-
```

Then run the following command:

```
> ldifde -v -i -f set_bridgehead_server.ldf
```

You can also set the preferred bridgehead server with AdMod, using the following syntax:

```
Admod -b cn=<DCName>,cn=servers,cn=<SiteName>,cn=sites,cn=configuration,↵
<ForestRootDN> bridgeheadTransportList:+:"cn=IP,cn=Inter-site transports,↵
cn=sites,cn=configuration,<ForestRootDN>"
```

Using PowerShell

You can set a preferred bridgehead server using the following syntax. Note that the transport can be set as IP or SMTP.

```
Set-ADObject -Identity "cn=<DCName>,cn=servers,cn=<SiteName>,cn=sites,↵
cn=configuration, <ForestRootDN>" -Add @{bridgeHeadTransportList="↵
cn=<Transport>,cn=Inter-site Transports,cn=sites,cn=configuration,↵
<ForestRootDN>"}
```

Discussion

Setting a preferred bridgehead server can give you more control over which domain controllers participate in inter-site replication, but it is also limiting. The KCC typically selects bridgehead servers dynamically, but if you set preferred bridgehead servers, the KCC will not select new ones if the preferred servers become unavailable. Therefore, you should ensure that if you do select preferred bridgehead servers, you select at least two for a given partition in a site.

As a general rule, you shouldn't set preferred bridgehead servers if at all possible.

See Also

"Active Directory Replication Concepts" (*http://bit.ly/15qGEJA*)

11.22. Listing the Servers

Problem

You want to list the `server` objects in the site topology.

Solution

Using a graphical user interface

1. Open the Active Directory Sites and Services snap-in (*dssite.msc*).
2. In the left pane, expand Sites and then expand the site where you want to list the servers.
3. Expand Servers under the site to list the servers in the site.

Using a command-line interface

```
> dsquery server [-site <SiteName>]
```

To list all servers in the site topology using AdFind, use the following syntax:

```
> adfind -config -rb cn=sites -f (objectcategory=server)
```

To restrict the results to a specific site, do the following:

```
> adfind -config -rb cn=<SiteName>,cn=sites -f (objectcategory=server)
```

Using PowerShell

To list all servers in the site topology by using PowerShell, use the following syntax:

```
Get-ADObject -SearchBase "cn=sites,cn=configuration,<ForestRootDN>" -Filter↵
{objectCategory -eq "server"} | Select Name
```

To list all servers in a specific site, use the following syntax:

```
Get-ADObject -SearchBase "cn=<SiteName>,cn=sites,cn=configuration,↵
<ForestRootDN>" -Filter {objectCategory -eq "server"} | Select Name
```

Discussion

Each Active Directory domain controller is represented in the site topology by a `server` object that is associated with a specific site. Replication decisions are made based on links from this site to other sites that contain domain controllers.

Other types of services can also add `server` objects to the site topology. The way you can distinguish which ones are domain controllers is the presence of an `NTDS Settings` (`nTDSDSA`) object that is a child of the `server` object. Only domain controllers will have that object.

11.23. Moving a Domain Controller to a Different Site

Problem

You want to move a domain controller to a different site.

Solution

Using a graphical user interface

1. Open the Active Directory Sites and Services snap-in (*dssite.msc*).
2. In the left pane, expand Sites, expand the site where the server you want to move is contained, and expand the `Servers` container.
3. Right-click on the server you want to move and select Move.
4. Select the site to move the server to.
5. Click OK.

 You can also drag and drop the `server` object from one site to another, if desired. To do so, drag the `server` object to the desired `Servers` container under the destination site.

Using a command-line interface

You can move a domain controller to a new site using either the built-in DSMove utility or AdMod. DSMove takes the following syntax:

```
> dsmove "cn=<ServerName>,cn=servers,cn=<CurrentSite>,↵
cn=sites,cn=configuration,<ForestRootDN>" -newparent "cn=servers,cn=<NewSite>,↵
cn=sites,cn=configuration,<ForestRootDN>"
```

To move a DC using AdMod, use the following syntax:

```
> admod -b "cn=<ServerName>,cn=servers,cn=<CurrrentSite>,↵
cn=sites,cn=configuration,<ForestRootDN> -move "cn=servers,cn=<NewSite>,↵
cn=sites,cn=configuration,<ForestRootDN>
```

Using PowerShell

To move a domain controller to a different site by using PowerShell, use the following syntax:

```
Move-ADObject -Identity "cn=<ServerName>,cn=servers,cn=<CurrentSite>,↵
cn=sites,cn=configuration,<ForestRootDN>" -TargetPath↵
 "cn=servers,cn=<NewSite>,cn=sites,cn=configuration,<ForestRootDN>"
```

Discussion

After you move a server to a new site, you might want to monitor replication to and from that server to make sure that any new connections that are needed get created and start replicating. See Recipe 12.2 for more on viewing the replication status of a server.

See Also

"Automatic detection of site membership for domain controllers" (*http://support.micro soft.com/kb/214677*)

11.24. Configuring a Domain Controller to Cover Multiple Sites

Problem

You want to configure a domain controller to cover multiple sites, which will cause clients in all of those sites to use that domain controller for authentication and directory lookups.

Solution

Using a graphical user interface

1. Run the Group Policy Management snap-in.
2. Locate the GPO that applies to the domain controller.
3. Right-click on the policy and then click Edit.
4. In the Group Policy Management Editor, browse to Computer Configuration→Administrative Templates→System→Net Logon→DC Locator DNS Records.

5. Double-click the "Specify sites covered by the DC Locator DNS SRV records" setting.

6. Click Enabled and then enter the sites that the DC should cover in the Sites dialog box. Each site should be separated by a space.

7. Click OK and then close the Group Policy Management Editor.

Discussion

In an Active Directory environment, it is perfectly valid to have a site that does not contain its own domain controller. In fact, if you model the site topology after your real network, some sites will lack their own domain controllers unless you've deployed a branch office architecture or have very few sites. If you create sites without any domain controllers, the site links between the sites will determine which domain controllers will *cover* or advertise their services to the site. When a domain controller covers for a remote site, it needs to publish site-specific DNS resource records that clients in the remote site can use to find the domain controller. Active Directory will select DCs to cover DC-less sites automatically, but you can hardcode the list of sites a specific domain controller should cover by using a Group Policy setting as described in the preceding section.

11.25. Viewing the Site Coverage for a Domain Controller

Problem

You want to view the sites that a domain controller covers.

Solution

Using a command-line interface

In the following command, replace *<DomainControllerName>* with the name of the domain controller you want to view site coverage for:

```
> nltest /server:<DomainControllerName> /DsGetSiteCov
```

Discussion

Recipe 11.24 describes how to configure a domain controller to cover multiple sites. Recipe 11.26 describes how you can prevent a domain controller from covering for any sites other than its own.

See Also

MSDN: DsGetDcSiteCoverage

11.26. Disabling Automatic Site Coverage for a Domain Controller

Problem

You want to prevent a domain controller from covering sites outside of the one in which it resides.

Solution

Using a graphical user interface

1. Run *regedit.exe* from the command line or select Start→Run.
2. Expand *HKEY_LOCAL_MACHINE\SYSTEM\CurrentControlSet\Services\Netlogon\Parameters*.
3. Right-click on Parameters and select New→DWORD Value.
4. For the name, enter AutoSiteCoverage.
5. Double-click on the new value, enter 0 under Value data, and click OK.

Using a command-line interface

```
> reg add HKLM\System\CurrentControlSet\Services\Netlogon\Parameters /v↵
AutoSiteCoverage /t REG_DWORD /d 0
```

Using PowerShell

```
$strRegPath = "HKLM:\System\CurrentControlSet\Services\Netlogon\Parameters"
set-ItemProperty -path $strRegPath -name "AutoSiteCoverage" -value 0
```

Discussion

If you want to reduce the load on a domain controller, one way is to prevent it from covering for other sites. Automatic site coverage happens when a site does not contain any domain controllers.

See Also

Recipe 11.25 for viewing the site coverage for a domain controller

11.27. Finding the Site for a Client

Problem

You want to find which site a client computer is located in.

Solution

Using a command-line interface

In the following command, replace *<HostName>* with the name of the host you want to find the site for:

```
> nltest /server:<HostName> /DsGetSite
```

 You'll use the /server: *<HostName>* parameter even if you are specifying a client computer.

Microsoft provides a DsGetSiteName method that can be used by languages such as Visual Basic and C++ to retrieve site coverage information. In fact, the nltest command shown in the CLI solution is a wrapper around this method.

The IADsTool interface provides a wrapper around this method:

```
set objIadsTools = CreateObject("IADsTools.DCFunctions")
strSite = objIadsTools.DsGetSiteName("<HostName>")
Wscript.Echo "Site: " & strSite
```

Discussion

Each domain controller has a server object that is contained within a site. Clients are different—they are associated with a site based on their IP address, and the corresponding subnet that it matches is in the Subnets container. The client site information is important because it determines the domain controller the client authenticates with. If the client's IP address does not match the subnet range of any of the subnets stored in Active Directory, it will randomly pick a site to use, which means it could authenticate against any domain controller in the domain. See Recipe 11.28 for a way to hardcode the site association for a client.

See Also

Recipe 11.28 for forcing a host into a particular site; MSDN: DsGetSiteName

11.28. Forcing a Host into a Particular Site

Problem

You want to force a host to be in a particular site.

Solution

Using a graphical user interface

1. Run *regedit.exe*.

2. Expand *HKEY_LOCAL_MACHINE\SYSTEM\CurrentControlSet\Services\Netlogon\Parameters*.

3. Right-click on Parameters and select New→String Value.

4. Enter SiteName for the name.

5. Double-click on the new value, enter the name of the site under Value data, and click OK.

Using a command-line interface

```
> reg add HKLM\System\CurrentControlSet\Services\Netlogon\Parameters↵
/v SiteName /t
REG_SZ /d <SiteName>
```

Using PowerShell

```
$strRegPath = "HKLM:\System\CurrentControlSet\Services\Netlogon\Parameters"
set-ItemProperty -path $strRegPath -name "SiteName" -value "<SiteName>"
```

Discussion

You can bypass the part of the DC Locator process that determines a client's site by hardcoding it in the Registry. This is generally not recommended and should primarily be used as a troubleshooting tool. If a client is experiencing authentication delays due to a misconfigured site or subnet object, you can hardcode its site so that it temporarily points to a more optimal location (and domain controller) to see whether this alleviates the problem. However, in a situation like this, your ultimate goal should be to properly configure your sites and subnets so that the DC Locator process can function without this kind of manual intervention.

 Unlike client computers, hardcoding a domain controller via this solution does not change the site of the domain controller.

See Also

Recipe 11.27 for finding the site for a client

11.29. Creating a connection Object

Problem

You want to create a connection object to manually set up replication between two servers.

Solution

Using a graphical user interface

1. Open the Active Directory Sites and Services snap-in (*dssite.msc*).
2. In the left pane, expand Sites, expand the site that contains the connection object you want to check, expand the Servers container, and expand the server for which you want to create the connection object.
3. Right-click on the NTDS Settings object, click New, and then click Connection.
4. Select the replication partner and click OK.
5. Enter the name for the connection and click OK.

Using a command-line interface

```
> repadmin /add <PartitionDN> <DC1DNSName> <DC2DNSName>
```

Discussion

Hopefully you will not need to create connection objects manually, since creating and maintaining connection objects is the job of the KCC. It can be a lot of work to keep your connection objects up to date by yourself, especially if you have a large topology. The KCC uses complex algorithms to determine the best partners for a domain controller to replicate with.

It is sometimes necessary to create connections manually if you find a replication problem and need to get replication going again between one or more sites. By creating a connection and forcing replication to occur over that connection, you can get servers back in sync quickly.

See Also

Recipe 11.30 for listing the connection objects for a server

11.30. Listing the connection Objects for a Server

Problem

You want to view the connection objects associated with a domain controller.

Solution

Using a graphical user interface

1. Open the Active Directory Sites and Services snap-in (*dssite.msc*).
2. In the left pane, expand Sites, expand the site that contains the connection object you want to check, expand the Servers container, expand the server that contains the connection object, and click on the NTDS Settings object.

   In the right pane, under the Name column, the snap-in will display which connection objects were automatically generated by the KCC and which ones were manually generated.

Using a command-line interface

```
> repadmin /showconn [<DomainControllerName>]
```

Using PowerShell

```
Get-ADObject -SearchBase "cn=<DCName>,cn=servers,cn=<SiteName>,cn=sites,↵
cn=configuration,<ForestRootDN>" -Filter {objectClass -eq↵
 "nTDSConnection"} -Properties * | FL Name,fromServer
```

Discussion

connection objects are used to replicate inbound changes to a domain controller. By viewing the connection objects for a server, you can see what domain controllers it receives updates from. connection objects are created automatically by the KCC, but they can be created manually if necessary.

See Also

Recipe 11.29 for creating a connection object

11.31. Finding the ISTG for a Site

Problem

You want to find the Inter-Site Topology Generator (ISTG) for a site.

Solution

Using a graphical user interface

1. Open the Active Directory Sites and Services snap-in (*dssite.msc*).
2. Click on the site you are interested in.
3. In the right pane, double-click on the `NTDS Site Settings` object.

   The ISTG will be displayed under Inter-Site Topology Generator if one is present.

Using a command-line interface

You can query for this information using *repadmin*:

```
> repadmin /istg
```

You can also use AdFind, as follows:

```
> adfind -config -rb "cn=ntds site settings,cn=<SiteName>,cn=sites"
intersitetopologygenerator
```

Using PowerShell

```
Get-ADObject -Identity "cn=NTDS Site Settings,cn=<SiteName>,cn=sites,
cn=configuration,<ForestRootDN>" -Properties interSiteTopologyGenerator |
 Select interSiteTopologyGenerator
```

Discussion

One domain controller in every site is picked as the ISTG for that site. While each domain controller is responsible for creating its own intra-site `connection` objects, the ISTG for a site is responsible for creating the inter-site `connection` objects for the bridgehead servers in the site.

The current ISTG for a site is stored in the `interSiteTopologyGenerator` attribute of the site's `NTDS Site Settings` object. The distinguished name of ISTG's `NTDS Settings` object is stored in the `interSiteTopologyGenerator` attribute.

Disabling inter-site topology generation is synonymous with disabling the KCC for a site. See Recipe 11.35 for more information on disabling the KCC.

See Also

Recipe 11.32 for moving the ISTG; Recipe 11.35; "The Role of the Inter-Site Topology Generator in Active Directory Replication" (*http://support.microsoft.com/kb/224815*)

11.32. Transferring the ISTG to Another Server

Problem

You want to move the ISTG for a site to another domain controller. This happens automatically if you take the current ISTG offline, but you may want to transfer the role to a server that is more optimal in your environment.

Solution

Using a graphical user interface

1. Open the Active Directory Sites and Services snap-in (*dssite.msc*).
2. Click on the site you are interested in.
3. In the right pane, double-click on the NTDS Site Settings object.
4. Open the Attribute Editor tab and then modify the interSiteTopologyGenerator attribute to include the DN of the NTDS Settings object of the domain controller you want to transfer the ISTG role to.
5. Click OK.

Using a command-line interface

```
> admod -b "cn=NTDS Site Settings,cn=<SiteName>,cn=sites,cn=configuration,↵
;<ForestRootDN>" interSiteTopologyGenerator::"cn=NTDS Site Settings, ↵
;cn=<NewISTGName>,cn=servers,cn=<SiteName>,cn=sites,cn=configuration,↵
<ForestRootDN>
```

Using PowerShell

You can modify the Inter-Site Topology Generator for an AD site by using PowerShell, as follows:

```
Set-ADObject -Identity "cn=NTDS Site Settings,cn=<SiteName>,cn=sites,↵
cn=configuration,<ForestRootDN>" -Replace @{interSiteTopologyGenerator=↵
"cn=NTDS Settings,<DCName>,cn=Servers,cn=<SiteName>,cn=Sites,cn=Configuration,↵
<ForestRootDN>"}
```

Discussion

The current ISTG for a site is stored as the DN of the ISTG's NTDS Settings object in the interSiteTopologyGenerator attribute of the site's NTDS Site Settings object.

Domain controllers communicate their presence as the ISTG by writing to the interSiteTopologyGenerator attribute at a set interval. If you want another domain controller to assume the role of the ISTG, you need to write the distinguished name of that domain controller's `NTDS Settings` object to the `interSiteTopologyGenerator` attribute of the `NTDS Site Settings` object for the site.

Two Registry settings govern the ISTG registration process, both of which are stored under the *HKEY_LOCAL_MACHINE\System\CurrentControlSet\Services\NTDS\Parameters* key. The interval (in minutes) in which the current ISTG should write to the `interSiteTopologyGenerator` attribute to inform the other DCs in the site that it is still the ISTG is stored in the `KCC site generator renewal interval (minutes)` value. The default is 30 minutes. The other value is named `KCC site generator fail over (minutes)` and contains the time in minutes that each domain controller in the site should wait for the `interSiteTopologyGenerator` attribute to be written to before attempting to register itself as the ISTG. The default is 60 minutes.

See Also

"The Role of the Inter-Site Topology Generator in Active Directory Replication" (*http://support.microsoft.com/kb/224815*)

11.33. Triggering the KCC

Problem

You want to trigger the KCC.

Solution

Using a graphical user interface

1. Open the Active Directory Sites and Services snap-in (*dssite.msc*).
2. In the left pane, browse to the `NTDS Settings` object for the server you want to trigger the KCC for.
3. Right-click on `NTDS Settings`, select All Tasks, and check Replication Topology.
4. Click OK.

Using a command-line interface

```
> repadmin /kcc <DomainControllerName>
```

Using PowerShell

```
$domain = [System.DirectoryServices.ActiveDirectory.Domain]::GetCurrentDomain();↵
foreach ($domaincontroller in $domain.FindAllDomainControllers())↵
{$domaincontroller.CheckReplicationConsistency()}
```

Discussion

The KCC runs every 15 minutes by default on all domain controllers to generate the intra-site topology connections. The KCC that runs on the server that is selected as the ISTG generates inter-site topology connections to other sites from the bridgehead servers in its site. In some situations—such as when you create new `site`, `siteLink`, or `subnet` objects—you may want to run the KCC immediately so that any new connections between domain controllers are created right away.

See Also

Recipe 11.34 for determining whether the KCC is completing successfully; "The Role of the Inter-Site Topology Generator in Active Directory Replication" (*http://support.microsoft.com/kb/224815*)

11.34. Determining Whether the KCC Is Completing Successfully

Problem

You want to determine whether the KCC is completing successfully.

Solution

Using a graphical user interface

1. Open the Event Viewer of the target domain controller.

2. Expand Applications and Services Logs.

3. Click on the Directory Service log.

4. In the right pane, click on the Source heading to sort by that column.

5. Scroll down to view any events with `Source: NTDS KCC`.

Using a command-line interface

The following command will check to see whether the KCC is completing without errors:

```
> dcdiag /v /test:kccevent /s:<DomainControllerName>
```

Using PowerShell

The following syntax will query the Directory Service log for all events that have a source of "NTDS KCC":

```
Get-EventLog "Directory Service" | Where-Object {$_.Source -eq "NTDS KCC" } | FL
```

Discussion

The main way to debug issues with the KCC is by looking for NTDS KCC events in the Directory Service event log. If you suspect a problem or perhaps are seeing errors, you can increase the amount of logging in the event log by enabling diagnostics logging for the KCC. When KCC diagnostics logging is enabled, each KCC exception logs a significant amount of information to the event log that may help you pinpoint the problem. See Recipe 15.1 for more information on enabling diagnostics logging.

11.35. Disabling the KCC for a Site

Problem

You want to disable the KCC for a site and generate your own replication connections between domain controllers.

Solution

Using a graphical user interface

1. Open the Active Directory Sites and Services snap-in (*dssite.msc*).
2. Click on the site you are interested in.
3. In the right pane, double-click on the NTDS Site Settings object.
4. Modify the options attribute. To disable only intra-site topology generation, enable bit 0 (decimal 1). To disable inter-site topology generation, enable bit 4 (decimal 16). To disable both, enable both bit 4 and bit 1 (decimal 17).
5. Click OK.

Using a command-line interface

You can disable the KCC for *<SiteName>* by using the *ldifde* utility and an LDIF file that contains the following:

```
dn: cn=NTDS Site Settings,<SiteName>,cn=sites,cn=configuration,<ForestRootDN>
changetype: modify
replace: options
options: <OptionsValue>
-
```

If the LDIF file were named *disable_kcc.ldf*, you would run the following command:

```
> ldifde -v -i -f disable_kcc.ldf
```

You can also perform this change using a combination of AdFind and AdMod, as follows:

```
> adfind -b "cn=NTDS Site Settings,cn=<SiteName>,cn=Sites,cn=configuration, ↵
;<ForestRootDN>" options -adcsv | admod options::{{.:SET:<OptionsValue>}}
```

 The *ldifde* solution simply overwrites the value of the options attribute without checking to see whether any current value may be in place. See Recipe 4.15, or use the AdFind/AdMod solution for a safer method to modify bitwise values.

Using PowerShell

The following command will update the options attribute. To disable only intra-site topology generation, enter the number 1 for the value. To disable inter-site topology generation, enter the number 16 for the value. To disable both, enter the number 17 as the value.

```
Set-ADObject "cn=NTDS Site Settings,cn=<SiteName>,cn=sites,cn=configuration, ↵
;<ForestRootDN>" -Replace @{Options="<OptionsValue>"}
```

Using PowerShell

To clear the attribute and revert to the <not set> default value, use the following command:

```
Set-ADObject "cn=NTDS Site Settings,cn=<SiteName>,cn=sites,cn=configuration, ↵
;<ForestRootDN>" -Clear Options
```

Discussion

In some cases, you may want to disable the KCC from generating the intra-site topology connections, inter-site topology connections, or both. The connection objects that the KCC dynamically creates determine how domain controllers replicate with each other. Disabling the KCC was sometimes necessary with legacy versions of Windows due to scalability issues with the KCC and very large topologies. Since Windows Server 2003, the KCC has been greatly improved, and it is unlikely that you will need to disable the KCC. If you disable the KCC, you will need to pay close attention to any domain controller or site topology changes and manually adjust the connection objects accordingly.

Disabling the KCC can be done only at the site level. You have to modify the NTDS Site Settings object of the site for which you want to disable the KCC. The options attribute (a bit flag) on this object determines whether the KCC runs. If the 00001 bit is enabled, intra-site topology generation is disabled; if the 10000 bit is enabled (16 in decimal), inter-site topology generation is disabled. See Recipe 4.15 for more on the proper way to set bit flags.

See Also

Recipe 4.15 for more on setting bit flags; Recipe 11.29 for creating a `connection` object manually

11.36. Changing the Interval at Which the KCC Runs

Problem

You want to change the interval at which the KCC runs.

Solution

Using a graphical user interface

1. Run *regedit.exe*.
2. Expand *HKEY_LOCAL_MACHINE\SYSTEM\CurrentControlSet\Services\NTDS \Parameters*.
3. Right-click on Parameters and select New→DWORD Value.
4. Enter the following for the name: `Repl topology update period (secs)`.
5. Double-click on the new value, and under "Value data" enter the KCC interval in number of seconds (900 is the default).
6. Click OK.

Using a command-line interface

```
> reg add HKLM\System\CurrentControlSet\Services\NTDS\Parameters↵
 /v "Repl topology
update period (secs)" /t REG_DWORD /d <NumberOfSeconds>
```

Using PowerShell

```
$strRegPath = "HKLM:\System\CurrentControlSet\Services\NTDS\Parameters";↵
set-ItemProperty -path $strRegPath -name "Repl topology update period (secs)"↵
 -value "<NumberOfSeconds>"
```

Discussion

By default, the KCC checks its connections every 15 minutes and makes changes as necessary. You can modify this interval by simply modifying the Registry.

There is another related Registry setting you should also be aware of. By default, the KCC waits five minutes after Active Directory starts up before it runs. You can change this delay by creating a `REG_DWORD` value called `Repl topology update delay` (`secs`) under the *HKLM\System\CurrentControlSet\Services\NTDS\Parameters* key. The data for the value should be the number of seconds to wait after startup before the KCC starts. The default is 300, which is five minutes.

See Also

MS KB 271988 (Replication Topology Updates)

## CHAPTER 12

Replication

12.0. Introduction

Replication is one of the most important and perhaps complex components of Active Directory. The infrastructure behind Active Directory replication, including the site topology, connection objects, and the KCC, was covered in Chapter 11. This chapter focuses strictly on some of the tasks and processes associated with replicating data and checking replication health. For an in-depth overview of how replication works in Active Directory, we suggest reading *Active Directory*, Fifth Edition by Brian Desmond et al. (O'Reilly).

12.1. Determining Whether Two Domain Controllers Are in Sync

Problem

You want to determine whether two domain controllers are in sync and you do not have objects to replicate to each other.

Solution

Using a command-line interface

By running the following command you can compare the up-to-dateness vector on DC1 and DC2:

```
> repadmin /showutdvec <DC1> <NamingContextDN>
> repadmin /showutdvec <DC2> <NamingContextDN>
```

Using PowerShell

By running the following command you can compare the up-to-dateness vector on a domain controller named DC1 and a domain controller named DC2:

```
Get-ADReplicationUpToDatenessVectorTable -Target DC1,DC2
```

Discussion

To determine whether two or more DCs are in sync from a replication standpoint, you need to compare their up-to-dateness vectors. Each domain controller stores what it thinks is the highest update sequence number (USN) for every DC that replicates a naming context. This is called the *up-to-dateness vector*. If you want to compare DC1 and DC2, you'd first want to get the up-to-dateness vector for DC1 and compare DC1's highest USN against what DC2 thinks DC1's highest USN is. If they are different, then you can deduce that DC2 has not yet replicated all the changes from DC1. Next, compare the reverse to see whether DC1 is in sync with DC2.

See Also

`Get-ADReplicationUpToDatenessVectorTable` cmdlet reference (*http://bit.ly/15raXQe*)

12.2. Viewing the Replication Status of Several Domain Controllers

Problem

You want to take a quick snapshot of replication activity for one or more domain controllers.

Solution

Using a command-line interface

The following command will show the replication status of all the domain controllers in the forest, as shown in the output that follows:

```
> repadmin /replsum

Replication Summary Start Time: 2012-11-29 20:09:22

Beginning data collection for replication summary, this may take awhile:
 .....
```

```
Source DC          largest delta  fails/total %% error
    DC1                15m:22s    0 /   3    0
    DC2                   :12s    0 /   3    0

Destination DC largest delta    fails/total %% error
    DC1                   :05s    0 /   3    0
    DC2                15m:22s    0 /   3    0
```

You can also use * as a wildcard character to view the status of a subset of domain controllers. The following command will display the replication status of the servers that begin with the name dc-rtp:

```
> repadmin /replsum dc-rtp*
```

Using PowerShell

The following PowerShell command will display the time of the last successful replication for the specified domain controller:

```
Get-ADReplicationPartnerMetadata <DomainController> | FL LastReplicationSuccess
```

Discussion

The /replsum option in *repadmin* is a great way to quickly determine whether there are any replication issues. This command should be your starting point if you suspect any replication problems. If you are running /replsum against a lot of domain controllers, you can use the /sort option to sort the returned table output by any of the table columns. You can also use the /errorsonly option to display only the replication partners who are encountering errors.

See Also

Get-ADReplicationPartnerMetadata cmdlet reference (*http://bit.ly/10gZaRJ*); "AD Replication Status Tool is Live" (*http://bit.ly/18Nmtlw*)

12.3. Viewing Unreplicated Changes Between Two Domain Controllers

Problem

You want to find the unreplicated changes between two domain controllers.

Solution

Using a command-line interface

Run the following commands to find the differences between two domain controllers. Use the /statistics option to view a summary of the changes.

```
> repadmin /showchanges <DC1Name> <NamingContextDN>
> repadmin /showchanges <DC2Name> <NamingContextDN>
```

Discussion

The solution shows how to display the current unreplicated changes between two domain controllers. This can be useful in troubleshooting replication on your network, particularly if you are finding inconsistent information between one or more domain controllers. The repadmin /showchanges command has several additional options you can use to display the changes, including saving the output to a file for later comparison. Also, with the /statistics option, you can view a summary of the changes.

See Also

"Using Repadmin.exe to troubleshoot Active Directory replication" (*http://support.microsoft.com/kb/229896*)

12.4. Forcing Replication from One Domain Controller to Another

Problem

You want to force replication between two partners.

Solution

Using a graphical user interface

1. Open the Active Directory Sites and Services snap-in (*dssite.msc*).

2. Browse to the NTDS Setting object for the domain controller you want to replicate to.

3. In the right pane, right-click on the connection object corresponding to the domain controller you want to replicate from and select Replicate Now.

Using a command-line interface

The following command will perform a replication sync from *<DC2Name>* to *<DC1Name>* of the naming context specified by *<NamingContextDN>*:

```
> repadmin /replicate <DC1Name> <DC2Name> <NamingContextDN>
```

Using PowerShell

```
$strDCname = <DomainDNSName>
$context = New-Object↵
System.DirectoryServices.ActiveDirectory.DirectoryContext('DirectoryServer',↵
$strDCname)
$dc =↵
[System.DirectoryServices.ActiveDirectory.DomainController]↵
::getDomainController($context)
$strPartDN = "<Partition DN>"
$dc.TriggerSyncReplicaFromNeighbors($strPartDN)
```

Discussion

Each solution shows how to replicate all unreplicated changes from a source domain controller to a destination domain controller. This sync is a one-way operation. If you want to ensure that both domain controllers are in sync, you'll need to follow the same procedure in the opposite direction, replicating both from DC1 to DC2 and from DC2 to DC1. It's important to remember that all replication takes place as a *pull* operation. For example, DC2 notifies DC1 that it has changes available, after which DC1 pulls the changes it needs from DC2. For replication to occur in the opposite direction, DC1 will notify DC2 that it has changes available, and DC2 will pull those changes from DC1.

 With *repadmin*, you can replicate a single object instead of all unreplicated objects in a naming context by using the /replsingleobj option.

Using PowerShell

The PowerShell method in this solution will prompt the DC to trigger replication for all of its configured replication partners, not just an individual remote domain controller.

See Also

Recipe 12.3 for viewing unreplicated changes between two domain controllers

12.5. Enabling and Disabling Replication

Problem

You want to enable or disable inbound or outbound replication on a domain controller.

Solution

Using a command-line interface

To disable outbound replication on a domain controller, use the following syntax:

```
> repadmin /options <DC Name> +DISABLE_OUTBOUND_REPL
```

To reenable outbound replication, enter the following:

```
> repamin /options <DC Name> -DISABLE_OUTBOUND_REPL
```

To disable inbound replication, use the following syntax:

```
> repadmin /options <DC Name> +DISABLE_INBOUND_REPL
```

To reenable inbound replication, use the following:

```
> repadmin /options <DC Name> -DISABLE_INBOUND_REPL
```

Discussion

When you are making major changes to Active Directory, particularly in cases where you are extending the schema, it is recommended that you disable outbound replication on the DC that you're modifying. This will allow you to test any changes that you've made on a single DC without propagating those changes to the remainder of your directory. If you make a mistake or find that the changes you've made are otherwise unacceptable, you can restore a single DC rather than being faced with the prospect of performing a disaster recovery operation on your entire domain.

It's important to note that disabling outbound replication on a domain controller will not have any effect on inbound replication; the DC in question will still receive updates from its other replication partners unless you disable inbound replication on them as well.

You can also disable replication for an entire forest by issuing the following command:

```
> repadmin /options * +DISABLE_INBOUND_REPL
```

See Also

"Turn Off Inbound Replication" (*http://bit.ly/13mrTn3*)

12.6. Changing the Intra-Site Replication Notification Interval

Problem

You want to change the number of seconds that a domain controller in a site waits before sending replication partner notification within the site.

Solution

Using a graphical user interface

1. Open ADSI Edit.

2. If an entry for the Configuration naming context you want to browse is not already displayed, do the following:

    a. Right-click on ADSI Edit in the right pane and click "Connect to".

    b. Fill in the information for the Configuration NC. Click on the Advanced button if you need to enter alternate credentials.

3. In the left pane, browse to cn=Configuration, *<ForestRootDN>*→cn=Partitions. Right-click on the domain partition designated by the short name of the domain (cn=ADATUM for *adatum.com*) and select Properties.

4. Double-click on the following attributes and modify their values as appropriate:

    - msDS-Replication-Notify-First-DSA-Delay
    - msDS-Replication-Notify-Subsequent-DSA-Delay

Using a command-line interface

Create a file called *modify_replication_interval.ldf* with the following contents:

```
dn: <DomainPartitionCrossRefDN>
changetype: modify
replace: msDS-Replication-Notify-First-DSA-Delay
msDS-Replication-Notify-First-DSA-Delay: <FirstDelayInSeconds>
-
replace: msDS-Replication-Notify-Subsequent-DSA-Delay
msDS-Replication-Notify-Subsequent-DSA-Delay: <NextDelayInSeconds>
```

Then import the changes into Active Directory using the following syntax:

```
ldifde -i -v modify_replication_interval.ldf
```

You can also make the changes using AdMod, as follows:

```
admod -b cn=<DomainPartition>,cn=Partitions,cn=Configuration,<ForestRootDN>↵
msDS-Replication-Notification-First-DSA-Delay::<FirstDelayInSeconds>↵
msDS-Replication-Notify-Subsequent-DSA-Delay::<NextDelayInSeconds>
```

Using PowerShell

The following commands are examples that modify the intra-site replication parameters to 10 seconds, in the *adatum.com* domain:

```
Set-ADObject "cn=Adatum,cn=Partitions,cn=Configuration,dc=adatum,dc=com"↵
  -Replace @{"msDS-Replication-Notify-First-DSA-Delay"="10"}

Set-ADObject "cn=Adatum,cn=Partitions,cn=Configuration,dc=adatum,dc=com"↵
  -Replace @{"msDS-Replication-Notify-Subsequent-DSA-Delay"="10"}
```

Discussion

Because Active Directory assumes that DCs within a site are connected by high-speed links, intra-site replication occurs as changes are made rather than adhering to a specific schedule. The intra-site replication initial delay interval is 15 seconds, after which a DC will notify its replication partners in three-second intervals. This greatly reduces the *convergence time* within a site—that is, the amount of time it takes for domain controllers within a site to synchronize with one another.

 Some updates are deemed to be sufficiently important that the initial 15-second delay does not apply. This is known as *urgent replication*, and it applies to critical directory updates such as locking out an account, changing the account lockout or password policy of a domain, and changing the password of a domain-controller computer account.

See Also

"How to Modify the Default Intra-Site Domain Controller Replication Interval" (*http://support.microsoft.com/kb/214678*)

12.7. Changing the Inter-Site Replication Interval

Problem

You want to set the replication schedule for a site link.

Solution

Using a graphical user interface

1. Open the Active Directory Sites and Services snap-in (*dssite.msc*).
2. Expand the Inter-Site Transport container.
3. Click on the IP container.
4. In the right pane, double-click on the site link you want to modify the replication interval for.
5. Enter the new interval beside "Replicate every".
6. Click OK.

Using a command-line interface

To change the replication interval, create an LDIF file named *set_link_rep_interval.ldf* with the following contents:

```
dn: cn=<LinkName>,cn=ip,cn=Inter-Site Transports,cn=sites,
cn=configuration,<ForestRootDN>
changetype: modify
replace: replInterval
replInterval: <NewInterval>
-
```

Then run the following command:

```
> ldifde -v -i -f set_link_rep_interval.ldf
```

You can also make this change using AdMod, as follows:

```
> admod -b cn=<LinkName>,cn=ip,cn=Inter-Site↵
Transports,cn=sites,cn=configuration,<ForestRootDN>↵
replInterval::<NewInterval>
```

Using PowerShell

The following PowerShell command will change the default IP site link replication interval to 15 minutes:

```
Set-ADReplicationSiteLink "DEFAULTIPSITELINK" -Replace @{"replInterval"=15}
```

Discussion

To configure the inter-site replication interval between two sites, you need to set the replInterval attribute on the site-link object that connects the two sites. The value of the attribute should be the replication interval in minutes. The default value is 180

---

minutes (three hours), and the minimum is 15 minutes. To view all site links, issue the following cmdlet:

```
Get-ADReplicationSiteLink -Filler *
```

These solutions assume the use of IP transport, but SMTP transport can be used as well. However, keep in mind that you cannot use an SMTP link to replicate the Domain naming context, only the Schema and Configuration NCs as well as global catalog information.

See Also

Set-ADReplicationSiteLink cmdlet reference (*http://bit.ly/11O0zvH*)

12.8. Disabling Inter-Site Compression of Replication Traffic

Problem

You want to disable inter-site compression of replication traffic.

Solution

You need to modify the options attribute of the site-link object that connects the sites you want to disable compression for. Site-link objects are stored in the following location:

```
cn=IP,cn=Inter-site Transports,cn=Sites,cn=Configuration,<ForestRootDN>
```

The options attribute is a bit flag. In order to disable compression, you must set bit 2, or 0100 in binary. If the attribute is currently unset, you can simply set it to 4.

Using a graphical user interface

1. Open the Active Directory Sites and Services snap-in (*dssite.msc*).
2. Expand the Inter-Site Transport container.
3. Right-click the IP container and select Properties.
4. Click the Attribute Editor tab and select the options attribute.
5. Click the Edit button and enter the value for the attribute.
6. Click OK twice.

Using a command-line interface

```
> admod -b "cn=IP,cn=Inter-Site Transports,cn=Sites,cn=Configuration,↵
<ForestDN>" options::<Interval>
```

Using PowerShell

To set the options bit value, use the following syntax:

```
Set-ADObject "cn=IP,cn=Inter-Site Transports,cn=Sites,cn=Configuration,↵
dc=adatum,dc=com" -Replace @{"options"="4"}
```

Discussion

By default, data replicated inter-site is usually compressed. By contrast, intra-site replication traffic is not compressed. It is useful to compress inter-site traffic if the traffic is going over a WAN on the assumption that the less traffic the better. The trade-off to reducing WAN traffic is increased CPU utilization on the bridgehead servers replicating the data. If CPU utilization is an issue on your bridgehead servers and you aren't as concerned about the amount of traffic being replicated, you should consider disabling inter-site compression.

See Also

Recipe 4.15 for setting bit-flag attributes

12.9. Checking for Potential Replication Problems

Problem

You want to determine whether replication is succeeding.

Solution

Using a command-line interface

The following two commands will help identify problems with replication on a source domain controller:

```
> dcdiag /test:replications
> repadmin /showrepl /errorsonly
```

Using PowerShell

The following command will identify replication failures for a specified domain controller:

```
Get-ADReplicationFailure "<DomainControllerName>"
```

Discussion

The Directory Service event log is an invaluable source of information on replication and KCC problems.

See Also

Recipe 12.2 for viewing the replication status of several domain controllers

12.10. Enabling Enhanced Logging of Replication Events

Problem

You want to enable enhanced logging of replication events.

Solution

Enable diagnostics logging for five replication events.

Discussion

See Recipe 15.1 for more information.

See Also

"How to configure Active Directory diagnostic event logging in Windows Server 2003 and in Windows 2000 Server" (*http://support.microsoft.com/kb/314980*)

12.11. Enabling Strict or Loose Replication Consistency

Problem

You want to enable strict or loose replication consistency.

Solution

Using a graphical user interface

1. Run *regedit.exe*.
2. Expand *HKEY_LOCAL_MACHINE\SYSTEM\CurrentControlSet\Services\NTDS \Parameters*.

3. If the `Strict Replication Consistency` value does not exist, right-click on Parameters and select New→DWORD Value. For the name, enter `Strict Replication Consistency`.

4. In the right pane, double-click on the value and enter 1 to enable strict consistency or 0 to enable loose consistency.

5. Click OK.

Using a command-line interface

To enable strict consistency, run the following command:

```
> reg add HKLM\System\CurrentControlSet\Services\NTDS\Parameters /v "Strict↵
Replication Consistency" /t REG_DWORD /d 1
```

To enable loose consistency, run the following command:

```
> reg add HKLM\System\CurrentControlSet\Services\NTDS\Parameters /v "Strict↵
Replication Consistency" /t REG_DWORD /d 0
```

You can also enable and disable strict replication using `repadmin`. You can either specify an individual domain controller in the *<DC Name>* field or use a * to enable or disable strict replication on every DC in the forest, as follows:

```
repadmin /regkey <DCName> +strict
repadmin /regkey <DCName> -strict
```

Using PowerShell

```
$strRegPath = "HKLM:\System\CurrentControlSet\Services\NTDS\Parameters"
Set-ItemProperty -Path $strRegPath -name "Strict Replication Consistency"↵
 -Value"1"
```

Discussion

Using *strict replication consistency*, a domain controller will stop replicating with a destination domain controller when it determines that the source is attempting to replicate a lingering object. Event ID 1084 will get logged in the Directory Service event log, indicating that the domain controller couldn't replicate the lingering object. Although strict replication can halt replication, it is the preferable method, and a good way to check that lingering objects do not infiltrate your forest. For this reason, you must monitor your domain controllers to ensure they are replicating on a regular basis and they do not have any 1084 events.

Using *loose replication consistency*, lingering objects could get reinjected into Active Directory and replicate among all the domain controllers. A *lingering object* is one that was previously deleted but got reintroduced because a domain controller did not successfully replicate for the duration of the time defined by the `tombStoneLifetime`

---

attribute, or because the object was restored using a backup older than the tombStone Lifetime. Domain controllers will replicate the lingering object throughout the naming context. Loose consistency thus has the potential to cause some security risks since an object you thought was deleted is now back in the forest again.

See Also

"Lingering Objects Prevent Active Directory Replication from Occurring" (*http://support.microsoft.com/kb/317097*); "Lingering objects may remain after you bring an out-of-date global catalog server back online" (*http://support.microsoft.com/kb/314282*)

12.12. Finding conflict Objects

Problem

You want to find conflict objects that are a result of replication collisions.

Solution

Using a graphical user interface

1. Open LDP.
2. From the menu, select Connection→Connect.
3. Click OK to connect to the closest domain controller over port 389.
4. From the menu, select Connection→Bind.
5. Click OK to bind as the currently logged on user or select the option to bind with credentials, enter the credentials, and then click OK.
6. From the menu, select Browse→Search.
7. For Base DN, type the base DN from where you want to start the search.
8. For Scope, select the appropriate scope.
9. For Filter, enter (name=*\0ACNF:*).
10. Click Run.

Using a command-line interface

The following command finds all conflict objects within the whole forest:

```
> dsquery * forestroot -gc -attr distinguishedName -scope subtree -filter↵
"(name=*\0ACNF:*)"
```

You can also perform this query with AdFind as follows:

```
> adfind -b -gc -f "(name=*\0ACNF:*)" -dn
```

Using PowerShell

The following command will search for `conflict` objects within a domain:

```
Get-ADObject -Filter {Name -eq "*\0ACNF:*"}
```

Discussion

Any distributed multimaster system has to deal with replication collisions, and Active Directory is no different. A collision can occur if an object is created on one domain controller and before that object has time to replicate out, an object with at least the same name is created on a different domain controller. So which object wins? With Active Directory, the following steps are used to determine which object is retained as is and which one is considered a `conflict` object:

1. AD will compare the version number of the objects. In Active Directory, version numbers are incremented every time you make a change to an object. The higher the version number, the more changes have been made to the object.

2. If the version numbers are the same, AD then compares the timestamps of when each object was created. The object that was created more recently will be retained and the older one will be renamed.

3. If the statistically improbable happens and two objects or attributes possess identical timestamps and version numbers, AD will take one final step to resolve the conflict by maintaining the object that originated from the DC with the higher GUID, and renaming the object that originated from the DC with the lower GUID.

When the losing object is renamed, the format of the renamed object is:

```
<ObjectName>\0ACNF:<ObjectGUID>
```

where *<ObjectName>* is the original name of the object, followed by a null termination character, followed by `CNF:`, followed by the object's GUID.

It is good to periodically scan your Active Directory tree to ensure you do not have a lot of `conflict` objects hanging around and to remove any that exist. It is a bit problematic to find `conflict` objects in a single query because the filter to find them is not optimized. In all three solutions, you have to perform a leading- and trailing-match pattern search (with *), and this can easily time out if you have a lot of objects. You may want to restrict your initial search to a few containers so that the search is quicker.

See Also

"Replication Collisions in Windows 2000" (*http://support.microsoft.com/kb/218614*); MS KB 297083 "How to rename an object after a replication collision has occurred" (*http://support.microsoft.com/kb/297083*)

12.13. Finding Orphaned Objects

Problem

You want to find orphaned objects within Active Directory.

Solution

Using a graphical user interface

1. Open the Active Directory Administrative Center.
2. Double-click the domain name in the left pane.
3. Double-click the LostAndFound container in the middle pane.

   You will see a list of any orphaned objects in the middle pane.

Using a command-line interface

You can query for orphaned objects using either the built-in DSQuery utility or AdFind. DSQuery takes the following syntax:

```
> dsquery * cn=LostAndFound,<DomainDN> -scope onelevel -attr *
```

To use AdFind, enter the following:

```
> adfind -default -rb cn=LostAndFound -s onelevel
```

Using PowerShell

```
Get-ADObject -SearchBase "cn=LostAndFound,<DomainDN>" -Filter *
```

Discussion

Because of the distributed nature of Active Directory, there exists the possibility that an administrator working on one DC can attempt to create or move a user into a container object such as an OU at the same time that another administrator *deletes* that OU from another DC. When this occurs, the leaf object becomes orphaned and is moved into the LostAndFound container within the Domain NC. You can view the lastKnownParent attribute of an object in this container to determine the OU or container that was deleted, and then delete the object or move it to a different container as appropriate.

From a procedural standpoint, objects being moved to the LostAndFound container should be a rare event. If it is happening frequently or if there are a large number of objects in the container, you should review the change-control procedures that are in place on your network to ensure that object moves and deletions are more tightly coordinated.

See Also

MSDN: Lost-And-Found Class [AD Schema]

12.14. Listing the Replication Partners for a DC

Problem

You want to find the replication partners for a particular DC.

Solution

Using a graphical user interface

1. Open the Active Directory Sites and Services snap-in (*dssite.msc*).

2. Browse to Sites→*<SiteName>*→Servers→*<DCName>*→NTDS Settings.

3. The replication partners that have been configured for the DC in question will appear in the right pane. Double-click on any connection object to view its properties.

Using a command-line interface

You can query for replication connections using either the built-in DSQuery utility or AdFind. DSQuery takes the following syntax:

```
> dsquery * "cn=NTDS Settings,cn=<DCName>,cn=Servers,cn=<SiteName>,↵
cn=Sites,cn=Configuration,<ForestRootDN> -filter↵
 (objectcategory=NTDSConnection) -attr *
```

To use AdFind, enter the following:

```
> adfind -config -rb "cn=NTDSSettings,cn=<DCName>,cn=Servers,cn=<SiteName>,↵
cn=Sites" -f (objectcategory=NTDSConnection)
```

Using PowerShell

```
Get-ADReplicationConnection -Server "<DCName>"
```

Discussion

By default, Active Directory's replication topology is created by the KCC, which runs on every DC to dynamically create and maintain connection objects. (The KCC will run every 15 minutes by default to determine whether there have been any changes to the site topology that require modifications to the connection objects the KCC has created.) Each connection object corresponds to an inbound replication connection— that is, a remote DC that will contact the local DC whenever it has changes available. Any connection object that is listed as <automatically generated> in Active Directory Sites and Services was created by the KCC. You can create additional connection objects manually, but these objects will not be kept up-to-date by the KCC in the event that a remote DC is relocated or taken offline.

See Also

Get-ADReplicationConnection cmdlet reference (*http://bit.ly/15rgKpa*); "Identify Replication Partners" (*http://bit.ly/18pDK6Z*)

12.15. Viewing Object Metadata

Problem

You want to view metadata for an object. The object's replPropertyMetaData attribute stores metadata information about the most recent updates to every attribute that has been set on the object.

Solution

Using a graphical user interface

1. Open LDP.
2. Click OK to connect to the closest domain controller over port 389.
3. From the menu, select Connection→Bind.
4. Click OK to bind as the currently logged on user or select the option to bind with credentials, enter the credentials, and then click OK.
5. From the menu, select Browse→Replication→View Metadata.
6. For Object DN, type the distinguished name of the object you want to view.
7. Click OK to view the metadata.

Using a command-line interface

In the following command, replace *<ObjectDN>* with the distinguished name of the object for which you want to view metadata:

```
> repadmin /showobjmeta <DomainControllerName> <ObjectDN>
```

You can also obtain object metadata for a single object using AdFind, as follows:

```
> adfind -sc objmeta:<ObjectDN>
```

To obtain the object metadata for all objects within a container, use the following syntax:

```
> adfind -sc objsmeta:<ContainerDN>
```

Using PowerShell

```
Get-ADReplicationAttributeMetadata -Object "<ObjectDN>" -Server "<DCName>"
```

Discussion

Object metadata can be an invaluable source of information when you need to troubleshoot replication problems or find out the last time an attribute was set for a particular object. In fact, a quick way to determine whether two domain controllers have the same copy of an object is to look at the metadata for the object on both servers. If they both have the same metadata, then they have the same version of the object. The following data is stored for each attribute that has been set on the object:

Attribute ID
Attribute that was updated.

Attribute version
Number of originating writes to the property.

Local USN
USN of the property on the local DC. This will be the same value as the originating DC if the originating DC and local DC are the same.

Originating USN
USN stored with the property when the update was made on the originating DC.

Originating DC
DC that the originating write was made on.

Time/Date
Time and date that the property was changed in UTC.

You also have access to the msDS-ReplAttributeMetaData and the msDS-ReplValueMetaData attributes, which provide much object metadata in XML-formatted output, as shown through this AdFind query (query output truncated):

```
> adfind -default -rb cn=administrator,cn=users msds-replattributemetadata

AdFind V01.46.00cpp Joe Richards (joe@joeware.net) March 2012

Using server: dc1.adatum.com:389
Directory: Windows Server 8
Base DN: cn=administrator,cn=users,dc=adatum,dc=com

dn:cn=Administrator,cn=Users,dc= adatum,dc=com
>msDS-ReplAttributeMetaData: <DS_REPL_ATTR_META_DATA>
        <pszAttributeName>lastLogonTimestamp</pszAttributeName>
        <dwVersion>6</dwVersion>
        <ftimeLastOriginatingChange>2012-11-29T20:18:49Z</ftimeLastOriginating⏎
Change>
        <uuidLastOriginatingDsaInvocationID>aae693c5-d0d9-497f-a1c4-f298aaec8a8b
</uuidLastOriginatingDsaInvocationID>
        <usnOriginatingChange>1056930</usnOriginatingChange>
        <usnLocalChange>1056930</usnLocalChange>
        <pszLastOriginatingDsaDN>cn=NTDS Settings,cn=dc1,cn=Servers,cn=Def
ault-First-Site-Name,cn=Sites,cn=Configuration,dc=adatum,dc=com</pszLastO
riginatingDsaDN>
</DS_REPL_ATTR_META_DATA>

>msDS-ReplAttributeMetaData: <DS_REPL_ATTR_META_DATA>
        <pszAttributeName>isCriticalSystemObject</pszAttributeName>
        <dwVersion>1</dwVersion>
        <ftimeLastOriginatingChange>2012-09-27T18:16:45Z</ftimeLastOriginating⏎
Change>
        <uuidLastOriginatingDsaInvocationID>c0e0fe92-685b-4e0e-863b-7067745d31f7
</uuidLastOriginatingDsaInvocationID>
        <usnOriginatingChange>8196</usnOriginatingChange>
        <usnLocalChange>8196</usnLocalChange>
        <pszLastOriginatingDsaDN></pszLastOriginatingDsaDN>
</DS_REPL_ATTR_META_DATA>

>msDS-ReplAttributeMetaData: <DS_REPL_ATTR_META_DATA>
        <pszAttributeName>objectCategory</pszAttributeName>
        <dwVersion>1</dwVersion>
        <ftimeLastOriginatingChange>2012-09-27T18:16:45Z</ftimeLastOriginating⏎
Change>
```

```
        <uuidLastOriginatingDsaInvocationID>c0e0fe92-685b-4e0e-863b-7067745d31f7
</uuidLastOriginatingDsaInvocationID>
        <usnOriginatingChange>8196</usnOriginatingChange>
        <usnLocalChange>8196</usnLocalChange>
        <pszLastOriginatingDsaDN></pszLastOriginatingDsaDN>
</DS_REPL_ATTR_META_DATA>

1 Objects returned
```

See Also

Get-ADReplicationAttributeMetadata cmdlet reference (*http://bit.ly/10CaaDu*); "Troubleshooting replication with repadmin" white paper (*http://bit.ly/ZLkqhg*)

## CHAPTER 13

DNS and DHCP

13.0. Introduction

Active Directory is tightly coupled with the Domain Name System (DNS) name resolution service. Windows clients and domain controllers alike use DNS to locate domain controllers that are housed in a particular site or that serve a particular function (such as a global catalog server). Each domain controller registers numerous resource records (RRs) in DNS to advertise its services as a domain controller, global catalog server, PDC Emulator, and so on.

One of the innovative uses of Active Directory is as a store for DNS data. Instead of using the primary and secondary zone transfer method, or even the more recent NOTIFY method (RFC 1996) to replicate zone data between non-AD integrated DNS servers, AD integrated zones store the zone data in Active Directory and use the same replication process used to replicate other data between domain controllers. The one catch with AD integrated zones is that the DNS server must also be a domain controller, and overloading DNS server responsibilities on your domain controllers may not be something you want to do if you plan to support a large volume of DNS requests. You can integrate forward lookup zones, reverse lookup zones, and stub zones into Active Directory. Stub zones are used to maintain information about remote DNS zones and to reduce zone transfer traffic across WAN links. Additionally, you can use a GlobalNamesZone (GNZ), a manually maintained zone that is used to provide short name resolution on a DNS network: GNZ allows clients to resolve a hostname such as *server1* via DNS instead of a fully qualified domain name such as *server1.adatum.com*. For a detailed description of resource records, zone types, and much more on DNS, see Chapter 8 of *Active Directory*, Fifth Edition, by Brian Desmond et al. (O'Reilly).

The Anatomy of a DNS Object

The only time DNS data is stored in Active Directory is if you have a zone that is AD integrated. When using standard primary and secondary zones that are not AD integrated, the DNS data is stored locally in the filesystem of each DNS server in *zone files*. If you have an AD integrated zone configured for legacy compatibility, a container is created in the following location: `cn=<ZoneName>,cn=MicrosoftDNS,cn=System,<DomainDN>`, where `<ZoneName>` is the name of the zone.

You can also use application partitions to store DNS data in an alternate location. By default, there are three replication options for DNS zones stored in Active Directory:

- Replicate DNS data to all domain controllers in a domain.
- Replicate DNS data to all domain controllers that are DNS servers in the domain.
- Replicate DNS data to all domain controllers that are DNS servers in the forest.

The default location for the second option is `dc=DomainDNSZones,<DomainDN>`; for the third option, it is `dc=ForestDNSZones,<ForestDN>`. These two locations are actually application partitions that are replicated only to the domain controllers that are DNS servers in the domain or forest, respectively.

Inside the `MicrosoftDNS` container is a `dnsZone` object for each AD integrated zone. Inside the `dnsZone` container are `dnsNode` objects that store all resource records associated with a particular node. In the following text representation of an A record, the *dc1.adatum.com* name is considered a node (generally the left side of the resource record):

```
dc1.adatum.com. 600 IN A 6.10.57.21
```

There could be multiple resource records associated with the *dc1.adatum.com* name, so Microsoft decided to implement each distinct name as a `dnsNode` object. The `dnsNode` object has a `dnsRecord` attribute, which is multivalued and contains all of the resource records associated with that node. Unfortunately, the contents of that attribute are stored in a binary format and are not directly readable.

Table 13-1 and Table 13-2 contain some of the interesting attributes that are available on `dnsZone` and `dnsNode` objects.

Table 13-1. Attributes of dnsZone objects

Attribute	Description
Dc	Relative distinguished name of the zone. For example, the dc=domaindnszones,dc=adatum,dc=com dnsZone object has a dc attribute value of *adatum.com*.
dnsProperty	Binary-formatted string that stores configuration information about the zone.
msDS-Approx-Immed-Subordinates	Approximate number of nodes contained within the zone.

Table 13-2. Attributes of dnsNode objects

Attribute	Description
dc	Relative distinguished name of the node.
dnsRecord	Binary-formatted multivalued attribute that stores the resource records associated with the node.
dnsTombstoned	Boolean that indicates whether the node is marked for deletion. FALSE means that it is not and TRUE means that it is.

13.1. Creating a Forward Lookup Zone

Problem

You want to create a forward lookup zone. A forward lookup zone maps FQDNs to IP addresses or other names.

Solution

Using a graphical user interface

1. Open the DNS Management snap-in (*dnsmgmt.msc*).

2. If an entry for the DNS server you want to connect to does not exist, right-click on DNS in the left pane and select Connect to DNS Server. Select "This computer" or "The following computer", then enter the server you want to connect to (if applicable) and click OK.

3. Expand the server in the left pane and click on Forward Lookup Zones.

4. Right-click on Forward Lookup Zones and select New Zone.

5. Click Next.

6. Select the zone type and click Next.

7. If you selected to store the zone data in Active Directory, next you will be asked which servers you want to replicate the DNS data to. Click Next after you make your selection.

8. Enter the zone name and click Next.

9. Fill out the information for the remaining screens. They will vary depending on whether you are creating a primary, secondary, or stub zone.

Using a command-line interface

The following command creates an AD integrated zone:

```
> dnscmd <DNSServerName> /zoneadd <ZoneName> /DsPrimary
```

Using PowerShell

The following PowerShell code will create an Active Directory–integrated forward lookup zone:

```
Add-DnsServerPrimaryZone -Name "<ZoneName>" -ReplicationScope "Domain"↵
 -DynamicUpdate "Secure"
```

Discussion

Using a command-line interface

When you create an AD integrated zone with the /DsPrimary switch, you can additionally include a /dp switch and specify an application partition to add the zone to. Here is an example:

```
> dnscmd /zoneadd "<ZoneName>" /DsPrimary /dp domaindnszones.adatum.com
```

Using PowerShell

Since PowerShell provides a built-in way to easily create any type of DNS zone, this method can be quicker and more efficient than using the graphical user interface:

```
Add-DnsServerPrimaryZone "<ZoneName>" -ReplicationScope Domain
```

See Also

Recipe 13.2 for creating a reverse lookup zone; "Add a Forward Lookup Zone" (*http://bit.ly/16c1egv*); MSDN: DNS WMI Provider; MSDN: CreateZone Method of the MicrosoftDNS_Zone Class

13.2. Creating a Reverse Lookup Zone

Problem

You want to create a reverse lookup zone. A reverse lookup zone maps IP addresses to names.

Solution

Using a graphical user interface

1. Open the DNS Management snap-in (*dnsmgmt.msc*).
2. If an entry for the DNS server you want to connect to does not exist, right-click on DNS in the left pane and select Connect to DNS Server. Select "This computer" or

"The following computer", then enter the server you want to connect to (if applicable) and click OK.

3. Expand the server in the left pane and click on Reverse Lookup Zones.

4. Right-click on Reverse Lookup Zones and select New Zone.

5. Click Next.

6. Select the zone type (Primary, Secondary, or Stub zone). To AD integrate the zone, place a checkmark next to "Store the zone in Active Directory (available only if DNS server is a writeable domain controller)" and click Next.

7. If you selected to store the zone data in Active Directory, next you will be asked which servers you want to replicate the DNS data to: all DNS servers in the forest, all DNS servers in the domain, all domain controllers in the domain, or all DCs that are hosting a particular application partition. Click Next after you make your selection.

8. Type the Network ID for the reverse zone or enter a reverse zone name to use.

9. Fill out the information for the remaining screens. They will vary depending on whether you are creating a primary, secondary, or stub zone.

Using a command-line interface

The following command creates an AD integrated reverse zone:

```
> dnscmd <DNSServerName> /zoneadd <ZoneName> /DsPrimary
```

Using PowerShell

The following PowerShell command will create an Active Directory–integrated reverse lookup zone:

```
Add-DnsServerPrimaryZone 0.168.192.in-addr.arpa -ReplicationScope "Domain"↵
 -DynamicUpdate "Secure"
```

Discussion

Creating a reverse zone is very similar to creating a forward zone. See Recipe 13.1 for more information.

See Also

"Add a Reverse Lookup Zone" (*http://bit.ly/16NlvJd*); MSDN: CreateZone Method of the MicrosoftDNS_Zone Class

13.3. Viewing a Server's Zones

Problem

You want to view the zones on a server.

Solution

Using a graphical user interface

1. Open the DNS Management snap-in (*dnsmgmt.msc*).
2. Right-click on DNS in the left pane and select Connect to DNS Server.
3. Enter the server you want to connect to and click Enter.
4. In the left pane, expand the server and click Forward Lookup Zones and Reverse Lookup Zones to view the hosted zones.

Using a command-line interface

```
> dnscmd <DNSServerName> /enumzones
```

Using PowerShell

```
Get-DnsServerZone
```

Discussion

Using a graphical user interface

When you click on either Forward Lookup Zones or Reverse Lookup Zones in the lefthand pane of the DMS MMC, the right pane contains a Type column that displays the zone type for each zone.

Using a command-line interface

When you use the /enumzones switch without additional parameters, it displays all of the zones on the server. You can specify additional filters that limit the types of zones returned, including the following:

`/Primary`
    Lists both standard and Active Directory–integrated primary zones

`/Secondary`
    Lists all standard secondary zones

/Forwarder
:   Lists all zones that forward unresolvable queries to another DNS server

/Stub
:   Lists all stub zones hosted on a server

/Cache
:   Lists zones that are loaded into cache on the server

/Auto-Created
:   Lists zones that were created automatically during the DNS server installation

/Forward
:   Lists all forward lookup zones

/Reverse
:   Lists all reverse lookup zones

/Ds
:   Lists all Active Directory–integrated zones

/File
:   Lists zones that are stored in text files

/DomainDirectoryPartition
:   Lists zones that are stored in the DomainDNSZones partition

/ForestDirectoryPartition
:   Lists zones that are stored in the ForestDNSZones partition

/CustomDirectoryPartition
:   Lists zones that are stored in a user-created directory partition

/LegacyDirectoryPartition
:   Lists zones that are stored in the domain NC

/DirectoryPartition <PartitionName>
:   Lists zones that are stored in a particular application partition

Using PowerShell

The Get-DnsServerZone cmdlet shows all DNS zones and some properties, including whether the zone is directory-integrated, if it is a forward or reverse lookup zone, as well as the zone type.

See Also

MSDN: MicrosoftDNS_Zone

13.4. Converting a Zone to an AD Integrated Zone

Problem

You want to convert a standard primary zone to an AD integrated zone. This causes the contents of the zone to be stored and replicated in Active Directory instead of in a text file on the local server.

Solution

Using a graphical user interface

1. Open the DNS Management snap-in (*dnsmgmt.msc*).
2. Right-click on DNS in the left pane and select Connect to DNS Server.
3. Enter the server you want to connect to and click Enter.
4. If you want to convert a forward zone, expand the Forward Lookup Zone folder. If you want to convert a reverse zone, expand the Reverse Lookup Zone folder.
5. Right-click on the zone you want to convert and select Properties.
6. Beside Type, click the Change button.
7. Check the box beside "Store the zone in Active Directory (available only if DNS server is a domain controller."
8. Click OK twice.

Using a command-line interface

```
> dnscmd <ServerName> /zoneresettype <ZoneName> /DsPrimary
```

Using PowerShell

```
ConvertTo-DnsServerPrimaryZone -Name "<ZoneName>" -ReplicationScope↵
 "<Forest|Domain|Legacy>" -Force
```

Discussion

See this chapter's Recipe 13.0; Recipe 13.5, and *Active Directory*, Fifth Edition by Brian Desmond et al. (O'Reilly) for more on AD integrated zones.

See Also

"Configure AD Integrated Zones" (*http://bit.ly/16Nm6KX*); MSDN: ChangeZoneType Method of the MicrosoftDNS_Zone Class

13.5. Moving AD Integrated Zones into an Application Partition

Problem

You want to move AD integrated zones into an application partition.

Solution

Using a graphical user interface

1. Open the DNS Management snap-in (*dnsmgmt.msc*).
2. If an entry for the DNS server you want to connect to does not exist, right-click on DNS in the left pane and select Connect to DNS Server. Select "This computer" or "The following computer", and then enter the server you want to connect to (if applicable) and click OK.
3. Expand the server in the left pane and expand either Forward Lookup Zones or Reverse Lookup Zones, depending on the type of zone you want to manage.
4. Right-click on the name of the zone and select Properties.
5. Click on the Change button beside Replication.
6. Select the application partition you want to move the zone into.
7. Click OK twice.

Using a command-line interface

The following command will move a zone to the default application partition that replicates across all domain controllers in the domain that are configured as DNS servers:

```
> dnscmd <DNSServerName> /zonechangedirectorypartition <ZoneName>↵
<ApplicationPartition>
```

Using PowerShell

```
Set-DnsServerPrimaryZone "<ZoneName>" -ReplicationScope "Custom"↵
-DirectoryPartitionName "<PartitionName>"
```

Discussion

Application partitions are user-defined partitions that can be configured to replicate with any domain controller in a forest. This provides flexibility for how you store and replicate your AD integrated zones. You could, in fact, have a few domain controllers from each domain act as DNS servers for all of your AD domains.

See Also

Chapter 17 for more information on application partitions

13.6. Configuring Zone Transfers

Problem

You want to enable zone transfers to specific secondary name servers.

Solution

Using a graphical user interface

1. Open the DNS Management snap-in (*dnsmgmt.msc*).
2. In the left pane, expand the server node and expand either Forward Lookup Zone or Reverse Lookup Zone, depending on the type of zone you want to manage.
3. Right-click on the zone and select Properties.
4. Select the Zone Transfers tab.
5. Select either the option to restrict zone transfers to those servers listed on the Name Servers tab or the option to restrict zone transfers to specific IP addresses. See this recipe's "Discussion" on page 471 for more on these two options.

Using a command-line interface

The following command enables zone transfers for the *test.local* zone and specifies they can only occur with servers that have NS records in the zone (i.e., servers listed within the Name Servers tab of the DNS snap-in):

```
> dnscmd <ServerName> /ZoneResetSecondaries test.local /SecureNs
```

The next command enables zone transfers for the same zone, but specifies they can only occur with hosts whose IP addresses are 172.16.11.33 and 172.16.11.34:

```
> dnscmd <ServerName> /ZoneResetSecondaries test.local /SecureList 172.16.11.33↵
172.16.11.34
```

Using PowerShell

```
Set-DnsServerPrimaryZone "<ZoneName>" -SecureSecondaries↵
 TransferToSecureServers -SecondaryServers "<IP Address>"
```

Discussion

Depending on your environment, your DNS implementation may require that you create secondary zones to allow for load balancing for busy DNS servers or remote sites connected by slow links. In this situation, you want to allow zone transfers to occur between your AD integrated DNS servers and your secondary servers, but you want to restrict which hosts can initiate zone transfers with your AD integrated name servers. Allowing anyone to initiate a zone transfer with your domain controllers could provide an attacker with information for mapping out your network; it is therefore critical that you limit which hosts can pull zone transfers from your servers.

If you are using only Active Directory–integrated zones, the Name Servers tab will be automatically populated with a list of all name servers that are authoritative for the selected zone, and this is the recommended choice when you have a large network with many name servers deployed. If any of your name servers are using standard zone files, however, you will need to populate this tab manually for any secondary name servers you deploy.

Specifying a list of IP addresses for hosts that can initiate zone transfers may be more secure since it is more specific, but this approach has the trade-off of creating the additional management overhead of keeping track of the IP addresses of all name servers on your network, so you should follow this approach only if your network is small and you have relatively few name servers deployed. Another disadvantage of this approach is that if you forget to add some IP addresses of name servers to your list, zone information stored on those servers could become stale, causing name resolution to fail for some of your clients. This could result in some of your users experiencing difficulties in accessing network resources.

DNS is secured, by default, because in the case of file-based zones, it is configured to allow zone transfers only with servers listed on the Name Servers tab of a zone. In the case of Active Directory integrated zones, DNS is configured to disallow zone transfers entirely—they generally aren't needed in an Active Directory environment because the data replicates through Active Directory replication.

See Also

"Understanding zones and zone transfer" (*http://bit.ly/10ea454*)

13.7. Configuring Forwarding

Problem

You want to configure forwarding to allow for name resolution outside of your corporate network.

Solution

Using a graphical user interface

1. Open the DNS Management snap-in (*dnsmgmt.msc*).

2. Connect to the DNS server you want to modify. In the left pane, right-click on DNS and select Connect to DNS Server. Select "The following computer" and enter the target server name. Click OK.

3. Right-click on the server and select Properties.

4. Click the Forwarders tab.

5. Click the Edit button.

6. Enter the IP address, or DNS name, of the destination DNS server.

7. Click OK twice.

Using a command-line interface

The following command sets the default forwarders. Replace *<IPsOfForwarders>* with a space-separated list of IP addresses for the name servers to forward requests to:

```
> dnscmd <ServerName> /resetforwarders <IPsOfForwarders>
```

For example:

```
> dnscmd dns01 /resetforwarders 10.22.3.4 10.22.3.5
```

The following command configures the default forwarder timeout:

```
> dnscmd <ServerName> /config /forwardingtimeout <NumSeconds>
```

The following command configures the forwarder timeout for a specific domain:

```
> dnscmd <ServerName> /config <DomainName> /forwardertimeout <NumSeconds>
```

Using PowerShell

```
Set-DnsServerForwarder -IPAddress "<IPAddress>" -Timeout "<Value>"
```

Discussion

Name servers have long supported the notion of *forwarders*. Rather than sending all unresolved queries to the root Internet name servers, you can use forwarders to send queries to a specific server or set of servers, perhaps hosted by your ISP or by a partner corporation. This allows you to better control the name resolution process on your network.

Using PowerShell

By using the -PassThru switch, you can see the object that you are working with and the values of the properties.

See Also

MS KB 304491 (Conditional Forwarding in Windows Server 2003); MS KB 811118 (Support WebCast: Microsoft Windows Server 2003 DNS: Stub Zones and Conditional Forwarding)

13.8. Configuring Conditional Forwarding

Problem

You want to configure forwarding for specific domain names.

Solution

Using a graphical user interface

1. Open the DNS Management snap-in (*dnsmgmt.msc*).
2. Connect to the DNS server that you want to modify. In the left pane, right-click on DNS and select Connect to DNS Server. Select "The following computer" and enter the target server name. Click OK.
3. Expand the DNS server and then right-click on Conditional Forwarders. Click New Conditional Forwarder.
4. Enter the DNS name of the domain you wish to forward.
5. Enter the IP address or DNS name of the destination DNS server.
6. Choose whether to store the forwarder in Active Directory or to modify the query timeout period, and then click OK.

Using a command-line interface

```
dnscmd <ServerName> /zoneadd <DomainName> /forwarder <IPsOfForwarders>
```

Using PowerShell

```
Add-DnsServerConditionalForwarderZone "<DomainName>" -MasterServers↲
 "<IPAddress>" -ReplicationScope <Forest|Domain|Legacy|Custom>↲
 -ForwarderTimeout "<Value>"
```

Discussion

With *conditional forwarding*, you can forward unresolved queries for specific domains to different name servers. The most common use of conditional forwarding is when you have two or more noncontiguous namespaces. Consider, for example, a merger between the *adatum.com* and *othercorp.com* corporations. Normally, for the name servers of *adatum.com* to resolve queries for *othercorp.com*, the queries would have to first be forwarded to the root Internet name servers. With conditional forwarding, you can configure the *adatum.com* DNS servers so that all requests for *othercorp.com* should be sent directly to the *othercorp.com* name servers and all other unresolved queries should be sent to the Internet, and vice versa. The trade-off for this feature is the additional CPU processing that's necessary to examine each query and forward it to the appropriate server, rather than just funneling all unresolved queries to a single external server.

13.9. Delegating Control of an Active Directory Integrated Zone

Problem

You want to delegate control of managing the resource records in a zone.

Solution

Using a graphical user interface

1. Open the DNS Management snap-in (*dnsmgmt.msc*).

2. If an entry for the DNS server you want to connect to does not exist, right-click on DNS in the left pane and select Connect to DNS Server. Select "This computer" or "The following computer", and then enter the server you want to connect to (if applicable) and click OK.

3. Expand the server in the left pane and expand either Forward Lookup Zones or Reverse Lookup Zones, depending on the type of zone.

4. Right-click on the name of the zone and select Properties.

5. Click on the Security tab.

6. Click the Add button.

7. Use the Object Picker to locate the user or group to which you want to delegate control.

8. Under Permissions, check the Full Control box.

9. Click OK.

Using a command-line interface

The following command grants full control over managing the resource records in an AD integrated zone:

```
> dsacls dc=<ZoneName>,cn=MicrosoftDNS,<DomainOrAppPartitionDN>↵
/G<UserOrGroup>:GA
```

Using PowerShell

The following script delegates full control of an AD integrated DNS zone to a particular user or group:

```
$Path = [ADSI]"LDAP://dc=<ZoneName>,cn=MicrosoftDNS,cn=System,↵
 <DomainOrAppPartitionDN>"
$Group = New-Object System.Security.Principal.NTAccount("<UserorGroup>")
$IdentityReference = $Group.Translate↵
([System.Security.Principal.SecurityIdentifier])
$Perms = New-Object System.DirectoryServices.ActiveDirectoryAccessRule↵
 ($IdentityReference,"GenericAll","Allow")
$Path.psbase.ObjectSecurity.AddAccessRule($Perms)
$Path.psbase.commitchanges()
```

Discussion

By default, members of the *DNSAdmins* group have control over DNS server and zone configuration. You can delegate control of individual AD integrated zones by modifying permissions on the zone object in AD. The solutions show examples for how to grant full control to an additional user or group over a particular zone.

See Also

MS KB 256643 (Unable to Prevent DNS Zone Administrator from Creating New Zones)

13.10. Creating and Deleting Resource Records

Problem

You want to create and delete resource records in a zone.

Solution

Using a graphical user interface

1. Open the DNS Management snap-in (*dnsmgmt.msc*).

2. If an entry for the DNS server you want to connect to does not exist, right-click on DNS in the left pane and select Connect to DNS Server. Select "This computer" or "The following computer," and then enter the server you want to connect to (if applicable) and click OK.

3. If you want to add or delete a record in a forward zone, expand the Forward Lookup Zone folder. If you want to add or delete a record for a reverse zone, expand the Reverse Lookup Zone folder.

To create a resource record, do the following:

1. In the left pane, right-click the zone and select the option that corresponds to the record type you want to create—for example, New Host (A).

2. Fill in all required fields.

3. Click OK.

To delete a resource record, do the following:

1. In the left pane, click on the zone the record is in.

2. In the right pane, right-click on the record you want to delete and select Delete.

3. Click Yes to confirm.

Using a command-line interface

To add a resource record, use the following command:

```
> dnscmd <DNSServerName> /recordadd <ZoneName> <NodeName> <RecordType> <RRData>
```

The following command adds an A record in the *adatum.com* zone:

```
> dnscmd dc1 /recordadd adatum.com Server01 A 192.168.52.2
```

To delete a resource record, use the following command:

```
> dnscmd <DNSServerName> /recorddelete <ZoneName> <NodeName> <RecordType>↵
  <RRData>
```

The following command deletes an A record in the *adatum.com* zone:

```
> dnscmd dc1 /recorddelete adatum.com wins01 A 192.168.52.2
```

Using PowerShell

There are several PowerShell cmdlets available to create resource records for DNS zones:

Add-DnsServerResourceRecord
> This cmdlet adds an available resource record for a given zone.

Add-DnsServerResourceRecordA
> This cmdlet adds an A type record for IPv4 hosts in a given zone.

Add-DnsServerResourceRecordAAAA
> This cmdlet adds an AAAA type record for IPv6 hosts in a given zone.

Add-DnsServerResourceRecordCName
> This cmdlet adds a CNAME type record for a given zone.

Add-DnsServerResourceRecordDnsKey
> This cmdlet adds a DNS Key record for DNSSEC zones.

Add-DnsServerResourceRecordDS
> This cmdlet creates a Delegation of Signing record for a signed zone file.

Add-DnsServerResourceRecordMX
> This cmdlet creates an MX record for mail records in a given zone.

Add-DnsServerResourceRecordPtr
> This cmdlet creates a PTR record for reverse DNS lookup.

The following will add an A record named Host01 that corresponds to the IP address 10.0.0.3, in the *adatum.com* zone:

```
Add-DnsServerResourceRecordA -Name "Host01" -IPv4Address "10.0.0.3"↵
 -ZoneName "adatum.com"
```

The following will delete an A record named Host01, without prompting for confirmation, from the *adatum.com* zone:

```
Remove-DnsServerResourceRecord -ZoneName "adatum.com" -Name "Host01"↵
 -RRType "A" -Force
```

Discussion

Using a graphical user interface

The DNS Management snap-in is good for creating a small number of records, but if you need to add or delete more than a couple of dozen, then we'd recommend writing a PowerShell script to automate the process.

Using a command-line interface

Adding A, CNAME, and PTR resource records is pretty straightforward in terms of the data you must enter, but other record types, such as SRV, require quite a bit more data. The help pages for /recordadd and /recorddelete display the required information for each record type. For example, to add an SRV record using *dnscmd*, you need to specify the priority, weight, port, and hostname of the record, as in the following example:

```
> dnscmd /recordadd adatum.com dc1.adatum.com SRV _kerberos 50 100 88
```

See Also

MSDN: MicrosoftDNS_ResourceRecord

13.11. Querying Resource Records

Problem

You want to query resource records.

Solution

Using a graphical user interface

1. Open the DNS Management snap-in (*dnsmgmt.msc*).

2. If an entry for the DNS server you want to connect to does not exist, right-click on DNS in the left pane and select Connect to DNS Server. Select "This computer" or "The following computer." and then enter the server you want to connect to (if applicable) and click OK.

3. Expand the lookup zone folder and then select the zone you wish to filter.

4. Right-click the zone name and select View→Filter.

5. Enter the filter parameters and then click OK.

6. Right-click the zone name again and click Refresh.

Using a command-line interface

In the following command, replace *<RecordType>* with the type of resource record you want to find (e.g., A, CNAME, SRV) and *<RecordName>* with the name or IP address of the record to match:

```
> nslookup -type=<RecordType> <RecordName>
```

Using PowerShell

```
Get-DnsServerResourceRecord -ZoneName "<ZoneName>" -RRType "A"
```

Discussion

Using a command-line interface

You can leave off the -type switch, and the command will find any A, PTR, and CNAME records that match *<RecordName>*.

You can also run *nslookup* from interactive mode, which can be entered by typing nslookup at a command prompt with no additional parameters, or you can switch back and forth between query types by using the set q=ANY command to reset *nslookup*. Interactive mode allows you to issue a series of queries with more efficiency because you don't have to type nslookup or wait for the initial connection to the DNS server.

See Also

MSDN: MicrosoftDNS_ResourceRecord; RFC 1035 (Domain Names—Implementation and Specification); RFC 1700 (DNS Parameters)

13.12. Modifying the DNS Server Configuration

Problem

You want to modify the DNS server settings.

Solution

Using a graphical user interface

1. Open the DNS Management snap-in (*dnsmgmt.msc*).
2. If an entry for the DNS server you want to connect to does not exist, right-click on DNS in the left pane and select Connect to DNS Server. Select "This computer" or "The following computer", and then enter the server you want to connect to (if applicable) and click OK.
3. Right-click on the server and select Properties.
4. Edit the server settings from the tabs that are displayed.
5. Click OK to commit the changes after you complete your modifications.

Using a command-line interface

With the following command, replace *<Setting>* with the name of the setting to modify and *<Value>* with the value to set:

```
> dnscmd <DNSServerName> /config /<Setting> <Value>
```

The following command enables the `EnableDnsSec` setting on *dns01*:

```
> dnscmd dns01 /config /EnableDnsSec 1
```

The following command disables the `NoTcp` setting on the local host:

```
> dnscmd /config /NoTcp 0
```

The following command sets the `DsPollingInterval` setting to 60 on *dns02*:

```
> dnscmd dns02 /config /DsPollingInterval 60
```

For the complete list of settings, run `dnscmd /config` from the command line.

Using PowerShell

There are several Windows PowerShell cmdlets that you can use to set DNS properties. To view a list of all available cmdlets that set DNS properties, use the following command:

```
Get-Command *Set-Dns*
```

Discussion

The Microsoft DNS server supports a variety of settings to configure everything from scavenging and forwarders to logging. With the DNS Management snap-in, the settings are spread over several tabs in the Properties page. You can get a list of these settings by simply running `dnscmd /config` from a command line.

See Also

MSDN: MicrosoftDNS_Server

13.13. Scavenging Old Resource Records

Problem

You want to scavenge old resource records. DNS scavenging is the process whereby resource records are automatically removed if they are not updated after a period of time. Typically, this applies only to resource records that were added via dynamic DNS (DDNS), but you can also scavenge manually created static records. DNS scavenging is a recommended practice so that your DNS zones are automatically kept clean of stale resource records.

Solution

The following solutions will show how to enable automatic scavenging on all AD integrated zones.

Using a graphical user interface

1. Open the DNS Management snap-in (*dnsmgmt.msc*).
2. If an entry for the DNS server you want to connect to does not exist, right-click on DNS in the left pane and select Connect to DNS Server. Select "This computer" or "The following computer", and then enter the server you want to connect to (if applicable) and click OK.
3. Click on the server, right-click on it, and select "Set Aging/Scavenging for all zones".
4. Check the box beside "Scavenge stale resource records".
5. Configure the No-Refresh and Refresh intervals as necessary, and click OK.
6. Check the box beside "Apply these settings to the existing Active Directory-integrated zones" and click OK.
7. Right-click on the server again and select Properties.
8. Select the Advanced tab.
9. Check the box beside "Enable automatic scavenging of stale resource records".
10. Configure the scavenging period as necessary.
11. Click OK.

Using a command-line interface

```
> dnscmd <DNSServerName> /config /ScavengingInterval <ScavengingMinutes>
> dnscmd <DNSServerName> /config /DefaultAgingState 1
> dnscmd <DNSServerName> /config /DefaultNoRefreshInterval <NoRefreshMinutes>
> dnscmd <DNSServerName> /config /DefaultRefreshInterval <RefreshMinutes>
> dnscmd <DNSServerName> /config ..AllZones /aging 1
```

Using PowerShell

```
Set-DnsServerScavenging -ScavengingState $True -RefreshInterval "<Value>"↵
 -ScavengingInterval "<Value>"
Start-DnsServerScavenging -Force
```

Discussion

There are four settings that you need to be aware of before enabling scavenging. You must use caution when enabling scavenging, because an incorrect configuration could lead to resource records getting deleted by mistake.

The first setting you have to configure is the *scavenging interval*. This is the interval in which the DNS server will kick off the scavenging process. It is disabled by default so that scavenging does not take place unless you enable this setting. The default value is seven days.

The second setting is the *default aging configuration setting* for new zones. If you want all new zones to be configured for scavenging, set this to 1.

The next two settings control how records get scavenged. The *no-refresh interval* determines how much time must pass before a dynamically updated record can be updated again. This setting is necessary to reduce how often a DNS server has to update its timestamp of the resource record. The default value is seven days. This means that after a resource record has been dynamically updated, the server will not accept another dynamic update for the same record for another seven days. However, if the IP address or some other data for the record changes, the server will still accept the new information. Static records have a timestamp of 0 and will not get scavenged in an automated scavenging process.

The *refresh interval* setting is the amount of time that must pass after the no-refresh interval during which a client can update its record before it is considered old or stale. The default value for this setting is also 168 hours (seven days). If you use the default values, the combination of the no-refresh interval and refresh interval would mean that a dynamically updated record would not be considered stale for up to 14 days after its most recent update. Combine this with the default scavenging interval, and it could be up to 21 days before a record is deleted if the record became stale immediately after the last scavenge process completed: 7 days (no refresh) + 7 days (refresh) + up to 7 days (scavenge process) = up to 21 days.

The solutions in this recipe show you how to configure these settings for all zones that are hosted on a server; however, you can configure these settings for individual zones as well. In the GUI solution, you would do this by accessing the Properties sheet of an individual zone rather than the server node; in *dnscmd*, simply specify the zone name after /aging, /scavenginginterval, /defaultagingstate, /defaultnorefreshin terval, or /defaultrefreshinterval.

13.14. Clearing the DNS Cache

Problem

You want to clear the DNS cache. The DNS cache contains resource records that are cached by the server or workstation for a period of time in memory so that repeated requests for the same record can be returned immediately. There are two types of DNS cache. One pertains to the cache on the Windows DNS *client* resolver (this can refer to both server and workstation operating systems when they are requesting DNS information from a server), and the other refers to the cache used by the Microsoft DNS *server* software.

Solution

To flush the client resolver cache, use the following command:

```
> ipconfig /flushdns
```

To flush the client resolver cache by using PowerShell, use the following cmdlet:

```
Clear-DnsClientCache
```

To flush the DNS server cache, use any of the following solutions.

Using a graphical user interface

1. Open the DNS Management snap-in (*dnsmgmt.msc*).
2. Right-click on DNS in the left pane and select Connect to DNS Server.
3. Enter the server you want to connect to and click Enter.
4. Right-click on the server and select Clear Cache.

Using a command-line interface

The following command will clear the cache on *<DNSServerName>*. You can leave out the *<DNSServerName>* parameter to simply run the command against the local server:

```
> dnscmd <DNSServerName> /clearcache
```

Using PowerShell

```
Clear-DnsServerCache -Force
```

Discussion

The client resolver cache is populated whenever a DNS lookup is performed on a workstation or server (e.g., by visiting a website in Internet Explorer, a DNS lookup is performed and cached). It's important to remember that this cache will store positive DNS responses as well as negative ones. For example, if lost network connectivity causes DNS queries for an external resource like a mail server to fail, those queries will continue to fail until the cache refreshes: the queries have been *negatively cached*.

The second type of cache is in place on Microsoft DNS servers and on some third-party DNS servers. It is a cache of all DNS requests that the server has made while processing queries from various clients. You can view this cache by browsing the Cached Lookups folder for a server in the DNS Management snap-in. This folder is not shown by default, so you'll need to select Advanced from the View menu.

With both the client and server cache, records are removed from the cache after the record's TTL value expires. The TTL is used to age records so that clients and servers will request an updated copy of the record at a later point in order to receive any changes that may have occurred.

13.15. Verifying That a Domain Controller Can Register Its Resource Records

Problem

You want to verify that DNS is configured correctly so that a domain controller can register its resource records, which are needed for clients to be able to locate various AD services.

Solution

Using a command-line interface

With the following *dcdiag* command, replace *<DomainName>* with the FQDN of the domain that the domain controller is in. This command has to be run from the domain controller you want to test, not from an administrative workstation:

```
> dcdiag /test:RegisterInDNS /DnsDomain:<DomainName>

Starting test: RegisterInDNS
   DNS configuration is sufficient to allow this domain controller to↵
dynamically register the domain controller
   Locator records in DNS.

   The DNS configuration is sufficient to allow this computer to dynamically↵
register the A record corresponding to its DNS name.
```

Using PowerShell

```
Test-DnsServer "<IPAddress>"
```

Discussion

With the default setup, domain controllers attempt to dynamically register the resource records necessary for them to be located by Active Directory clients and other domain controllers. Domain controllers must have their resource records populated in DNS in order to function, but it can be very tedious and error-prone to register all of the records manually. This is why allowing the domain controllers to use DDNS to automatically register and update their records can be much easier from a support standpoint.

The *dcdiag* command provides a `RegisterInDNS` switch that allows you to test whether the DC can register its records. In the solution, we showed the output if the domain controller passes the test.

Here is the output if an error occurs:

```
Starting test: RegisterInDNS
   This domain controller cannot register domain controller Locator DNS
records. This is because it cannot locate a DNS server authoritative for the
zone adatum.com. This is due to one of the following:

   1. One or more DNS servers involved in the name resolution of the adatum.com
name are not responding or contain incorrect delegation of the DNS zones; or

   2. The DNS server that this computer is configured with contains incorrect
root hints.

   The list of such DNS servers might include the DNS servers with which this
computer is configured for name resolution and the DNS servers responsible
for the following zones: adatum.com

   Verify the correctness of the specified domain name and contact your
network/DNS administrator to fix the problem.

   You can also manually add the records specified in the
%systemroot%\system32\config\netlogon.dns file.
```

As you can see, the output of *dcdiag* offers some options for resolving the problem. The information provided will also vary depending on the error encountered.

See Also

Recipe 13.17 for registering a domain controller's resource records

13.16. Enabling DNS Server Debug Logging

Problem

You want to enable DNS debug logging to troubleshoot issues related to DNS queries or updates.

Solution

Using a graphical user interface

1. From the Administrative Tools, Open the DNS Management snap-in (*dnsmgmt.msc*).

2. Connect to the DNS Server you want to modify. In the left pane, right-click on DNS and select Connect to DNS Server. Select "The following computer" and enter the target server name. Click OK.

3. Right-click on the server and select Properties.

4. Click on the Debug Logging tab.

5. Select what you want to log and the location of the logfile.

6. Click OK.

Using a command-line interface

Use the following four commands to enable debug logging. For the log level, you have to add together the event codes you want logged and specify the result in hex. The available event codes can be found in Table 13-3.

```
> dnscmd <ServerName> /Config /LogLevel <EventFlagSumInHex>
```

Use the following command to specify the location of the logfile:

```
> dnscmd <ServerName> /Config /LogFilePath <DirectoryAndFilePath>
```

Use the following command to log only entries that pertain to certain IP addresses:

```
> dnscmd <ServerName> /Config /LogIPFilterList <IPAddress1>[,<IPAddress2>...]
```

Use the following command to specify the maximum logfile size:

```
> dnscmd <ServerName> /Config /LogFileMaxSize <NumberOfBytesInHex>
```

Use the following command to disable debug logging:

```
> dnscmd <ServerName> /Config /LogLevel 0
```

Using PowerShell

```
Set-DnsServerDiagnostics -SaveLogsToPersistentStorage $True↵
 -LogFilePath "<LogFilePath>"
```

Discussion

With the DNS Server debug log, you can record all DNS operations received and initiated by the server, including queries, updates, zone transfers, etc. If you need to troubleshoot a particular host, you can use the LogIPFilterList setting in *dnscmd* or the WMI DNS Provider to restrict the log to operations performed only for or by that host.

The most important debug log setting is the log level. With the DNS snap-in, you can select from a list of available options. The DNS snap-in provides an intuitive interface for selecting the required options. Table 13-3 contains all of the event codes with their hexadecimal and decimal values for the command-line options.

Table 13-3. DNS debug logging event codes

Hexadecimal value	Decimal value	Descriptions
0x0	0	No logging. This is the default.
0x1	1	Query transactions.
0x10	16	Notifications transactions.
0x20	32	Update transactions.
0xFE	254	Nonquery transactions.
0x100	256	Question packets.
0x200	512	Answer packets.
0x1000	4096	Send packets.
0x2000	8192	Receive packets.
0x4000	16384	UDP packets.
0x8000	32768	TCP packets.
0xFFFF	65535	All packets.
0x10000	65536	AD write transactions.
0x20000	131072	AD update transactions.
0x1000000	16777216	Full packets.
0x80000000	2147483648	Write-through transactions.

DNS debug logging can come in handy if you want to look at the dynamic update requests a particular DNS server is processing. For example, if a client or DHCP server is attempting to dynamically register records, you can enable the Update Transactions log category on the DNS server you think should be processing the updates. If you don't see any update transactions, this can indicate that another server is processing the dynamic update requests.

 Transactions are not immediately written to the debug logfile as they occur. They are buffered and written to the file after a certain number of requests are processed.

See Also

MSDN: MicrosoftDNS_Server

13.17. Registering a Domain Controller's Resource Records

Problem

You want to manually force registration of a domain controller's resource records. This may be necessary if you've made some configuration changes on your DNS servers to allow your domain controllers to start dynamically registering resource records.

Solution

Using a command-line interface

```
> nltest /dsregdns /server:<DomainControllerName>
```

Discussion

With the *nltest* command, a /dsregdns switch allows you to force registration of the domain-controller-specific resource records. You can also force reregistration of its resource records by restarting the NetLogon service on the domain controller. The NetLogon service automatically attempts to reregister a domain controller's resource records every hour, so if you can wait that long, you do not need to use *nltest*.

See Also

Recipe 13.15 for verifying whether a domain controller is registering its resource records

13.18. Deregistering a Domain Controller's Resource Records

Problem

You want to manually deregister a domain controller's resource records.

Solution

Using a command-line interface

With the following *nltest* command, replace *<DomainControllerName>* with the FQDN of the domain controller you want to deregister and *<DomainDNSName>* with the FQDN of the domain of which the domain controller is a member:

```
> nltest /dsderegdns: <DomainControllerName> /dom:<DomainDNSName>
```

Discussion

When a domain controller is demoted from a domain, it dynamically deregisters its resource records. This is a nice feature of the demotion process because it means you do not have to manually remove all of the resource records or wait for scavenging to remove them. If, however, you have a domain controller that crashes and you do not plan to bring it back online, you'll need to remove the records manually or wait for the scavenging process to take place.

You can use the DNS Management MMC snap-in and even the *dnscmd.exe* utility to manually remove them one by one, or you can use *nltest*, as shown in the solution.

The /dsderegdns switch also has /DomGUID and /DsaGUID options if you want to delete the records that are based on the domain GUID and DSA GUID, respectively. You need to know the actual GUIDs of the domain and domain controller to use those switches, so if you don't have them handy, it would be easier to delete them using the DNS Management MMC snap-in.

13.19. Preventing a Domain Controller from Dynamically Registering All Resource Records

Problem

You want to prevent a domain controller from dynamically registering its resource records using DDNS. If you manually register a domain controller's resource records, you'll want to prevent those domain controllers from attempting to dynamically register them. If you do not disable them from sending dynamic update requests, you may see annoying error messages on your DNS servers that certain DDNS updates are failing.

Solution

Using a command-line interface

```
> reg add HKLM\System\CurrentControlSet\Services\Netlogon\Parameters /v↵
UseDynamicDNS /t REG_DWORD /d 0
The operation completed successfully.

> net stop netlogon
The Net Logon service is stopping.
The Net Logon service was stopped successfully.

> del %SystemRoot%\system32\config\netlogon.dnb

> net start netlogon
The Net Logon service is starting.......
The Net Logon service was started successfully.
```

Using PowerShell

```
$strRegPath = "HKLM:\System\CurrentControlSet\Services\Netlogon\Parameters"
new-ItemProperty -path $strRegPath -name "UseDynamicDNS" -type DWORD
set-ItemProperty -path $strRegPath -name "UseDynamicDNS" -value "0"

Stop-Service netlogon
$strPath = join-path (get-content env:SystemRoot) system32\config\netlogon.dnb
Remove-Item $strPath
Start-Service netlogon
```

Discussion

By default, domain controllers attempt to dynamically register their Active Directory
–related resource records every hour via the NetLogon service. You can prevent a domain controller from doing this by setting the UseDynamicDNS value to 0 under
HKEY_LOCAL_MACHINE\System\CurrentControlSet\Services\Netlogon\Parameters.
After you set that value, you should stop the NetLogon service, remove the *%SystemRoot
%\system32\config\netlogon.dnb* file and then restart NetLogon. It is necessary to remove the *netlogon.dnb* file because it maintains a cache of the resource records that are
dynamically updated. This file will get re-created when the NetLogon service restarts.

See Also

Recipe 13.20 for preventing certain resource records from being dynamically registered;
MS KB 198767 (How to Prevent Domain Controllers from Dynamically Registering
DNS Names)

13.20. Preventing a Domain Controller from Dynamically Registering Certain Resource Records

Problem

You want to prevent a domain controller from dynamically registering certain resource
records. It is sometimes advantageous to prevent certain resource records from being
dynamically registered. For example, if you want to reduce the load on the PDC Emulator for a domain, you can prevent some of its SRV records from being published, which
would reduce the amount of client traffic the server receives.

Solution

Using a graphical user interface

1. Open the Group Policy Management snap-in (*gpmc.msc*).

2. Create a GPO linked to the Domain Controllers OU, or else edit an existing GPO.

3. Select Computer Configuration→Policies→Administrative Templates→System→Net Logon→DC Locator DNS Records.

4. Enable the "Specify DC Locator DNS records not registered by the DCs" setting, and list one or more of the following record types that should not be registered:

- Dc
- DcAtSite
- DcByGuid
- Gc
- Gc
- GcAtSite
- GcIpAddress
- GenericGc
- Kdc
- Ldap
- LdapIpAddress
- Rfc1510Kdc
- Rfc1510Kpwd
- Rfc1510UdpKdc
- Rfc1510UdpKpwd

Using a command-line interface

This command will disable the Ldap, Gc, and GcIpAddress resource records from being dynamically registered:

```
> reg add HKLM\System\CurrentControlSet\Services\Netlogon\Parameters↵
/v DnsAvoidRegisterRecords /t REG_MULTI_SZ /d Ldap\0Gc\0GcIpAddress

> net stop netlogon

> del %SystemRoot%\system32\config\netlogon.dnb

> net start netlogon
```

Using PowerShell

```
$strRegPath = "HKLM:\System\CurrentControlSet\Services\Netlogon\Parameters"
$arrValues = "Ldap", "Gc", "GcIpAddress"
```

```
New-ItemProperty -Path $strRegPath -Name "DnsAvoidRegisterRecords" -Type↵
MultiString
Set-ItemProperty -Path $strRegPath -Name "DnsAvoidRegisterRecords" -Value↵
$arrValues

Stop-Service netlogon
$strPath = Join-Path (Get-Content env:SystemRoot) system32\config\netlogon.dnb
Remove-Item $strPath
Start-Service netlogon
```

Discussion

The procedure to disable registration of certain resource records is very similar to that described in Recipe 13.19 for preventing all resource records from being dynamically registered; however, in this case you need to create a value called `DnsAvoidRegisterRe` cords under the *HKEY_LOCAL_MACHINE\System\CurrentControlSet\Services\Net logon\Parameters* key. The type for `DnsAvoidRegisterRecords` should be REG_MUL TI_SZ, and the data should be a whitespace-separated list of mnemonics. Mnemonics are used to represent various resource records that domain controllers register. The complete list of mnemonics is included in Table 13-4.

 You can also control these values using Group Policy, in *Computer Con figuration\Policies\Administrative Templates\System\Netlogon.*

Table 13-4. Registry mnemonics for resource records

Registry mnemonic	Resource record type	Resource record name
LdapIpAddress	A	*<DnsDomainName>*
Ldap	SRV	_ldap._tcp.*<DnsDomainName>*
LdapAtSite	SRV	_ldap._tcp.*<SiteName>*._sites.*<DnsDomainName>*
Pdc	SRV	_ldap._tcp.pdc._msdcs.*<DnsDomainName>*
Gc	SRV	_ldap._tcp.gc._msdcs.*<DnsForestName>*
GcAtSite	SRV	_ldap._tcp.*<SiteName>*._sites.gc._msdcs.*<DnsForest Name>*
DcByGuid	SRV	_ldap._tcp.*<DomainGuid>*.domains._msdcs.*<DnsForest Name>*
GcIpAddress	A	_gc._msdcs.*<DnsForestName>*
DsaCname	CNAME	*<DsaGuid>*._msdcs.*<DnsForestName>*
Kdc	SRV	_kerberos._tcp.dc._msdcs.*<DnsDomainName>*
KdcAtSite	SRV	_kerberos._tcp.dc._msdcs.*<SiteName>*._sites.*<DnsDo mainName>*

Registry mnemonic	Resource record type	Resource record name
Dc	SRV	_ldap._tcp.dc._msdcs.<DnsDomainName>
DcAtSite	SRV	_ldap._tcp.<SiteName>._sites.dc._msdcs.<DnsDomain Name>
Rfc1510Kdc	SRV	_kerberos._tcp.<DnsDomainName>
Rfc1510KdcAtSite	SRV	_kerberos._tcp.<SiteName>._sites.<DnsDomainName>
GenericGc	SRV	_gc._tcp.<DnsForestName>
GenericGcAtSite	SRV	_gc._tcp.<SiteName>._sites.<DnsForestName>
Rfc1510UdpKdc	SRV	_kerberos._udp.<DnsDomainName>
Rfc1510Kpwd	SRV	_kpasswd._tcp.<DnsDomainName>
Rfc1510UdpKpwd	SRV	_kpasswd._udp.<DnsDomainName>

If you configure DCs not to register these domain-wide SRV records, such as in a branch office environment, your branch office clients will still fail over to DCs in your hub site if their local DC becomes unavailable. Clients will continue to use the hub site DCs until they are rebooted, even if the local DC comes back online. MS KB 939252 provides a hotfix for Windows XP and Windows Server 2003 that will improve client failover behavior in this scenario. In Windows operating systems since Windows XP, there is improvement and built-in control available. See TechNet (*http://bit.ly/11bLAkp*) for more details.

See Also

Recipe 13.19 for preventing all resource records from being dynamically registered

13.21. Allowing Computers to Use a Domain Suffix That Is Different from Their AD Domain

Problem

You want to allow computers to use a domain suffix that is different from their AD domain.

Solution

Using a graphical user interface

1. Open ADSI Edit.
2. Connect to the domain you want to edit.

---

3. Right-click on the `domainDNS` object and select Properties.

4. Edit the `msDS-AllowedDNSSuffixes` attribute and the DNS suffix you want to add.

5. Click OK.

Using a command-line interface

Create an LDIF file called *add_dns_suffix.ldf* with the following contents:

```
dn: <DomainDN>
changetype: modify
add: msDS-AllowedDNSSuffixes
msDS-AllowedDNSSuffixes: <DNSSuffix>
-
```

Then run the following command:

```
> ldifde -v -i -f add_dns_suffix.ldf.ldf
```

You can also make this change using AdMod, as follows:

```
> admod -b <DomainDN> msDS-AllowedDNSSuffixes:+:<DNSSuffix>
```

Using PowerShell

You can modify the list of allowed DNS suffixes for a domain using PowerShell, as follows:

```
Set-ADObject "<DomainDN>" -Add @{"msDS-AllowedDNSSuffixes"="<Suffix>"}
```

Discussion

Windows Server and client domain members dynamically maintain the `dNSHostName` and `servicePrincipalName` attributes of their corresponding `computer` object in Active Directory with their current hostname. By default, those attributes can only contain hostnames that have a DNS suffix equal to the Active Directory domain the computer is a member of.

If the computer's DNS suffix is not equal to the Active Directory domain, as may be the case during a domain migration or a corporate merger or consolidation, 5788 and 5789 events will be generated in the System event log on the domain controllers the clients attempt to update. These events report that the `dnsHostName` and `servicePrincipal Name` attributes could not be updated due to an incorrect domain suffix. You can avoid this by adding the computer's DNS suffix to the `msDS-AllowedDNSSuffixes` attribute on the domain object (e.g., `dc=adatum,dc=com`).

See Also

MS KB 258503 (DNS Registration Errors 5788 and 5789 When DNS Domain and Active Directory Domain Name Differ)

13.22. Authorizing a DHCP Server

Problem

You want to permit (i.e., authorize) a DHCP server to process DHCP requests from clients. This is necessary only if the DHCP server is a member of an Active Directory domain.

Solution

Using a graphical user interface

1. Open the DHCP snap-in (*dhcpmgmt.msc*).
2. If necessary, in the left pane, right-click on DHCP and select Add Server. Type in the name of the DHCP server you want to target and click OK.
3. Click on the server entry in the left pane.
4. Right-click on the server and select Authorize.

 If the DHCP server is not a member of an Active Directory domain, you will not see the Authorize option.

Using a command-line interface

The following command authorizes a DHCP server in Active Directory:

```
> netsh dhcp add server <DHCPServerName> <DHCPServerIP>
```

This example shows how to authorize the DHCP server named *dhcp01.adatum.com* with IP 192.168.191.15:

```
> netsh dhcp add server dhcp01.adatum.com 192.168.191.15
```

Using PowerShell

The following PowerShell command will authorize a DHCP server in Active Directory:

```
Add-DhcpServerInDC -DnsName "<ServerName>"
```

Discussion

Windows-based DHCP servers that belong to an Active Directory domain must be authorized before they can give leases to clients. This feature helps reduce the danger of a rogue Windows DHCP server that an end user sets up, perhaps even unintentionally.

However, this still doesn't prevent someone from plugging in a non-Windows DHCP server (e.g., a Linksys router with the DHCP server enabled) and causing clients to receive bad leases. A rogue DHCP server can provide incorrect lease information or deny lease requests altogether, ultimately causing a denial of service for clients on your network.

A DHCP server that is a member server of an Active Directory domain performs a query in Active Directory to determine whether it is authorized. If it is, it will respond to DHCP requests; if not, it will not respond to requests.

A standalone Windows DHCP server that is not a member of an Active Directory domain sends out a DHCPINFORM message when it first initializes. If an authorized DHCP server responds to the message, the standalone server will not respond to any further DHCP requests. If it does not receive a response from a DHCP server, it will respond to client requests and distribute leases.

DHCP servers are represented in Active Directory as objects of the dhcpClass class, in the cn=NetServices,cn=Services,cn=Configuration,<ForestRootDN> container. The relative distinguished name of these objects is the IP address of the DHCP server. There is also an object in the same container named cn=dhcpRoot, which is created after the first DHCP server is authorized. It has an attribute named dhcpServers that contains all authorized servers. By default, only members of the *Enterprise Admins* group can authorize DHCP servers. However, you can delegate the rights to authorize a DHCP server. Do the following to delegate the necessary permissions to a group called *DHCP Admins*:

1. Open ADSI Edit from the Support Tools while logged on as a member of the *Enterprise Admins* group.

2. In the left pane, expand the Configuration Container→cn=Configuration→cn=Services→cn=NetServices.

3. Right-click on cn=NetServices and select Properties.

4. Select the Security tab.

5. Click the Advanced button.

6. Click the Add button.

7. Use the object picker to select the *DHCP Admins* group.

8. Check the boxes under "Create dHCPClass objects" and "Delete dHCPClass objects."

9. Click OK until all dialog boxes are closed.

10. Back in ADSI Edit, right-click on cn=dhcpRoot (if you've previously authorized DHCP servers) and select Properties.

11. Select the Security tab.

12. Click the Advanced button.

13. Click the Add button.

14. Use the object picker to select the *DHCP Administrators* group.

15. Check the boxes under Allow for Write All Properties.

16. Click OK until all dialog boxes are closed.

 If the *DHCP Administrators* group does not exist, run the following command on a DHCP server or on a computer with the DHCP management tool installed:

```
netsh dhcp add securitygroups
```

Using a graphical user interface

You can quickly determine whether a DHCP server has been authorized by looking at its server node in the left pane of the DHCP snap-in. If the icon has a little red flag, it isn't authorized; if the flag is green, it is authorized.

Using a command-line interface

To see the list of authorized servers using the command line, run the following command:

```
> netsh dhcp show server
```

Using PowerShell

```
Get-DhcpServerInDC
```

See Also

"Controlling DHCP Active Directory Authorization" (*http://bit.ly/17HUqoZ*)

13.23. Restricting DHCP Administrators

Problem

You want to restrict who can administer your DHCP servers in your domain.

Solution

Using a graphical user interface

1. Open the Active Directory Users and Computers MMC snap-in (*dsa.msc*).

2. In the console tree, click Active Directory Users and Computers→*<Domain Name>*→Users.

3. In the Details pane, click DHCP Administrators.

 If the *DHCP Administrators* group does not exist, run the following command:

    netsh dhcp add securitygroups

4. Click Action→Properties→Members.

5. Remove all users and groups you do not want to have administering your DHCP server by clicking their names and then clicking Remove.

6. To add new DHCP administrators, click Add, provide the user or group name, and then click OK.

7. Click OK.

Using a command-line interface

Add a member to a group with DSMod by passing the -addmbr option:

    > dsmod group "<GroupDN>" -addmbr "<MemberDN>"

To add a group member with AdMod, use the following syntax:

    > admod -b "<GroupDN>" member:+:"<MemberDN>"

Remove a member from a group with DSMod by passing the -rmmbr option:

    > dsmod group "<GroupDN>" -rmmbr "<MemberDN>"

To remove a group member with AdMod, use the following syntax:

    > admod -b "<GroupDN>" member:-:"<MemberDN>"

Replace the complete membership list with DSMod by passing the -chmbr option:

    > dsmod group "<GroupDN>" -chmbr "<Member1DN Member2DN ...>"

To replace the membership of a group with AdMod, use the following command:

    > admod -b "<GroupDN>" member:+-:"<Member1DN>;<Member2DN>;<Member3DN>"

Using PowerShell

You can add a user or group to the membership of the *DHCP Administrators* group using the Add-ADGroupMember command as follows:

```
Add-ADGroupMember "DHCP Administrators" "<User/Group>"
```

Discussion

In Active Directory, most roles can be assigned independently of one another rather than just by making a user a Domain Admin or an Enterprise Admin. This is great for security administrators who want to ensure that users have only enough rights to perform their assigned tasks. For example, a user *Fred* might need to modify an enterprise-wide object. You could just add *Fred* to the *Enterprise Admin* groups to solve the problem. However, *Fred* now has access to virtually any object in the entire forest and could cause irreparable harm to your network, not to mention compromising all security in place. Instead, you can grant *Fred* access to just that object.

This can be done in different ways. One method is to use the Delegation of Control Wizard. Another way is to use the several built-in groups in Windows that are created and populated when specific services are installed. One such group is *DHCP Administrators*, which is created when the first DHCP server is brought up in a domain. You can control administrative access to the DHCP function of these servers through this group membership.

 Nondomain joined computers also have a *DHCP Administrators* group. This is a local group on each computer and must be managed separately on each server.

See Also

"DHCP Groups" (*http://bit.ly/16NrC0j*)

## CHAPTER 14

Security and Authentication

14.0. Introduction

The default Windows 2000 installation of Active Directory was not as secure as it could have been out of the box. It allowed anonymous queries to be executed, which could take up valuable processing resources, and it did not place any requirements on encrypting or signing traffic between clients and domain controllers. As a result, usernames, passwords, and search results could be sent over the network in clear text. Fortunately, beginning with Windows Server 2003, things tightened up significantly. LDAP traffic is signed by default, and anonymous queries are disabled by default. Additionally, Transport Layer Security (TLS), the more flexible cousin of Secure Sockets Layer (SSL), is supported, allowing for end-to-end encryption of traffic between domain controllers and clients.

Active Directory's ACL model provides ultimate flexibility for securing objects throughout a forest; you can restrict access down to the attribute level if you need to. With this flexibility comes increased complexity. An object's ACL is initially generated from the default ACL for the object's class, inherited permissions, and permissions directly applied on the object.

An ACL is a collection of ACEs, which defines the permission and properties that a security principal can use on the object to which the ACL is applied. Defining these entries and populating the ACL is the foundation of Active Directory security and delegation.

In this chapter, we will explore some of the common tasks of managing permissions in Active Directory. If you are looking for a detailed guide to Active Directory permissions, we suggest reading *Active Directory*, Fifth Edition, by Brian Desmond et al. (O'Reilly).

In order for ACLs to be of use, a user must first authenticate to Active Directory. *Kerberos* is the primary network authentication system used by Active Directory. Kerberos is a standards-based system originally developed at MIT that has been widely implemented at universities. We will also be covering some Kerberos-related tasks in this chapter that you will likely encounter in an Active Directory environment. For a complete review of Kerberos, we recommend *Kerberos: The Definitive Guide* by Jason Garman (O'Reilly).

14.1. Enabling SSL/TLS

Problem

You want to enable SSL/TLS access to your domain controllers so that clients can encrypt LDAP traffic to the servers.

Solution

Using a graphical user interface (solution specific to Windows Server 2012)

1. Open Server Manager.

2. Click Manage, then click Add Roles and Features, and then click Next.

3. Click Next, which will select a role-based or featured-based installation.

4. Click Next to select the local server as the destination server.

5. Check the box beside Active Directory Certificate Services and then click Next.

6. The Add Roles and Features Wizard will appear. Maintain the option to include the management tools, and then click the Add Features button to add the required features to the role installation. Click Next.

7. On the features screen, click Next.

8. On the AD CS screen, click Next.

9. On the Role services screen, click Next.

10. Review the installation options and then click Install to begin the installation.

11. Upon completion of the installation, click Close.

12. Go back to Server Manager and click the notifications. In the Post-deployment Configuration notification for AD CS, click the "Configure Active Directory Certificate Services on the destination server" link.

13. On the Credentials screen, enter administrative credentials if needed and then click Next.

14. On the Role Services screen, click Certification Authority and then click Next.

15. Select the setup type that you want and click Next.

16. Select the CA type that you want the server to be and click Next.

17. The "Specify the type of the private key" screen appears. Click Next to create a new private key.

18. The Cryptography for CA screen will appear. Click Next.

19. On the CA Name screen, click Next.

20. On the Validity Period screen, click Next.

21. Enter the location for the certificate database and logs, and then click Next.

22. Click Configure and then click Close when the installation completes.

Discussion

The GUI solution example installs AD CS on an existing domain controller. (While this works, it is a good practice to separate AD DS and AD CS to separate servers when possible.) Because the example installs AD CS on a domain controller, the domain controller automatically acquires a certificate after the installation is complete. If you install AD CS on member server(s), you will need to acquire a certificate for each domain controller. One way to do this is to create an auto-enrollment GPO for all domain controllers. After Active Directory domain controllers obtain certificates, they automatically listen on ports 636 and 3269. Port 636 is for LDAP over SSL/TLS and port 3269 is used for global catalog queries performed over SSL/TLS. See Recipe 14.2 for more information on how to query a domain controller using SSL/TLS.

See Also

"How to Enable Secure Socket Layer [SSL] Communication over LDAP for Windows 2000 Domain Controllers" (*http://support.microsoft.com/kb/247078*); "How to enable LDAP over SSL with a third-party certification authority" (*http://support.micro soft.com/kb/321051*)

14.2. Securing LDAP Traffic with SSL, TLS, or Signing

Problem

You want to secure LDAP traffic using SSL, TLS, or signing.

Solution

Using a graphical user interface

Most of the GUI-based tools running on both client computers and server computers will automatically sign and encrypt traffic between the server and client. This includes the following tools:

- Active Directory Domains and Trusts

- Active Directory Sites and Services

- Active Directory Schema

- Active Directory Users and Computers

- Active Directory Administrative Center

- ADSI Edit

- Group Policy Management snap-in

- Object Picker

With ADSI Edit, you can also specify the port number to use when browsing a partition. View the settings for a connection by right-clicking on the partition and selecting Settings. Click the Advanced button and enter 636 for LDAP over SSL or 3269 for the global catalog over SSL.

Using a command-line interface

The DS command-line tools support LDAP signing and encryption. This includes DSAdd, DSMod, DSrm, DSMove, DSGet, and DSQuery. The *joeware* utilities also support connecting using SSL security.

Discussion

It is a good idea to test whether traffic is being encrypted. If you run Network Monitor (*netmon.exe*) while using tools that perform simple LDAP binds, you'll see LDAP requests, usernames, and passwords going over the network in plain text. Obviously this is not the most secure configuration. If you use some of the tools listed in the preceding section, you will notice that you aren't able to see the requests, usernames, or passwords. Don't take encryption for granted.

See Also

Recipe 14.1 for enabling SSL/TLS; Recipe 14.3; MSDN: ADS_AUTHENTICA-TION_ENUM

14.3. Disabling LDAP Signing

Problem

You want to disable LDAP signing.

Solution

Using a graphical user interface

To temporarily disable LDAP encryption or signing for troubleshooting purposes, use the following steps on a client computer:

1. Create a new GPO. Edit the GPO and select Computer Configuration→Policies→Windows Settings→Security Settings→Local Policies, and then highlight Security Options.
2. In the right pane, double-click the policy titled "Network security: LDAP client signing requirements".
3. Click the checkbox to define the policy setting and then select None as the setting.
4. Click OK.
5. Link the GPO to the container that contains the desired computer object(s).

Discussion

If the target domain controllers require signing, then disabling the client signing will result in the client administrative tools not being able to communicate with the domain controllers. To disable LDAP signing on domain controllers, follow the preceding steps but modify the policy titled "Domain controller: LDAP server signing requirements" in the Default Domain Controllers policy.

See Also

Recipe 14.2 to enable LDAP signing and encryption

14.4. Enabling Anonymous LDAP Access

Problem

You want to enable anonymous LDAP access for clients. Anonymous queries are disabled by default except for querying the RootDSE.

Solution

Using a graphical user interface

1. Open ADSI Edit.

2. In the Configuration partition, browse to cn=Services→cn=Windows NT→cn=Directory Service.

3. In the left pane, right click on the Directory Service object and select Properties.

4. Double-click on the dSHeuristics attribute.

5. If the attribute is empty, set it with the value 0000002.

6. If the attribute has an existing value, make sure the seventh digit is set to 2.

7. Click OK twice.

Using PowerShell

```
$root = [ADSI]"LDAP://RootDSE"
$obj  = [ADSI]("LDAP://cn=Directory Service,cn=Windows NT,cn=Services," +↲
        $root.configurationNamingContext)

$dsHeuristics = $obj.dsHeuristics.value
if ($dsHeuristics -eq $null)
{
    "dsHeuristics was null (not previously set)"
    $dsHeuristics = "0000000"     # seven zeroes
}

$len = $dsHeuristics.Length
if ($len -lt 7)
{
    $dsHeuristics = $dsHeuristics + ("0000000").SubString(0, (7 - $len))
    $len = 7
}

# we've ensured that $dsHeuristics is AT LEAST seven chars long now
# it may be 13 chars or more. we really don't care about that!

$char = $dsHeuristics.SubString(6, 1)
if ($char -eq "2")
{
    "Anonymous query mode already set to 2"
}
else
{
    $upd =  $dsHeuristics.SubString(0, 6) + "2"
    if ($dsHeuristics.Length -gt 7)
    {
        $dsHeuristics.SubString(7, $len)
    }

    $obj.dsHeuristics = $upd
    $obj.SetInfo()

    "Anonymous query mode set to 2"
```

```
    "New value of dsHeuristics equal to $upd"
}
```

Discussion

To enable anonymous access, you have to modify the dSHeuristics attribute of the cn=Directory Service,cn=Windows NT,cn=Services,ConfigurationDN object. The dSHeuristics attribute is an interesting attribute used to control certain behavior in Active Directory. For example, you can enable List Object Access mode (see Recipe 14.17) by setting the dSHeuristics flag.

The dSHeuristics attribute consists of a series of digits that, when set, enable certain functionality. To enable anonymous access, the seventh digit must be set to 2. By default, dSHeuristics does not have a value. If you set it to enable anonymous access, the value would be 0000002.

After enabling anonymous access, the assumption is that you'll want to grant access for anonymous users to retrieve certain data from Active Directory. To do that, grant the ANONYMOUS LOGON user access to the parts of the directory you want anonymous users to search. You must grant the access from the root of the directory down to the object of interest. See MS KB 320528 for an example of how to enable the anonymous user to query the email addresses of user objects.

See Also

Recipe 14.17; "How to configure Active Directory to allow anonymous queries" (*http://support.microsoft.com/kb/320528*); MSDN: DS-Heuristics attribute

14.5. Using the Delegation of Control Wizard

Problem

You want to delegate control over objects in Active Directory to a user or group.

Solution

Using a graphical user interface

1. Open the Active Directory Users and Computers snap-in (*dsa.msc*) or Active Directory Sites and Services snap-in (*dssite.msc*), depending on the type of object you want to delegate.

2. In the left pane, browse to the object on which you want to delegate control.

3. Right-click on the object and select Delegate Control. Only certain objects support the Delegation of Control Wizard, so this option will not show up for every type of object.

4. Click Next.

5. Click the Add button and use the object picker to select the users or groups to which you want to delegate control.

6. Click Next.

7. If the task you want to delegate is an option under "Delegate the following common tasks," place a checkmark next to it and click Next. If the task is not present, select "Create a custom task to delegate" and click Next. If you selected the latter option, you will need to perform four additional steps:

   a. Select the object type you want to delegate.

   b. Click Next.

   c. Select the permissions you want to delegate.

   d. Click Next.

8. Click Finish.

Using a command-line interface

To grant permissions from the command line, use the following syntax:

```
> dsacls <ObjectDN> /g <Permissions>
```

For example, the following syntax will delegate the permission to read and write information to the `description` property:

```
> dsacls <ObjectDN> /g RPWP;description;
```

Discussion

The Delegation of Control Wizard is Microsoft's attempt to ease the pain of trying to set permissions for common tasks. Because Active Directory permissions are so granular, they can also be cumbersome to configure. The Delegation of Control Wizard helps in this regard, but it is still limited in functionality. The default tasks that can be delegated are fairly minimal, although you can add more tasks as described in Recipe 14.6. Another limitation is that you can only add new permissions; you cannot undo or remove permissions that you previously set with the wizard. To do that, you have to use the ACL Editor directly as described in Recipe 14.8.

See Also

Recipe 14.6 for customizing the Delegation of Control Wizard; Recipe 14.7 for more on using *dsrevoke*

14.6. Customizing the Delegation of Control Wizard

Problem

You want to add or remove new delegation options in the Delegation of Control Wizard.

Solution

Open the Delegation of Control Wizard INF file (*%SystemRoot%\System32\Dele gwiz.inf* in Windows Server 2008 and later) on the computer for which you want to modify the wizard.

Under the [DelegationTemplates] section, you'll see a line similar to the following:

```
Templates = template1, template2, template3, template4, template5, template6,
template7, template8, template9,template10, template11, template12, template13
```

You need to append a new template name. In this case, we'll follow the same naming convention and create a template named template14. The line should now look like this:

```
Templates = template1, template2, template3, template4, template5, template6,
template7, template8, template9,template10, template11, template12, template13,
template14
```

Scroll to the end of the file and append a new template section. You can use the other template sections as examples. Here is the generic format:

```
[<TemplateName>]
AppliesToClasses = <CommaSeparatedListOfObjectClassesInvokedFrom>

Description = "<DescriptionShownInWizard>"

ObjectTypes = <CommaSeparatedListOfObjectClassesThatAreSet>

[<TemplateName>.SCOPE]<Permission entries for Scope>

[<TemplateName>.<ObjectClass1>]<Permission entries for ObjectClass1>

[<TemplateName>.<ObjectClass2>]<Permission entries for ObjectClass2>

...
```

<TemplateName> is the same as what we used in the [DelegationTemplates] section— that is, template14.

In the `AppliesToClasses` line, replace *<CommaSeparatedListOfObjectClassesInvo kedFrom>* with a comma-separated list of LDAP display names of the classes that can be delegated. This delegation action will show up on the classes listed here only when you select Delegate Control from a snap-in. To make our new template entry apply to domain objects, OUs, and containers, we would use this line:

```
AppliesToClasses = domainDNS,organizationalUnit,container
```

In the `Description` line, replace *<DescriptionShownInWizard>* with the text you want shown in the wizard that describes the permissions being delegated. Here is a sample description for delegating full control over `inetOrgPerson` objects:

```
Description = "Create, delete, and manage user and inetOrgPerson accounts"
```

In the `ObjectTypes` line, replace *<CommaSeparatedListOfObjectClassesThatAre Set>* with a comma-separated list of object classes to be delegated. In this example, permissions will be modified for `user` and `inetOrgPerson` objects:

```
ObjectTypes = user,inetOrgPerson
```

Next, define the actual permissions to set when this action is selected. You can define two different types of permissions. You can use a *[<TemplateName>.*`SCOPE`*]* section to define permissions that are set on the object that is used to start the wizard. This will be one of the object classes defined in the `AppliesToClass` line. This is commonly used in the context of containers and organizational units to specify, create, modify, or delete child objects of a particular type. For example, to allow the granting of create (CC) or delete (DC) permissions for `user` and `inetOrgPerson` objects, you would use the following:

```
[template14.SCOPE]
user=CC,DC
inetOrgPerson=CC,DC
```

As you can see, each permission (e.g., create child) is abbreviated to a two-letter code (e.g., CC). Table 14-1 lists the valid codes.

Table 14-1. Permissions and abbreviated codes

Abbreviated code	Permission
RP	Read Property
WP	Write Property
CC	Create Child
DC	Delete Child
GA	Full Control

It is perfectly valid to leave out a `SCOPE` section if it is not needed. The rest of the lines are used to specify permissions that should be set on the object classes defined by the `ObjectTypes` line.

To allow the granting of full control over all existing user and inetOrgPerson objects, we'll use these entries:

```
[template14.user]
@=GA

[template14.inetOrgPerson]
@=GA
```

This is very similar to the previous example, except that here SCOPE is replaced with the names of the object classes the permissions apply to. The @ symbol is used to indicate that the permission applies to all attributes on the object. You can get more granular by replacing @ with the name of the attribute the permission applies to. For example, this would allow the granting of read and write permissions on the department attribute for inetOrgPerson objects:

```
[template14.inetOrgPerson]
department=RP,WP
```

You can also enable control access rights using the CONTROLRIGHT designator instead of @ or an attribute name; you just need to specify the LDAP display name of the control access right you want to enable. The following section enables the Reset Password right on inetOrgPerson objects and enables read and write access to the pwdLastSet attribute:

```
[template14.inetOrgPerson]
CONTROLRIGHT="Reset Password"
pwdLastSet=RP,WP
```

Discussion

You can completely customize the tasks that can be delegated with the Delegation of Control Wizard, but you still have the problem of getting the *Delegwiz.inf* file, on all the clients that need to use the new settings. You can manually copy it to the computers that need it, or you can use Group Policy to automate the distribution of it.

Microsoft offers a prebuilt delegation file that allows you to delegate more than 70 administrative tasks. The file can be used to replace the existing *Delegwiz.inf* file or it can be used as a starting point if you only wanted to use a subset of the file. See the file at TechNet (*http://bit.ly/16c3Par*) for more information.

See Also

Recipe 14.5 for more on using the Delegation of Control Wizard

14.7. Revoking Delegated Permissions

Problem

You want to remove permissions that you've delegated to a domain or an OU.

Solution

Using a graphical user interface

1. Open the Active Directory Users and Computers MMC snap-in (*dsa.msc*). Right-click on the object that you wish to modify and select Properties.

2. From the Security tab, highlight the permissions entry that you wish to revoke and click Remove, and then click OK.

Using a command-line interface

The following command will remove any permissions that have been delegated directly to the ADATUM\jsmith user over the Finance Organizational Unit:

```
> dsrevoke /remove "/root:ou=Finance,dc=adatum,dc=com" ADATUM\jsmith
```

Discussion

While the Delegation of Control Wizard makes it trivial to grant permissions to objects within Active Directory, one thing that it lacks is an Undo button. To help address this, Microsoft has made the *dsrevoke* command-line utility a free download from its website (*http://bit.ly/15rrzaL*). Note that the tool is dated as it was created originally for Windows 2000. It has been a bit spotty on Windows Server 2008 and Windows Server 2008 R2, but we've used it successfully with Windows Server 2012. The *dsrevoke* utility will remove any permissions that have been delegated to a security principal on a domain or an OU, with the following limitations:

- You can use *dsrevoke* only on a domain or an OU; if you've delegated permissions over individual objects, you'll need to remove them manually.

- *dsrevoke* removes only object permissions; if you've assigned any user rights through Group Policy, they'll need to be removed separately.

- You can't use *dsrevoke* to remove any permissions that have been delegated to the Schema or Configuration NCs.

See Also

"Best Practices for Delegating Active Directory Administration" (*http://bit.ly/15rrKCZ*)

14.8. Viewing the ACL for an Object

Problem

You want to view the ACL for an object.

Solution

Using a graphical user interface

1. Open the ACL Editor. You can do this by viewing the properties of an object (right-click on the object and select Properties) with a tool such as ADUC or ADSI Edit. Select the Security tab. To see the Security tab with ADUC, you must select View→Advanced Features from the menu.

2. Click the Advanced button to view a list of the individual ACEs.

Using a command-line interface

```
> dsacls <ObjectDN>
```

Using PowerShell

```
(Get-Acl "ad:\<ObjectDN>").Access | FL
```

Discussion

Viewing an object's ACL is a common task and should already be familiar to most administrators. The ACL Editor is useful for checking the permissions that have been set on objects, especially after running the Delegation of Control Wizard. In addition to viewing permissions, the options available in the GUI include viewing auditing settings and the owner of the object. Knowing the owner of an object is important because ownership confers certain inherent rights.

Because the ACL Editor is the same for NTFS permissions and properties as it is for Active Directory objects, you should feel comfortable with the look and feel of the interface; it is exactly the same as file and folder permissions. We also highly recommend getting familiar with the Advanced view of the ACL Editor, as this is truly the view in which you can determine what is going on with permissions. The Basic view presents a list of security principals that have permissions configured, but it will not always show every configured ACE entry. The Advanced view will show the complete picture, including the scope of permissions for ACEs down to the object and even the attribute level.

See Also

Recipe 14.12 for changing an ACL; Recipe 15.13 for auditing of object access

14.9. Customizing the ACL Editor

Problem

You want to set permissions on attributes that do not show up in the default Active Directory Users and Computers ACL Editor.

Solution

The ACL Editor in ADUC and in the Active Directory Administrative Center shows only a subset of the object's attributes on which permissions can be set. Most attributes can be seen in the ACL Editor by clicking the Advanced button, adding or editing a permission entry, and selecting the Properties tab.

An attribute can have a read permission, a write permission, or both, either of which can be set to Allow or Deny. If the attribute you want to secure is not in the list, you will need to modify the *dssec.dat* file on the computer that you're running the ACL Editor from. On Windows Server 2012, the *dssec.dat* file is located in the *%SYSTEMROOT% \System32* folder.

There are sections for each object class represented in square brackets—for example, [user]. Underneath that heading is a list of attributes that you can configure to display or not display in the ACL Editor.

These are the first few lines for the [user] section:

```
[user]
aCSPolicyName=7
adminCount=7
allowedAttributes=7
```

The value to the right of the attribute determines whether it is shown in the ACL Editor. The valid values include the following:

0

Both the Read property and the Write property are displayed for the attribute.

1

The Write property is displayed for the attribute.

2

The Read property is displayed for the attribute.

7

No entries are displayed for the attribute.

If the attribute is not defined, then the default value (specified by @, if present) is used.

Discussion

Much like the Delegation of Control Wizard, you can customize the attributes that are shown in the ACL Editor, but you still need to distribute the *dssec.dat* file to all computers that need to see the change.

After making the changes to *dssec.dat*, close ADUC and/or the Active Directory Administrative Center and then reopen them.

See Also

MS KB 296490 (How to Modify the Filtered Properties of an Object); MS KB 294952 (How to Delegate the Unlock Account Right)

14.10. Viewing the Effective Permissions on an Object

Problem

You want to view the effective permissions that a user or group has for a particular object.

Solution

Using a graphical user interface (solution specific to Windows Server 2012)

1. Open the ACL Editor. You can do this by viewing the properties of an object (right-click on the object and select Properties) with a tool such as ADUC or ADSI Edit. Select the Security tab. To see the Security tab with ADUC, you must select View→Advanced Features from the menu.

2. Click the Advanced button.

3. Select the Effective Access tab.

4. Click the "Select a user" button to bring up the Object Editor.

5. Find the user or group for which you want to see the effective permissions.

6. Click the "View effective access" button.

The results will be shown in the bottom of the window.

 The Effective Access tab is the new name for the Effective Permissions tab since Windows Server 2008.

Using a command-line interface

```
> acldiag <ObjectDN> /geteffective:<UserOrGroupDN>
```

Discussion

Viewing the permissions on an object does not tell the whole story as to what the actual translated permissions are for a user or group on that object. The *effective permissions* of an object take into account all group membership and any inherited permissions that might have been applied farther up the tree. While this is a useful tool to analyze permissions, it is unfortunately only a best guess; there are still some situations in which certain permissions will not be reflected.

The *AclDiag* tool is from the Windows Server 2003 Service Pack 2 32-bit Support Tools. It is a free download (*http://bit.ly/ZBehAJ*), and it installs and works successfully up to Windows Server 2012.

See Also

AclDiag overview (*http://bit.ly/16c4c4M*)

14.11. Configuring Permission Inheritance

Problem

You want to configure permission inheritance on an Active Directory container to configure whether a child object should automatically receive any permissions that you've granted to its parent object.

Solution

1. Open the ACL Editor. You can do this by viewing the properties of an object (right-click on the object and select Properties) with a tool such as Active Directory Users and Computers (ADUC) or ADSI Edit. Select the Security tab. If the Security tab is not visible within ADUC, you must select View→Advanced Features from the menu.

2. Click the Advanced button to view a list of the individual ACEs.

3. To turn off inheritance, click the "Disable inheritance" button.

4. You will be given the option to "Convert inherited permissions into explicit permissions on this object", to "Remove all inherited permissions from this object", or to cancel. Click the desired option.

5. To reenable permission inheritance from objects farther up the directory structure, click the "Enable inheritance" button in the Advanced Permissions window.

Using a command-line interface

To disable permission inheritance (i.e., to configure an object such that only explicitly assigned permissions apply), use the following syntax:

```
> dsacls <ObjectDN> /P:Y
```

To enable permission inheritance, do the following:

```
> dsacls <ObjectDN> /P:N
```

Using PowerShell

The following syntax will prevent an object from receiving inherited permissions that have been applied at a higher level in the tree:

```
$acl = Get-Acl -Path "AD:<ObjectDN>"
$acl.SetAccessRuleProtection($true,$true);Set-Acl -AclObject $acl "AD:<ObjectDN>"
```

The following syntax will configure an AD object so that it will receive inherited permissions that have been applied at a higher level in the directory tree:

```
$acl = Get-Acl -Path "AD:<ObjectDN>"
$acl.SetAccessRuleProtection($false,$false);Set-Acl -AclObject $acl↵
  "AD:<ObjectDN>"
```

Discussion

Similar to NTFS permissions on the filesystem, Active Directory permissions on container objects can be set to inherit or trickle down to objects farther down the directory structure. This process can greatly simplify assigning permissions, as you can assign a common set of permissions high up in the directory structure and have those permissions filter down to all of the OUs and objects below. In some cases, though, you might want to turn off permission inheritance to configure an entirely different set of permissions for a child object or container.

One thing to keep in mind when enabling or disabling inheritance is that there are a number of AD security principals protected by the AdminSDHolder process that will receive a specific set of permissions regardless of the inheritance settings you configure.

These groups include *Enterprise Admins*, *Schema Admins*, *Domain Admins*, *Administrators*, *Account Operators*, *Server Operators*, *Print Operators*, *Backup Operators*, and *Cert Publishers*. In addition, some Active Directory–aware applications depend on inheritance being in place in order to function efficiently.

See Also

"AdminSDHolder—or where did my permissions go?" (*http://bit.ly/18pGCkc*); "Description and Update of the Active Directory AdminSDHolder Object" (*http://support.microsoft.com/kb/232199*)

14.12. Changing the ACL of an Object

Problem

You want to change the ACL on an object to grant or restrict access to it for a user or group.

Solution

Using a graphical user interface

1. Open the ACL Editor. You can do this by viewing the properties of an object (right-click on the object and select Properties) with a tool such as ADUC, Active Directory Administrative Center, or ADSI Edit. Select the Security tab. To see the Security tab with ADUC, you must select Views→Advanced Features from the menu.

2. Click the Advanced button to view a list of the individual ACEs.

3. Click Add to specify a new user or group, and then place checkmarks next to the permissions that you want to assign and click OK.

4. To remove an ACE, highlight the entry and click Remove. If the Permissions entry is inherited from farther up the directory tree, the option to remove the permission will not be available unless you disable inheritance. With inheritance enabled, you will only have the option to remove any permissions that have not been inherited.

Using a command-line interface

To grant permissions from the command line, use the following syntax:

```
> dsacls <ObjectDN> /g <Permissions>
```

To deny permissions, replace /g with /d.

Using PowerShell

To add an entry for Full Control to the ACL of an object, use the following syntax:

```
$Path = [ADSI]"LDAP://<ObjectDN>"
$Group = New-Object System.Security.Principal.NTAccount("<GroupName>")
$IdentityReference = $Group.Translate↵
([System.Security.Principal.SecurityIdentifier])
$Perms = New-Object System.DirectoryServices.ActiveDirectoryAccessRule↵
 ($IdentityReference,"GenericAll","Allow")
$Path.psbase.ObjectSecurity.AddAccessRule($Perms)
$Path.psbase.commitchanges()
```

Discussion

Changing the ACL of an object is a common task for administrators in any but the most basic AD implementations because, as shown in Recipe 14.5 and Recipe 14.6, the Delegation of Control Wizard is limited and cumbersome to extend and deploy. The GUI and command-line methods are useful for one-off changes to permissions, but for making global changes to a number of objects, you should consider using a script to automate the process.

See Also

Recipe 7.10; Recipe 8.2; Recipe 13.9; Recipe 14.5; Recipe 14.6; Recipe 17.9

14.13. Changing the Default ACL for an Object Class in the Schema

Problem

You want to change the default ACL for an object class in the schema.

Solution

Using a graphical user interface

1. Open the Active Directory Schema snap-in.
2. In the left pane, browse to the class you want to modify.
3. Right-click on it and select Properties.
4. Select the Default Security tab.
5. Use the ACL Editor to change the ACL.
6. Click OK.

Discussion

Each instantiated object in Active Directory has an associated structural class that defines a default security descriptor (the defaultSecurityDescriptor attribute). When an object is created and a security descriptor isn't specified, the default security descriptor is applied to it. This, along with inheritable permissions from the parent container, determines how an object's security descriptor is initially defined. If you find that you are modifying the default security descriptor on a particular type of object every time it is created, you may want to modify its default security descriptor. Another option would be to use a script that would modify the individual object's ACL at the same time that the object was created.

See Also

Recipe 10.1 for more on registering the Active Directory Schema snap-in; Recipe 14.14 for comparing the ACL of an object to the default defined in the schema; Recipe 14.15 for resetting the ACL of an object to the default defined in the schema

14.14. Comparing the ACL of an Object to the Default Defined in the Schema

Problem

You want to determine whether an object has the permissions defined in the schema for its object class as part of its ACL.

Solution

Using a command-line interface

```
> acldiag <ObjectDN> /schema
```

Discussion

For more on the default security descriptor (SD), see Recipe 14.13. *AclDiag* will determine whether the object possesses the security descriptor that's defined in the schema —if you've modified the security descriptor, *AclDiag* will compare the object's SD against the currently defined SD, not the Active Directory default.

See Also

Recipe 14.15 for resetting an object's ACL to the default defined in the schema

14.15. Resetting an Object's ACL to the Default Defined in the Schema

Problem

You want to reset an object's ACL to the one defined in the schema for the object's object class.

Solution

Using a graphical user interface

1. Open the ACL Editor. You can do this by viewing the properties of an object (right-click on the object and select Properties) with a tool such as ADUC, Active Directory Administrative Center, or ADSI Edit. Select the Security tab. To see the Security tab with ADUC, you must select View→Advanced Features from the menu.

2. Click the Advanced button.

3. Click the "Restore defaults" button.

4. Click OK twice.

Using a command-line interface

```
> dsacls <ObjectDN> /S
```

 The /S parameter is case-sensitive.

Discussion

For more on the default security descriptor, see Recipe 14.13.

14.16. Enabling Strong Domain Authentication

Problem

You want to ensure that users can only authenticate to Active Directory using strong authentication protocols.

Solution

Using a graphical user interface

1. Open the Group Policy Management snap-in (*gpmc.msc*).

2. In the left pane, expand the Forest container, expand the Domains container, browse to the domain you want to administer, and expand the Group Policy Objects container.

3. Right-click on the GPO that controls the configuration of your domain controllers and select Edit. (By default, this is the Default Domain Controller Policy, but it may be a different GPO in your environment.) This will bring up the Group Policy Object Editor.

4. Browse to Computer Configuration→Policies→Windows Settings→Security Settings→Local Policies→Security Options.

5. Double-click on "Network security: LAN Manager Authentication Level". Place a checkmark next to "Define this policy setting".

6. Select "Send NTLMv2 response only. Refuse LM & NTLM." Click OK.

7. Wait for Group Policy to refresh, or run the gpupdate /force command from the command prompt.

Discussion

Microsoft operating systems have supported different flavors of LM and NT LAN Manager (NTLM) authentication since the earliest days of Windows. LM authentication is an extremely old and weak authentication protocol that should no longer be used in production environments unless absolutely necessary. By default, Windows 2000 Active Directory supported client authentication attempts using LM, NTLM, or NTLMv2; Windows Server 2003 and later support only NTLM and NTLMv2 out of the box.

The strongest NTLM authentication scheme you can select is to refuse LM and NTLM authentication from any client, and to respond only to clients using NTLMv2. Depending on your client configuration, though, enabling this option may require changes on the client side as well. You can apply the same setting to a GPO linked to your Active Directory domain to ensure that all of your clients will use NTLMv2 instead of older, weaker protocols.

Windows Server 2008, Windows Server 2008 R2, and Windows Server 2012 Active Directory have a default value of "Send NTLMv2 response only" for this GPO setting. This is more secure than previous versions of the operating system but still allows domain controllers to accept weaker authentication methods.

See Also

"Introducing the Restriction of NTLM Authentication" (*http://bit.ly/13cP3gx*); "Purging Old NT Security Protocols" (*http://bit.ly/13mFeM9*)

14.17. Enabling List Object Access Mode

Problem

You want to prevent any authenticated user from being able to browse the contents of Active Directory by default. Enabling List Object Access mode means that users will need explicit permissions to see directory listings of containers.

Solution

Using a graphical user interface

1. Open ADSI Edit.
2. In the Configuration partition, browse to cn=Services→cn=Windows NT→cn=Directory Service.
3. In the left pane, right-click on the Directory Service object and select Properties.
4. Double-click on the dSHeuristics attribute.
5. If the attribute is empty, set it with the value 001. If the attribute has an existing value, make sure the third digit (from the left) is set to 1.
6. Click OK twice.

Using VBScript

```
On Error Resume Next ' necessary if dsHeuristics is not
                     ' already set

' This code enables or disables list object mode for a forest.
' ------ SCRIPT CONFIGURATION -----
boolEnableListObject = 1 ' e.g. 1 to enable, 0 to disable
' ------ END CONFIGURATION --------

set objRootDSE = GetObject("LDAP://RootDSE")
set objDS = GetObject( _
            "LDAP://cn=Directory Service,cn=Windows NT,cn=Services," ↵
          & objRootDSE.Get("configurationNamingContext") )
strDSH = objDS.Get("dSHeuristics")
if len(strDSH) = 1 then
    strDSH = strDSH & "0"
end if
```

```
strNewDSH = Left(strDSH,2) & boolEnableListObject
if len(strDSH) > 3 then
    strNewDSH = strNewDSH & Right(strDSH, len(strDSH) - 3)
end if

WScript.Echo "Old value: " & strDSH
WScript.Echo "New value: " & strNewDSH

if strDSH <> strNewDSH then
    objDS.Put "dSHeuristics", strNewDSH
    objDS.SetInfo
    WScript.Echo "Successfully set list object mode to " & ↵
                 boolEnableListObject
else
    WScript.Echo "List object mode already set to " & boolEnableListObject
end if
```

Discussion

List Object Access mode is useful if you want your users to view only a subset of objects when doing a directory listing of a particular container, or you do not want them to be able to list the objects in a container at all. This mode was originally intended for multitenant environments and should undergo thorough testing in an environment before deploying to production. By default, the *Authenticated Users* group is granted the List Contents access control right over objects in a domain. If you remove or deny this right on a container by modifying the ACL, users will not be able to get a listing of the objects in that container using tools such as ADUC or ADSI Edit.

To limit the objects that users can see when they pull up an object listing, you first need to enable List Object Access mode as described in the solution. You should then remove the List Contents access control right on the target container. Lastly, you'll need to grant the List Object right to the objects that the users or groups should be able to list.

Enabling List Object Access mode can significantly increase the administration overhead for configuring ACLs in Active Directory. It can also impact performance on a domain controller since it will take considerably more time to verify ACLs before returning information to a client.

Using VBScript

This script requires the On Error Resume Next command in order to function. Without this line in place, the script will throw an error if the dsHeuristics attribute is not set.

See Also

Ask the Directory Services Team blog (*http://bit.ly/15kFAXP*)

14.18. Modifying the ACL on Administrator Accounts

Problem

You want to modify the ACL for user accounts that are members of one of the administrative groups.

Solution

Using one of the methods described in Recipe 14.12, modify the ACL on the `cn=Ad minSDHolder,cn=Systems,<DomainDN>` object in the domain that the administrator accounts reside in. The ACL on this object gets applied every hour to all user accounts that are members of the administrative groups.

Discussion

If you've ever tried to directly modify the ACL on a user account that was a member of one of the administrative groups in Active Directory, or you modified the ACL on the OU containing an administrative account, and then wondered why the account's ACL was overwritten later, you've come to the right place. The Admin SD Holder feature of Active Directory is one that many administrators stumble upon after much grinding of teeth. However, after you realize the purpose for it, you'll understand it is a necessary feature.

Once an hour, a process on the PDC Emulator that we'll refer to as the Admin SD Holder process compares the ACL on the `AdminSDHolder` object to the ACL on the accounts that are in administrative groups in the domain as well as the groups themselves. If it detects a difference, it will overwrite the account or Group ACL and disable inheritance.

 If you later remove a user from an administrative group, you will need to reapply any inherited permissions and enable inheritance if necessary. The Admin SD Holder process will not take care of this for you.

The Admin SD Holder process is intended to subvert any malicious activity by a user that has been delegated rights over an OU or container that contains an account that is in one of the administrative groups. An OU administrator could, for example, modify permissions inheritance on an OU to attempt to lock out the *Domain Admins* group; this permission change would be reverted the next time the `AdminSDHolder` thread runs.

These groups are included as part of Admin SD Holder processing:

- *Administrators*
- *Account Operators*

- *Cert Publishers*
- *Backup Operators*
- *Domain Admins*
- *Enterprise Admins*
- *Print Operators*
- *Schema Admins*
- *Server Operators*

The *administrator* and *krbtgt* user accounts are also specifically checked during the Admin SD Holder process.

See Also

"Description and Update of the Active Directory AdminSDHolder Object" (*http://support.microsoft.com/kb/232199*); "Five common questions about AdminSdHolder and SDProp" (*http://bit.ly/10hbguh*)

14.19. Viewing and Purging Your Kerberos Tickets

Problem

You want to view and purge your Kerberos tickets.

Solution

The *kerbtray* utility can be found in the Windows Server 2003 Resource Kit. The *kerbtray* utility works through Windows Server 2012. *Klist* is built into the Active Directory Domain Services role.

Using a graphical user interface

1. Run *kerbtray.exe* from the command line or from Start→Run.
2. A new icon (green) should show up in the system tray. Double-click on that icon. This will allow you to view your current tickets.
3. To purge your tickets, right-click on the *kerbtray* icon in the system tray and select Purge Tickets.
4. Close the *kerbtray* window and reopen it by right-clicking on the *kerbtray* icon and selecting List Tickets.

Using a command-line interface

Run the following command to list your current tickets:

```
> klist tickets
```

Run the following command to purge your tickets:

```
> klist purge
```

Discussion

Active Directory uses Kerberos as its preferred network authentication system. When you authenticate to a Kerberos Key Distribution Center (KDC), which in Active Directory terms is a domain controller, you are issued one or more tickets. These tickets identify you as a certain principal in Active Directory and can be used to authenticate you to other Kerberized services. This type of ticket is known as a *ticket-granting ticket*, or TGT. Once you've obtained a TGT, the client can use the TGT to gain access to a Kerberized service by querying the Ticket Granting Service on the KDC; if the KDC verifies that the user is authorized to access the service in question, it will issue a *service ticket* that allows the client to use the particular service.

Kerberos is a fairly complicated system, and we can't do it justice in a single paragraph. If you want more information on tickets and how the Kerberos authentication system works, see *Kerberos: The Definitive Guide* by Jason Garman (O'Reilly).

See Also

RFC 1510 (The Kerberos Network Authentication Service V5); "Kerberos Authentication Overview" (*http://bit.ly/16c4Tel*)

14.20. Forcing Kerberos to Use TCP

Problem

Clients are experiencing authentication problems, and you've determined it is due to UDP fragmentation of Kerberos traffic. You want to force Kerberos traffic to use TCP instead. Perform the solution on all computers that are experiencing the issue (client computers, server, domain controllers).

Solution

Using a graphical user interface

1. Run *regedit.exe* from the command line or from Start→Run.

2. In the left pane, expand HKEY_LOCAL_MACHINE→System→Current-ControlSet→Control→Lsa→Kerberos→Parameters.

3. Right-click on Parameters and select New→DWORD value. Enter `MaxPacket Size` for the value name.

4. In the right pane, double-click on MaxPacketSize and enter 1.

5. Click OK.

Using a command-line interface

```
> reg add "HKLM\SYSTEM\CurrentControlSet\Control\Lsa\Kerberos\Parameters" /v↵
"MaxPacketSize" /t REG_DWORD /d 1
```

Using VBScript

```
' This code forces Kerberos to use TCP.
' ------ SCRIPT CONFIGURATION -----
strComputer = "<ComputerName>" ' e.g. rallen-w2k3
' ------ END CONFIGURATION --------

const HKLM = &H80000002
strRegKey = "SYSTEM\CurrentControlSet\Control\Lsa\Kerberos\Parameters"
set objReg = GetObject("winmgmts:\\" & strComputer & ↵
                        "\root\default:StdRegProv")
objReg.SetDwordValue HKLM, strRegKey, "MaxPacketSize", 1
WScript.Echo "Kerberos forced to use TCP for " & strComputer
```

Using PowerShell

```
$strRegPath = "HKLM:\System\CurrentControlSet\Lsa\Kerberos\Parameters"
New-ItemProperty -path $strRegPath -name "MaxPacketSize" -type DWORD
Set-ItemProperty -path $strRegPath -name "MaxPacketSize" -value "1"
```

Discussion

If you have users that are experiencing extremely slow logon times (especially over VPN) or they are seeing the infamous "There are currently no logon servers available to service the logon request" message, then they may be experiencing UDP fragmentation of Kerberos traffic. This occurs because UDP is a *connectionless protocol*, so UDP packets that arrive out of order will be dropped by the destination router.

A source of information is the System event log on the clients. Various Kerberos-related events are logged there if problems with authentication occur.

See Also

"How to force Kerberos to use TCP instead of UDP in Windows" (*http://support.micro soft.com/kb/244474*)

14.21. Modifying Kerberos Settings

Problem

You want to modify the default Kerberos settings, such as maximum ticket lifetime.

Solution

Using a graphical user interface

1. Open the Default Domain Group Policy Object, or another domain-linked GPO, in the Group Policy Management Console.
2. Navigate to Computer Configuration→Policies→Windows Settings→Security Settings→Account Policies→Kerberos Policy.
3. In the right pane, double-click on the setting you want to modify.
4. Enter the new value and click OK.

Discussion

There are several Kerberos-related settings you can customize, most of which revolve around either increasing or decreasing the maximum lifetime for Kerberos user and service tickets. In most environments, the default settings are sufficient, but the ones you can modify are listed in Table 14-2.

 Change the default Kerberos policy settings with caution, as doing so can cause operational problems and compromise security if done incorrectly.

Table 14-2. Kerberos policy settings

Setting	Default value
Enforce user logon restrictions	Enabled
Maximum lifetime for service ticket	600 minutes
Maximum lifetime for user ticket	10 hours
Maximum lifetime for user ticket renewal	7 days
Maximum tolerance for computer clock synchronization	5 minutes

See Also

"Kerberos Policy" (*http://bit.ly/15kG2FB*)

14.22. Viewing Access Tokens

Problem

You want to view the access tokens that are created for a user account that has authenticated to Active Directory.

Solution

Using a command-line interface

```
> tokensz /compute_tokensize /package:negotiate /target_server:host/<DCName>↵
/user:<Username> /domain:<DomainName> /password:<Password> /dumpgroups
```

Discussion

When an Active Directory security principal receives a TGT from the Kerberos Key Distribution Center, the TGT contains a Privilege Attribute Certificate (PAC). This PAC contains several pieces of authentication data, such as the groups that a user belongs to (including all nested group memberships). In the majority of AD environments, this PAC is created without issue, but some larger environments can run into instances of token bloat. This occurs when a user belongs to a large number of groups (estimates start at around 70 to 120), and the size of the PAC becomes too large for the TGT to handle. This issue can manifest itself through authentication issues or through Group Policy Objects not applying properly. You can download (*http://bit.ly/13YMJse*) and use the *tokensz.exe* utility to compute the token size for a user relative to the maximum allowable size, as well as to list the groups that a user belongs to.

You can resolve this issue by streamlining the number of groups that the user or users belong to, which has the added benefit of simplifying the process of assigning permissions and applying Group Policy Objects. If this isn't possible, you can apply the hotfix referenced in MS KB 327825 or modify the `HKLM\System\CurrentControlSet\Control\Lsa\Kerberos\Parameters\MaxTokenSize` DWORD value on your domain computers. This issue is most relevant on legacy domain controllers, since modern versions of Windows have made a number of improvements to alleviate the need to modify this value. Additional details about the recent improvements are in the following "See Also" section.

If you determine that you need to modify the `MaxTokenSize` value, use the following formula as an approximate guideline:

```
1200 + 40d + 80s
```

In this equation, 1200 denotes a suggested amount of overhead that's used by the PAC; you can use the *tokensz* utility to determine the size for the domain in question. d refers to the number of domain local security groups that a representative user is a member of, plus any universal security groups in other domains that the user belongs to, plus any groups represented in the user's sIDHistory attribute. s refers to the number of global security groups a representative user belongs to, plus any universal security groups within the user's own domain.

See Also

"MaxTokenSize and Windows 8 and Windows Server 2012" (*http://bit.ly/12KInCx*); "Whoami" (*http://bit.ly/11bPPfT*) (note that a new /CLAIMS parameter exists but is not documented on the Whoami site at the time of this writing)

14.23. Creating a Claim Type

Problem

You want to create a new claim type for Dynamic Access Control.

Solution

Using a graphical user interface

1. Launch the Active Directory Administrative Center.
2. Select Dynamic Access Control and then click Claim Types.
3. From the Tasks menu, click New→Claim Type.
4. Select an Active Directory attribute to use as a source and modify the name and description, if desired.
5. Select whether to use the claim type for Users, Computers, or both class types.
6. Click OK to create the claim type.

Using PowerShell

The following PowerShell command will create a new claim type:

```
New-ADClaimType -DisplayName "<DisplayName>" -SourceAttribute "<ADAttribute>"↵
 -AppliesToClasses "<ClassType>"
```

Discussion

Claim types are associated with an Active Directory attribute and are then associated with the object class. Claim types can be associated with the following Active Directory classes:

- User
- Computer
- InetOrgPerson
- msDS-ManagedServiceAccount
- msDS-GroupManagedServiceAccount

See Also

"Dynamic Access Control: Scenario Overview" (*http://bit.ly/15rwqbO*); New-ADClaimType cmdlet reference (*http://bit.ly/15rwwjS*); *Active Directory*, Fifth Edition, by Brian Desmond et al. (O'Reilly)

14.24. Creating a Resource Property

Problem

You want to create a resource property for Dynamic Access Control.

Solution

Using a graphical user interface

1. Launch the Active Directory Administrative Center.
2. Select Dynamic Access Control and then click Resource Properties.
3. From the Tasks menu click New→Resource Property.
4. Enter a display name for the resource property.
5. Select a value type from the drop-down list to use for the resource property.
6. If required by the value type, click Add in suggested values.
7. Add a value and display name, and then click OK twice.

Using PowerShell

```
New-ADResourceProperty -DisplayName "<DisplayName>"↵
  -ResourcePropertyValueType "<ValueType>"
```

Discussion

Resource properties are used to authorize access to data. They can be used to describe and classify files through a manual or automatic classification process. Here is a list of built-in resource property value types:

- `MS-DS-SingleValuedChoice`
- `MS-DS-YesNo`
- `MS-DS-Number`
- `MS-DS-DateTime`
- `MS-DS-OrderedList`
- `MS-DS-Text`
- `MS-DS-MultiValuedText`
- `MS-DS-MultiValuedChoice`

See Also

"Deploy a Central Access Policy (Demonstration Steps)" (*http://bit.ly/106GTVv*); `New-ADResourceProperty` cmdlet reference (*http://bit.ly/YA82lI*); and *Active Directory, Fifth Edition*, by Brian Desmond et al. (O'Reilly)

14.25. Configuring a Central Access Rule

Problem

You want to configure a central access rule for Dynamic Access Control.

Solution

Using a graphical user interface

1. Launch the Active Directory Administrative Center.
2. Select Dynamic Access Control and then click Central Access Rules.
3. From the Tasks menu, click New→Central Access Rule.
4. Enter a name for the rule.
5. If necessary, edit the target resources to customize the scope.
6. If necessary, modify the permissions that will apply to the central access rule.

7. Click OK to create the central access rule.

Using PowerShell

```
New-ADCentralAccessRule -Name "<RuleName>" -ResourceCondition "<Conditions>"↵
    -CurrentAcl "<ACL>"
```

Discussion

A central access rule assigns permissions to resources under the conditions set on the target resource. Central access rules are used in central access policies, which are then applied on a resource, such as a shared folder.

See Also

"Deploy a Central Access Policy (Demonstration Steps)" (*http://bit.ly/106GTVv*); New-ADCentralAccessRule cmdlet reference (*http://bit.ly/11bQYnG*); *Active Directory, Fifth Edition*, by Brian Desmond et al. (O'Reilly)

14.26. Creating a Central Access Policy

Problem

You want to create a central access policy.

Solution

Using a graphical user interface

1. Launch the Active Directory Administrative Center.
2. Select Dynamic Access Control and then click Central Access Policies.
3. From the Tasks menu, click New→Central Access Policy.
4. Enter a name for the central access policy.
5. Click Add and select the central access rules to add to the policy by selecting the rule and clicking the double-arrow icon.
6. Click OK twice to create the policy.

Using PowerShell

```
New-ADCentralAccessPolicy -Name "<PolicyName>"
Add-ADCentralAccessPolicyMember "<PolicyName>" -Members "<CentralAccessRule>"
```

Discussion

A central access policy is a collection of central access rules. The policy can be applied to the resource that will be protected. In the PowerShell solution, first we create the access policy and then we add in the central access rules as necessary.

See Also

"Deploy a Central Access Policy (Demonstration Steps)" (*http://bit.ly/106GTVv*); *Active Directory*, Fifth Edition, by Brian Desmond et al. (O'Reilly)

14.27. Applying a Central Access Policy

Problem

You want to apply a central access policy by using Group Policy.

Solution

1. Launch the Group Policy Management console.
2. Create and link a GPO, or select an existing GPO to apply the central access policy.
3. Right-click the GPO and click Edit.
4. Navigate to Computer Configuration→Policies→Windows Settings→Security Settings→File System.
5. Right-click Central Access Policy and select Manage Central Access Policies.
6. Select the central access policy you wish to apply and then click Add. Click OK to close the configuration dialog box.

Discussion

Central access policies complement existing discretionary access control lists (DACLs) by providing another layer of permissions for resource access. You can use Group Policy to effectively and efficiently deploy a central access policy to the specific servers that need the central access policy settings.

See Also

Recipe 14.27; "Deploy a Central Access Policy (Demonstration Steps)" (*http://bit.ly/106GTVv*); *Active Directory*, Fifth Edition, by Brian Desmond et al. (O'Reilly)

14.28. Enabling Domain Controller Support for Claims and Compound Authentication

Problem

You want to allow domain controllers to provide claims or device authorization.

Solution

1. Launch the Group Policy Management console (gpmc.msc).

2. Select the Default Domain Controllers Policy or another GPO that applies to all domain controllers. Right-click the GPO and click Edit.

3. Navigate to Computer Configuration→Policies→Administrative Templates→System→KDC.

4. Right-click KDS Support for claims, compound authentication, and Kerberos armoring and select Edit.

5. Click Enabled to enable the configuration and then select Supported from the "options" drop-down list.

6. Click OK to close the properties dialog box.

 KDC support for claims, compound authentication, and Kerberos armoring has a couple of options ("Always provide claims" and "Fail unarmored authentication requests") that require that the domain be set to the Windows Server 2012 domain functional level.

Discussion

For domain controllers to provide claims or device authorization, they must be configured to support Dynamic Access Control. Changing this setting through the Default Domain Controllers Policy allows you to modify this setting for all domain controllers efficiently and effectively.

See Also

Recipe 14.26; Recipe 14.27; "Deploy a Central Access Policy (Demonstration Steps)" (*http://bit.ly/106GTVv*); *Active Directory*, Fifth Edition, by Brian Desmond et al. (O'Reilly)

14.29. Enabling Claims for Devices in a Domain

Problem

You want to enable claims for devices within a domain.

Solution

1. Launch the Group Policy Management console (gpmc.msc).
2. Select the Default Domain Policy or another GPO that applies to all domain devices. Right-click the GPO and click Edit.
3. Navigate to Computer Configuration→Policies→Administrative Templates→System→Kerberos.
4. Right-click Kerberos Support for claims, compound authentication, and Kerberos armoring and select Edit.
5. Click Enabled to enable the configuration and then select Supported from the "options" drop-down list.
6. Click OK to close the properties dialog box, and then close the Group Policy Management console.
7. Launch the Active Directory Administrative Center.
8. Select Dynamic Access Control and then double-click Claim Types.
9. Right-click the claim that you want to modify and then select Properties.
10. Place a checkmark next to Computer and then click OK.

 Kerberos support for claims, compound authentication, and Kerberos armoring requires that there be at least one domain controller running Windows Server 2012 to support devices running Windows 8.

Discussion

For devices to provide claims, they must be configured to support Dynamic Access Control. The two-step process described in this recipe allows you to configure claims for devices within a domain.

See Also

Recipe 14.28; "Deploy a Central Access Policy (Demonstration Steps)" (*http://bit.ly/106GTVv*); *Active Directory*, Fifth Edition, by Brian Desmond et al. (O'Reilly)

## CHAPTER 15

Logging, Monitoring, and Quotas

15.0. Introduction

This chapter deals with tracking the activity and usage of various Active Directory components. When you need to troubleshoot a problem, often the first place you look is the logfiles. With Active Directory, there are several different logfiles, and each has different ways to increase or decrease the verbosity of the information that is logged. Viewing log messages can be a useful troubleshooting step, but you should also look at *performance metrics* to determine whether system hardware or a particular service is being overutilized. In this chapter, we'll review a couple of ways you can view performance metrics, as well as monitor Active Directory performance. For more extensive monitoring, we suggest looking at Microsoft System Center Operations Manager (OpsMgr) (*http://bit.ly/YA9K6C*), or similar products from other vendors such as NetIQ and Quest. In addition to the typical items that you would monitor on a Windows server (e.g., disk space usage, physical and virtual memory errors, processor utilization), you should also monitor AD-specific performance metrics. This extends to monitoring replication activity and Event Log information.

We'll also cover a somewhat-related topic called *quotas*, which allow you to monitor and limit the number of objects that a security principal (user, group, or computer) can create within a partition. This feature closes a hole that allowed users who had access to create as many objects in Active Directory as they wanted. These users could cause a denial-of-service attack by creating objects until the disk drive on the domain controllers filled to capacity. This kind of attack is not likely to happen in most environments, but you should still consider the possibility and protect against it.

The Anatomy of a Quota Object Container

Quota objects are stored in the NTDS Quotas container of the naming contexts and application partitions except for the schema naming context. (Quotas cannot be associated with the schema NC.) By default, this container is hidden from view within tools such as Active Directory Users and Computers, but you can see it by selecting View→Advanced Features from the menu. The quota object container has an object Class of msDS-QuotaContainer and contains several attributes that define default quota behavior. Table 15-1 lists some of the important attributes of msDS-QuotaContainer objects.

Table 15-1. Attributes of msDS-QuotaContainer objects

Attribute	Description
cn	RDN of quota container objects. By default, this is equal to NTDSQuotas.
msDS-DefaultQuota	The default quota applied to all security principals that do not have another quota specification applied. See Recipe 15.18 for more details.
msDS-QuotaEffective	A constructed attribute that contains the effective quota of the security principal that is viewing the attribute. See Recipe 15.19 for more details.
msDS-QuotaUsed	A constructed attribute that contains the quota usage of the security principal that is viewing the attribute. See Recipe 15.19 for more details.
msDS-TombstoneQuotaFactor	Percentage that tombstone objects count against a quota. The default is 100, which means a tombstone object has equal weighting to a normal object. See Recipe 15.17 for more details.
msDS-TopQuotaUsage	Multivalued attribute that contains information about the security principals with the top quota usage. See Recipe 15.19 for more details.

The Anatomy of a Quota Object

Quota objects have an objectClass of msDS-QuotaControl, which defines three attributes that relate to quotas. Table 15-2 contains these attributes and provides a description for each.

Table 15-2. Attributes of msDS-QuotaControl objects

Attribute	Description
cn	RDN of the quota object.
msDS-QuotaAmount	Number of objects that can be created by the security principals that the quota applies to. See Recipe 15.15 for more information.
msDS-QuotaTrustee	SID of the security principal that the quota applies to. This can be a user, group, or computer SID. See Recipe 15.15 for more information.

15.1. Enabling Diagnostics Logging

Problem

You want to enable diagnostics event logging because the current level of logging is not providing enough information to help pinpoint the problem you are troubleshooting.

Solution

Using a graphical user interface

1. Run *regedit.exe* from the command line or from Start→Run.
2. In the left pane, expand the following Registry key: *HKEY_LOCAL_MACHINE* \System\CurrentControlSet\Services\NTDS\Diagnostics.
3. In the right pane, double-click on the diagnostics logging entry you want to increase, and enter a number (0–5) based on how much you want logged.
4. Click OK.

Using a command-line interface

```
> reg add HKLM\SYSTEM\CurrentControlSet\Services\NTDS\Diagnostics /v↵
"<LoggingSetting>" /t REG_DWORD /d <0-5>
```

Using PowerShell

```
Set-ItemProperty -Path "HKLM:\SYSTEM\CurrentControlSet\Services\NTDS\↵
Diagnostics" -Name "<LoggingSetting>" -Value "<FlagValue>"
```

Discussion

A useful way to troubleshoot specific problems you are encountering with Active Directory is to increase the diagnostics logging level. Diagnostics logging can be enabled for individual components of AD. For example, if you determine the KCC is not completing every 15 minutes, you can enable diagnostics logging for the "1 Knowledge Consistency Checker" setting.

These settings are stored under *HKLM\SYSTEM\CurrentControlSet\Services\NTDS* \Diagnostics. By default, all settings are set to 0, which disables diagnostics logging, but you can increase it by setting it to a number from 1 through 5. As a general rule, a value of 1 is used for minimum logging, 3 for medium logging, and 5 for maximum logging. It is a good practice to ease your way up to 5 because some diagnostics logging settings can generate a bunch of events in the event log, which may make it difficult to read, along with increasing resource utilization on the domain controller.

Here is the complete list of diagnostics logging settings:

```
1 Knowledge Consistency Checker
2 Security Events
3 ExDS Interface Events
4 MAPI Interface Events
5 Replication Events
6 Garbage Collection
7 Internal Configuration
```

```
 8 Directory Access
 9 Internal Processing
10 Performance Counters
11 Initialization/Termination
12 Service Control
13 Name Resolution
14 Backup
15 Field Engineering
16 LDAP Interface Events
17 Setup
18 Global Catalog
19 Inter-site Messaging
20 Group Caching
21 Linked-Value Replication
22 DS RPC Client
23 DS RPC Server
24 DS Schema
25 Transformation Engine
26 Claims-Based Access Control
```

See Also

"Active Directory Diagnostic Logging" (*http://bit.ly/166jhF1*)

15.2. Enabling NetLogon Logging

Problem

You want to enable NetLogon logging to help with troubleshooting client account logon, lockout, or domain controller location issues.

Solution

Using a command-line interface

To enable NetLogon logging, use the following command:

```
> nltest /dbflag:0x2080ffff
```

To disable NetLogon logging, use the following command:

```
> nltest /dbflag:0x0
```

Discussion

The *netlogon.log* file located in *%SystemRoot%\Debug* can be invaluable for trouble-shooting client logon and related issues. When enabled at the highest setting (0x2080ffff), it logs useful information such as the site the client is in, the domain controller the client authenticated against, additional information related to the DC Locator process, account password expiration information, account lockout information, and even Kerberos failures.

The NetLogon logging level is stored in the following Registry value:

```
HKLM\System\CurrentControlSet\Services\Netlogon\Parameters\DBFlag
```

 If you set that Registry value manually instead of using *nltest*, you'll need to create the string value, adjust the value, and then restart the NetLogon service for it to take effect.

One of the issues with the *netlogon.log* file is that it can quickly grow to several megabytes, which makes it difficult to peruse. The command-line tool *nlparse* can filter the contents of the *netlogon.log* file so that you'll see only certain types of log entries. The *nlparse* tool is part of the Account Lockout and Management Tools (*http://bit.ly/16NCdbq*).

See Also

MS KB 109626 (Enabling Debug Logging for the Netlogon Service); MS KB 247811 (How Domain Controllers Are Located in Windows); MS KB 273499 (Description of Security Event 681); "Troubleshooting Netlogon Error Codes" (*http://bit.ly/128gPtt*)

15.3. Enabling GPO Client Logging

Problem

You want to troubleshoot GPO processing issues on a client or server by enabling additional logging in the Application event log.

Solution

Using a graphical user interface

1. Run *regedit.exe* from the command line or from Start→Run.
2. In the left pane, expand the appropriate key from the table in this recipe's "Discussion" section.
3. Create and populate the appropriate key value.
4. Click OK.

Using a command-line interface

```
> reg add "<Key Value>" /v "<ValueName>" /t REG_DWORD /d <Value>
```

Using PowerShell

```
Set-ItemProperty -Path "<RegistryKeyPath>" -Name "<ValueName>" -Value "<Value>"
```

Discussion

If you experience problems with client GPO processing, such as a GPO not getting applied even though you think it should, there are a number of different Registry keys that can help you troubleshoot the problem. One way to get detailed information about which GPOs are applied on a client computer is by enabling additional GPO event logging. Table 15-3 lists a number of Registry settings that can be configured to enable Group Policy logging, as well as the files that are created when the settings are enabled.

Table 15-3. Registry settings to enable Group Policy logging

Logging for the CSE	Location	Enable verbose logging by adding this key or value ...	...to this Registry key
Security CSE	%windir%\security \logs\winlogon.log	ExtensionDebugLevel=REG_DWORD 0x2	HKEY_LOCAL_MACHINE\Software \Microsoft\Windows NT \CurrentVersion\Winlogon \GpExtensions \{827d319e-6eac-11d2-a4ea-00c04f79f83a}\
Folder Redirection CSE	windir%\debug \usermode \fdeploy.log	FdeployDebugLevel = Reg_DWORD 0x0f	HKEY_LOCAL_MACHINE\Software \Microsoft\Windows NT \CurrentVersion\Diagnostics
Software Installation CSE	%windir%\debug \usermode \appmgmt.log	Appmgmtdebuglevel=dword:0000009b	HKEY_LOCAL_MACHINE\Software \Microsoft\Windows NT \CurrentVersion\Diagnostics
Windows Installer (deployment-related actions)	%windir%\temp \MSI*.log	Logging = voicewarmup Debug = DWORD: 00000003	HKEY_LOCAL_MACHINE\Software \Policies\Microsoft\Windows\Installer
Windows Installer (user-initiated actions)	%temp%\MSI*.log	Logging = voicewarmup Debug = DWORD: 00000003	HKEY_LOCAL_MACHINE\Software \Policies\Microsoft\Windows\Installer

See Also

"Fixing Group Policy problems by using log files" (*http://bit.ly/Yq6CYK*); "Troubleshooting Group Policy Using Event Logs" (*http://bit.ly/10hhoTa*); "Userenvlog for Windows Vista/2008/Win7" (*http://bit.ly/YAawQV*)

15.4. Enabling Kerberos Logging

Problem

You want to enable Kerberos logging on a domain controller to troubleshoot authentication problems.

Solution

Using a graphical user interface

1. Run *regedit.exe* from the command line or from Start→Run.
2. In the left pane, expand *HKEY_LOCAL_MACHINE\System\CurrentControlSet \Control\Lsa\Kerberos\Parameters*.
3. If the LogLevel value doesn't already exist, right-click on Parameters and select New→DWORD value. Enter LogLevel for the value name and click OK.
4. In the right pane, double-click on LogLevel and enter 1.
5. Click OK.

Using a command-line interface

```
> reg add HKLM\SYSTEM\CurrentControlSet\Control\Lsa\Kerberos\Parameters↵
/v "LogLevel" /t REG_DWORD /d 1
```

Using PowerShell

```
Set-ItemProperty -Path↵
  "HKLM:\SYSTEM\CurrentControlSet\Control\Lsa\Kerberos\Parameters" -Name↵
  "LogLevel" -Value "1"
```

Discussion

If you are experiencing authentication problems or would like to determine whether you are experiencing any Kerberos-related issues, enabling Kerberos logging will ensure that Kerberos errors will be logged in the System event log. The Kerberos events can point out if the problem is related to clock skew, an expired ticket, an expired password, etc. For a good overview of some of the Kerberos error messages, see MS KB 230476.

Here is a sample event:

```
Event type:  Error
Event source:  Security-Kerberos
Event ID:  3

A Kerberos error message was received:
```

```
on logon session user5@adatum
ClientTime
ServerTime 19:34:26.0000 12/17/2012 Z
ErrorCode 0x17
ErrorMessage 0x19 KDC_ERR_PREAUTH_REQUIRED
ExtendedError
ClientRealm
ClientName
ServerRealm ADATUM.COM
ServerName krbtgt/ADATUM.COM
TargetName krbtgt/ADATUM.COM@ADATUM.COM
ErrorText
File e
Line d3a
Error Data is in record data.
```

See Also

"How to enable Kerberos event logging" (*http://support.microsoft.com/kb/262177*)

15.5. Viewing DNS Server Performance Statistics

Problem

You want to view DNS server performance statistics.

Solution

Using a graphical user interface

1. Open the Performance Monitor.

2. Click on Performance Monitor in the left pane.

3. In the right pane, click the + button. This will bring up the page to add counters.

4. Under "Select counters from computer", enter the DNS server you want to target.

5. Select the DNS performance object.

6. Select the counters you want to add and click the Add button.

7. Click Close.

Using a command-line interface

```
> dnscmd <DNSServerName> /statistics
```

Using PowerShell

```
Get-EventLog "DNS Server"
```

Discussion

The Microsoft DNS Server keeps track of dozens of performance metrics. These metrics include the number of queries, updates, transfers, directory reads, and directory writes processed by the server. If you can pump these metrics into an enterprise management system, you can track DNS usage and growth over time.

These statistics can also be useful to troubleshoot load-related issues. If you suspect a DNS server is being overwhelmed with DNS update requests, you can look at the Dynamic Update Received/sec counter and see whether it is processing an unusually high number of updates.

Using a command-line interface

You can obtain a subset of the statistics by providing a *statid* after the /statistics option. Each statistics category has an associated number (i.e., statid). For a complete list of categories and their statids, run the following command:

```
> dnscmd /statistics /?
```

Here is an example of viewing the Query (statid = 2) and Query2 (statid = 4) statistics:

```
> dnscmd /statistics 6
DNS Server . statistics:

Queries and Responses:
----------------------
Total:
    Queries Received =    14902
    Responses Sent   =    12900
UDP:
    Queries Recvd    =    14718
    Responses Sent   =    12716
    Queries Sent     =    23762
    Responses Recvd  =        0
TCP:
    Client Connects  =      184
    Queries Recvd    =      184
    Responses Sent   =      184
    Queries Sent     =        0
    Responses Recvd  =        0

Queries:
--------
Total       =    14902
    Notify  =        0
```

```
Update    =   2207
TKeyNego  =    184
Standard  =  12511
A         =   1286
NS        =     29
SOA       =   2263
MX        =      0
PTR       =      1
SRV       =   8909
ALL       =      0
IXFR      =      0
AXFR      =      0
OTHER     =     23
```

```
Command completed successfully.
```

See Also

MSDN: MicrosoftDNS_Statistic

15.6. Monitoring the Windows Time Service

Problem

You want to verify the correct functioning of the Windows Time Service.

Solution

Using a command-line interface

The following syntax verifies that the Windows Time Service is functioning on *dc1.ada-tum.com* and *dc2.adatum.com*:

```
> w32tm /monitor /computers:dc1.adatum.com,dc2.adatum.com
```

Discussion

Because Active Directory relies on Kerberos for authentication, it's critical that all of your domain controllers, member servers, and client computers maintain a consistent time across the network; if any computer's clock is off by more than five minutes, then by default, it will not be able to authenticate to Active Directory. You can use the *w32tm* utility to verify time synchronization on one or more computers using the /monitor switch, as well as using the /resync switch to prompt a computer to immediately re-synchronize its clock with its authoritative time source.

See Also

"Configuring a Time Source for the Forest" (*http://bit.ly/Yq6R5Y*); "How to configure an authoritative time server in Windows Server" (*http://support.microsoft.com/kb/816042*)

15.7. Enabling Inefficient and Expensive LDAP Query Logging

Problem

You want to log inefficient and expensive LDAP queries to the Directory Services event log.

Solution

To log a summary report about the total number of searches, total expensive searches, and total inefficient searches to the Directory Services event log, set the 15 Field Engineering diagnostics logging setting to 4. This summary is generated every 12 hours during the garbage collection cycle.

To log an event to the Directory Services event log every time an expensive or inefficient search occurs, set the 15 Field Engineering diagnostics logging setting to 5.

See Recipe 15.1 for more on enabling diagnostics logging.

Discussion

A search is considered *expensive* if it has to visit a large number of objects in Active Directory. The default threshold for an expensive query is 10,000. That means any search that visits 10,000 or more objects would be considered expensive. A search is considered *inefficient* if it returns fewer than 10 percent of the total objects it visits. If a query visited 10,000 objects and only returned 999 of them (less than 10 percent), it would be considered inefficient. The default bottom limit for an inefficient query is 1,000. If the query returned 1,000 instead, it would not be considered inefficient. To summarize, with 1,000 as the default bottom threshold, no search that visits fewer than 1,000 entries (even if it visited 999 and returned 0) would be considered inefficient.

Here is a sample summary report event that is logged when 15 Field Engineering is set to 5:

```
Log Name:      Directory Service
Source:        Microsoft-Windows-ActiveDirectory_DomainService
Date:          12/21/2012 11:38:32 PM
Event ID:      1643
Task Category: Field Engineering
```

```
Level:          Information
Keywords:       Classic
User:           ANONYMOUS LOGON
Computer:       adatum-dc.adatum.com
Description:
Internal event: Active Directory Domain Services performed the following number⤶
 of search operations within this time interval.

Time interval (hours):
0
Number of search operations:
38529

During this time interval, the following number of search operations were⤶
 characterized as either expensive or inefficient.

Expensive search operations:
7
Inefficient search operations:
22
```

If you set 15 Field Engineering to 5, the summary event is logged during the garbage collection cycle, and event 1644 is generated every time an expensive or inefficient search occurs. Setting this value can provide useful information if you are running applications that regularly generate expensive or inefficient queries. Notice that this event provides details on all aspects of the search, including the authenticating user, search base DN, search filter, attributes, controls, number of entries visited, and number of entries returned. The following entry is from a Windows Server 2012 domain controller:

```
Log Name:       Directory Service
Source:         Microsoft-Windows-ActiveDirectory_DomainService
Date:           12/22/2012 1:19:05 AM
Event ID:       1644
Task Category: Field Engineering
Level:          Information
Keywords:       Classic
User:           SYSTEM
Computer:       dc1.adatum.com
Description:
Internal event: A client issued a search operation with the following options.

Client:
SAM
Starting node:
dc=adatum,dc=com
Filter:
( & (userAccountControl&2) (objectClass=user)
(objectCategory=cn=Person,cn=Schema,cn=Configuration,dc=adatum,dc=com) )
Search scope:
subtree
```

```
Attribute selection:
[shortnames]objectSid,sAMAccountName,userAccountControl
Server controls:

Visited entries:
51443
Returned entries:
3513
```

With the default settings, the query shown in the preceding event is considered both expensive and inefficient. It is expensive because it visited more than 10,000 entries. It is inefficient because it returned fewer than 10 percent of those entries.

You can customize what a domain controller considers *expensive* and *inefficient* by creating a couple of Registry values under the *HKLM\SYSTEM\CurrentControlSet \Services\NTDS\Parameters* key. You can create a value named Expensive Search Re sults Threshold of type DWORD and specify the number of entries a search would need to visit to be considered expensive. Similarly, you can create a value named Inefficient Search Results Threshold of type DWORD and specify the minimum number of entries visited where a match returning fewer than 10 percent would be considered inefficient.

 If you want to see all the LDAP queries that are being sent to a domain controller, a quick way to do that would be to set the 15 Field Engineering setting to 5 and Expensive Search Results Threshold to 0. This would cause the domain controller to consider every search as expensive and log all the LDAP searches. While this can be very useful, you should use it with care as it could quickly fill your event log. Be sure to allow sufficient disk space for your event logs to avoid any issues with low disk space on your domain controllers.

See Also

Recipe 15.1 for enabling diagnostics logging

15.8. Using the STATS Control to View LDAP Query Statistics

Problem

You want to use the STATS LDAP control to test the efficiency of a query.

Solution

Using a graphical user interface

1. Launch *LDP.exe*.

2. From the menu, select Connection→Connect.

3. For Server, enter the name of a domain controller.

4. For Port, enter 389.

5. Click OK.

6. From the menu, select Connection→Bind.

7. Enter the credentials of a user to perform the search or accept the default and bind as the currently logged on user.

8. Click OK.

9. From the menu, select Options→Controls.

10. From the Load Predefined drop-down, select Search Stats.

11. Click OK.

12. From the menu, select Browse→Search.

13. Enter your search criteria and then click the Options button.

14. Under Search Call Type, be sure that Extended is selected.

15. Click OK and then click Run. The status will be shown at the top of the search results.

Using a command-line interface

The AdFind command-line utility has four switches that will display efficiency statistics for any query:

`-stats`
: Enables the STATS control to return statistics about the query, along with the actual results of the query

`-statsonly`
: Returns *only* the statistics about the query, and suppresses the actual query results

`-stats+`
: Similar to `-stats`, but also displays additional advanced analysis about the query

`-stats+only`
: Just like `-stats+`, but will suppress the actual results of the query and display only the query statistics

---

Discussion

The STATS control is a useful way to obtain statistics about the performance of an LDAP query. With the STATS control, you can find out information such as the amount of time it took the server to process the query, how many entries were visited versus returned, what the search filter expanded to, and whether any indexes were used. Here is an example of what the STATS control returns for a search for all `group` objects in the `cn=Users` container:

```
Statistics
======================================================
Elapsed time: 0 (ms)
Returned 18 of 23 visited - (78.26%)

Used Filter:
  (objectCategory=cn=Group,cn=Schema,cn=Configuration,cn=adatum,cn=com

Used Indices:
  Ancestors_index:23:N

Pages referenced: 332
Pages read from disk: 0
Pages pre-read from Disk: 0

Analysis
--------------------------------------------------

Indices used:

Index name: Ancestors_index
Record count: 23 (estimate)
Index type: Normal attribute index
Ancestor index used, possibly inefficient, verify filter
```

A couple of things are worth noting here. You can also see that the filter used, (`object category=group`), was expanded to:

```
(objectCategory=cn=Group,cn=Schema,cn=Configuration,dc=adatum,dc=com)
```

The syntax of the `objectCategory` attribute is a distinguished name, but Active Directory provides a shortcut so that you need to use only the LDAP display name of the class instead. Internally, Active Directory converts the display name to the distinguished name, as shown here. Finally, we can see that our search used an index, `INTERSECT_IN DEX:17:I`.

Let's look at another example, except this time we'll perform an ANR search for `Jim Smith`:

```
***Searching ...
ldap_search_ext_s(ld, "ou=Sales,dc=adatum,dc=com", 2, "(anr=Jim Smith)",
attrList, 0, svrCtrls, ClntCtrls, 20, 1000 ,&msg)
```

```
Result <0>:
Matched DNs:
Stats:
        Call Time:         20 (ms)
        Entries Returned:      1
        Entries Visited:       2
        Used Filter:          ( | (displayName=Jim Smith*) (givenName=Jim Smith*)
(legacyExchangeDN=Jim Smith)  (msDS-AdditionalSamAccountName=Jim Smith*)
(physicalDeliveryOfficeName=Jim Smith*)  (proxyAddresses=Jim Smith*) (name=Jim
Smith*)  (sAMAccountName=Jim Smith*)
(sn=Jim Smith*)  ( & (givenName=Jim*)  (sn=Smith*) )  ( & (givenName=Smith*)
(sn=Jim*) ) )
        Used Indexes:
idx_givenName:10:N;idx_givenName:10:N;idx_sn:9:N;idx_
sAMAccountName:8:N;idx_name:7:N;idx_proxyAddresses:6:N;idx_
physicalDeliveryOfficeName:5:N;idx_msDS-AdditionalSamAccountName:4:N;idx_
legacyExchangeDN:3:N;idx_givenName:2:N;idx_displayName:1:N;
```

You can see from the second line that we used a very simple filter, (`anr=Jim Smith`). If
you look down a little farther at `Used Filter:` you can see a better example of search-
filter expansion. Like the `objectCategory` example earlier, ANR is a shorthand way to
do something complex. A simple one-term search filter expands into a multiterm filter
that searches across numerous attributes. (For more on the behavior of ANR, see
Recipe 10.12.) The point of showing this is to illustrate that the STATS control is very
powerful and can be an invaluable tool when trying to troubleshoot or optimize LDAP
queries.

See Also

Recipe 4.4 for using LDAP controls; Recipe 4.8 for searching for objects; Recipe 10.12
for more on ANR; Recipe 15.7 for more on expensive and inefficient searches

15.9. Monitoring the Performance of Active Directory

Problem

You want to use the Performance Monitor to examine the performance of Active
Directory.

Solution

Using a graphical user interface

1. Open the Performance Monitor (*perfmon.exe*).

2. Click on Performance Monitor in the left pane.

3. Click the + button. This will bring up the page to add counters.

4. Under "Select counters from computer", enter the name of the domain controller you want to target.

5. Select the NTDS performance object.

6. Select the counters that you want to monitor.

7. After you're done with your selections, click Close.

Using PowerShell

To retrieve a continuous counter for a performance object, use the following PowerShell command:

```
Get-Counter -Counter "<PerformanceObject>" -Continuous
```

For example, to view the performance counter for the DS Directory Searches/sec object, run the following command:

```
Get-Counter -Counter "\NTDS\DS Directory Searches/sec" -Continuous
```

Discussion

There are several Performance Monitor counters that can be very valuable for monitoring and troubleshooting Active Directory. The NTDS performance object has counters for address-book lookups; inbound and outbound replication; LDAP reads, writes, and searches; and the Security Account Manager (SAM).

Here is a list of some of the most useful NTDS counters. We've also included their Performance Monitor explanation, which you can view by clicking on the Explain button in the Add Counters dialog box.

DRA Inbound Bytes Total/sec
Shows the total number of bytes received through replication. It is the sum of the number of uncompressed bytes (never compressed) and the number of compressed bytes (after compression).

DRA Inbound Objects/sec
Shows the number of objects received from neighbors through inbound replication. A *neighbor* is a domain controller from which the local domain controller replicates locally.

DRA Inbound Values Total/sec
Shows the total number of object property values received from inbound replication partners. Each inbound object has one or more properties, and each property has zero or more values. A zero value indicates property removal.

DRA Outbound Bytes Total/sec
Shows the total number of bytes replicated out. It is the sum of the number of uncompressed bytes (never compressed) and the number of compressed bytes (after compression).

DRA Outbound Objects/sec
Shows the number of objects replicated out.

DRA Outbound Values Total/sec
Shows the number of object property values sent to outbound replication partners.

DRA Pending Replication Synchronizations
Shows the number of directory synchronizations that are queued for this server but not yet processed.

DS Client Binds/sec
Shows the number of *ntdsapi.dll* binds per second serviced by this DC.

DS Directory Reads/sec
Shows the number of directory reads per second.

DS Directory Searches/sec
Shows the number of directory searches per second.

DS Directory Writes/sec
Shows the number of directory writes per second.

LDAP Bind Time
Shows the time, in milliseconds, taken for the last successful LDAP bind.

LDAP Client Sessions
Shows the number of currently connected LDAP client sessions.

LDAP Searches/sec
Shows the rate at which LDAP clients perform search operations.

LDAP Successful Binds/sec
Shows the number of LDAP binds per second.

LDAP Writes/sec
Shows the rate at which LDAP clients perform write operations.

15.10. Using Perfmon Trace Logs to Monitor Active Directory

Problem

You want to enable Trace Logs to view system-level calls related to Active Directory.

Solution

Using a graphical user interface

1. Open the Performance Monitor (*perfmon.exe*).

2. In the left pane, expand Data Collector Sets.

3. Right-click Event Trace Sessions and click New→Data Collector Sets.

4. In the Name: field, enter `AD Trace Log`. Click Next.

5. Click Add. In the Event Trace Providers screen, click Active Directory Domain Services: Core. Click OK.

6. Click Next, note the directory to be used for the log, and then click Next again.

7. Click the "Start this data collector set now" radio button and click Finish.

8. Open a command prompt and run the following command:

   ```
   tracerpt <LogFileName>
   ```

Discussion

Trace Logs capture detailed system- and application-level events. Applications support Trace Log capability by developing a Trace Log Provider. Active Directory supports several providers that log low-level system calls related to Kerberos, LDAP, and DNS, to name a few. This can be an extremely valuable tool for debugging or just exploring the inner workings of Active Directory. Trace Logs can be resource-intensive, so you should enable them with care.

The `tracerpt`/`tracedmp` commands generate a *summary.txt* file that summarizes all of the events by total. A second file called *dumpfile.xml* is created by default, but the dump format can be changed by specifying the `-of` switch, with a *CSV*, *EVTX*, or *XML* value.

Here is an example of what the *summary.txt* file looks like on a domain controller that had all of the Active Directory–related Trace Log Providers enabled:

```
Files Processed:
    AD Trace Log.etl
```

```
Total Buffers Processed 18
Total Events  Processed 720
Total Events  Lost      0
Start Time              Saturday, December 22, 2012
End Time                Saturday, December 22, 2012
Elapsed Time            51 sec
+---------------------------------------------------------------------------+
|Event Count Event Name    Task   Opcode      Version    Guid
+---------------------------------------------------------------------------+
|          1 EventTrace     0      DbgIdRSDS   2          {68fdd900-4a3e-11d1↵
|                                                         -84f4-0000f80464e3}|
|          1 EventTrace     0      BuildInfo   2          {68fdd900-4a3e-11d1↵
|                                                         -84f4-0000f80464e3}|
|          1 EventTrace     0      Header      2          {68fdd900-4a3e-11d1↵
|                                                         -84f4-0000f80464e3}|
|          2 DsDrsReplGtChg 0      End         4          {14f8aa24-7f4b-11d2↵
|                                                         -b389-0000f87a46c8}|
|          2 DsDrsReplGtChg 0      Start       4          {14f8aa24-7f4b-11d2↵
|                                                         -b389-0000f87a46c8}|
|        125 LdapRequest    0      End         4          {b9d4702a-6a98-11d2↵
|                                                         -b710-00c04fb998a2}|
+---------------------------------------------------------------------------+
```

Here you can see that over a 51-second period, there was one Event Trace request (EventTrace), two directory replication change requests (DsDrsReplGtChg), and 125 total LDAP requests (LdapRequest).

The *dumpfile.csv* file contains entries for every event that was generated during the time period. Here is an example of an entry for one of the DsDrsReplGtChg requests (note that the lines will wrap due to their length, so we've added a blank line in between for separation):

```
DsDrsReplGtChg,    Start,          0,         4,        0,         0,
        1,         0, 0x0000000000000000, 0x00000240, 0x00001388,
                   0,              ,                  ,
   {00000000-0000-0000-0000-000000000000},
,   130006457569095598,       15,        0, "DS", 4, 8, 3506765888,       0,
"e5a1b109-4add-4503-a909-66e55820265c (DC2.adatum.com)", "dc=adatum,dc=com",
"250469",
"250469", "2147483760", "536", "5363998", "0",
  0x00000000000000000000A7E12200CD00

DsDirGtNcChg,      Start,          0,         4,        0,         0,
        1,         0, 0x0000000000000000, 0x00000240, 0x00001388,
                   0,              ,                  ,
   {00000000-0000-0000-0000-000000000000},
,   130006457569097056,       15,        0, "DS", 4, 6, 805568576,        0,
"e5a1b109-4add-4503-a909-66e55820265c (DC2.adatum.com)", "dc=adatum,dc=com",
"250469", "80000070", "0", "0",   0x47D92200CD000000A820303D
```

Based on those two lines, you can see Active Directory Domain Services replication commutation occur from this server to another server named *dc2.adatum.com*.

15.11. Creating an Administrative Alert

Problem

You want to define a threshold for a performance counter that should cause an alert to be generated.

Solution

Using a graphical user interface

1. Open the Performance Monitor (*perfmon.exe*).
2. Expand Data Collector Sets. Right-click User-Defined and click New→Data Collector Set.
3. In the Name text box, enter AD Performance Alert. Select the "Create manually" radio button and click Next.
4. Click the Performance Counter Alert radio button and click Next.
5. Click Add. Select the counter that you wish to be alerted about. Click Add and click OK.
6. In the "Alert when:" drop-down box, click Above or Below. In the Limit text box, enter the threshold value that you wish to monitor. Click Next.
7. Click the "Start this data collector now" radio button. Click Finish.

Discussion

There are a number of options for monitoring the ongoing performance of the Windows operating system, whether the machine in question is a domain controller, member server, or client computer. For larger environments, you can look into add-on tools such as the Microsoft System Center Operations Manager (OpsMgr) or third-party utilities from NetPro, NetIQ, and others. For a built-in solution, however, the Performance Monitor MMC snap-in can monitor performance metrics and send various administrative alerts.

See Also

"Windows Performance Monitor" (*http://bit.ly/106KHWQ*)

15.12. Emailing an Administrator on a Performance Alert

Problem

You want to create an alert that will notify an administrator via email if a performance alert is generated.

Solution

Using PowerShell

You can create a Windows scheduled task that runs the following PowerShell command. Then, the task can be called from a performance counter alert in Performance Monitor.

```
Send-MailMessage -SmtpServer "<ServerName>" -From "<FromAddress>"↵
  -To "<ToAddress>" -Subject "<MessageSubject>" -Body "<MessageBody>"
```

Discussion

A common request among Windows system administrators is to have the ability to email an on-call administrator when a critical performance alert is generated—for example, when a domain controller is experiencing a critical hardware failure. It is a relatively simple matter to send email through PowerShell using the sample command shown in the solution. You can either hardcode the appropriate alert messages into the email message and maintain multiple scripts for the various alerts that you create, or include counter information in each message by using a generic email message (see Recipe 15.9). Using the Performance Monitor MMC, you can submit one or more of the following as command-line arguments to a script that's been fired in response to an alert:

- Date/time
- The value that was measured by the alert
- The name of the alert
- The name of the counter being measured
- The value of the limit that was exceeded
- A manually defined text string

  You can also use a number of third-party tools to implement this solution, such as the open-source Blat SourceForge project (*http://www.blat.net*), which allows you to send SMTP or NNTP messages from a command line.

See Also

Send-MailMessage cmdlet overview (*http://technet.microsoft.com/library/hh849925*)

15.13. Enabling Auditing of Directory Access

Problem

You want to enable auditing of directory access and modifications. Audit events are logged to the Security event log.

Solution

Using a graphical user interface

1. Open the Group Policy Management snap-in (*gpmc.msc*) and edit the Default Domain Controllers Policy.

2. In the left pane, expand Computer Configuration→Policies→Windows Settings→Security Settings→Local Policies and click on Audit Policy.

3. In the right pane, double-click "Audit directory service access."

4. Make sure the box is checked beside "Define these policy settings."

5. Check the box beside Success and/or Failure.

6. Click OK.

Alternatively, you can also use the Advanced Audit Policy Configuration settings, which allow for a bit more granularity:

1. Open the Group Policy Management snap-in (*gpmc.msc*) and edit the Default Domain Controllers Policy.

2. In the left pane, expand Computer Configuration→Policies→Windows Settings→Security Settings→Advanced Audit Configuration Policy and click on Audit Policies.

3. In the right pane, double-click "DS access."

4. In the right pane, enable "Success and/or Failure auditing" for the Audit Directory Service Access and the Audit Directory Service Changes subcategories.

Discussion

You can log events to the Security event log for every successful and/or failed attempt to access or modify the directory, which is referred to as *auditing*. Auditing is enabled via the Security Settings section of a GPO that's linked to the Domain Controllers OU, using either the "Audit directory service access" setting or the "Advanced Audit Policy Configuration" settings. Once either is enabled, you need to use the ACL Editor to define auditing in the SACL of the objects and containers you want to monitor.

By default, the domain object has an inherited audit entry for the *Everyone* security principal for all object access and modifications. That means once you enable auditing in the Domain Controller Security Policy and this configuration change replicates out, domain controllers will log events for any directory access or modification to any part of the directory. As you can imagine, auditing every access to Active Directory can generate a lot of events, so you'll either want to disable auditing of the *Everyone* group and use the Advanced Audit Policy Configuration settings instead, or else keep a close eye on your domain controllers to ensure that they are not adversely affected while auditing is enabled.

Here is a sample event that was logged after the *Administrator* account created a user object called foobar in the Sales OU:

```
Event Type:        Audit Success
Event Source:      Microsoft Windows security
Task Category:     User Account Management
Event ID:          4720
Date:              12/26/2012
Time:              7:24:10 PM
User:              N/A
Computer:          DC1
A user account was created.

Subject:
    Security ID:        ADATUM\administrator
    Account Name:        administrator
    Account Domain:          ADATUM
    Logon ID:        0x36BFF

New Account:
    Security ID:        ADATUM\foobar
    Account Name:        foobar
    Account Domain:          ADATUM

Attributes:
    SAM Account Name:        foobar
    Display Name:        foobar
    User Principal Name:  foobar@adatum.com
    Home Directory:        -
    Home Drive:        -
    Script Path:        -
    Profile Path:        -
    User Workstations: -
    Password Last Set: <never>
    Account Expires:    <never>
```

```
        Primary Group ID:   513
        Allowed To Delegate To:    -
        Old UAC Value:        0x0
        New UAC Value:        0x15
        User Account Control:
            Account Disabled
            'Password Not Required' - Enabled
            'Normal Account' - Enabled
        User Parameters:    -
        SID History:        -
        Logon Hours:        <value not set>

    Additional Information:
        Privileges     -
```

 It can also be useful to enable Audit Account Management in the GPO that's linked to the Domain Controllers OU. This provides additional information about account-management operations—for example, finding what account deleted a certain object.

Once you have enabled auditing of Directory Service Changes and configured auditing on the relevant objects or containers, the Directory Services Event Viewer will record detailed entries whenever an AD object is created, modified, moved, or deleted, as follows:

- Event 4738 will be logged when an object is modified. In the case of a modify event, you will see the old value (e.g., the old description attribute) and the new value (e.g., the new description attribute).
- Event 4720 will be logged when an object is created.
- Event 4725 will be logged when an object is disabled.
- Event 4740 will be logged when an object is locked out.
- Event 4726 will be logged when an object is deleted.

See Also

"Advanced Security Audit Policy Settings" (*http://bit.ly/1710NbT*); "Planning and Deploying Advanced Security Audit Policies" (*http://bit.ly/11bXuL1*)

15.14. Enabling Auditing of Registry Keys

Problem

You want to enable auditing of any changes to one or more Registry keys.

Solution

Using a graphical user interface

To enable auditing of a Registry key on an individual domain controller, do the following:

1. Create a Group Policy Object (or edit an existing GPO) that enables settings under the following path: Computer Configuration→Policies→Windows Settings→Security Settings→Local Policies→Audit Policy:

   - Audit object access: Success
   - Audit object access: Failure

2. Link the GPO to the OU containing the DC that you wish to audit.

3. On the DC that you want to audit, open *regedit.exe*.

4. Navigate to the Registry key that you want to enable auditing on.

5. Right-click on the key and select Permissions. Click Advanced and select the Auditing tab.

6. Click Add to select a user or group to audit, then click OK. For Apply Onto, select "This key only," "This key and subkeys," or "Subkeys only."

7. Under Access, select the actions that should be audited, and click OK.

If you need to enable auditing of the same Registry keys on multiple computers, a much more efficient solution would be to use a GPO as follows:

1. Create a Group Policy Object (or modify an existing GPO) that enables the following settings under Computer Configuration→Policies→Windows Settings→Security Settings→Local Policies→Audit Policy:

   - Audit object access: Success
   - Audit object access: Failure

2. Navigate to Computer Configuration→Policies→Windows Settings→Security Settings→Registry.

3. Right-click on Registry and select "Add key." On the "Select Registry key" screen, navigate to the key that you want to audit and click OK.

4. Right-click on the key and select Permissions. Click Advanced and select the Auditing tab.

5. Click Add to select a user or group to audit, then click OK. For Apply Onto, select "This key only," "This key and subkeys," or "Subkeys only."

6. Under Access, select the actions that should be audited, and click OK.

7. Link the GPO to the container containing the computers that you wish to audit.

 The Advanced Audit Policy Configuration settings offer another way to audit the Registry. This method allows you to use a global object access audit policy, which provides for auditing without having to specify security access control lists (SACLs). For additional information, check out the "See Also" section of this recipe.

Discussion

Before you can enable auditing on specific Registry keys, you must create an audit policy that enables auditing of object access events, both Success and Failure events. You can enable auditing by modifying an existing GPO or by creating a new GPO created expressly for this purpose. Maintaining a number of single-purpose GPOs can make for easier Group Policy troubleshooting but can lead to performance implications if clients need to process too many GPOs at logon and during the background refresh of Group Policy. As is usually the case, the definition of "too many" will vary from one environment to the next; it's important to monitor the performance of your clients to determine which approach is appropriate for your environment. Once you've enabled auditing of a specific key or keys, information about the activity that you've chosen to audit will appear in the Security event log of the computer where the event took place.

See Also

"Advanced Security Audit Policy Step-by-Step Guide" (*http://bit.ly/16NI9kR*)

15.15. Creating a Quota

Problem

You want to limit the number of objects a security principal can create in a partition by creating a quota.

Solution

Using a command-line interface

```
> dsadd quota -part <PartitionDN> -qlimit <QuotaLimit> -acct <PrincipalName>↵
[-rdn <QuotaName>]
```

The following command creates a quota specification that allows the *ADATUM\rallen* user to create only five objects in the dc=adatum,dc=com partition:

```
> dsadd quota -part dc=adatum,dc=com -qlimit 5 -acct ADATUM\rallen
```

Discussion

Quotas allow an administrator to limit the number of objects that a user (or group of users) can create. A quota applies not just to a user object, but also to the creation of any object type in Active Directory. Three things need to be set when creating a quota specification:

Partition
>   Currently, quotas can apply only to an entire partition. You cannot create a quota that pertains only to a subtree in a partition. You can create quotas for any partition, including application partitions, except for the schema naming context. The reasoning behind this restriction is that the schema is a highly protected area of the directory, and you shouldn't need to restrict how many objects get created there.

Target security principal
>   A quota can be defined for any type of security principal. The msDS-QuotaTrustee attribute on the quota object stores the target principal in the form of an SID.

Limit
>   This determines how many objects the target security principal can create.

The quota limit is a combination of the new objects that a user creates plus any tombstone objects that are created by that user. If a user creates an object and then deletes another object, that would still count as two objects toward any quotas that apply to the user. This is because when an object is deleted, it isn't removed; it is simply marked as tombstoned. Once the tombstone object is removed from Active Directory, the user's quota will be decremented accordingly. By default, a tombstone object counts as one object, but that is configurable. See Recipe 15.17 for more on changing the tombstone quota factor.

Since quotas can be assigned to both users and groups, it is conceivable that multiple quotas may apply to a user. In this case, the quota with the highest limit will be in force for the user. You can also create a default quota for a partition that applies to all security principals. See Recipe 15.18 for more information on configuring the default quota.

Quotas do not apply to members of the *Enterprise Admins* and *Domain Admins* groups. Even if you've configured a default quota for all users, members of those administrative groups will not have any restrictions.

See Also

Recipe 8.13 for more on the computer object quota; this chapter's Recipe 15.0 section for more on the attributes of quota objects; Recipe 15.16 for finding the quotas assigned to a security principal; Recipe 15.17 for changing the tombstone quota factor; Recipe 15.18 for setting a default quota

15.16. Finding the Quotas Assigned to a Security Principal

Problem

You want to find the quotas that have been configured for a security principal (i.e., user, group, or computer).

Solution

Using a command-line interface

```
> dsquery quota <PartitionDN> -acct <PrincipalName>
```

The following command searches for quotas that have been assigned to the *ADATUM* *rallen* user in the dc=adatum,dc=com partition:

```
> dsquery quota dc=adatum,dc=com -acct ADATUM\rallen
```

Using PowerShell

The following command searches for all quotas in a domain:

```
Get-ADObject -Filter {objectClass -eq "msDS-QuotaControl"} | FL Name
```

Discussion

The DSQuery solution will find only quotas that have been directly assigned to a security principal; it will not list quotas that have been assigned to any group objects that the principal may be a member of. The msDS-QuotaTrustee attribute on quota objects defines an SID that the quota applies to. The dsquery quota command will look up the SID for the specified account and match that against quota objects that reference that SID. Unfortunately, this doesn't quite show the whole picture. A user could have a quota assigned directly, which the DSQuery command would show, but the user could also be part of one or more groups that have quotas assigned. These won't show up using

DSQuery. The PowerShell solution lists all quotas, including groups, for the Active Directory domain. However, it does not show a relation between the user object and any groups returned.

A more robust solution would entail retrieving the tokenGroups attribute of the user, which contains a list of SIDs for all expanded group memberships, and then querying each of those groups to determine whether any of them have quotas assigned. This is actually the type of algorithm that is used to determine a user's effective quota, as shown in Recipe 15.19.

See Also

Recipe 15.15 for creating a quota; Recipe 15.19

15.17. Changing How Tombstone Objects Count Against Quota Usage

Problem

You want to change the relative weight of tombstone objects in quota calculations.

Solution

Using a graphical user interface

1. Open ADSI Edit.
2. Connect to the partition on which you want to modify this setting. (This setting must be changed for each partition that you want to configure.)
3. In the left pane, expand the root of the partition.
4. Right-click on cn=NTDS Quotas and select Properties.
5. Set the msDS-TombstoneQuotaFactor attribute to a value between 0 and 100.
6. Click OK.

Using a command-line interface

Create an LDIF file called *change_ tombstone_quota.ldf* with the following contents:

```
dn: cn=NTDS Quotas,<PartitionDN>
changetype: modify
replace: msDs-TombstoneQuotaFactor
msDs-TombstoneQuotaFactor: <1-100>
-
```

Then run the following command:

```
> ldifde -v -i -f change_tombstone_quota.ldf
```

You can also make the change using DSMod or AdMod. DSMod takes the following syntax:

```
> dsmod partition <PartitionDN> -qtmbstnwt <1-100>
```

You can make the change with AdMod, as follows:

```
> admod -b <PartitionDN> msDs-TombstoneQuotaFactor::<0-100>
```

Using PowerShell

You can modify the tombstone quota factor by using PowerShell, as follows:

```
Set-ADObject "<PartitionDN>" -Replace↵
@{"msDS-TombstoneQuotaFactor"="<QuotaValue>"}
```

Discussion

The tombstone quota factor is a percentage that determines how much each tombstone object counts against a security principal's quota usage. By default, tombstone objects count as one object. This means if a user's quota is set to 10 and the user deletes 10 objects, that user will not be able to create or delete any other objects until those tombstone objects have been purged from Active Directory.

The msDs-TombstoneQuotaFactor attribute on the NTDS Quota container for each partition defines the tombstone quota factor. As mentioned previously, the default is that tombstone objects count 100 percent of a normal object; thus, the attribute msDs-TombstoneQuotaFactor contains 100 by default. If you modify this attribute to contain a value of 50 and a user has a quota limit of 10, then that user could delete a maximum of 20 objects (i.e., create 20 tombstone objects) because 20×50 percent = 10. As another example, you may not care about how many objects your users delete; in this case, you'd want to set the tombstone quota factor to 0 so that tombstoned objects would not count against a user's NTDS quota at all.

See Also

MSDN: ms-DS-Tombstone-Quota-Factor attribute [AD Schema]; MSDN: ms-DS-Quota-Container class [AD Schema]; "Active Directory Quotas" (*http://bit.ly/12bAJm4*)

15.18. Setting the Default Quota for All Security Principals in a Partition

Problem

You want to set a default quota for all security principals.

Solution

Using a graphical user interface

1. Open ADSI Edit.
2. Connect to the partition you want to modify. (This setting must be changed for each partition that you want to configure.)
3. In the left pane, expand the root of the partition.
4. Right-click on cn=NTDS Quotas and select Properties.
5. Set the msDS-DefaultQuota attribute to the number of objects that security principals should be allowed to create if they are not assigned another quota.
6. Click OK.

Using a command-line interface

Create an LDIF file called *set_default_quota.ldf* with the following contents:

```
dn: cn=NTDS Quotas,<PartitionDN>
changetype: modify
replace: msDs-DefaultQuota
msDs-DefaultQuota: <NumberOfObjects>
-
```

Then run the following command:

```
> ldifde -v -i -f set_default_quota.ldf
```

You can also make the change using DSMod or AdMod. DSMod takes the following syntax:

```
> dsmod partition <NTDS Quotas DN> -qdefault <DefaultQuota>
```

You can make the change with AdMod, as follows:

```
> admod -b <NTDS Quotas DN> msDs-DefaultQuota::<DefaultQuota>
```

Using PowerShell

You can modify the tombstone quota factor using PowerShell, as follows:

```
Set-ADObject "cn=NTDS Quotas,<PartitionDN>"↵
 -Replace @{"msDS-DefaultQuota"="<QuotaValue>"}
```

Discussion

The easiest way to apply a default quota to all of your users is to modify the msDS-DefaultQuota attribute on the NTDS Quotas container for the target partition. This attribute contains the default quota limit that is used if no other quotas have been assigned to a security principal. A value of –1 means that no quota exists; security principals can create and/or tombstone as many objects as they wish.

You should be careful when setting the default quota because it applies to every non-administrator security principal. If you set the default to 0, for example, computers would not be able to dynamically update their DNS records in an AD integrated zone because that creates an object. This may not be applicable in your environment, but the point is that you need to consider the impact of the default quota and test it thoroughly before implementing it.

15.19. Finding the Quota Usage for a Security Principal

Problem

You want to find the quota usage for a certain security principal.

Solution

Using a command-line interface

The quota usage of a security principal can be determined a few different ways. First, you can use DSGet. Here is an example:

```
> dsget user "<UserDN>" -part <PartitionDN> -qlimit -qused
```

This displays the effective quota limit and how much of the quota has been used for a particular user. You can use similar parameters with dsget computer and dsget group to find the quota usage for those types of objects.

Users can find their own quota usage by querying the msDs-QuotaUsed and msDs-QuotaEffective attributes on the cn=NTDS Quotas container for a partition. These two attributes are constructed, which means they are dynamically calculated based on the user that is accessing them (see Recipe 10.14 for more on constructed attributes). The msDs-QuotaUsed attribute returns how much of the quota has been used by the user, and the msDs-QuotaEffective attribute contains the quota limit.

Using PowerShell

Alternatively, view the `msDs-TopQuotaUsage` attribute on a partition's `cn=NTDS Quo tas` container, which contains the users with the top quota usage. This attribute is multivalued, with each value being XML-like text that contains the SID and how much of the quota the principal has used. To view the quota usage, use the following command:

```
Get-ADObject "cn=NTDS Quotas,<PartitionDN>" -Properties msds-TopQuotaUsage
```

Discussion

If you implement quotas, you'll certainly need to tell users what their quotas are (or provide instructions on how they can find out for themselves). Currently, there are a few ways to determine quota usage, as outlined in this recipe's "Solution" section.

Perhaps the most interesting is obtaining the top-quota usage. Note that it contains quota usage for all objects, even if the objects don't have a quota. Each value of the `msDs-TopQuotaUsage` attribute contains an entry that details the top quota users in the database, listed in decreasing order of quota usage. Each value of the `msDs-TopQuotaUsage` attribute contains blocks of data formatted in an XML-like language. Each block has the SID of the security principal (`<ownerSID>`), quota used (`<quo taUsed>`), number of tombstone objects created (`<tombstonedCount>`), and number of objects that are still active (`<liveCount>`) (i.e., not tombstoned). Here is an example of what the attribute can contain:

```
DistinguishedName  : cn=NTDS Quotas,dc=adatum,dc=com
msds-TopQuotaUsage : {
                     <MS_DS_TOP_QUOTA_USAGE>
                         <partitionDN> dc=adatum,dc=com </partitionDN>
                         <ownerSID> S-1-5-32-548 </ownerSID>
                         <quotaUsed> 10003 </quotaUsed>
                         <deletedCount> 7 </deletedCount>
                         <liveCount> 10001 </liveCount>
                     </MS_DS_TOP_QUOTA_USAGE>
                     ,
                     <MS_DS_TOP_QUOTA_USAGE>
                         <partitionDN> dc=adatum,dc=com </partitionDN>
                         <ownerSID>↵
        S-1-5-21-1553546772-1433447814-1030694943-512 </ownerSID>
                         <quotaUsed> 240 </quotaUsed>
                         <deletedCount> 14 </deletedCount>
                         <liveCount> 237 </liveCount>
                     </MS_DS_TOP_QUOTA_USAGE>
                     ,
                     <MS_DS_TOP_QUOTA_USAGE>
                         <partitionDN> dc=adatum,dc=com </partitionDN>
                         <ownerSID> S-1-5-18 </ownerSID>
                         <quotaUsed> 37 </quotaUsed>
                         <deletedCount> 32 </deletedCount>
                         <liveCount> 32 </liveCount>
```

```
                     </MS_DS_TOP_QUOTA_USAGE>
                     ,
                     <MS_DS_TOP_QUOTA_USAGE>
                         <partitionDN> dc=adatum,dc=com </partitionDN>
                         <ownerSID> S-1-5-32-544 </ownerSID>
                         <quotaUsed> 21 </quotaUsed>
                         <deletedCount> 0 </deletedCount>
                         <liveCount> 21 </liveCount>
                     </MS_DS_TOP_QUOTA_USAGE>
                     ...}
Name           : NTDS Quotas
ObjectClass    : msDS-QuotaContainer
ObjectGUID     : c4bad721-caa3-4893-9bf5-cf399edca9aa
```

Additionally, AdFind has switches that can decode this output in a much friendlier format, as follows:

```
adfind -b "cn=NTDS Quotas, <PartitionDN>" msDs-TopQuotaUsage;binary -resolvesids
```

This command will return results similar to the following:

```
cn=NTDS Quotas,dc=adatum,dc=com
> msDs-TopQuotaUsage;binary: NC: dc=adatum,dc=com Owner: ADATUM\Domain Admins
Used:175 Tombstone: 0 LiveCount: 175
cn=NTDS Quotas,dc=adatum,dc=com
> msDs-TopQuotaUsage;binary: NC: dc=adatum,dc=com Owner: NT AUTHORITY\SYSTEM↵
 Used:
62 Tombstone: 29 LiveCount: 33
> msDs-TopQuotaUsage;binary: NC dc=adatum,dc=com Owner: BUILTIN\Administrators
Used: 14 Tombstone: 0 LiveCount: 14
```

See Also

Recipe 15.16 for more on finding the quotas that are assigned to a security principal

## CHAPTER 16

Backup, Recovery, DIT Maintenance, and Deleted Objects

16.0. Introduction

The AD Directory Information Tree (DIT) is implemented as a transactional database using the Extensible Storage Engine (ESE). The primary database file is named *ntds.dit* and is stored in the *%SystemRoot%\NTDS* folder by default, but it can be relocated during the initial promotion process or manually via *ntdsutil* (see Recipe 16.11 for more details).

Each database write transaction is initially stored in a logfile named *edb.log*, which is stored in the same directory as *ntds.dit* by default, though you can modify this either during or after the initial promotion process. That logfile can grow to 10 MB in size, after which additional logfiles are created (e.g., *edb00001.log*), each of which can also grow to up to 10 MB in size. After the transactions in the logfiles are committed to the database, the logfiles are purged, beginning with the log containing the oldest transactions. This process is referred to as *circular logging*. These logfiles are useful when a domain controller is shut down unexpectedly because when the DC comes back online, Active Directory can replay the logfiles and apply any transactions that might not have been written to disk before the DC shut down. The *edb.chk* file stores information about the last transaction that was actually committed to the database; AD uses this information to determine which transactions in the logfiles still need to be committed. Finally, two 10 MB files called *edbres00001.jrs* and *edbres00002.jrs* are used as placeholders in case the disk runs out of space; if this happens, these files are deleted to free up enough space to allow Active Directory to commit any final changes before the DC is shut down.

In order to recover portions of Active Directory, or the entire directory itself, you need to have a solid backup strategy in place. You can back up Active Directory while it is online, which means you do not need to worry about scheduling regular downtime simply to perform backups. Restoring Active Directory is also a relatively simple process. You can restore a single object, an entire subtree, or the entire database if necessary. For a detailed discussion on backing up and restoring Active Directory, see *Active Directory*, Fifth Edition, by Brian Desmond et al. (O'Reilly).

You also need to be familiar with how deleted objects are treated in Active Directory, which can affect your backup procedures. By default, the Active Directory Recycle Bin is not enabled. When the Active Directory Recycle Bin is not enabled and an object is requested to be deleted, it is actually marked as a tombstone and moved to the `Deleted Objects` container. This *tombstone object* has most of the original object's attribute values removed to save space in the *NTDS.DIT* file. These objects are stored in the `cn=Deleted Objects` container in the naming context that the original object was located in. The deleted object is named using the following format: `<OrigName>\0ADEL: <Object GUID>`, where `<OrigName>` is the original RDN of the object, `<ObjectGUID>` is the GUID of the object, and `\0A` is a null-terminated character. For example, if you deleted the `jsmith` user object, its tombstone object would have a distinguished name similar to the following:

```
cn=jsmith\0ADEL:fce1ca8e-a5ec-4a29-96e1-c8013e533d2c,cn=Deleted↵
Objects,dc=adatum,dc=com
```

If the Active Directory Recycle Bin is enabled, a deleted object becomes logically deleted while the link-valued and non-link-valued attributes are maintained. Thus, during the deleted object lifetime, deleted objects can be restored to the exact state that they were in prior to the deletion. (This includes group membership information, too.) The restore process for deleted objects becomes much simpler and cleaner with the Active Directory Recycle Bin.

In Windows Server 2012, the AD DS service can be stopped to perform some (but not all) maintenance operations without needing to reboot the domain controller into DSRM. Some of the operations you can perform on a 2012 DC while the AD DS service is stopped include:

- Performing an offline defragmentation.
- Moving the AD database files.
- Performing a nonauthoritative restore. However, performing an authoritative restore still requires a full reboot into DSRM.

You can stop the Active Directory Domain Services service using familiar interfaces such as the Services MMC snap-in, Server Manager, the `net stop` command-line utility, or the `Stop-Service` PowerShell cmdlet. Be aware that when you stop the Active Directory Domain Services service, one or more of the following dependent services will be stopped as well; you will need to take this into consideration when restarting the AD DS service so that all associated services are also restarted:

- File Replication
- Kerberos Key Distribution Center
- Intersite Messaging
- DNS Server (on DCs that are running the DNS Server service)
- DFS Replication

After a period of time known as the *tombstone lifetime* (180 days is the default for Windows Server 2012), the tombstone object is finally removed from Active Directory. At that point, remnants of the former object do not exist in Active Directory.

Tombstone objects are important to understand with regard to your backup strategy because you should not keep backups longer than the tombstone lifetime. If you attempt to restore a backup that is older than the tombstone lifetime, it may introduce objects that were deleted but for which a tombstone object no longer exists. Under normal conditions, if you do a nonauthoritative restore from backup, objects that were valid when the backup was taken but that were subsequently deleted will be deleted during the first replication cycle after the DC is rebooted normally. If the tombstone object has already expired (e.g., the backup is older than 180 days), Active Directory has no way to determine whether the object was previously deleted and will read it. Reinjected deleted objects are referred to as *lingering* or *zombie objects*.

The tombstone lifetime value is stored in the `tombstoneLifetime` attribute on the following object: `cn=Directory Service,cn=Windows NT,cn=Services,cn=Configura tion,` *<ForestRootDN>*.

The Anatomy of a Deleted Object

Deleted objects are generally stored in the respective `Deleted Objects` container of their naming context. You can view deleted objects by using the Active Directory Administrative Center and browsing to the `Deleted Objects` container. Table 16-1 contains some of the attributes that are stored with deleted objects.

 The attributes that are preserved in tombstone objects are determined by `attributeSchema` objects that have bit 3 enabled (8 in decimal) in the `searchFlags` attribute.

Table 16-1. Useful attributes of deleted objects

Attribute	Description
isDeleted	The value for this attribute is TRUE for deleted objects
isRecycled	The value for this attribute is TRUE for deleted objects that have had their deleted object lifetime expire.
lastKnownParent	Distinguished name of container the object was contained in.
Name	RDN of the object's current location.
userAccountControl	This attribute is retained when the original object is deleted. This applies only to user and computer objects.
objectSID	This attribute is retained when the original object is deleted. This applies only to user and computer objects.
sAMAccountName	This attribute is retained when the original object is deleted. This applies only to user and computer objects.
sidHistory	This attribute is retained when the original object is deleted. This applies only to user and computer objects.

To aid in Active Directory backup and recovery, Windows Server 2012 includes a *snapshot* feature that allows you to take point-in-time snapshots of the Active Directory database and then mount those snapshots to view the contents and compare them to the current contents of the AD database. Using scripts or third-party tools, you can even copy information from an Active Directory snapshot directly into the live AD database without needing to reboot the domain controller to perform a traditional restore operation.

16.1. Backing Up the Active Directory Database

Problem

You want to back up the Active Directory database.

Solution

Using a command-line interface

```
> wbadmin start systemstatebackup -backuptarget:"<BackupTarget>"
```

Using Windows PowerShell

The following PowerShell example will start a one-time System State backup, saving the backup data on the E:\ volume.

```
$wbPolicy = New-WBPolicy
Set-WBSchedule -Policy $wbPolicy -Schedule 23:59
Add-WBSystemState -Policy $wbPolicy
```

```
$wbTarget = New-WBBackupTarget -VolumePath E:
Add-WBBackupTarget -Policy $wbPolicy -Target $wbTarget
Start-WBBackup -Policy $wbPolicy
```

Discussion

The wbadmin command can be used to create a System State backup of the Active Directory database. In addition, there is a Windows Server Backup GUI tool that can be used to perform the backup. Alternately, Windows PowerShell cmdlets are available to configure one-time and scheduled backup jobs. The steps in this recipe assume that you have installed the Windows Server Backup feature. To install the Windows Server Backup feature using PowerShell, run the following command.

```
Add-WindowsFeature Windows-Server-Backup -IncludeAllSubFeature
```

See Also

Recipe 16.2 for information on creating Active Directory snapshots; Recipe 16.3 for more on mounting and using snapshots

16.2. Creating an Active Directory Snapshot

Problem

You want to create a snapshot of the Active Directory database.

Solution

Using a command-line interface

```
> ntdsutil
> activate instance ntds
> snapshot
> create
```

Discussion

The Active Directory Domain Services snapshot feature leverages the Volume Shadow Copy Service (VSS) to allow administrators to create "shadow copies" of the Active Directory database. Once a snapshot has been created, you can use the *ntdsutil* and *dsamain* command-line utilities to mount the snapshot as a read-only copy of the Active Directory database. Once the snapshot is mounted, you can view it using customary tools such as ADSI Edit and LDP, as well as using third-party tools to copy information from a snapshot into a live Active Directory database.

See Also

Recipe 16.3 for more on mounting and using snapshots

16.3. Mounting an Active Directory Snapshot

Problem

You want to mount a snapshot of the Active Directory database that you created previously using either *ntdsutil* or a System State backup.

Solution

Using a command-line interface

If you want to view a snapshot in *ntdsutil*, you must first mount the snapshot within *ntdsutil* as follows:

```
> ntdsutil
> activate instance ntds
> snapshot
> list all
```

The `list all` command generates a list of snapshots that have been created on the domain controller in question, each with a corresponding number. You will then issue the `mount<Number>` command to mount the snapshot that you want. Once the snapshot is mounted, *ntdsutil* will list the physical path that the database has been mounted to, such as *C:\$SNAP_200808011002_VOLUMEC$*.

Once you have mounted the snapshot you want, you'll use the `dsamain` command to expose the snapshot as an LDAP server. When using `dsamain`, you will need to provide an alternate LDAP port since 389 is in use by the live AD database. You can also specify an alternate LDAPS port, Global Catalog port, and secure Global Catalog port. Use the *dsamain* tool as follows:

```
> dsamain /dbpath "<Path to database file>" /ldapport <Port Number>
```

The mounted snapshot will be exposed as an LDAP server as long as the command window remains open. Use Ctrl-C to "switch off" the snapshot functionality.

Discussion

The *dsamain* utility can be used to expose an Active Directory snapshot that has been created using *ntdsutil*, or it can use the contents of a System State backup that has been restored to an alternate location on the local hard drive. Network or UNC paths are not supported. Once a snapshot or restored backup is exposed using *dsamain*, it can be accessed in a read-only manner using Active Directory tools such as LDP or ADSI Edit, as well as scripts and PowerShell.

See Also

Recipe 16.2 for more on creating snapshots; Recipe 16.4 for more on accessing and manipulating information contained in a snapshot

16.4. Accessing Active Directory Snapshot Data

Problem

You want to access data contained within a snapshot of the Active Directory database that you created previously using either *ntdsutil* or a System State backup.

Solution

Using a graphical user interface

1. Launch *LDP.exe* and then connect to the server with a snapshot mounted, using the appropriate port number.
2. Select Connection→Bind and then click OK.
3. Click View→Tree. Select the Base DN you would like to view snapshot data from.
4. Expand the snapshot tree to view the containers and objects available in the snapshot.

Using Windows PowerShell

```
Get-ADObject -Identity "<ObjectDN>" -Server <ServerName>:<PortNumber>↵
   -Properties * | FL
```

Discussion

An Active Directory snapshot provides a read-only view of the Active Directory database as it existed at a particular point in time, whether the snapshot was created using *ntdsutil* or whether you are using *dsamain* to mount the *ntds.dit* contained in a System State backup. While Windows does not provide a method to perform a simple GUI "cut-and-paste" to insert values from a snapshot into a live Active Directory database, you can do so using scripting, PowerShell, or a third-party tool. You can also view the contents of a snapshot using tools such as ADSI Edit by simply indicating the alternate LDAP port number that you specified when you mounted the snapshot.

See Also

Recipe 16.3 for more on mounting and using snapshots; "Active Directory Explorer v1.14" (another tool for working with snapshots) (*http://bit.ly/10hvtJp*)

16.5. Restarting a Domain Controller in Directory Services Repair Mode

Problem

You want to restart a domain controller in DS Repair Mode.

Solution

To enter DS Repair Mode, press F8 after the power-on self-test (POST), which will bring up a menu, as shown in Figure 16-1. From the menu, select Directory Services Repair Mode.

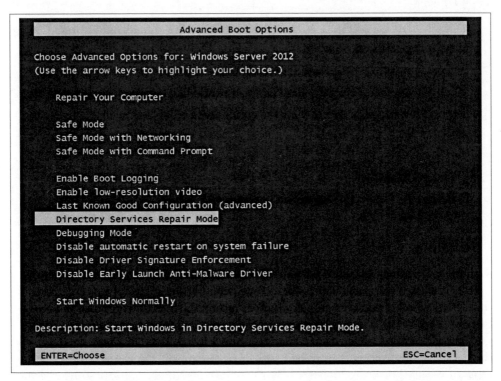

Figure 16-1. Boot options

Using a graphical user interface

1. Run *msconfig.exe* and then select the Boot tab.

2. Place a checkmark in the Safe Boot option and then select the Active Directory repair option.

3. Click OK. You will be prompted to restart the server.

Using the command-line interface

You can also enable DSRM prior to rebooting a server by entering the following command:

```
> bcdedit /set safeboot dsrepair
```

Once you have completed the maintenance on the DC and wish to return to a normal startup mode, enter the following prior to rebooting:

```
> bcdedit /deletevalue safeboot
```

Discussion

The Active Directory database is live and locked by the system whenever a domain controller is booted into normal mode. In DS Repair Mode, Active Directory does not start up and the database files (e.g., *ntds.dit*) are not locked. The restartable AD DS service allows you to perform certain maintenance tasks, such as performing an offline defrag, without needing to reboot the domain controller into DSRM. However, certain critical operations, such as an authoritative restore, still need to be performed in Directory Services Repair Mode.

It is not always practical to be logged in to the console of the server when you need to reboot it into DS Repair Mode. You can use Remote Desktop Connection to log on to the machine remotely while it is in DSRM mode.

 Directory Services Repair Mode was referred to as Directory Services Restore Mode in previous versions of Windows.

See Also

"Restart the Domain Controller in Directory Services Restore Mode Remotely" (*http://bit.ly/18NXE90*)

16.6. Resetting the Directory Services Repair Mode Administrator Password

Problem

You want to reset the DS Repair Mode administrator password. This password is set individually (i.e., not replicated) on each domain controller and is initially configured when you promote a server to a domain controller.

Solution

Using a command-line interface

Using *ntdsutil*, you can change the DS Repair Mode administrator password of a domain controller while it is live (i.e., not in DS Repair Mode). Another benefit of this option is that you can run it against a remote domain controller. Use the following command sequence to reset the password on a domain controller named DC1:

```
> ntdsutil
> set dsrm password
> reset password on server DC1
```

However, if you are already in DSRM and would like to change the password, the *ntdsutil* option is not available. To change the DSRM password once you are already logged in, use the following command:

```
net user Administrator "<Password>"
```

Discussion

You may be thinking that having a separate DS Repair Mode administrator password can be quite a pain. Yet another thing you have to maintain and update on a regular basis, right? But if you think about it, you'll see that it is quite necessary.

Generally, you boot a domain controller into DS Repair Mode when you need to perform some type of maintenance on the Active Directory database. To do this, the database needs to be offline. But if the database is offline, then there is no way to authenticate against it. Because of this, the system has to use another authentication repository, so it reverts back to the legacy SAM database. The DS Repair Mode administrator account and password are stored in the SAM database, just as with standalone Windows servers.

The one disadvantage to the solutions presented in this recipe is that you have to reset the DSRM password on one machine at a time. To automate this process on all domain controllers, the following PowerShell command will synchronize the DSRM password with the current password of the domain Administrator account:

```
Get-ADDomainController -Filter * | ForEach-Object {Invoke-Command↵
-ComputerName $_.Name -ScriptBlock {ntdsutil "set dsrm password"↵
"sync from domain account Administrator" "Q" "Q"}}
```

See Also

TechNet Article cc754363, "set DSRM password" for resetting the DSRM password on a domain controller (*http://bit.ly/Z7G01c*)

16.7. Performing a Nonauthoritative Restore

Problem

You want to perform a nonauthoritative restore of a domain controller. This can be useful if you want to quickly restore a domain controller that failed due to a hardware problem.

Solution

Using a command-line interface

To perform a system state recovery, you will need to know the date and timestamp of the system state backup that you want to recover from. You can perform a nonauthoritative restore by rebooting the DC into DSRM or by stopping the Active Directory Domain Services service; you can stop this service from the Services MMC snap-in, from Server Manager, or by using the `net stop` command-line utility. The following command syntax performs a system state recovery:

```
> wbadmin start systemstaterecovery -version:<BackupDate>-<BackupTime>
```

Discussion

If you encounter a failed domain controller that you cannot bring back up (e.g., multiple hard disks fail), you have two options for restoring it. One option is to remove the domain controller completely from Active Directory (as outlined in Recipe 3.10) and then promote it back in. This is known as the *restore from replication* method, because you are essentially bringing up a brand-new domain controller and letting replication restore all the data on the server. After performing the steps described in Recipe 3.10, you can also use the Install From Media option described in Recipe 3.5 to expedite this process.

The other option is described in this recipe's solution. You can restore the domain controller from a good backup. This method involves restoring the System State and any necessary system drive(s) and then rebooting. As long as the domain controller comes up clean, it should start participating in Active Directory replication once again and replicate any changes that have occurred since the backup was taken. This method is generally the fastest for restoring a domain controller, particularly if the server is the only DC located in a remote site.

For a detailed discussion of the advantages and disadvantages of each option, see *Active Directory*, Fifth Edition, by Brian Desmond et al. (O'Reilly).

See Also

Recipe 16.5 for getting into Directory Services Repair Mode

16.8. Performing an Authoritative Restore of an Object or Subtree

Problem

You want to perform an authoritative restore of one or more objects, but not the entire Active Directory database. For the GUI solution, this recipe assumes that the Active Directory Recycle Bin was enabled prior to the deletion. If you have not enabled the AD Recycle Bin, you can do so from the Tasks pane in the Active Directory Administrative Center.

Solution

Using a graphical user interface (steps specific to Windows Server 2012)

1. Launch Active Directory Administrative Center.
2. Select the domain and navigate to the Deleted Objects container.
3. Locate the deleted object in the container.
4. Right-click the object and select Restore.

Using a command-line interface

To restore a single object, run the following commands:

```
> ntdsutil
> activate instance ntds
> auth restore
> restore object cn=jsmith,ou=Sales,dc=adatum,dc=com
> q
```

To restore an entire subtree, run the following commands:

```
> ntdsutil
> activate instance ntds
```

```
> auth restore
> restore subtree ou=Sales,dc=adatum,dc=com
> q
```

Restart the computer.

There are some issues related to restoring user, group, computer, and trust objects that you should be aware of. See MS KB 216243 and MS KB 280079 for more information.

Using PowerShell

```
Get-ADObject -Filter {isDeleted -eq $true} -IncludeDeletedObjects |↵
  Where-Object {$_.DistinguishedName -match "<GroupName>"} | Restore-ADObject
```

Discussion

If an administrator or user accidentally deletes an important object or entire subtree from Active Directory, you can restore it. Fortunately, the process isn't very painful. The key is to have a good backup that contains the objects you want to restore.

Using a command-line interface

To restore one or more objects, you need to follow the same steps as when performing a nonauthoritative restore. The only difference is that after you do the restore, you need to use *ntdsutil* to mark the objects in question as authoritative on the restored domain controller. After you reboot the domain controller, it will then receive information from its replication partners and process updates for any objects that have been changed since the backup that was restored on the machine, except for the objects or subtrees that were marked as authoritative. For those objects, Active Directory modifies the restored objects in such a way that they will become authoritative and replicate out to the other domain controllers.

> Performing an authoritative restore of user or group objects will require additional considerations, as detailed in MS KB 280079. (Authoritative restore of groups can result in inconsistent membership information across domain controllers.)

You can also use *ntdsutil* without first doing a restore in situations where an object has accidentally been deleted, but the change has not yet replicated to all domain controllers. The trick here is that you need to find a domain controller that has not had the deletion replicated yet, and either stop it from replicating or make the object authoritative before it sends its replication updates. Take a look at Recipe 12.5 for more information on controlling inbound and outbound replication on a domain controller.

Using PowerShell

If the Active Directory Recycle Bin is not enabled, then the PowerShell solution will restore the object without the link-valued and some of the non-link-valued attributes. However, if the Active Directory Recycle Bin was enabled prior to the object deletion, then the PowerShell solution will restore the object to its original state, which includes the link-valued and the non-link-valued attributes.

See Also

Recipe 16.5 for booting into Directory Services Repair Mode; Recipe 16.22 for restoring a deleted object; MS KB 216243 (Authoritative Restore of Active Directory and Impact on Trusts and Computer Accounts); MS KB 280079 (Authoritative Restore of Groups Can Result in Inconsistent Membership Information Across Domain Controllers)

16.9. Performing a Complete Authoritative Restore

Problem

You want to perform a complete authoritative restore of the Active Directory database because a significant failure has occurred.

Solution

First, reboot into Directory Services Repair Mode (DSRM)—see Recipe 16.5 for more information. Then, once in DSRM, run the following command to restore the entire database:

```
> wbadmin start systemstaterecovery -version:<BackupDate>-<BackupTime>↵
-authsysvol
```

For example, to restore a backup from 02/14/2013 at 08:56pm, run the following command:

```
> wbadmin start systemstaterecovery -version:02/14/2013-20:56 -authsysvol >↵
activate instance ntds
```

Restart the computer.

Discussion

In a production environment, you should never have to perform an authoritative restore of the entire Active Directory database unless you have encountered a drastic situation such as a forest recovery scenario. It is a drastic measure, and you will almost inevitably lose data as a result. Before you even attempt such a restore, you may want to contact Microsoft Support to make sure that all options have been exhausted. However, you should still test the authoritative restore process in a lab environment and make sure that you have the steps properly documented in case you ever do need to use it.

See Also

Recipe 16.5 for getting into Directory Services Repair Mode; MB KB 216243 (Authoritative Restore of Active Directory and Impact on Trusts and Computer Accounts); MS KB 280079 (Authoritative Restore of Groups Can Result in Inconsistent Membership Information Across Domain Controllers)

16.10. Checking the DIT File's Integrity

Problem

You want to check the integrity and semantics of the DIT file to verify that there is no corruption or bad entries.

Solution

Using a command-line interface

This recipe can be performed while the Active Directory Domain Services service is in a stopped state; it is not necessary to reboot the DC into DSRM. To stop the AD DS service, use *services.msc*, or issue the net stop command.

Once the DC is prepared as needed, run the following commands:

```
> ntdsutil
> activate instance ntds
> files
> integrity
> quit
> semantic database analysis
> verbose on
> go
> quit
> quit
```

Discussion

The Active Directory DIT file (*ntds.dit*) is implemented as a transactional database. Microsoft uses the ESE database (also called JET Blue) for Active Directory, which has been used for years in other products such as Microsoft Exchange.

Since the Active Directory DIT is ultimately a database, it can suffer from many of the same issues as traditional databases. The ntdsutil integrity command checks for any low-level database corruption and ensures that the database headers are correct and

---

the tables are in a consistent state. It reads every byte of the database and can take quite a while to complete, depending on how large the DIT file is.

Whereas the `ntdsutil integrity` command verifies the overall structure and health of the database files, the `ntdsutil semantics` command looks at the contents of the database. It will verify, among other things, reference counts, replication metadata, and security descriptors. If any errors are reported back, you can run `go fixup` to attempt to correct them. You should have a recent backup handy before doing this and perform this step only as a troubleshooting option, preferably under the direction of a Microsoft PSS engineer, since in the worst case the corruption cannot be fixed or the state of your AD database may even become worse after the `go fixup` command completes.

See Also

Recipe 16.5 for booting into Directory Services Repair Mode; MS KB 315136 (How to Complete a Semantic Database Analysis for the Active Directory Database by Using Ntdsutil.exe)

16.11. Moving the DIT Files

Problem

You want to move the Active Directory DIT files to a new drive to improve performance or capacity.

Solution

Using a command-line interface

This recipe can be performed while the Active Directory Domain Services service is in a stopped state; it is not necessary to reboot the DC into DSRM. Once the service is stopped, run the following commands, in which `<DriveAndFolder>` is the new location where you want to move the files (e.g., *d:\NTDS*):

```
> ntdsutil
> activate instance ntds
> files
> move db to "<DriveAndFolder>"
> move logs to "<DriveAndFolder>"
> q
> q
```

Discussion

You can move the Active Directory database file (*ntds.dit*) independently of the logfiles. The first command in the solution moves the database, and the second moves the logs.

You may also want to consider running an integrity check against the database after you've moved it to ensure that nothing went wrong during the move. See Recipe 16.10 for more details.

See Also

Recipe 16.5 for booting into Directory Services Repair Mode; Recipe 16.10 for checking DIT file integrity

16.12. Repairing or Recovering the DIT

Problem

You need to repair or perform a soft recovery of the Active Directory DIT because a power failure or some other failure caused the domain controller to enter an unstable state.

Solution

Using a command-line interface

This recipe can be performed while the Active Directory Domain Services service is in a stopped state; it is not necessary to reboot the DC into DSRM. Once the service is stopped, run the following commands:

```
> ntdsutil
> activate instance ntds
> files
> recover
> q
> q
```

If the recover operation is successful, you should then check the integrity of the AD database (see Recipe 16.10).

Discussion

Hopefully, you will never need to recover or repair your Active Directory database. However, a recovery may be needed after a domain controller unexpectedly shuts down, perhaps due to a power loss, and certain changes were never committed to the database. When it boots back up, a soft recovery is automatically done in an attempt to reapply any changes that were contained in the transaction logfiles. Since Active Directory does this automatically, it is unlikely that running the ntdsutil recover command will be of much help.

We recommend that you use extreme caution when performing a repair and you may wish to engage Microsoft Support first in case something goes wrong. If you try the repair, and it makes things worse, you should consider rebuilding the domain controller from scratch. See Recipe 3.10 for forcibly removing a failed domain controller from your domain.

See Also

Recipe 16.10 for checking the integrity of the DIT file

16.13. Performing an Online Defrag Manually

Problem

You want to initiate an online defragmentation to optimize the disk space that's being used by the *ntds.dit* file.

Solution

Using a graphical user interface

1. Open *LDP.exe.*

2. From the menu, select Connection→Connect.

3. For Server, enter the name of the target domain controller.

4. For Port, enter 389.

5. Click OK.

6. From the menu, select Connection→Bind.

7. Enter the credentials of an administrative user or accept the default and log on with the current user credentials.

8. Click OK.

9. From the menu, select Browse→Modify.

10. Leave the Dn blank.

11. For Attribute, enter `DoOnlineDefrag`.

12. For Values, enter `180`.

13. For Operation, select Add.

14. Click Enter.

15. Click Run.

Using a command-line interface

Create an LDIF file called *online_defrag.ldf* with the following contents:

```
dn:
changetype: modify
replace:DoOnlineDefrag
DoOnlineDefrag: 180
-
```

Then run the following command:

```
> ldifde -v -i -f online_defrag.ldf
```

You can also perform an online defrag using AdMod:

```
> admod -b "" doOnlineDefrag::180
```

Using PowerShell

```
$rootDSE = [ADSI] "LDAP://<DomainControllerName>/RootDSE"
$rootDSE.put("DoOnlineDefrag", "180")
$rootDSE.SetInfo()
```

Discussion

By default, the online defrag process runs every 12 hours on each domain controller after the garbage collection process completes. This process defrags the Active Directory database (*ntds.dit*) by combining whitespace generated from deleted objects but does not reduce the size of the database file.

To start an online defrag, simply write the `DoOnlineDefrag` attribute to the RootDSE with a value equal to the maximum time the defrag process should run (in seconds). You must be a member of the *Domain Admins* group in the domain controller's domain in order to write to this attribute.

See Also

Recipe 16.17 for performing an offline defrag; MS KB 198793 (The Active Directory Database Garbage Collection Process)

16.14. Performing a Database Recovery

Problem

You want to perform a recovery of the Active Directory database when other methods have failed.

Solution

Using a command-line interface

This recipe can be performed while the Active Directory Domain Services service is in a stopped state; it is not necessary to reboot the DC into DSRM. Once the service is stopped, to perform an integrity check of the Active Directory database, enter the following:

```
> esentutl /g "<PathToNTDS.DIT>"/!10240 /8 /o
```

To perform a recovery of the AD database, enter the following:

```
> esentutl /r "<PathToNTDS.DIT>" /!10240 /8 /o
```

To perform a repair of the database, use the following syntax:

```
> esentutl /p "<PathToNTDS.DIT>" /!10240 /8 /o
```

Discussion

When attempting to recover the *ntds.dit* database, you may occasionally encounter a situation where *ntdsutil* is unable to repair whatever damage has occurred. You may run into error messages similar to the following:

```
Operation failed because the database was inconsistent.

Initialize jet database failed; cannot access file.

Error while performing soft recovery.
```

Because the AD database is based on the ESE, you also have access to the *esentutl* database utility, which can perform a number of operations against the *ntds.dit* file, including defragmentation, database recovery or repair, and integrity checks. (For a complete description of each operation, type `esentutl /?` at the command line.)

If the *ntdsutil* recovery options listed elsewhere in this chapter fail, you can attempt to repair AD using this ESE utility. Many of the operations that you can perform with *esentutl* have the potential to exacerbate data loss, so be certain that you have a viable backup in place before attempting any of them. In fact, in some cases it may actually be easier and quicker to simply restore from a known good backup to get your domain or forest back online again.

See Also

MS KB 305500 (Cannot Repair the Active Directory Database by Using the Ntdsutil Tool); MS KB 280364 (How to Recover from Event ID 1168 and Event ID 1003 Error Messages)

16.15. Creating a Reserve File

Problem

You want to create another reserve file on the disk containing the *ntds.dit* file to guard against AD failures caused by running out of disk space.

Solution

Using a command-line interface

The following command will create an empty reserve file, 250 MB in size, in the same directory as the *ntds.dit* file:

```
> fsutil file createnew <PathToNTDS.DIT>\reservefile 256000000
```

For example, the following will create the reserve file in *c:\windows\ntds*:

```
> fsutil file createnew c:\windows\ntds\reservefile 256000000
```

Discussion

By default, Active Directory creates two files called *ebdres00001.jrs* and *ed bres00002.jrs* in the same directory as the *ntds.dit* database. Each of these files is 10 MB in size and is used to hold in reserve the last 20 MB of space on the drive hosting the AD database files. If a domain controller runs out of space on that drive, Active Directory will use the space being held by *ebdres00001.jrs* and *edbres00002.jrs* to commit any uncommitted transactions before shutting down so that no information is lost. If you wish to set aside more space than this, you can create a reserve file to set aside additional space; this reserve file can then be manually deleted to free up disk space. This can provide an additional safeguard against a user or administrator inadvertently filling up the drive that's hosting the *ntds.dit* file, or guard against a virus or a malicious user performing a denial-of-service attack by intentionally filling up the drive.

 To prevent accidental or malicious bloating of the *ntds.dit* file itself, you can also establish quotas to restrict the number of objects that can be created by a user.

See Also

Recipe 15.15 for more on creating Active Directory quotas; Recipe 15.17 for configuring how tombstoned objects affect quotas

16.16. Determining How Much Whitespace Is in the DIT

Problem

You want to find the amount of whitespace in your DIT. A lot of whitespace in the DIT may mean that you could regain enough space on the disk to warrant performing an offline defrag.

Solution

Using a graphical user interface

1. Run *regedit.exe* from the command line or from Start→Run.

2. Expand *HKEY_LOCAL_MACHINE\SYSTEM\CurrentControlSet\Services\NTDS \Diagnostics*.

3. In the right pane, double-click on 6 Garbage Collection.

4. For Value data, enter 1.

5. Click OK.

Using a command-line interface

```
> reg add HKLM\System\CurrentControlSet\Services\NTDS\Diagnostics /v "6 Garbage↵
Collection" /t REG_DWORD /d 1
```

Using Windows PowerShell

```
$strRegPath = "HKLM:\System\CurrentControlSet\Services\NTDS\Parameters"
Set-ItemProperty -Path $strRegPath -Name "6 Garbage Collection" -value "1"
```

Discussion

By setting the 6 Garbage Collection diagnostics logging option, event 1646 will get generated after the garbage collection process runs. Here is a sample 1646 event:

```
Event Type:        Information
Event Source:      NTDS Database
Event Category:    Garbage Collection
Event ID:          1646
Date:              11/25/2012
Time:              9:52:46 AM
User:              NT AUTHORITY\ANONYMOUS LOGON
Computer:          DC1
Description:
Internal event:    The Active Directory database has the following amount of↵
free hard disk space remaining.
```

```
Free hard disk space (megabytes): 100
Total allocated hard disk space (megabytes): 1024
```

This shows that domain controller Dc1 has a 1 GB DIT file with 100 MB that is free (i.e., whitespace).

See Also

Recipe 16.17 for performing an offline defrag

16.17. Performing an Offline Defrag to Reclaim Space

Problem

You want to perform an offline defrag of the Active Directory DIT to reclaim whitespace in the DIT file.

Solution

Using a command-line interface

This recipe can be performed while the Active Directory Domain Services service is in a stopped state; it is not necessary to reboot the DC into DSRM.

1. Once the AD DS service is stopped, check the integrity of the DIT as outlined in Recipe 16.10.

2. Now, you are ready to perform the defrag operation. Run the following command to create a compacted copy of the DIT file. You should check to make sure the drive on which you create the copy has plenty of space. A rule of thumb is that it should have at least 115 percent of the size of the current DIT available:

    ```
    > ntdsutil "activate instance ntds" files "compact to <TempDriveAndFolder>"↵
    q q
    ```

3. Delete the transaction logfiles in the current NTDS directory:

    ```
    > del <CurrentDriveAndFolder>\*.log
    ```

4. You may want to keep a copy of the original DIT file for a short period of time to ensure that nothing catastrophic happens to the compacted DIT. This does not replace the need for a System State backup and a backup of the domain controller's system drive; it is simply a temporary measure to provide a fallback if the move process itself goes wrong. If you are going to copy or move the original version, be sure you have enough space in its new location:

    ```
    > move <CurrentDriveAndFolder>\ntds.dit <TempDriveAndFolder>\ntds_orig.dit
    > move <TempDriveAndFolder>\ntds.dit <CurrentDriveAndFolder>\ntds.dit
    ```

5. Repeat the steps in Recipe 16.10 to ensure that the new DIT file is not corrupted. If it is clean, reboot into normal mode and monitor the event log. If no errors are reported in the event log, make sure the domain controller is backed up as soon as possible.

Discussion

Performing an offline defragmentation of your domain controllers can reclaim disk space if you've deleted a large number of objects from Active Directory. You should perform an offline defrag when (and if) this occurs only if you actively require the disk space back—for example, when following a spin-off in which you've migrated a large number of objects into a separate domain. The database will reuse whitespace and grow organically as required. Typically, the database grows year over year as more objects are added, so an offline defrag should seldom be required. An offline defrag always carries a small element of risk, so it should not be done unnecessarily.

The key thing to plan ahead of time is your disk space requirements. If you plan to create the compacted copy of the DIT on the same drive as the current DIT, you need to make sure that drive has 115 percent of the size of the DIT available. If you plan to store the original DIT on the same drive, you'll need to make sure you have at least that much space available.

See Also

Recipe 16.10 for checking the integrity of the DIT; MS KB 198793 (The Active Directory Database Garbage Collection Process); MS KB 229602 (Defragmentation of the Active Directory Database); MS KB 232122 (Performing Offline Defragmentation of the Active Directory Database)

16.18. Changing the Garbage Collection Interval

Problem

You want to change the default garbage collection interval.

Solution

Using a graphical user interface

1. Open ADSI Edit.
2. In the left pane, expand cn=Configuration→cn=Services→cn=Windows NT.
3. Right-click on cn=Directory Service and select Properties.

4. Edit the `garbageColPeriod` attribute and set it to the interval in hours that the garbage collection process should run (the default is 12 hours).

5. Click OK.

Using a command-line interface

Create an LDIF file called *change_garbage_period.ldf* with the following contents:

```
dn: cn=Directory Service,cn=Windows NT,cn=Services,cn=Configuration,↵
<ForestRootDN>
changetype: modify
replace: garbageCollPeriod
garbageCollPeriod: <IntervalInHours>
-
```

Then run the following command:

```
> ldifde -v -i -f change_garbage_period.ldf
```

You can also modify the garbage collection period using AdMod:

```
> adfind -config -rb "cn=Directory Service,cn=Windows NT,cn=Services" -s base↵
 -dsq | admod garbageCollPeriod::<IntervalInHours>
```

Using Windows PowerShell

```
Set-ADObject "cn=Directory Service,cn=Windows NT,cn=Services,cn=Configuration,↵
 <ForestRootDN>" -Replace @{"garbageCollPeriod"="1"}
```

Discussion

In an environment where the Active Directory Recycle Bin is not enabled, when an object is deleted from the Configuration naming context, a Domain naming context, or an application partition, the object is *tombstoned* by renaming the object, moving it to the `Deleted Object` container, and clearing the value of most of its attributes to save space in the *ntds.dit* file. This tombstone object remains in Active Directory for the duration of the tombstone lifetime (180 days for Windows Server 2012) before it gets completely removed. See Recipe 16.24 for more information on the tombstone lifetime.

A garbage collection process runs on each domain controller that automatically removes expired tombstone objects. This process runs every 12 hours by default, but you can change it to run more or less frequently by setting the `garbageCollPeriod` attribute on the following object to the frequency in hours:

```
"cn=Directory Service,cn=Windows NT,cn=Services,cn=Configuration,<RootDomainDN>"
```

See Also

Recipe 16.19 for logging the number of tombstones that get garbage-collected; Recipe 16.24 for modifying the tombstone lifetime; MS KB 198793 (The Active Directory Database Garbage Collection Process)

16.19. Logging the Number of Expired Tombstone Objects

Problem

You want to log the number of expired tombstone objects that are removed from Active Directory during each garbage collection cycle.

Solution

Using a graphical user interface

1. Run *regedit.exe* from the command line or from Start→Run.
2. Expand *HKEY_LOCAL_MACHINE\SYSTEM\CurrentControlSet\Services\NTDS \Diagnostics*.
3. In the right pane, double-click on 6 Garbage Collection.
4. For Value data, enter 3.
5. Click OK.

Using a command-line interface

```
> reg add HKLM\System\CurrentControlSet\Services\NTDS\Diagnostics /v "6 Garbage↵
Collection" /t REG_DWORD /d 3
```

Using PowerShell

```
$strRegPath = "HKLM:\System\CurrentControlSet\Services\NTDS\Parameters"
Set-ItemProperty -Path $strRegPath -Name "6 Garbage Collection" -value "3"
```

Discussion

Here is a sample event that is logged when the 6 Garbage Collection diagnostics logging level is set to 3 or higher:

```
Event Type:         Information
Event Source:       NTDS General
Event Category:     Garbage Collection
Event ID:           1006
Date:               11/24/2012
Time:               11:29:31 AM
```

```
User:                   NT AUTHORITY\ANONYMOUS LOGON
Computer:               DC1
Description:
Internal event: Finished removing deleted objects that have expired (garbage
collection). Number of expired deleted objects that have been removed: 229.
```

See Also

Recipe 15.1 for more on diagnostics logging; Recipe 16.18 for more on the garbage collection process

16.20. Determining the Size of the Active Directory Database

Problem

You want to determine the size of the Active Directory database.

Solution

Using a command-line interface

This recipe can be performed while the Active Directory Domain Services service is in a stopped state; it is not necessary to reboot the DC into DSRM. Once the service is stopped, you can display file information using the following syntax:

```
> ntdsutil
> activate instance ntds
> files
> info
> quit
> quit
```

When you are finished, don't forget to restart the AD DS service, as well as any dependent services that halted when you stopped Active Directory Domain Services.

Discussion

The size of the Active Directory database on a domain controller is the size of the *ntds.dit* file. This file can vary slightly in size between domain controllers, even within the same domain, due to unreplicated changes, differences with nonreplicated data, and whitespace from purged objects.

You should monitor the size of this file on one or more domain controllers in each of your domains to ensure that you have adequate disk space. Also, by knowing the average size of your DIT, you can quickly recognize if it spikes dramatically, perhaps due to a new application that is writing data to the directory.

If you find that you are running out of disk space, you have a couple of options. You could move the Active Directory files to a new drive with more capacity. Alternatively, you can perform an offline defragmentation if the DIT file contains a lot of whitespace.

See Also

Recipe 16.11 for moving the DIT files; Recipe 16.16 for determining how much whitespace is in the DIT; Recipe 16.17 for performing an offline defragmentation of the Active Directory database

16.21. Searching for Deleted Objects

Problem

You want to search for deleted objects.

Solution

Using a graphical user interface

1. Launch the Active Directory Administrative Center.
2. Select the domain and then navigate to the `Deleted Objects` container.
3. Use the filter search bar to search through the deleted objects.

Using a command-line interface

To view all of the deleted objects in the current domain, use the following syntax:

```
> adfind -default -rb "cn=Deleted Objects" -showdel
```

You can also use the *adrestore.exe* utility from the Microsoft website by simply typing `adrestore` from the command line.

Using PowerShell

You view all of the deleted objects in the current domain, use the following PowerShell command:

```
Get-ADObject -Filter {isDeleted -eq $True} -IncludeDeletedObjects |↲
    FT Name,objectCLass
```

Discussion

When an object is deleted in Active Directory, it is not really deleted, at least not immediately. The object is renamed, most of its attributes are cleared, and it is moved to the Deleted Objects container within the naming context that it was deleted from. See this chapter's Recipe 16.0 for more on tombstone objects.

 Not all objects are moved to the Deleted Objects container. If you are unable to find a given deleted object, open the search scope to the whole naming context the object previously existed in.

Both the Deleted Objects container and tombstone objects themselves are hidden by default in tools such as ADUC and ADSI Edit. Only members of the administrator groups can perform searches for tombstone objects.

See Also

MSDN: Retrieving Deleted Objects

16.22. Undeleting a Single Object

Problem

You want to undelete an object that has been deleted from your Active Directory domain. This recipe assumes that the Active Directory Recycle Bin has been enabled. If you have not enabled the AD Recycle Bin, you can do so from the Tasks pane in the Active Directory Administrative Center.

Solution

Using a graphical user interface

1. Launch the AD Administrative Center.
2. Select the domain and navigate to the Deleted Objects container.
3. Locate the deleted object in the container.
4. Right-click the object and select Restore.

Using Windows PowerShell

To restore all deleted user objects, run the following PowerShell command:

```
Get-ADObject -Filter {(isDeleted -eq $true) -and (ObjectClass -eq "user") -and
  (ObjectClass -ne "computer")} -IncludeDeletedObjects | Restore-ADObject
```

The filter option can be expanded to reduce the number of objects returned, or to return only specific objects.

Discussion

Another option when restoring a single object is to perform a System State restore on a domain controller, and then to use *ntdsutil* to mark the individual object as *authoritative*. This has the downside of causing downtime on a domain controller, since you'll need to reboot it into Directory Services Repair Mode to perform the restore.

Microsoft also offers the *adrestore* command-line utility that will enumerate the deleted objects in a domain and give you the option to undelete them.

See Also

"Step 2: Restore a Deleted Active Directory Object" (*http://bit.ly/128qCPW*); the other recipes in this chapter for more on AD backups, restores, snapshots, and disaster recovery

16.23. Undeleting a Container Object

Problem

You want to undelete a container object such as an OU that contained other objects when it was deleted.

Solution

Using a graphical user interface

Use the steps in Recipe 16.22 to first undelete the container object. Then undelete each individual child object that was contained within the container, specifying the container's DN in the restored object's DN. Alternately, perform a System State restore and use *ntdsutil* to mark the restored OU as authoritative, as described in Recipe 16.8.

Performing an authoritative restore of user or group objects will require additional considerations, as detailed in MS KB 280079 (Authoritative Restore of Groups Can Result in Inconsistent Membership Information Across Domain Controllers).

Using a command-line interface

```
> adfind -default -rb "cn=Deleted Objects" -f "(name=<ContainerRDN>*)"↵
 -showdel -dsq | admod -undel
> adfind -default -rb "cn=Deleted Objects" -f↵
("lastKnownParent=<ParentContainerDN>") -showdel -dsq | admod -undel
```

Using Windows PowerShell

To restore all child objects of an organizational unit named Accounts, use the following command:

```
Get-ADObject -Filter {(isDeleted -eq $True) -and (lastKnownParent -eq↵
 "ou=Accounts,dc=adatum,dc=com")} -IncludeDeletedObjects | Restore-ADObject
```

Discussion

When you delete an Active Directory container object, it also deletes any child objects that are housed within that container. Restoring an OU and all of the child objects, for example, therefore requires you to restore both the container itself as well as all of the child objects contained within it. This is relatively simple to perform using Windows PowerShell since you can restrict your query to those objects that have the appropriate value listed in the lastKnownParent attribute.

See Also

MSDN: Restoring Deleted Object [Active Directory]

16.24. Modifying the Tombstone Lifetime for a Domain

Problem

You want to change the default tombstone lifetime for a domain.

Solution

Using a graphical user interface

1. Open ADSI Edit.
2. In the left pane, expand cn=Configuration→cn=Services→cn=Windows NT.

3. Right-click on cn=Directory Service and select Properties.

4. Set the tombstoneLifetime attribute to the number of days that tombstone objects should remain in Active Directory before getting removed completely.

5. Click OK.

Using a command-line interface

Create an LDIF file called *change_tombstone_lifetime.ldf* with the following contents:

```
dn: cn=Directory Service,cn=Windows NT,cn=Services,cn=Configuration,↵
<ForestRootDN>
changetype: modify
replace: tombstoneLifetime
tombstoneLifetime: <NumberOfDays>
-
```

Then run the following command:

```
> ldifde -v -i -f change_tombstone_lifetime.ldf
```

You can also make this change using AdMod, as follows:

```
> admod -b "cn=Directory Service,cn=WindowsNT,↵
cn=Services,cn=Configuration,<ForestRootDN>" tombstoneLifetime::<NumberOfDays>
```

Using PowerShell

```
Set-ADObject "cn=Directory Service,cn=Windows NT,cn=Services,cn=Configuration,↵
 <ForestRootDN>" -Replace @{"tombstoneLifetime"="<NumberOfDays>"}
```

Discussion

The default tombstone lifetime for Windows 2008 and later is set to 180 days. It is not recommended that you decrease the tombstone lifetime unless you have a very good reason for doing so, since decreasing this value below the 180-day default also decreases the length of time a backup of Active Directory is good for. See this chapter's Recipe 16.0 and Recipe 16.21 for more information on tombstone (deleted) objects and the tombstone lifetime.

See Also

Recipe 16.18 for more on the garbage collection process; MS KB 198793 (The Active Directory Database Garbage Collection Process); MS KB 314282 (Lingering Objects May Remain After You Bring an Out-of-Date Global Catalog Server Back Online)

## CHAPTER 17

Application Partitions

17.0. Introduction

Active Directory domain controllers, when first installed, host three predefined partitions. The *Configuration naming context* is replicated to all domain controllers in the forest, and it contains information that is needed forest-wide, such as the site topology and LDAP query policies. The *Schema naming context* is also replicated forest-wide and contains all of the schema objects that define how data is stored and structured in Active Directory. The third partition is the *Domain naming context*, which is replicated to all of the domain controllers that host a particular domain.

There is another partition type that is called an *application partition*, which is very similar to the other naming contexts except that you can configure which domain controllers in the forest will replicate the data that's contained within it. Examples include the `DomainDnsZones` partition, which is replicated across all AD integrated DNS servers in the same domain, and `ForestDnsZones`, which is replicated across all AD integrated DNS servers in the forest. This capability gives administrators much more flexibility over how they can store and replicate the data that is contained in Active Directory. If you need to replicate a certain set of data to only two different sites, for example, you can create an application partition that will only replicate the data to the domain controllers in those two sites rather than replicating the data to additional DCs that have no need for it.

See Chapter 13 for more on DNS-related management tasks, as well as *Active Directory*, Fifth Edition, by Brian Desmond et al. (O'Reilly), for more details on application partitions.

The Anatomy of an Application Partition

Application partitions are stored in Active Directory in a similar fashion as a Domain NC. In fact, application partitions and Domain NCs consist of the same two types of objects: a `domainDNS` object and a `crossRef` object that resides under the `Partitions` container in the Configuration naming context (CNC). Application partitions have a similar naming convention as domains and can be named virtually anything you want. You can create an application partition that uses the current namespace within the forest. For example, in the *adatum.com* (`dc=adatum,dc=com`) forest, you could create an *apps.adatum.com* (`dc=apps,dc=adatum,dc=com`) application partition. Alternatively, a name that is part of a new tree can also be used; for example, *apps.local* (`dc=apps,dc=local`). Application partitions can also be subordinate to other application partitions.

Table 17-1 and Table 17-2 contain some of the interesting attributes of `domainDNS` and `crossRef` objects as they apply to application partitions.

Table 17-1. Attributes of domainDNS objects

Attribute	Description
dc	Relative distinguished name of the application partition.
instanceType	This attribute must be set to 5 when creating an application partition. See Recipe 17.1 for more information.
msDs-masteredBy	List of nTDSDSA object DNs of the domain controllers that replicate the application partition. See Recipe 17.4 for more information.

Table 17-2. Attributes of crossRef objects

Attribute	Description
cn	Relative distinguished name of the `crossRef` object. This value is generally a GUID for application partitions.
dnsRoot	Fully qualified DNS name of the application partition.
msDS-NC-Replica-Locations	List of nTDSDSA object DNs of the domain controllers that replicate the application partition. See Recipe 17.4 for more information.
msDS-SDReferenceDomain	Domain used for security descriptor translation. See Recipe 17.8 for more information.
nCName	Distinguished name of the application partition's corresponding `domainDNS` object.
systemFlags	Bit flag that identifies whether the `crossRef` represents an application. See Recipe 17.2 for more information.

17.1. Creating and Deleting an Application Partition

Problem

You want to create or delete an application partition. Application partitions are useful if you need to replicate data to a subset of locations where you have domain controllers. Instead of replicating the application data to all domain controllers in a domain, you can use an application partition to replicate the data to only the domain controllers of your choosing.

Solution

Using a command-line interface

Use the following command to create an application partition on a domain controller:

```
> ntdsutil
> activate instance ntds
> partition management
> connections
> connect to server <DomainControllerName>
> quit
> create nc <AppPartitionDN> NULL
> quit
> quit
```

Use the following command to delete an application partition:

```
> ntdsutil
> activate instance ntds
> partition management
> connections
> connect to server <DomainControllerName>
> quit
> delete nc <AppPartitionDN>
> quit
> quit
```

Discussion

To create an application partition, you create a `domainDNS` object that serves as the root container for the partition. A `crossRef` object is automatically created in the `Partitions` container in the Configuration NC. Conversely, when removing an application partition, you only need to remove the `crossRef` object and the `domainDNS` is automatically deleted. When you delete an application partition, all objects within the partition also get deleted. Tombstone objects are not created for any of the objects within the application partition or for the application partition itself.

See Also

MSDN: Creating an Application Directory Partition; MSDN: Deleting an Application Directory Partition

17.2. Finding the Application Partitions in a Forest

Problem

You want to find the application partitions that have been created in a forest.

Solution

Using a graphical user interface

1. Open LDP.
2. From the menu, select Connection→Connect.
3. Click OK to connect to the closest domain controller over port 389.
4. From the menu, select Connection→Bind.
5. Click OK to bind as the currently logged on user or select the option to bind with credentials, enter the credentials, and then click OK.
6. From the menu, select Browse→Search.
7. For Base DN, type the DN of the Partitions container (e.g., `cn=parti tions,cn=configuration,dc=adatum,dc=com`).
8. For Filter, enter:

       (&(objectcategory=crossRef)(systemFlags:1.2.840.113556.1.4.803:=5))

9. For Scope, select One Level.
10. Click the Options button.
11. For Attributes, enter dnsRoot.
12. Click Run.

Using a command-line interface

Use the following command to find all of the application partitions in a forest:

```
> dsquery * cn=partitions,cn=configuration,<ForestDN> -filter↵
"(&(objectcategory=crossRef)(systemFlags:1.2.840.113556.1.4.803:=5))"↵
-scope onelevel -attr dnsRoot
```

You can also find application partitions in a forest using AdFind:

```
> adfind -sc appparts+
```

Using PowerShell

The following example will search for application partitions within an Active Directory domain:

```
Get-ADObject -SearchBase "cn=partitions,cn=configuration,<ForestDN>" -Filter↵
{(objectCategory -eq "crossref") -and (systemFlags -eq "5")}
```

Discussion

To get the list of application partitions in this recipe's solution, we queried all cross Ref objects in the Partitions container that have the systemFlags attribute with the bits 0 and 2 set (5 in decimal). To do this, a logical AND bitwise filter was used. See Recipe 4.12 for more on searching with a bitwise filter.

You can take a shortcut by not including the bitwise OID in the search filter, and changing it to systemFlags=5. This currently produces the same results in the test forest as with the bitwise filter, but there are no guarantees since it is a bit-flag attribute. You may encounter circumstances in which an application partition would have another bit set in systemFlags that would yield a different value.

In each solution, the dnsRoot attribute was printed for each application partition, which contains the DNS name of the application partition. You can also retrieve the nCName attribute, which contains the distinguished name of the application partition.

See Also

Recipe 4.12

17.3. Adding or Removing a Replica Server for an Application Partition

Problem

You want to add or remove a replica server for an application partition. After you've created an application partition, you should make at least one other server a replica server in case the first server fails.

Solution

Using a graphical user interface

To add a replica server to an application partition, follow these steps:

1. Open ADSI Edit.
2. If necessary, connect to the Configuration naming context of the forest the application partition is in.
3. Expand the Configuration naming context and click on cn=Partitions.
4. In the right pane, right-click on the crossRef object that represents the application partition and select Properties.
5. Under Attributes, select the msDS-NC-Replica-Locations attribute and click Edit.

6. In the "Value to add" field, enter the following:

```
cn=NTDS Settings,cn=<DCName>,cn=Servers,cn=Default-First-Site-Name,↵
cn=Sites,cn=Configuration,<ForestDN>
```

7. Click Add, and then OK twice.

To remove a replica server from an application partition, follow these steps:

1. Open ADSI Edit.

2. If necessary, connect to the Configuration naming context of the forest the application partition is in.

3. Expand the Configuration naming context and click on cn=Partitions.

4. In the right pane, right-click on the crossRef object that represents the application partition and select Properties.

5. Under Attributes, select the msDS-NC-Replica-Locations attribute and click Edit.

6. Select the value to remove and then click Remove.

7. Click OK twice.

Using a command-line interface

Use the following command to add a replica server for an application partition:

```
> ntdsutil
> activate instance ntds
> partition management
> connections
> connect to server <DomainControllerName>
> quit
> add nc replica<AppPartitionDN> <DomainControllerName>
> quit
> quit
```

Use the following command to remove a replica server from an application partition:

```
> ntdsutil
> activate instance ntds
> partition management
> connections
> connect to server <DomainControllerName>
> quit
> remove nc replica <AppPartitionDN> <DomainControllerName>
> quit
> quit
```

Using PowerShell

The following command will add DC2 to the list of replica locations for *app1.adatum.com*, while leaving the rest of the list intact:

```
Get-ADObject -SearchBase "cn=Partitions,cn=Configuration,dc=adatum,dc=com"↵
-Filter {dnsroot -eq "app1.adatum.com"} | Set-ADObject↵
-Add @{"msDS-NC-Replica-Locations"="cn=NTDS Settings,cn=DC2,cn=Servers, ↵
cn=Default-First-Site-Name,cn=Sites,cn=Configuration,dc=adatum,dc=com"}
```

The following command will remove DC2 from the replica location list for *app1.adatum.com*, without removing any other entries:

```
Get-ADObject -SearchBase "cn=Partitions,cn=Configuration,dc=adatum,dc=com"↵
-Filter {dnsroot -eq "app1.adatum.com"} | Set-ADObject↵
-Remove @{"msDS-NC-Replica-Locations"="cn=NTDS Settings,cn=DC2,cn=Servers,↵
cn=Default-First-Site-Name,cn=Sites,cn=Configuration,dc=adatum,dc=com"}
```

Discussion

When you initially create an application partition, there is only one domain controller that hosts the application partition, namely the one you created the application partition on. You can add any other domain controllers in the forest as replica servers. The list of replica servers is stored in the msDS-NC-Replica-Locations attribute on the cross Ref object for the application partition in the Partitions container. That attribute contains the distinguished name of each replica server's nTDSDSA object. To add a replica server, simply add the DN of the new replica server's nTDSDSA object. To remove a replica server, remove the DN corresponding to the server's nTDSDSA object that you want to remove. Behind the scenes, the KCC gets triggered anytime there is a change to that attribute, at which point it will either cause the application partition to get replicated to the target domain controller or remove the replica from the target DC. When a domain controller is demoted, it should automatically remove itself as a replica server for any application partitions that it replicated.

See Also

Recipe 17.4 for finding the replica servers for an application partition

17.4. Finding the Replica Servers for an Application Partition

Problem

You want to find the replica servers for an application partition.

Solution

Using a graphical user interface

1. Open ADSI Edit.
2. Connect to the Configuration naming context of the forest the application partition is in, if it is not already present in the left pane.
3. Expand the Configuration naming context and click on the `Partitions` container.
4. In the right pane, right-click on the `crossRef` object that represents the application partition and select Properties.
5. Under Attributes, select the `msDS-NC-Replica-Locations` attribute and then click View.

Using a command-line interface

```
> ntdsutil
> activate instance ntds
> partition management
> connections
> connect to server <DomainControllerName>
> quit
> list nc replicas <AppPartitionDN>
> quit
> quit
```

Using PowerShell

```
Get-ADObject -SearchBase "cn=Partitions,cn=Configuration,dc=adatum,dc=com"↵
  -Filter; {dnsroot -eq "<PartitionFQDN>"} -Properties msDS-NC-Replica-Locations
```

Discussion

The list of replica servers for an application partition is stored in the multivalued `msDS-NC-Replica-Locations` attribute on the `crossRef` object for the application partition. This object is located in the `Partitions` container in the Configuration naming context.

See Also

Recipe 17.3 for adding and removing replica servers

17.5. Finding the Application Partitions Hosted by a Server

Problem

You want to find the application partitions that a particular server is hosting. Before you decommission a server, it is good to check to see whether it hosts any application partitions and, if so, to add another replica server to replace it.

Solution

Using a graphical user interface

1. Open LDP.

2. From the menu, select Connection→Connect.

3. Click OK to connect to the closest domain controller over port 389.

4. From the menu, select Connection→Bind.

5. Click OK to bind as the currently logged on user or select the option to bind with credentials, enter the credentials, and then click OK.

6. From the menu, select Browse→Search.

7. For Base DN, type the DN of the `Partitions` container (e.g., `cn=partitions,cn=configuration,dc=adatum,dc=com`).

8. For Filter, enter:

   ```
   (&(objectcategory=crossRef)(systemFlags:1.2.840.113556.1.4.803:=5)↵
   (msDS-NC-Replica-Locations=cn=NTDS Settings,cn=<DomainControllerName>,↵
   cn=servers,cn=<SiteName>,cn=sites,cn=configuration,<ForestDN>))
   ```

9. For Scope, select One Level.

10. Click the Options button.

11. For Attributes, enter dnsRoot.

12. Click OK.

13. Click Run.

Using a command-line interface

Use the following command to find all of the application partitions hosted by a domain controller. To run this command, you need the distinguished name of the forest root domain (`<ForestDN>`), the common name of the DC's server object (`<DomainControllerName>`), and the common name of the site object the server is in (`<SiteName>`).

```
> dsquery * "cn=partitions,cn=configuration,<ForestDN>" -scope onelevel -attr↵
dnsRoot -filter "(&(objectcategory=crossRef)↵
(systemFlags:1.2.840.113556.1.4.803:=5)
(msDS-NC-Replica-Locations=cn=NTDS Settings,cn=<DomainControllerName>,↵
cn=servers,cn=<SiteName>,cn=sites,cn=configuration,<ForestDN>))"
```

You can also display the application partitions hosted by a particular DC using AdFind:

```
> adfind -partitions -s onelevel -bit -f↵
"(&(objectcategory=crossRef)(systemFlags:AND:=5)↵
(msDS-NC-Replica-Locations=cn=NTDS
Settings,cn=<DomainControllerName>,cn=servers,cn=<SiteName>,↵
cn=sites,cn=configuration,<ForestRootDN>))"
```

Using PowerShell

```
Get-ADObject -SearchBase "cn=Partitions,cn=Configuration,dc=adatum,dc=com"↵
 -Filter {(objectCategory -eq "crossRef") -and (systemFlags -eq "5") -and↵
 (msDS-NC-Replica-Locations -eq "cn=NTDS Settings,cn=<DCName>,cn=servers,↵
cn=<SiteName>,cn=sites,cn=configuration,<ForestDN>")}
```

Discussion

As described in Recipe 17.3 and Recipe 17.4, the msDS-NC-Replica-Locations attribute on crossRef objects contains the list of replica servers for a given application partition. Each of the solutions illustrates how to perform a query using this attribute to locate all of the application partitions a particular domain controller is a replica server for. For the GUI and CLI solutions, you need to know the distinguished name of the nTDSDSA object for the target domain controller.

See Also

Recipe 17.3 and Recipe 17.4 for finding the replica servers for an application partition

17.6. Verifying Application Partitions Are Instantiated Correctly on a Server

Problem

You want to verify that an application partition is instantiated on a replica server. After you add a domain controller as a replica server for an application partition, the data in the application partition needs to fully replicate to that domain controller before it can be used on that domain controller.

Solution

Using a command-line interface

Use the following command to determine whether there are any problems with application partitions on a domain controller:

```
> dcdiag /test:checksdrefdom /test:verifyreplicas /test:crossrefvalidation↵
/s:<DomainControllerName>
```

You can also verify the state of a particular application partition by using *ntdsutil* as follows:

```
> ntdsutil
> activate instance ntds
> partition management
> connections
> connect to server <DCName>
> quit
> list nc replicas <PartitionDN>
> quit
> quit
```

Discussion

The *dcdiag* CheckSDRefDom, VerifyReplicas, and CrossRefValidation tests can help determine whether an application partition has been instantiated on a server and whether there are any problems with it. Here is the *dcdiag* help information for those three tests:

CrossRefValidation
    This test looks for cross-references that are in some way invalid.

CheckSDRefDom
    This test checks that all application directory partitions have appropriate security descriptor reference domains.

VerifyReplicas
    This test verifies that all application directory partitions are fully instantiated on all replica servers.

Another way you can check to see whether a certain application partition has been instantiated on a domain controller is to look at the msDS-HasInstantiatedNCs attribute for the server's nTDSDSA object. That attribute has DN with Binary syntax and contains a list of all the application partitions that have been successfully instantiated on the server. Unfortunately, tools such as ADSI Edit and DSQuery do not interpret DN with Binary attributes correctly, but it can be viewed with LDP. In addition, you can use AdFind as follows:

```
adfind -b "cn=NTDS Settings,cn=<DCName>,cn=Servers,cn=<SiteName>,cn=Sites,↵
cn=Configuration,<ForestDN>" -f↵
  "msds-HasInstantiatedNCs=B:8:0000000D:<ParitionDN>" -dn
```

This will return results similar to the following:

```
AdFind V01.47.00cpp Joe Richards (joe@joeware.net) October 2012

Using server: adatum-dc.adatum.com:389
Directory: Windows Server 2012

dn:cn=NTDS Settings,cn=DC2,cn=Servers,cn=Default-First-Site-Name,cn=Sites
cn=Configuration,dc=adatum,dc=com

1 Objects returned
```

See Also

MSDN: ms-DS-Has-Instantiated-NCs attribute [AD Schema]

17.7. Setting the Replication Notification Delay for an Application Partition

Problem

You want to set the replication notification delay for an application partition. Two replication-related settings that you can customize for application partitions (or any naming context for which change notification is enabled) include the first and subsequent replication delays after a change to the partition has been detected. The first replication delay is the time that a domain controller waits before it notifies its first replication partner that there has been a change. The subsequent replication delay is the time that the domain controller waits after it has notified its first replication partner before it will notify its next partner. You may need to customize these settings so that replication happens as quickly as you need it to for data in the application partition.

Solution

Using a graphical user interface

1. Open ADSI Edit.
2. Connect to the Configuration naming context of the forest that the application partition is in if a connection is not already present in the left pane.
3. Expand the Configuration naming context and click on the Partitions container.
4. In the right pane, right-click on the crossRef object that represents the application partition and select Properties.

5. Set the `msDS-Replication-Notify-First-DSA-Delay` and `msDS-Replication-Notify-Subsequent-DSA-Delay` attributes to the number of seconds you want for each delay (see this recipe's "Discussion" for more details).

6. Click OK.

Using a command-line interface

To change the settings using the command line, run the following command:

```
> repadmin /notifyopt "<DCName>" "<AppPartitionDN>"↵
/first:<FirstDelayInSeconds>
/subs:<NextDelayInSeconds>
```

You can also change both of these parameters using AdMod, as follows:

```
> admod -b <AppPartitionCrossRefDN>↵
msDS-Replication-Notify-First-DSA-Delay::<FirstDelayInSeconds>↵
 msDS-Replication-Notify-Subsequent-DSA-Delay::<NextDelayInSeconds>
```

Using PowerShell

To modify the initial and subsequent notification delays, you can use the following PowerShell commands:

```
Set-ADObject "<PartitionDN>" -Replace↵
 @{"msDS-Replication-Notify-First-DSA-Delay"="<Interval>"}

Set-ADObject "<PartitionDN>" -Replace↵
 @{"msDS-Replication-Notify-Subsequent-DSA-Delay"="<Interval>"}
```

Discussion

The settings that control the notification delay are stored in the `msDS-Replication-Notify-First-DSA-Delay` and `msDS-Replication-Notify-Subsequent-DSA-Delay` attributes on the application partition's `crossRef` object in the `Partitions` container. The time values are stored as seconds. The default for application partitions is 15 seconds for the first delay and three seconds for each subsequent delay.

See Also

MSDN: Application Directory Partition Replication [Active Directory]; MSDN: Modifying Application Directory Partition Configuration [Active Directory]; MSDN: ms-DS-Replication-Notify-First-DSA-Delay; MSDN: ms-DS-Replication-Notify-Subsequent-DSA-Delay

17.8. Setting the Reference Domain for an Application Partition

Problem

You want to set the reference domain for an application partition. Whenever you create an object in Active Directory, the default security descriptor that's defined in the schema for the object's class is applied to the object. This default security descriptor may reference specific groups, such as *Domain Admins*, but it is not specific to a domain. This makes a lot of sense for domain naming contexts, where the *Domain Admins* group in question would be the one that's defined in the domain in question. But for application partitions that don't contain a *Domain Admins* group, it is not so straightforward. Which domain's *Domain Admins* group do you use? To work around this issue, you can set a default security descriptor reference domain for an application partition by setting the msDS-SDReferenceDomain attribute of the partition's crossRef object. The default value of the msDS-SDReferenceDomain attribute is the domain that the application partition was created in.

Solution

Using a graphical user interface

1. Open ADSI Edit.
2. Connect to the Configuration naming context of the forest the application partition is in if it is not already present in the left pane.
3. Expand the Configuration naming context and click on the Partitions container.
4. In the right pane, right-click on the crossRef object that represents the application partition and select Properties.
5. Under Attributes, select the msDS-SDReferenceDomain attribute.
6. Enter the Distinguished Name for the appropriate domain and click OK.

Using a command-line interface

```
> ntdsutil
> activate instance ntds
> partition management
> connections
> connect to server <DomainControllerName>
> quit
> set nc ref domain<AppPartitionDN> <DomainDN>
> quit
> quit
```

You can also set the reference domain using AdMod:

```
> adfind -partitions -f "(dnsRoot=<PartitionDNSName>)" -dsq |↵
  admod msDS-SDReferenceDomain::"<DomainDN>"
```

Using PowerShell

```
Set-ADObject "<PartitionDN>" -Replace @{"msDS-SDReferenceDomain"="<DomainDN>"}
```

Discussion

If you don't set the msDS-SDReferenceDomain attribute for an application partition, then a specific hierarchy will be followed to determine the default security descriptor domain. These are the guidelines:

- If the application partition is created as part of a new tree, the forest root domain is used as the default domain.
- If the application partition is a child of a domain, the parent domain is used as the default domain.
- If the application partition is a child of another application partition, the parent application partition's default domain is used.

See Also

Recipe 10.18 for more on setting the default security descriptor for a class; Recipe 17.1 for creating an application partition

17.9. Delegating Control of Managing an Application Partition

Problem

You want to delegate control over the management of an application partition.

Solution

Using a graphical user interface

1. Open ADSI Edit.
2. Connect to the Configuration naming context of the forest the application partition is in if it is not already present in the left pane.
3. Expand the Configuration naming context and click on the Partitions container.

4. In the right pane, right-click on the crossRef object that represents the application partition and select Properties.

5. Click the Security tab.

6. Click the Advanced button.

7. Click the Add button.

8. Use the object picker to find the user or group you want to delegate control to and click OK.

9. Under Properties, check the boxes beside Write msDS-NC-Replica-Locations, Write msDS-SDReferenceDomain, Write msDS-Replication-Notify-First-DSA-Delay, and Write msDS-Replication-Notify-Subsequent-DSA-Delay.

10. Click OK.

Using a command-line interface

```
> dsacls <AppPartitionCrossRefDN> /G <UserOrGroup>:RPWP;msDS-NC-Replica-Locations
> dsacls <AppPartitionCrossRefDN> /G <UserOrGroup>:RPWP;msDS-SDReferenceDomain
> dsacls <AppPartitionCrossRefDN> /G <UserOrGroup>:RPWP;msDS-Replication-↵
Notify-First-DSA-Delay
> dsacls <AppPartitionCrossRefDN> /G <UserOrGroup>:RPWP;msDS-Replication-↵
Notify-Subsequent-DSA-Delay
```

 As is the case with most permissions, you should exercise care when delegating the ability to create or modify application partitions. Because application partitions reside within Active Directory, allowing them to be placed indiscriminately or setting the initial and subsequent replication delays too low can bring your network to a grinding halt.

Discussion

If you want to delegate control of management of application partitions, you must grant control over four key attributes. Here is a description of each attribute and what can be accomplished by having control over it:

msDS-NC-Replica-Locations
A user can add replica servers for the application partition. See Recipe 17.3 for more information.

msDS-SDReferenceDomain
A user can define the default security descriptor domain for the application partition. See Recipe 17.8 for more information.

msDS-Replication-Notify-First-DSA-Delay
See Recipe 17.7 for more information.

`msDS-Replication-Notify-Subsequent-DSA-Delay`
    See Recipe 17.7 for more information.

If you want to delegate control over managing objects within the application partition, you need to follow the same procedures you would when delegating control over objects in a domain naming context. See Recipe 13.9 for more information on delegating control.

See Also

Recipe 13.9; Recipe 14.5 for delegating control; Recipe 17.3 for more on adding and removing replica servers; Recipe 17.7 for more on the replication delay attributes; Recipe 17.8 for more on the default security descriptor domain

Active Directory Lightweight Directory Service

18.0. Introduction

Active Directory Application Mode (ADAM) was released in November 2003 on the Microsoft website. With the release of Windows Server 2008, along with several other technologies, Microsoft renamed ADAM. The new name for ADAM is Active Directory Lightweight Directory Service (AD LDS). AD LDS is a lightweight LDAP platform that allows developers and administrators to work with AD objects such as users, groups, and organizational units, without worrying about the overhead of running a full-blown copy of the Active Directory Domain Services. AD LDS can run on Windows Server 2012 and Windows 8 computers, and you can run multiple instances of AD LDS on a single machine. Because AD LDS runs as a standalone service, you can start, stop, install, or remove AD LDS instances without affecting or interfering with any underlying AD infrastructure. AD LDS can leverage domain authentication, local machine users, and groups, or it can authenticate users based on security principals that you've created within AD LDS itself. (It's important to note that these are separate from Active Directory security principals, which cannot be created within an AD LDS instance.)

AD LDS includes the following features:

Server Core support
> AD LDS can be installed on computers that are running Server Core, the reduced-footprint installation option that was introduced with Windows Server 2008.

Auditing for AD LDS changes
> The Directory Services Changes audit policy subcategory allows you to view old and new values when changes are made to AD LDS objects.

Database Mounting Tool (Dsamain.exe)
> Similar to Active Directory Domain Services, you can use *dsamain* to mount snap-shots of AD LDS partitions to view and compare information from previous points in time.

Support for Active Directory Sites and Services
> You can now use the AD Sites and Services MMC to manage replication between AD LDS instances.

18.1. Installing AD LDS

Problem

You want to install a new instance of AD LDS.

Solution

Using a graphical user interface

To install AD LDS on a Windows Server 2012 server, do the following:

1. Launch Server Manager.
2. Click Manage and then click Add Roles and Features.
3. Click Next three times.
4. Place a checkmark next to Active Directory Lightweight Directory Services.
5. Click Add Features and then click Next three times.
6. Click Install.

Using Windows PowerShell

To perform a Windows PowerShell install of AD LDS on Windows Server 2012, run the following command:

```
Install-WindowsFeature -Name "ADLDS" -IncludeAllSubFeature↵
  -IncludeManagementTools
```

Discussion

At its most basic level, an AD LDS installation will simply copy the necessary program files and DLLs to the machine in question without creating an AD LDS instance or performing any other configuration steps. This can be useful if you want to include AD LDS as part of a base image that you deploy to your application developers, while allowing them to create their own instances and configuration sets as they see fit.

If the installation process encounters any errors, these will be logged in the *%windir%\Debug\adamsetup.log* file.

See Also

Recipe 18.2; Recipe 18.3

18.2. Creating a New AD LDS Instance

Problem

You want to create a new AD LDS instance.

Solution

Using a graphical user interface

1. From Administrative Tools, launch the Active Directory Lightweight Directory Services Setup Wizard and then click Next.

2. Select the radio button next to "A unique instance" and click Next.

3. Enter the name of the instance and click Next.

4. Enter the LDAP and SSL port numbers that will be used to access this instance; these default to 50000 and 50001 on a domain controller or any computer that is already listening on the default LDAP port. Otherwise, the LDAP and SSL ports that AD LDS chooses during the installation will be 389 and 636.

   If you've already installed an AD LDS instance on ports 50000 and 50001, the AD LDS installer will choose the next two ports available; the second AD LDS instance would choose ports 50002 and 50003, then 50004 and 50005, and so on.

5. Click Next to continue.

6. Specify whether you want to create an Application Directory partition for this instance. You can use any partition name that isn't already being used, such as cn=In tranetApplication,dc=adatum,dc=com. Click Next to continue.

7. Specify the directory that will house the instance data as well as its data recovery files. These will both default to *c:\Program Files\Microsoft ADAM\<instance name>\data*. Click Next.

8. On the Service Account Selection screen, configure the account under whose security context this instance will run. By default, `Network Service Account` is selected, or you can click the radio button next to "This account" and specify a different account.

9. On the AD LDS administrator's screen, specify the user or group account that will have administrative rights to this AD LDS instance. This defaults to the currently logged-on user, or you can click the radio button next to "This account" and specify a different user or group. Click Next.

10. Specify whether you want to import additional LDIF files into this instance. See Recipe 18.7 for more information.

11. Click Next twice and then click Finish to create the new instance.

Using a command-line interface

Create an answer file similar to the one listed here. Save it as *adlds_install.txt*:

```
[ADAMInstall]

  Install a unique AD LDS instance
InstallType=Unique

  Specify the name of the new instance
InstanceName=IntranetApplication

  Specify the ports to be used by LDAP.
LocalLDAPPortToListenOn=50000
LocalSSLPortToListenOn=50001

  Create a new application partition
NewApplicationPartitionToCreate="cn=IntranetApplication,dc=adatum,dc=com"

  The following line specifies the directory to use for ADAM data files.
DataFilesPath=C:\Program Files\Microsoft ADAM\IntranetApplication\data
  The following line specifies the directory to use for ADAM log files.
LogFilesPath=C:\ADAM Log Files\IntranetApplication\logs

  The following line specifies the .ldf files to import into the ADAM schema.
ImportLDIFFiles="ms-inetorgperson.ldf" "ms-user.ldf"
```

Then enter the following command at the Run line or from the Windows command prompt:

```
> adaminstall.exe /answer:<driveletter>:\<pathname>\<answerfile.txt>
```

The default location of *adaminstall.exe* is *<driveletter>:\Windows \ADAM*. You must run this command from this location in the command prompt.

Discussion

An AD LDS *instance* refers to a single installation of AD LDS on a particular server or workstation. A single Windows computer can host multiple instances of AD LDS simultaneously; they are all independently managed and use different LDAP and LDAPS ports to communicate. Just as you can have multiple web servers operating on the same computer, with one using TCP port 80 and one using TCP port 8081, you can also have multiple AD LDS instances running simultaneously on different ports.

When you create an AD LDS instance, you also have the option to create an application directory partition to associate with the instance. An AD LDS instance can have zero, one, or multiple application partitions associated with it that will be used to store application data such as security principals as well as user and group information.

See Also

Recipe 18.7; MSDN: Binding to an Instance [ADAM]; "Create a New AD LDS Instance" (*http://bit.ly/13YZRgY*); *Active Directory*, Fifth Edition, by Brian Desmond et al. (O'Reilly)

18.3. Creating a New Replica of an AD LDS Configuration Set

Problem

You want to create a new replica of an existing AD LDS configuration set.

Solution

Using a graphical user interface

1. From Administrative Tools, launch the Active Directory Lightweight Directory Services Setup and then click Next.
2. Select the radio button next to "A replica of an existing instance" and click Next.
3. Enter the name of the instance that you want to create and click Next.
4. Enter the LDAP and SSL port numbers that will be used to access this instance; these default to 50000 and 50001 on a domain controller or any computer that is

already listening on the default LDAP port. Otherwise, the LDAP and SSL ports that AD LDS chooses during the installation will be 389 and 636.

 If you've already installed an ADAM instance on ports 50000 and 50001, the ADAM installer will choose the next two ports available; the second ADAM instance would choose ports 50002 and 50003, then 50004 and 50005, and so on.

5. On the Join a Configuration Set screen, enter the name of a server hosting an existing replica of this instance, and the port number used to connect to it. Click Next to continue.

6. On the Administrative Credentials for the Configuration Set screen, specify a user or group account that has administrative rights to this AD LDS instance. This defaults to the currently logged-on user, or you can click the radio button next to "This account" and specify a different user or group. Click Next.

7. On the Copy Application Partitions screen, select the application directory partitions that you would like to replicate to the local server. Use the Add, Remove, Select All, and Remove All buttons to select the appropriate partitions. Click Next to continue.

8. Specify the directory that will house the instance data as well as its data recovery files. These will both default to *c:\Program Files\Microsoft ADAM\<instance name>\data*. Click Next.

9. On the Service Account Selection screen, configure the account under whose security context this instance will run. By default, `Network Service Account` is selected, or you can click the radio button next to "This account" and specify a different account.

10. On the AD LDS Administrators screen, specify the user or group account that will have administrative rights to this instance. This defaults to the currently logged-on user, or you can click the radio button next to "This account" and specify a different user or group. Click Next.

11. Click Next and then Finish to create the new AD LDS replica.

Using a command-line interface on all versions

Create an answer file similar to the one listed here. Save it as *new_replica_install.txt*.

```
[ADAMInstall]

[ADAMInstall]
 Install a replica of an existing AD LDS instance.
InstallType=Replica
```

```
  Specify the name of the new replica.
InstanceName=IntranetApplication
  Specify the ports used for LDAP and SSL.
LocalLDAPPortToListenOn=50000
LocalSSLPortToListenOn=50001
  The following line specifies the directory to use for
  ADAM data files.
DataFilesPath=C:\Program Files\Microsoft ADAM\IntranetApplication\data
  The following line specifies the directory to use for ADAM log files.
LogFilesPath=C:\ADAM Log Files\IntranetApplication\logs
  Specify the name of the a computer hosting an existing replica
SourceServer=servername
SourceLDAPPort=389
```

Then enter the following command at the Run line or from the Windows command prompt:

```
> adaminstall.exe /answer:<driveletter>:\<pathname>\<answerfile.txt>
```

 The default location of *adaminstall.exe* is *<driveletter>:\Windows \ADAM*. You must run this command from this location in the command prompt.

Discussion

Similar to Active Directory itself, AD LDS use *multimaster replication* that allows multiple computers to host, read, and make updates to one or more *configuration sets*. An AD LDS *replica* is a computer that is hosting one instance of a particular configuration set. Unlike Active Directory, you can host replica instances on computers that run any version of Windows since Windows XP (including client operating systems and server operating systems). You are not restricted to replicating data to *all* of your AD LDS servers unnecessarily; this can be quite useful in the case of data that is locally interesting but that doesn't need to be replicated throughout your entire environment.

See Also

Recipe 18.2 for creating a new AD LDS instance; "Create a Replica AD LDS Instance" (*http://bit.ly/16cgTwd*)

18.4. Stopping and Starting an AD LDS Instance

Problem

You want to start or stop an AD LDS instance.

Solution

Using a graphical user interface

1. Open the Services MMC snap-in (*services.msc*).
2. Select the name of the AD LDS instance that you want to manage.
3. Right-click on the instance name and select Start, Stop, Pause, Resume, or Restart, as needed.

Using a command-line interface

To stop an AD LDS instance, enter the following:

```
> net stop <instance_name>
```

To start an AD LDS instance, enter the following:

```
> net start <instance_name>
```

Using PowerShell

```
Start-Service "<AD LDS Instance Name>"
Stop-Service "<AD LDS Instance Name>"
```

Discussion

When you install an AD LDS instance on a computer (regardless of whether it is a new or replica instance), the instance will advertise itself as a typical Windows service. The service name naming convention is ADAM_*<InstanceName>*, where *<InstanceName>* is the name you specified when you installed the instance. The display name of the service will be just the *<InstanceName>*, where *<InstanceName>* is the name you specified when you installed the instance. If you need to modify the display name of the service after you've installed the AD LDS instance, you can use the built-in sc utility as follows:

```
> sc \\<servername> config <servicename> displayname = "<display name>"
```

See Also

Recipe 18.6 for listing the AD LDS instances installed on a computer; "Start, Stop, or Restart an AD LDS Instance" (*http://bit.ly/15sfUs3*)

18.5. Changing the Ports Used by an AD LDS Instance

Problem

You want to change the LDAP or LDAP over SSL ports that are being used by a particular AD LDS instance.

Solution

```
> dsdbutil
    > activate instance <instancename>
    > LDAP port <port>
    > SSL port <port>
> quit
```

Discussion

If you need to change the LDAP and/or LDAP over SSL port that an instance is using to communicate, you must first stop the instance using one of the methods specified in Recipe 18.4. Once the instance has stopped, use *dsdbutil* as shown in this recipe's solution.

See Also

Recipe 18.4 for more on starting and stopping AD LDS instances; "Modify the Communication Ports Used by an AD LDS Instance" (*http://bit.ly/11OmmU6*)

18.6. Listing the AD LDS Instances Installed on a Computer

Problem

You want to list all of the AD LDS instances installed on a computer.

Solution

Using a command-line interface

To list all AD LDS instances installed on a computer, enter the following:

```
> dsdbutil
```

From the dsbutil: prompt, enter the following:

```
> list instances
```

Using PowerShell

The following command will list all AD LDS instances whose name begins with "ADAM_" on the local computer:

```
Get-Service -Include "ADAM_*"
```

Discussion

As we discussed in Recipe 18.4, a single computer can host multiple AD LDS instances running on different ports, each of which will advertise itself as a typical Windows service. These services will have a service name naming convention of ADAM_*<Instan ceName>*, where *<InstanceName>* is the name that you specified when you installed the instance. The name of the service will remain the same even if you change the display name or description of the service at a later time, which can make the *services.msc* snap-in a less-than-desirable option for stopping and starting AD LDS instances if you make a habit of renaming them. By querying for service names that include the string "ADAM" using something like '%ADAM_%' in the WQL query, you can return the AD LDS instances that are installed on a local or remote computer. The method discussed in this recipe will not help you, however, if someone has modified the Registry key containing the name of the AD LDS instance. Locating AD LDS services can be a difficult task if someone in your organization is trying to hide their AD LDS instance(s). One possible solution, if you are having difficulty with this type of information gathering, would be to perform a port scan on one or more target computers; once you've obtained a list of listening ports, you can connect to each one in turn and look for an LDAP response.

In Windows Server 2008 and later, the "ADAM_" prefix was dropped from the service display name, which makes the dsbutil option the most appropriate option for listing AD LDS instances on a Windows Server 2008 instance.

See Also

Recipe 18.4; MSDN: Querying with WQL [WMI]; MSDN: WQL Operators [WMI]; "List the AD LDS Instances Installed on a Computer" (*http://bit.ly/10hEqcw*)

18.7. Extending the AD LDS Schema

Problem

You want to extend the AD LDS Schema with new classes or attributes.

Solution

Using a command-line interface

To extend the AD LDS Schema from the command line, you'll need to create an LDIF file containing the necessary schema extensions and then import it using the LDIFDE command, or use a tool like AdMod to perform the changes. AD LDS comes with a number of such LDIF files preinstalled that you can import during the AD LDS installation process. If you did not import these files during installation, you can do so after the fact using the following syntax:

```
> ldifde -i -f <driveletter>:\<pathname>\<Name of LDIF (.ldf) file>↵
  -s <servername>:<portnumber> -k -j . -c "<Schema DN>" #schemaNamingContext
```

Discussion

The schema that you receive when you install AD LDS contains a subset of the classes and attributes that exist in the Active Directory Schema. You have the same ability to extend the schema in AD LDS as you do in AD, which means that you can expand and modify the schema to be the same as the AD Schema, or to match any changes made by your third-party or home-grown applications. Because of this, AD LDS is a great place to test potential schema modifications that you want to make in Active Directory. Because the schema extension process works the same in both AD and AD LDS, and because you can easily install, uninstall, and reinstall AD LDS instances, you can use AD LDS to quickly test new extensions, tweaking the definitions until you get exactly what you want.

Every instance of AD LDS will have at least two partitions: the Configuration partition and the Schema partition; you can create additional application partitions during or after installation, as described in *Active Directory*, Fifth Edition, by Brian Desmond et al. (O'Reilly). Similar to the Active Directory Schema NC, the AD LDS Schema partition contains definitions of classes and attributes that can be used to create objects within a particular AD LDS instance. An AD LDS Schema is unique to an individual AD LDS instance or configuration set; changes to the schema in one instance or configuration set will not affect the schema in other, separate instances or configuration sets. AD LDS comes with a number of preconfigured LDIF files that you can import to create common object types such as `user`, `contact`, and `inetOrgPerson` objects. You can import these LDIF files during the initial creation of an AD LDS instance as well as after the instance has been created.

Using a command-line interface

When updating the AD LDS Schema, be sure to use the version of *ldifde* that came with AD LDS rather than any earlier versions of the utility.

See Also

Recipe 18.2; MSDN: Adding User Classes [ADAM]; MSDN: Adding Contact Classes [ADAM]; MSDN: Extending the Active Directory Application Mode Schema [ADAM]; "Create an Application Directory Partition" (*http://bit.ly/ZLzDPl*); "Delete an Application Directory Partition" (*http://bit.ly/10hEJ7h*); *Active Directory*, Fifth Edition, by Brian Desmond et al. (O'Reilly)

18.8. Managing AD LDS Application Partitions

Problem

You want to add or remove an application partition.

Solution

Using a graphical user interface

To add an application partition, do the following:

1. From the run prompt, open *ldp.exe*.
2. Click Connection→Connect to connect to the desired instance.
3. Click Connection→Bind to provide credentials to bind to the instance.
4. Click on Browse→Add child.
5. For DN, enter a distinguished name for the application partition.
6. Under "Edit entry", enter `ObjectClass` in the Attribute box and `container` in the Values box and then click Enter.
7. Under "Edit entry", enter `instanceType` for the Attribute and `5` in the Values box, and then click Enter.
8. Click Run.

To remove an application partition, do the following:

1. Open ADSI Edit. If necessary, create and bind to a connection of your AD LDS instance.
2. Browse to the `Partitions` container (`cn=Partitions`). Right-click on the application directory partition that you want to delete and then click Delete.
3. Click Yes to confirm.

Using a command-line interface

Use the following sequence of commands to create an AD LDS application partition:

```
> dsmgmt
    > Partition Management
    > create nc <ApplicationPartitionDN> container <ComputerName>:<PortNumber>
    > quit
> quit
```

Use the following command to delete an application partition:

```
> dsmgmt
    > Partition Management
    > delete nc <ApplicationPartitionDN>
    > quit
> quit
```

Discussion

An AD LDS installation creates up to three partitions by default: Configuration, Schema, and an application. The Configuration and Schema partitions get created automatically during the creation of a new AD LDS instance; you can create application partitions during the initial installation or after the instance has been created. If you're installing a replica of an existing configuration set, the existing Schema and Configuration partitions are automatically replicated to the new instance. The Configuration partition stores information about AD LDS replication and partitions, while the Schema partition contains definitions for the types of objects that you can create within the instance. Note that these partitions correspond quite closely to the Configuration and Schema naming contexts within Active Directory.

When you create a new application directory partition, you need to specify a *distinguished name* for the partition; this name needs to be unique within your environment.

See Also

MSDN: Using Application Directory Partitions [ADAM]; MSDN: Creating an Application Directory Partition [ADAM]; MSDN: Deleting an Application Directory Partition [ADAM]; Chapter 20 of *Active Directory*, Fifth Edition, by Brian Desmond et al. (O'Reilly)

18.9. Managing AD LDS Organizational Units

Problem

You want to create or delete OUs within an AD LDS instance.

Solution

Using a graphical user interface

1. Open ADSI Edit. If necessary, create and bind to a connection of your instance.

2. Right-click on the instance and select New→Object.

3. Under "Select a class", click on `organizationalUnit` and click Next.

4. For the value of the `ou` attribute, type `ADLDSUsers` and click Next.

5. Click Finish.

6. To delete an OU, right-click on the object in question and select Delete.

Using a command-line interface

To create an ADAM OU from the command line, use the following syntax:

```
> admod -h <ComputerName>:<PortNumber> -b <OU DN>↵
  objectClass::organizationalUnit -add
```

To delete an OU, replace the –add switch with –del in the previous statement.

> A useful option in AdFind and AdMod for working with AD LDS is the ability to create environment variables to specify long or often-used switches. In this example, it would be quite useful to define an environment variable of `adam-h` that has a value of `<ComputerName>:<Port Number>` and then that portion of the command can be shortened to `-e adam`. See the AdFind usage screens for more information. If you work with multiple instances, you can specify multiple environment variables, such as `adam1-h`, `adam2-h`, and `adam3-h`, and then specify `-e adam1`, `-e adam2`, or `-e adam3` to access the different instances. You can even specify `adamx-u` and `adamx-up` environment variables to specify alternate credentials to connect to the various instances.

Using PowerShell

To create an organizational unit using Windows PowerShell, use the following syntax:

```
New-ADObject -Name "<OUName>" -Type OrganizationalUnit↵
  -Server "<ComputerName>:<PortNumber>" -Path "<ParentContainerDN>"
```

To remove an organizational unit using Windows PowerShell, use the following syntax:

```
Remove-ADObject "<ObjectDN>" -Server "<ComputerName>:<PortNumber>"↵
  -Confirm:$false
```

Discussion

Creating OUs in AD LDS is identical to creating them within Active Directory. Just like in AD, AD LDS OUs are containers that can contain other objects such as users, groups, contacts, or other OUs. You can also delegate permissions to an OU, allowing a user or group to have rights to the OU itself and to objects within that OU.

Using a command-line interface

A useful feature of AdFind and AdMod is that, if you are working on ADAM or AD on the local machine, you can use a period (.) for the hostname and it will expand that into *localhost* for you.

See Also

Recipe 18.20 for more on managing AD LDS permissions; Chapter 5 for more on managing Active Directory OUs; "Add an Organizational Unit to the Directory" (*http://bit.ly/YqhxSe*)

18.10. Managing AD LDS Users

Problem

You want to create or delete user objects within an AD LDS instance.

Solution

Using a graphical user interface

1. Open ADSI Edit. If necessary, create a connection and bind to the necessary AD LDS instance.
2. Right-click on the container that should house the user and select New→Object.
3. Under "Select a class", click on "user" and click Next.
4. For the value of the cn attribute, type Joe Smith and click Next.
5. Click Finish.

Using a command-line interface

```
> admod -h <ComputerName>:<PortNumber> -b <User DN>objectClass::user -add
```

Using PowerShell

To create an AD LDS user with PowerShell, use the following syntax:

```
New-ADUser -Name "John Doe" -Server "<ComputerName>:<Port Number>"↵
  -Path "<Application/Parent DN>" -AccountPassword (ConvertTo-SecureString↵
  -AsPlainText "<PlainTextPassword>" -Force)
```

To remove an AD LDS user with PowerShell, use the following syntax:

```
Remove-ADUser "<User DN>" -Server "<ComputerName>:<Port Number>" -Confirm:$false
```

Discussion

Creating users in AD LDS is quite similar to creating users in Active Directory. The most significant difference is that AD LDS users do not have the sAMAccountName attribute. You could conceivably define such an attribute within AD LDS and associate it with the user class, but it will not have the same properties that it does in Active Directory, particularly the AD constraint in which sAMAccountName uniqueness is enforced across a domain. AD LDS also would not be able to use a manually created attribute like that for user logons the way that sAMAccountName is used in AD.

 If you create an AD LDS user without creating a password for it, the object will be disabled until you enable it.

See Also

Recipe 18.11 to configure the password for an AD LDS user; MSDN: Managing Users [ADAM]; MSDN: Set or Modify the Password of an ADAM User [ADAM]; "Add an AD LDS User to the Directory" (*http://bit.ly/10eqQkv*)

18.11. Changing the Password for an AD LDS User

Problem

You want to change the password for an AD LDS user.

Solution

Using a graphical user interface

1. Open ADSI Edit. If necessary, create a connection and bind to the necessary AD LDS instance.

---

2. Navigate to the container that houses the user.

3. Right-click the user and click Reset Password.

4. Enter the new password twice and click OK.

Using PowerShell

```
Set-ADAccountPassword "<User DN>" -Server "<ComputerName>:<PortNumber>"↵
 -NewPassword (ConvertTo-SecureString -AsPlainText "<PlainTextPassword>" -Force)
```

Discussion

To create user objects within an AD LDS instance, you first need to import the optional LDIF files that are provided with the AD LDS installer into the AD LDS schema, including *ms-User.ldf, ms-InetOrgPerson.ldf,* and *ms-UserProxy.ldf.* The *ms-user.ldf* file allows you to create Person, organizational-Person, and User objects. Any AD LDS user objects that you create will adhere to whatever local or domain password and account lockout policies are in place on the server that's hosting the instance. You can use the procedures listed here to change the password for an AD LDS user, or to set a password for an AD LDS user that was created without specifying an initial password.

Using a command-line interface

You can also use *ldifde* to set or change an ADAM or AD LDS user's password, but it requires a 128-bit SSL connection with a certificate installed on the computer that's running the instance.

You can also perform this using the -kerbenc switch in admod, as follows:

```
> admod -h . -b cn=jsmith,o=test userpassword::mypasswordQ1 -kerbenc
```

See Also

MSDN: Setting User Passwords [ADAM]; "Modify the Password of an AD LDS User" (*http://bit.ly/106UoVi*)

18.12. Enabling and Disabling an AD LDS User

Problem

You want to enable or disable an AD LDS user object.

Solution

Using a graphical user interface

1. Open ADSI Edit. If necessary, create and bind to a connection of your AD LDS instance.

2. Navigate to the user in question, right-click, and select Properties.

3. Scroll to the msDS-UserAccountDisabled attribute and click Edit.

4. Click True and then click OK.

5. To reenable the AD LDS user account, modify the msDS-UserAccountDisabled attribute to have a value of False.

Using a command-line interface

To disable an AD LDS user from the command line, enter the following syntax:

```
> admod -h <ComputerName>:<PortNumber> -b <User DN>↵
  msDS-UserAccountDisabled::TRUE
```

To enable or reenable a user account, change TRUE to FALSE in the previous command.

> When configuring this attribute, TRUE and FALSE are case-sensitive and must be specified using all uppercase letters.

Using PowerShell

To enable an AD LDS user account, use the following syntax:

```
Set-ADUser <User DN> -Replace @{"msDS-UserAccountDisabled"=$false}↵
  -Server "<ComputerName>:<Port Number>"
```

To disable an AD LDS user account, use the following syntax:

```
Set-ADUser <User DN> -Replace @{"msDS-UserAccountDisabled"=$true}↵
  -Server "<ComputerName>:<Port Number>"
```

Discussion

AD LDS users can be enabled or disabled by modifying the msDS-UserAccountDisabled property. A new user will be enabled by default when you first create it, unless the password you've assigned for it doesn't meet the requirements of the password policy, which is in effect on the machine.

See Also

Recipe 18.11 for more on setting the password of an AD LDS user; MSDN: ms-DS-User-Account-Disabled Attribute [AD Schema]; "Disable or Enable an AD LDS User" (*http://bit.ly/11OnYgM*)

18.13. Creating AD LDS Groups

Problem

You want to create or delete a group object within AD LDS.

Solution

Using a graphical user interface

1. Open ADSI Edit. If necessary, create and bind to a connection of your AD LDS instance.
2. Right-click on the instance and select New→Object.
3. Under "Select a class," click on group and click Next.
4. For the value of the cn attribute, type ADLDSGroup and click Next.
5. For the sAMAccountName attribute, enter ADLDSGroup and then click Next.
6. Click Finish.
7. To delete a group object, right-click on the object in question and select Delete.

Using PowerShell

To create a group object using Windows PowerShell, use the following syntax:

```
New-ADGroup -Name "<Name>" -GroupScope "<Scope>" -Path "<Parent DN>"↵
 -Server "<ComputerName>:<PortNumber>"
```

To remove a group object using Windows PowerShell, use the following syntax:

```
Remove-ADGroup -Identity "<Object DN>" -Server "<ComputerName>:<PortNumber>"↵
 -Confirm:$false
```

Discussion

Group objects in AD LDS are greatly simplified compared to their Active Directory counterparts, since the notion of security and distribution groups as two separate entities does not exist. In addition, all AD LDS groups have the same scope: a group that has been created within an application partition can only be used within that partition, whereas a security principal that's been created in the Configuration NC can be used in all naming contexts in that instance. This means that a group or user that was created in Instance1 cannot be used to assign permissions on objects in Instance2 or be added to a group in Instance2 (unless Instance1 and Instance2 are members of the same configuration set). Windows security principals can be assigned permissions in any application partition. And just like AD LDS user objects, AD LDS group objects do not contain the sAMAccountName attribute.

 When you first install an AD LDS instance, you have three default groups that are installed in the cn=Roles container: *Administrators, Readers*, and *Users*.

See Also

MSDN: Enumerating Users and Groups [ADAM]; MSDN: Creating Groups [ADAM]; "Add an AD LDS Group to the Directory" (*http://bit.ly/10erAWV*); MSDN: Deleting Groups [MSDN]; *Active Directory*, Fifth Edition, by Brian Desmond et al. (O'Reilly)

18.14. Managing AD LDS Group Memberships

Problem

You want to manage the groups that an AD or AD LDS user is a member of.

Solution

Using a graphical user interface

1. Open ADSI Edit. Connect and bind to the instance you want to manage.

2. Navigate to the group in question, right-click, and select Properties.

3. Scroll to the member attribute and click Edit.

4. To add a Windows user to the group, click Add Windows Account and enter the name of the Windows account. To add an AD LDS user, click Add DN and then enter the DN of the user that you want to add. Repeat this to add additional users.

5. To remove members, click on the CN of the object you wish to remove and then click Remove. Repeat this to remove additional users from the group.

Using a command-line interface

To add a Windows user to a group from the command line, enter the following syntax:

```
> admod -h <ComputerName>:<PortNumber> -b <GroupDN> member:+:<UserDN>
```

To add multiple users at one time, change + to ++ in the previous command and separate the User DNs with a semicolon.

To remove a single user, change + to – in the previous command.

To remove multiple users, change + to –– in the previous command and separate the User DNs with a semicolon.

Using PowerShell

To add users to AD LDS groups using PowerShell, use the following syntax:

```
Add-ADGroupMember -Identity "<GroupDN>" -Members "<UserDN>"↵
 -Server "<ComputerName>:<PortNumber>" -Partition "<PartitionDN>"
```

To remove users from AD LDS groups using PowerShell, use the following syntax:

```
Remove-ADGroupMember -Identity "<GroupDN>" -Members "<UserDN>"↵
 -Server "<ComputerName>:<PortNumber>" -Partition "<PartitionDN>"↵
 -Confirm:$false
```

Discussion

AD LDS group objects can contain both AD LDS users and Windows security principals, which allows you to assign permissions to data stored in AD LDS instances using a consistent method. In the case of groups that were created within a specific application partition, they can only be assigned permissions within that partition; groups that were created within the Configuration partition can be assigned permissions to objects in any partition within the instance.

Using a command-line interface

To insert a Windows principal into an ADAM/AD LDS group, you need to know either the ForeignSecurityPrincipal or the userProxy object that the Windows user is tied to within the instance; otherwise, you need to add the user by its DN as done here.

See Also

MSDN: Adding a User to a Group [ADAM]; MSDN: Removing Members from Groups [ADAM]; "Add or Remove Members to or from an AD LDS Group" (*http://bit.ly/ 13Z3jIA*)

18.15. Viewing and Modifying AD LDS Object Attributes

Problem

You want to view the attributes of an object within an AD LDS instance.

Solution

Using a graphical user interface

1. Open ADSI Edit. If necessary, connect and bind to a connection of your AD LDS instance.

2. Navigate to the object in question, right-click, and select Properties. To view only the mandatory attributes for an object, click Filter and then remove the checkmark next to Optional. To view only the optional attributes for an object, place a checkmark next to Optional and remove the checkmark next to Mandatory.

3. Scroll through the object's properties. To modify a particular property, select the property and select Edit.

4. To insert a value into a single-valued attribute, enter the value and click OK. To remove a value from a single-valued attribute, click Clear.

5. To insert one or more values into a multivalued attribute, enter each value and click Add. To remove one or more values from a multivalued attribute, select the value and click Remove.

Using a command-line interface

To view the attributes of an object, enter the following:

```
> adfind -h <ComputerName>:<PortNumber> -b <ObjectDN> -s base
```

 To restrict the AdFind output to only a few attributes, specify the name of each attribute you want to view after the ObjectDN; to view multiple attributes, separate each one with spaces in between. You can also use the -excl switch to display all but one or two attributes.

To insert a value into a single-valued attribute, enter the following syntax:

```
> admod -h <ComputerName>:<PortNumber> -b <ObjectDN> <AttributeName>::<Value>
```

To insert multiple values into a multivalued attribute, change *<AttributeName>::* to "*<AttributeName>:++:<Value>;<Value>*" in the previous command.

To clear an attribute's value (whether a single- or a multivalued attribute), enter the following:

```
> admod -h <ComputerName>:<PortNumber> -b <ObjectDN> <AttributeName>:-
```

To remove a single value from a multivalued attribute, change - to - - in the previous command and then add the value that you want to remove.

Using PowerShell

To view an AD LDS object's properties using Windows PowerShell, use the following syntax:

```
Get-ADObject -Identity "<Object DN>" -Server "<ComputerName>:<Port Number>"↵
  -Properties *
```

To modify an AD LDS object's properties using Windows PowerShell, use the following syntax:

```
Set-ADObject -Identity "<Object DN>" -Server "<ComputerName>:<Port Number>"↵
  -Add @{"<Attribute"="<Value>"}
```

Discussion

Just like in Active Directory, each AD LDS instance possesses a schema that defines what types of objects you can create and what sorts of attributes those objects possess. One of the major advantages of working with AD LDS is that you can make changes to the schema of an AD LDS instance without affecting the AD schema, thus allowing for more flexible application development that doesn't run the risk of making permanent or far-reaching changes to an entire Active Directory forest. Similar to AD, object classes can have both *mandatory* and *optional* attributes that you can view.

See Also

MSDN: Active Directory Application Mode Schema [ADAM]; MSDN: Extending the Active Directory Application Mode Schema [ADAM]

18.16. Importing Data into an AD LDS Instance

Problem

You want to perform a bulk import of object data into an AD LDS instance.

Solution

Using a command-line interface

To import objects using the *ldifde* utility, you must first create an LDIF file with the objects to add, modify, or delete. Here is an example LDIF file that adds three users to an AD LDS application partition:

```
dn: cn=Joe Smith,cn=users,ou=AdamUsers,o=adatum,c=us
changetype: add
objectClass: user
cn: Joe Smith
name: Joe Smith

dn: cn=Richard Mahler,cn=users,ou=AdamUsers,o=adatum,c=us
changetype: add
objectClass: user
cn: Richard Mahler
name: Richard Mahler

dn: cn=Doug Martin,cn=users,ou= AdamUsers,o=adatum,c=us
changetype: add
objectClass: user
cn: Doug Martin
name: Doug Martin
```

Once you've created the LDIF file, you just need to run *ldifde* to import the new objects:

```
> ldifde -i -f c:\import.ldf -s <servername>:<portnumber> -k
```

 Be sure to use the most current version of *ldifde* available.

Discussion

For more information on the LDIF format, check RFC 2849.

Using a command-line interface

To import with *ldifde*, simply specify the -i switch to turn on import mode and -f <filename> for the file. It can also be beneficial to use the -v switch to turn on verbose mode to get more information in case of errors. The -j switch can be used to specify the path of the logfile location.

See Also

Recipe 4.29 for information on importing data using LDIF files; RFC 2849 (The LDAP Data Interchange Format [LDIF]—Technical Specification); "Import or Export Directory Objects Using Ldifde" (*http://bit.ly/16O8oaL*)

18.17. Configuring Intra-Site Replication

Problem

You want to create a replication schedule for an AD LDS application partition that is hosted on multiple computers within a single site.

Solution

Using a graphical user interface

1. Open Active Directory Sites and Services (*dssite.msc*). If necessary, connect and bind to a connection of your AD LDS instance.

    In order to use the AD Sites and Services MMC snap-in to manage AD LDS replication, you must use the *MS-ADLDS-DisplaySpecifiers.LDF* file to extend the schema of the configuration set that you are managing.

2. Navigate to the `Sites` container and click the name of the site you need to modify.

3. Right-click `cn=NTDS Site Settings` and then click Properties.

4. Click Change Schedule. Select the block of time that should be available for replication. For every available block of time, you can configure the replication frequency to None, Once per Hour, Twice per Hour, or Four Times per Hour. Click OK when you're finished.

Discussion

Like Active Directory, AD LDS uses multimaster replication to copy information between replicas of each member of a configuration set. By default, all AD LDS instances that you create will be placed within a single site, `Default-First-Site-Name`. Similar to AD, AD LDS's intra-site replication takes place through *update notifications*, where replication partners are notified as changes occur.

See Also

MSDN: Active Directory Application Mode Schema [ADAM]; MSDN: Using Application Directory Partitions [ADAM]; "Configure Replication Frequency Within a Site" (*http://bit.ly/ZLBbsL*)

18.18. Forcing AD LDS Replication

Problem

You want to force immediate replication of an AD LDS application partition.

Solution

Using a graphical user interface

1. Open Active Directory Sites and Services (*dssite.msc*). If necessary, connect and bind to a connection of your AD LDS instance.

2. Navigate to the Site container and then expand the Servers container. Expand the server name and click NTDS Settings.

3. Right-click the connection and click Replicate Now. Click OK.

Using a command-line interface

```
> repadmin /syncall <servername>:<port> <AppPartitionDN>
```

Discussion

The *repadmin* command-line tool that comes with both AD and AD LDS is primarily used to display and manage the replication topology of multiple directory servers. But *repadmin* can do much more, such as allowing you to view object metadata, update Service Principal Names (SPNs), and display information on trust relationships. You can see all of the basic options that are available by typing repadmin /? at a command prompt. Once you've familiarized yourself with these switches, you can then start learning about the more advanced features available by typing repadmin /experthelp. *repadmin* is one of those indispensable tools for an AD or AD LDS administrator; it's well worth the time to learn its ins and outs to help you monitor and troubleshoot your network.

See Also

MS KB 229896 (Using Repadmin.exe to Troubleshoot Active Directory Replication); MS KB 905739 (TechNet Support WebCast: Troubleshooting Active Directory replication using the Repadmin tool)

18.19. Managing AD LDS Replication Authentication

Problem

You want to manage the security of AD LDS replication.

Solution

Using a graphical user interface

1. Open ADSI Edit. Connect and bind to the `Configuration` container of the AD LDS instance that you wish to manage.
2. Double-click on `Configuration [<ComputerName>:<PortNumber>]`.
3. Right-click on `cn=Configuration,cn=<GUID>` and click Properties.
4. Scroll to `msDS-ReplAuthenticationMode`. Double-click on the attribute and enter one of the following values:

   2
   > Mutual authentication with Kerberos

   1
   > Negotiated authentication

   0
   > Negotiated pass-through authentication

Using a command-line interface

```
> admod -h <ComputerName>:<PortNumber> -b <ConfigDN>↵
  msDS-ReplAuthenticationMode::<AuthenticationMode>
```

Using PowerShell

```
Set-ADObject -Identity "<ConfiguratoinDN>" -Partition "<PartitionDN>"↵
 -Replace @{"msDS-ReplAuthenticationMode"="<AuthenticationMode>"}↵
 -Server "<ComputerName>:<Port Number>"
```

Discussion

To ensure replication security, AD LDS will authenticate replication partners within a configuration set before replication begins. The method used for replication authentication will depend on the value of the `msDS-ReplAuthenticationMode` attribute on the configuration directory partition. After replication partners have successfully authenticated, all replication traffic between the two partners is encrypted. AD LDS uses Security Support Provider Interface (SSPI) to establish the appropriate authentication security level between replication partners, and replication authentication always occurs over a secure channel.

Table 18-1 lists the security levels for replication authentication in Windows Server 2008, Windows Server 2008 R2, and Windows Server 2012. The default replication security level for a new, unique AD LDS instance is 1, unless a local workstation user account is specified as the AD LDS service account, in which case the replication security level is set to 0.

Table 18-1. Description of the msDS-ReplAuthenticationMode values

Value	Description
0— Negotiated pass-through	All AD LDS instances in the configuration set use an identical account name and password as the AD LDS service account. Using this replication authentication value, a configuration set can include computers that are joined to one or more workgroups and/or computers that are joined to one or more untrusted domains or forests. This is the default value if a local user account is specified as the AD LDS service account for the configuration set.
1— Negotiated	Kerberos authentication (using SPNs) is attempted first. If Kerberos fails, NTLM authentication is attempted. If NTLM fails, the AD LDS instances will not replicate. This is the default value for a configuration set, unless it is configured with a local account as the AD LDS service account.
2—Mutual authentication with Kerberos	Kerberos authentication, using service principal names (SPNs), is required. If Kerberos authentication fails, the AD LDS instances will not replicate. If this value is selected, the configuration set must be fully contained within an AD DS domain or within computers belonging to trusted domains or forests.

See Also

MSDN: Active Directory Application Mode Schema [ADAM]; MSDN: Using Application Directory Partitions [ADAM]; "Modify the Replication Security Level of a Configuration Set" (*http://bit.ly/13Z3Bzc*)

18.20. Managing AD LDS Permissions

Problem

You want to manage permissions within an AD LDS instance.

Solution

Using a graphical user interface

1. Launch *LDP.exe*. Connect and bind to the object or container that you wish to modify.
2. Right-click on the object or container and select Advanced→Security Descriptor.
3. To display and edit auditing information in addition to the Discretionary Access Lists (DACLs) associated with the object, place a checkmark next to SACL. Click OK.
4. To delete an Access Control Entry (ACE), highlight the entry and click Delete.
5. To add an entry, click Add.
6. In the Trustee text box, enter the name of the user or group object that you wish to apply permissions to. In the ACE mask section, select whether you are creating *Allow ACE* or *Deny ACE*.
7. In the Access mask section, place checkmarks next to the permissions that you are allowing or denying.
8. Click OK when you are finished.

Using a command-line interface

To view the effective permissions on an AD LDS object, use the following syntax:

```
> dsacls \\<servername>:<port>\<ObjectDN>
```

To grant permissions on an AD LDS object, use the following:

```
> dsacls "\\<servername>:<port>\<ObjectDN>"↵
  /G <User or Group ReceivingPermissions>:<Permission Statement>
```

To deny permissions on an AD LDS object, use the following:

```
> dsacls "\\<servername>:<port>\<ObjectDN>"↵
  /D <User or Group ReceivingPermissions>:<Permission Statement>
```

Discussion

The LDP utility provides you the ability to modify both DACL and SACL entries at an extremely granular level. You also have the familiar *dsacls* utility that will allow you to delegate permissions from the command line. When delegating permissions, you must first determine whether you are delegating permission over an entire container and all objects contained therein, or whether you are only going to delegate control over specific child objects. (For example, you can delegate control over all AD LDS user objects within an OU.) Once you've made this determination, you'll then designate the specific permissions that you're delegating; you can delegate anything from full control of the entire object down to granting read permissions on a single attribute.

Using a command-line interface

dsacls requires a specific syntax for the permission statement used to grant or deny permissions, formatted in this manner:

```
[PermissionBits];[{Object|Property}];[InheritedObjectType]
```

[PermissionBits] here refers to any of the values listed in Table 18-2; you can specify one or more together with no spaces between them.

Table 18-2. Description of the PermissionBits values

Value	Description
GR	Generic read
GE	Generic execute
GW	Generic write
GA	Generic all (FULL CONTROL)
SD	Delete
DT	Delete an object and all its child objects (DELETE TREE)
RC	Read security information
WD	Change security information
WO	Change owner information
LC	List child objects
CC	Create child objects
DC	Delete child objects
WS	Write to self
RP	Read property
WP	Write property
CA	Control access
LO	List object access

The [Object | Property] option allows you to delegate permissions for an entire object, or for only specific properties of that object. For example, you can delegate the Write Property permission for all properties of an object, or only one or two specific properties.

See Also

"View or Set Permissions on a Directory Object" (*http://bit.ly/17Ibs6e*)

18.21. Enabling Auditing of AD LDS Access

Problem

You want to enable auditing of directory access and modifications. Audit events are logged to the Security event log.

Solution

Using a graphical user interface

1. Open the Group Policy Object (GPO) that is linked to the computer(s) hosting the AD LDS instance that you wish to audit.
2. In the left pane, expand Windows Settings→Security Settings→Local Policies and click on Audit Policy.
3. In the right pane, double-click "Audit directory service access".
4. Check the box beside Success and/or Failure.
5. Click OK.

Using a command-line interface

To modify the audit policy, use the following syntax:

```
auditpol /set /category:"<category>" /success:enable /failure:enable
```

To view the list of categories, use the following syntax:

```
auditpol /list /category
```

Discussion

Since Windows Server 2008, additional auditing functionality is enabled, which allows auditing of Directory Services events, including capturing `"before"` and `"after"` values on changes and deletions to Active Directory objects. You can enable this functionality using the *auditpol.exe* tool discussed earlier, using syntax similar to the following:

```
auditpol /set /subcategory:"directory service changes"
```

Here is a sample event that was logged after the *Administrator* account created a user object called JSmith in the Sales OU:

```
Log Name:      Security
Source:        Microsoft Windows security auditing
Date:          11/13/2012 3:50:58 AM
Event ID:      5137
Task Category: Directory Service Changes
```

```
Level:         Information
Keywords:      Audit Success
User:          N/A
Computer:      dc01.adatum.us
Description:
A user account was created.

Subject:
    Security ID:        ADATUM\Administrator
    Account Name:       Administrator
    Account Domain:     ADATUM
    Logon ID:           0xb3405

Directory Service:
    Name:       ADAM_Partition1
    Type:       Active Directory Lightweight Directory Services
Object:
    DN:    cn=JSmith,cn=Container1,cn={61E04C68-5582-494D-9F0A-1E0B970Db2D3}
    GUID:       {7c427193-64f6-476f-9cf4-748d850f02f8}
    Class:      User
Operation:
    Correlation ID:         {dbae9153-eae6-49cd-b641-fbef24d19cee}
    Application Correlation ID:    -
```

 In an Active Directory environment it can also be useful to enable Audit Account Management in the GPO that's linked to the Domain Controllers OU. This provides additional information about account management operations—for example, finding what account deleted a certain object.

## CHAPTER 19

Active Directory Federation Services

19.0. Introduction

Active Directory Federation Services (AD FS) was introduced in Windows Server 2003 R2 as version 1.0, updated for Windows Server 2008 (version 1.1), released as a stand-alone product in version 2.0, and then updated for Windows Server 2012 (2.1). It is used to allow single sign-on (SSO) capabilities to web applications hosted by multiple organizations without the need to configure an Active Directory trust relationship between them. This task is performed by using AD FS servers to separate the process of *authentication* (proving who a user *is*) from that of *authorization* (specifying what a user can *do*). AD FS allows this separation by configuring *account partners* to authenticate users and groups, and then providing *claims* to *resource partners* that control the actual access to resources.

This relationship between account partners and resource partners is called a *federated trust*. This verbiage can sometimes lead to confusion, since it seems to imply that AD FS requires an Active Directory trust relationship to exist between account and resource partners. In this case, the word *trust* merely refers to a business agreement between two organizations that have agreed to this type of distributed authentication and authorization arrangement. A federated trust refers to a scenario in which the AD FS Federation Service has been properly configured by both the organization that performs user authentication and the organization that controls access to web resources.

There are two AD FS 2.0 designs. One design, the *Web SSO* design, is used for authenticating access to web applications in a perimeter network environment. This design is typically used when there isn't a partner organization and all users are external. The other common AD FS design, *Federated Web SSO*, is commonly used by two separate organizations (most notably in a B2B relationship) for whom an Active Directory forest trust would create too much access for users on both sides of the equation or where Selective Authentication would require too much ongoing maintenance.

19.1. Installing AD FS Prerequisites

Problem

You want to preinstall the necessary prerequisites before installing AD FS. The GUI steps are specific to Windows Server 2012 but also very close to what is found in Windows Server 2008 and Windows Server 2008 R2.

Solution

Using a graphical user interface

To install IIS on a server, follow these steps:

1. Launch Server Manager.
2. Click Manage and then click Add Roles and Features.
3. Click Next twice.
4. Place a checkmark next to Web Server (IIS). If prompted, click Add Required Features. Click Next twice.
5. Place a checkmark next to ASP.NET and Windows Authentication. If prompted, click Add Required Role Services.
6. Click Next and then click Install.
7. When the installation completes, click Close.

To enable SSL for the Default Web Site, do the following:

1. Open the Internet Information Service (IIS) Manager snap-in (*iis.msc*).
2. Drill down to *<server name>*. In the right-hand pane, double-click on Server Certificates.
3. Click on Create Certificate Request. Enter the identifying information for the certificate request. Click Next.
4. Select the desired Cryptographic Service Provider and Bit length, and then click Next.
5. Specify a name for the Certificate request and then click Next.

Once you have submitted the certificate request to a Certification Authority and have received a *.cer* file in return, use these steps to install the certificate:

1. Navigate to *<server name>* if you have not done so already. Click "Complete certificate request."

2. Browse to the appropriate CER file, and enter the FQDN of the server in the Friendly name field. Click OK.

3. Browse to Sites→Default Web Site. Right-click on Default Web Site and click Edit Bindings.

4. Click Add. In the Type: drop-down box, select *https*. In the IP Address: drop-down box, select the IP address of the server. Confirm that the Port text box reads 443. In the "SSL certificate:" drop-down box, select the SSL certificate that you installed in steps 1 and 2.

5. Click OK and then click Close.

6. In the middle pane, double-click on SSL Settings. On the SSL Settings page, place a checkmark next to Require SSL. In the "client certificates:" radio buttons, select Accept. Click Apply.

Using a command-line interface

To generate a certificate request via the command line, you must first create a *request.inf* file similar to the following:

```
;---------------- request.inf ----------------

[Version]

Signature="$Windows NT$"

[NewRequest]

Subject = "cn=<DC FQDN>" ; replace with the FQDN of the DC
KeySpec = 1
KeyLength = 2048
; Can be 1024, 2048, 4096, 8192, or 16384.
; Larger key sizes are more secure, but have
; a greater impact on performance.
Exportable = TRUE
MachineKeySet = TRUE
SMIME = False
PrivateKeyArchive = FALSE
UserProtected = FALSE
UseExistingKeySet = FALSE
ProviderName = "Microsoft RSA SChannel Cryptographic Provider"
ProviderType = 12
RequestType = PKCS10
```

```
KeyUsage = 0xa0

[EnhancedKeyUsageExtension]

OID=1.3.6.1.5.5.7.3.1 ; this is for Server Authentication

;------------------------------------------------
```

Once you have created the appropriate *request.inf* file, issue the following *certreq.exe* command:

```
> certreq -new request.inf request.req
```

Once you have submitted the certificate request to a Certification Authority and have received a *.cer* file in return, use the following command to install the certificate:

```
> certreq -accept newcert.cer
```

Discussion

You need to install an SSL certificate on the IIS server before configuring AD FS. You can configure a certificate from a commercial CA or one internal to your environment, or else you can install a self-signed certificate if you are operating in a test environment. Self-signed certificates should not be used in a production or public-facing server environment.

Note that the installation of the AD FS Federation Service will automatically install prerequisites. For many administrators, this makes it more efficient. However, some organizations prefer to split up the different phases of the installation due to change control requirements or segmented administration teams controlling different parts of the environment.

See Also

"How to enable LDAP over SSL with a third-party certification authority" (*http://support.microsoft.com/kb/321051*)

19.2. Installing the AD FS Federation Service

Problem

You want to install the AD FS Federation Service on a server.

 Installing the Federation Service presumes that the server in question is joined to an Active Directory domain.

Solution

Using a graphical user interface

1. Launch Server Manager.

2. Click Manage and then click Add Roles and Features.

3. Click Next. Select the server to install the role on and then click Next.

4. Place a checkmark next to Active Directory Federation Services. If prompted, click Add Features. Click Next three times.

5. Ensure that a checkmark is next to Federation Service.

6. Click Next three times and then click Install.

7. When the installation completes, click Close.

Using PowerShell

```
Install-WindowsFeature ADFS-Federation -IncludeAllSubFeature↵
    -IncludeManagementTools
```

Discussion

The functionality of the AD FS Federation Service in Windows Server 2012 is fundamentally identical to AD FS 2.0 running on a 2008 R2 server. However, note that Windows Server 2008 R2 comes with AD FS version 1.1 built in. Version 2.0 has to be downloaded and installed. Since AD FS 2.1 comes as a role in Windows Server 2012, you get an enhanced installation experience (validation checks during installation and dependency checks during installation).

See Also

Recipe 19.1; "Best Practices for Secure Planning and Deployment of AD FS 2.0" (*http://bit.ly/15kZS3w*)

19.3. Configuring an LDAP Attribute Store

Problem

You want to configure AD FS to use an instance of LDAP for attributes.

Solution

Using a graphical user interface

1. Open the AD FS MMC snap-in (*adfs.msc*).
2. From the Actions menu, select Add Attribute Store.
3. Enter a name in the Display name field.
4. Select LDAP as the Attribute store type.
5. In "Connection string", enter the string to be used for the connection for the attribute store; for example, dc=adatum,dc=com.
6. Click OK to add the LDAP attribute store.

Using Windows PowerShell

```
Add-ADFSAttributeStore -Name "<Name>" -StoreType LDAP↵
  -Configuration @{"Name"="<Description>"; "Connection"="<AD LDS DN>"}
```

Discussion

LDAP attribute stores are configured quite similarly to Active Directory stores; you can configure multiple LDAP attribute stores on a given federation server. You can also modify the default timeout period for searches; the default is five seconds. In addition, you can enable SSL/TLS to encrypt the connection between the federation server and the web server hosting the application.

See Also

Chapter 18 for more on configuring LDAP instances and application partitions

19.4. Configuring a Microsoft SQL Server Attribute Store

Problem

You want to configure AD FS to use a Microsoft SQL Server attribute store for attributes.

Solution

Using a graphical user interface

1. Open the AD FS MMC snap-in (*adfs.msc*).
2. From the Actions menu, select Add Attribute Store.

3. Enter a name in the Display name field.

4. Select SQL as the Attribute store type.

5. In "Connection string", enter the string to be used for the connection to the attribute store; for example, `Server=adatum-sql;Database=userDatabase;Integrated Se curity=True`

6. Click OK to add the SQL attribute store.

Using Windows PowerShell

```
Add-ADFSAttributeStore -Name "<Name>" -StoreType SQL↵
 -Configuration @{"Name"="<Description>"; "Connection"=↵
"<SQL Connection String>"}
```

Discussion

SQL attribute stores allow you to use a SQL database to store attributes.

19.5. Creating Claim Descriptions

Problem

You want to add a new type of claim that can be used by claims-aware applications.

Solution

Using a graphical user interface

1. Open the AD FS MMC snap-in (*adfs.msc*). Navigate to AD FS→Service→Claim Descriptions.

2. From the Actions menu, click Add Claim Description.

3. Enter a name for the claim description and then enter a claim identifier.

4. Add a description and then select the publishing options.

5. Click OK to create the claim description.

Using Windows PowerShell

```
Add-ADFSClaimDescription -Name "<Name>" -ClaimType "<ClaimURI>" -IsAccepted↵
 $True -IsOffered $True
```

Discussion

AD FS *claims* are the foundation of authentication and authorization in federated applications. Administrators in account partners will configure organizational claims that will be presented by users when accessing applications that are hosted by resource partners.

See Also

Recipe 19.6 for more on configuring an account partner; Recipe 19.7 for more on configuring a claims provider trust

19.6. Creating a Relying Party Trust

Problem

You want to configure a relying party trust to allow your organization's users to access applications that are managed by an AD FS resource partner.

Solution

Using a graphical user interface

1. Open the AD FS MMC snap-in (*adfs.msc*).
2. From the Actions menu, click Add Relying Party Trust.
3. Click Start to begin the Add Relying Party Trust Wizard.
4. To create a relying party manually, click "Enter data about the relying party manually" and then click Next.
5. On the Specify Display Name screen, enter the display name and notes of the relying party, and then click Next.
6. On the Choose Profile screen, select the appropriate AD FS profile and then click Next.
7. On the Configure Certificate screen, specify a token encryption certificate that will be used to encrypt outgoing requests and then click Next.
8. On the Configure URL screen, select the appropriate protocols and enter the respective URLs, if necessary.
9. On the Configure Identifiers screen, enter the relying party's trust identifier and then click Add. Click Next to continue.
10. On the Choose Issuance Authorization Rules screen, select the authorization rule for the relying party trust.

11. Click Next and then Close to complete the wizard.

Using Windows PowerShell

```
Add-ADFSRelyingPartyTrust -Name "<Name>" -Identifier "<URI>"↵
  -ProtocolProfile WsFed-SAML -EncryptionCertificate "<CertificatePath>"
```

Discussion

When configuring AD FS, you'll start by configuring one or more relying party trusts to represent the organization that houses user accounts, which requires access to applications hosted by one or more partners. The AD FS Federation Server in the partner's organization will create security tokens or claims that can be processed by the Federation Service and used to make authorization decisions.

 You can think of a relying party trust as being analogous to a trusted domain or forest in an Active Directory trust relationship; however, it is not necessary for an Active Directory trust relationship to be configured for AD FS to function in this manner.

In addition to configuring the relying party trust, you also need to determine which types of claims will be sent by the account partner to the federation server hosted by the partner. You can send any combination of UPN, E-Mail, Common name, Group, or Custom claims. (Claim types are discussed further in Recipe 19.5.)

See Also

Recipe 19.5 for more on creating group or custom claims; Recipe 19.7 for information on configuring a trust partner; Add-ADFSRelyingPartyTrust cmdlet reference (*http://bit.ly/16cly1q*)

19.7. Configuring a Claims Provider Trust

Problem

You want to configure a claims provider trust to allow a partner organization to access a resource in your environment.

Solution

Using a graphical user interface

1. Open the AD FS MMC snap-in (*adfs.msc*).
2. From the Actions menu, click Add Claims Provider Trust.
3. Click Start to begin the wizard.
4. To add a claims provider manually, click "Enter claims provider trust data manually" and then click Next.
5. Enter a display name and notes, and then click Next.
6. Select the appropriate AD FS profile and then click Next.
7. If necessary, select the additional protocols for the claims provider and then click Next.
8. Enter the claims provider trust URI and then click Next.
9. Click Add to specify a token-signing certificate. Browse to the appropriate certificate and click Open. Click Next to continue.
10. Click Next and then Close to complete the wizard.

Using Windows PowerShell

```
Add-ADFSClaimsProviderTrust -Name "<Name>" -MetadataUrl "<URI>"↵
  -ProtocolProfile WsFed-SAML
```

Discussion

A claims provider trust is the necessary second piece of the AD FS puzzle, and is the organization that is hosting the resources that need to be accessed by the account partner. It's important to note that claims provider trusts do not actually authenticate users from the account partner's organization; rather, they simply process the claims that are forwarded to them after the account partner has performed any necessary authentication. This process cuts very much to the heart of AD FS—the resource partner trusts the account partner to perform whatever authentication is needed, after which the claims trust provider performs the authorization portion of the process using the claims that were produced by the account partner.

See Also

Recipe 19.5 for more on configuring a claim; Recipe 19.6 for more on creating a party trust; Add-ADFSClaimsProviderTrust cmdlet reference (*http://bit.ly/10eumLR*)

19.8. Configuring an Alternate UPN Suffix

Problem

You want to modify or add a new UPN suffix for the users in an Active Directory forest.

Solution

Using a graphical user interface

1. Open the Active Directory Domains and Trusts snap-in (*domain.msc*).
2. In the left pane, right-click Active Directory Domains and Trusts and select Properties.
3. Under Alternate UPN suffixes, type the name of the suffix you want to add.
4. Click Add and OK.

Using a command-line interface

```
> admod -config -rb cn=Partitions uPNSuffixes:+:treyresearch.com
```

 The *attributeName* :+: *attributeValue* syntax will add an additional value to an existing list of values in a multivalued attribute. Using *at tributeName::attributeValue* would add the value you specify and remove all other values.

Using PowerShell

```
Set-ADObject "cn=Partitions,cn=Configuration,<ForestRootDN>"↵
 -Add @{"uPNSuffixes"="<Suffix>"}
```

Discussion

The UPN allows users to log on with a friendly name that may or may not correspond to their email address. Also, UPN logons do not require the domain to be known, so it can be abstracted away from the user. You may need to create an additional UPN suffix (e.g., *@adatum.com*) if you want UPNs to map to email addresses when your AD forest is rooted at a different domain name (e.g., *ad.adatum.com*) from the domain name used in email addresses (e.g., *adatum.com*). In the case of AD FS, only one UPN claim can be used for a given application, so it may also be necessary to configure additional UPN suffixes to meet this requirement as well.

Using a command-line interface

Like many command-line recipes in this book, this recipe references the AdMod utility that can be downloaded from joeware (*http://www.joeware.net*).

See Also

"HOW TO: Add UPN Suffixes to a Forest" (*http://support.microsoft.com/kb/243629*)

19.9. Configuring AD FS 2.x and AD FS 1.x Interoperability

Problem

You want to configure AD FS 2.x and AD FS 1.x interoperability for AD FS 1.x security tokens.

Solution

Using a graphical user interface

The first step in configuring AD FS interoperability is to extract the User Principle Name from Active Directory. To create a claim rule, follow these steps:

1. Launch the AD FS management console.
2. Expand AD FS→Trust Relationships→Claims Provider Trusts.
3. Right-click on the Claims Provider Trust you wish to configure and click Edit Claim Rules.
4. On the Acceptance Transform Rules tab, click the Add Rule button.
5. On the Choose Rule Type screen, verify that Send LDAP Attributes as Claims is selected from the drop-down box and then click Next.
6. From the Attribute Store drop-down box, select the appropriate attribute store.
7. From the LDAP Attribute drop-down box, select User-Principal-Name.
8. From the Outgoing Claim Type drop-down box, select UPN.
9. Name the claim rule appropriately and then click Finish.

The second step in configuring AD FS interoperability is to transform the claim to the AD FS 1.x format, Name ID. To transform the claim, follow these steps:

1. Launch the AD FS management console.
2. Expand AD FS→Trust Relationships→Claims Provider Trusts.

3. Right-click on the Claims Provider Trust you wish to configure and click Edit Claim Rules.

4. On the Acceptance Transform Rules tab, click the Add Rule button.

5. On the Choose Rule Type screen, select Transform an Incoming Claim.

6. From the Incoming claim type drop-down box, select UPN.

7. From the Outgoing claim type drop-down box, select Name ID.

8. From the name ID format drop-down box, select UPN.

9. Verify that "Pass through all claim values" is selected.

10. Name the claim rule appropriately and then click Finish.

The third step in configuring AD FS interoperability is to extract the attribute store information as AD FS 1.x claim types. To configure the claim rule, follow these steps:

1. Launch the AD FS management console.

2. Expand AD FS→Trust Relationships→Claims Provider Trusts.

3. Right-click on the Claims Provider Trust you wish to configure and click Edit Claim Rules.

4. On the Acceptance Transform Rules tab, click the Add Rule button.

5. On the Choose Rule Type screen, verify that Send LDAP Attributes as Claims is selected from the drop-down box and then click Next.

6. From the Attribute Store drop-down box, select the appropriate attribute store.

7. From the first LDAP Attribute drop-down box, select User-Principal-Name.

8. From the first Outgoing claim type drop-down box, select AD FS1.x UPN.

9. From the second LDAP Attribute drop-down box, select E-Mail-Addresses.

10. From the second Outgoing Claim Type drop-down box, select AD FS 1.x E-Mail Addresses.

11. Name the claim rule appropriately and then click Finish.

The final step in configuring AD FS interoperability is to pass through the claim types to the Relying Party Trust. Note that this claim rule is created on the Relying Party Trust. To configure the claim rule, follow these steps:

1. Launch the AD FS management console.

2. Expand AD FS→Trust Relationships→Relying Party Trusts.

3. Right-click the relying party trust you wish to configure and click Edit Claim Rules.

4. On the Issuance Transform Rules tab, click Add Rule.

5. From the Claim rule template drop-down box, select Pass Through or Filter an Incoming Claim.

6. From the Incoming claim type drop-down, select AD FS 1.x UPN.

7. Ensure that "Pass through all claim values" is selected.

8. Name the claim rule appropriately and then click Next.

9. Repeat these steps for the AD FS 1.x E-Mail Addresses claim type.

Using Windows PowerShell

To create the Claims Provider Trust rules using PowerShell, first create a text file named *CPTrust.txt* with the following information:

```
@RuleTemplate = "LdapClaims"
@RuleName = "Extract UPN"
c:[Type == "http://schemas.microsoft.com/ws/2008/06/identity/claims/↵
windowsaccountname", Issuer == "AD AUTHORITY"]
 => issue(store = "Active Directory", types =↵
("http://schemas.xmlsoap.org/ws/2005/05/identity/claims/upn"),↵
 query = ";userPrincipalName;{0}", param = c.Value);

@RuleTemplate = "MapClaims"
@RuleName = "Transform UPN to Name ID"
c:[Type == "http://schemas.xmlsoap.org/ws/2005/05/identity/claims/upn"]
 => issue(Type = "http://schemas.xmlsoap.org/ws/2005/05/identity/claims/↵
nameidentifier", Issuer = c.Issuer, OriginalIssuer = c.OriginalIssuer,↵
 Value = c.Value, ValueType = c.ValueType, Properties[↵
"http://schemas.xmlsoap.org/ws/2005/05/identity/claimproperties/format"]↵
 = "http://schemas.xmlsoap.org/claims/UPN");

@RuleTemplate = "LdapClaims"
@RuleName = "Extract AD as 1.x"
c:[Type == "http://schemas.microsoft.com/ws/2008/06/identity/claims/↵
windowsaccountname", Issuer == "AD AUTHORITY"]
 => issue(store = "Active Directory", types = ("http://schemas.xmlsoap.org/↵
claims/UPN", "http://schemas.xmlsoap.org/claims/EmailAddress"),↵
 query = ";userPrincipalName,mail;{0}", param = c.Value);
```

After the text file has been created, append the current acceptance transform rules to the file with the following commands:

```
$CPTrust = Get-ADFSClaimsProviderTrust
Add-Content C:\temp\CPTrust.txt $CPTrust.AcceptanceTransformRules
```

Failure to append the current acceptance transform rules to the file will overwrite all existing transform rules for the party trust.

To set the claims provider trust with the claim rule sets, issue the following command:

```
Set-ADFSClaimsProviderTrust -TargetName "<CPTName>"↵
 -AcceptanceTransformRulesFile "C:\temp\CPTrust.txt"
```

Next, to create the Relying Party Trust rules, create a text file named *RPTrust.txt* with the following content:

```
@RuleTemplate = "PassThroughClaims"
@RuleName = "Pass through UPN"
c:[Type == "http://schemas.xmlsoap.org/claims/UPN"]
 => issue(claim = c);

@RuleTemplate = "PassThroughClaims"
@RuleName = "Pass through email"
c:[Type == "http://schemas.xmlsoap.org/claims/EmailAddress"]
 => issue(claim = c);
```

After the text file has been created, append the current issuance transform rules to the file with the following commands:

```
$RPTrust = Get-ADFSRelyingPartyTrust
Add-Content C:\temp\RPTrust.txt $RPTrust.IssuanceTransformRules
```

 Failure to append the current issuance transform rules to the file will overwrite all existing transform rules for the party trust.

Apply the transform rule set to the relying party trust:

```
Set-ADFSRelyingPartyTrust -TargetName "<RPTName>"↵
 -IssuanceTransformRulesFile "C:\temp\RPTrust.txt"
```

Discussion

For situations that require you to communicate from AD FS 2.x to AD FS 1.x, you must configure claim rules to send claims in a way that AD FS 1.x can comprehend. To do this, create the claim rules as shown in the solution. Default and custom claims can be extracted from attribute stores to send to the AD FS 1.x servers.

See Also

"Planning for Interoperability with AD FS 1.x" (*http://bit.ly/15l26jz*)

19.10. Configuring Logging for AD FS

Problem

You want to configure the logging level captured in the Windows Event Log for AD FS.

Solution

Using Windows PowerShell

```
Set-ADFSProperties -LogLevel Errors,Warnings,Information
```

Discussion

By default, AD FS performs verbose logging of all events related to the AD FS service. To lower the logging level of the AD FS service, you must set the AD FS `LogLevel` properties to the logging levels you wish to capture. Available log levels are `FailureAu dits`, `SuccessAudits`, `Errors`, `Information`, `Warnings`, `Verbose`, and `None`. You can configure multiple logging levels with one command as shown in the solution. Note that you cannot configure the AD FS logging level through the AD FS management console.

See Also

"Configuring Computers for Troubleshooting AD FS 2.0" (*http://bit.ly/10jYtm0*)

## CHAPTER 20

Microsoft Exchange Server 2013

20.0. Introduction

Microsoft Exchange Server is Microsoft's flagship messaging and collaboration server application. Exchange manages email messages through a proprietary MAPI protocol for rich use with Microsoft Outlook clients as well as the Internet standard protocols POP3, IMAP4, and SMTP. It is a scalable enterprise solution from gateway to mailbox with expected functionality including backup and recovery, message hygiene, and mailbox management. Several features that have evolved over the years are still present in the latest version, including Outlook Web App (OWA), Public Folders, cached Exchange mode, and mobile device synchronization with ActiveSync (the primary mechanism for Windows RT devices to communicate with Exchange. Other features have been added or improved significantly for 2013, such as a single unified management console, Data Loss Prevention (DLP), and OWA optimization for smartphones and tablets.

Exchange has a set of APIs that can be used to integrate custom applications or access specific Exchange data. Exchange can be an important component of a business collaboration system. We are not going to cover every single PowerShell cmdlet or all possible recipes for configuring Exchange, but we will introduce a good cross section of common tasks that Exchange implementers or administrators may need to perform their duties.

20.1. Exchange Server and Active Directory

Even with the major changes in Exchange, one of the mainstays over the past few versions is the use of Windows Active Directory as the Directory Services provider. Exchange 2000 Server was one of the first AD-aware applications. Indeed, AD is partly based on the Exchange directory used in Exchange 5.5 and earlier. Installing Exchange requires first extending the AD schema with Exchange-specific attributes. A successful implementation of Microsoft Exchange Server is dependent therefore on a successful implementation of Active Directory. In addition, Exchange routing is now dependent on AD Site topology instead of its own routing engine, as was present in 2003.

This deep integration also means that AD topology design should also consider Exchange messaging requirements. The AD and Exchange relationship also makes an Exchange chapter a suitable addition to this book.

20.2. Exchange Server 2013 Architecture

Microsoft has made significant changes to Exchange Server with Exchange 2013. Some of the architecture for the latest version is different from Exchange 2010 and other earlier versions, and as a result, so are the mechanisms for deploying and administering Exchange. Exchange 2013 requires Windows Server 2008 R2 or Windows Server 2012. Exchange 2013 has reverted some of the modularity found in Exchange 2010 by separating functionality into just two different server roles.

There are two Exchange roles to choose from at installation:

- Client Access Server
- Mailbox Server

Only the selected role(s) are installed. Other installation options include Clustered Mailbox Roles and the Management Tools. The roles can share residence on a single server or be placed on separate servers as part of a deployment strategy.

Exchange Server Tools

Exchange administration is shared between the Exchange Management Shell (EMS) and the Exchange Administration Center (EAC); however, the EAC is built upon the EMS. Every configuration performed in the console has an equivalent command-line entry using the shell.

Exchange Management Shell

As we have seen in the previous chapters, PowerShell revolutionizes the command-line experience in Windows. With Exchange 2013, there are more than 900 cmdlets to assist with Exchange management.

PowerShell uses an XML file as a console definition file to identify snap-ins to be loaded with PowerShell. For the EMS, this file is named *exshell.psc1* and is called with the parameter -PSConsoleFile. The Exchange Management Shell is an extension of PowerShell. The shortcut for the EMS actually uses the following command:

```
C:\WINDOWS\system32\windowspowershell\v1.0\powershell.exe -PSConsoleFile
   "C:\Program Files\Microsoft\Exchange Server\bin\exshell.psc1" -noexit
   -command ".'C:\Program Files\Microsoft\Exchange Server\bin\Exchange.ps1'"
```

Exchange Administration Center

The EAC is a web-based management center that allows you to easily manage multiple Exchange servers. It is a graphical representation of underlying shell commands in the EMS. The EAC replaces the Exchange Management Console that existed in Exchange 2007 and Exchange 2010. The EAC allows you to manage the Exchange Server environment, regardless of whether it is a local on-premises installation, in the cloud, or in a hybrid Exchange deployment scenario.

The EAC can be accessed from a web browser by navigating to **https://<CASServer-Name>/ecp**.

Exchange Scripts Folder

Not to be overlooked in terms of Exchange administration is the *scripts* folder. Installed with Exchange Server, the folder includes several PowerShell scripts that can be used to easily make specific changes or that can be amended to customize components:

```
C:\Program Files\Microsoft\Exchange Server\V15\Scripts\
```

For example, in the *scripts* folder, there are PowerShell scripts to enable anti-malware scanning on a Mailbox server and to export Message Classifications for distribution to Outlook clients. Administrators can also add their own custom Exchange scripts to this folder as it is added to the Windows Path environment variable when Exchange is installed. It is not necessary, therefore, to remember the entire path to the *scripts* folder when executing scripts from the command line.

Third-Party Tools

Sometimes third parties create innovative utilities that can accomplish a task with greater ease than the native tools. There are numerous products, both free and commercially available, that can assist with Exchange management. joe Richards maintains several Active Directory and Exchange utilities through his website (*http://www.joeware.net*). A few tools that we use in this chapter, including ExchMbx, AdFind, and AdMod, are available as freeware (*http://bit.ly/12bOwJl*).

20.3. Finding Exchange Server Cmdlets

Problem

You want to generate a reference list of all the Exchange Server cmdlets available in the Exchange Management Shell.

Solution

Using PowerShell

PowerShell has a cmdlet that can list all the available cmdlets in PowerShell or the EMS, called `Get-Command`. A subset of this cmdlet, called `Get-ExCommand`, returns only the cmdlets added to PowerShell with the installation of the EMS. To get a list of all the EMS cmdlets, execute the following cmdlet:

```
Get-ExCommand | FL Name,Definition >> c:\ExCommandList.txt
```

This will generate a formatted list of all of the EMS cmdlets and their definitions in a text file on the *C:* drive.

Discussion

The purpose of the `Get` cmdlets is really to serve as a search and query tool. When specific cmdlet properties are designated, `Get-Command` will return only the cmdlets representing the filter properties requested. `Get-ExCommand` is actually `Get-Command` with a built-in filter for cmdlets, called `Microsoft.Exchange.Management.Power Shell.Admin`, that are part of the PSSnapin, which we know as the Exchange Management Shell. For example, we can show all EMS cmdlets with the word *mailbox* as part of the object, as follows:

```
Get-ExCommand *mailbox*
```

See Also

The Exchange Management Shell Quick Reference (*http://bit.ly/13nqSuN*)

20.4. Preparing Active Directory for Exchange

Problem

You want to prepare your Active Directory forest and domains for the installation of your first Exchange server.

Solution

Using a graphical user interface

Exchange Server requires that the Active Directory forest schema be extended before installation. Exchange extends AD with new attributes. This step is done automatically through the GUI setup process. Running setup from the GUI therefore requires Schema Admin rights (in addition to Enterprise Admin and Domain Admin rights, which are discussed in more detail in "Discussion" on page 678).

There is no separate mechanism to apply schema extensions or prepare the domain independent of installing the Exchange Server binaries when using the GUI. This makes the GUI a reasonable option for smaller shops; however, larger businesses with division of administrative duties will certainly want to use the command-line option instead.

Using a command-line interface

Exchange Server uses *Setup.exe* at the root of the installation media to control aspects of preparation, installation, and even recovery. *Setup.exe* can be run from the command line with the appropriate parameters applied. The command line allows for easier separation of administrative duties based on permission level. The Exchange administrator may not have schema admin rights in AD. For AD preparation, there are several parameters to be applied in order.

/PrepareSchema
> This switch updates the Active Directory schema by importing a set of *.ldf* files for Exchange.

/PrepareAD
> This switch creates the Exchange configuration container in AD, creates the Exchange-related universal security groups (USGs), and applies the appropriate permissions. The /PrepareAD switch will also run the /PrepareSchema switch if it has not been run.

/PrepareDomain
> This switch configures the necessary permissions and configuration of the domain in preparation for installation of Exchange Server.

/PrepareAllDomains
> This switch prepares all the domains in the forest at once.

/IAcceptExchangeServerLicenseTerms
> This switch is required for all command-line operations, and is required each time a command is issued.

/OrganizationName
> This switch accepts input to specify the name of the Exchange organization. This switch has a 64-character limit, including letters, numbers, spaces, hyphens, and dashes.

/DomainController
> This switch allows you to specify the domain controller that *setup.exe* will use to read from and write to Active Directory.

/ActiveDirectorySplitPermissions
> This switch allows you to enable Active Directory split permissions mode when preparing the Active Directory topology.

This series of setup steps is sequential. The schema needs to be extended before AD is configured, and that must complete prior to the domains being prepared. Especially in a wide area topology, you should leave sufficient time in between steps to allow for AD replication between domain controllers.

Discussion

Microsoft Exchange will not run in an Active Directory forest unless the forest and the domain have been properly prepared. Microsoft did not make the assumption that everyone or every AD forest would use Exchange and therefore did not include all of the Exchange attributes and classes in the base Active Directory schema. The ability to dynamically extend the schema for Active Directory makes it possible to require only those people running Exchange to install the Exchange infrastructure and only in the AD forests where they need Exchange.

In addition to schema changes, you have to make security changes to Active Directory and the domain policy, as well as create some basic Exchange infrastructure objects. All of this is completed in the AD and Domain preparation processes for Exchange. Do not confuse these with the Active Directory *ForestPrep* and *DomainPrep* processes (using the adprep command); the concept is the same but the specific changes are different.

You need to run the *PrepareSchema* and *PrepareAD* processes once per forest to make the schema changes, create the Exchange organization structure in the Configura tion container, and set up Exchange-specific permissions. We recommend that you create a security group in your root domain for this delegation. You could use a domain local group in a single domain forest in which you will never create another domain. In a multidomain forest, you must use a global group or a universal group. The group is used to assign rights to objects in the Configuration container. Whether you use a global or universal group is up to you—either will do the job.

You need to run the *PrepareDomain* processes in the root domain of the forest and for every domain that will contain mail-enabled objects. Normally, *PrepareDomain* is run on every domain in an Active Directory forest. The process creates Exchange security principals, modifies the domain security policy, creates some Exchange-specific infrastructure objects, and assigns permissions for Exchange-specific objects. The *Prepare-Domain* processes require the person running the process to be a member of the *Domain Admins* group of the domain being prepared. Thankfully, Exchange Server has a / PrepareAllDomains switch allowing this step to be run once and have it apply to all accessible domains. However, when running the /PrepareAllDomains step, the person running the process must be a member of the *Enterprise Admins* group of the forest being prepared.

Due to the depth of changes made to the overall structure of Active Directory, the *PrepareAD* processes require Schema Admin and Enterprise Admin rights, and *Pre-pareDomain* requires Domain Admin rights. This usually prevents anyone but the centralized administration group responsible for the overall Active Directory forest from preparing the forest and domain(s) for Exchange.

For a more in-depth discussion of the Exchange deployment requirements, considerations, and specifics of what the preparation processes do, please see "Planning and Deployment" (*http://bit.ly/11cmG4e*).

See Also

Chapters 7 and 11 for more on groups and the AD schema

20.5. Installing the First Exchange Server 2013 Server in an Organization

Problem

You want to install the first Exchange server for a new Exchange organization.

Solution

Using a graphical user interface

1. Log on to a server that is a member of an Exchange-prepared domain with an account that is a member of the delegated group in Recipe 20.4.
2. From the Exchange 2013 media, launch *setup.exe*.
3. Choose whether to check and download updates or continue without checking, and then click Next.
4. Click Next on the Introduction screen.
5. On the License Agreement screen, read through the agreement, and if you agree, click "I accept the terms in the license agreement" and click Next.
6. On the error reporting screen, select the desired error reporting setting and then click Next.
7. Select the Exchange Server roles for this installation by placing a checkmark next to the roles you wish to install, and then click Next.
8. If necessary, specify a different path for the Exchange Server installation. Or, accept the default and then click Next.
9. As the first Exchange server in a new organization, enter the new organization name. This value cannot be changed later. Place a checkmark in the Apply Active Directory split permissions security model to the Exchange organization if needed, and then click Next.

10. The next screen asks whether you would like to enable malware scanning. Malware scanning is enabled by default; if you would like to disable it, click Yes, and then click Next.

11. Setup works through a set of Readiness Checks. Click Install if there are no issues to correct.

12. Installation progress is shown in the GUI; when it is done, the Completion screen will be presented. Click Finish to close the window.

Using a command-line interface

You can also install Exchange Server from the command line. *Setup.exe*, found in the root of the Exchange Server installation media, has several switches to break down installation into its components. We already covered the preparatory switches in Recipe 20.4. The other command-line switches for *setup.exe* are shown in the following list. Note that *setup.com*, used with previous versions of Exchange, is now part of *set up.exe*.

/Mode
> The mode for *setup.exe* identifies whether you are performing an install, uninstall, or recovery. The default mode is Install.

/Roles
> These are the main roles that you can select for a custom installation in the GUI. The roles are Mailbox, Client Access, and Management Tools.

/OrganizationName
> This value is required for the first Exchange server in a new organization.

/IAcceptExchangeServerLicenseTerms
> This switch is required for all command-line operations, and is required each time a command is issued.

/TargetDir
> This is the destination directory for binary installation. By default, this is found in *%ProgramFiles%\Microsoft\Exchange Server*.

/DomainController
> This switch allows you to specify the domain controller that *setup.exe* will use to read from and write to Active Directory.

/AnswerFile
> Setup is directed to a text file with preset properties to apply during installation.

/DoNotStartTransport

This switch prevents Exchange Server from automatically routing email when it first starts. This is usually used in case there is additional software to install or configure before Exchange is enabled.

/CustomerFeedbackEnabled

As we saw in the GUI, Microsoft is interested in making the product better by automating error reports submitted to the company. This is optional, and the default is set to True.

/DisableAMFiltering

This option disables the Exchange server anti-malware feature.

/InstallWindowsComponents

This option installs all required Windows Server roles and features.

/OrganizationName

This switch accepts input to specify the name of the Exchange organization. This switch has a 64-character limit, including letters, numbers, spaces, hyphens, and dashes.

/UpdatesDir

This switch specifies the directory in which Exchange Server updates are located and will be installed during installation.

/ActiveDirectorySplitPermissions

This switch allows you to enable Active Directory split permissions mode when preparing the Active Directory topology.

/DbFilePath

This switch allows you to specify the full directory path for the mailbox database if the Mailbox server role is installed.

/LogFolderPathUse

This switch allows you to specify the full directory path for the mailbox database logfiles if the Mailbox server role is installed.

/MdbName

This switch allows you to specify the Mailbox server role database name.

/TenantOrganizationConfig

This switch allows you to specify the file that contains the configuration for an Office 365 tenant.

For example, to install the Mailbox and Client Access roles on a new server run:

```
setup.exe /Mode:Install /Roles:Mailbox,ClientAccess↵
  /IAcceptExchangeServerLicenseTerms /InstallWindowsComponents
```

Using PowerShell

For small installations, PowerShell does not offer great benefits for running the setup. *Setup.exe* can be run from a classic command prompt or a PowerShell prompt. For larger organizations, especially with multiple simultaneous Exchange Server installations, PowerShell affords some opportunities to simplify the process, such as identifying Exchange servers on the network based on specific hostname policies or confirming target directory availability.

Discussion

If this is the first Exchange server in a new organization, additional parameters are needed at installation. For example, the administrator must specify a name for the new Exchange organization.

The Exchange installation has a few prerequisites before installing on Windows Server 2012, which are presented in the UI as follows:

- Microsoft Unified Communications Managed API 4.0, Core Runtime 64-bit
- Microsoft Office 2010 Filter Pack 64 bit, with SP 1

A Custom installation provides us with the opportunity to select individual roles or a combination. The Management Tools are listed as a separate option, but they are automatically installed with any of the other roles. They are listed separately for installation on an administration client computer or on a server.

Exchange performs readiness checks based on the roles selected. Should a readiness check fail, the offending situation must be resolved and, if you're using the GUI, the setup must be restarted.

See Also

The deployment section of the Exchange Server technical library (*http://bit.ly/ 10evMpC*)

20.6. Creating Unattended Installation Files for Exchange Server

Problem

You want to create an unattended installation file to minimize the administrative effort of installing several Exchange servers while also ensuring a consistent deployment across servers.

Solution

Using a command-line interface

Exchange 2013 can be installed in unattended mode simply using the command-line setup options. Some of the *setup.exe* switches can be listed within a text file that in turn is called by the /AnswerFile parameter. The *setup.exe* switches that can reside in an unattended installation answer file are TargetDir, SourceDir, UpdatesDir, DomainCon troller, MdbName, LogFolderPath, and more. See the full list of switches mentioned previously in the chapter. These switches are listed in a text file without the backslash and are saved as a text file such as *UnattendParams.txt*.

Setup.exe references the answer file as follows:

```
Setup.exe /Mode:Install /Roles:ClientAccess,Mailbox↵
  /AnswerFile:C:\UnattendParams.txt
```

Discussion

Using unattended installation is a great way to install Exchange on many servers, deploy the Exchange tools to many admin workstations, update service packs for Exchange on many servers, or maintain consistency in installation configurations.

To see a complete list of options, run the *setup* or *update* executable with the /? option. In Exchange 2010, the parameter is /AnswerFile and is formed using parameters available with *Setup.com*. After you create an unattended installation answer file, you can use it to install additional Exchange servers.

See Also

Recipe 20.7 for more on installing the Exchange Management Tools; "Install Exchange 2013 Using Unattended Mode" (*http://bit.ly/16OgSP5*)

20.7. Installing Exchange Management Tools

Problem

You want to install Exchange Management Tools onto a client computer or onto a server that isn't running Exchange.

Solution

Using a graphical user interface

1. Follow the standard installation steps outlined in Recipe 20.5, except bypass the step that creates a new organization.
2. Select the defaults for the remainder of the installation and complete the wizard.

Using a command-line interface

Setup.exe provides a switch to select the roles to install. The `ManagementTools` or `MT` role is one of the options. After the prerequisites are applied, the Exchange Management Tools can be installed as follows:

```
setup.exe /Mode:Install /Role:ManagementTools /IAcceptExchangeServerLicenseTerms
```

Discussion

Installing the Exchange Management Tools on a client computer or on a server that is not running Exchange Server is an alternative to using Remote Desktop administration of Exchange. The tools install the following components:

- Exchange Administration Center
- Exchange Management Shell
- Exchange Help files

Exchange Management Tools are supported on Windows 7 64-bit, Windows 8 64-bit, Windows Server 2012, and Windows Server 2008 R2. Windows 7 installations require the IIS 6 Management Console, as well as .NET Framework 4.5, Windows Management Framework 3.0, and Windows Identify Foundation. The Windows 7 prerequisites must be installed in that order.

See Also

Recipe 20.6 for more on unattended installation

20.8. Stopping and Starting Exchange Server

Problem

You want to stop or start Exchange Server.

Solution

Using a graphical user interface

1. Launch the Services management console (*services.msc*).
2. Locate the services that begin with "Microsoft Exchange."
3. Right-click the service and select the appropriate action.

Using a command-line interface

To start a service using the command line, issue the following command:

```
net start "<ServiceName>"
```

To stop a service using the command line, issue the following command:

```
net stop "<ServiceName>"
```

Using PowerShell

Stopping and starting Exchange Server services is a little easier because almost every service has the term *Exchange* in its name. For a list of all of the services on the server with *Exchange* in their display name, issue the following command:

```
Get-Service *Exchange* | FT Name, Status
```

 PowerShell will return the services in alphabetical order. The results can be further piped to the Sort-Objects cmdlet to control how the list is presented.

To start an Exchange service using PowerShell, use the following command:

```
Start-Service "<ServiceName>"
```

To stop services that are running and have *Exchange* in the display name, use the following command:

```
Get-Service *Exchange* | Where {$_.Status -eq "Running"} | Stop-Service
```

Discussion

Several services are involved with Exchange Server, and stopping different services will accomplish different things. Typically, it is not necessary to stop services manually. The services are interdependent, so when you stop or start various services, you may see a message about having to stop dependent services. If you do stop dependent services, don't forget to restart them again when you restart the service that you began with.

Different servers could be running a combination of different services based on the complexity of the environment and the specific function of the server. Not all Exchange servers will run all Exchange services.

For the long list of Exchange Server services, see Table 20-1.

Table 20-1. Exchange services

Exchange service	Description
Microsoft Exchange POP3 (MSExchangePOP3)	Supplies POP3 protocol message server functionality. This is available only on a Client Access Server.
POP3Backend (MSExchangePOP3BE)	Runs on Exchange servers with the Mailbox role installed and is required when POP3 is being used to access Exchange.
Microsoft Exchange IMAP4 (MSExchangeIMAP4)	Supplies IMAP4 protocol message server functionality. This is available only on a Client Access Server.
IMAP 4 Backend (MSExchangeIMAP4BE)	Runs on Exchange servers with the Mailbox role installed and is required when IMAP is being used to access Exchange.
Microsoft Exchange Information Store (MSExchangeIS)	Is used to access the Exchange mail and public folder stores. If this service is not running, users will not be able to use the Exchange server.
Microsoft Exchange Active Directory Topology (MSExchangeADTopology)	Queries Active Directory and returns configuration information and other data.
Anti-spam Update service (MSExchangeAntiSpamUpdate)	Automatically downloads anti-spam filter updates from Microsoft.
Mailbox Assistants (MsExchangeMailboxAssistants)	Manages the calendar, resource booking, Out-of-Office, and managed folder assistants.
Monitoring (MSExchangeMonitoring)	Allows diagnostics using an RPC server.
Replication (MSExchangeRepl)	Performs replication services for highly available environments.
Transport (MSExchangeTransport)	Manages SMTP.
Transport Log Search (MSExchange-TransportLogSearch)	Powers the Message Tracking functionality in Exchange.
Unified Messaging (MSExchangeUM)	Manages the Unified Messaging engine for Outlook Voice Access.
Mailbox Transport Delivery (MSExchangeDelivery)	Relays messages from the Transport service to the respective mailbox by using a remote procedure call (RPC).
Diagnostics (MSExchangeDiagnostics)	Monitors the Exchange server health.
Search (MSExchangeFastSearch)	Handles indexing and search queries for the Exchange server.
Frontend Transport (MSExchangeFrontEndTransport)	Relays SMTP connecting to and from hub servers.
Health Manager (MSExchangeHM)	Manages the Exchange server health.
Mailbox Replication (MSExchangeMailBoxReplication)	Manages and processes mailbox move requests.
RPC Client Access (MSExchangeRPC)	Manages client RPC connections for Exchange Server.
ServiceHost (MSExchangeServiceHost)	Manages services for applications.

Exchange service	Description
Mailbox Transport Submission (MSExchangeSubmission)	Runs on Mailbox servers and processes messages by converting from MAPI to MIME, and then relays them to the hub transport server.
Throttling (MSExchangeThrottling)	Limits the rate of user operations that could affect Exchange performance.
Unified Messaging Call Router (MSExchangeUMCR)	Enables the Unified Messaging Call Router features.
Tracing Service for Search (SearchExchangeTracing)	Enables trace logs for searching in Exchange Server.
Extension for Windows Server Backup (wsbexchange)	Allows Windows Server Backup to perform backup and recovery operations for Exchange Server.

See Also

"What's New in Exchange 2013" (*http://bit.ly/YqmASp*)

20.9. Mail-Enabling a User

Problem

You want to mail-enable an existing user.

Solution

Using a graphical user interface

1. Sign in to the Exchange Administration Center (EAC). To launch the EAC, open a web browser and navigate to **https://<CASServerName>/ecp**.
2. From the Recipients screen, click Contacts on the top menu.
3. Click the arrow on the plus sign (+) and then click "Mail user."
4. Ensure that the existing user is selected. Click Browse and select the user account to create the mailbox for, and then click OK.
5. Enter a unique alias for the mailbox and an external email address, and then click Save.

This entry now represents a mail-enabled user. This user does not have a mailbox. The external SMTP address we entered can be seen in the E-mail Addresses tab in the user properties looking from the EAC. The mail-enabled user can be found in the Recipients Configuration container in the Mail Contacts folder, and this entry represents the primary SMTP address in the multivalued attribute called proxyAddresses.

Using PowerShell

This is one of those tasks that is simple on the surface but makes significant changes beneath. PowerShell and Exchange Server reduce mail-enabling an existing user to a simple one-line cmdlet:

```
Enable-MailUser -Identity "<user_ID_parameter>" -Alias "<Alias_Name>"↵
-ExternalEmailAddress "<SMTP:proxy_SMTP_Address>"
```

An example of the cmdlet might look like this:

```
Enable-MailUser -Identity 'adatum.com/Users/Elias Mereb' -Alias 'Elias'↵
-ExternalEmailAddress 'SMTP: emereb@widetechconsulting.com'
```

Discussion

With Exchange Server, these controls are available in the Exchange Administration Center (EAC) and the Exchange Management Shell (EMS). The `Enable-MailUser` cmdlet mail-enables an existing user; however, the EAC can also be used to configure new users. Note that while a mail-enabled user is similar to a mail-enabled contact, the key difference is that a mail-enabled user can log on to Active Directory and access resources, whereas a mail-enabled contact cannot log on to Active Directory.

20.10. Mail-Disabling a User

Problem

You want to mail-disable a user.

Solution

Using a graphical user interface

1. Sign in to the EAC
2. From the Recipients screen, click Contacts from the top menu.
3. Select the user to mail-disable.
4. Click the arrow next to the trashcan icon and then click Disable.
5. Select Yes to confirm.

The mail-disabled user then disappears from the `Recipient Contact` container view; however, it still resides as a regular user in AD, stripped of the Exchange properties.

Using PowerShell

The cmdlet to mail-disable a user is as follows:

```
Disable-MailUser -Identity "<user_ID_parameter>"
```

An example of the cmdlet might look like this:

```
Disable-MailUser -Identity "Elias Mereb"
```

or:

```
Disable-MailUser "emereb@widetechconsulting.com"
```

The -Identity parameter can use the Distinguished Name, the User Principal Name, the Domain\Account name, the GUID, or other identifying information (see TechNet (*http://bit.ly/10hQI4A*) for a complete list). This cmdlet also only removes the Exchange properties for the user; it does not remove the user from AD. Because it is a significant change, there is a confirmation step after entering the preceding code. The administrator will be prompted to complete the action, requiring a Yes, Yes to all, No, No to all, Suspend, or Help. This prompt can be suppressed or selected by assigning one of those values in the original cmdlet by using the -Confirm parameter.

Discussion

This recipe removes the Active Directory Exchange attributes for a previously mail-enabled user. This is a simple process from EAC or PowerShell, but behind the scenes, several attributes are being updated.

Mail-disabling a user requires Exchange View-Only Administrator or higher permissions, as well as Read and Write permissions to a number of object attributes. See the Microsoft Exchange Tech Center on the Microsoft website for a list of all necessary attributes.

See Also

Recipe 20.7; Recipe 20.9 for more on mail-enabling a user

20.11. Mailbox-Enabling a User

Problem

You want to create a mailbox for a user. This is also known as mailbox-enabling a user.

Solution

Using a graphical user interface

1. Sign in to the EAC by navigating to **https://<CASServer>/ecp**.
2. From the Mailboxes screen, click the plus sign (+).

3. Enter a unique alias for the mailbox.

4. Select whether this is a new user or whether to add a mailbox for an existing Active Directory user.

5. If enabling a mailbox for an existing user, click Browse and select the user. Click OK and then Save.

6. If creating a new user, click the "new user" radio button.

7. Complete the new user information form and then click Save.

Using PowerShell

In the EMS, we use the `Enable-Mailbox` cmdlet to apply the appropriate Exchange attributes to an existing user. A mailbox has to have an associated storage location, which is the message store where it will reside:

```
Enable-Mailbox -Identity "<User_ID_Parameter>" -Alias "<Name>"↵
  -Database "<DatabaseName>"
```

An example of this cmdlet might read as follows:

```
Enable-Mailbox -Identity "Alberto Contador" -Alias "Alberto" -Database "DB01"
```

To mailbox-enable a group of users, this command can be piped from a `Get-User` filter parameter as well:

```
Get-User -RecipientType User | Enable-Mailbox -Database "Mailbox Database"
```

This command retrieves all users with the Recipient Type of User and mail-enables them. After `Enable-Mailbox` is successfully applied to an object, the Recipient Type will show as `UserMailbox`.

If you have a set of users within an OU that need to be mailbox-enabled, it is just a matter of applying a different filter parameter to the `Get-User` cmdlet:

```
Get-User -OrganizationalUnit "Sales" | Where-Object{$_.RecipientType -eq↵
  "User"} | Enable-Mailbox -Database "DB01"
```

Discussion

A mailbox-enabled user is a `user` object that has a mailbox defined in the Exchange organization that the `user` object exists in. This is one of the most common objects in an Exchange organization.

 Mailbox-enabling a user requires Exchange View-Only Administrator or higher permissions, as well as Read and Write permissions to a number of object attributes. See the Microsoft Exchange Tech Center on the Microsoft website for a list of all necessary attributes.

When you create a mailbox for a user, in the background, the specific changes occur on the user object in Active Directory and include changes to the following attributes:

- mDBUseDefaults
- msExchUserAccountControl
- homeMTA
- msExchHomeServerName
- homeMDB
- mailNickname
- msExchMailboxGuid
- msExchMailboxSecurityDescriptor
- legacyExchangeDN
- mail
- msExchPoliciesIncluded
- msExchRecipientDisplayType
- msExchRecipientTypeDetails
- msExchVersion
- proxyAddresses
- showInAddressBook

You can view the attributes before and after the Enable-Mailbox cmdlet is run to see the different attributes of the object to which values have been added. Right-click on the user in the Active Directory Administrative Center and select properties and then scroll down to the Attribute Editor. Click on the Filter button and enable "Show only attributes that have values" to display the attributes in use for that user object. Doing this before and after engaging the Enable-Mailbox cmdlet will allow you to visualize the changes.

See Also

Recipe 20.7; Recipe 20.13

20.12. Deleting a User's Mailbox

Problem

You want to delete a user's mailbox. This is also known as mailbox-disabling a user.

Solution

Using a graphical user interface

1. Sign in to the EAC by navigating to **https://<CASServer>/ecp**.
2. From the Recipient screen, select the user to mailbox-disable.
3. Click the arrow next to the trashcan icon and click Disable.
4. Select Yes to confirm.

This process disconnects the mailbox from the user object by removing the Exchange-specific attributes. In the EAC drop-down, there is the option to Disable and also Delete. The latter will disconnect the mailbox and also delete the user from AD.

Using PowerShell

```
Disable-Mailbox -Identity <User_ID_Parameter>
```

A basic example might be:

```
Disable-Mailbox ray@adatum.com
```

As with the some other cmdlets, the -Identity parameter is assumed and does not need to be typed out in the command as long as it is the first parameter after the cmdlet. The mailbox for *ray@adatum.com* will be disconnected from the user.

To delete mailboxes from a set of users, just pipe the output of a Get-Mailbox filter to the Disable-Mailbox cmdlet, similar to the examples in Recipe 20.11.

Discussion

Although the recipe title is "Deleting a User's Mailbox," these solutions don't really delete the mailbox. They actually just clear the Exchange attributes from the user object, and that disassociates the mailbox from the user; the mailbox itself will still exist in the Exchange store. The length of time it will exist depends on the mailbox retention period, which is 30 days by default. While the mailbox exists in that state, it can be reconnected to the same or a different user object.

 Deleting a user requires Exchange View-Only Administrator or higher permissions, as well as Read and Write permissions to a number of object attributes. See the Microsoft Exchange Tech Center on the Microsoft website for a list of all necessary attributes.

See Also

Recipe 20.7; Recipe 20.10

20.13. Moving a Mailbox

Problem

You want to move a mailbox to a new database or server.

Solution

Using a graphical user interface

1. Sign in to the EAC by navigating to **https://<CASServer>/ecp**.
2. From the Recipients screen, select the mailbox that you want to configure.
3. From the right panel, scroll to the bottom, and under Move Mailbox, click "to another database."
4. Name the migration job and then select whether to move the primary mailbox, archive mailbox, or both.
5. For the target database, click Browse and select the database that you want to move the mailbox to. Repeat the process for the archive database, if necessary, and then click Next.
6. If necessary, change the batch report recipient by clicking Browse and then selecting a user.
7. Choose whether to automatically or manually start the batch, and whether to automatically complete the migration, and then click New.
8. To view the migration job, click Migration from the top menu.
9. Double-click the job name from the list to view the progress or results.

Using PowerShell

There is a simple PowerShell command to accomplish the same feat. The command to move a mailbox is as follows:

```
New-MoveRequest "<Mailbox>" -TargetDatabase "<MailboxDB>"
```

An example of such a move might be:

```
New-MoveRequest "User5" -TargetDatabase "DB02"
```

Again, the -Identity parameter is assumed, so typing the actual parameter is optional. There are many times where you will have to move groups of mailboxes to new storage or a new database. There are several ways of accomplishing this. The easiest is probably to pipe the output from a Get-Mailbox cmdlet with the appropriate filters to the New-MoveRequest cmdlet. For example:

```
Get-Mailbox | Where {$._<Property> -eq "<Value>"} |↵
New-MoveRequest -TargetDatabase "<Database>"
```

You can also assemble the mailboxes in an array that PowerShell can loop through using a foreach command. This works well if the array is loaded at the beginning of the script. If not, the mailboxes are then moved in serial—the next mailbox isn't moved until the previous one is completed. That is not the most efficient method. The array itself can be piped to the New-MoveRequest cmdlet to work through the items in a multithreaded fashion:

```
$array = "UserA","UserB","UserC","UserD","UserE"
$array | New-MoveRequest -TargetDatabase <Database> -Confirm:$false
```

The source can also be a CSV file with a list of usernames and the intended destination store for their mailbox. These are the two required values for the New-MoveRequest cmdlet. If all the mailboxes are to be moved to the same destination database, then the target database is best specified as part of the cmdlet and not pulled from the CSV for each mailbox. The Import-CSV cmdlet calls the *.csv* file by name and pipes the output to the New-MoveRequest command.

Assuming we have a *.csv* file with a column heading of Username and the users with mailboxes to be moved are listed in the column, then we can import those values and move their mailboxes as follows:

```
Import-CSV <file_name>.csv | foreach {New-MoveRequest -Identity $_.Username↵
-TargetDatabase <Database> -Confirm:$false}
```

Discussion

Mailbox moves are commonly performed in many Exchange organizations due to servers getting upgraded, server hardware issues, users changing locations, or if the administrators want to readjust the mailbox location for load distribution.

Moving a mailbox in Exchange requires Read and Write permissions to the following attributes:

- msexchhomeservername
- homemdb
- homeMTA
- msExchOmaAdminWirelessEnable
- msExchOmaAdminExtendedSettings
- targetAddress

A mailbox move is an odd operation in terms of permissions. Logically, moving a mailbox is basically a combination of create and delete operations, which is something a typical Exchange administrator has permissions to do. See MS KB 842033 for details of the permissions needed.

Using a graphical user interface

The new Local Mailbox Move Wizard allows you to perform the move(s) immediately or at some point later (by manually starting the move[s] later). This is obviously a handy feature for mailbox moves because it isn't something you tend to want to do in the middle of the day. This allows Exchange administrators who like to sleep at night to schedule the work to be done and then go home with everyone else.

Using PowerShell

After a move, you may notice that the source mailbox is in a disconnected state. This is helpful in the case of an unsuccessful move or a problem with the new destination mailbox. The disconnected mailbox can be removed by using the Remove-StoreMailbox cmdlet, or it will automatically be removed based on the retention period. There are several ways to perform this task using PowerShell, depending on the number of mailboxes to move. Looping through an array, importing a CSV file, and applying a cmdlet filter and piping the result to the New-MoveRequest command are all good options.

Like the other solutions, PowerShell does not have a mechanism to migrate the recoverable items folder. This is a consideration for companies that require access to the recoverable items folder for compliance reasons. You may need to keep the last backup available prior to the mailbox move.

See Also

Recipe 20.7; Recipe 20.11

20.14. Viewing Mailbox Sizes and Message Counts

Problem

You want to view the sizes and message counts of all mailboxes on a server.

Solution

Using PowerShell

Again, this is another scenario where the EMS simplifies Exchange management. An important reporting cmdlet for mailbox reporting is Get-MailboxStatistics. It quantifies mailbox size, item count, last logon time, and more. (See this recipe's "Discussion" for the list.) To get summary statistics for a specific server, run the following:

```
Get-MailboxStatistics -Server <Server_name>
```

This lists the mailboxes and their size and message counts on the server specified. Data is easily sorted in ascending or descending order by any value in the Get-MailboxStatistics output. For example, to sort the list by mailbox size and easily identify the largest mailboxes, we can use:

```
Get-MailboxStatistics -Server <Server_name> | Sort-Object StorageLimitStatus↵
-Descending | FT
```

Administrators often need to act on this information and need it in a timely manner. It is easy to write this information to a file and attach it to a scheduled email using a PowerShell script.

This script assigns parts of the email message to variables, collects the data with Get-MailboxStatistics values, writes the report to a *.txt* file, and attaches it to an email to the administrator. It specifies only a Recipient Type of UserMailbox, which is a mailbox-enabled user. This also requires that the sending SMTP server can relay for the host sending the request:

```
$FromAddress = "reports@adatum.com"
$ToAddress = "administrator@adatum.com"
$MessageSubject = "Daily Mailbox Size Report"
$MessageBody = "The Daily Mailbox Size Report is attached."
$SendingServer = "EX01"

Get-MailboxStatistics -Server "EX01"| Sort-Object StorageLimitStatus↵
-Descending | FT DisplayName, ItemCount | Out-File "C:\temp\mbxreport.txt"

Send-MailMessage -To $ToAddress -From $FromAddress -Subject $MessageSubject↵
-SmtpServer $SendingServer -Body $MessageBody↵
-Attachments "C:\temp\mbxreport.txt"
```

Save the script as a PowerShell file such as *MbxReportSend.ps1* and schedule it to run every morning so that it is sitting in your inbox when you get to the office.

Discussion

Mailbox sizes and message counts are items on Exchange systems that administrators routinely want to know about for the purposes of reporting and metrics. Administrators want to know whether their mail system is balanced and whether users are spread across the mailbox stores evenly. Knowing the number of users and the size of their mailboxes in each mailbox store, the administrator can make better decisions about where new user mailboxes should be placed or if some leveling of mailboxes is required.

Using PowerShell

The Get-MailboxStatistics cmdlet is a powerful reporting resource. It can be used as a standalone command to review a snapshot of mailbox properties, or it can be used as a filter for other queries. The output can be saved on a regular basis to compare values over time and identify trends of how users leverage their mailboxes.

By running the cmdlet with the Format List option at the end, the full set of variables captured by Get-MailboxStatistics is displayed:

```
Get-MailboxStatistics "user5" | FL

RunspaceId                      : 2d75e969-834f-4eee-9897-73cdd0f4abb8
AssociatedItemCount             : 12
DeletedItemCount                : 0
DisconnectDate                  :
DisconnectReason                :
DisplayName                     : User5
ItemCount                       : 3
LastLoggedOnUserAccount         :
LastLogoffTime                  :
LastLogonTime                   : 12/26/2012 1:41:24 AM
LegacyDN                        : /o=AdatumExchange/ou=Exchange Administrative↵
                                  Group
                                  (FYDIBOHF23SPDLT)/cn=Recipients/cn=60f0b069318↵
                                  a4edca0b06bfe11b9170d-User5
MailboxGuid                     : 4ea903e2-fd9d-49ec-9ae8-b51dd0015a05
MailboxType                     : Private
ObjectClass                     : Unknown
StorageLimitStatus              :
TotalDeletedItemSize            : 0 B (0 bytes)
TotalItemSize                   : 829.94 MB (870,255,165 bytes)
MailboxTableIdentifier          :
Database                        : MailboxDB2
ServerName                      : EX01
DatabaseName                    : MailboxDB2
MoveHistory                     :
IsQuarantined                   : False
PersistableTenantPartitionHint  : 00-00-00-00-00-00-00-00-00-00-00-00-00-00-00-↵
                                  00
IsArchiveMailbox                : False
IsMoveDestination               : False
DatabaseIssueWarningQuota       : 1.899 GB (2,039,480,320 bytes)
DatabaseProhibitSendQuota       : 2 GB (2,147,483,648 bytes)
DatabaseProhibitSendReceiveQuota : 2.3 GB (2,469,396,480 bytes)
Identity                        : 4ea903e2-fd9d-49ec-9ae8-b51dd0015a05
MapiIdentity                    : 4ea903e2-fd9d-49ec-9ae8-b51dd0015a05
OriginatingServer               : ex01.adatum.com
IsValid                         : True
ObjectState                     : Unchanged
```

Any of these output values can be used to filter another cmdlet or be saved to file or database for reporting over time. The `LastLogonTime` is valuable in identifying stale mailboxes that have not been archived and deleted. Be wary of the `LastLogonTime` if you have third-party software (such as archiving software) that logs on to mailboxes, as the date and time may not be accurate.

See Also

`Get-MailboxStatistics` cmdlet reference (*http://bit.ly/12bPTYj*)

20.15. Configuring Mailbox Limits

Problem

You want to enable storage limits for user mailboxes on an Exchange server.

Solution

Using a graphical user interface

To configure storage quota settings on a database, follow these steps:

1. Sign in to the EAC by navigating to **https://<CASServer>/ecp**.
2. Navigate to Servers→Databases.
3. Double-click the database that needs to have quota limits changed.
4. Click on the Limits link.
5. Set the values for the storage quota.

To configure storage quota settings on a mailbox, follow these steps:

1. Open the EAC by navigating to **https://<CASServer>/ecp**.
2. Double-click the mailbox that needs to have quota limits changed.
3. Click on the "Mailbox usage" link.
4. Click "More options," and then select "Customize the settings for this mailbox."
5. Set the storage quota values as required for the user.

Using PowerShell

To set the different quota levels on a database, use the following command:

```
Set-MailboxDatabase "<Database>" -IssueWarningQuota "<Value>"↵
  -ProhibitSendQuota "<Value>" -ProhibitSendReceiveQuota "<Value>"
```

An example of this command is as follows:

```
Set-MailboxDatabase "DB01" -IssueWarningQuota "3GB" -ProhibitSendQuota "4GB"↵
 -ProhibitSendReceiveQuota "5GB"
```

To set the different quota levels on a mailbox, use the following command:

```
Set-Mailbox "<MailboxAlias>" -UseDatabaseQuotaDefaults <$true|$False>↵
 -IssueWarningQuota  "<Value>" -ProhibitSendQuota "<Value>"↵
 -ProhibitSendReceiveQuota "<Value>"
```

Discussion

It's not uncommon for administrators to want to set reasonable size limits on individual users' mailboxes. You can configure this globally at the mailbox store level. Since you can have multiple stores on a single server, this allows you to create multiple stores with multiple storage limits for departments or groups that have greater storage needs. You can also override the mailbox store defaults for individual user accounts by program-matically modifying the same three attributes and then setting the mdBUseDefaults attribute to FALSE. In Exchange Server, this is an EMS parameter on the Set-Mailbox cmdlet called -UseDatabaseQuotaDefaults. The following explains each quota setting and its default values:

"Issue warning at"
> Warns users that they have exceeded the storage limit, but their mailbox will con-tinue to function. The default value is 1.9 GB.

"Prohibit send at"
> Warns users that they have exceeded the storage limit and then prevents them from sending new messages until their mailboxes are brought back underneath the con-figured storage limit. Users can still receive messages. The default value is 2 GB.

"Prohibit send and receive at"
> Warns users that they have exceeded the storage limit and then prevents them from both sending and receiving messages until they have corrected the situation. The default value is 2.3 GB.

You can set the quota values using PowerShell to KB, MB, GB, or even TB. The quota levels are relative to each other. The IssueWarningQuota value should not be greater than the ProhibitSendQuota value, which in turn should not be greater than the Pro hibitSendReceiveQuota value.

See Also

Set-Mailbox cmdlet reference (*http://bit.ly/YAyGL7*)

20.16. Creating an Address List

Problem

You want to create an address list.

Solution

Using a graphical user interface

1. Sign in to the EAC by navigating to **https://<CASServer>/ecp**.
2. Navigate to Organization→Address lists.
3. Click the plus sign (+) to create a new address list.
4. Enter a name for the new list.
5. Select the container for the address list.
6. If necessary, identify the recipient types to include in this address list.
7. To further define the recipient list, click "add a rule" and then select the attribute from the drop-down list.
8. Click Save to create the new address list.

Using PowerShell

There is a simple cmdlet for creating address lists in Exchange Server, as follows:

```
New-AddressList -Name "<AddressList_Name>" -Container↵
 "<AddressListIDParameter>"-IncludedRecipients
```

Here is an example of this cmdlet creating a new address list container named `Regions`:

```
New-AddressList -Name "Regions" -Container "\" -IncludedRecipients "None"
```

In addition, there is an `Update-AddressList` to generate members independent of list creation or to apply any changes in list membership:

```
Update-AddressList -Identity "<AddressListIDParameter>"
```

A custom address list placed in the new `Regions` container based on a state, in this case Nevada, might read as follows:

```
New-AddressList -Name "Nevada" -IncludedRecipients "MailboxUsers, MailContacts,↵
 MailGroups, MailUsers" -ConditionalStateOrProvince "NV"↵
 -Container "\Regions"
```

After the list is created, it needs to be applied. This is done with a separate command as follows:

```
Update-AddressList -Identity "\Regions\Nevada"
```

Discussion

Address lists are special groupings of email accounts that allow users to quickly find specific email users that are part of some logical grouping in the GAL. In essence, they are a subset of the GAL. Exchange Server provides some precanned address lists and allows for more complete Opath filter creation with the Recipient Filter option.

Address lists should employ friendly and descriptive names, as they are options for users to query in finding other users through Outlook. In addition, address lists should be added after consideration. Too many address lists can confuse users as to which one they should be using.

Using a graphical user interface

Using the GUI for this process is straightforward and is the most likely way you'll want to create address lists unless you need to create a lot of them on the fly or you are importing them from a test lab.

Using PowerShell

There is a set of cmdlets to manage address lists in Exchange Server. First the New-AddressList cmdlet is used to create the list. Subsequently, Update-AddressList is used to populate the address list or specifically apply the filters and build the list, and even schedule when it should be updated. For larger enterprises with tens of thousands or hundreds of thousands of Active Directory recipients, address list generation is not trivial.

See Also

"Email Addresses and Address Books" (*http://bit.ly/13nxbP6*)

20.17. Creating a Database Availability Group

Problem

You want to create a new Database Availability Group (DAG) for automatic database-level recovery.

Solution

Using a graphical user interface

1. Sign in to the EAC by navigating to **https://<CASServer>/ecp**.

2. Navigate to Servers→Database Availability Groups.

3. Click the plus sign (+) to open the new DAG window.

4. Enter a name for the DAG.

5. If you would like a specific server to be the witness server, specify it in the Witness Server field; otherwise, leave it blank.

6. If you need to designate a specific directory for the witness server, specify it in the Witness Directory field; otherwise, leave it blank.

7. Enter one or more IP addresses to be used for the DAG. Leave this field blank to use DHCP.

8. Click Save to create the DAG.

Using PowerShell

```
New-DatabaseAvailabilityGroup -Name "<DAGName>" -WitnessServer "<ServerName>"
```

An example of this command might be as follows:

```
New-DatabaseAvailabilityGroup -Name "DAG01" -WitnessServer "EX01"
```

Discussion

Database Availability Groups (DAGs) are used to automatically recover at the database level, regardless of whether the failure is database-, server-, or network-related. In addition, DAGs are useful for supporting server maintenance because they allow administrators to perform maintenance without causing downtime for users. Mailbox servers are added to a DAG to provide automatic recovery. A common deployment for a DAG provides high availability at the primary data center and disaster recovery capability at a remote site (often a DR site). You can add up to 16 Exchange mailbox servers to a DAG. If you plan to create a DAG in an environment where there are still Windows Server 2008 R2 domain controllers, you must pre-stage the object in Active Directory. For more information, see the TechNet article "Pre-Stage the Cluster Network Object for a Database Availability Group" (*http://bit.ly/Z7GtQL*).

The witness server parameter for both the GUI and the PowerShell solutions is optional. By default, the witness server is applied only on an Exchange server with the Client Access Server role installed, but not the Mailbox Server role. This can be overridden by specifying the witness server manually.

See Also

"High Availability and Site Resilience" (*http://bit.ly/10exnvM*)

20.18. Creating a Mailbox Database

Problem

You want to create a mailbox database.

Solution

Using a graphical user interface

1. Sign in to the EAC by navigating to **https://<CASServer>/ecp**.
2. Navigate to Servers→Databases.
3. Click the plus sign (+) to add a new database.
4. Assign the mailbox database a relevant name.
5. Click Browse and select the server to create the database on.
6. The default database file path is generated. Choose whether to mount the new database.
7. Click Save to create the database.

Using PowerShell

Here is the command for creating a new mailbox database:

```
New-MailboxDatabase -Name <Name_ID_Parameter> -Server <ServerName>
```

An example of this command is as follows:

```
New-MailboxDatabase -Name "DB07" -Server "EX01"
```

A final step for the PowerShell-generated database is to mount it if needed:

```
Mount-Database "DB07"
```

Discussion

Mailbox databases are where mailboxes are located. There are quite a few configuration settings for mailbox databases that are beyond the scope of this chapter, but going through the EAC when manually creating a mailbox store should give you an idea of what can be configured.

In Exchange Server, depending on the version (Standard or Enterprise) of Exchange, you can have up to five mailbox databases mounted. EAC and EMS enforce these limits, but it is possible to directly modify Active Directory to exceed these limits. If you create more databases or storage groups than are allowed, the additional databases will not mount. Exchange Server allows for up to 50 databases with the Enterprise edition (this was reduced from a maximum of 100 databases in Exchange 2010).

Mailbox databases are represented in Active Directory by the `msExchPrivateMDB` class. This class is not as simple as some of the other classes used by Exchange. In addition, several of the attributes hold binary data, so working with these Active Directory objects directly can be difficult. One of the more notable attributes of the mailbox store objects is a backlink attribute called `homeMDBBL`. This is a multivalued attribute linking back to all of the `user` objects that have mailboxes in this mailbox store.

See Also

"Manage Mailbox Databases in Exchange 2013" (*http://bit.ly/17Igyzk*)

20.19. Enabling or Disabling Anti-Malware Scanning

Problem

You want to enable Exchange Server anti-malware scanning.

Solution

Using PowerShell

Within the *scripts* folder on any Exchange server, there is a precanned PowerShell script to enable anti-malware scanning. This is found in the *scripts* folder located by default at *C:\Program Files\Microsoft\Exchange Server\V15\scripts*. You can enable anti-malware scanning by running the script as follows:

```
& $env:ExchangeInstallPath\Scripts\Enable-Antimalwarescanning.ps1
```

 Changing the anti-malware scanning settings requires the transport service to be restarted before the settings will take place. Running the built-in PowerShell scripts will automatically restart this service without prompting.

Discussion

To confirm the installation, run the `Get-MalwareFilteringServer` cmdlet, which will also show the anti-malware settings. To disable anti-malware filtering, run the following command:

```
& $env:ExchangeInstallPath\Scripts\Disable-Antimalwarescanning.ps1
```

See Also

"Disable or Bypass Anti-Malware Scanning" (*http://bit.ly/10CAxZX*)

20.20. Enabling Message Tracking

Problem

You want to enable message tracking on Exchange Server.

Solution

Using a graphical user interface

Message tracking in Exchange can be set on servers running with the Mailbox role installed. To enable message tracking on an Exchange server, follow these steps:

1. Sign in to the EAC by navigating to **https://<CASServer>/ecp**.
2. Navigate to Servers→Servers.
3. Double-click the server that you want to configure and then click the "Transport logs" link.
4. Select or deselect the checkbox next to "Message Tracking logging" to enable or disable the feature.
5. Accept the default message tracking log path or specify an alternate path.
6. Click Save to close the window and save the settings.

Using PowerShell

To enable the message tracking log for an Exchange server, use the following syntax:

```
Set-MailboxServer <Server_Name> -MessageTrackingLogEnabled $True
```

There are a few other parameters that are easily configured with the cmdlet. These include:

MessageTrackingLogPath
> This parameter is used to set a nondefault local path for the message tracking logs. The default location is *C:\Program Files\Microsoft\Exchange Server\TransportRoles \Logs\MessageTracking*.

MessageTrackingLogSubjectEnabled
> By default, message subjects are logged in message tracking; however, a privacy or compliance policy may require subjects be omitted from logging content.

`MessageTrackingLogMaxDirectorySize`

> Controlling the directory size where message tracking logs are stored can prevent unexpected drive space usage.

`MessageTrackingLogMaxFileSize`

> The default file size for message tracking logs is 10 MB. To control the frequency of new logfiles and the total number of files, it may be beneficial to increase or decrease the individual file size.

`MessageTrackingLogMaxAge`

> For policy, compliance, or storage reasons, it may benefit a company to have logs expire.

A full example of this configuration is:

```
Set-MailboxServer EX01 -MessageTrackingLogEnabled:$True -MessageTrackingLogPath↲
"e:\Logs\" -MessageTrackingLogMaxDirectorySize 1GB
```

Discussion

Message tracking logs are an invaluable aid when troubleshooting message delivery in any Exchange environment. A message can be tracked from submission to the Information Store all the way through to its departure out of the Exchange environment. As long as the administrator doing the tracking has the rights to and can resolve the Net-BIOS name of each server along the message path, the administrator will be able to see how a particular message traveled through the network and how long it took to go through each server.

Message tracking is enabled by default on all Exchange servers running the Mailbox role. The EMS allows for full configuration of message tracking.

When changing the location of the message tracking logs, the existing logs are not automatically transferred to the new location.

See Also

"Message Tracking Role" (*http://bit.ly/1070q8k*)

## CHAPTER 21

Microsoft Forefront Identity Manager

21.0. Introduction

Microsoft Forefront Identity Manager (FIM) is the successor to Microsoft Identity Lifecycle Manager (ILM). The core focus areas of FIM are managing policy, managing credentials, managing and provisioning users and groups, access control, and compliance. The product includes a Credential Management (CM) feature for use in environments that have a Public Key Infrastructure (PKI) and need to provide self-service and policy-based certificate management. While FIM is typically thought of as a solution for smart-card enrollment and life-cycle management, it excels at providing policy management for any certificate type. In light of the new product name, the community has struggled to differentiate between what was the synchronization engine and the product itself, not wishing to drag CM into what has typically been an MIIS/ILM/FIM conversation. In cases where differentiation is important, the two server products are usually referred to as the "sync engine" and Certificate Lifecycle Manager (CLM); however, for the purposes of simplification in this chapter, we will use the term *ILM* to refer to the sync engine.

FIM is a robust .NET application platform built on Microsoft's highly successful database platform—SQL Server. FIM provides services for the synchronization and reconciliation of identity data, and in some cases passwords, between multiple disparate repositories, including (but not limited to):

- Enterprise directories
  - Active Directory/Active Directory Application Mode
  - Novell eDirectory
  - Sun Directory Server
  - IBM Tivoli Directory Server

- Databases
  - Microsoft SQL
  - Oracle
  - IBM DB2
- Email
  - Microsoft Exchange Server
  - Lotus Notes
- Flat text files
  - DSML
  - LDIF
  - Attribute Value Pair
  - CSV
  - Delimited
  - Fixed width

FIM is considered to be in a class of products known as *metadirectory synchronization* tools. This is in contrast to other products like virtual directories that have no central reconciliation or synchronization mechanism.

For an up-to-date list of supported FIM management agents, visit TechNet (*http://bit.ly/YqoK4K*).

While the depth of connector coverage for identity management products is often a popular topic, it is typically irrelevant for two reasons:

- FIM is a SQL Server application, and with SQL Server comes connectivity via ODBC, Linked Servers, and Integration Services, all of which provide access to databases and systems that do not have native management agent support.

- FIM has what is known as the Extensible MA for Connectivity (XMA or ECMA), which is a framework for writing your own MA to proprietary applications and platforms; the XMA allows you to write the connectivity components and hand them back to FIM using its standard interface.

Given the options for aggregating data sources through SQL Server or creating an XMA to consume a custom interface or web service, FIM provides an extremely flexible platform on top of which to develop an identity management solution.

While the term *MA* is fairly common in the Microsoft community, the generic term *connector* is also commonly used across multiple identity management products.

Requirements for FIM 2010 R2

Each FIM component has a specific set of prerequisite software, with the high-level pieces listed here:

Windows Server 2008 Standard or Enterprise Edition (x64) or Windows Server 2008 R2 Standard or Enterprise
  All of the FIM components rely on Windows Server 2008 at a minimum.

SQL Server 2008 (x64) Standard or Enterprise Edition with SP1 or later
  Either version or edition is sufficient; however, x64 editions are supported only if the SQL server and the FIM server are loaded onto separate servers.

Windows SharePoint Services 3.0 Service Pack 2 (SP2) or Microsoft SharePoint Foundation 2010
  SharePoint is used for the FIM Portal, FIM Password Registration portal, and FIM Password Reset portal.

While not strictly required, most deployments make use of Visual Studio 2008 or later to build and compile rules extensions.

SQL and FIM collocation

In previous versions of FIM (e.g., ILM/MIIS), there was sometimes a performance benefit when collocating with SQL. However, with FIM 2010 R2, it is recommended that you separate SQL onto a dedicated server (or cluster) and avoid collocating FIM components with SQL.

While FIM itself does not officially support failover clustering of the application, some users have noted that it works using a Cluster Generic Script resource. For most deployments, deploying a supported topology is the best course of action. FIM does support Network Load Balancing (NLB), which can distribute the processing load of the FIM Service.

FIM Primer

The really attractive thing about FIM is that it is a streamlined .NET engine for synchronizing and reconciling identity information. That, in effect, is all it does, and it does it really well. What makes the product so versatile is that at pretty much any point in a data flow you can "go to code" via an extension, resolve the issue in your preferred .NET language, and return the manipulated data back to your data flow. All the product does is take information from one source, and transform it or flow it to another source. We're hoping the power of the tool will begin to make itself more apparent as you read on.

The synchronization engine is an application that relies completely on SQL Server, and all data, code, rule sets, attribute flows, and consolidated data sets are stored within SQL tables (see Figure 21-1).

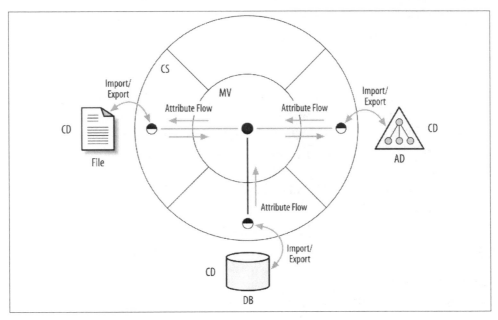

Figure 21-1. FIM architecture

Since FIM is a complex application and not something most AD administrators have experience with, we are going to discuss the basic features and terminology in more depth.

Importing data

There are several terms that you will hear attributed to a data source within FIM: *data source*, *directory*, and *connected directory (CD)*. "CD" can refer to a database, a flat file, or a full-fledged directory such as Active Directory.

There are two ways we can get data into the product for processing: full imports and delta imports. Since AD exposes delta changes natively via *DirSync*, you are spoiled into thinking you can do delta imports with any CD, but that is not the case. When data is brought in for processing, it's stored in a special location called the Connector Space (CS).

Full imports (stage only)

Also called "staging," full imports read the entire CD every time. Full imports can be scoped or limited to specific containers or organizational units, and the entire MA can be scoped to process only specific object types.

Delta imports (stage only)

If the CD is capable of differentiating changes like AD is, you can ask the CD for objects that have changed since your last full import. The caveat here is that you always have to start with at least one *error-free* full import in order to get a delta import.

 You get data into FIM by "staging" the data into a special area called the Connector Space (CS) through a full import. Subsequent imports may be able to utilize delta imports if the CD supports it.

In Figure 21-2, the (A) actions depict the import process from CD to CS. While this could be a full or a delta import, the very first import should always be a full import.

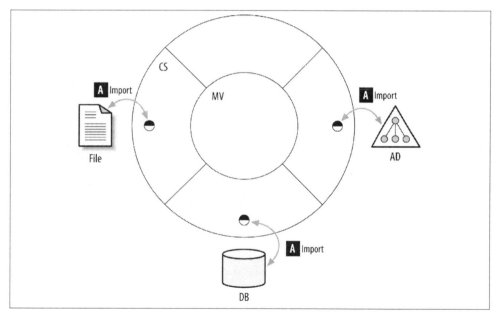

Figure 21-2. Importing data

The connector space

Technically speaking, the connector space is just a table in SQL, but the important concepts to understand here are that the CS is where objects go once they've been staged (through either a full or delta import) and that the CS effectively becomes a localized copy of the CD you're connecting to. From that point on, all of the processing happens against the objects in the CS—not directly against the CD; this is an important distinction between a metadirectory product, like FIM, and a Virtual Directory. This is a good thing because you can grab a copy of the data and then build and validate your rules against it without risking data corruption, access rights, or network traffic. Getting objects staged into the CS takes minutes to set up and is limited only by your rights to read the directory and the time it takes to iterate through the directory and create the entries in SQL.

Now, this is very important: before you can read from an Active Directory connected directory, the account you will use to connect must have at least the Replicating Directory Changes right. For information on how to set that up, refer to the KB article (*http://support.microsoft.com/kb/303972/en-us*).

Beyond this detail, any authenticated user can read public attributes; however, sooner or later you may run into areas of the directory that require greater access rights.

Once objects have been staged into the connector space, they can synchronize with another section of the engine called the *metaverse*.

The metaverse

The metaverse (MV) holds the consolidated representation of identities from each connector space. For instance, if you have an account in AD LDS and an account in an AD domain, and both have been staged into their respective connector spaces, you can choose to represent those objects either independently through a process called *projection*, or as a single object through a process called a *join*. As a general practice, the MV holds a single object representing the consolidated identity information mined from objects in the individual data sources; think of it as a many (CS) to one (MV) relationship. Most importantly, the way data is synchronized from one CS to another CS is through the MV. Without an MV object, you cannot flow information between one CS and another. So what's this we were saying about projection and joins?

Projection and joins

One of the immutable laws of FIM is that *every MV object has to start out its life cycle as a projection from one CS object*. Incidentally, the converse is also true: *once all of your CS objects are disconnected from an MV object, that MV object will cease to exist*. A projection rule simply states, "Create an MV object of a specific type for this specific CS object."

Once you've projected a set of CS objects into the MV, you can set up some rules for objects in another CS to *join* the MV object. There are tons of ways you can specify this, but once you have two CS joined via a common MV object, you can then synchronize data between the respective CS and MV objects, creating a "bridge" of sorts.

After using a full or delta import to stage data into the CS, we can then project those objects into the MV using a projection rule. Objects in a separate CS can be connected through an MV object through the join process, which allows for the synchronization of data between connected objects.

Now, projecting an object into the MV doesn't mean that any of its data goes with it. On the contrary, we have to create attribute flow rules to tell the engine exactly which CS attribute goes to which MV attribute. Before we can discuss how synchronization works, we need to talk briefly about connectors, what states they can be in, and how we can filter them.

In Figure 21-3, action (1) depicts the *projection* of a CS object into the metaverse, which results in the creation of the MV object, while action (2) depicts inbound attribute flow.

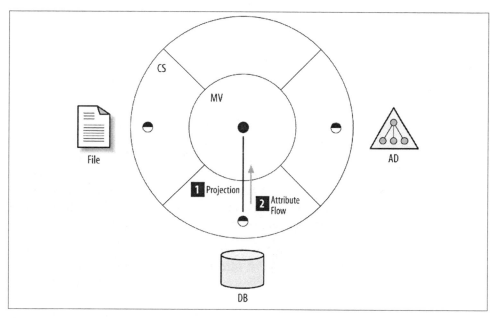

Figure 21-3. Projection

In Figure 21-4, actions (3) and (5) depict *joins* occurring between CS objects in the file and AD, respectively, while actions (4) and (6) depict inbound and outbound attribute flow.

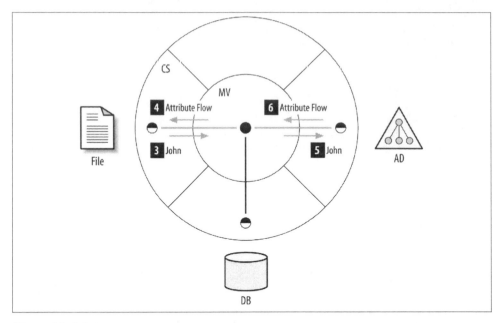

Figure 21-4. Joins

The many faces of the connector

Whenever you project a CS object into the MV, a *connector* is created. Of particular importance is the type of that connector—in this case it is considered a *normal connector*. You can also create connectors of type *explicit*, and you can remove a connector by disconnecting it. When an object is first staged into the CS, it is a *normal disconnector*. If that object is joined or projected, it becomes a *normal connector*. Suffice it to say that normal disconnectors can become connectors again, whereby if it is explicit then it must be manually made a connector or disconnector.

If you disconnect an existing connector, you can place that *disconnector* as one of two types: a *normal disconnector* or an *explicit disconnector*. A connector is really just a special relationship between CS and MV objects that absolves the need to reevaluate the relationship every time a sync is run, which makes the connector a static entity within the engine. This is an important concept to understand, as join rules for a particular CS object are evaluated only under two conditions: the CS object is not currently connected, and the CS object is not assigned as an explicit disconnector. Once a join is made the rule is never executed again for that CS object.

The bottom line here is *never to create anything that is explicit, and your life will be much easier*—explicit disconnectors are designed to provide a temporary state until information can be "breadcrumbed" back into the originating system, and are not intended to be a permanent solution (although for many people, they are nonetheless a permanent problem).

State-based synchronization

There are two basic types of Identity Management (IdM) products on the market today: state-based and event-based. FIM is a state-based product, which simply means that *things happen when an object or attribute changes state*. Where event-based systems are concerned, an event is generated based upon some predefined threshold or application trigger that tells the IdM system to do something. Without devolving into a religious discussion regarding which is better, the first truth you need to understand is that all systems on the market today have aspects of both systems. While one system may claim to be one or the other, all products include both state- and event-based aspects. The important thing to note is how you approach a problem with one system versus another. The only thing you need to understand is that as a synchronization engine, the product will process each object in turn (serially) and resolve the state of that object (and all of its attributes) completely each and every time that object is touched. This is probably the most difficult concept to understand with the product, and it generally confounds people trying to understand why full or delta synchronizations cause extensions in other management agents to fire. (Don't worry, we're not there yet.)

The problem facing any IdM product vendor is that if you change the set of rules for synchronization of data, then how do you reapply those new rules to objects that have not been triggered by an event or state change? We'll come back to this, but suffice it to say that this product enforces the current set of rules against *all* objects when a *full synchronization* is run; so full synchronization reconciles every connector. Running a *delta synchronization* applies the current rule set to objects that have changed, or are currently disconnected, since the last full or delta import (i.e., the state changed).

Full synchronization
> Forces all rules and attribute flows to process every object in the CS. This ultimately will flow data from the CS to the MV and out to any other CS that is joined to the MV object in question.

Delta synchronization
> Forces all rules and attribute flows to process only the objects in the CS that have changed since the last synchronization. This will flow data from the CS to the MV only for changed objects.

It is important to recognize that the process of reconciliation is critical for issues of compliance. Products that do not ensure full reconciliation for all objects are not telling you the whole story.

We use full or delta imports to stage data into the CS, but we also do full or delta syncs to copy data between the CS and the MV. The important thing to note is that while imports are always one-way (import, not export), synchronizations are always two-way (import and export). There is simply no way around this—if you have export attribute flow rules set up, they must be processed to complete the state evaluation of every object, even if you only intend for this to happen in one place. If that CS object is tied to a CS object through an MV object (through a join), then a sync run on one CS will process changes all the way to the other CS object.

Figure 21-5 depicts normal synchronization convergence. Running a full or delta sync will cause synchronization to occur across all three connectors; however, *inbound attribute flow only occurs on the management agent that the synchronization was triggered from* (depicted as the DB-connected directory).

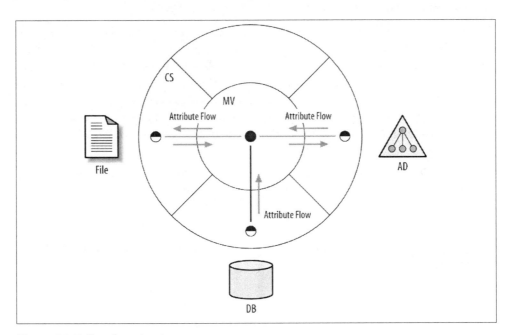

Figure 21-5. Synchronization

Now that we've talked about how to get data into the CS and sync it with an MV object, we need to talk more about management agents. We will touch on attribute flow in a moment.

Management Agents

The management agent (MA) is a set of processes comprising the native APIs of the product we are connecting to combined with a nice little GUI to configure it. All the stuff we talked about—imports and syncs, joins and projections, and connector filters —is part of the management agent itself. In fact, it is not an agent at all—at least not in the sense that you have to install anything on the CD. This is a fundamental difference between state-based and event-based products: event-based systems require some sort of agent or driver that must reside on the system or application in question, whereas state-based systems require nothing but a local instance of the APIs in question.

 To get the APIs needed for connectivity to Lotus Notes, the Lotus Notes client needs to be installed on the FIM server. The same can be said for Oracle connectivity requiring the Oracle client, SQL connectivity requiring the SQL client, and so on.

The MA is responsible for determining how you connect to the CD, which object types you want to see (e.g., user, group, or computer), and which attributes you care to have copied to the CS. Only selected attributes can flow into the MV through attribute flow.

Sometimes the terms *MA* and *CS* are used interchangeably, but while they represent the entirety of the CS relative to the CD, they are much more. The MA is where you store the credentials for connecting to the CD, as well as all of the connectivity, scopes, filters, join and projection rules, attribute flows, deprovision rules, extension configuration, and password sync setup. Suffice it to say that you will have one MA for every CD you want to talk to, which will be represented by its own CS.

MAs also provide a way to store and represent sets of potentially schedulable operation profiles, called *run profiles*.

Run profiles

You tell FIM that you want to perform a full import or a delta sync by creating a series of run profiles that contain at least one of the following prebuilt operations:

- Full import (stage only)
- Delta import (stage only)
- Full synchronization
- Delta synchronization
- Full import and delta synchronization
- Delta import and delta synchronization

- Export

The export operation is solely for exporting pending changes in the CS out to the CD. This is critical for actually sending the changes back to the directory. You should feel reassured to know that the product cannot automatically affect the CD simply by manipulating objects in the MV or the CS. You *must* do an export to send changes out. Consequently, if the credentials you supplied to the MA do not have rights to modify the requested attributes or create a newly provisioned user, for example, the exports will fail. The credentials in the MA must have all of the appropriate rights to affect the pending changes.

You can also string combinations of operations together in one profile. For instance, you might want to start with a delta import and delta synchronization and follow that immediately with an export, followed by a delta import. That would get data in, process it, and send it back out with the changes, all in one run.

At this point, don't worry too much about the "special" run profiles; you'll touch on them more if you begin working with the full product. But suffice it to say that they pretty much do what you'd think, with one exception. The "delta import delta synchronization" profile will only synchronize changes that were imported as part of the current delta import. This is *not* the same as performing the same two operations in separate steps.

Now, before we talk about attribute flow we need to talk briefly about the Metaverse Designer.

The Metaverse Designer

Suppose you have an attribute in your AD called `extensionAttribute3`, but it really represents your cost center. What you'd really like to do is just call it "Cost Center" in the MV so that it actually makes sense when you decide to flow this to some other CS. With the Metaverse Designer you can create custom object types and attributes as needed and you don't have to have OID numbers like you do in AD. You can create a `costCenter` of type `String (indexable)`, make it multivalue or not, index it if you want to, and assign it to the `person` object class. You can then flow data into that from any CS as long as it is of type `String`.

The Metaverse Designer is what you use when you want to add custom attributes to objects in the metaverse.

Attribute flow rules

Simply stated, an *attribute flow rule* is a mapping between a CS attribute (such as `extensionAttribute3`) and an MV attribute (such as `costCenter`). An attribute flow can be either import or export, and either direction can be one of the following mapping types:

Direct

Flowing data from a CS attribute to an MV attribute of the same type (e.g., `String`/`String`). The attribute names can be completely different, but you just want to flow the data over unaltered—for example, flow `EIN` into `employeeID`.

Advanced

There are three types of advanced flows:

Extension

Flows data from *one or more* CS attributes to a single MV attribute, whereby the data needs to be transformed or concatenated in some way. The attributes can even be of different types, as long as you perform the type conversion within the code. The term *extension* implies that we have to write code to accomplish this mapping. For example, take a user's last name and add the first character of the first name to form the logon ID.

Constant

Flows a constant or arbitrary `String` to a single MV object of type `string`. Since it's a constant, the data is not originating from any CS attribute. No code is required; however, if you want to "blank" out an attribute (flow a null), you have to do this with an *extension*—as of SP1, this was not an option available in the GUI. For example, everyone's company attribute is "My Company."

Distinguished name

Flows a component of a DN into an MV object of type `string`. You can pick apart a large DN by choosing which section of the string to flow across. No code is required, unless you want to transform the component itself, and then you're back to the extension. For example, you know that the second component of the DN is always the department name, so flow that information unaltered into the department attribute.

 This is available only for importing attribute flows into the metaverse; it cannot be used to export components of a DN to another CS. To do that, you need to flow the component into an MV attribute and then set up a direct export attribute flow to the CS.

With any rules extension, you have the opportunity to resolve the situation in any .NET language. The good news is that if you are a VB.NET or C# programmer, FIM will create the entire project template for you. You will find the greatest number of examples online in VB.NET, and that is the language we will use in this chapter.

MAs are used to connect natively to a CD; they define the objects in which you are interested, whether those objects should be filtered, how they are joined or projected, and what attribute flow rules exist between the CS and MV. You can create custom attributes to flow information into the MV through the Metaverse Designer, and run profiles are used to bundle together various methods to pull data into the CS and synchronize it with the MV.

FIM also supports password management via a web-based application and password synchronization from AD to other systems. Many additional scenarios are covered in the Microsoft Identity and Access Management Series (refer to "See Also" on page 721).

The scenario

Figure 21-6 outlines the example scenario of synchronizing AD from an HR database, which is used throughout this chapter. The numbered points will be referenced in later recipes.

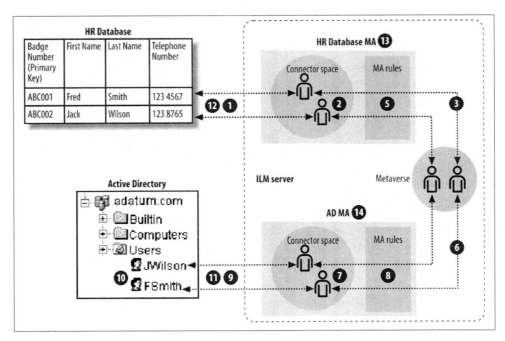

Figure 21-6. Example scenario

We'll start with an employee database that runs on SQL Server, referred to from now on as the HR Database.

Let's walk through how FIM will synchronize the HR Database with Active Directory and define some of the specialized terms Microsoft uses to describe the process. The numbers in parentheses refer to the numbered points in the diagram.

First, we will *import* or *stage* (1) records from the HR Database into the HR Database MA connector space. The import process creates connector space objects (2).

Next, we will *synchronize* the data in the HR Database MA connector space. The first time we do this, and any time FIM discovers a new user record in the MA connector space, FIM will *project* (3) a new object (4) into the metaverse, and *join*, or link, the HR Database MA object to the metaverse object. FIM will then *flow* attribute data from the HR Database MA connector space object to the *joined* metaverse object through the MA's rules (5).

Synchronizing the HR Database MA will also *provision* (6) a new connector space object (7) in the Active Directory MA's connector space and join the new Active Directory connector space object to the metaverse object (4). FIM will then flow the appropriate attribute information from the metaverse object (4) into the AD connector space object (7) through the Active Directory MA's rules (8).

We will *export* (9) objects (7) from the AD connector space into Active Directory itself to create Active Directory user objects (10).

We will also import (11) the `telephoneNumber` attribute from AD user objects (10) into the related AD connector space objects (7) and synchronize the AD management agent. This will flow attribute data through the ADMA rules (8) and into the joined metaverse object (4); from there, attribute data will flow through the HR Database MA's rules (5) to the joined HR Database MA connector space object (2). At this stage, the updated HR Database MA connector space object (2) will be exported (12) to the HR Database, resulting in the [`telephoneNumber`] column being updated.

We also will test deprovisioning by deleting a row in the HR Database and then importing (1) objects from the HR Database into the HR Database connector space. This will result in the related connector space object (2) being marked as deleted. Synchronizing the HR Database MA will cause the joined metaverse object (4) to be deleted. This will, in turn, cause the joined AD connector space object (7) to be deleted. Finally, the delete operation is exported to Active Directory, resulting in the deletion of an Active Directory user object (10).

See Also

Microsoft provides a great deal of useful documentation for MIIS on its website. This section lists some of the most useful documents:

The FIM help file

FIM comes with a very useful and complete help file. You can find it in the FIM Synchronization Service installation folder, typically at *C:\Program Files\Microsoft Forefront Identity Manager\2010\Synchronization Service\UIShell\Helpfiles*. The file is named *mms.chm*, and it contains general help for configuring and running FIM.

The FIM home page

The FIM home page (*http://bit.ly/10722il*) is the starting point for all the current information about FIM, including recent releases and other news.

Microsoft TechNet: FIM product page

The first stop for technical and training information for FIM can be found at the product page (*http://bit.ly/ZBLCLT*).

Microsoft TechNet: Forums - Forefront Identity Manager 2010

Here you can find the link to the FIM forum, which is frequented by the product team as well as many of the FIM MVPs (*http://bit.ly/YABw2C*).

FIM 2010 Technical Overview

This document provides an overview of FIM and describes core scenarios of the product features. Visit the FIM 2010 Technical Overview (*http://bit.ly/13Zcetm*).

FIM Installation Guide

The guide contains a series of articles covering the requirements and installation of FIM (*http://bit.ly/15sMY3l*).

FIM 2010 R2 Documentation Roadmap

The Documentation Roadmap (*http://bit.ly/13nBU3p*) contains a series of links that include an overview of the newest features and a complete series of links walking through the various features and functions.

TechNet Virtual Labs: Forefront Security

There are several virtual labs for FIM that are available as free downloads (*http://bit.ly/12LDBEV*). Each download includes FIM and a manual, along with a 90-minute block of lab time.

21.1. Creating a SQL Server Management Agent

Problem

You want to get employee records from a SQL Server database to FIM so that they can be used as the source for new accounts in AD.

Solution

You need to start by creating a management agent (MA) for the SQL Server database:

1. Open the Synchronization Service Manager.
2. Click the Management Agents button on the toolbar.
3. In the Actions pane on the right, click Create.
4. In the Create Management Agent Wizard, select SQL Server from the "Management Agent for" drop-down list.
5. Type HR Database into the Name text box.
6. Type a description in the Description field—this is where you can be creative.
7. Click Next.
8. In the Connect to Database pane on the right side:
    a. Type the SQL server name into the Server Name text box.
    b. Type the name of the database in the Database text box.
    c. Type the name of the table or view that contains the employee records in the Table/View text box.
    d. Leave the Delta View and Multivalue Table text boxes blank.
    e. Select the radio button for the type of authentication the SQL server is set up to use.
    f. Fill in the User Name, Password, and Domain text boxes with the credentials of a user who has permissions to read and update the table we will create.
9. Click Next.
10. On the Configure Columns page:
    a. Click the Set Anchor button. This will display the Set Anchor dialog box.
    b. In the Set Anchor dialog box, select Badge Number and click the Add button.
    c. Click OK to save the anchor attribute definition and then click Next.
11. On the Configure Connector Filter page, click Next.
12. On the Configure Join and Projection Rules page, click Next.
13. On the Configure Attribute Flow page, click Next.
14. On the Configure Deprovisioning page, click the "Make them disconnectors" radio button.
15. Click Next.
16. On the Configure Extensions page, click Finish.

Discussion

Following these steps will create a SQL Server management agent. Associated with the MA is a namespace known as the *connector space*. FIM will store the data from the relevant columns of the database here and use them to provision, synchronize, and deprovision user accounts in Active Directory. Creating the SQL Server management agent is the first of several steps to get the data into FIM. You should now see a management agent in the Management Agents pane of the Synchronization Service Manager with the name and comments displayed.

See Also

Recipe 21.2 for more on creating a SQL Server MA

21.2. Creating an Active Directory Management Agent

Problem

You want to provision user accounts into Active Directory from the records in a SQL database.

Solution

The first step to accomplish this is to create an Active Directory management agent (in Recipe 21.1, see (13) of Figure 21-6):

1. Open the Synchronization Service Manager.
2. Click the Management Agents button on the toolbar.
3. In the Actions pane on the right side, click Create.
4. In the Create Management Agent Wizard, select Active Directory Domain Services from the "Management Agent for" drop-down list.
5. In the Name box, type a name. The forest name is usually a good choice.
6. If you feel creative, type a meaningful description into the Description text box.
7. Click Next.
8. In the Connect to Active Directory Forest pane on the right side:
   a. Type the fully qualified DNS name of the forest into the Forest Name text box.
   b. Fill in the username, password, and domain name of an appropriate user account. The account must have sufficient access permissions. See this recipe's "Discussion" on page 725 for more details.
   c. Click Next.

9. In the Configure Directory Partitions pane on the right side:

    a. Select the domain(s) you wish to manage in the Select Directory Partitions field.

    b. Click the Containers button in the lower-right portion of the dialog box.

    c. In the Select Container dialog, select the containers you wish to manage.

    d. Click OK.

    e. Click Next.

10. On the Configure Provisioning Hierarchy screen, click Next.

11. On the Select Object Types screen, select the user object type and then click Next.

 FIM requires that the organizationUnit, domainDNS, and con
tainer object types always be selected. FIM uses these objects to
maintain the hierarchical structure of Active Directory in the MA's
connector space.

12. In the Select Attributes pane on the right side, select the attributes you wish to manage from the Attributes field. You can check the Show All checkbox to display a full list of all attributes in the AD. Some AD attributes are mandatory; a typical minimal list would be cn, displayName, employeeID, givenName, sAMAccount Name, sn, userAccountControl, userPrincipalName, and unicodePwd. (You need to select the Show All checkbox to see the unicodePwd attribute.) Click Next to save the selected attributes.

13. On the Configure Connector Filter page, click Next.

14. On the Configure Join and Projection Rules page, click Next.

15. On the Configure Attribute Flow page, click Next.

16. On the Configure Deprovisioning page, click "Stage a delete on the object for the next export run" and then click Next.

17. On the Configure Extensions page, click Finish.

Discussion

The account used to connect to AD must have the following rights to the containers that you intend to write to:

*   Standard
*   Read
*   Write

- Advanced
- Delete
- Replicate directory changes
- Create all child objects
- Delete all child objects
- List contents
- Read all properties
- Write all properties
- Delete subtree
- Read permissions
- All validated writes

A popular question that surfaces in the discussion boards has to do with why FIM doesn't support the use of anonymous binds to LDAP directories. While there is quite a bit of development involved in connecting to a given directory's change log for the purposes of being able to process deltas, there was obviously a hard choice made during the original product planning to avoid direct support for binding anonymously. Most of the use cases involving FIM have to do with ongoing delta processing, so supporting an anonymous bind provides little or no value except for the small percentage of cases where a quick solution precipitates the need for an anonymous bind. If you find yourself in the latter situation, consider using *ldifde* or another tool to extract the directory to an LDIF file for processing or build an extensible MA (XMA).

See Also

Recipe 21.1; Recipe 21.5; Recipe 21.8

21.3. Setting Up a Metaverse Object Deletion Rule

Problem

You have decided on a single authoritative source for new employees: a SQL Server database. When a user record is deleted from it, you want FIM 2010 R2 to delete the corresponding Active Directory account.

Solution

One of the configuration options required to have deletions propagated from a SQL Server database to Active Directory is the *metaverse object deletion rule*:

1. Open the Synchronization Service Manager.

2. Click the Metaverse Designer button on the toolbar.

3. In the Actions pane on the far-right side, click Configure Object Deletion Rule.

4. Select the "Delete metaverse object when connector from this management agent is disconnected" radio button and ensure that the SQL Server database MA has a checkmark in the box next to the name.

5. Click OK.

Discussion

The object deletion rule informs FIM of when to delete metaverse objects. Deleting a metaverse object does not necessarily cause anything to happen in the connected data source, but it *does* disconnect any connected objects in all of the connector spaces. This will cause the deprovisioning rule to fire for each disconnected object. The deprovisioning rule is configured for each management agent in the Configure Deprovisioning page for the management agent.

It is critical to plan accordingly for the life cycle of every object. In many cases, deleting the MV object is not desirable if not all of the connectors are to be deleted. If you find yourself needing to maintain objects in other connected directories even after an authoritative source object has changed to an inactive status or been removed entirely, consider leaving the connectors in place and allowing the default metaverse object deletion rule to prevail. This is incredibly helpful if you are doing any sort of reporting based off of aggregated identity data derived from the metaverse.

See Also

Recipe 21.1; Recipe 21.28 for deleting data in the connector space and metaverse; Recipe 21.15 for the provisioning run profile

21.4. Setting Up a Simple Import Attribute Flow

Problem

You have already created the MAs you need, but you want to flow the column data from a SQL Server database to attributes in Active Directory.

Solution

You need to configure the AD MA's attribute flow rules page (in Recipe 21.1, refer to (5) in Figure 21-6):

1. Open the Synchronization Service Manager.

2. Click the Management Agents button on the toolbar.

3. In the Management Agents pane, double-click the SQL Server database MA.

4. In the Management Agent Designer pane on the lefthand side, select Configure Attribute Flow.

5. Ensure that "person" is selected in the data source object type drop-down list.

6. Ensure that "person" is selected in the metaverse object type drop-down list.

7. In the Data Source attribute list, select the attribute whose data you wish to flow into the metaverse. (See "Discussion" for some suggestions.)

8. In the Metaverse attribute list, select the attribute you want the data to flow into. (See "Discussion" for some suggestions.)

9. In the Mapping Type section of the dialog, select Direct.

10. In the Flow Direction section of the dialog, select Import.

11. Click New. The new attribute mapping will appear in the attribute mapping list, with an arrow indicating that it is an import attribute flow.

12. Click OK.

Discussion

FIM has been configured to flow an attribute from the SQL Server database MA's connector space into the metaverse. In general, we can map any attribute from the connected system to any attribute in the metaverse. However, if a Mapping Type of Direct is issued, the attributes in the MA and the metaverse must be of the same data type (e.g., string or integer). To map from one data type to another, configure the advanced attribute flow (see Recipe 21.6).

Here are some typical simple mappings:

- `FirstName→givenName`
- `LastName→sn`
- `Dept→department`
- `StaffNumber→employeeID`
- `TelNo→telephoneNumber`

You need to make your own decisions about what data in the SQL Server database maps onto what data in the metaverse attributes, but these are usually fairly obvious. If you want to construct a name—for example, you'd like the `sAMAccountName` to be derived from the first character of the first name prepended to the last name—you need an advanced flow.

As a rule of thumb (and personal preference), it is generally better to do advanced flows to assemble data on the inbound flow so that the correct information is contributed to the metaverse. This approach scales better since syncs process only the inbound attribute flow for the MA that the run profile was executed from, and having direct flows on all outbound attribute rules translates to less overhead for converging a single identity. So consider moving as many of your advanced rules to import flows as possible, and use advanced rules only when necessary for export flows.

See Also

Recipe 21.1; Recipe 21.5 for setting up a simple export attribute flow to AD; Recipe 21.6 for defining a more advanced attribute flow; Recipe 21.7 for writing a rules extension to take the advanced flow even further (all these flows are eventually exported to AD)

21.5. Setting Up a Simple Export Attribute Flow to Active Directory

Problem

You want to flow attributes in the metaverse to attributes in AD. For example, the givenName field in the metaverse needs to map to the givenName field in AD.

Solution

You need to configure the attribute flow pages on the AD MA (in Recipe 21.1, refer to (8) in Figure 21-6):

1. Open the Synchronization Service Manager.
2. Click the Management Agents button on the toolbar.
3. In the Management Agents pane, double-click the AD MA.
4. In the Management Agent Designer pane on the lefthand side, select Configure Attribute Flow.
5. Ensure that "user" is selected in the data source object type drop-down list.
6. Ensure that "person" is selected in the metaverse object type drop-down list.
7. In the data source attribute list, select the connector space attribute you want to flow data into. See "Discussion" on page 730 for some suggestions.
8. In the Metaverse attribute list, select the attribute you want to flow data from. See "Discussion" on page 730 for some suggestions.

9. In the Mapping Type section of the dialog, select Direct.

10. In the Flow Direction section of the dialog, select Export.

11. Click New. The new attribute mapping will appear in the attribute mapping list, with an arrow indicating that it is an export attribute flow.

12. Click OK.

Discussion

This will configure a simple export attribute flow from the metaverse to the AD MA. You need to determine what attributes in the metaverse should flow to AD attributes.

Here are some typical simple mappings:

- givenName→givenName
- sn→sn
- department→department
- employeeID→employeeID
- telephoneNumber→telephoneNumber
- cn→displayName
- cn→cn
- uid→sAMAccountName

In many FIM scenarios, data is manipulated on its way *into* the metaverse, and then copied on its way out to other connected systems. In this example, the cn comes from the displayName. This is because you will later create an advanced import flow that will write the first name followed by a space and the last name into the displayName in the metaverse. Something similar will be done for uid, only you will take the first character of the first name and append the last name; for example, Fred Smith gets an sAMAccountName of *FSmith*.

See Also

Recipe 21.1; Recipe 21.4; Recipe 21.6; Recipe 21.7 (these recipes are interesting because most of the data you are exporting to AD in this recipe was first imported from them)

21.6. Defining an Advanced Import Attribute Flow

Problem

You want to create an Active Directory username using the first and last names from a SQL Server database. Simple attribute-to-attribute mapping is not sufficient. You need to take partial strings from different attributes and combine them to form a new name.

Solution

This will involve writing some VB or C# code for an advanced attribute flow, which is covered in Recipe 21.7. To start, you must define the *flow rule*—an entity that connects the UI elements to the coding we will do later (refer to (5) in Figure 21-6):

1. Open the Synchronization Service Manager.
2. Click the Management Agents button on the toolbar.
3. In the Management Agents pane, double-click the HR Database MA.
4. In the Management Agent Designer pane on the lefthand side, select Configure Attribute Flow.
5. Ensure that "person" is selected in the data source object type drop-down list.
6. Ensure that "person" is selected in the metaverse object type drop-down list.
7. In the Mapping Type section of the dialog, select Advanced.
8. In the Flow Direction section of the dialog, select Import.
9. Select FirstName and LastName from the data source attributes text box. (To select multiple entries, hold down the Ctrl key.)

 FirstName and LastName in this example are the names of fields in the SQL Server database. Your available field options will depend on the database used.

10. Select cn from the Metaverse attribute list.
11. Click New.
12. In the Advanced Import Attribute Flow Options dialog, delete the default name, type cn, and then click OK. The flow rule name you defined here will appear in the VB or C# code you will write later. A convention among MIIS developers is to use the name of the destination attribute (in this case, cn).

13. Notice that in the Type column in the upper pane, the newly created attribute mapping is detailed as Rules-Extension. A rules extension is a unit of managed .NET code.

14. Select `FirstName` and `LastName` from the Data Source attribute mapping list. (Remember to use the Ctrl key to select multiple attributes.)

15. Select `uid` from the Metaverse attribute mapping list.

16. Click New.

17. In the Advanced Import Attribute Flow Options dialog, type **uid** into the "Flow rule name" text box and click OK.

18. Notice in the Type column in the upper pane the newly created attribute mapping is detailed as Rules-Extension.

19. Select Configure Extensions in the lefthand pane.

20. Type `HR DatabaseExtension` into the Rules Extension Name text box.

21. Click OK.

Discussion

In this recipe, an advanced attribute flow rule was defined. The rule extension is implemented in managed .NET code in Recipe 21.7.

There are two additional types of advanced attribute flow. One is where a constant is defined that will always be written to the selected attribute. The other is used if you are flowing a distinguished name (the source attribute must be defined as a *Reference DN*) and only wish to flow a specific component of the DN and not the entire DN itself into a string attribute in the metaverse. No rules extension code is required for either type of advanced attribute flow. However, if you need to manipulate the attributes being flowed using code, you must define an advanced attribute flow and provide a flow rule name. Even though you may not have created the DLL that will be used at this stage, you still have to put a name in the dialog to exit the MA designer.

See Also

Recipe 21.1; Recipe 21.4 for setting up a simple import attribute flow; Recipe 21.5; Recipe 21.7 for creating a rules extension to further extend advanced attribute flow; Recipe 21.8 to export data to AD

21.7. Implementing an Advanced Attribute Flow Rules Extension

Problem

You want to perform advanced attribute flow from a SQL Server database.

Solution

You've already defined an advanced attribute flow rule for the MA in the Identity Manager console. You now need to write the code and produce the DLL that implements that flow rule (refer to (5) in Figure 21-6):

1. Open the Synchronization Service Manager.

2. Click the Management Agents button on the toolbar.

3. Right-click the SQL Server MA in the Management Agents pane and select Create Extension Projects→Rules Extension.

4. Ensure that the dialog box is filled in similar to Figure 21-7. (You can specify your own name and location.)

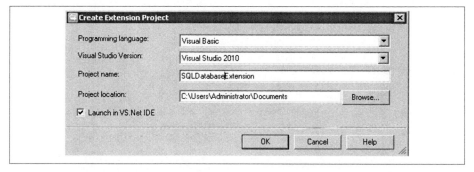

Figure 21-7. Create Extension Project dialog

5. Click OK. This will launch Visual Studio.

This recipe assumes that you have already installed Visual Studio 2008 or later on the machine running FIM. If you are doing your development on another machine, you have two choices. You can map a drive to the FIM server and modify the code through the mapped drive, or you can copy the entire project to your development machine and work on it there. In any case, you will have to be sure to copy the resultant DLL back to the server any time you make a code change.

6. In the Solution Explorer in the far-righthand pane in Visual Studio, double-click the *HR DatabaseExtension.vb* node. This file contains the source code for your rules extension.

7. The main code window should show the automatically generated code. (This auto-code generation is provided for VB and C#.) The first few lines of code should look like this:

```
Imports Microsoft.MetadirectoryServices
Public Class MAExtensionObject
    Implements IMASynchronization
```

8. Scroll to the code section that looks like this:

```
Public Sub MapAttributesForImport(ByVal FlowRuleName As String, ByVal↵
 csentry As
    CSEntry, ByVal mventry As MVEntry) Implements
    IMASynchronization.MapAttributesForImport
        ' TODO: write your import
attribute flow code
        Select Case FlowRuleName
            Case "uid"
                ' TODO: remove the following statement and add your scripted
                    ' import attribute flow here
                Throw New EntryPointNotImplementedException()

            Case "cn"
                ' TODO: remove the following statement and add your scripted
                    ' import
attribute flow here
                Throw New EntryPointNotImplementedException()

            Case Else
                ' TODO: remove the following statement and add your default
                    ' script here
                Throw New EntryPointNotImplementedException()

        End Select
End Sub
```

9. Edit this section to make the code look like this (the bold sections are new code that we typed in):

```
Select Case FlowRuleName
Case "uid"If Not csentry("Last Name").IsPresent Then          Throw New↵
 UnexpectedDataException("No Last Name!")End If
If Not csentry("First Name").IsPresent Then          Throw New↵
 UnexpectedDataException("No First Name!")End If
mventry("uid").Value = csentry("First Name").StringValue.Substring(0, 1)↵
 + csentry("Last Name").Value

Case "cn"If Not csentry("Last Name").IsPresent Then          Throw New↵
 UnexpectedDataException("No Last Name!")    End If
If Not csentry("First Name").IsPresent Then          Throw New↵
 UnexpectedDataException("No First Name!")    End If
mventry("cn").Value = csentry("First Name").Value + " "↵
;+ csentry("Last Name").Value

Case Else
    ' TODO: remove the following statement and add your default script here
        Throw New EntryPointNotImplementedException

End Select
```

 First Name and Last Name in this example are the names of fields in the SQL Server database. Your available field options will depend on the database used.

10. Go to the Build menu and select Build Solution. Ensure that in the output panel at the bottom of the screen you see a message that looks like this:

```
--------------------- Done ---------------------

    Build: 1 succeeded, 0 failed, 0 skipped
```

11. Close Visual Studio.

12. Open Windows Explorer and browse to *C:\Program Files\Microsoft Forefront Identity Manager\2010\Synchronization Service\Extensions* (this assumes you installed FIM 2010 R2 on the *C:* drive in the default location; if you didn't, substitute the relevant parts of the path), and ensure that the DLL is present. The DLL will be called *<SQL Server MA>.dll*.

13. To be absolutely sure you have the correct rules extension selected in FIM, open the Synchronization Service Manager.

14. Click the Management Agents button.

15. In the Management Agents pane, double-click the SQL Server MA.

16. In the lefthand pane of the Management Agent Designer, click Configure Extensions.

17. Click the Select button.

18. Select *HR DatabaseExtension.dll* and click OK.

19. Click OK to close Management Agent properties.

20. Close the Synchronization Service Manager.

Discussion

This code does some fairly simple string manipulation. This chapter doesn't venture into the world of advanced FIM coding, but there are many examples in the Developer Reference off the help menu in the Synchronization Service Manager.

The FIM development environment is so flexible that human-driven digital identity business processes can be encapsulated in extension rules. However, there is no workflow engine, which means you may have to call workflow processes on another engine, such as BizTalk.

See Also

Recipe 21.1; Recipe 21.8 for setting constants on certain attributes

21.8. Setting Up Advanced Export Attribute Flow in Active Directory

Problem

Simple attribute-to-attribute mapping is not flexible enough to create the attribute values you want. You want to set constant values on some attributes. In this case, there is a bit mask of great interest: the mask used to set properties for accounts, such as whether the account is disabled.

Solution

This will involve writing some VB or C# code, like the script for advanced attribute flow covered in Recipe 21.9, but we must set up flow rule names for the code in this section (refer to (8) in Figure 21-6):

1. Open the Synchronization Service Manager.

2. Click the Management Agents button on the toolbar.

3. In the Management Agents pane, double-click the AD MA.

4. In the Management Agent Designer pane on the lefthand side, select Configure Attribute Flow.

5. Ensure that "user" is selected in the data source object type drop-down list.

6. Ensure that "person" is selected in the metaverse object type drop-down list.

7. In the Mapping Type section of the dialog, select Advanced.

8. In the Flow Direction section of the dialog, select Export.

9. Select userAccountControl from the Data Source attributes list.

10. Click New.

11. In the Advanced Attribute Flow Options dialog, select Constant.

12. Type 512 into the Value text box and then click OK.

13. Notice that in the Type column in the upper pane, the newly created attribute mapping is detailed as Constant, with an arrow indicating export attribute flow.

14. Click OK to close the Management Agent Designer.

Discussion

Active Directory requires a minimal set of attributes in order to create normal, usable, enabled accounts. In this recipe we have set the required attributes. We set the userAccountControl flag to 512 (bit 9 set), which indicates that this account is a normal account. In other cases we might use a rules extension and set bit 1 to disable the account; for example, if there was an employee status field in the SQL Server database that indicated the employee was inactive.

See Also

Recipe 21.1; Recipe 21.9; Recipe 21.14 for writing a rules extension to provision user objects to the AD MA from objects in a SQL Server MA

21.9. Configuring a Run Profile to Do an Initial Load of Data from a SQL Server Management Agent

Problem

You need to get the data from the SQL Server database to its connector space.

Solution

Before you can run a management agent, you must create a *run profile* for it (refer to (9) in Figure 21-6, which shows data being loaded from AD to the AD connector space):

1. Open the Synchronization Service Manager.

2. Click the Management Agents button on the toolbar.

3. In the Management Agents pane, click the SQL Server MA.

4. In the Actions pane on the far-right side, click Configure Run Profiles.

5. In the Configure Run Profiles for "<MA Name>" dialog box, click New Profile.

6. In the Name text box, type `Full Import (Stage Only)` and then click Next.

7. Ensure that Full Import (Stage Only) is selected in the Type drop-down list and then click Next.

8. Ensure that "default" is showing in the Partition drop-down list and then click Finish.

9. Click OK to create the run profile.

Discussion

Three steps are required to get data into the SQL Server MA connector space:

1. Create the MA.

2. Create a run profile to run the MA.

3. Execute the run profile. In this recipe you have created the run profile.

It is generally a good idea to give the run profiles exactly the same names as the step type they represent. You will later create scripts that call run profiles. It is possible to give a run profile a name such as "Complete Cycle" and combine many steps in the run profile. However, when calling such entities from scripts, the calling script isn't self-documenting, in that it hides what it is doing. It is also much easier to debug scripts when you know exactly what step is being called. Hence, you have created a run profile called Full Import (Stage Only), which consists of a single step of type Full Import (Stage Only). The one exception to this general rule is discussed in Recipe 21.17.

See Also

Recipe 21.10 for more on how to use the run profile to load data; Recipe 21.17

21.10. Loading Initial SQL Server Database Data into FIM 2010 R2 Using a Run Profile

Problem

With the MA and run profile created, you now want to load the data into FIM 2010 R2.

Solution

You need to execute the run profile to load the data (refer to (1) in Figure 21-6, which shows data being loaded from the SQL Server database to the SQL Server database MA connector space):

1. Open the Synchronization Service Manager.
2. Click the Management Agents button on the toolbar.
3. In the Management Agents pane, click the SQL Server MA.
4. In the Actions pane on the far-right side, click Run.
5. In the Run Management Agent dialog, select Full Import (Stage Only) and click OK.

   You'll have to be quick if there is only a small amount of data in the database. Notice the MA says "Running" in the State column of the Management Agents pane.

6. In the Synchronization Statistics pane in the bottom-lefthand corner, statistics showing the number of adds are displayed. If you click the hyperlink, you can navigate to the information that was loaded.

The SQL Server database you are importing from must have records in it before FIM can import any data.

Discussion

When designing a large system, work with a very small, representative set of data during development (maybe 10 records). This is because you will frequently find errors in your rules and set about deleting everything in FIM, reconfiguring your rules, and starting again. It is much better to do these initial data loads with 10 or so records rather than 100,000 records, which will take a long time to load. When you are convinced your rules are good, start working with larger data sets.

See Also

Recipe 21.1; Recipe 21.9 for more on how this run profile was configured

21.11. Configuring a Run Profile to Load the Container Structure from Active Directory

Problem

Before you can provision and synchronize data in the AD connector space, you need to build the container structure in the connector space to reflect the container structure of Active Directory.

Solution

To do this, you have to create an appropriate run profile for the AD MA and import the AD container structure into the connector space.

 The fact that you have to separately import the container structure from AD into the MA's connector space is not obvious and is frequently overlooked by even the most experienced FIM developers. If you fail to perform this step, the synchronization process will fail when it tries to provision new objects into the AD connector space.

Refer to (9) in Figure 21-6, which shows data being loaded from AD to the AD connector space:

1. Open the Synchronization Service Manager.
2. Click the Management Agents button on the toolbar
3. In the Management Agents pane, click the AD MA.
4. In the Actions pane on the far-right side, click Configure Run Profiles.
5. In the Configure Run Profiles dialog, click New Profile.
6. In the Name text box, type **Full Import (Stage Only)** and then click Next.
7. Ensure that Full Import (Stage Only) is selected in the Type drop-down list and then click Next.
8. Ensure that the correct domain partition is showing in the Partition drop-down list and then click Finish.
9. Ensure that the details in the Step Details field look like Figure 21-8.

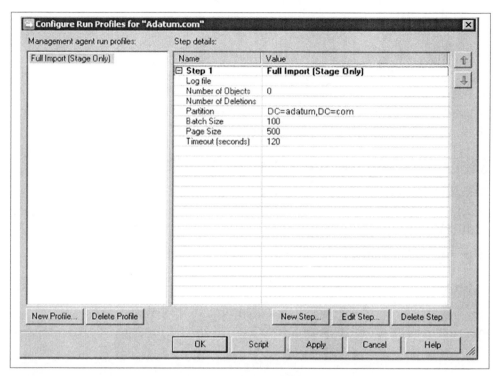

> Your partition name may be different.

10. Click OK.

Figure 21-8. Configure Run Profiles dialog for the AD MA

Discussion

Three steps are required to get data into the AD MA connector space:

1. Create the MA.

2. Create the run profile.

3. Execute the run profile. In this recipe you created the run profile.

When you create an AD MA, you specify which partitions (naming contexts) you wish to synchronize. When creating a run profile, you must be careful to select the correct partition (Naming Context in AD terms, which will usually be after the domain NC) from which to load the container structure.

A common mistake among FIM novices is to get "object does not have a parent" errors when running a synchronization step. This is because the container structure for Active Directory isn't loaded into the AD MA's connector space.

FIM can create missing containers based on rules, but you need to configure and write those rules. That is beyond the scope of this book.

See Also

Recipe 21.1; Recipe 21.12 for more on how to use the run profile that was configured in this recipe; the TechNet FIM 2010 R2 Forum for many discussion threads on programming techniques for the creation of missing containers (search for "OU creation" after you have joined the forum (*http://bit.ly/16crFTp*))

21.12. Loading the Initial Active Directory Container Structure into FIM 2010 R2 Using a Run Profile

Problem

With the AD MA and run profile created, you need to get the data into FIM.

Solution

You now need to run the AD MA run profile to import the AD container structure (refer to (9) in Figure 21-6, which shows the data being loaded from AD into the AD connector space):

1. Open the Synchronization Service Manager.
2. Click the Management Agents button on the toolbar.
3. In the Management Agents pane, click the AD MA.
4. In the Actions pane on the far-right side, click Run.
5. In the Run Management Agent dialog, select Full Import (Stage Only) and click OK.
6. You'll have to be quick if there is only a small amount of data in AD. Notice the MA briefly says "Running" in the State column of the Management Agents pane.
7. Notice the Synchronization Statistics pane in the bottom-lefthand corner, where statistics showing the number of adds are displayed. If you click the hyperlink, you can navigate to the information that was loaded.

Discussion

The first time you load the container structure into FIM, you need to use a full import step. Once the container structure is loaded, subsequent imports can use delta import steps, which in normal daily operations will be considerably faster to execute and will consume fewer resources on the FIM server, the AD domain controller, and the network.

See Also

Recipe 21.1; Recipe 21.11 for more on how to configure the run profile that was used in this recipe

21.13. Setting Up a SQL Server Management Agent to Project Objects to the Metaverse

Problem

The objects in the SQL Server MA's connector space now need to be projected into the metaverse. There are three steps:

1. Configuring the MA for projection
2. Creating a synchronization run profile
3. Executing the synchronization run profile

Solution

Refer to (3) in Figure 21-6, which shows objects being provisioned from the SQL Server MA's connector space to the metaverse:

1. Open the Synchronization Service Manager.
2. Click the Management Agents button on the toolbar.
3. In the Management Agents pane, double-click the SQL Server MA.
4. In the Management Agent Designer pane on the lefthand side, select Configure Join and Projection Rules.
5. Click the New Projection Rule button.
6. In the Projection dialog, ensure that Declared is selected and that the drop-down list shows "person", and then click OK.
7. Notice in the "Join and Projection Rules for person" frame, the columns are detailed thusly:

- Mapping Group: 1
- Action: Project
- Metaverse Object Type: person

8. Click OK.

Discussion

The synchronization process *projects* (or creates) metaverse objects that are *joined* to objects in the SQL Server MA connector space. When projected, FIM can *provision* new objects to the AD MA's connector space. Hence, in our demonstration it is *projection* that initiates *provisioning*; however, it is perfectly legal for changes in attribute states to trigger provisioning if you have written your provisioning extensions to observe such workflows. The most common example would be looking for a change in an HR employee status attribute to trigger creation of a new account in AD. While novices often use the terms *project* and *provision* interchangeably, they mean quite different things.

From the FIM perspective, *provision* means "to create a new CS object in a CS where there was no object previously." From an AD administrator's perspective, provision generally means creation of an AD account complete with all of the standard accoutrements (home directory, terminal server profile, etc.), so it is important to be clear, depending on your audience.

Table 21-1 clarifies this and introduces some new terminology: csentry for connector space objects and mventry for metaverse objects.

Table 21-1. Synchronization process

HR Database connector space	Action	Metaverse	Action	AD connector space
csentry objects →	Project to metaverse →	mventry objects →	Provision to connector space →	csentry objects

See Also

Recipe 21.1; Recipe 21.14 for more on provisioning

21.14. Writing a Rules Extension to Provision User Objects

Problem

This recipe specifically covers writing a rules extension to provision user objects to the AD MA from objects in the SQL Server MA. You want FIM to provision objects to the AD MA's connector space based on objects in the SQL Server MA.

Solution

There are three steps to *provisioning*:

1. Write a rules extension.
2. Configure a run profile.
3. Execute the run profile.

In this recipe, you will write a Provisioning-Rules-Extension. FIM will help you with the initial project creation. Refer to (6) in Figure 21-6, which shows objects being provisioned from the metaverse to the AD connector space:

1. Open the Synchronization Service Manager.
2. From the Tools menu, select Options.
3. In the Options dialog, place a checkmark next to "Enable metaverse rules extension".
4. Click the Create Rules Extension Project button.
5. Ensure that the Create Extension Project dialog looks like Figure 21-9.

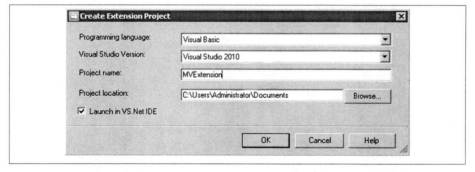

Figure 21-9. Dialog for creating the metaverse Provisioning-Rules-Extension

6. Click OK.
7. In Visual Studio, double-click *MVExtension* in the Solution Explorer.
8. The first few lines of the code pane should look like this:

```
Imports Microsoft.MetadirectoryServices

Public Class MVExtensionObject
    Implements IMVSynchronization
```

9. Navigate to the section that looks like this:

```
Public Sub Provision(ByVal mventry As MVEntry) Implements
IMVSynchronization.Provision
        ' TODO: Remove this throw statement if you implement this method
```

```
                Throw New EntryPointNotImplementedException()
            End Sub
```

10. Modify it to contain the following code:

```
    Public Sub Provision(ByVal mventry As MVEntry) Implements ↵
    IMVSynchronization.Provision

        Dim container As String
        Dim rdn As String
        Dim ADMA As ConnectedMA
        Dim numConnectors As Integer

        Dim myConnector As CSEntry
        Dim csentry As CSEntry
        Dim dn As ReferenceValue

        ' Ensure that the cn attribute is present.
        If Not mventry("cn").IsPresent Then
            Throw New UnexpectedDataException("cn attribute is not present.")
        End If
        ' Calculate the container and RDN.↵
        container = "cn=users,DC=adatum,DC=com"
        rdn = "cn=" & mventry("cn").Value
        ADMA = mventry.ConnectedMAs("adatum.com")
        dn = ADMA.EscapeDNComponent(rdn).Concat(container)

        numConnectors = ADMA.Connectors.Count

        ' create a new connector.
        If numConnectors = 0 Then
            csentry = ADMA.Connectors.StartNewConnector("user")
            csentry.DN = dn
          csentry("unicodePwd").Value = "Password1"
            csentry.CommitNewConnector()

        ElseIf numConnectors = 1 Then
            ' If the connector has a different DN rename it.
            myConnector = ADMA.Connectors.ByIndex(0)
            myConnector.DN = dn
        Else
            Throw New UnexpectedDataException("Error: There are" + ↵
            numConnectors.ToString + " connectors")
        End If
    End Sub
```

11. Notice the highlighted entries "cn=users,DC=adatum,DC=com". You will need to enter your own domain and container information here.

12. Notice the highlighted entry mventry.ConnectedMAs("adatum.com"). You will need to modify this to your own AD MA name.

13. From the File menu, select Build→Build Solution.

14. Open the Synchronization Service Manager.

15. From the menu select Tools→Options.

16. In the Options dialog, click Browse.

17. Select *MVExtension.dll* and click OK to close the Options dialog.

Discussion

Because you can use any .NET programming language, FIM is very flexible in a multi-team environment. As with many modern systems, it is not great programming skills that help you build good rules extensions with FIM: it is experience and familiarity with the object model. It is well worth getting to know the FIM object model. Many novices spend hours or days coding a function, only to find there is already a method on the object that does the thing they have spent all their time on.

If you are working on distributing the workload for provisioning to multiple systems (e.g., each MA is assigned to a developer or team), consider adopting the MV Router model whereby each MA is compartmentalized into its own project DLL and controlled by a single "router" DLL. In this manner, you reduce the amount of testing involved whenever code for a single MA is changed, since you are not affecting code in other projects.

See Also

Recipe 21.1; Recipe 21.4 for a description of how the code in this recipe is triggered; Recipe 21.13 for setting up a SQL Server MA to project objects to the metaverse (remember, in this demonstration it is *projection* that triggers *provisioning*)

21.15. Creating a Run Profile for Provisioning

Problem

You need to synchronize data using the management agent to provision new accounts in the AD connector space. Before you can run the MA, you have to create a run profile that will synchronize the MA's connector space with the metaverse.

Solution

You now need to create a provisioning run profile for a SQL Server MA to synchronize user objects from it to the AD MA's connector space. The run profile step is of type *synchronization*:

1. Open the Synchronization Service Manager.

2. Click the Management Agents button on the toolbar.

3. In the Management Agents pane, click the SQL Server MA.

4. In the Actions pane on the far-right side, click Configure Run Profiles.

5. In the Configure Run Profiles dialog, click New Profile.

6. In the Name text box, type **Full Synchronization** and then click Next.

7. Ensure that Full Synchronization is selected in the Type drop-down list and then click Next.

8. Ensure that "default" is showing in the Partition drop-down list and then click Finish.

9. Ensure that the details in the Step Details field look like Figure 21-10.

10. Notice in the Management Agent run profiles list that the Full Import (Stage Only) profile you created earlier is still there.

11. Click OK.

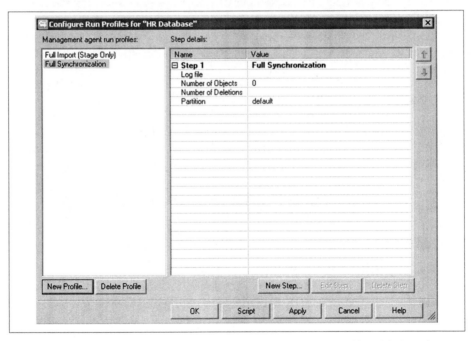

Figure 21-10. Dialog showing a Full Synchronization run profile added to the SQL Server MA

Discussion

There are two types of synchronization run profiles: full and delta. A *full synchronization* will process every object in the connector space. This is obviously necessary when it is the very first synchronization on the data. But in normal daily operations, you only want to perform *delta synchronization* steps because they process only objects that have changed since the last synchronization.

Full synchronization is also used when you have made a change to the management agent configuration; for example, you have added a new attribute flow. Usually you will want to run the reconfigured MA against all of the objects in the connector space. A delta synchronization would apply the rule only to objects that had changed since the last synchronization.

See Also

Recipe 21.13 for setting up a SQL Server MA to project objects to the metaverse; Recipe 21.14 for writing a rules extension to provision user objects to the AD MA from objects in a SQL Server MA; Recipe 21.16 for executing the run profile created in this recipe

21.16. Executing the Provisioning Rule

Problem

You need to *provision* new objects to the AD connector space.

Solution

You need to run the provisioning run profile. The provisioning run profile triggers projection ((3) in Figure 21-6). The arrival of new objects in the metaverse ((4) in Figure 21-6) in turn triggers provisioning ((6) in Figure 21-6) and creates new objects ((7) in Figure 21-6) in the AD connector space. Follow these steps:

1. Open the Identity Manager.
2. Click the Management Agents button on the toolbar.
3. In the Management Agents pane, click the HR Database MA.
4. In the Actions pane on the far-right side, click Run.
5. In the Run Management Agent dialog, select Full Synchronization and click OK.
6. Notice that the MA says "Running" in the State column of the Management Agents pane and then says "Idle."

7. Notice that in the Synchronization Statistics pane in the bottom-lefthand corner, statistics showing the number of projections and provisioned entries are displayed. If you click one of the hyperlinks, you can navigate to the information that was projected and provisioned.

Discussion

Inbound attribute flow is processed only on the MA that the run profile is executed against. That includes joins and projections, and since we have to have an MV object from which to provision, we will need to run a synchronization run profile against the HR MA in order to trigger provisioning to create the objects in the AD MA. If you were to run a synchronization run profile against the AD MA at this stage, nothing would be provisioned.

See Also

Recipe 21.13 for setting up the HR Database MA to project objects to the metaverse; Recipe 21.14 for writing a rules extension to provision user objects to the AD MA from objects in the HR Database MA; Recipe 21.15 for creating the run profile that was executed in this recipe

21.17. Creating a Run Profile to Export Objects from the AD MA to Active Directory

Problem

You want to create the new accounts in Active Directory.

Solution

There are two steps to get the data from an MA to a connected system: creating an *export* run profile and executing the profile. This is the first step (the second step is in Recipe 21.18):

1. Open the Synchronization Service Manager.
2. Click the Management Agents button on the toolbar.
3. In the Management Agents pane, click the AD MA.
4. In the Actions pane on the far-right side, click Configure Run Profiles.
5. In the "Configure Run Profiles for" pane, click New Profile.
6. In the Name text box, type Export and then click Next.

7. Ensure that Export is selected in the Type drop-down list and then click Next.

8. Ensure that the correct domain partition is showing in the Partition drop-down list and then click Finish.

9. Click New Step.

10. In the Configure Step dialog, ensure that Delta Import (Stage Only) is selected in the Type drop-down list and then click Next.

11. Ensure that the correct domain is selected in the Partition drop-down list and then click Finish.

12. Ensure that the details in the Step Details field look like Figure 21-11.

 Your partition name may be different.

13. Click OK.

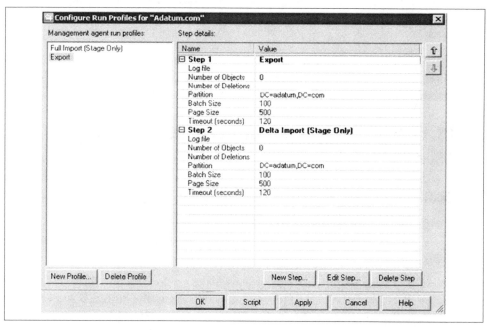

Figure 21-11. AD MA Export run profile showing an Export step followed by a Delta Import (Stage Only) step

Discussion

We mentioned earlier that it is a good idea to name the run profiles you create exactly the same as the run profile steps; that is, a run profile of type Full Import (Stage Only) is named Full Import (Stage Only). The one exception to this general rule applies to export run profiles. When an export is completed, the only way the MA can truly know the data was successfully written to the target data store is to reimport the changes and compare them to what it believes was written out. This is known as a *confirming import*. In AD, for example, if we programmatically create a user account without a password, AD will automatically disable the user account by setting a flag in the `userAc` `countControl` attribute. For FIM to maintain knowledge of this state, the confirming import brings this knowledge back into FIM. Therefore, exports need to include a confirming import stage. If the system we are exporting to supports some form of change logging (as AD does through USNs), then the type of confirming import can be a delta import (stage only). If the system doesn't expose any form of change logging (e.g., Novell eDirectory), a full import (stage only) step will be necessary.

FIM's sync engine performs delta imports using the Active Directory DirSync control. You need to assign the "Replicate Directory Changes" right to the user associated with the AD MA for delta imports to work (see MS KB 303972 for instructions).

See Also

Recipe 21.18 for more on how to use this run profile to export objects to AD; MS KB 303972 (How to Grant the "Replicating Directory Changes" Permission for the Microsoft Metadirectory Services AD MA Service Account)

21.18. Exporting Objects to Active Directory Using an Export Run Profile

Problem

You need to execute the export run profile.

Solution

The second step is executing the export run profile to get the data into AD (the first step is in Recipe 21.17). Refer to (9) in Figure 21-6, which shows the objects being exported to AD; (10) in the same figure shows the objects created in AD. Follow these steps:

1. Open the Identity Manager.
2. Click the Management Agents button on the toolbar.
3. In the Management Agents pane, click the AD MA.

4. In the Actions pane on the far-right side, click Run.

5. In the Run Management Agent dialog, select Export and click OK.

6. You'll have to be quick if there is only a small amount of data in the AD MA. Notice that the MA says "Running" in the State column of the Management Agents pane.

7. Notice that in the Synchronization Statistics pane in the bottom-lefthand corner, statistics showing the number of adds are displayed. If you click a hyperlink, you can navigate to the information that was written to AD.

8. Open Active Directory Users and Computers.

9. Navigate to the Users container.

10. Ensure that the user objects have been created.

Discussion

User accounts in Active Directory may be flagged as disabled even though you think they should be active. Assuming you set the userAccountControl attribute correctly, the usual reason for this is that some other attribute has not been set correctly and Active Directory has disabled the account. For example, if you do not set a password on an account, or the password you set does not meet the domain password requirements, Active Directory will disable the account.

> If you do not set a password on a user object using the Active Directory Users and Computers MMC snap-in, you will receive a warning. If you do it programmatically, as FIM does, the account will be disabled.

By performing all the previous recipes successfully, you have provisioned user accounts from records in the SQL Server database to AD.

See Also

Recipe 21.1; Recipe 21.17 for how to configure the run profile that was used in this recipe

21.19. Creating a Run Profile Script

Problem

It is impractical to continually use the UI every time you wish to execute a run profile. You want to automate the process by calling FIM run profiles to perform the required actions.

Solution

You need to create a run profile script:

1. Open the Synchronization Service Manager.
2. Click the Management Agents button on the toolbar.
3. In the Management Agents pane, click the SQL Server MA.
4. In the Actions pane on the far-right side, click Configure Run Profiles.
5. In the Configure Run Profiles dialog, select the Export run profile.
6. Click the Script button.
7. Browse to a location to save the script files.
8. In the "File name" text box, type `SQL Server MA Export`.
9. In the "Save as type" text box, select VB Script.
10. Click the Save button.
11. Repeat steps 3–9 for the other run profiles in the SQL Server MA and the AD MA. Follow the same file-naming convention.

Discussion

The scripts free you from the UI and can also form the building blocks of a FIM implementation that runs unattended. You have several options, including:

- Submit the scripts to the Windows Task Scheduler Service to run on a specified daily schedule. To do this, open the Task Scheduler, double-click Add Scheduled Task, and follow the steps in the wizard.
- Create a Windows service that calls the scripts according to your own criteria, perhaps by submitting them to the Task Scheduler using its APIs.
- Use the SQL Server Agent process to invoke run profiles on the FIM server. This approach is especially useful if you are using a SQL Server cluster and need your profiles to follow the active node in case of a failure condition.
- If you already have a script execution environment, incorporate the new scripts.

See Also

Recipe 21.20 to create a controlling script; the MSDN walkthrough about creating a Windows Service Application (*http://bit.ly/13dguqg*); the Task Scheduler API reference (*http://bit.ly/18q57hh*)

21.20. Creating a Controlling Script

Problem

You want a self-contained script that controls an entire sequence of operations; for example, import the SQL Server database records, synchronize, and then export to AD.

Solution

Before you start this recipe, you may want to make sure you have the *GroupPopulator Sync.cmd* and *RunMA.vbs* files available. Refer to "See Also" on page 760 for the URLs.

1. Open Notepad.

2. Type this script (or copy and paste the contents of the *GroupPopulatorSync.cmd* file from the MIIS Scenarios, referenced in this recipe's "See Also" on page 760):

```
@echo off
rem
rem Copyright (c) Microsoft Corporation. All rights reserved.
rem

setlocal
set zworkdir=%~dp0
pushd %zworkdir%

set madata=" C:\Program Files\Microsoft Forefront Identity Manager\2010\↵
Synchronization Service\MaData"

rem Full Import of SQL Database Records
rem --------------------------------------------
cscript runMA.vbs /m:"<SQL Server MA Name>" /p:"Full Import (Stage Only)"
if {%errorlevel%} NEQ {0} (echo Error[%errorlevel%]: command file failed) ↵
& (goto exit_script)

rem Full Sync of SQL Database Records
rem --------------------------------------------
cscript runMA.vbs /m:"<SQL Server MA Name>" /p:"Full Sync"
if {%errorlevel%} NEQ {0} (echo Error[%errorlevel%]: command file failed) ↵
& (goto exit_script)

rem Export users in to AD
rem -------------------
cscript runMA.vbs /m:"<Domain FQDN>" /p:"Export"
if {%errorlevel%} NEQ {0} (echo Error[%errorlevel%]: command file failed) ↵
& (goto exit_script)

:exit_script
popd
endlocal
```

3. In this case, insert the SQL Server MA name and domain FQDN where appropriate. This example also shows Full Import (Stage Only), which is the name of the run profile. If you named the steps differently, replace them with the appropriate name here.

4. Save the file with a *.cmd* file extension.

5. Close Notepad.

6. Open Notepad.

7. Type the following script (or copy and paste the contents of the *RunMA.vbs* file in the FIM scenarios, referenced in the "See Also" section):

```
option explicit
on error resume next


'=-=-=-=-=-=-=-=-=-=-=-=-=-=-=-=-=-=-=-=-=-=-=-=-=-=-=-=-=-=-=-=-=-=-=-=-=-=
'SCRIPT:        runMA.vbs
'DATE:          2003-02-05
'=-=-=-=-=-=-=-=-=-=-=-=-=-=-=-=-=-=-=-=-=-=-=-=-=-=-=-=-=-=-=-=-=-=-=-=-=-=
'= Copyright (C) 2003 Microsoft Corporation. All rights reserved.
'=
'***************************************************************************
'* Function: DisplayUsage
'*
'* Purpose:  Displays the usage of the script and exits the script
'*
'***************************************************************************
Sub DisplayUsage()
        WScript.Echo ""
        WScript.Echo "Usage: runMa </m:ma-name> </p:profile-name>"

        WScript.Echo "                      [/s:mms-server-name]"
        WScript.Echo "                      [/u:user-name]"
        WScript.Echo "                      [/a:password]"
        WScript.Echo "                      [/v] Switch on Verbose mode"
        WScript.Echo "                      [/?] Show the Usage of the script"
        WScript.Echo ""
        WScript.Echo "Example 1: runMa /m:adma1 /p:fullimport"
        WScript.Echo "Example 2: runMa /m:adma1 /p:fullimport /u:domain\user
/a:mysecret /v"
            WScript.Quit (-1)
End Sub


'***************************************************************************
' Script Main Execution Starts Here
'***************************************************************************
'--Used Variables-------------------------
dim s
dim runResult
dim rescode
dim managementagentName
```

```
dim profile
dim verbosemode
dim wmiLocator
dim wmiService
dim managementagent
dim server
dim username
dim password
'----------------------------------------

rescode = ParamExists("/?")
if rescode = true then call DisplayUsage
verbosemode = ParamExists("/v")

managementagentName = ParamValue("/m")
if managementagentName = "" then call DisplayUsage

profile = ParamValue("/p")
if profile = "" then call DisplayUsage

if verbosemode then wscript.echo "%Info: Management Agent and Profile is ↵
<"& managementagentName &":"& profile &">"
if verbosemode then wscript.Echo "%Info: Getting WMI Locator object"

set wmiLocator = CreateObject("WbemScripting.SWbemLocator")
if err.number <> 0 then
        wscript.echo "%Error: Cannot get WMI Locator object"
        wscript.quit(-1)
end if

server = ParamValue("/s")
password = ParamValue("/a")
username = ParamValue("/u")

if server = "" then server = "." ' connect to WMI on local machine

if verbosemode then

        wscript.Echo "%Info: Connecting to MMS WMI Service on↵
 <" & server &">"
        if username <> "" then wscript.Echo _
        "%Info: Accessing MMS WMI Service as <"& username &">"
end if

if username = "" then
        set wmiService = wmiLocator.ConnectServer _
        (server, "root/MicrosoftIdentityIntegrationServer")
else
        set wmiService = wmiLocator.ConnectServer_
        (server, "root/MicrosoftIdentityIntegrationServer", username,↵
 password)
end if
```

```
if err.number <> 0 then
        wscript.echo "%Error: Cannot connect to MMS WMI Service <" ↵
        & err.Description & ">"
        wscript.quit(-1)
end if

if verbosemode then wscript.Echo "%Info: Getting MMS Management Agent↵
 via WMI"

Set managementagent = wmiService.Get( "
MIIS_ManagementAgent.Name='" & _
managementagentName & "'")
if err.number <> 0 then
        wscript.echo _
        "%Error: Cannot get Management Agent with specified WMI Service <"↵
        & err.Description & ">"
        wscript.quit(-1)
end if

wscript.echo "%Info: Starting Management Agent with Profile <"& ↵
managementagent.name &":"& profile &">"
runResult = managementagent.Execute(profile)
if err.number <> 0 then
        wscript.Echo "%Error: Running MA <"& err.Description & ↵
        ">. Make sure the correct profile name is specified."
        wscript.quit(-1)
end if

wscript.Echo "%Info: Finish Running Management Agent"
wscript.Echo "%Result: <" & CStr(runResult) & ">"
wscript.quit(0)

'**************************************************************************
'* Function: ParamValue
'*
'* Purpose: Parses the command line for an argument and
'*          returns the value of the argument to the caller
'*          Argument and value must be seperated by a colon
'*
'* Arguments:

'* [in]      parametername      name of the parameter
'*
'* Returns:
'*           STRING      Parameter found in commandline
'*           ""          Parameter NOT found in commandline
'*
'**************************************************************************
Function ParamValue(ParameterName)

Dim i                      '* Counter
```

```
Dim Arguments              '* Arguments from the command-line command
Dim NumberofArguments      '* Number of arguments from the command-line
Dim ArgumentArray          '* Array to store arguments from command-line
Dim TemporaryString        '* Utility string

        '* Initialize Return Value to e the Empty String
        ParamValue = ""

        '* If no ParameterName is passed into the function exit
        if ParameterName = "" then exit function

        '* Check if Parameter is in the Arguments and return the value

Set Arguments = WScript.Arguments
        NumberofArguments = Arguments.Count - 1

        For i=0 to NumberofArguments
                TemporaryString = Arguments(i)
                ArgumentArray = Split(TemporaryString,":",-1,vbTextCompare)

                If ArgumentArray(0) = ParameterName Then
                    ParamValue = ArgumentArray(1)
                    exit function
                End If
        Next
end Function

'****************************************************************************
'* Function: ParamExists
'*
'* Purpose:  Parses the command line for an argument and
'*           returns the true if argument is present
'*
'* Arguments:
'* [in]      parametername       name of the paramenter
'*
'* Returns:
'*           true        Parameter found in commandline
'*           false       Parameter NOT found in commandline
'*
'****************************************************************************

Function ParamExists(ParameterName)

Dim i                      '* Counter

Dim Arguments              '* Arguments from the command-line command
Dim NumberofArguments      '* Number of arguments from the command-line
Dim ArgumentArray          '* Array to store arguments from command-line
Dim TemporaryString        '* Utility string

        '* Initialize Return Value to e the Empty String
```

```
            ParamExists = false

            '* If no ParameterName is passed into the function exit
            if ParameterName = "" then exit function

            '* Check if Parameter is in the Arguments and return the value
            Set Arguments = WScript.Arguments
            NumberofArguments = Arguments.Count - 1

            For i=0 to NumberofArguments
                    TemporaryString = Arguments(i)
                    If TemporaryString = ParameterName Then
                        ParamExists = true
                        exit function
                    End If
            Next
    end Function
```

8. Save the file in the same folder as the previous script we created and name it *run MA.vbs.*

9. Close Notepad.

Discussion

A script to control these operations, known as a *controlling script*, is required. You could simply create a script that called each of your other scripts in turn, but managing large numbers of scripts as the solution gets more complex becomes a problem.

Using the *RunMA.vbs* script inside a batch file to create a wrapper around your run profile execution is a common way to control when profiles get called. In a majority of solutions, you will find yourself needing to halt the processing of one run profile should a preceding run profile end in an error condition. By using this process, you ensure that any `errorlevel` other than 0 is an error, and you can either choose to halt processing altogether or branch accordingly.

See Also

FIM 2010 R2 Developer Reference (*http://bit.ly/16OxNRB*); the *runMA.vbs* and *Group PopulatorSync.cmd* script files in the Group Management folder in the ILM scenarios (*http://bit.ly/YAGuMU*)

21.21. Enabling Directory Synchronization from Active Directory to the HR Database

Problem

You want AD to become the authoritative source for the `telephoneNumber` attribute of Active Directory users.

Solution

You need to configure both the import attribute flow from the AD MA connector space to the metaverse, as well as the export attribute flow from the metaverse to the SQL Server MA connector space (refer to (5) and (8) in Figure 21-6, which show where the rules will be configured):

1. Open the Synchronization Service Manager.
2. Click the Management Agents button on the toolbar.
3. In the Management Agents pane, double-click the AD MA.
4. In the Management Agent Designer pane on the lefthand side, highlight Select Attributes.
5. In the Attributes pane on the righthand side, select "telephoneNumber."
6. In the Management Agent Designer pane on the lefthand side, highlight Configure Attribute Flow.
7. In the Mapping Type section of the dialog, select Direct.
8. In the Flow Direction section of the dialog, select Import.
9. Ensure that "user" is selected in the data source object type drop-down list.
10. Ensure that "person" is selected in the metaverse object type drop-down list.
11. In the data source object type attribute list, select "telephoneNumber."
12. In the metaverse object type attribute list, select "telephoneNumber."
13. Click New.
14. Notice that in the Attribute Flow pane, the arrow for this mapping indicates an import attribute flow. Click OK.
15. In the Management Agents pane, double-click the SQL Server MA.
16. In the Management Agent Designer pane on the lefthand side, highlight Configure Attribute Flow.
17. In the Mapping Type section of the dialog, select Direct.
18. In the Flow Direction section of the dialog, select Export.

19. Ensure that "person" is selected in the data source object type drop-down list.

20. Ensure that "person" is selected in the metaverse object type drop-down list.

21. In the data source object type attribute list, select "telephoneNumber."

 This assumes that the SQL Server database contains a field called "telephoneNumber."

22. In the metaverse object type attribute list, select "telephoneNumber."

23. Click New.

24. Notice that in the Attribute Flow pane, the arrow for this mapping indicates an export attribute flow. Click OK.

Discussion

You configured import attribute flow (IAF) from the AD MA to the metaverse and export attribute flow (EAF) to the SQL Server MA. Notice that these flows only dealt with attribute data. The object-level operations of projection and provisioning were not required because the objects already exist.

To put the new configuration to work, you will need to configure run profiles to import, synchronize, and export the data. These steps are covered in Recipe 21.22.

See Also

Recipe 21.1; Recipe 21.22

21.22. Configuring a Run Profile to Load the telephoneNumber from Active Directory

Problem

You need to get the AD `telephoneNumber` attribute into FIM and synchronize it.

Solution

Configure a run profile that combines import and synchronization as demonstrated in this recipe, and then execute it (see Recipe 21.23):

1. Open the Synchronization Service Manager.

2. Click the Management Agents button on the toolbar.

3. In the Management Agents pane, click the AD MA.

4. In the Actions pane on the far-right side, click Configure Run Profiles.

5. In the Configure Run Profiles for "adatum.com" (the name in quotes will reflect the name you chose when creating the AD MA), click New Profile.

6. In the Name text box, type **Delta Import** and **Delta Synchronization** and then click Next.

7. Ensure that Delta Import and Delta Synchronization is selected in the Type drop-down list and then click Next.

8. Ensure that the correct domain partition is showing in the Partition drop-down list and then click Finish.

9. Ensure that the details in the Step Details field look like Figure 21-12.

 Your partition name may be different, and the assumption is that you have completed the previous recipes.

10. Click OK.

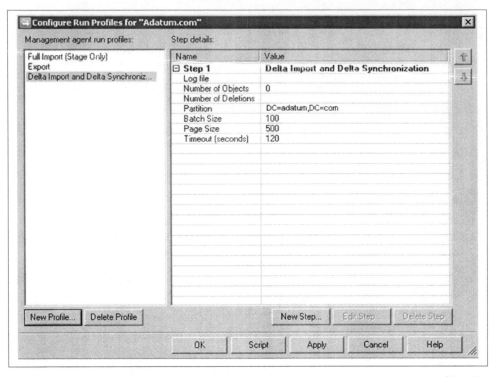

Figure 21-12. Dialog showing Delta Import and Delta Synchronization run profile added to the existing AD MA run profiles

Discussion

Because a previous import step was completed in an earlier recipe, you can use the combined Delta Import and Delta Synchronization step so that FIM imports and synchronizes changes that have occurred in AD since the last time it connected. You can use this run profile from now on since it keeps track of changes internally using the DirSync control.

The Delta Import (Stage Only) step in the AD Export run profile (the confirming import from Recipe 21.17) also imports changes, which suggests you could simply configure a delta synchronization run profile to process those changes in this recipe. Such an approach will work. The decision about which approach to use will depend on the service-level agreements you make. If it is two hours since the last AD import, your service-level agreement might force you to import and synchronize the changes that have occurred over the past two hours and feed them to the SQL Server database; however, you may only need to export to AD every four hours. If you only rely on the changes detected in the confirming import step, you will only be able to update the SQL Server database with changes every four hours.

See Also

Recipe 21.17; Recipe 21.23 for how to use the run profile configured in this recipe

21.23. Loading telephoneNumber Changes from AD into FIM Using a Delta Import/Delta Sync Run Profile

Problem

You need to pull the data from AD into FIM.

Solution

With the MA and run profile created, you can now load telephoneNumber attribute data into FIM by executing the run profile.

In Recipe 21.1, (11) in Figure 21-6 shows the telephoneNumber data being loaded into the AD connector space. The synchronization process then flows the data to the metaverse ((6) in Figure 21-6) and from there to the AD connector space ((3) in Figure 21-6).

1. Open Active Directory Users and Computers.
2. Navigate to a user in the container you are managing with FIM.
3. Double-click the user object.
4. Ensure that the General tab is selected and then type a telephone number into the Telephone Number text box and click OK.
5. Open the Synchronization Service Manager.
6. Click the Management Agents button on the toolbar.
7. In the Management Agents pane, click the AD MA.
8. In the Actions pane on the far-right side, click Run.
9. In the Run Management Agent dialog, select Delta Import and Delta Synchronization and click OK.
10. Because you have changed the rules but not yet run a full synchronization on all the existing objects, a Run Step Warning dialog appears, as shown in Figure 21-13. Click No.
11. Notice that the MA briefly says "Running" in the State column of the Management Agents pane.

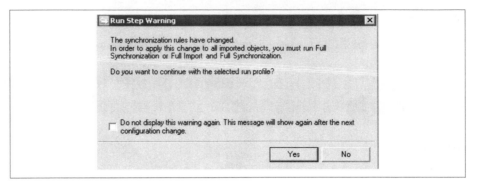

Figure 21-13. Run Step Warning dialog box

12. Notice that the Synchronization Statistics pane in the bottom-lefthand corner displays statistics showing the number of updates and connectors with flow updates. If you click one of the hyperlinks, you can navigate to the information that was loaded.

Discussion

The Run Step Warning dialog will pop up to annoy you any time you change any of the FIM rules or configuration settings. Even changing (adding, updating, or deleting) files in the *Extensions* directory will cause this warning to pop up on all run profile executions until every MA undergoes a full synchronization. This is done to force you into reconciling the state of every connector whenever there is a policy change. In this manner, FIM is one of the few Identity Management products that places such a serious emphasis on complete reconciliation and convergence of identity—often at the cost of some performance.

If you ignore the warning, the updates will apply only to connectors processed by the run profile (in our case, only the records we changed). However, the warning will continue to generate FIMSynchronizationService Event ID 6127 Warning messages in the Application Event log until you do so. This is also a cheap but effective method of monitoring for unscheduled changes to your FIM server.

With respect to the `telephoneNumber` data that already exists in the connector space, that data won't be subjected to those new rules. The warning is asking whether you'd like to apply the new rules to the existing objects. Essentially, you ignored the warning because if you have followed these recipes exactly, you should have only one new object in the AD MA's connector space with a telephone number, and that is the only one that will be synchronized.

See Also

Recipe 21.1; Recipe 21.18 for exporting objects to AD using an export run profile, which contains information about the confirming import (a Delta Import [Stage Only] step type)

21.24. Exporting telephoneNumber Data to a SQL Server Database

Problem

You need to export the data from a SQL Server MA connector space into a SQL Server database.

Solution

You need to configure and execute an export run profile. First, create the run profile:

1. Open the Synchronization Service Manager.
2. Click the Management Agents button on the toolbar.
3. In the Management Agents pane, click the SQL Server MA.
4. In the Actions pane on the far-right side, click Configure Run Profiles.
5. In the "Configure Run Profiles for" pane, click New Profile.
6. In the Name text box, type Export and then click Next.
7. Ensure that Export is selected in the Type drop-down list and then click Next.
8. Ensure that "default" is showing in the Partition drop-down list and then click Finish.
9. Click New Step.
10. In the Configure Step dialog, ensure that Full Import (Stage Only) is selected in the Type drop-down list and then click Next.
11. Ensure that "default" is selected in the Partition drop-down list and then click Finish.
12. Ensure that the details in the Step Details field look like Figure 21-14.

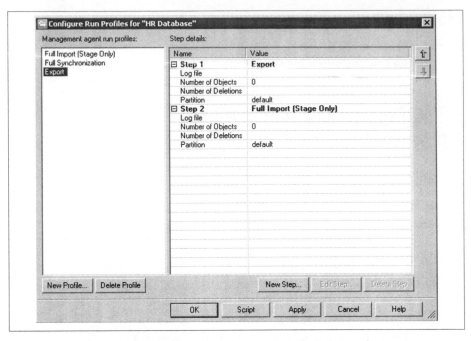

Figure 21-14. Export Run Profile added to the existing HR Database MA run profiles

13. Click OK.

Discussion

You had to select Full Import (Stage Only) for the confirming import step in this run profile because the SQL Server MA hasn't been configured to provide deltas.

See Also

Recipe 21.17 for similarities in how a run profile is configured to export objects to AD

21.25. Using a SQL Server MA Export Run Profile to Export the telephoneNumber to a SQL Server Database

Problem

The run profile is configured, but you need to actually move the data from FIM to a SQL Server database.

Solution

You need to execute the run profile (refer to (12) in Figure 21-6, which shows the telephoneNumber data being exported to a SQL Server database):

1. Open the Synchronization Service Manager.
2. Click the Management Agents button on the toolbar.
3. In the Management Agents pane, click the SQL Server MA.
4. In the Actions pane on the far-right side, click Run.
5. In the Run Management Agent dialog, select Export and click OK.
6. Notice that the MA briefly says "Running" in the State column of the Management Agents pane.
7. Notice that in the Synchronization Statistics pane in the bottom-lefthand corner, statistics showing the number of updates are displayed.

Discussion

Now is a good time to add the last two run profiles you created to the controlling script in Recipe 21.20. Then we can make multiple changes to AD and the SQL Server database and watch the effects by simply running the script. We could even put a simple loop into the script so that it is executing continuously and watch new users, deleted users, and telephoneNumber change as they propagate around the systems.

See Also

Recipe 21.1; Recipe 21.18 for similarities in how a run profile is used to export objects to AD; Recipe 21.20

21.26. Searching Data in the Connector Space

Problem

You have started to use FIM, but things aren't going according to plan. You want to see if the changes you made to either the SQL Server database or AD have made it into the associated connector space.

Solution

1. Open the Synchronization Service Manager.
2. Click the Management Agents button on the toolbar.

3. In the Management Agents pane, click the MA you wish to search.

4. In the Actions pane on the far-right side, click Search Connector Space.

5. In the Search Connector Space dialog, click the Search button.

   You will notice records returned in the main search pane.

   If this is the SQL Server MA, the DN of each record will be the primary key in the database that ensures uniqueness in the record set. If this is the AD MA, the DN will be the object's DN in LDAP format (e.g., cn=Steve Plank,OU=Users,DC=adatum,DC=com).

6. Record the RDN of a record from the previous step. If it's the SQL Server MA, the RDN is the same as the DN. If it's the AD MA, it's the element that contains the least-significant object in the DN (e.g., cn=Steve Plank).

7. Select RDN in the Scope drop-down list.

8. Type the RDN you have recorded into the text box (e.g., cn=Steve Plank).

9. Click Search.

   You will notice a single record returned, which matches the RDN you have specified.

10. If you double-click any of the returned records, you can examine the object in detail.

Discussion

You will see in the Scope drop-down list that there are more entries than just Subtree and RDN. The error collections are useful when trying to debug records that give errors from a large connector space with many thousands of objects in it. We find it particularly useful to use the Pending Export scope to look at outbound changes whenever we are performing a change to a production system. The Pending Export scope allows you to filter additionally by selecting Add, Modify, or Delete to include in the result set. It's very reassuring to verify that there are no delete operations pending when you make a new change.

Also, once you have double-clicked a record and are viewing its properties, you will notice a Lineage tab at the top of the page. On it, there is a Metaverse Object Properties button. This will show you the properties held on the related metaverse object as well as when the last change was imported from the connected directory. Validating when the last change was seen by FIM can be extremely helpful when troubleshooting why FIM didn't process a change.

See Also

Recipe 21.27 for searching data in the metaverse; MSDN: How to: Find Specified Connector Space Objects (*http://bit.ly/15sZRua*)

21.27. Searching Data in the Metaverse

Problem

You are troubleshooting and want to view a metaverse object.

Solution

You need to search the metaverse:

1. Open the Synchronization Service Manager.
2. Click the Metaverse Search button on the toolbar.
3. Click the Search button.

   Records from the metaverse are returned in the Search Results pane.

4. Double-click a record in the Search Results pane.
5. You can see which MA contributed data to this metaverse object. If you double-click the object that you added a `telephoneNumber` to in AD, you should see its attributes detailed in the pane below the Attributes tab.
6. Click the Connectors tab.

   You can see which MAs this metaverse object is joined to.

Discussion

The Connectors tab highlights the difference between projection and provisioning. You should see that the link between the metaverse object and the connector space entries was created because of projection rules for the SQL Server MA and provisioning rules for the AD MA. That is because you configured the SQL Server MA to project objects to the metaverse, and then you wrote a rules extension to provision objects from the metaverse to the AD connector space.

See Also

Recipe 21.26 for searching data in the connector space; TechNet: Create a Metaverse Search Query (*http://bit.ly/19URIvj*)

21.28. Deleting Data in the Connector Space and Metaverse

Problem

You want to clear out the connector space or the metaverse, perhaps so that you can perform another complete run-through of all these recipes to consolidate learning.

Solution

1. Open the Synchronization Service Manager.

2. Click the Metaverse Designer button on the toolbar.

3. In the Actions pane on the far-right side, click Configure Object Deletion Rule.

4. Ensure that the "Delete metaverse object when connector from this management agent is disconnected" radio button is selected.

5. Place a checkmark next to the SQL Server MA in the list and then click OK.

6. Click the Management Agents button on the toolbar.

7. In the Management Agents pane, click the MA you wish to delete objects from— do the AD MA first.

8. In the Actions pane on the far-right side, click Delete.

 This is important: you risk deleting the whole MA if you do not perform the following step correctly.

9. Ensure that the "Delete connector space only" radio button is selected.

10. When prompted that you are sure you want to delete the connector space, click Yes.

11. A message box will appear with details of how many records were deleted. Click OK.

12. Perform steps 7–11 again on the HR Database MA.

Discussion

You configured the metaverse object deletion rule so that when objects from the SQL Server MA were deleted, the related metaverse objects would also be deleted. That is why you deleted objects from the AD MA first. When you performed steps 7–11 the second time, the metaverse objects were also deleted. You can prove this by searching the metaverse in between delete operations.

There is no metaverse delete; FIM ensures that objects in the metaverse *always* have a join to at least one object in a connector space from at least one MA. The object deletion rule is the configuration that tells FIM what to do with metaverse objects when connector space objects get deleted.

For more control, you can specify that a rules extension should be used to make the decision for you.

It is impossible to end up in the situation where FIM has an object in the metaverse but no corresponding object in any connector space.

See Also

TechNet: Configuring Management Agents (*http://bit.ly/18bXkT2*)

21.29. Extending Object Types to Include a New Attribute

Problem

You want to add a new attribute to an existing object type in the metaverse so that you can hold data specific to your implementation.

Solution

1. Open the Synchronization Service Manager.
2. Click the Metaverse Designer button on the toolbar.
3. In the "Object type" pane, select the object type you wish to modify (e.g., Person).
4. In the lower Actions pane, click the Add Attribute listing.
5. In the Add Attribute To Object Type dialog box, click the "New attribute" button.
6. In the New Attribute dialog box, fill in the following properties:

   a. Attribute name (the name of the attribute as you will see it in the metaverse attributes list)

    Choosing a nonindexed value will let you store a much larger value here, but it cannot be indexed and should never be used for purposes of a join.

   b. Attribute type (the type of attribute data you can store; it defaults to String (indexable))

   c. Multi-values (check this if you intend this attribute to be multivalued)

    d. Indexed (check this if you intend the value to be used during join operations)

  7. Click the OK button twice to accept the changes.

Discussion

Once an attribute is created and attached to an object type, it can be linked to any other object type by following steps 1–4 and then checking off the attribute(s) that you wish to add. Choosing a multivalued attribute type will automatically configure the attribute to also be indexed, if supported by the chosen attribute type.

21.30. Previewing Changes to the FIM Configuration

Problem

You want to make changes to one or more flows and you would like to confirm the exact effect the change will have before you roll it out.

Solution

The solution involves the use of the *Preview* function, which is accessed as a property of an individual connector space object:

1. Open the Synchronization Service Manager.

2. Locate the connector space object you would like to preview changes against by using the recipe for searching the connector space—you need to pick the connector in the MA that you would run the full or delta synchronization against.

3. On the Connector Space Object Properties dialog, click the Preview button (see Figure 21-15).

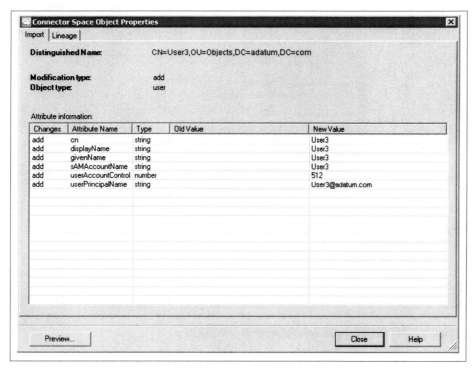

Figure 21-15. Connector Space Object Properties dialog—Preview

4. On the Preview dialog, under the "Select preview mode" section, select between a Full Synchronization or a Delta Synchronization; select the radio button accordingly and then click the Generate Preview button (see Figure 21-16).

5. In the contents pane, you can now browse each step and follow from Source Object Details all the way through provisioning to Export Attribute flow on individual connectors.

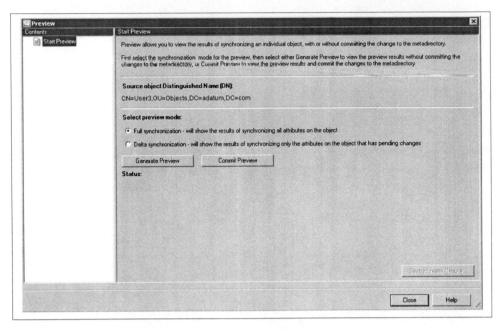

Figure 21-16. Preview dialog—Select preview mode

Discussion

Preview is one of the most useful aspects of the FIM product; it allows you to do *what if* scenarios and ascertain the exact effect any configuration change will have on the state of all identities. Incidentally, the Preview function is actually a side effect of basing FIM on SQL Server. Under normal circumstances, any given run profile step is wrapped in a SQL transaction (one transaction for every connector space object in the MA of the run profile), and as each identity is converged across all connectors, that transaction is committed to the database. In the event of an exception, only that transaction is rolled back and the next identity is processed. Given this feature, the Preview ability simply rolls back the transaction for the given object. This means that FIM is not simply simulating what a run would look like; it's actually executing the process exactly as it would be under normal circumstances, with the exception that the changes are not committed.

 Since Preview is executing every step and rolling back the transaction, be extremely careful in your rules extensions that you are not performing actions that can't be undone. Anything you do through a rules extension to any source outside of FIM *will not be rolled back* because it is outside of the scope of the SQL transaction. You should use the `Utils.InPreviewMode()` property to determine when you are in Preview mode, and gate certain functions of your flow.

See Also

TechNet: Using Metaverse Search (*http://bit.ly/12oLgKq*)

21.31. Committing Changes to Individual Identities Using the Commit Preview Feature

Problem

You want to make changes to a rules extension or flow but you would like to confirm the exact effect the change will have before you roll it out. In addition, you want to commit the changes to only a handful of records that need the changes to go into effect right away and you can't afford to run a full synchronization to get them.

Solution

1. Open the Synchronization Service Manager.

2. Locate the connector space object you would like to preview changes against by using the recipe for searching the connector space—you need to pick the connector in the MA that you would run the full or delta synchronization against.

3. On the Connector Space Object Properties dialog, click the Preview button (see Figure 21-15).

4. On the Preview dialog, under the Select preview mode section, select between a Full Synchronization or a Delta Synchronization; select the radio button accordingly and then click the Commit Preview button (see Figure 21-16).

5. In the contents pane, you can now browse each step and follow from Source Object Details all the way through provisioning to Export Attribute flow on individual connectors!

Discussion

Commit Preview functions like the Preview button; however, it actually commits the transaction at the end for the given connector. This allows you to automatically apply new policies to specific connectors; you should use this strategy only when you absolutely cannot afford (from a time perspective) to run a full sync. Using Commit Preview during testing and certification is recommended when you want to follow a change across data sources.

See Also

Recipe 21.26 for searching data in the connector space

21.32. Passing Data Between Rules Extensions Using Transaction Properties

Problem

You are tracking an event that occurs in an authoritative data source and want to pass a message or a data element to one of the other extensions.

Solution

1. Open Visual Studio and open your rules extension project solution.

2. You first need to set a transaction property, and while these properties can be set anywhere, you will most likely set them in ShouldProjectToMV, MapAttributes ForJoin, ResolveJoinSearch, MapAttributesForImport, MapAttributesForEx port, and Deprovision, or within the Provisioning rules extensions. The following example shows two ways of setting different types of transaction properties:

   ```
   ' String
   Dim strWF As String = "foobar"
   Utils.TransactionProperties.Add("WORKFLOW", strWF)

   ' Boolean
   Utils.TransactionProperties.Add("DELETE", True)
   ```

3. Once you have one or more properties set, you can query for them elsewhere:

   ```
   If (Utils.TransactionProperties.Contains("DELETE") AndAlso
   Utils.TransactionProperties("DELETE").Equals(True)) Then
   ' This allows for a typesafe way to query for the existence of a property
   End If

   If (Utils.TransactionProperties.Contains("WORKFLOW") AndAlso
   Utils.TransactionProperties("WORKFLOW").ToString.Contains("foo")) Then
   ' This allows you to search the contents of a string property
       ' You can then do an assignment
         Dim strWFResponse As String =↵
    Utils.TransactionProperties("WORKFLOW").ToString
   End If

   If (Utils.TransactionProperties.Contains("WORKFLOW") AndAlso
   Utils.TransactionProperties("WORKFLOW").Equals("foobar")) Then
       ' This allows you to do a simple comparison
   End If
   ```

Discussion

A transaction property is only good for as long as the current FIM transaction is running. This makes it relevant only to the identity you are processing, and it is available across all extensions that are touched as part of the synchronization of that identity; when the next identity is loaded for processing, all transaction properties are destroyed.

See Also

Recipe 21.30; Recipe 21.31

21.33. Using a Single Rules Extension to Affect Multiple Attribute Flows

Problem

You have several attributes that you would like to apply the same block of code to, and you don't want to duplicate the same block of code or call the same function from multiple case statements.

Solution

1. Open Visual Studio and open your rules extension project solution.

2. Add a code block similar to this (before your main `select case FlowRuleName` statement):

```
If FlowRuleName.StartsWith("Trim:") Then
' Trim String
'
' Reusable code to convert an attribute to its string format
' FlowRuleName will be passed as "Trim:srcAttribute,destAttribute"
'
Dim strAttributeName, strSrcAttribute, strDestAttribute, arrAttribs() _
As String

' Replace the beginning of the flowrulename with nothing
strAttributeName = FlowRuleName.Replace("Trim:", "")
arrAttribs = strAttributeName.Split(",","c")    ' Splits the string
                                                ' on a comma
trSrcAttribute = arrAttribs(0)                  ' Assigns the first value
strDestAttribute = arrAttribs(1)                ' Assigns the second value

' Now we can assign the value and trim any whitespace at the front and back
mventry(strDestAttribute).Value =_
 csentry(strSrcAttribute).Value.ToString.Trim

Else If FlowRuleName.StartsWith("MyFunction:") Then
```

```
' Apply custom function
'
' Reusable code to apply a custom function to an attribute
' FlowRuleName will be passed as
"MyFunction:sourceAttribute,destinationAttribute"
'
Dim strAttributeName, strSrcAttribute, strDestAttribute, arrAttribs()
As String

' Replace the beginning of the flowrulename with nothing
strAttributeName = FlowRuleName.Replace("MyFunction:", "")
arrAttribs = strAttributeName.Split(",","c")   ' Splits the string on a comma
strSrcAttribute = arrAttribs(0)                ' Assigns the first value
strDestAttribute = arrAttribs(1)               ' Assigns the second value

' Now we can apply your custom function prior to the assignment
Dim strSrcAttributeValue As String
strSrcAttributeValue = MySharedCodeLib.MyFunction↵
(csentry(strSrcAttribute).Value) mventry(strDestAttribute).Value =↵
 strSrcAttributeValue

Else
' Continue on as you normally do
Select case FlowRuleName
```

3. Open the Synchronization Service Manager.

4. Apply the rule.

Discussion

Using this approach allows you to create several reusable code sections and apply them to new advanced flows without the need for code changes or recompiles. This approach is valid in both the import and export flow sections.

21.34. Flowing a Null Value to a Data Source

Problem

You need to delete or "flow a null" to an attribute in another data source.

Solution

1. Open the Synchronization Service Manager.

2. Click the Management Agents button on the toolbar.

3. In the Management Agents pane, double-click the AD MA.

4. In the Management Agent Designer pane on the lefthand side, select Configure Attribute Flow.

5. Ensure that "user" is selected in the data source object type drop-down list.

6. Ensure that "person" is selected in the metaverse object type drop-down list.

7. In the Mapping Type section of the dialog, select Advanced.

8. In the Flow Direction section of the dialog, select Export and then check the box to Allow Nulls.

 If you don't check the box to Allow Nulls, the rule value will never be contributed.

9. Select telephoneNumber from the data source attributes list.

10. Select *<object-id>* from the Metaverse attributes list.

11. Selecting *<object-id>* here ensures that the source value will always be present; otherwise, the rule will not fire if the source value in the metaverse is null.

12. Click New.

13. In the Advanced Export Attribute Flow Options dialog, type Delete:telephone Number.

14. Open Visual Studio and open your rules extension project solution.

15. If you are using Recipe 21.33, insert the following before the final Else; otherwise, only the final line is needed in a standard Case block:

```
Else If FlowRuleName.StartsWith("Delete") Then
    '
    ' Reusable code to delete the referenced attribute
    ' FlowRuleName will be passed as "Delete:Attribute"
    '
    Dim strAttributeName As String

    ' Replace the beginning of the flowrulename with nothing
    ' to find the attribute to be deleted
    strAttributeName = FlowRuleName.Replace("Delete:", "")

    ' This is whre we delete the value
    csentry(strAttributeName).Dclete()
```

Discussion

You never have to actually set a "null value" to contribute a delete to another data source. This is partially due to the fact that different systems handle null values differently and in order to contribute the proper value, the `Delete()` property is used to handle that translation for you.

To process any Advanced Rules extension, you need to have a value in the source attribute. A common problem occurs when the source attribute is null in the metaverse, preventing the rule from firing on that identity. An advanced flow will fire if an existing value is deleted (by contributing a null), but it will never fire if the value is null to begin with. In addition, while using a fixed value like *<object-id>* ensures that the value will never be null, this value will never change and therefore you will require a full synchronization run to trigger this rule; however, you can use Recipe 21.31 to force a full synchronization on an individual identity and commit the changes.

See Also

Recipe 21.8; Recipe 21.31; Recipe 21.33

21.35. Importing and Decoding the accountExpires Attribute

Problem

You want to import the `accountExpires` attribute into the metaverse as a string-formatted date/time value. This could be any of the Large Integer/Interval syntax attributes, such as `accountExpires`, `badPasswordTime`, `lastLogoff`, `lastLogon`, `lastLogonTimestamp`, `lockoutTime`, or `pwdLastSet`.

Solution

1. Open the Synchronization Service Manager.
2. See Recipe 21.29 to add a new metaverse attribute if necessary.
3. Click the Management Agents button on the toolbar.
4. In the Management Agents pane, double-click the AD MA.
5. In the Management Agent Designer pane on the lefthand side, select Configure Attribute Flow.
6. Ensure that "user" is selected in the data source object type drop-down list.
7. Ensure that "person" is selected in the metaverse object type drop-down list.
8. In the Mapping Type section of the dialog, select Advanced.
9. In the Flow Direction section of the dialog, select Import.
10. Select `accountExpires` from the data source attributes list.

---

11. Select the attribute created in step 2 or an existing `String` attribute from the Metaverse attributes list (e.g., `AccountExpirationDate`).

12. Click New.

13. In the Advanced Import Attribute Flow Options dialog, type `ConvertFileTime:ac countExpires,AccountExpirationDate`, and then click OK twice.

14. Open Visual Studio and open your rules extension project solution.

15. If you are using Recipe 21.33 insert the following before the final `Else`; otherwise, only the final line is needed in a standard `Case` block:

```
ElseIf FlowRuleName.StartsWith("ConvertFileTime:") Then
    '
    ' Reusable code to convert generalized time into string format
    ' FlowRuleName will be passed as
"ConvertFileTime:sourceAttribute,destinationAttribute"
    '
    Dim strAttributeName, strSourceAttribute, strDestinationAttribute,↵
 arrAttribs()
As String

    ' Replace the beginning of the flowrulename with nothing to find↵
the attribute to be deleted
    strAttributeName = FlowRuleName.Replace("ConvertFileTime:", "")
    arrAttribs = strAttributeName.Split(","c)
    strSourceAttribute = arrAttribs(0)
    strDestinationAttribute = arrAttribs(1)

    ' NOTE: The value will be invalid if it was never set
    ' (9223372036854775807 (0x7FFFFFFFFFFFFFFF))
    ' or 0 if it was set and then later cleared

    Const AD_ACCOUNT_NO_EXPIRATION As Long = 9223372036854775807

    If (strSourceAttribute = "accountExpires") Then
        If (csentry(strSourceAttribute).Value = 0 OrElse
csentry(strSourceAttribute).Value = AD_ACCOUNT_NO_EXPIRATION) Then
            ' The value was cleared or never set
            mventry(strDestinationAttribute).Value = "Never"
        Else
            ' The value has been set
            Dim dtFileTime As DateTime =
DateTime.FromFileTime(DateTime.Parse(csentry↵
(strSourceAttribute).Value).ToFileTme)

mventry(strDestinationAttribute).Value = Format(dtFileTime, "yyyy-MM-dd")
End If
Else
' We are not dealing with the accountExpires attribute, just decode it
Dim dtFileTime As DateTime =
DateTime.FromFileTime(DateTime.Parse(csentry(strSourceAttribute).Value)↵
```

```
          .ToFileTime)

          mventry(strDestinationAttribute).Value = Format(dtFileTime, "yyyy-MM-dd")
          End If
```

Discussion

The Large Integer/Interval syntax in Active Directory can be decoded by using the `DateTime.FromFileTime()` function in the .NET Framework. By using the `DateTime.Parse().ToFileTime` property, you are ensuring that the value you are getting is a valid date/time.

 If you are concerned with data integrity here, consider wrapping this in a `Try/Catch` block.

See Also

Recipe 21.29; Recipe 21.33

21.36. Exporting and Encoding the accountExpires Attribute

Problem

You want to export to the `accountExpires` attribute from a string-formatted date/time value in the metaverse. This could be any of the Large Integer/Interval syntax attributes, such as `accountExpires`, `badPasswordTime`, `lastLogoff`, `lastLogon`, `lastLogonTimestamp`, `lockoutTime`, or `pwdLastSet`.

Solution

1. Open the Synchronization Service Manager.
2. Click the Management Agents button on the toolbar.
3. In the Management Agents pane, double-click the AD MA.
4. In the Management Agent Designer pane on the lefthand side, select Configure Attribute Flow.
5. Ensure that "user" is selected in the data source object type drop-down list.
6. Ensure that "person" is selected in the metaverse object type drop-down list.

7. In the Mapping Type section of the dialog, select Advanced.

8. In the Flow Direction section of the dialog, select Export.

9. Select `accountExpires` from the data source attributes list.

10. Select an existing String attribute from the Metaverse attributes list (e.g., `AccountExpirationDate`).

11. Click New.

12. In the Advanced Export Attribute Flow Options dialog, type `ConvertFileTime:accountExpires,AccountExpirationDate`, and then click OK twice.

13. Open Visual Studio and open your rules extension project solution.

14. If you are using Recipe 21.33, insert the following before the final `Else`; otherwise, only the final line is needed in a standard `Case` block:

```
ElseIf FlowRuleName.StartsWith("ConvertFileTime:") Then
    '
    ' Reusable code to convert generalized time into string format
    ' FlowRuleName will be passed as
"ConvertFileTime:sourceAttribute,destinationAttribute"
    '
    Dim strAttributeName, strSourceAttribute, strDestinationAttribute,↵
arrAttribs()
As String

    ' Replace the beginning of the flowrulename with nothing to find↵
the attribute to be deleted
    strAttributeName = FlowRuleName.Replace("ConvertFileTime:", "")
    arrAttribs = strAttributeName.Split(","c)
    strSourceAttribute = arrAttribs(0)
    strDestinationAttribute = arrAttribs(1)

    ' NOTE: The value will be invalid if it was never set
    ' (9223372036854775807 (0x7FFFFFFFFFFFFFFF))
    ' or 0 if it was set and then later cleared

    Const AD_ACCOUNT_NO_EXPIRATION As Long = 9223372036854775807

    If (strDestinationAttribute = "accountExpires") Then
        If (mventry(strSourceAttribute).IsPresent = False) Then
            ' The value in the metaverse is empty so remove the account
expiration
            csentry(strDestinationAttribute).IntegerValue = 0
        Else
            ' We should have a date value present to enforce
            Dim dtFileTime As DateTime =
DateTime.Parse(mventry(strSourceAttribute).Value)

            csentry(strDestinationAttribute).IntegerValue =
dtFileTime.ToFileTimeUtc()
        End If
```

```
        Else
                ' We are not dealing with the accountExpires attribute,↵
    just encode it
                Dim dtFileTime As DateTime =
        DateTime.Parse(mventry(strSourceAttribute).Value)

                csentry(strDestinationAttribute).IntegerValue =↵
          dtFileTime.ToFileTimeUtc()
            End If
```

Discussion

The Large Integer/Interval syntax in Active Directory can be encoded by using the `DateTime.ToFileTime()` function in the .NET Framework. By using the `Date Time.Parse()` property, you are ensuring that the value you are getting is a valid date/time.

 If you are concerned with data integrity here, consider wrapping this in a `Try/Catch` block.

See Also

Recipe 21.29; Recipe 21.33; Recipe 21.35

Index

returning distinguished name of server object, 78
searching for objects in a domain, 120
searching the global catalog, 123
searching with bitwise filter, 129
viewing an attribute, 358
viewing class attributes, 362
viewing created and last-modified timestamps of an object, 156
viewing object's attributes, 107
-attr option, 110
dsrevoke utility, revoking delegated permissions, 512
DSRM (Directory Services Restore Mode), 17
nonauthoritative restore by rebooting DC in, 585
rebooting into, during complete authoritative restore, 588
resetting administrator password, 584
restarting domain controller in, 582–584
stopping and starting of AD DS, 576
dsrm utility
deleting a computer, 278
deleting a subnet, 406
deleting a user, 201
deleting an OU, 174
deleting container with child objects, 155
deleting objects in an OU, 173
Dynamic Access Control
configuring central access rule, 533
creating central access policy, 534
creating new claim type for, 531
creating resource property for, 532
dynamic DNS (see DDNS)
Dynamic Host Configuration Protocol (see DHCP)
dynamic objects
creating, 140
modifying default TTL settings, 144
refreshing, 142
dynamicObjectDefaultTTL attribute, 141

E

EAC (see Exchange Administration Center)
effective permissions of an object, 516
email
configuring mailbox limits, 698
creating a mailbox database, 703
creating an address list, 700

deleting a user's mailbox, 691
enabling message tracking on Exchange Server, 705
mail-disabling a user, 688
mail-enabling a user, 687
mailbox-enabling a user, 689
moving a mailbox, 693
viewing mailbox sizes and message counts, 695
EMS (see Exchange Management Shell)
EMT (Exchange Management Tools), installing, 683
entryTTL attribute, 141, 143
enumprop command, 3
ESE (Extensible Storage Engine), 575
esentutl database utility, 594
event codes for DNS debug logging, 486
Event Viewer MMC
checking Directory Services Event Log for global catalog server, 89
determining if KCC completes successfully, 433
event-based synchronization, identity management products, 714
EventCombMT utility, 212
Everyone security principal, 353
Exchange Administration Center (EAC), 674
accessing, 675
configuring mailbox limits, 698
creating a Database Availability Group (DAG), 701
creating a mailbox database, 703
creating an address list, 700
deleting a user's mailbox, 692
enabling message tracking, 705
mail-disabling a user, 688
mail-enabling a user, 687
mailbox-enabling a user, 689
moving a mailbox, 693
Exchange Management Shell (EMS), 674
finding Exchange Server cmdlets, 675
Exchange Server 2013, 673–706
architecture, 674
configuring mailbox limits, 698
creating a mailbox database, 703
creating an address list, 700
creating Database Availability Group (DAG), 701
creating unattended installation files for, 682

migrating a group, 258
modifying a bit flag attribute, 137
modifying an object, 135
modifying an OU, 180
modifying attribute for several users at once, 200
modifying attributes copied during user duplication, 366
modifying attributes included with ANR, 367
modifying computer object's attributes, 293
modifying cost for a site link, 412
modifying default display name for users created in ADUC or ADAC, 192
modifying default security of a class, 379
modifying DNS server configuration, 480
modifying GPO settings, 314
modifying group attributes, 262
modifying list of allowed DNS suffixes for domain, 494
modifying replication schedules, 414
modifying sites associated with a site link, 411
modifying tombstone lifetime for a domain, 606
moving a group within a domain, 256
moving a mailbox, 693
moving AD integrated zones into application partition, 469
moving an OU, 178
moving computer within same domain, 281
moving domain controller to different site, 78, 423
moving object to different domain, 148
moving object to different OU or container, 146
moving objects to different OU, 176
moving Schema FSMO to another domain controller, 387
moving users, 204
parameters, replaceable text in, 6
performance monitoring for Active Directory, 555
performing online defrag, 593
preventing domain controller from dynamically registering certain resource records, 492
preventing user from changing a password, 229

preventing user's password from expiring, 231
promoting a server as RODC, 60
promotion or demotion of domain controllers, automating, 67
protecting an OU against accidental deletion, 186
protecting computer against accidental deletion, 303
protecting group against accidental deletion, 270
protecting user against accidental deletion, 246
querying DNS resource records, 479
raising domain functional level to Windows Server 2012, 27
refreshing a dynamic object, 143
refreshing GPO settings on a computer, 341
remotely installing domain controller, 68
removing all group memberships from user, 223
renaming a computer, 284
renaming a site, 396
renaming an object, 152
renaming an OU, 179
renaming user objects, 207
requiring user to change password at next logon, 230
resetting computer's secure channel, 288
resolving primary group for a user, 265
restoring a deleted group, 269
restoring a GPO, 337
restoring all child objects of OU, 605
restoring deleted domain controller in Windows Server 2012, 81
retrieving current forest functional level, 29
reviewing GPO settings, 313
running Exchange Server 2013 setup.exe, 682
scavenging old DNS resource records, 481
scripts in Exchange scripts folder, 675
searching for deleted objects, 602
searching for large number of objects, 125
searching for objects in a domain, 121
searching the global catalog, 123
searching with attribute-scoped query, 127
searching with bitwise filter, 129
seizing a FSMO role, 100

user objects, 15
    accountExpires attribute, 237
    attributes changed when creating a mailbox
        for, 691
    attributes of, 189
    converting to or from inetOrgPerson ob-
        jects, 198
    creating, 192
    linked attributes, 375
    logonHours attribute, 242
    provisioning in AD MA from objects in SQL
        Server MA, 744–747
    retrieving SAM account name for all in a do-
        main, 120
    userAccountControl attribute, 130, 235
User Principal Name (see UPN)
userAccountControl attribute, 130, 138, 219
    disabled user accounts, 221
    disabling expiration of user's password, 231
    properties defined in
        ADS_USER_FLAG_ENUM, 235
    setting user's account options, 234
userAccountControl flag, 737
USERDOMAIN environment variable, 25
userProxy objects, 645
users, 189–246
    adding additional fields to AD Users and
        Computers, 52
    anatomy of, 189
    applying fine-grained password policy to
        user object, 216
    changing password for AD LDS user, 640
    changing primary group for, 224
    converting user object to or from inetOrg-
        Person object, 198
    copying, 208
    copying user's group membership to another
        user, 225
    creating, 192
    creating a computer for specific user, 276
    creating inetOrgPerson user, 196
    creating large number of, 194
    creating UPN suffix for a forest, 243
    deleting, 201
    determining last logon time, 238
    disabling user settings in a GPO, 322
    duplication of, modifying attributes copied
        during, 365
    enabling and disabling, 218

    enabling and disabling AD LDS user, 641
    finding disabled users, 220
    finding locked-out users, 209
    finding passwords nearing expiration, 232
    finding users who haven't logged on recently,
        239
    mail-disabling, 688
    mail-enabling, 687
    mailbox-disabling (deleting the mailbox),
        691
    mailbox-enabling, 689
    managing AD LDS users, 639
    modifying attribute for several users at once,
        200
    modifying default display name for users
        created in ADUC or ADAC, 191
    moving, 203
    moving mailbox for, 693
    preventing from changing a password, 228
    preventing password from expiring, 231
    protecting against accidental deletion, 245
    redirecting to alternative OU, 205
    removing all group memberships from, 223
    renaming, 206
    requiring password change at next logon,
        229
    resolving primary group ID for, 264
    restoration of, issues with, 587
    restoring deleted user, 245
    setting account options (userAccountCon-
        trol), 234
    setting account to expire, 236
    setting password for, 227
    setting profile attributes, 202
    troubleshooting account lockout problems,
        211
    unlocking, 210
    viewing and modifying permitted logon
        hours for, 241
    viewing domain-wide account lockout and
        password policies, 213–215
    viewing effective POS for, 345
    viewing fine-grained password policy for
        user account, 217
    viewing group membership for, 221
    viewing RODCs that cached user's password,
        233
    viewing user's managed objects, 242
Users container of a domain, 15

About the Authors

Brian Svidergol specializes in Microsoft infrastructure and cloud-based solutions around Windows, Active Directory, Microsoft Exchange, System Center, virtualization, and MDOP. He holds the MCT, MCITP (EA), MCITP (VA), MCITP (Exchange 2010), and several other Microsoft and industry certifications. Brian authored Microsoft Official Curriculum (MOC) course 6426C - Configuring and Troubleshooting Identity and Access Solutions with Windows Server 2008 Active Directory. He has also worked on Microsoft certification exam development and related training content for several years. When he isn't working on technology projects, he enjoys family time, basketball, and gaming.

Robbie Allen is a technical leader at Cisco Systems, where he has been involved in the deployment of Active Directory, DNS, DHCP, and several network management solutions. Robbie was named a Windows Server MVP in 2004 and 2005 for his contributions to the Windows community and the publication of several popular O'Reilly books. Robbie is currently studying at MIT in its System Design and Management program. For more information, see Robbie's website (*http://www.rallenhome.com*).

Colophon

The animal on the cover of *Active Directory Cookbook*, Fourth Edition is a bluefin tuna (*Thunnus thynnus*), also known as a horse mackerel. It inhabits both the Atlantic and Pacific Oceans in temperate and subtropical waters. The body of a bluefin tuna is a metallic, deep blue on top, while the undersides and belly are silvery white. The first dorsal fin is yellow or blue; the second is red or brown. The rear fin and finlets are yellow, edged with black. The central caudal keel is black.

The bluefin tuna is one of the largest and fastest species of marine fish. An adult can weigh as much as 1,500 pounds (680 kilograms) and can swim up to speeds of 55 miles per hour (88.5 kilometers per hour). A bluefin tuna can swim across the Atlantic Ocean in 40 days. Recent pop-up satellite tracking has revealed that the bluefin tuna can dive to depths greater than 3,000 feet in a matter of minutes and still maintain a body temperature of 77 degrees Fahrenheit (25 degrees Celsius), even in near-freezing water.

Commercial fishing has reduced the stock of bluefin tuna to the extent that a single fish, once caught, can be worth up to $40,000. However, the situation is reversible, and the numbers of tuna could increase if the guidelines of the International Commission for the Conservation of Atlantic Tuna (ICCAT), an intergovernmental fishing organization that oversees tuna, are followed.

The cover image is from *Dover Pictorial Archive*. The cover font is Adobe ITC Garamond. The text font is Adobe Minion Pro; the heading font is Adobe Myriad Condensed; and the code font is Dalton Maag's Ubuntu Mono.

Have it your way.

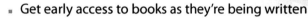

Get even more for your money.

Join the O'Reilly Community, and register the O'Reilly books you own. It's free, and you'll get:

- $4.99 ebook upgrade offer
- 40% upgrade offer on O'Reilly print books
- Membership discounts on books and events
- Free lifetime updates to ebooks and videos
- Multiple ebook formats, DRM FREE
- Participation in the O'Reilly community
- Newsletters
- Account management
- 100% Satisfaction Guarantee

Signing up is easy:

1. **Go to: oreilly.com/go/register**
2. **Create an O'Reilly login.**
3. **Provide your address.**
4. **Register your books.**

Note: English-language books only

To order books online:
oreilly.com/store

For questions about products or an order:
orders@oreilly.com

To sign up to get topic-specific email announcements and/or news about upcoming books, conferences, special offers, and new technologies:
elists@oreilly.com

For technical questions about book content:
booktech@oreilly.com

To submit new book proposals to our editors:
proposals@oreilly.com

O'Reilly books are available in multiple DRM-free ebook formats. For more information:
oreilly.com/ebooks

Spreading the knowledge of innovators   oreilly.com

CPSIA information can be obtained at www.ICGtesting.com
Printed in the USA
BVOW01s1019071013

333092BV00006B/143/P

9 781449 361426